Philosophy and memory traces defends two theories of autobiographical memory. One is a bewildering historical view of memories as dynamic patterns in fleeting animal spirits, nervous fluids which rummage through the pores of brain and body. The other is new connectionism, in which memories are 'stored' only superpositionally, and reconstructed rather than reproduced. Both models, argues John Sutton, depart from static archival metaphors by employing distributed representation, which brings interference and confusion between memory traces. Both raise urgent issues about control of the personal past, and about relations between self and body. Sutton demonstrates the role of bizarre body fluids in moral physiology, as philosophers from Descartes and Locke to Coleridge struggled to control their own innards and impose cognitive discipline on 'the phantasmal chaos of association'. Going on to defend connectionism against Fodor and against critics of passive mental representations, he shows how problems of the self are implicated in cognitive science.

Philosophy and memory traces

Philosophy and memory traces

Descartes to connectionism

John Sutton

UNIVERSITY OF SYDNEY

CAMBRIDGE
UNIVERSITY PRESS

PUBLISHED BY THE PRESS SYNDICATE OF THE
UNIVERSITY OF CAMBRIDGE
The Pitt Building, Trumpington Street, Cambridge CB2 2RU United Kingdom

CAMBRIDGE UNIVERSITY PRESS
The Edinburgh Building, Cambridge CB2 2RU, United Kingdom
40 West 20th Street, New York, NY 10011-4211, USA
10 Stamford Road, Oakleigh, Melbourne 3166, Australia

First published 1998

Printed in the United Kingdom at the University Press, Cambridge

Typeset in Quadraat 9.5/12.5, in QuarkXPress™   [SE]

A catalogue record for this book is available from the British Library

Library of Congress Cataloguing in publication data
Sutton, John.
Philosophy and memory traces:
Descartes to Connectionism / John Sutton.
    p.   cm.
Includes bibliographical references and index.
ISBN 0 521 59194 5 (hardback)
1. Memory (Philosophy) – History.   2. Autobiographical memory.
3. Connectionism.   I. Title.
BD181.7.S88   1997
128'.3–dc21   97–8909   CIP

ISBN 0 521 59194 5 hardback

For Doris

One day the soul did not exist,
neither did the mind,
as for consciousness,
no-one had ever thought of it,
but where, for that matter, was thought,
in a world made up solely of warring elements
no sooner destroyed than recomposed,
for thought is a luxury of peacetime.
              (Antonin Artaud, 'Van Gogh, The Man Suicided by Society')

Cognitive science is a body of research . . .
pathetically out of contact with its own history.
                              (Jerry Fodor, 'The Modularity of Mind')

Each memory is many memories . . .
                      (Matt Keoki Matsuda, *The Memory of the Modern*)

Contents

Figures

Preface

This book describes and defends a set of theories of autobiographical memory, both historical and contemporary, which view memories as dynamic patterns rather than static archives, fragmentary traces to be reconstructed rather than coherent things to be reproduced. It adds historical and philosophical flavour to clichés about the fragility of memory by telling odd tales of the motions and disappearance of fleeting animal spirits, by revivifying fears of 'the phantasmal chaos of association', and by defending distributed models of memory against critics' complaints about loss of cognitive discipline. Although I do not here move far in contributing to broader models in cognitive science which are sensitive to context and culture, I clear the ground for so doing by demonstrating that theories of memory do not have to be blind to society and history.

Readers can easily pursue independent, interest-driven routes through the book. After an introductory chapter, it falls into four parts. Parts I and II are primarily historical, part III deals with historical and contemporary problems about associationism together, and part IV is primarily about modern theories of memory. Each part begins with a brief introduction which outlines its contents and motivations.

The shape of the book is historically heavy: it is anchored in part I by a long rereading of Descartes' dynamic physiology of memory, which exemplifies the range of questions about mechanism, self, and body taken up in other contexts in the rest of the book. But this is not an exhaustive or even continuous narrative history: my studies of neglected early modern neurophilosophical controversies end with Reid and Coleridge, and I deal neither with traditions outside France and England nor with theories of memory between 1817 and the 1980s. I rely on authority throughout, citing experts extensively. The detailed historical studies are my own: but they inevitably build on and twist existing research.

Contemporary debates about interference and order in connectionist models of memory traces, which I sketch in the introduction, are taken up again in detail only in parts III and IV. But those attuned to current concerns about the catastrophic effects of superposition, about truth in memory, and about the difficulties of cognitive control over mental contents will find surprisingly clear resonances in forgotten older contexts. The bizarre detail of historical schemes in moral physiology for the disciplining of the neural fluids which roam the body is quite alien to us: this distance allows sharper vision of the way theories of memory are inevitably entangled in wider problems of self, society, and the past.

I wrote the penultimate draft as an Ahmanson/Getty Fellow in the UCLA Center for Seventeenth and Eighteenth Century Studies. I am grateful to Peter Reill and the Clark Library staff for making me welcome. The book was finished under the Australian Research Council's postdoctoral fellowship scheme.

Many people have engaged closely with this work over a number of years, and I am delighted to be able to thank some of them. Doris McIlwain has seen it through from inception, providing incalculable help in theory and practice as we have carried it round for so long. Her exuberant science, her moral physiology, her easy ability to take time seriously, and many of her choice phrases have improved it immensely: I dedicate the product to her with love.

Gerard O'Brien sparked my interest in philosophy of psychology and has often talked over the implications of distributed representation with me. For his own work and his careful attention to mine, Stephen Gaukroger deserves many thanks. Jamie Kassler discussed her views on historical topics close to my own, and provided important feedback. I have been encouraged tremendously by the enthusiasm of John Yolton, and spurred by his detailed comments. Keith Campbell, Frank Jackson, and two anonymous readers for Cambridge University Press also read the whole typescript and made many useful suggestions.

Audiences at various seminars and conferences in philosophy, history, cognitive science, history and philosophy of science, and psychology have commented, criticised, and often provoked new thoughts on this material, as did the students in two Honours courses on memory at Macquarie University. My thanks to them, and especially to the following people who through example, specific suggestions, help, or goodwill have guided and improved my work: Peter Anstey, David Armstrong, Kim Atkins, Michael Ayers, Judith Ayling, Maggie Boden, Derek Brookes, John Campbell, Betsy Colwill, Max Deutscher, Ros Diprose, Antony Duff, Lisabeth During, Brian Ellis, Robyn Ferrell, Robin Lane Fox, Jim Franklin, Hilary Gaskin, Jonathan Glover, Catherine Hunt, Keith Lehrer, Genevieve Lloyd, Tony Lynch, J. J. MacIntosh, Catriona Mackenzie, Sandra Marshall, Charlie Martin, Michael Mascuch, Joel Michell, Graham Nerlich, Marguerite Nesling, David Oldroyd, Agnes Petocz, Ross Poole, Huw Price, David Raynor, Tim Reiss, Julius Rocca, Dory Scaltsas, Jochen Schulte-Sasse, Roland Smith, Daniel Stoljar, Steve Straker, Will Sutton, Mary Terrall, Udo Thiel, Elizabeth Wilson, and John Wright.

Abbreviations

Quotations retain original spelling

A   René Descartes, *Descartes: oeuvres philosophiques*, vol. 1: 1618–1637, ed. F. Alquié (Paris: Editions Garnier Frères, 1963). Reference to editorial notes by page number, e.g. A 479.

AA   Henry More, *An Antidote against Atheism* (first published 1653), in More, *A Collection of Several Philosophical Writings* (1662; repr. New York and London: Garland, 1978), vol. 1, with book, chapter, paragraph, and page number, e.g. AA 1.11.2: 33.

AAA   Henry More, *An Appendix to the foregoing Antidote against Atheism*, in More, *A Collection of Several Philosophical Writings* (1662; repr. New York and London: Garland, 1978), vol. 1, with chapter, paragraph, and page number, e.g. AAA 10.2: 169.

AT   René Descartes, *Oeuvres de Descartes*, ed. C. Adam and P. Tannery (12 vols., repr, Paris: Vrin, 1996).

BL   Samuel T. Coleridge. *Biographia literaria* (first published 1817), in H. J. Jackson (ed.), *Samuel Taylor Coleridge* (Oxford University Press, 1985), 155–482. References are to chapter and page number, e.g. BL VII: 218.

CSM   René Descartes, *The Philosophical Writings of Descartes*, trans. J. Cottingham, R. Stoothoff, and D. Murdoch (2 vols., Cambridge University Press, 1985).

CSM-K   *The Philosophical Writings of Descartes*, vol. III: *Correspondence*, trans. J. Cottingham, R. Stoothoff, D. Murdoch, and A. Kenny (Cambridge University Press, 1991) (incorporating K with amendments).

EACP   Joseph Glanvill, *Essay against Confidence in Philosophy*, in *Essays on Several Important Subjects in Philosophy and Religion* (London: John Baker & Henry Mortlock, 1676); repr. in Joseph Glanvill, *The Vanity of Dogmatizing*, edited with an introduction by Stephen Medcalf (Brighton: Harvester Press, 1970).

Essay   John Locke, *An Essay concerning Human Understanding* (first published 1690), ed. P. H. Nidditch (Oxford: Clarendon, 1975). References are to book, chapter, and paragraph number, e.g. Essay IV.21.4.

Essays   Thomas Reid, *Essays on the Intellectual Powers of Man* (1785), in *The Works of Thomas Reid*, ed. W. Hamilton (Edinburgh: MacLachlan,

Stewart, & Co., 1849). References are to essay, chapter, page, and column number, e.g. *Essays* III.7: 354a.

H   René Descartes, *Treatise of Man: René Descartes* (first published 1662), trans. T. S. Hall (Cambridge, MA: Harvard University Press, 1972). Reference to editorial notes by page number, e.g. H 87.

IS   Henry More, *The Immortality of the Soul* (first published 1659), in *A Collection of Several Philosophical Writings* (1662: repr. New York and London: Garland 1978), vol. II, with book, chapter, paragraph, and page number, e.g. *IS* II.2.7: 68.

K   René Descartes, *Descartes: Philosophical Letters*, trans. A. Kenny (Oxford: Clarendon, 1970).

L'Homme René Descartes, *L'Homme* (first published 1662 (Latin) and 1664 (French)). References are to page numbers of AT, of the English translation in H and (for the small portion included in CSM I) of CSM, e.g. AT xi.120, H 4, CSM 1.99.

LL   Robert Hooke, *Lectures of Light*, in *The Posthumous Works of Robert Hooke*, ed. Richard Waller (London, 1705). I use the reprint with an introduction by T. M. Brown (London: Frank Cass & Co., 1971). The lecture on memory is lecture 7, pp. 138–48. Reference is to lecture, paragraph, and page number, e.g. LL 7.1: 140.

LO   Nicolas Malebranche, *The Search After Truth* (first published 1674), 6th edn (1712), trans. T. M. Lennon and P. J. Olscamp (Columbus, OH: Ohio State University Press). References are to page number, book, part, chapter, and section number, e.g. LO 93, II.1.2.iii. The structure of the books in LO varies considerably: in books I and V there is only one 'part', so references are to book and chapter numbers, with section numbers where they existed within chapters, e.g. LO 49, 1.10.ii.

OM   David Hartley, *Observations on Man, His Frame, His Duty, and His Expectations* (first published London, 1749; repr. New York: Garland, 1971). References are to page, part, chapter, section, and proposition number, e.g. OM 7, 1.i.2, prop. 11.

Passions René Descartes, *Passions of the Soul* (first published 1649). References are to part and paragraph number, and to AT and CSM, e.g. *Passions* 1.32, AT xi.352, CSM 1.340.

Principles René Descartes, *Principles of Philosophy* (first published 1644). References are to part and paragraph number, and to AT and CSM, e.g. *Principles* 1.74, AT viii(a).38, CSM 1.221.

SS   Joseph Glanvill, *Scepsis scientifica* (London: Henry Eversden, 1665); repr. in Joseph Glanvill, *The Vanity of Dogmatizing*, edited with an introduction by Stephen Medcalf (Brighton: Harvester Press, 1970).

Treatise David Hume, *A Treatise of Human Nature* (first published 1739), ed.

L. A. Selby-Bigge and P. H. Nidditch (Oxford: Clarendon, 1978). References are to book, part, and section numbers, followed by page number, e.g. *Treatise* I.vi.6: 259.

Tristram Shandy   Laurence Sterne, *The Life and Opinions of Tristram Shandy, Gentleman* (first published 1759), ed. I. C. Ross (Oxford University Press, 1983). References are to volume, chapter, and page number, e.g. *Tristram Shandy* I.1: 5.

TT   Kenelm Digby, *Two Treatises: in the one of which, the nature of bodies; in the other, the nature of mans soule; is looked into; in way of discovery, of the immortality of Reasonable Soules* (Paris: Gilles Blaizot, 1644; repr. New York and London: Garland, 1978). All references are to book I ('Of Bodies'), and include chapter and page number, e.g. TT 32: 282.

VOD   Joseph Glanvill, *The Vanity of Dogmatizing* (London: Henry Eversden, 1661); repr. edited with an introduction by Stephen Medcalf (Brighton: Harvester Press, 1970). References are to page number, e.g. VOD: 35.

I

Introduction: traces, brains, and history

... it can easily happen that we cannot simultaneously store many ... structures in a connectionist memory without getting intrusions of undesired memories during the retrieval of a given memory ... (Paul Smolensky 1991: 218)

... how much similarity must there be between the two moments in order for the one to count as a memory of the other? How much of the content of the experience must be reproduced and how accurately? How many portions of the past is the present connected to in a condensed memory, and how is this determined? (Marya Schechtman 1994: 9–10)

1.1 Porous memory
Beyond the archive

Porous memories fuse and interpenetrate. Fragments of song mingle in hot remembered afternoons, mysterious angers return at a flush with a chance forgotten postcard. Such memories were once the motions of old fluids, animal spirits which meandered and rummaged through the pores of the brain. They held experience and history in bodies which were themselves porous, uncertainly coupled across tissues and skin with their air, their ethics, their land. Now they are patterns of activation across vast neural networks, condensing and compressing innumerable possible trajectories into the particular vectors of flashing or torpid memories. Dynamic cognitive systems coevolving with the physiological, environmental, and social systems in which they are embedded (van Gelder and Port 1995: 27–30) need the wishful mixings of absence which interfering traces bring.

These studies in the history of theories of memory are grounded in new interpretations of strange, neglected old French and English neurophilosophy. But only late twentieth-century worries about memory, science, and truth make sense of indulgent attention to 'seventeenth-century French connectionism' (Diamond 1969), and to bizarre historical beliefs about interactive relations between self, body, mind, and coursing nervous fluids. This kind of historical cognitive science aims to demonstrate that it is possible to attend to contexts and to brains at once.

It is no big deal now to claim that human memory is not a set of static records in cold storage, that the subtle smack of the organic opens remembering to decay and confusion, affect-ridden association, the pains of time. Not all theories have taken memory to be a place where dead parts of the past sit passive

I

until recalled to full presence. But, across the bewildering range of disciplines in which models of memory are constructed and criticised, vast gulfs between brains and society (felt even, or especially, by those who deny them) limit moves beyond the archive. The fact that, say, neurobiology and narrative theory, as well as cognitive psychology (Roediger 1996: 79), describe the constructive functions of errors or lapses in the fidelity of memory is not sheer accident. But, in the frantic rush of new research in all of memory's fields, it is impossible to consider the physiological, the cognitive, and the cultural at once. Old, rejected theories offer a feeling for the shape of some debates about control of the personal past which pre-date our debilitating, tedious battles between 'science' and 'humanism'. It would be nice to entwine philosophical, social, psychological, and neuroscientific accounts of memory in modern contexts alone, in wild anthropological fables about the phenomenology of neural nets: but the frameworks are still too disjointed, and so only history affords the requisite pretence of distance.

I undertake both the description and the defence of related theories of memory, from animal spirits to connectionism, which employ *superpositional storage*: memories are blended, not laid down independently once and for all, and are reconstructed rather than reproduced. In dissolving old and new lines of attack on such theories, I suggest that they exemplify the sensitivity to culture and history which good psychological science can exhibit. Working between historical and contemporary material suggests that wider issues about the self and psychological control are also implicated in current debates. The models of memory distributed through these studies, in mosaic from Descartes to connectionism, hint at a more reckless algebra, an understanding of how complex self-organising physical systems like us can be so psychologically plastic, attuned to the configurations of culture in which cognition and remembering are situated.

I cannot, of course, even begin to fulfil this promise: these studies are mere groundwork, trying to undermine various patterns of hostility to neuro-philosophical theory. In too many spots I only sketch approaches to difficult puzzles, leaving detail undone. And yet there is a tenuous continuity between the studies, a faint order which might justify the threadbare juxtapositions. The active use of history in bringing culture into science and in undermining easy present-centredness requires a certain obliviousness, in theory as in practice. I hope that there is enough in these studies to excuse their shortcomings with respect to that relentless erudition which the genealogy of concepts and theories demands.

Interdisciplinarity
My account of these theories of memory both complicates and implicitly defends a set of philosophical positions crudely characterisable as mech-

anism, naturalism, associationism, determinism, and reductionism. These attitudes seem to signify thrall to matter, foolish scientism or misplaced physics-envy, blinkered materialism, the lack not so much of spiritual orientation as of embedding in culture. I do indulge overenthusiastic gestures and unlikely promises in these pages, through an untidy preference for proliferation over prudence in difficult domains. But I want to temper the repugnance which swells when wise humanists encounter cognitive sciences and neuromyths, by adding a sense of history, culture, and play to my reductionist neurophilosophy. Amidst the vast literature on memory, specific and insistent interdisciplinarity aligns this book with other approaches, histories, and ideas which are not usually put together. Detailed historical analysis of theories of memory in medicine, neuroscience, and philosophy sits, at least, in unusual combination with gullible faith in the new sciences of complexity, memory, and brain.

Theories of memory are a test case for the wish to connect cognition and culture. In breaking down educational and cultural divides between arts and sciences, it must be possible to trace interactions between minds and their social surround, or between particular bodies and the worlds in which they grow. Even if the shared backgrounds and forms of life in which individuals develop can never be fully articulated, this means not that science or theory is restricted to the repeatable and isolable, barred from dealing with complexity and change, but that the social permeation of the psychological is the most puzzling and urgent of areas for attempts, at once scientific and cultural, at theory. Only thus can the sciences of the mind/brain ever usefully spill out of their institutional limits and tell those on the outside things they want to know.

So I seek to show how mechanists can also be holists, how determinists can also be contextualists, how naturalists can accept their engagement within frameworks, how bodies too can have narrative flows. Existing taxonomies of theories of memory (Belli 1986) are disrupted by these models of memory. The point is not just that science itself (as activity and as product) is in time and culture, but that it also comfortably deals with the time-bound and the context-dependent. Memory is both a natural and a human kind (Hacking 1994). Its operation, in species, society, or individual, does not alter easily, and it cannot be moulded at will, for the body and the past both resist arbitrary voluntary manipulation: but neither is it forever fixed, its processes or its contents shaped beyond change by preordained, pre-social forces. The various sciences of memory still display a puzzling lack of overlap (Hacking 1995: 199), and the one material world in which memories exist looks increasingly disunified and promiscuous. How in practice, in detail, do complexity and explanation co-exist?

To sceptics about the very idea of cognitive sciences, the 'memories' of our computers furnish only ludicrous analogies for human remembering.

The point of the information storage systems which permeate our life is to retain static items, unchanged unless manipulated. If brains and bodies are introduced, they are more likely as hardware than as wetware, as containers and conduits of independent information than as noisy or sedimented transformers. But anti-scientific zeal is too easily promoted by mocking reductionists as inconsistent every time they speak a language other than fundamental physics. For matter is in culture and time, nature is in history, the brains through which experience piles are not isolated. Memory bridges not just past and present, but outside and inside, machine and organism, dreams and reason, invention and sadness, creation and loss.

Morals affect physiology

And so the archive caricature of the cognitive scientific view of memory must be displayed, questioned, and lampooned. But challenges to rigid approaches to memory do not rule out all scientific study of remembering. Interference too has its patterns and constraints, confusion its formal operations. Clearer tracing of historical and contemporary debates reveals important distinctions not so much between scientific and non-scientific methods as between explanatory polarities of order and chaos, discipline and anarchy. Within scientific models the gulf between new connectionist and classical symbolic approaches to cognitive science is only the most recent manifestation of older divisions. Early modern moral physiologists did not need to abandon the discourses of natural philosophy or 'science' in order to make their recommendations on the pursuits of virtue and truth. So when I describe 'tension' between neurophilosophy and ethics, or show how physiological theories were revised to fit social demands, I am not enforcing a model of inevitable conflict in which the 'scientific' must pull against the normative. Unease about the body and the traces it conceals provoked crises within the best theoretical systems, for 'knowledge' of mind and brain often had to serve as both truth and morality (Smith 1992: 231–8). Interdisciplinarity is here easy to spot if difficult to carry off, for knowledge-that in theories of memory is always also knowledge-how, moral and practical at the same time as scientific.

For cognitive scientists, especially new connectionists, this embedding of mind, brain, and memory in body and culture is urgent. 'Neurophilosophy' (Churchland 1986a) may have sprung from frustration at philosophy of mind and from excitement at the wonders of computational neuroscience. But, despite critics' laments at the 'pervasive gloom' of asocial materialist orthodoxy (Eccles 1994: x; Sharpe 1991), neurophilosophy would never work as 'austere scientific abstract theory' alone, and requires revisions of social, political, and historical understanding to run along with the revisionary philosophy of psychology (Churchland 1993: 218–19, 1995: 286–94).[1] Few have been both willing and equipped to embark on the task despite increasing recognition of its necessity (Hatfield 1988a: 732; van Gelder 1991a: 93). It is no use simply to complain that neurophilosophy is 'philosophically inadequate because it does not deal with the ethical dimension of the mind' (Stent 1990: 539, 556): but the new connectionist ethics being developed in response (Clark 1996) can be enriched with cultural and historical counter-theory to add to the brain-work and the morality. There is no moral theory in this book: but it does start to connect connectionists with dead revisionary allies and fellow wantons.

1.2 Distribution and dynamics

I invoke throughout a distinction or (better) a spectrum between *local* or archival models of memory as unchanging items in storage spaces, and *distributed* or reconstructive models of memory as blending patterns in shifting mixture. History and rhetoric pitch reproductive models of remembering against reconstructive, fidelity against fragility. Both old and new distributed models describe *dynamic* systems. Animal spirits theory, like some connectionist models, fits Tim van Gelder's description of a class of possible dynamical cognitive models, in which cognitive systems are 'complexes of continuous, simultaneous, and mutually determining change' (1995: 373):

> the cognitive system is not just the encapsulated brain; rather, since the nervous system, body, and environment are all constantly changing and simultaneously influencing each other, the true cognitive system is a single unified system embracing all three . . . interaction between the inner and the outer is . . . a matter of coupling, such that both sets of processes continually influence each other's direction of change.

My attention, then, is on two versions of that subset of dynamic models which employ superpositional storage. In an appendix to this introductory chapter (pp. 19–20), I sketch the connectionist framework for readers unfamiliar with it. Here I introduce significant issues linked with the local/distributed distinction to explain why those outside cognitive science should care, then focus on this key notion of superposition.

1 Churchland and Sejnowski (1992: 445, n. 5) accept the importance of the social level for the neurophilosopher, while acknowledging that 'it has not been the main focus' of their book. The case for extending the relevant levels of research from synapses, networks, and maps to social interaction *between* organisms and their brains is that 'the interaction between brains is a major factor in what an individual brain can and does do'. I add that bringing in the social enriches neurophilosophy also by opening interaction with disciplines which *start* from the social, and thus newly moulding the explananda for a mature neurophilosophy. My project is to probe potential historical and theoretical advantages of some models of memory which allow for and invite such extensions.

Total recall

Surprising personal and social consequences flow quickly from unthinking acceptance of a local model of passive items in independent cells, splayed on the spirals of memory, at the beck and call of the executive individual who possesses them. I am unsure if the idea that all memories somewhere remain ordered and unblemished has ever been part of 'folk psychology' (it had, for example, to be enforced powerfully by the English Restoration philosophers I discuss in chapter 5). But British Telecom invest vast millions in a 'Soul Catcher' project, which aims at 'memory transfer' by picking out and playing back individual traces in another brain (*Guardian*, 18 July 1996, p. 1): this is not the gorgeous fantasy of interpersonal dreaming which drives Wim Wenders' film *Until the End of the World* (1991), but a sad, expensive rerun of old 'bizarre memory experiments' which fed RNA from one worm or rat, in so-called 'informational macromolecules', to another so that the recipient could learn from the donor's experience (Rose 1993: 189–99). Yet in one survey 84 per cent of psychologists and 69 per cent of others believed that 'everything we learn is permanently stored in the mind' and is potentially recoverable (Loftus and Loftus 1980: 430).

If atomic items did remain impermeable to further change after encoding, access to a desired memory in court or in therapy might be difficult, but would always be possible in principle. As both recovered-memory controversies and science fiction teach, the quest to *reproduce* the content of an original experience would often fail to comfort: the personal past would be tyrannical, events preserved in aspic always returning to haunt us (Spence 1988: 320–1). But whatever evidence of memory malleability, suggestibility, and distortion psychologists produce in response to moral panic about repressed memories of abuse (Loftus, Feldman, and Dashiell 1995; Schacter 1996: 248–79), it cannot be proven that *some* memories do not sit fixed in awful archives (Bowers and Farvolden 1996; Brewin 1996). But note also the immediate implication of views about the self in theories of memory. Local memories are kept in a storage system which is distinct from ongoing processing, in a dusty corner from which a possessive individual must try to remove them on request. Such a theory of memory is but a minor part of a theory of cognition, in which problem-solving and abstract reasoning can take precedence.

Distributed memories, in contrast, are troubling just because their content *can* change over time.[2] If traces are composites, superimposed over long experience, what emerges in retrieval may be noisy, ambiguous, or systematically

---

2 Philosophers are sometimes sceptical about memory traces because, they realise, many factors other than brain states contribute to remembering. It is worth stating at the outset for their benefit that, obviously, theorists concerned with social aspects of memory must acknowledge that demands of specific situations affect the *content* as well as the expression of a memory. There is *no* reason to attribute to trace theorists the view that remembering is

distorted (Metcalfe Eich 1982: 611). Storage is naturally entwined with processing, and a theory of memory is central to a theory of mind. It is not that there are no secret angles of the mind, for in superpositional psychodynamics there is no easy conscious access to the forces driving representational change: but any 'inner walls of secrecy' where discontinuous systems coexist (Lingis 1994a: 148) in such models are immanent to the memory landscape, not imposed by executive decision.

As the anthropologists Michael Lambek and Paul Antze suggest, resistance to this idea that the sources of distortion may be internal and unavoidable is shared by those on both 'sides' of the false-recovered-memory controversies: 'such is the need to shore up a space of organic innocence that its absence can only be imagined in terms of a deliberate and violent despoiling on the part of corrupt adults' (1996: xxx n. 7). But they deny that the cognitive psychology of memory can help in encouraging acceptance of the complicated and inconsistent roles of remembering as a practice, on the ground that psychology inevitably constructs memory as 'objective and objectified' and omits 'the relation to a self, agent, or community that bears memory' (1996: xi–xii). In contrast, I show that cultural studies of memory too can find material of interest in dynamic models within connectionist cognitive science.

Confusion and mixture

On top of the basic, familiar connectionist propaganda outlined again in the appendix to this chapter, I examine more closely the central notion of superposition and its consequences. In true distributed models, memory traces are both *extended* and *superposed*, many traces piled or layered in the same physical system, with many 'representations' in one 'representing' (van Gelder 1991b, 1992a; Haugeland 1991; Schreter 1994). 'Each memory trace is distributed over many different connections, and each connection participates in many different memory traces': the traces of different memories 'are therefore superimposed in the same set of weights' (McClelland and Rumelhart 1986: 176). A trace is *extended* when it is spread across a number of elements or parts of a system, with many elements required for any one pattern. But extendedness is not enough for distribution, since every trace could still be quite distinct, entirely independent of the set of elements composing every other trace: such a model would still be local. *Superposition*, then, is also needed.

'Two representations are superposed if the resources used to represent item 1 are coextensive with those used to represent item 2' (Clark 1993: 17). Most

determined by the properties of the stored item (compare chapter 16 below). Mainstream psychology deals in detail with factors other than the nature of the trace: research on Tulving's 'synergistic ecphory' (1983: 12–14), for instance, describes the conspiratorial interaction of the cue (in the context of retrieval) with the trace (Schacter 1982: 181–9, 1996: 56–71). I am concerned primarily not with encoding or retrieval, or with cueing effects, but with alterations in traces during other ordinary ongoing processing.

distributed representations in practice are only partially superposed, on this definition. Superposition gives traces an internal structure. Patterns of activity grouped around a central prototype are subtly different from each other, but are similar to varying degrees in various objective respects.

Many philosophies of mind have trouble dealing with 'difference': the models they concoct reveal minds endlessly assimilating multiplicity to identity, turning threatening or challenging variation into safe and comprehensible repetition. But distributed models, in contrast, have problems with *sameness*.[3] Public representations like sentences may be frozen, relatively memorable, 'context-resistant', and thus relatively stable (Clark 1997: 210; but compare Sperber 1996: 25, 58, 100–6). But every occurrence of a mental representation is different, because every explicit tokening of a pattern of activation is a reconstruction: this leads connectionists, in the extreme, to say that we never create the same concept twice (Barsalou 1988: 236–7; Clark 1993: 91–4).[4] In connectionism, says Elman (1993: 89),

> once a given pattern has been processed and the network has been updated, the data disappear. Their effect is immediate and results in a modification of the knowledge state of the network. The data persist only implicitly by virtue of the effect they have on what the network knows.

Thinking of mind as text, of mental representation as language-like, made it easy to assume that sameness of meaning is unproblematically transferred across contexts. Words, normally, retain their meanings across different instantiations: 'apple' is easily recognisable whether scrawled misshapenly in a recipe notebook or printed in neat Palatino font in crisp poetry. The difference between tokens rarely challenges the sameness of type. The same information can thus be drawn on in many different circumstances, and is multiply usable without degradation. The point of language, or of a language of thought, is to be context-insensitive (Serres 1982; Kirsh 1990: 342–60; Clark 1993: 121–7).

---

3 There is one sense in which this is an issue for any materialist theory of memory, given the incessant motion of matter. Critics are led to reject physicalism: Straus (1970: 50) notes that 'in physics and physiology events are not repeated', and concludes from a phenomenological examination of memory that 'experience, then, transcends the realm of physical events'. But distributed models have specific problems with sameness, since superposed traces have not even the kind of imperfect but enduring material continuity possible for single stored items like books, bags, and birds.

4 This is the key sense of 'reconstruction' in my talk throughout of reconstructive memory. It *does not* mean that the deliverances of memory are always false, or that the fragility of remembering should override common-sense trust in memory or testimony: I do not want to belabour 'that banal topic, the indeterminacy of memory' (Hacking 1995: 234). Obviously, as Coady (1992: 268) observes about eyewitness testimony, 'neither the picture of wholly passive registration nor that of furiously active invention' tells the complete story. Rather the notion of reconstruction marks the content-addressable nature of memories, and the context-constrained nature of every act of remembering: the extent to which the picture of highly nuanced mental episodes, specifically indexed to the cognitive system, body, history, and current cues in which they occur, is alien to 'common sense' is disputable. See O'Brien 1991, and on reconstruction McCauley 1988.

But thinking of mind as process, with representations in distributed rather than linguistic form, means that current context is built into the particular reconstruction of any one pattern.

This feature arises directly from superposition. Since many traces are 'stored' in the same physical system, no single one of them can be continually explicitly active. Memory cannot be the permanent conservation of discrete unchanging informational atoms. But what then is the memory trace? Where does the trace disappear to between experience and recall, between past and present? There is only one set of connections in any system, only one set of weights between connections, while there are many traces. So traces are affected on reconstruction by the other traces implicitly present in the system, and may blend one with another, leading potentially to distortion or error.

Some connectionists try to exclude interference and the potential confusion between traces which it brings. Patterns of activity are set up to be independent enough to minimise blending between different traces encoded in the same representational resources: 'if the patterns are sufficiently dissimilar (i.e. orthogonal), there is no interference between them at all. Increasing similarity leads to increased confusability during learning' (McClelland and Rumelhart 1986: 185). A priori legislation against confusability, in favour of non-destructive overwriting (Tryon 1993: 344), is tempting: 'By "superpositional storage" I mean the property that one network of units and connections may be used to store a number of representations, so long as they are sufficiently distinct (the term used is "orthogonal") to coexist without confusion' (Clark 1989: 100).

Motivation for thus excluding confusion from distributed representations comes from fear of 'catastrophic interference' when models are realistically scaled up (McCloskey and Cohen 1989; Ratcliff 1990). This occurs when the learning of a new set of data wipes out memory of previous data and successful reconstruction becomes impossible, when the mixture's ingredients will not reseparate. 'Catastrophic forgetting is a direct consequence of the overlap of distributed representations and can be reduced by reducing this overlap' (French 1992: 366).

Unleashing interference

The specific sources of such disastrous interference in distributed models are disputed (Lewandowsky 1991). But neither this debate nor the slightly moral tone of some false-memory research on suggestion and misinformation illusions should blind us to the startling productive role of interference which fuelled connectionist enthusiasm as soon as data on interference in human memory (Anderson 1995: 247–65; Rubin 1995: 147–55) was modelled in neural nets. The same mechanisms which induce false recognition of plausible information (Roediger and McDermott 1995) also drive flexible generalisation and the capacity to 'extract the central tendencies of a set of experiences' (McClelland and Rumelhart 1986: 193; Clark 1989: 99). Composite traces blur and fuzz the memories of specific episodes, but render salient the overlapping, prototypical features of a set of exemplars:

> Each time an event occurs in a different context (time, place, and so on) a new trace is formed, but soon there are so many different contexts that none can individually be retrieved. What is common among the several exemplars is the knowledge, which we call abstract, but by default, by the massive interference attached to any individual context. (Crowder 1993: 156)

Even traumatic memories of repeated or persisting events may be filtered through later emotions: in such cases, memory is often accurate enough for the general character of the events, but awry in specific instances, mixing together the thoughts, perceptions, and emotions of different occasions (Schacter 1996: 205–12). It may be dangerous to unleash interference in contexts where historical truth matters terribly: but the fact that, like neural nets, humans often fail 'to separate information that arises from different sources' (McClelland 1995: 73) is also a powerful fund of pleasure and creativity.

These historical studies investigate the consequences of thinking interference freely. Rhetoric against confusion and mixture drives critics of distributed models of associative memory from the Cambridge Platonists to Jerry Fodor. It springs not only from technical concerns about how such models perform, but also from assumptions about just how confused human memory really is. Should extensive blending effects be built into our model of memory, or should order and independence among traces be taken as the natural state or competence to be explained, from which performance deviates? What features of human cognition, exactly, are defended in attacks on alleged chaos?

1.3 Historical cognitive science
Philosophical amnesia and the uses of history
D. G. C. Macnabb laconically comments (1962: 360) that 'The unsatisfactory nature of Hume's account of memory is noticed by nearly all his commentators. It is a fault however which he shares with nearly all other philosophers.' Aaron (1955: 136) likewise laments Locke's 'slight and superficial' treatment of memory. One does not need to think Locke or Hume got everything right to question the modern hostility to neurophilosophy which such historical judgements typify. Most early modern philosophers accepted specific accounts of the physical processes underlying and constraining cognition: modern analytic philosophers, in contrast, preferred to have no theory of memory than to rely on neurospeculations. The first full English translation of Descartes' *L'Homme*, which includes his weird philosophy of the body and

the elements of his distributed model of memory, was not published until 1972, when its translator commented that Descartes' 'mechanism for explaining association is not very convincing' (H 90, n. 138). In turn, the many physiological references in Locke's *Essay* just disappear from some modern editions: A. D. Woozley's often reprinted edition (1964/1977), for example, omits without acknowledgement Locke's reference to tension between his account of personal identity and the animal spirit psychophysiology of memory (chapter 7 below).[5] Philosophers in both 'analytic' and 'continental' traditions have long suffered historical amnesia in suppressing and ignoring neurophilosophy. A more nuanced history of early modern attempts to deal with uncertain territory between memory and body needs to be reclaimed.

The damaging anti-naturalist desire for principled divisions between philosophy and science (Kitcher 1992: 53–9) left little room to acknowledge neurological connections in the history of philosophy. Old references to cognitive or brain processes were too easily explained away as pre-Fregean confusion of the logical with the empirical, the mistaken offering of psychological or (worse) neuropsychological answers to epistemological questions. Pitching in for further bouts of Descartes-bashing, more recent combative critics of modernity latch on to the lovely historical narrative which spies 'the original sin of modern philosophy' (Rorty 1980: 60, n. 32) in the seventeenth-century 'invention' of ideas as dubious reflections or representations of the world which cut us off from a newly veiled reality.

Naturalistic history, in contrast, does not seek the roots of unfortunate modern fallacies, but traces complex development in old cognitive theories before returning to parallel contemporary problems (Meyering 1989; Hatfield 1990). Neither naturalism nor reductionism necessarily derives from philistine carelessness about the complexity and sophistication of human history and culture. Stephen Straker suggests a negative answer to his own question: 'The problem should take the form: "could a true and coherent history of theories of perception be written from the point of view of the triumph of the reductionist vision?"' (Straker 1985: 256, n. 30).[6]

---

5 The 1977 paperback edition went through ten impressions by 1981. Woozley's own discussion of memory occurs, significantly, in a widely read textbook called *Theory of Knowledge* (1949). For those who saw theory of memory as but a branch of epistemology, early modern neurophilosophy of memory made no sense: Macnabb (1962: 106, n. 15) puzzles over Hume's reference to the animal spirits theory of memory at *Treatise* I.ii.5, wondering 'why Hume thought that an excursion into physiology was more necessary in this context'.

6 Straker thinks that 'only historical studies can "rescue" philosophy from present infelicities' (1985: 272). He complains, for example, that Paul Churchland's proposals for revolution in our self-conception reveal only a failure 'to appreciate the depth and richness of the question' of the historical dimensions of subjectivity and perceptual theory (1985: 256, n. 30).

But detailed history (of a sort perhaps more familiar in the microstudies of historians of science, or in new historicist literary criticism, than in history of philosophy) can attend to contradiction, to internal fragmentation in our traditions, to the arbitrary confluences of factors driving conceptual change, and must itself be thoroughly naturalistic. The model of explanation with which the reductionist flirts is explanation which reduces, or explains in terms of something else, without explaining away. Temperature does not cease to exist just because it is reduced to mean kinetic energy of molecules.[7] Alleged dichotomies between reductionism and the crowning glories of our species' achievements fail to justify either humanist resistance to reduction or blind scientistic hostility to culture.[8] It is precisely because history (especially the history of aberrant bodily fluids and wriggling spirits) is so resistant to reduction that it is less important strategically to beware naturalism than to deflate claims that mind and self run along autonomous from nature. Reductionism and general commitment to the 'unity of science' can coexist with acknowledgement of and pleasure in the disunity of historical and physical phenomena.

This is not of course to deny the existence of crude atheoretical technologism with no ear for history. The sensible rejection of scientism need not force us inevitably to use history *against* naturalism. Those who resist the encroach of science on mind, fearing that it will swamp historical awareness, are attacking a 1950s ghoul, a dreich behaviourism without laughter.

7 I use the term 'neurophilosophy' to catch common features of the two models of memory I discuss, animal spirits and connectionism, one forgotten and one fashionable. It is neutral, in my usage, on metaphysics: Descartes and Hartley gave physiological accounts of memory, but thought that some mental events were non-physical. The key is belief that 'lower-level' descriptions and processes constrain, affect, and permeate the description and functioning of psychological capacities. Although I am happy to talk about reduction (because successful reduction precisely rules out elimination), those whose metaphysics turns on supervenience-without-reduction can think of supervenience: the point is that, rather than inevitably implying eliminativism, neurophilosophy is compatible with many different views of relations between levels of explanation (Sutton 1995). Distributed models can be and often are pitched at some level of abstraction from the neural: thus weird neurological detail in Descartes or Hartley can be treated as 'brain-style' modelling, with distributed traces being neither purely psychological nor purely neurobiological.

8 In an instructive exchange with Patricia Churchland, Keith Campbell (1986) argued against the requirements of reducibility which strong naturalism imposes on particular discourses, because such requirements threaten to force the abandonment of history, literature, moral talk, and social thought. But one does not have to use Campbell's confidence in the 'human truths' of 'humanistic works of (chiefly) literature' to isolate human achievement and cognition from neurophilosophy: Shakespearean, Joycean, or Humean psychologies need not oppose sciences which wonder about strange places in the brain. Equally, Churchland's rejection of the need to understand motive, emotion, and the passions when studying brains and internal geometries (1986b: 271, n. 1) unnecessarily resists genuine pluralism in psychology, which would require history, culture, and literature too.

Metaphors and the historiography of theories of memory

Spatial descriptions of the organisation of memory, reliant on current external recording technology, defend against cultural and psychological fear about loss of control. Talk of memory as rooms, palaces, or purses, as a bottle or a dictionary, as tape recorder or junk box (Roediger 1980: 233) incorporates into body and mind ways of keeping items safe, retaining control over fluid memories. Notions about selves in relation to natural and social worlds are already implicated in theorising about memory. Ancient and medieval arts of local or place memory, for example, supplemented weak natural memory with diverse techniques for rigidly fixing items in secure artificial locations, random access systems of images for the executive self to extract at its pleasure (Sutton 1997). Psychological language assimilates descriptions of body and external world, and the process artificially sediments cultural residues in descriptions and then experiences of memory (Jaynes 1976; Scarry 1988; Johnson 1991; Richards 1992: 54–66, 104–34; Derrida 1996: 15). Quite different thoughts and actions are opened up with metaphors of memory motions and dynamic traces than with metaphors of secure independent traces located firmly in a memory bank.

It is easy for us to enjoy picaresque old accounts of animal spirits roaming the 'crankling turnings and windings', the 'folds and lappets' of the brain (Thomas Willis, in Brown 1977: 49), less so to pick up high-level assumptions already implicit in our own sciences. The 'hardest', least society-driven neurobiology still requires theoretical input from other levels of explanation at which metaphor and culture have a purchase. Donald Hebb believed that those who complain at the use of physiology in psychology still possess 'an infantile neurology in [their] unconscious' (in Colville-Stewart 1975: 410). Neuroscientists need to find out what to ask, what to look for, what to do with their data.[9] Brain research into memory, concludes Sandra Colville-Stewart in her vast survey of memory metaphors and models (1975: 417) 'is not so much trying to find the answer to a problem, as to discover what the problem is'.

History encourages distrust of judgements which praise certain 'theories' of memory for their sober freedom from metaphor, denigrating the overly metaphorical nature of others. The point is not just that metaphor is generative rather than inevitably obstructive to the pursuit of truth, or that psychology in particular must necessarily adopt and adapt familiar terms (Wilkes 1975, 1988a: 198–229, 1990; Kearns 1987; Hoffman, Cochran, and Nead 1990): it is that memory is a domain in which there are peculiar problems in drawing even provisional lines between metaphorical and literal descriptions (Colville-Stewart 1975: 415). The specific difficulty in distributed models of internally

9 'Neurophysiology contains as an essential component a certain abstract level of description of the functional organization of the nervous system' (Enc 1983: 298).

distinguishing memory and imagination is part cause of our general difficulty in separating the literal and the figural.

Strange continuity in metaphor and model from ancient wax tablets and aviaries is often noticed: 'most current models of memory have been discussed under different names in earlier periods' (Berrios 1990: 198; compare 1996: 208). Does this erode confidence in contemporary science, or reveal the pointlessness of studying historical theories? Some lament science's lack of progress: David Krell (1990: 5, xi), describing 'the staying-power of the ancient model for memory', hopes to expose 'the failure of neurophysiological research to render plausible accounts of long-term memory'.[10] Others buttress current science, displacing genuine historical difference: dead scholars who had to rely merely on 'natural observation and intuition' are applauded for successfully identifying, 'without the use of experiment . . . the same topics' as those studied by psychologists after Ebbinghaus (Herrmann and Chaffin 1988: 1, 3). Psychology's 'old past' disappears: one psychologist, overtly aiming at a 'critical survey of the various hypotheses [about memory traces] proposed during the past 2500 years', devotes only six pages to theories before 1900, justifying the brevity in his treatment of 'the days before physiology was established on a firm scientific basis' by dismissing most prior hypotheses as 'at worst idle speculations and at best lucky guesses' (Gomulicki 1953: vii). It should, surely, be possible to avoid both the use of history merely to undermine science, and the use of science as battering-ram to rubbish history.

Early modern theories of memory suffer terribly in historical surveys. There are clear philosophical analyses of ancient views (Sorabji 1972; Lang 1980; Krell 1990: ch. 1; Annas 1992), wonderful detailed histories of the 'premodern' technologies of local memory (Yates 1966; Carruthers 1990; Bolzoni 1991), of medieval memory practices (Fentress and Wickham 1992; Geary 1994) and theories of voluntary reminiscence (Coleman 1992). But then there is a gulf: Wyschograd's (1970) account of 'memory in the history of philosophy' moves straight from Augustine to Bergson, Herrmann and Chaffin's anthology (1988) jumps from Bacon across Hume and Reid to Kant, and the attention of good historians of psychology naturally focuses (often after brief 'background' sections on Aristotle and association) on memory research in

---

10 'To my own astonishment, I have found that modern scientific accounts of the earlier theories of thinking and remembering are not only oversimplified and inaccurate . . . the modern theories . . . despite their experimental, scientific, jargon, often are rather more unsophisticated than some medieval ones' (Coleman 1992: xv, see also pp. 600–14). Coleman's rejection of modern psychology of memory is taken further by the anthropologist Maurice Bloch, who complains that psychologists' overt attempts to acknowledge social aspects of memory are thwarted by their use of a 'much too simple notion of a person' and their 'failure to grasp the full complexity of the engagement of the mind in culture and history' (Bloch 1996: 229, 216).

the last two centuries (Murray 1976; Marshall and Fryer 1978; Schacter 1982; Morris 1994).

Recently, late nineteenth-century French medical and philosophical theories of memory have been richly contextualised (Roth 1989, 1991, 1992; Matsuda 1993; Terdiman 1993; Hacking 1995). I seek to do the same for the period between Descartes and Coleridge. In doing so, I show that Ian Hacking's claim (1995: 203) that there was no depth knowledge sought about memory and self, 'no systematic attempt to discover facts about memory', until the 1870s is too strong. In particular, there is a longer background to more dynamic views of memory than is usually acknowledged: it is not the case that 'the attempt to conceive of memory in active terms is a relatively recent philosophical project' (Melion and Kuchler 1991: 3). Historians think of non-linear transformations more easily in the history of chemistry, where affinities, for instance, were 'forces "of a different order" than mechanical forces of impact', since the forces of affinity 'inhere in matter but are not absolute quantities; the strength of the affinity binding two substances together may change with the advent of a third substance' (Terrall 1996: 224). But precisely this kind of retroactive interference in prior associative bonds was at stake in animal spirits theory. Theories of memory in the early modern period and the late twentieth century may be more neurological in orientation than those of intervening periods (compare Rousseau 1969/1991: 4): but both cases confirm that caring for natural and bodily constraints is not condemning memory to a passive store.

Marshall and Fryer (1978: 21) asked whether, among the 'small number of metaphors' in the history of theories of memory, there is anything new or promising in recent talk, not of stores, libraries, or records, but of optical holographs as models for memory, models which allow for interference between memories and for redundancy of coding. How do connectionist models relate to traditional accounts of storage? In the early days of new connectionism, Rumelhart and Norman (1981: 2) wondered if distributed models of memory might 'offer an *alternative* to the "spatial" metaphor of memory storage and retrieval'. In using history actively to address these issues, offering retrospective analyses of old theories on the basis of new alternatives (compare Patton 1994: xi), I hope to find more subtle views in the past than are perceptible with the eyes of a straight historian of memory.

In a study of nineteenth-century views of 'the double brain', Anne Harrington acknowledges that her historical perspective could be immediately relevant to contemporary studies of hemispheric specialisation. But she retreats, noting that 'the historian must make every human effort to discipline his or her culturally colored subjectivity and take the historical evidence on its own terms' (1987: 5). I refuse this sensible historian's caution, and must flirt throughout with the twin dangers of nostalgia and present-centredness.

1.4 Self, body, memory, control

As I show in part II, early modern philosophers, aware of but disturbed by the dynamics of memory, held strange beliefs about the relation between self and body.[11] Like contemporary researchers on intentional forgetting but with extra attention to memory's bodily bases, they thought that training in the search after truth, the inculcation of cognitive discipline, can teach us to influence or directly act upon our own brains and spirits, to achieve true virtue by the exercise of moral dominion over our own bodily fluids. After the Fall, we cannot simply 'erase the brain's images' and 'instantaneously arrest the disturbance in the brain's fibers and the agitation of its spirits merely by considering [our] duty': our efforts 'to combat licentiousness' must now be indirect, through a neurological ethics (Malebranche, LO v. 4: 360, 357). Animal spirits tended to violate the moral agent's decency, and philosophers aware of the threat could not afford to ignore the microphysics of human nature. Moral physiologists attended intensely to methods and stratagems for gaining control over their own body processes. Memory may *seem* isolated from mechanisms of social control (Richards 1992: 102): but ways of remembering (as well as ways of thinking about memory) efficiently internalise norms in the body (Connerton 1989: 102; Strathern 1996: 28–36).[12]

After Wittgenstein, many philosophers mock these beliefs, just as they deny that action requires us to will our own body to move. They deny the intermediate steps of representation between intention and action, and blame the passive mechanistic conceptions of the body invented in seventeenth-century philosophy for such errors. But the body theorised by early modern neurophilosophers was never just an inert house for a ghostly soul. The body's fluids and spirits, and the traces it conceals, were always active, always escaping notice, always exceeding the domain of the will, always giving shape and flavour to the soul's plans.

It is too easy simply to say that there is no problem about the relation of self to body, or of self to memory. Dropping the dualists' ghostly soul acting behind and through dead flesh does not deliver up a final easy naturalistic view of action. All the difficult issues remain. We *do* seek to change relations between self and mental contents, and between self and body. Even if we *are*, in part, our

---

11 Compare Kihlstrom and Barnhardt (1993) on the 'prospects for strategic control of memory'. It is not that the idea of the self-regulation of memory is incoherent: remembering is, as they point out (1993: 114) a skilled activity, powerfully affected by early narrative training (Fivush and Reese 1992), and is constantly modified. But *control* of those modifications is desperately difficult.

12 Initial anthropological interest in connectionist models of memory is due to a desire to understand individual differences in response to cultural norms, without seeing social systems as monolithic hidden forces: socialisation is not the loading of a set of instructions, but the gradual build-up of specific, nuanced associative links into more stable representational structures. See, for example, Lawson 1993: 202–5; D'Andrade 1995: 136–49.

memories, and do not merely possess them, there are still dislocations between our parts, fragmentations, requiring philosophical and practical attention. So to think of memory as not archival but reconstructive is not to think of simple subjective 'spontaneous, alive and internal experience': instead, control in or of memory is always problematic, as Derrida suggests in calling the psychic archive 'a prosthesis of the inside' (Derrida 1996: 11, 19).

So philosophical theories of personal identity need not rigorously divide psychological from physical criteria for sameness of personhood over time. Memory requires the body's role in psychological continuity too: both historically, as early modern philosophers were less forgetful of physiology than Nietzsche thought, and theoretically, in attending to empirical constraints on the extent and nature of executive control. It is hard both to take psychophysiology seriously and to see rational inference as the basic characteristic of human cognition. Something has to give. Molly Bloom, not Sherlock Holmes, is the fictional figurehead for the neurophilosopher (chapter 11 below; contrast Fodor 1985b/1991: 39–41, 1987: 18).

I have no positive account of the true link between memory and personal identity. Marya Schechtman (1994) argues persuasively that facts about autobiographical memory disrupt philosophers' accounts of continuity of self, accounts commonly used to buttress theories of agency and moral responsibility. She argues that 'the immense complexity of the relation "memory of"' (1994: 9) challenges the Lockean assumption that all we, courts, or gods have to do in deciding problem cases about sameness of personhood is to check up on simple connections between two well-defined (past and present) moments of consciousness. Schechtman finds in empirical work on reconstructive personal memory more realistic pictures of the roles of narrative continuity in personal identity, acknowledging the ways we construct and change the past to make it 'more smooth and comprehensible'.

> It is precisely insofar as our memories smooth over the boundaries between the different moments in our lives, interpreting and reinterpreting individual events and experiences in the context of the whole, that we are able to produce a coherent life history. It is by summarising, condensing, and conflating the different temporal portions of our lives in memory that we are able to see them as parts of an integrated whole, and this integration blurs the distinction between different moments of our lives. (Schechtman 1994: 13)

Revised notions of self, which do not impose unity and continuity in advance, are obviously desirable. But I do not pursue this project here. I am less concerned with new decentred conceptions of subjectivity, with deciding in the abstract whether 'the subject' should be discarded or merely fragmented and dissolved, than with firming up historical and conceptual connections between certain accounts of memory and certain pictures of control. Only if memories are local items waiting to be scanned and dealt with is there need for a strong conception of an active, evaluating, transcendent self.

Some of these remarks may seem irrationalist, and they are certainly intended to undermine logicist overconfidence in the 'natural order' of cognition and memory. But there are still, I repeat, constraints on confusion. Not everything is equally interconnected, in memory or in the self (compare Cherniak 1986: 49–71 on memory holism and rationality). It is never a matter just of doubting at will, rather of acknowledging existing cracks in cultural consensus, reclaiming forgotten alternatives, buttressing independently motivated revisions with new ideas in cognition. The ways that representational spaces in memory get partitioned are not chosen by a self which transcends them, but neither are they entirely chance, for they are the sediment of a particular past in a specific brain and body. Alien memories, like feelings, can also be our own, and strangeness can lie inside (Lingis 1994b: 99–103). This is why memory has its sadness: because remembering is reconstructive, it is also destructive. Like anatomy, memory mangles and transforms its materials, tending to obliterate as well as construct. It is not only in repression and the organised forgetting imposed by oppressive regimes that memory is continuous with violence: there is also, as Francis Barker argues (1994: 85–6), a 'more rarely noted violence of recall'. Science does not inevitably neglect such cares.

I should say, finally, which of the many forms of memory distinguished by some psychologists I am concerned with. Superposition and distributed representation are particular mechanisms of persistence which need not apply across *every* domain of memory, with the extent of their application to be decided only by empirical research in neuropsychology across various systems and subsystems: the 'general theoretical proposals and ideas about the nature of memory' put forward by the authors I discuss can be suitably restricted when the range of superposition is decided (Schacter and Tulving 1994: 1). My interest is primarily in the subcategory of episodic memory which includes autobiographical remembering of specific episodes from a personal past (Larsen 1992). But I do not restrict attention to those personal recollective memories which are 'a "reliving" of the individual's phenomenal experience during that earlier moment' (Brewer 1996: 60), since many important effects of the personal past operate outside immediate awareness: thus these theories also cover implicit memory, the unconscious influence of past experience when the past, so to speak, leaks into, or contaminates, behaviour and ongoing cognition (Schacter 1995: 19). Further, I include passive remembering, in which events come to mind unrequested (Spence 1988). Autobiographical memories are not necessarily marked as such, nor do they come neatly dated (Larsen, Thompson, and Hansen 1996): there is room for the idea that some memories *become* autobiographical in use and improvisation, on the basis of both cultural and individual narrative norms (Barclay and Smith 1992: 75; Barclay 1996).

Appendix: memory and connectionism

For readers with little previous exposure to connectionism, I append a tiny simplified sketch (good introductions to connectionism and memory include McClelland and Rumelhart 1986; Smolensky 1988; Clark 1989: ch. 5; Churchland and Sejnowski 1989, 1992: chs. 3–4; Bechtel and Abrahamsen 1991: chs. 2–3; Rumelhart 1992; O'Brien 1993; Collins and Hay 1994; McClelland 1995).[13] I do not distinguish among its many varieties, but should note that some recognisably connectionist models do not use distributed representation: I ignore them here.

Minimal distributed connectionist memory networks involve the following ingredients. First, processing *units* have a continuous range of activation values, for instance between −1 and 1. Second, a (physical) *pattern of connectivity* between these units determines which units send output and receive input from which others. The pattern of connectivity can be unidirectional (feedforward nets) or can allow for feedback, via mutual input/output connections between units or through introducing extra context layers of units. Third, *weights* on each individual connection play a part in determining the transformation of the net output from one unit into input to another.

These connection weights between units change in the course of processing, usually after a stable *activity pattern* is achieved, according to one of a variety of learning algorithms. A unit's *activation value* is computed from the net input values communicated to the unit from the other units to which it is connected. This net input can either simply become the new activation value, or, more interestingly, can combine with the current activation value of the unit, the combination perhaps including a bias or threshold function, allowing nonlinearity or 'squashing functions' (Churchland and Sejnowski 1992: 62–5,109–12), by which small changes in input can cause large-scale shifts in activity. The gross activity pattern of a simple network (the whole set of individual activation values) is determined by the combination of the existing pattern of connectivity, the weights on these individual connections, the present activation values of the units, and the present inputs to the system.

Simple *computation* in such a network is the processing of continuous inputs so that the pattern of connectivity weights changes to produce a global pattern of activation which satisfies as many of the mutual constraints between units as possible. The network 'relaxes' into a stable state, settling into a solution through iterative operations performed in parallel by units which are only locally

13 As I am not defining differences between 'classical' and connectionist models of memory, I do not mean to overdo contrasts between them. The strategy is to develop on its own terms a connectionist approach to cognition, to see what such a thing might possibly be (van Gelder 1991c). Apart from the treatment of Fodor in part III below, I contribute to direct criticism of 'logicist cognitive science' merely by showing that connectionist-style theory was once common, submerged only by contingent historical changes.

connected to others and are under no global executive control. 'Remembering' is, like other operations, 'a process for producing an output' (Wiles 1994: 80).

How does memory occur in these mechanisms? When inputs are continually presented, patterns of activation come and go. But the shifting patterns leave traces behind them (McClelland 1995: 69–70):

> Forming a memory trace for something – say, an episode or event – begins with the construction of a pattern of activity over the processing units, with the experience itself strongly influencing the pattern. But the existing connections among the units will also influence the pattern constructed, thereby introducing the possibility of additions, omissions, and distortions. Storage of a trace of the episode or event then occurs through the modification of the strengths of the connections among the units.

Traces are in the interrelations between units rather than fixed to individual units, and ongoing processing takes place in the very same (parts of a) system as 'storage'.

New input is not just accumulated, preserved in an unprocessed form, but is filtered through existing representational space in which many traces are compacted (Touretzky and Pomerleau 1989; Elman 1993: 79; Wiles and Ollila 1993). So 'search' through memory cannot be a systematic scanning from a transcendent command viewpoint of many independent memory locations. Memories do not need specific addresses in order to be successfully retrieved. The indexing schemes of the traditional spatial metaphor break down if there is any error in the retrieval cue. But in connectionist models, the same activation pattern can be achieved in response to a number of different partial input descriptions, even if noisy or degraded: if some part of a distributed trace becomes active, the whole trace will tend to activate (Anderson and Hinton 1981; McClelland, Rumelhart, and Hinton 1986: 25–9). Without having to fix external context tags to every trace, context effects are built into the system of co-occurring units.[14]

Distributed models thus naturally exhibit *causal holism*. The representations or traces 'stored' in the same physical system are all automatically causally implicated in all the system's behaviour (O'Brien 1993). This is just because they are all in the same space and any reconstruction of one activity pattern is affected by everything else that has happened in that space. No network acts in freedom from its history. In part 1, I show how this causal holism operated in the brains and bodies described by animal spirits theory.

14 It is worth noting, in addition, the importance of the *absences* in connectionist models. The lack of central executives, explicit rules, explicit prototypes, discrete memory addresses, and external context tags has given these models at least some appeal even to philosophers who have been scathing about the claims of classical artificial intelligence to model human cognition (Dreyfus and Dreyfus 1988).

PART I

Animal spirits and memory traces

It would have made for clarity had Descartes and others discarded the phrase 'animal spirits', since it was difficult to disinfect the words of connotations wholly at variance with the assumptions of their physiology.

(Albert Balz 1951: 54)

The history of parallel distributed processing has itself been a case of parallel distributed processing.   (Elizabeth Valentine 1989: 355)

The descendants of Descartes comprise both theoreticians and fantasists; but Descartes himself is neither one nor the other, for there was no structure in 1640 that could prise and hold those categories apart.

(Catherine Wilson 1995: 34)

Introduction

The two long chapters in part I introduce my central themes, suggesting the virtues and pleasures of superficially silly old theories. Chapter 2 outlines the long background of animal spirits theory, questions the assumption that spirits were inevitably detrimental to the development of sciences of brain and mind, and describes strange 'pre-modern' human bodies, filled with turbulent fluids and rummaging spirits. In chapter 3 I reinterpret Descartes' 'philosophy of the brain'. Descartes used animal spirits flowing through brain pores in tentatively suggesting a distributed model of memory employing superpositional storage. I defend this anachronistic reading against four strong objections, and articulate surprising conclusions about dynamics and the body in Cartesian mechanism. This model of memory was much less common than animal spirits theory, which most accepted.[1] But its historical influence was powerful, as I show in part II.

Animal spirits, those 'ultimate oxymorons' (Krell 1990: 5), were neither animals nor spirits. Coursing through brain and nerves, they long remained candidates for the role of bearers of neural information: in philosophy, neurology, and medicine, this old physiological psychology was still all but ubiquitous in the early eighteenth century. Here is a first example of how spirits operate in remembering, which reveals how they were 'terrifically personified' (Rousseau 1989: 41) as contrary agents causing discomfort to the self in bewildering internal environments. A character in popular dialogues by a literary physician (Mandeville 1711/1976: 130) describes how animal spirits, 'volatil Messangers' seeking images 'from the dark Caverns of Oblivion' in the brain, will roam 'flying through all the *mazes* and *meanders*', and 'rommage the whole Substance of the medullary Labyrinth, whilst others ferret through the inmost Recesses of it with so much Eagerness and Labour, that the Difficulty they meet with sometimes makes us uneasie'. This indicates how spirits touched feeling as well as theory, in odd early modern experiences of uneasy innards. What some lament as 'confusions and contaminations' across discourses and levels

---

1 Spirits theory did not entail distributed representation: many who had quite different accounts of memory believed in animal spirits, while Hartley did not use animal spirits in his detailed distributed model (chapter 13). Distribution is conceptually independent of its specific physical instantiation. Yet there were looser suggestive connections: even those who officially attacked distribution often described the workings of animal spirits in terms of superposition and interference.

of explanation involving the spirits (Walker 1984: 223) can instead be seen as rare proximity between theory, culture, and phenomenology. The bodies in which spirits flowed are quite alien to us: the 'kinesthetic model of oriented flows' (Duden 1993: 85) was both hypothesis and lived reality.

I follow Gary Hatfield (1995: 185–6) in assuming that 'psychology' was as much a 'natural science' as any other by the seventeenth century, once we reject a false dichotomy between metaphysical conceptual work and truly scientific quantitative experiment. Theories of memory, for instance, were often independent of theology and yet were closely connected to deep concerns about self, society, and the past. The web of discourses around memory and brain was fruitfully extensive, the language of spirits theory spreading easily from feelings to fibres, pores to passions, between personal and subpersonal psychology. Spirits' liminal status, 'uncertainly poised between the medical and the metaphysical' (Myer 1984: 104), seems more enabling when we acknowledge a need for our own psychological theories to spread again, to encompass wider explananda and constraints. Cognitive science can no longer retain immunity to the subpersonal or to the social: stress-related hormones like epinephrine intensify the power of traumatic memories (Schacter 1996: 214–17), neuropeptides are coupled with context (Levin and Solomon 1990). Hanging round old texts and recalling the strangeness of our own cultural past, animal spirits help us listen to urgent old debates about the relations of body and self which customary historiographies have drowned out.

The outstanding scholarship on ancient, medieval, and Renaissance spirits theories on which I draw in chapter 2 is not matched for spirits in early modern science or culture. Knowledge of earlier, more holistic physiological traditions implicitly licenses an easy but false assumption that animal spirits disappeared during the rationalising scientific revolution of the seventeenth century. I discuss Descartes' spirits at such length not just to analyse his puzzling model of memory, but to query his talismanic place in philosophy and cultural studies alike as the demonic source of modern alienation. The permeation of psychology by context, culture, and body which spirits promoted (chapter 2) did not cease with the sudden fracture of self from matter with which Descartes is supposed to have urged on new scientists to master and possess passive nature. Mechanistic bodies are *also* dynamic (chapter 3).

2

Wriggle-work: the quick and nimble animal spirits

... and all that has been said about animal spirits, through more than fifteen
centuries, is mere conjecture. (Thomas Reid, *Essays* II.3: 248)

These vinegar tart spirits are too pearcing ...
Finde they a chinke, they'll wriggle in and in
(John Marston, *Antonio's Revenge* (1600) IV.2)

In one sense the worst accident that ever befell physiology was its intimate
association with animal spirits. (G.S. Rousseau 1989: 40)

They will forcibly gett into the porousnesse of it, and passe with violence betweene
part and part. (Kenelm Digby TT 4: 28)

2.1 Introduction: wriggle-work

Even if the 'ill-defined "animal spirits"' (Porter 1987: 177) were too charged
with imaginary values to achieve 'the specificity of a true scientific concept'
(Starobinski 1966: 179), their usage has its patterns and constraints. 'These
quick and nimble spirits', as the Cambridge Platonist John Smith called them
(1660/1979: 116), were meshed in a 'lush jungle of metaphor' (Rousseau 1989:
41). They failed 'to satisfy the spirit [l'esprit]' of one of their historians, Dr
Maurice Mignon (1934: 12): but, as their study proves, there is more than one
style of spirit.

Don't wriggle!

Ludwig Wittgenstein, ridiculing the neurophilosophical associationism of
William James and other 'scientific' psychologists, complained at the metaphysical machinations to which, he thought, the confused new discipline was
prone.

How needed is the work of philosophy is shown by James' psychology.
Psychology, he says, is a science, but he discusses almost no scientific questions. His movements are merely (so many) attempts to extricate himself from
the cobwebs of metaphysics in which he is caught. He cannot yet walk, or fly at
all he only wriggles. Not that that isn't interesting. Only it is not a scientific
activity. (Wittgenstein MS 165: 150–1, in Hilmy 1987: 196–7)

But why, I want to ask Wittgenstein, must scientists not wriggle? When it
seems possible to theorise and model the fuzzy, the fluid, the volatile, as now

through new connectionism and other sciences of complexity, such bans on questions on the fringes of science are puzzling. Sciences of the messy and the particular just do not fit a division between 'genuine' empirical accounts of repeatable and predictable observable phenomena, and, on the other hand, metaphysically tainted and prejudice-driven speculation.

Like Aphrodite, animal spirits would not be among those hypothetical entities which meekly hang around waiting to be observed (Feyerabend 1988, 1989). Making sense of the bits of the world which move might require a certain shimmying. Just as in late twentieth-century sciences 'nothing is less static than the nervous system' (Wilkes 1980: 115), so the baroque internal edifices of the early modern neurophysiology of spirits were maintained only by motion. The intervening nineteenth-century nervous system, in contrast, was less dynamic (Clarke 1968: 139–41; Changeux 1985: 29–30, 67). It is the sense that difficult mind/brain sciences are now returning to more uncertain explananda, taking time seriously, acknowledging the changing nature of their object, which motivates attention to earlier, stranger agendas.

Wriggle-work

'Wriggle-work', or 'wriggled-work', was a late seventeenth-century English style of engraving, for example on pewter, with (what would later be called) zigzag lines, fashioned by engravers known as 'wrigglers', which developed after the 'Glorious Revolution' of 1688 (OED, s.v. 'wriggle', 6a). Later, Hogarth (1753/1971: 39) praised the multiple encodings of the serpentine line which 'by its waving and winding at the same time different ways ... may be said to inclose (tho' but in a single line) varied contents'. This aesthetics of wriggling signals distributed memory, many traces sedimented in a single fold of the brain, where representation works neither linguistically nor by simple resemblance, neither by word nor by image.

I take wriggling as symptom and symbol of early modern sinuous paths imagined for animal spirits in the brain's memory folds; of the squirming discomfort which drove philosophers to advance tortuous evasive techniques against the unpredictable spirits; of intense attention in the early Royal Society to forms of writhing in nature, to eels, animalcules, insects in pieces, lizards and fish, and to the fluid mixtures inside bodies; of historical acknowledgement of somatopsychic and psychosomatic phenomena in which animal spirits easily united cognition and emotion (jealousy, says a Tourneur character, 'makes the spirit of the flesh begin to wriggle in my blood' (1611/1976 IV.i)); of inevitable spillage of language about memory, brain, and culture across disciplines and domains, between rhetoric and science, which violated seventeenth-century desire for linguistic purity and literality; of, generally, piercing awareness of constraints on freedom and control. Thomas Burnet wrote in 1690 that 'men will wriggle any way to get from under the force of a text' (in

OED, s.v. 'wriggle'): I generalise this into an image of men fleeing from memory, squirming to wrest back a semblance of control from the supplements (textual, artefactual, and physiological) used by and using the self.

Wriggling spirits

Theoretical 'wriggle-work' hints at how discourses of the spirits disregarded later boundaries, both between disciplines which came to be distinct (like neurophysiology and philosophy) and between apparent classes of phenomena (such as solid and fluid, or natural and supernatural) which these theoretical entities, being imaginary, never had to respect. Spirits traversed easy early modern passages between life sciences and literature, physics and philosophy, cognition and cosmology, pneumatology and poetry.

This is not yet the comprehensive empirical study of the mass of primary source material on spirits which Rousseau has requested (1969/1991: 5–7, 20–1), though it brings up many questions for such a study to address. But the difficulty of the multidisciplinary history required is severe, and I leap over possible microstudies of the uses, connections, and implications of spirits theories in specific times and places.

2.2 The dustbin theory of animal spirits

The prevailing account of animal spirits in the history of physiology might be called the 'dustbin theory'. On this view, spirits theorists, repeatedly committing category mistakes, concocted a spurious unity to what was in fact a hopelessly heterogeneous collection of phenomena. For one historian, *spiritus* was 'an inherently self-contradictory concept ... so to speak, a dustbin into which you threw fundamental antinomies' (Walker 1953/1985: 150). Another was confident enough to complain of the spirits' 'almost paralysing effect' on neuroscientific progress (Brazier 1958: 198).[1]

If animal spirits were disastrous for science, then nothing, or nothing worth remembering, was lost in the replacement of such an over-inclusive concept by tightly defined alternatives. We can now see spirits, it seems, as useless catch-all constructs, suggesting deceptively simple accounts of problems which should have been kept in the 'too hard' basket. Walker, the pre-eminent historian of Renaissance spirits theories, rejects as incoherent Descartes' mechanical accounts of imagination and memory (where spirits 'function like

---

1 Examples of this disdain can be multiplied. It was all too easy in difficult explanation to resort to *spiritus*, 'that most adaptable category of theoretical entities'; various uses of that 'quasi-magical fluid' animal spirit simply 'lent an air of science' to primitive and folkloric, or rationalist and metaphysical speculations (Copenhaver 1991: 379; Rousseau 1976: 147; DePorte 1974: 5; compare Miller 1978: 292–4). There could be no 'good explanation' in the life sciences, judged G.S. Rousseau (1969/1991: 5), until the nineteenth century (when animal spirits were finally consigned to the dustbin in which they always belonged).

transmission in a car'), but allows that medical and animal spirits did no harm when 'used merely as a stop-gap, and a scientist's attention was not concentrated on them'. He praises Vesalius, in contrast to Bacon and Descartes, for wasting little time on the spirits (Walker 1985a: 126).[2]

Was the heyday of the animal spirits then just an aberrant episode in the history of science? Cannot this venerable theory, 'that most firmly entrenched of Galen's fancies' (Wightman 1958: 135), embedded in myth, religion, and antiquated pseudo-sciences, be reasonably neglected? I suggest that it is dismissed on peril of missing important, alien aspects of the world-views we have lost.

A test case in conceptual change

Further, spirits theory poses problems about conceptual change and about the reference of theoretical terms as sharp as the familiar cases of phlogiston and caloric. What are we to say spirits theorists were talking about? What decides, in practice, whether terms which (seek to) designate theoretical entities are jettisoned or retained, eliminated or smoothly reduced (by identification) to terms for new hypothetical constructs? This is important because the absence of a typical set of overlapping causes (whether 'internal' and 'rational' or simply sociological, political, and rhetorical) for historical cases of elimination and radical theory-change seems to leave us at sea as to how current and future change might (let alone should) occur (Stich 1996: 63–82, 199). Philosophers of pragmatist bent who are sensibly pessimistic about rationalistic accounts of the history of science run the risk of denying that radical conceptual change can ever happen, or instead, sensibly (Heilbron 1982; Hacking 1983) reject general theory in favour of attention to technological and practical change in science.

The dustbin theory, constructing animal spirits as a historical accident, suggests that any empirical advances which did occur in early modern neurophysiology must have been independent of the faulty theoretical commitment to animal spirits. Philip Kitcher's careful defence of scientific progress in the face of historicising criticism (1993a, 1993b) relies on just this kind of result from the history of science. Discovery and conceptual progress require the *narrowing* of the 'reference potential' (Kitcher 1978: 536–46) of central concepts so as to exclude old metaphysical and moral associations, and hone in on the genuine explananda in new fields. Historical investigation is meant to show that, where past theories were partly successful despite their use of non-

---

2 Walker's historiography illustrates the need for sensitivity to modern difficulties in these domains, to acknowledge current disagreements about neuro/psycho/philosophical problems, let alone solutions. He complains, for example, that Campanella's use of spirits in psychology was not explanatory, because spirits blur the mind/body divide (1958/1975: 230–1). What position on dualism, or on levels of explanation in psychology, is assumed here? It is significant that, in rejecting spirits or nervous fluids, Vesalius ruled out the whole project of connecting neural and cognitive functions (*Fabrica* (1543) VII, in Singer 1952: 1–6, 39–40, 49–50).

referential terms like animal spirits (Kitcher's example, following Laudan, is ether), 'the failures of reference and the false claims do not contribute to the successes' (Kitcher 1993b: 174).

Simplicity is an epistemic virtue in almost every philosophy of science. Yet it is precisely the narrowing of neurological reference which remains at issue in comparing spirits theory with its successors. The question can be put by asking which side spirits lie on Adrian Cussins' distinction, in a wonderful paper on eliminativism, between 'conflations' and 'misplaced composites'. Conflations are relatively harmless, imprecise but not incoherent yokings of two concepts from the same explanatory domain, as 'weight' conflates mass and force (Cussins 1993: 243–4). Misplaced composites, in contrast, are unnatural and confused hybrids which arise 'where the early theory employs concepts which are a combination of components of other concepts which come from distinct explanatory domains, or which subserve quite different functional interests' (1993: 244). Misplaced composites like mermaids serve no useful function in ontology and should be eliminated from conceptual schemes which seek contact with reality. Phrenologists' concept of physiology illegitimately mixed brain anatomy with 'a mix of psychological, social and evaluative notions' which 'from the perspective of a successor neuropsychology . . . belong to distinct explanatory domains' (1993: 244–6).

But how do we know which explanatory domains are distinct? As the phrenology example shows, Cussins is clear: 'which concepts belong to the same explanatory domain is determined from the point of view of the successor theory' (1993: 243). In conceptual crisis, successors have to be fought for: the notion of Man is, Cussins suggests (1993: 246), 'from a feminist successor perspective . . . a misconceived composite formed from the idea of universal humankind and the idea of certain masculine qualities. It licenses illegitimate inferences to the form or nature of humanity. And again the proper response is eliminativist: in that sense of Man, there is no Mankind.'

For some two hundred years, it has been clear that the concept of animal spirit united domains which should be kept isolated, and thus that a good theory's constructs ought to be narrower, less wriggly, than were those imaginary fluids. The conviction of a concept as a 'misplaced composite' from the successor perspective leaves no links intact or, more strongly, thinkable across domains which were once intimately interlaced.[3] These studies, then,

---

3 The kind of incommensurability at stake here is close to that called 'dissociation' by Ian Hacking (1983: 69–72), rather than the general incommensurability across different theories sometimes thought to result from meaning holism. Dissociation, in Hacking's Feyerabendian sense (his example is a comparison of Laplace and Paracelsus), occurs when it is hard to know, from the successor perspective, how to even approach settling the truth-value of sentences (or the rationality of methods) in the earlier world. We cannot easily assert or deny the earlier sentences, or can only start talking and thinking the old way if we become 'alienated or dissociated from the thought of our own time' (1983: 71).

challenge the natural view that the over-adaptable spirits were such hopeless composites. The replacement of the strange old world in which they existed with tighter, more isolated concepts was also a loss.

Spirits and the historiography of neuroscience

References to the disastrous paralysis of physiology in the years when it 'was for a long time tributary to the representation of animal spirits' (Starobinski 1966: 176) sanction continuing triumphalist evaluations in histories of neurophysiology. Clarke and Jacyna claim, remarkably, that every idea of 'nerve force, fluid, spirit, or whatever' before Jiri Prochaska's concept of nerve conduction was an 'untestable hypothesis that obstructed progress' (1987: 163).

Such historical brashness assumes considerable current consensus, as if the relation (or lack of relation) between the domains which animal spirits were thought to connect is transparent to us. There is no doubt that the dropping of explicit philosophical baggage did encourage the neurosciences, though it is harder than most histories allow to work out exactly how and why this happened. There's no doubt too that new techniques and methods in the utterly different world of modern neurological investigation, immersed in new institutional and social practices, have produced both new knowledge and new ways of intervening successfully in the domain under investigation. I do not advocate replacing brain research with interdisciplinary animal spirits projects: nostalgia fails, and anyway, in our world, nothing quite like animal spirit exists to be studied.

My point here is that, in late twentieth-century mind/brain sciences, it is often difficult to say for sure that historical links across what now seem disparate domains were just wrong. It is important, for example, to wonder again whether historical meshing of the explanatory domains of reproduction and reasoning (2.3.7 and chapter 9 below) really does show that animal spirit was a misplaced composite: the domains which our best theories connect do change. Many feel the need again to connect cognition and culture, to question the boundaries which keep apart not just neuroscience and philosophy of mind, but also psychology and history.

The uncertain status of present and future mind/brain sciences, then, should motivate resistance to easy dismissals of weird old views. Two of the best historians of neuroscience operate by showing how 'outmoded' ideas were replaced by 'revolutionary' ones, while giving some space to ideas 'of less lasting importance' (Clarke and Jacyna 1987: 1). The integration of modern knowledge into historical contexts may make sense for the lower-level

Immersion in the details of weird old theories makes it clear that this is not an all-or-nothing matter: a certain dissociation of this sort is often in place anyway, especially among historians, and occasionally it can be used to make better sense of strange words from the past about bodies, nerves, memory, or whatever.

neuroscience (from the cerebrospinal axis to the vegetative nervous system) which is the focus of their indispensable work. But in the more neurophilosophical context of nerve and brain function, there is no clear end of inquiry in the present to which history could show the past inevitably leading. The relevant consensus just does not exist. Careful observation with wonderful technology has provided astonishingly detailed maps of the brain, and incomparably more raw material for explanation. But beyond neuroanatomy and the neurophysiology of the individual cell, it is not that easy to point now to a developed corpus of successful theory against which historical shifts could be evaluated. Approaches to the dynamic systems of brain and body which could conceivably influence and alter our crude high-level, common-sense-inspired macroscopic psychologising are barely visible under the weight of experimental data.[4] So following Canguilhem (1977), I treat history of science, especially of these sciences, as not itself a science, for it demands unbalanced judgement, polemic, and selective evaluation. The cast of any meta-narrative of the history of physiological psychology depends in part on its picture of the present.

2.3 Spirits, bodies, and souls

Multiple connotations already pervaded ancient concepts of spirit,[5] and few associations had disappeared by the seventeenth century (Armogathe 1984): the repertoire of problems for spirits theorists evolved by accretion and eclectic superposition, in complex processes of transmission traced by outstanding historians of ideas (Verbeke 1945; Putscher 1973; Rist 1985). I deliberately flatten disputes and differences across the tangled history of ancient, medieval,

---

4 Churchland and Sejnowski acknowledge (1992: 16) that the old description of the neurosciences as data-rich but theory-poor 'remains true . . . inasmuch as we do not yet know how to explain how brains see, learn, and take action'. They spell out (1992: 157–63) contingent reasons for the long dominance of research on individual cells, claiming that the advent of distributed representation may foreshadow the end of 'the era of the single neuron'. In fact, in the case of memory at least, many theorists have always accepted that groups, networks, or paths of cells are more likely than single neurons to be the functionally relevant unit (Colville-Stewart 1975: 200–12): but the point remains that larger-scale dynamics are desperately difficult. Interpretations of the gorgeous results of new brain imaging techniques reveal the difficulty of generalising across the brains of different subjects (Lloyd 1996).

5 Delatte, Govaerts, and Denooz (1984), in a neat semi-quantitative study of spiritus in classical Latin, describe a chronological shift from concrete/physical contexts, to moral usage, and on to spiritual senses. Ideas on the sources of Greek usage (Tanner 1985; Young 1991/1993: xxi–xxiv, 381–7) need closer integration with anthropological studies of intermediary entities and their functions (Boyer 1993; Strathern 1996: 153–76). One place to start is Kuriyama's marvellous cross-cultural study of concepts of breath and spirit in ancient Greece and China (Kuriyama 1995). My work remains, with other studies of spirits in history of philosophy and medicine, over-confined to intellectual history, unable to address the contexts of use of the concepts.

and Renaissance traditions in order briefly to convey the complexity of the conceptual inheritance of early modern spirits theorists. In its broad outlines, the physiology of spirits commonly attributed to Galen was, with its varied versions and internal tensions, somehow rendered compatible with much medieval philosophy and theology (Bono 1984: 93). The diversity and adaptability of these doctrines is the point, for there are no clear lines between the strands which developed into intelligible later theory in theology or physiology and those which resonate only with pre-modern mentalities. Use of the same word for 'those spirits which are methylated and those which are angelic' (Davie 1963: 48) was both awkward and productive. 'Spirit' forces difference on the historian, since the 'physiological use of the word is probably the most obscure to the modern reader, who is most likely to encounter it in a bar or a church' (Kemp 1990: 26).

A surprising number of the specific spirit doctrines discussed here survived the apparent or rhetorical overthrow of their ancient theoretical contexts. It is much too simple to say that great scientific advances of the sixteenth and seventeenth centuries 'left the old medical theories derelict', old ideas concerning spirit going by the board with 'the wrecking of the Galenic physiology' in the scientific revolution (Singer and Underwood 1962: 137–8). But I stress again that there are many other histories of spirits. I omit, for example, classifications and applications of chemical spirits in alchemical and Paracelsian traditions (Davis 1973; Debus 1984), which significantly transformed the concepts (Clericuzio 1994): but, I submit, use of spirits in alchemy and chemistry is not as surprising as their continued presence in supposedly austere mechanical philosophies.[6] Condensing an extraordinary conceptual range at least hints at the difficulty of articulating the strangeness of 'pre-modern' bodies and the fluids which whirled through them.

I sketch the spirits' associations under nine headings: etymology, theology, cosmobiology, the occult traditions, the message, medicine and the body, reproduction and reasoning, physiology, and moral neurophilosophy.

2.3.1 Etymology

The richly ambiguous noun phrase 'animal spirit' derives from Greek *pneuma psychikon*. But the link (via Latin *anima*) to *psyche* as principle of life could easily be neglected. Swift caricatures the brain's mechanical spirits as a 'Crowd of

---

6 The 'metamorphosis of meaning' which Clericuzio (1994: 51, 72) thinks distanced English chemical notions of spirit from Descartes' scheme in fact involved a set of principles about holism and the interactions of bodily spirits with celestial and chemical spirits which, I argue, was also present in mechanical physiology. Although clearly Paracelsian and chemical notions of volatility and nitrous spirits were alien to Descartes, the consequences for cognitive theories were not necessarily great. From my perspective, Clericuzio (1994: 68) underestimates the possible complexity of 'purely mechanical' processes in Cartesianism.

little Animals, but with Teeth and Claws extremely sharp' (1704/1984: 173). The satire is sharp, for rather than the soft associations with wind, breath, and life which animal spirits might have retained from both *pneuma* and *psyche*, more telling in practice were wilder, harsher metaphorical connotations of violence, randomness, and transience. Early modern spirits would be regularly person-ified as animalistic agents mischievous in the innards, or as combining into a vicious mob, scratchy and hard to control, ill-disciplined beasts lacerating the self from the inside.

The qualification 'animal' applied primarily to spirits in natural philosoph-ical contexts. Crudely, between Galen and Descartes animal spirits were but the 'highest' of three spirits in living things. Natural spirits had their 'seat' in the liver, vital spirits in the heart, and animal spirits in the brain.[7] Despite uncer-tainty about just how the nervous system related to veins and arteries, in most accounts animal spirits were elaborated from blood by some filtering process. The tradition included no clear distinction between the life functions and the cognitive functions of physiological spirits.

2.3.2 Theology

'Spirit' alone could refer, not just to the Holy Spirit (a concept indebted to the pneumatic tradition (Rist 1985)), but also to the individual soul as locus of moral evaluation, or to the immortal soul, locus of personal survival beyond bodily death. 'Animal spirits', though, traditionally operated *between* body and soul. Medieval theologies of spirits (Putscher 1973; Bono 1984) rarely remained detached from natural philosophy in this context. One function of animal spirits was to relate ontology to moral theology by elucidating the connection between organic individuals and supra-individual cosmic and/or divine forces. The ambiguous human is located between disembodied intelli-gences (angelic spirits) and animals (full of bodily spirits but, on most views, lacking individual souls).[8] The communication of spirits between our corpo-real and incorporeal aspects is a microcosmic enactment of macrocosmic transmissions between mortal and immortal realms.

Ontological uncertainty Divisions between soul, spirit, and body could in-volve three ontologically distinct substances, with scholastic and Renaissance

---

7 See the OED, s.v. 'animal spirits'. In a 1543 description of the 'thre kindes of spirites', for example, the 'animal spirite' gives 'facultie of movynge, and felynge' and is so called 'bycause it is the first instrument of the soule, whyche the Latins call *animam*'. It is unclear whether this tripartite scheme was Galen's or was developed later (Temkin 1951/1977, 1973; Wilson 1959; Siegel 1973: 134–9).

8 Our nature is 'not simple but multiple, not certain but ambiguous, in between mortal and immortal things' (Pomponazzi 1516/1948: 282–3). This thought might glorify us cuspy creatures on the cosmic up, as in Pico della Mirandola, or, as for Pomponazzi, remind that we have 'not intellect but the trace and shadow of intellect' (1516/1948: 322). Attitudes depended on views of free will (Sutton 1991).

theorists often taking spirits to be the first instrument of the soul. Medievalists are right to complain (Bynum 1995a: 13–14) that the use of trinary (not binary) categories is one respect in which modern attributions of dualism and denigration of the body to the entire Western Christian philosophical past are too swift. But the tripartite metaphysics too was unstable.

Some, like Albertus Magnus, sought ontological economy by placing spirits with body on the physical side of a single metaphysical dichotomy: animal spirits were intermediaries only in that the non-physical acts more easily or more directly on them than on grosser matter. Others, comfortable with Neoplatonic hierarchies of superimposed entities, conflated medical spirits (in linguistics and ontology) with transcendent spiritual forces, exhorting the moral ideal of ascent on the scale of emanations by spirituous imitation of the divine (Bono 1984: 112). But recurrent drives for theoretical simplicity left spirits theologically problematic. It was an ancient suggestion, probably Praxagoras' (Rist 1985), that spirits or *pneuma* should be identified with *psyche*. But when others argued that the spirits were physical, the way was open for medical materialists to combine these moves and heretically identify the soul itself with corporeal spirits (Walker 1958/1975).

Spiritual vehicles   One other theological complication lies in the connection of animal spirits to astral vehicles. Something in humans responds to, or is in sympathy with, cosmic 'vehicles' between the corrupt earth and the untainted realm of wholly disembodied intelligences. Even outside suspect demonological contexts, in which unguents and ointments were used to aid the passage of spirits through the skin to join their supernatural kin (IS 11.15.8; Ginzburg 1966/1983: 17–18), this could speak to a desire to surrender individuality. The spirit realm, from the physiological to the astral, promised merging, the swallowing-up of the soul in the divine, ecstatic rebirth through being purged of the longing to retain separateness (Walker 1985b; Screech 1980: 158–73). Theorists from Renaissance Averroists (Skulsky 1968; Pine 1986) and Ficinian Platonists through the English atomist Nicholas Hill (Jacquot 1974: 113) and on to Cambridge Platonist Henry More (Walker 1984) sought the dispersion of their spirits into a larger reservoir. These world-soul beliefs, challenging individualistic conceptions of the person from a mystic point of view, are the theological counterparts of cosmobiological links in natural philosophy with spirits outside the body.

2.3.3 Cosmobiology

Animal spirits linked the human body to the cosmos in natural philosophy and medicine as well as in theological contexts. Bodily spirits took pleasure in uniting with the sky (Donio, in Walker 1958/1975: 193–4). The tradition offered naturalistic images of the human body embedded in earthly, astronomical, and astrological environments, a vulnerable container, the boundaries between physiological and celestial processes incessantly breached.

Aristotle had denied the identity of *pneuma* and cosmic ether or quintessence while being brief about both (Reiche 1960; Nussbaum 1978: 143–64; Annas 1993: 18–20; Freudenthal 1995: 106–48). Stoics, at least by the time of Chrysippus, aligned biology and cosmology by taking *pneuma* to pervade inert matter as a creative principle: *pneuma* is ether, a mix of air and fire. Proper life and cognitive functions depend on the difficult maintenance of *krasis*, the appropriate blending of elements which require *pneuma* for coherence. Death, then, is the conflagration or relaxation of *pneuma*, for the cosmos as for the individual (Sambursky 1959; Hahm 1977: 136–74; Rist 1985).

The traditions promoted a picture of the body permeated by the world, a temporary pocket of stability in a fluid cosmos (for Aristotle on physiological and moral blending, see Tracy 1969: 157–333). Before Erasistratus, medical theorists thought *pneuma* enters the body through the skin: Erasistratus' claim that it all derives from inhaled air retained the wholly external origin (Wilson 1959). Galen took psychic *pneuma* to have an internal source, in blood exhaled with our innate heat, and to be maintained by respiration: but subsequent pneumatic theory in both Neoplatonism (Tarrant 1985) and medical naturalism (Klibansky, Panofsky, and Saxl 1964) stressed the body's openness to cosmic ethers.

In the work of Henry of Langenstein in the fourteenth century, 'the movement of spirits and humors throughout the body parallels the sweating world of meteorological exhalations and vapors' (Steneck 1976: 137). Motions of body fluids are described, in this tradition, in various quasi-circulation metaphors: both nervous fluids and blood move to the rhythms of ebbing and shifting external forces, compared to irrigation or to the specific directional flows of waters in the Euripus channel (Bitbol-Hespériès 1990: 158–73). Medical views of bodily mixtures as dependent on local environment (2.3.6 below) required in turn the larger cosmic context of criss-crossing ethers and fluids, the twin threats of turbulence and stagnation always barely kept at bay (Barkan 1975: 8–60).

2.3.4 Spirits and the occult traditions

In cultures which have not valued impermeable ontological barriers, when 'the categories of material, mental, and spiritual are meaningless' (Hesse 1961/1970: 36–8), even physiological animal spirits are entwined in quite other histories of spirit. *Pneuma* can still be seen as the key to 'the origin of the sacred' (Young 1991/1993). In addition to the bewildering array of spirits in early modern folklore (West 1969), they retained privileged roles in the occult sciences of Renaissance elites.

Most obvious is the special association between animal spirits and evil spirits. Melanchthon gave prototypical moral advice about controlling the unruly fluids: 'when devils occupy the heart, by their blowing they trouble the spirits in the heart and brain . . . Let us therefore look to our nature and diligently rule it' (in Walker 1984: 228). Technique and theory, knowing how and knowing that, meshed in spiritual and demonic magic, since understanding of the networks of forces criss-crossing the spirit realm was necessary for any attempt to control or intervene.[9]

Animal spirits were also susceptible to spirits of wine, and the aerial spirits which carry melody, thus explaining physiological responses to alcohol and to music. Advice on diet and regimen in the care of the spirits was given in medical texts relying on the spirits' openness to environmental changes. But as Walker's (1953/1975) account of Ficino and his influence shows, there was a continuum between commonplace physiological and secretive magico-metaphysical uses of spirits. Ficino's notorious advice on animating statues required dormant spirits to be activated by other forms of spirituous input. The Neoplatonic revival of the association between melancholy and genius from the pseudo-Aristotelian *Problemata* (Babb 1951: 58–67; Klibansky, Panofsky, and Saxl 1964) was not independent of physiological theory: Ficino explains the vulnerability of intellectuals to melancholy as the result of constant usage of animal spirits in cognition (Walker 1953/1985: 133). Careful managing of spirits might allow privileged access to supra-natural phenomena. Those in the know hoped and strove for ecstasy (rather than possession), scholar's melancholy (as opposed to the constant threats of mania and madness), or inspired contact with the Holy Spirit (rather than the encroach of Satan, wriggling snakily into animal spirits).

One common factor in a number of occult uses of the diverse spirits is the attempt to deal with action at a distance, by (in different contexts) understanding, encouraging, or preventing it. The notorious weapon-salve cure in which ointments are applied not to a wound but to the weapon which inflicted it, popularised by Kenelm Digby in the seventeenth century, depended on streams of spirituous particles flowing across the distance between weapon and wound (Dobbs 1971: 5–10). It was the power of music to operate on its listeners without apparent contact which rendered it so mysteriously powerful, and so susceptible to spirituous explanation. The sympathies and correspondences of Renaissance occult knowledge-systems (which so appalled the seventeenth-century mechanists who allowed causation only by impulse) were loosely reliant on nested systems of spirits in the cosmos, the environment, the human body, and in inanimate objects, with the animal spirits of medical theory holding a crucial microcosmic position. In chapter 4, I examine how the spirits came to play parallel

---

9 Good overviews of the many contexts of 'magic' in Renaissance and early modern periods include Webster 1982; Copenhaver 1990; Henry 1990.

roles even for those mechanists, in explaining *away* apparent action at a distance. Differences of ontological detail notwithstanding, spirits in many systems had the privileged capacity of connecting present to absent, bridging spatial or temporal gulfs by somehow holding or reaching objects or information which would otherwise be inaccessible or lost. (Summers (1987: 110–24) sketches the operation of this principle in Renaissance aesthetics.) This is a source of the necessary role animal spirits played in explanations of memory.

2.3.5 The message: animal spirits as analogue angels

As unobservable intermediaries, animal spirits carried messages between realms otherwise irretrievably distinct. In this particular logic of the liminal, the bearers of information between natural and supernatural, visible and invisible, body and soul, periphery and centre, muscles and brain focused concerns about the integrity of the message, on its way in from sinner or senses, or on its way out from God, soul, or will. Informational purity was in doubt, the fickle spirits transforming or condensing their contents, opening up dangerous distortion and confusion. This was a fascinating problematic: John Donne, suggests Carey (1990: 253), found animal spirits alluring just because, like angels, they bridged divided worlds.

It is not surprising, then, that leading Renaissance spirits theorists were also interested in cryptography. Problems of the message preoccupied the occultists Trithemius and Agrippa, who saw ciphers as more predictable substitutes or supplements for spirits in the representation and processing of information. Better mechanisms of transmission and decoding might augment the magician's powers, and allow the tapping of angelic communication across the spirit realm (Walker 1958/1975: 85–96). I argue elsewhere that systems for the external selection, compression, and storage of information, such as shorthand, brachygraphy, and tachygraphy, were intimately related to changing Renaissance models of mental representation (Sutton 1997).[10] Here I am interested in a more specific informational role of spirits, in transmitting messages from body, senses, and muscles to the deep interior and back again.

It is in this sense that animal spirits functioned as analogue angels. Each fleeting pattern of spirit motions was a scheming Hermes scooting between soul and body, authority and executive. As bearers of neural information, spirits had to negotiate the same risks of noise and interference whether the end and source of their journey was soul or brain. Ontology matters less than the problem of control over processes of transmission, the fear of losing order in the message. Communication depends on the independence of an abstract code from the vagaries of its instantiation, the possibility of extracting

---

10 Seventeenth-century cryptographers also invoked Trithemius: for Hooke see Henry 1989a: 171–8. Generally see Salmon 1972: 60–7, 110–16, 144–5; and Slaughter 1982: 135–40.

sameness out of a confused background of difference (Serres 1982). But repetition was never the animal spirits' strong point.

Animal spirits were traditionally the first instruments of the soul, shuttling between thought and bodily sense. They functioned as 'Internuncii' even in post-Cartesian physiological psychology, when the 'exquisitely small Particles' were taken to be themselves corporeal (Mandeville 1711/1976: 131, 125). As the 'tye or medium' between soul and body (Burton 1621/1989: 140–1), these threshold beings patrolled an uncertain boundary which had to be continually crossed in all cognition and action. If reason is 'but *Harmony*; a certain modification and tuning of the parts, (either the Spirits, or the Filaments,) that are the immediate instruments of cogitation' (Burthogge 1694/1976: 134), then distemper or jarring in the spirits could pervert commands of the will.

These angels of the microcosm were even, it turns out, occasionally so-called. Where Henry More saw animal spirits only as 'congenerous to the ethereal Vehicles of the Angels or Genii' (IS II. 18. I: 139),[11] Anne Conway identified them. For her, physiological spirits are only barely contained in the body, always on the verge of breaching its boundaries. Ministering bodily spirits are derived from food, and eventually the most subtle, those which may flow out and carry off something of the self, are 'the proper angels of a man' and can be good or bad. 'Subtile' animal spirit is a 'volatile Body' (1690/1982: 210–11, 217–19).

The uncertainty of transmission in such a tricksy fluid medium was one motivation for attempts to guarantee control. The thirteenth-century Platonist Alfred of Sarashel, for instance, saw the irradiation of light as a perfect model for the operation of spirits in the body because of the (apparent) non-temporality of transmission (compare chapter 5 below on Hooke's use of the metaphysics of light in describing memory and centralised control). The unleashing of spirits into time would produce error, so the gaps across which messages need to be brought are closed or denied. Albertus Magnus, in contrast, committed to the corporeality of spirits, rejected celestial analogies and likened spirit instead to smoke or vapour (Bono 1984: 116–18). This medieval debate over physiological metaphors raises just the right questions, for there is no guarantee that the medium which memory and neural messages alike seem to require will be transparent, securely transmitting an original encoding. Not every angel, after all, is immune to darkness.

2.3.6 Medicine and the body

Animal spirits, like other old fluids, ran through the pores (*poroi*) of humoral bodies. Historians of medicine sketch patterns of transmission of ancient

---

11   This connection is pervasive in More's work. Yet one bewildered biographer, noting that Walker 'emphasizes the relation between More's concept of spirit and the spirits of physiology', complains 'I confess inability to see the force of this argument' (Hall 1990: 282)!

medical theory through Arab and medieval sources, and seek a basis for understanding the relation of theory to medical practice in dealing with 'pre-modern' bodies (Temkin 1973; Pouchelle 1983/1990; Siraisi 1990; Park 1992). Some use anthropological evidence, notably from Melanesian and European folk biomedicine, to ask whether the open bodies of these old learned theories might also be detected in the practices and beliefs of quite other and much later societies (Duden 1991: 34–7, 45; Strathern 1996: 53, 107–38). Of course it is misleading to isolate the spirits from the vast systems of fluid exchange within the body and between the body and the world: but here, by using the spirits alone, I seek to convey that body history for Western medicine reveals not only the spongy, thrown, fragile bodies documented by these historians, but also the survival of various forms of body holism into much later physiological schemes as spirits were incorporated into pulsing body-machines. If philosophers did help to isolate the human body as a mere container, they did so much later.

Spirits and medical holism In the broadly 'Galenist' tradition (tied only loosely to specific Galenic texts), animal spirits were among the 'naturals', body parts like blood, elements, and humours common to all. The term 'contra-naturals' then covered pathological conditions. The theoretical division most interesting here is 'non-natural'. A rough consensus was that the 'six things non-natural' were air or climate, food and drink, sleep and wake, motion and rest, evacuation and repletion, and passions or perturbations of mind (Rather 1968; Niebyl 1971; Jackson 1986: 11–12). 'A dynamic body deserves an expectant medicine' (Canguilhem 1994: 129), and (as in the Hippocratic treatise *Airs, Waters, Places* (Lloyd 1978: 148–69)) attention to individuals' non-naturals motivated medical advice on regimen, diet, sexual behaviour, travel, and responses to stress and distress. As Kuriyama shows, the earlier meaning of *pneuma* as wind pervades Hippocratic writings, bequeathing to later theories of spirit the twin problems of environmental influence and radical contingency (Kuriyama 1995: 7–14).[12] The state of the naturals, the humours and spirits, depended directly on influences picked up, usually through the blood but also directly through the skin, from climate, environment, nutrition, and emotion. So, as Vivian Nutton argues (1995: 141), highly individualised schemes of therapy could fit on to the holistic framework. In practice, the scheme allowed for multicausal accounts of disease. In continual interaction with the *krasis* (blend) of internal fluids, the non-naturals combined to produce an individual's current, fragile balance against imminent

---

12 Kuriyama's remarkable argument about *pneuma*'s shift from 'wind' to 'breath' deserves far more attention than is possible here. For him, the shift marks not so much an internalisation of the obscure dynamics inherent in contingent environmental influence, as the creation of autonomous volitional agents in isolated bodies (Kuriyama 1995: 13–27).

stagnation or excess. Only those who denied animal spirits and their influence by airs and places, like William Harvey, would 'cut man off from his environment' (Frank 1980: 40).

An individual's fluid balance was always specific. It depended not only on an initial, biological temperament (by which some were predisposed, for example, to melancholy and domination by Saturn), for this temperament *was* just the dynamic mixture of fluids in different proportions and conditions, changing over time in accordance with external influences as well as the drying or cooling rhythms of the life-cycle. Theories of individual *complexio* were at once medical and cultural, supporting particularised narratives of what Nancy Siraisi endorses as 'the history of human life' (1990: 101–4, 109–14; compare Babb 1951: 1–20). The departure of internal mixture from its (relative, changing) 'proper blend' (the narrower meaning of *krasis*) due to excessive or insufficient environmental or psychological input was a framework for explaining not only disease (Richardson 1985) but also the varieties of health (Cook 1990: 405–11). Individual differences in personality and in cognition were acknowledged in linked medieval theories of astrology and humours, which did not rely exclusively on either biological temperament or social influence (Kemp 1990: 89–110).

These psychophysiological frameworks were dynamic in the sense that they assumed the importance of what modern dynamicists in cognitive science call 'continuous reciprocal causation' (Clark 1997: 163). Andy Clark's powerful recent synthesis of work on embodied cognition is particularly suggestive in the light of this sketch of the history of the old fluid physiologies. There are 'mutually modulatory influences linking brain, body, and world', with causal coupling between all the components (1997: 163). As in jazz improvisation, the behaviour of every part of the system changes continuously as the patterns of input within a dense web of causal complexity alter (Clark 1997: 165). But in these old physiological systems, it was also assumed that the cultural environment was as influential a part of such conspiracies of causes as was the physical world. Cognitive theorists are dreaming again of being able to integrate language and culture into such a dynamic theoretical framework, as forms of mental scaffolding which supplement 'fundamentally short-sighted, special-purpose, internally fragmented minds' (Clark 1997: 33). So if both 'premodern' and post-connectionist theories assume a vision of mind as 'a leaky organ, forever escaping its "natural" confines and mingling shamelessly with body and with world' (Clark 1997: 53), we should care about the fate of the vanished tradition. Was it not just overthrown in the course of the Scientific Revolution of the seventeenth century?

The end of holism? According to the historians, the concepts of these theories, like spirits, humours, and proper blending, led 'continuous lives from the Greeks to the nineteenth century' (Siraisi 1990: 97). Harold Cook argues (1990: 423) that the patchy development of alternative models in the 'scientific revolution' barely displaced in practice older traditions of temperament-based physic, which 'continued in different guises' through the eighteenth century.[13] It was only, suggests L.J. Rather (1968: 342), the rise of cellular pathology and bacteriology in the nineteenth century which led to a diminished interest 'in any but single efficient causes of disease'. It is worth overemphasising this consensus among medical historians, to avoid being taken in by seventeenth-century rhetorics of discontinuity: only relatively recently medical theory's picture of the human body and its operations changed into that of a static, solid container, only rarely breached, in principle autonomous from culture and environment, tampered with only by diseases and experts. Owsei Temkin concluded his history of Galenism (1973: 181) by claiming that, through reinterpretations, the non-naturals, the animal spirits, and the temperaments, 'which provided a medically useful classification of man, and a somatic theory of human behavior, were preserved into the nineteenth century'.

The pronounced materialism of 'pre-modern' medical theory is not its only attraction for medical historians: that alone can just as easily be coupled with culturally blind reductionism and a refusal to countenance complex causes. But materialist explanatory models which were also resolutely holistic do encourage a certain nostalgia. In seeking also to remember the strangeness of these old theories, we can point out the ease with which they lent themselves to the inculcation of forms of bodily surveillance, from Greek temple physicians to Victorian popular hygiene literature: if the non-naturals dictate health, then expert advice about sex, food, and passion has a direct claim to turn cultural norms into medical models.

Body, phenomenology, control But just as useful as pursuing the implication of various technologies of the body in supporting micromechanisms of power is the realisation of just how hard it is to form any sense of the bodily experience of those who lived with belief in spirits and other internal fluids (Duden 1993; Hahn 1995). Thinking of the body as 'nothing but a congeries of canals', as George Cheyne recommended in 1701 (in Wear 1995: 358), seems

---

13 Compare Wear 1995: 360: 'Regimen, the way to lead a healthy life, continued to be structured well into the eighteenth century in terms of the traditional "six non-naturals"'. Michael Macdonald (1981: 178–98) does locate the shift in the seventeenth century. Arguing that 'Restoration medicine was less comprehensive and less consistent than Renaissance medicine', he claims that 'physicians paid less and less attention to the holistic facets of their craft' (1981: 197). But Macdonald, focusing here on psychological healing alone, equates the 'secularization of the elite's beliefs about insanity' in the late seventeenth century (1981: 10) with a move away from multicausal understanding. In my view, even anti-supernaturalist iatromechanical medicine of spirits assumed the continual openness of bodies to multiple environmental and cultural exchanges.

just conceivable. But how do we displace trust in our school anatomy pictures enough to know how to sense 'an unstructured osmotic space' of multiple fluxes beneath the skin (Duden 1991: 127)? In her wonderful book *The Body Embarrassed*, Gail Paster mounts a powerful case against seeing medical theory as autonomous from phenomenology. Physiology in its theoretical forms is also part of social history, she argues (1993: 2–4), part of the obviousness of a culture, of what is lived as true. The persisting symbolic representations which partly compose a body *image* in turn influence the preconscious continuous body *schema* which supports and constrains action and thought (Gallagher 1995): both image and schema are historical. The bodies Paster writes of, glimpsed through texts of English Jacobean drama, were (not only theorised as but lived as) semipermeable irrigated containers, moist sponges filled with interchangeable fluids. They supported, and produced, narratives of open internal tumult, dramatic tales of regulation and release, in which strangely affective internal agencies are barely amenable to personal or medical control. Even though the early seventeenth century saw the emergence of stronger civilising ideologies of refinement and bodily self-mastery, in which volatility was slowly silenced, the residually dominant medical theories still authorised experiences of somatic lacks and losses of control (1993: 14).[14]

Wriggling spirits, then, were phenomenologically felt. Even in remembering, their sensed tracks and trails could make one uneasy. Bakhtin's (1984) nostalgia for the indiscriminate openness of the 'grotesque' porous body to all and any external influence, its resistance to singular authoritarian will, has been sharpened by recent body historians (Stewart 1984/1993: 104–11; Stallybrass 1987; Paster 1993). Marie-Christine Pouchelle sees the whole man described in medieval fluid physiologies as immersed 'in a flask of his own excretions', his spirits, blood, and humours in endless whirling circulation with the fluids outside him (1983/1990: 137). She details forms of defence against such openness, the stratagems of containment which language could attempt. In these imaginary anatomies, inner 'precincts and enfoldments' are theoretically used to guarantee the security of fluid contents. Images of boxes and purses provide but uncertain security, however: all dangerous passages between inside and outside must be policed. Orifices and even skin must be imaged as windows and doors to be controlled in the two-way traffic which

---

14 An intriguing case study of a life of excessive turbulence which invites analysis in Paster's terms is F.F. Blok's (1976) biography of the Dutch poet and philosopher Caspar Barlaeus (1584–1648), the likely model for Descartes' notorious account in the First Meditation of the madman who thinks he is made of glass. Not only did Barlaeus live out in awful experience the theoretically sanctioned chimeras and physiological disruptions of the extreme melancholic (1976: 46–7, 105–21); poignantly, during his depressions he taught his students an extreme Platonic dualism in which the rampant body can only erupt squallingly to cloud and envelop the mind (1976: 67–9).

regulates the coction and metamorphoses of the internal fluids (1983/1990: 140–54; see Whigham 1988 on containment and contamination).

Exactly parallel worries about memory fluids, I will suggest, fuel early modern (neuro)philosophy of mind. How could items in memory be kept secure and ordered, immune to the promiscuous blending characteristic of the fluid motions on which they depended? The metaphorical profusion of these earlier schemes was compressed into the animal spirits, charged with the care of cognitive boundaries. Rhetoric about order and chaos in connection with the animal spirits is unlikely to be merely philosophical: it touched deeply the way body processes were experienced in banal or extreme conditions. More ordered models for the physiology of memory would eventually be required. Science, religion, and language were used in the Renaissance, argued Elaine Scarry (1988: 95–6, 101–2; compare Sutton 1997), to enter the body and 'revise it to be volitional'. Memory, like the body, had to be *forced* to submit to conscious control.

2.3.7 Reproduction and reasoning

The ancient association between reproduction and reasoning is a pertinent example of the tradition's persistence. It had many functions, allowing men to impose their own, intellectual form of conception in having an idea/Idea in the womb (Huet 1993). Specifically, a long-standing (though far from unanimous) analogy or even identity between semen and foamy ethereal quintessence was easily extended to the whole spirit realm, so that the same spirits operate in the brain and in the seed (Putscher 1973: 20–6; Rist 1985; Jacquart and Thomasset 1985/1988: 52–60). Through the tortuous history of embryological theory (Lloyd 1983; MacLean 1980: 28–46), many retained Aristotle's suggestion that *pneuma* carries the sensitive soul (*Parts of Animals* 652b8–13), giving vital urgency to the informational problems of ensuring that ruffled spirits could accurately transmit encoded form (as Tristram Shandy would discover to his cost). Combined with the belief that the brain was the origin not only of animal spirits, but also of semen (Jacquart and Thomasset 1985/1988: 55), this encouraged the assumption of an equivalence between intellectual and sexual capacities, at least in men.[15]

Precious male liquors were in short supply in the fluid internal environment, always tending to be swamped, consumed, diluted, or polluted by chance or immorality. Theoretical attempts to understand the connections between desire, as a cognitive capacity, and the physiology of sex inevitably had recourse to ani-

---

15 Polemic about the existence, function, and nature of female semen continued from ancient until very recent times (Jacquart and Thomasset 1985/1988; Laqueur 1990). More directly analogous to concerns about male expenditure of spirits in a double psychological and libidinal economy were theories of the maternal imagination's powers to imprint on the foetus via the animal spirits: see chapter 9 below.

mal spirits, indiscriminately transitive agents wheeling between memory and action, pneumatically encoding and releasing psychic virtues (Jacquart and Thomasset 1985/1988: 82–4). In particular, in Renaissance self-ascriptions of genius from Ficino onwards, it was accepted that scholarship consumes the spirits (Babb 1951: 23–8). As I show in chapter 9 below, the advent of mechanical philosophy and physiology not only retained these beliefs, but provided newly explicit mechanisms to explain why those partial to the expense of spirits in sexual activity would inevitably lose their intellectual vigour.

2.3.8 Physiology

Spirits, roaming through systems of 'secret canals', were in Francis Bacon's natural philosophy 'the agents and workmen that produce all the effects in the body' (Wallace 1967: 23–39; Jardine 1974: 88–94). Surveys of physiological texts (Rothschuh 1958; Putscher 1973; Jacyna 1995) reveal that the ubiquitous popularity of animal spirits in the second half of the seventeenth century was not due to a period of long neglect followed by a miraculous 'reappearance in Cartesian physiology' (Riese 1959: 51).

Yet, for all the continuity with the mixed traditions I have sketched (see also Frank 1980: 1–16), there was a new reliance on animal spirits in seventeenth-century physiological explanation. In the work of Vesalius and other sixteenth-century theorists *spiritus* 'rarely plays a conspicuous part', concluded Walker (1953/1985: 150), contrasting the explanatory profligacy of Bacon and Descartes. This can be partly explained as sixteenth-century prudery about hypothetical entities, associated with rhetoric about a new restriction of anatomy to observation (Kemp 1997). But, against the grain of slack Whiggish assumptions of progress from folklore to precise science, there was a seventeenth-century shift *towards* animal spirit explanations, revealing simultaneously both increased explanatory ambition and wild speculation. It is hard to disagree with Alan Gabbey's judgement that seventeenth-century mechanists 'tried to explain everything, which was too much by a long chalk' (1985: 13): but, in the uncertain domain of psychosomatic and neurophilosophical phenomena, such overreaching has its compensatory justifications.

Ontology Descartes, jettisoning natural and vital spirits, resolutely corporealised animal spirits: 'what I am calling "spirits" here are merely bodies' (*Passions* 1.10, AT xi.335, CSM 1.331). Confusion arising from the identification with matter of something called 'animal *spirit*' was merely verbal.[16] Comparisons with 'a certain very subtle wind, or rather a very lively

---

16 Descartes acknowledges that someone might object 'to the term "spirits" being applied to particles of terrestrial matter that are separated from each other and driven about at great speed', but retorts that he would be surprised if such a critic was doing anything other than merely 'questioning the name' (to Vorstius 19 June 1643, in Descartes CSM-K 226).

and very pure flame' (L'Homme H 19, AT xi.129, CSM 1.100) place spirits firmly within Cartesian matter theory, as fine bodies which 'never stop for a single moment in any place' (L'Homme H 79, AT xi.171–2).

Later mechanical philosophers adopted and adapted animal spirits theory to give accounts in terms of the motions of material fluids of all but the very highest rational functions. Evidence assembled by John Yolton in Thinking Matter (1984b: 153–89) suggests that, at least by the early eighteenth century, writers of diverse metaphysical persuasions had accepted the Cartesian materialisation of spirits.[17]

The ontology of physiological spirits did, of course, still differ across the natural philosophical schools, with many (notably chemical philosophers) still seeing spirits and ethers as sharing in incorporeality.[18] But they were still grosser than pure soul, and could still be recalcitrant, resisting the command of the will and escaping the attention of reason. So it is not clear, in the contexts which concern me, that ontology had as much importance as the issue of control. When insubstantial subtle fluids came into fashion in eighteenth-century Newtonian sciences, animal spirits were still, for one clear reason, more firmly linked by association in theorists' minds with matter than were other ethereal substances. Spirits, on almost all accounts, derived in some way from blood. This belief had been transformed from old general parallels between nerves and veins (Bitbol-Hespériès 1990: 204–9) into accounts of specific mechanical processes by which the finest particles of blood separated out in the brain to form animal spirit (Mazzolini 1991; see chapter 3 below on Descartes' version). So even if physiological spirits were kin with subtle quintessences and chemical ethers, their formation brought them bubbling through thickly material fluids.[19] Further, their role in neural transmission made consideration of physical processes unavoidable.

Muscular motion A relatively respectable history of animal spirits might be possible if one looked only at their explanatory role in theories of muscular

17 Malebranche vigorously announces the Cartesian line: everyone agrees that the animal spirits are 'the most refined and agitated parts of the blood' (LO 91, 11.1.2.i). Yolton quotes descriptions of material spirits in Hoffman, Cheyne, Mandeville, Chambers, Langrish, Watts and others.

18 Roger French (1981: 114) contends that in England the corporealisation of spirits never really took hold because of 'the absence of a Cartesian physiological revolution'; Patricia Churchland (1986a: 15–17) recognises that, even though 'there was nothing very spiritual about [Descartes'] "animal spirits"', nevertheless 'orthodoxy continued to pronounce animal spirits and vital forces as immaterial and ghostly and to see nervous activity as requiring vital forces'. I am not sure about this: corporeal animal spirits were by no means confined to Cartesian theorists. At the very least, spirits were always aligned with general matter theory, even in iatrochemical traditions. Thanks to Anita Guerrini for pressing me on the ontology of spirits.

19 It was because he could not see how they could be easily separated from blood that one leading Newtonian physiologist, Archibald Pitcairne, took a stand against the use of hypothetical spirits (Guerrini 1987: 74–5).

motion. It is not that this primary problem of early modern neurophysiology (Brazier 1984) was independent of metaphysics, for it had to explain the proper action of the will in producing movements instantaneously. But books about, and theories of, muscular motion look roughly continuous with post-Galvani accounts of animal electricity in nineteenth-century physiology. One idea of muscle contraction was that a motion of animal spirits is transmitted from the brain, so that a small influx of spirit from the nerve causes the spirits already in the muscle to open a valve into its antagonist, from which more spirits flow, causing the relaxation of the antagonist and the contraction of the first muscle (Descartes L'Homme, AT xi.134–7, H 24–9; Passions, 1.11, AT xi.335–6, CSM 1.332). Though a number of early modern physiologists rejected this account of muscle inflation, there was no feasible alternative (Nayler 1993: 225–6, 334, 583). We do not believe this balloon theory, but it looks appropriately proto-scientific, and it is gratifying to find that various experiments were performed in the second half of the seventeenth century to test it (chapter 8 below). Might this briefly delay conviction of the concept of animal spirit as one of Cussins' misplaced composites?

But, if anything is of the essence of the wriggling animal spirits, it is that they did not tidily restrict themselves to the occasional inflation of muscle tissue at the behest of the will. This is why muscular motion is subordinated in my tale of spirits to memory and other hopelessly mixed psychophysiological ex-plananda.

2.3.9 Neurophilosophy, memory, and moral physiology

Spirits were requisite theoretical entities in accounts not only of muscular motion, but also of memory, dreaming, and imagination, and of emotion, moods, and madness. Long before the Cartesian philosophy of the brain, Renaissance theorists of mind, in what Burton called 'those tedious tracts de Anima' (1621/1989: 140), employed animal spirits to embed cognitive function in the body. Stoic pneuma theory had long merged with Aristotelian accounts of the internal senses (Sepper 1996: 13–28), so that reason had to draw on the fluid support of memory in manipulating representations.

For Descartes (here as elsewhere following Renaissance spirits theorists in range, if not in detail), the scope of spirits theory extended from the physiological to the emotional. Differences in the abundance, coarseness, agitation, and uniformity of the particles of spirits alter our humours or 'natural inclina-tions'. Unusual abundance excites movements that give evidence of generos-ity, liberality, and love; coarseness or strength of the spirits gives rise to confidence or courage, agitation to promptness, diligence, and desire, and so on (Descartes L'Homme, AT xi.166–7, H 72–3). In The Passions of the Soul, Descartes gives physiological-fantastical accounts of peculiarities of spirit motions in various psychological states: in hatred, for example, gall entering the blood from the liver boils up and causes spirits going to the brain to 'have very unequal parts' and to 'move very strangely' (11.103, AT xi.404–5, CSM 1. 364).[20]

Turbulence, then, could easily spread from the physical to the psychological, and spirits featured in abnormal psychology from ancient times (Putscher 1973: 26–9; Kemp 1990: 114–21, 148–51). They had to be kept pure to ensure cognitive propriety and health, and Renaissance moral physiologists developed a psychological medicine of cognitive transparency in describing the dangers. The state of the spirits suffers when the body is out of joint, and this in turn causes awful deviations from cognitive, and cultural, norms.

Historians of melancholy have described how fumes of the melancholy humour were thought to blacken images carried in animal spirits. Bright, Platter, du Laurens, Wright and others warn of the effects of discoloured spirits (Babb 1951: 16–17; Klibansky, Panofsky, and Saxl 1964; Lyons 1971). Just as anger is spirits burning, boiling the blood, so more subtle psychoemotional shifts and disorders proceed from the taint or discolouring of the spirits. The rising of the melancholy humour to the brain 'counterfetteth terible objects to the fantasie, and polluting both the substance, and spirits of the brayne, causeth it without externall occasion, to forge monstrous fictions' (Timothy Bright in Jackson 1986: 85). In their quintessential nature, spirits yearned to be united with celestial ether, but they could contrarily be turned from the light and break links with reality.[21] Melancholics, horribly, see backwards into their own brains, befogged by 'the vapors of the animal spirits turned smoky by the black bile' (du Laurens, in Jobe 1976: 220).

These beliefs imply a peculiar ideal of transparency. The animal spirits, warned Platter, which are clouded and darkened by an excess of black bile, 'ought to be bright clear lucid and most pure' (in Jackson 1986: 93–4). There is here an implicit theory of mental representation in which images can be sustained only under dazzlingly bright physiological conditions. In later, mechanised versions of spirits theory, when the norm of resemblance between representation and reality had been jettisoned, the physiological dangers to morality remained: insufficient care of body fluids and the multiple factors which influence them could drag the mind down into darkness, away from the security of contact with the real world, into a spectral world of spirit-driven fantasies in flux (chapter 9 below). Moral physiology, in this context, was the disciplined mastery of the self and of the body by the self. Theoretical knowledge about the body was required in moral training, for example in internalising the

---

20 This possibility of the gall 'regorg[ing] into the veins the matter it contains' and thus causing the spirits to be 'more lively and more unevenly agitated withal' had been raised in the earlier L'Homme (AT xi.169, H 75).

21 'Unpure and naughtie blood', distributed through the body when passages are blocked, distorts the clarity of the spirits which derive from it (Philip Barrough, in Babb 1951: 27).

rigid architectural loci of place-memory systems (Yates 1966; Carruthers 1990): there was no clear line here between practice and science, between knowing how and knowing that.[22]

The immediate presence of objects, events, and other people to mind was lost at the Fall. Post-lapsarian gaps between representation and reality were imperfectly bridged by sense organs, nerves, and brain. After the Greek discovery of the nerves (Solmsen 1961), the spirits which filled them were usually thought to derive from the ventricles in the brain, fluid-filled reservoirs which seemed sufficiently isolable to serve as localised seats for cognitive functions (Woollam 1958; Pagel 1958; Harvey 1975; Bruyn 1982; Park 1988).

With little differentiation of the solid brain parts (Dewhurst and Clarke 1973), memory had long been fixed by internal sense theorists in the posterior ventricle, where a drier environment was meant to aid the preservation of the past in the fluid spirituous medium. Too much moisture in the back of the brain will 'confound / All the impressions which the Sences give' (John Davies of Hereford, in R. L. Anderson 1927: 18). Remembering, on a popular account, required the dislodging of *species* stored in the memory (Steneck 1976: 136). But the eclectic tradition encompassed two different pictures of the operation of memory, which would increasingly come into conflict. Thinking of spirits and fluids made memories seem like motions: but thinking of memory as a collection of stored items, analogous to the images placed in artificial memory loci in the arts of memory, made memories seem like individual bodies. The increased popularity of animal spirits theory, and its applications to memory in the seventeenth century, gave the former option the theoretical, though not the moral, advantage.[23]

Memories 'stored' in a fluid medium characterised by incessant motion could not easily be thought of as located in a single place. Spirits theories of memory are unlikely to be literalist storehouse models, in which static items

22 I pursue this point in connection with medieval and Renaissance memory arts in Sutton 1997. Ian Hacking (1995: 198–209), arguing that 'the sciences of memory were new in the latter part of the nineteenth century', claims that architectural mnemonics, like all disciplines of memory before Janet's time, were only or primarily techniques or technologies, not part of a search for knowledge about memory. I suggest, in contrast, that practical methods for imposing rigidity on the mind, for avoiding spillage or catastrophic interference between memory items, were intimately entwined with theoretical quests for facts about memory (Sutton 1997: sect. 2). Indeed models for examining historical technologies of the self on which Hacking builds (Foucault 1985, 1986, 1988) include abundant analysis of the close interplay between philosophical knowledge-claims and mundane bodily and psychological practice. The civilising process of learning to tame one's own body was not just a matter of maintaining appropriate habits at table: it required also intense attention to psychophysiology.

23 It was possible, though, to accept animal spirits and still have a localist model of memory items as independent bodies at specific addresses. This works when, as for Digby (chapter 5 below), spirit motions themselves are only the instruments which rouse separate memory bodies, rather than identified with the representations themselves.

are piled up in a place called 'the memory'. The background of dynamic physiological psychology left the absent past to be reconstructed: temporal continuity
could only be provided by recurring patterns of fluid motions across new contexts. Indeed, an intuition of memory as motions is implicit in general spirits
theory, for animal spirits are always bearers of history in the body, their condition and flow already marked by the past as well as by present context. They
gesture towards the external world, with no guarantee of catching it either
representationally or analogically. They make it hard both to get enough
memory, to reproduce what is absent, and not to get too much, to keep the past
in order and available in moderation for rational scrutiny. Theories of memory
thus confront issues of psychological control, working out how to pin down
and hold on to faint temporal order within material flux.

So tensions between moral physiology and these general medical theories
are obvious: control of brain, body, and memory was a difficult enterprise.
'Tension', however, is too simple a word for the symbiotic relation of theory
and practice here: physiology, intruding inevitably into the psychological
realm, opened an intensely attractive space for debate, for moral, didactic,
tragic, puzzled, and simply entertaining discussion of the various disjunctions
between the fluidity of spirits and the solid, rigid order required in cognition
and morality. Rhetorical invocation of desired order could leave descriptive
space for tantalising, horrid, and seductive accounts of the confusion and
chaos to which disordered spirits were prone.

The Cartesian version of animal spirits theory was extraordinarily popular
across medicine and culture for close on a century after Descartes. His follower
Malebranche (LO 134, II.ii.2) affirms the centrality of the spirits for psychological explanation: 'all the changes occurring in the imagination and the mind are
only the consequences of those encountered in the animal spirits and the
[brain] fibres'. Perhaps animal spirits were, as William Harvey complained, 'a
common subterfuge of ignorance' (1649/1990: 117). Perhaps the concept of
animal spirit, 'physiology's most embarrassing object' (Boissier de Sauvages,
in Mignon 1934: 6), like other misplaced composites, did promote mystifica-
tion, delay the inevitable advance of science, and fool a lot of people. But I hope
so far to have shown that animal spirits, 'these dubious entities' (Macdonald
1981: 182) soaking up the (cultural and natural) environment, are at least an
intriguing historical subject, condensing fears and desires about body and
memory.

3
Memory and 'the Cartesian philosophy of the brain'

In the true art of memory . . . by the leading back of things to causes, when all those things are finally led back to a single one, there will be no need of memory for any science.　　　(René Descartes, *Cogitationes Privatae* (1619–21), AT x.230)

There is a remarkable Story to confirm the Cartesian philosophy of the Brain. A Man hurt by the fall of a Horse forgot about twenty Years of his Life, and remember'd what went before in a much more lively manner than usual.
　　　　　　　　　　　　　　　(David Hume's early memoranda, Hume 1948: 502)

It is a big mistake to accept the principle that no body moves of itself. For it is certain that a body, once it has begun to move, has in itself for that reason alone the power to continue to move. . .
　　　　　　　(Descartes to Mersenne, 28 October 1640, AT iii.213, CSM-K 155)

Our machines are disturbingly lively, and we ourselves frighteningly inert.
　　　　　　　　　　　　　　　　　　　(Donna Haraway 1991a: 152)

3.1 Introduction

Descartes' psychophysiology is notoriously absurd, 'a little fantastical' (A 479), 'a baroque ruse' (Metraux 1996: 67) betraying exuberant rationalist disdain for observation. His neuromechanical speculations on the dramatic whirl of invisible spirits in hollow nerves are at best 'quaint', separable from his true metaphysical and epistemological achievements (Wilson 1978: viii; Schouls 1989: 154), at worst 'particularly uncontrolled' (Mackenzie 1992: 136; Hatfield 1992: 347–8). Reducing the phenomenological complexity of lived bodily experience to the atomic combinations of mythical particles, Descartes bypasses 'the concrete life of feeling' which he 'had done his best to avoid' (Grene 1985: 52). Since he barred the thinking subject from its body, which was just another object in a world 'not of meaning and love and laughter and tears . . . but of material particles going about their lonely business', it is no surprise that 'twentieth-century approaches to subjectivity are dominated by the anxiety not to be Descartes' (Rée 1995: 205–6). Specific microreductions of emotions and temperaments to diverse motions of animal spirits are 'intuitive but extraordinarily simplistic' (Gaukroger 1995: 273), and the physiological treatment of memory is 'particularly incoherent' (Richards 1992: 41). Descartes revels in wild hypotheses about body processes, entranced by the *ébranlement* ('commotion, disturbance') of nervous fluids through the folded mesh of the brain.

It is true that modern physiologist-historians, neuroscientists, and memory theorists have repeatedly looked to Descartes for inspiration. The father of modern philosophy was already there (wherever present theory stands) in neurophysiology too! With a few swiftly exchanged terms, old language is revivified: according to Karl Lashley (1950/1988: 59), a mere substitution of nerve impulse for animal spirit, and of synapse for brain pore results in 'the doctrine of learning as change in resistance of synapses'.[1] Now computational neuroscience, announces Patricia Churchland in *Scientific American* (1989: 100), is modernising Descartes' vision of reflex action in neural nets.

Obviously, such heroic nostalgia answers no better to historical or philosophical complexity than does easy vilification of Descartes as source of 'the original sin of modern philosophy' (Rorty 1980: 60). Canguilhem (1955/1977: 138–42 (= 1994: 52–6)) marvellously undermined rhetoric of Descartes' 'paternity' by analysing the specific political circumstances in which Descartes was 'anointed' an illustrious precursor for 'discovering' the reflex by du Bois-Reymond in the 1850s. In such myths, invocation of the oddly absent father (as hero or villain) distorts and distracts from important current polemics (Tomaselli 1984a; Williams 1994).

Safety, then, requires historians to avoid compressing old and new, wary of the dangers of reducing an alien past to the present. But I have a different agenda, in which a skewed historical slant on one topic, memory, can open conceptual space in modern sciences of mind. I am interested neither (though a materialist) in another anti-dualist exposure of 'Descartes' error', nor (though agreeing with Churchland that neural networks are not just new fashion) in identifying Descartes as exuberant neurophilosopher. My retrospective reading, on the basis of current concerns about memory, is none the less situated within a growing body of work on Descartes' natural philosophy which seeks to counteract historiographical obsession with metaphysics (and I extend to memory the new approaches to internal sense developed by Baker and Morris (1996) and by Sepper (1996), whose books appeared too late for me to use them fully). Anti-naturalist history either neglected Descartes' science or treated it only as an adjunct to first philosophy (Kenny 1968; Frankfurt 1970; Williams 1978; Wilson 1978; Cottingham 1986; Dicker 1992). Neither the Descartes of undergraduate courses nor that of psychoanalytic and anti-humanist polemic answers to the more interesting, weirder texts in natural philosophy (Irigaray 1974/1985a and Kofman 1976/1991, for example, focus on metaphysics and the *Meditations* in particular).

What happens if we take seriously Descartes' advice that meditation on metaphysical principles is 'very harmful' since it impedes us from imagination

---

1 Descartes' memory traces are Semon's engrams (Riese 1958: 125–6); his 'system of tubes' can be replaced by 'the present system of concatenated neurons' (Foster 1901/1970: 268, in Carter 1983: 19).

and the senses (to Princess Elizabeth, 28 June 1643, AT iii.695, CSM-K 228), and note that about 90 per cent of his surviving correspondence is on scientific matters (Gaukroger 1993a)? Descartes did not set out implausibly to derive the whole of physics from the *cogito*: early modern followers and critics alike treated Cartesianism as over-hypothetical and speculative, rather than a priorist and deductivist. Descartes' place as anti-hero in neat schematic battles between rationalism and empiricism was imposed by nineteenth-century historians (Gaukroger 1993a, 1995: 5–6): earlier readers were as likely to study the psychophysiology of *L'Homme* as the *Meditations* (Wright 1983: 5–9). In describing the neurophilosophical model of memory, I assume Descartes' interest in knowledge gained a posteriori (Larmore 1980). On this reading Descartes was a mechanical philosopher who was as interested in the motions of matter as in the supernatural realm carefully separated from it (Hutchison 1983; Schuster 1990; Tamny 1990): although a dualist, he was uninterested in metaphysical dualism (MacIntosh 1983: 328; Clarke 1982).

It is not that Descartes was a pure empiricist either. Although the popular view that 'Descartes shunned experiment with Jesuitical disdain' (Miller 1978: 295) is quite wrong in *general*, the physiology seems particularly ridiculous just because of the gap between accounts of inner fluid machinations and any conceivable observation. There is still disagreement on how Descartes *did* see the relations between metaphysics and scientific practice (Hatfield 1985, 1990: 111–17; Gaukroger 1993a; Schuster 1993); and scholars still convict Descartes of inconsistency for not adhering firmly in practice to his methodological 'order of reasons'. His speculations on the physiology of memory are a useful test case in assessing the significance of Descartes' own neglect of Cartesian method.

Descartes outlined the rudiments of a distributed model of memory, where memories are 'stored' only superpositionally. 'Memory' is neither a repository for images nor an inner lexicon. Distributed representation can be theorised at a level of abstraction from the specific (historically and technologically dependent) material in which it is thought to be implemented. Descartes was not the origin of such a model: the key questions about interference and mixture in memory which these models bring up were discussed in the long traditions of the memory arts (Sutton 1997). But Descartes was hostile to the cognitive technology of place-memory systems (Sepper 1993; Gaukroger 1995: 273–4), rejecting humanist schemes for the classification and rearrangement of already existing knowledge (Judowitz 1988: 25–32; Gaukroger 1989: 31–8, 46ff.). Architectural mnemonics (Carruthers 1990) was designed to supplement weak, confused natural memory with rules for maintaining rigorous order. Descartes instead examines sources of this 'natural' confusion in memory. The psychophysiological ideas he draws on were not intended to locate memory's seat in the brain, but to model the mechanisms of retention and storage. To the extent that his neurophilosophy is absurd, it is partly because of his hidden reliance on sources with which we have no illusion of familiarity. But he takes seriously as explananda holistic associative processes, phenomena of blending and interference, and the uncertain relation of memory and imagination.

This reappropriation of Descartes is the deliberate antithesis of uses of Descartes-the-rationalist by Chomsky and Fodor to buttress the language of thought hypothesis and 'Cartesian linguistics' (Chomsky 1966). Rather than taking the defining feature of Cartesianism to be the stress on rationality, linguistic generativity, and innate ideas, I point underneath to Descartes' (much more extensive) work on the many capacities which we share with other animals. What Fodor denigrates as babble and mere mental causation (chapter 11 below) is as central to Descartes' concerns as deduction, intuition, or meditation.

I begin by outlining evidence for distributed representation in Descartes (section 3.2), and develop the theme in answering a series of objections to my reading. The objections are powerful, and will occur to readers immediately, so I mention them here at the outset before addressing them in turn in sections 3.3 to 3.6.

1 Intellectual memory: notoriously, Descartes believed in an incorporeal intellectual memory: does this not vitiate my stress on his physiology of memory?

2 Memory, soul, and automatism: notoriously, Descartes denied that animals have souls: does this not vitiate my assumption that his physiological works alone, describing soul-less machines, could even address problems of memory and cognition at all? How can a dualist have a neuroscientific theory of memory? More specifically, behaviour without the soul as cause is for Descartes, notoriously, purely automatic, the mere product of reflex arcs: does his restriction of physical behaviour to reflex action (accepted even in Churchland's search for precursors to connectionism) not vitiate my claim that complex and flexible action occurs even when the soul is not involved?

3 Mechanism, matter, and active bodies: notoriously, Descartes' mechanical philosophy requires that matter (including the human body) be passive, pure extension in motion: does this not vitiate my picture of a dynamic physiology in which the body is always active, always escaping the soul's command? Is mechanism not an intrinsically authoritarian natural philosophy, in which isolated atomic elements combine only through external intervention, rather than the anarchic holism of my account? Is the Cartesian body not inert, closed, a forgotten container, rather than the highly theorised, permeable temporary pocket of stability embedded in social and physical worlds which I attribute to Descartes?

4 Memory, method, and metaphysics: notoriously, Cartesian method requires the subject to doubt opinion and easy belief in starting anew with only clear and distinct ideas. As Tim Reiss (1996) shows, Descartes does not claim (as Gassendi thought he did) that old ideas are simply erased, obliterated in the process of destruction and rebuilding: is he not then acknowledging the permanence of stored items in a way which vitiates my claim that memories, for Descartes, must be reconstructed?

These issues overlap in their relevance to memory but together touch an enormous range of Cartesian problems. My answers come at a small set of claims from different perspectives, trying to get across unusual points of view about Cartesian automata, about Descartes' conception of the body, and about the place of the past in Cartesian method.

Even if my responses to these objections are adequate, Descartes remains not just historically but conceptually distant from modern distributed-memory theorists. Unable to integrate his psychophysiology of memory into his general philosophy, Descartes is least clear and least convincing on issues of cognitive control: not just about familiar problems of the non-physical soul, but on the independent issue of the need for an executive centre in the brain, whether hooked up to a soul or not (Dennett 1991a). I conclude by briefly drawing together the various threats to psychological control and mental autonomy, challenging 'Descartes' relentless optimism about the autonomy and power of the will' (Rorty 1992: 384), which are posed by memory and the body, and sketching a more positive Cartesian account of self-mastery based on moral neurology.

In two appendices I fill in background to this Cartesian philosophy of the brain. The first spells out the general physiological psychology of L'Homme to show how the theory of memory is embedded in it. The second examines Malebranche's more explicit distributed model of memory, which supports the attribution of distributed representation to Descartes, as does the horror expressed at its consequences by English critics (chapter 5 below). In the late seventeenth and early eighteenth centuries, both supporters and critics of Cartesianism were aware of, and concerned about, the implications and dangers of these views of memory and brain. These accounts are unfamiliar now, hidden under the weight of commentary on scepticism, the cogito, and foundational epistemology; but it is naive to ascribe this to progress in separating truly philosophical questions about knowledge and mind from truly empirical questions about brain traces.

This long chapter cuts new paths through many strands of Descartes scholarship, at the cost of starting from a highly specific concern with memory. The neglected memory models map on to slants on surrounding issues that deserve attention. Relations between body and world, between psychology and physiology, between forgetting and moving on are at stake in memory, and

Descartes hinted at much more interesting views on all these topics than our textbooks admit.

3.2 Distributed representation in Descartes' neurophilosophy of memory

Remembering, for Descartes, is (or at least requires) the reconstructing of patterns of motion in the animal spirits flowing through particular brain pores. This reconstruction is possible in retrieval because of physical dispositions in these pores: these dispositions or memory traces are *superpositional* in that there can be many in one part or fold of the brain. He describes associative mechanisms which allow not only for redundant coding and graceful degradation, but also for causal holism in the effects of implicit memory representations. They chime with his interest in external forms of condensed representation, such as the distorted images of anamorphotic art which required reconstruction from specific points of view (Decyk forthcoming). I do not deal with the aesthetics of superposition, and here merely introduce the model of memory to exemplify distributed representation.

L'Homme

In April 1630, soon after starting anatomical studies, Descartes told Mersenne that he was studying chemistry and anatomy simultaneously: 'every day I learn something that I cannot find in any book' (AT i.137, CSM-K 21; compare to Mersenne, 18 December 1629, AT i.102, and 20 February 1639, AT ii.525, CSM-K 134). In late 1632 he was 'dissecting the heads of various animals, so that [he could] explain what imagination, memory, etc. consist in' (AT i.263, CSM-K 40).[2] Reading and observation resulted in revisions of his earlier views on sensation and cognition.[3] L'Homme (the Treatise

2 The claim to be discovering facts unavailable in any book should not be taken at face value; in fact Descartes told Mersenne in 1637 that his anatomical assumptions were those accepted generally (AT i.378). Hall's commentary details Descartes' sources. But here as elsewhere, in Alquié's words (1966: 27), information read by Descartes entered 'une mémoire déformant ce qu'elle rappelle, et toujour mêlée à la création'. This lovely description of Descartes' own memory also applies to his theoretical conception of memory. It is quoted by Annie Bitbol-Hespériès, who throws new light on Descartes' physiological reading, demonstrating the particular importance of the early seventeenth-century work of Caspar Bauhin (1990: 36, 195–202, 214–18). Not much of her new material relates directly to memory and other internal senses, but I hope it is clear that my narrative, playing with a new myth of Descartes' 'discovery' of distributed representation, skates over a more complex past. Provocative accounts of Descartes' anatomical contacts and practices in Leiden and Amsterdam include Lindeboom 1979: ch. 3; Barker 1984: 73–85; Rupp 1990, 1992; and Sawday 1995: 146–58.

3 I cannot address here the account of cognition in the earlier *Regulae*, where Descartes assumes that objects stamp imprints on sense-organs which are instantaneously transmitted through the *sensus communis* into *phantasia*, where they are recognised by the *vis cognoscens*. On this psychophysiology see Sepper 1996: 28–35 (compare Sepper 1988, 1989,

on Man)[4] resulted. Though it was published only in the 1660s (Descartes 1662, 1664), it was almost complete by July 1633, when, on hearing of the condemnation of Galileo, Descartes prudently decided not to risk antagonising the Church by publishing *Le Monde*, of which it was part. I give some background to *L'Homme*'s strange general physiology in appendix 1 to this chapter, but here move straight to memory.

L'Homme describes a soul-less world in which earthen machines imitate our bodily functions. But these 'statues' are animated, these machines dream. The capacities of the self-moving automata are many, though they depend only on the disposition of the organs (AT xi.120, H 4, CSM 1.99; AT xi.201–2, H 113, CSM 1.108):[5] there is no life/body dualism to accompany Descartes' mind/body dualism (Mackenzie 1975; Wright 1990: 253–4). Cartesian cyborgs can not only walk, breath, sleep and wake, nourish themselves, digest, and reproduce: they also have what are *to us* mental capacities like sensation, imagination, memory, and emotion. Descartes' fable seeks to catch at the very pulse of the machine.

All this is accomplished (thanks to God's skilled craft)[6] by means of the whooshing animal spirits, shaking through brain tissues. The spirits incessantly undergo *criblage* or *tamisage* (sifting, filtering, sieving) in the textured porous net, forming and retracing patterns across the inner surfaces of a filamentous mesh. They connect the deepest interior, the pineal gland, to the world in numerous ways. It is not just that muscular motion requires appropriate spirituous input from brain to periphery. Rather, interior and world are always already connected, for the state of the body at a time results from the history of its interactions. The condition of animal spirits shifts with context: changes in environment, climate, diet, bodily practices, in the condition of the

---

1993); Foti 1986b: 634–7; Gaukroger 1995: 158–72. These writers do not draw attention to the absence of animal spirits in the *Regulae*: without the spirits, no dynamics of memory could be even implicit.

4 The gender-specificity of the subject of Descartes' inquiry is uncertain. Where Stephen Voss (1994: 273) translates Descartes' 'unhappy usage' as 'man', I retain the French, and hope to show that the gendered body-machines in Descartes' overtly universalising text are in fact all particular, context-bound, and marked by bodily differences. I do not address Descartes' views of gender explicitly here: but my revised interpretations of bodies and memory may help such projects. See also Sutton 1998, and chapter 9 below on how animal spirits focus Cartesian men's fears that psychological and libidinal energies were mutually exclusive.

5 For *L'Homme*, in addition to the editions cited, I have used Alquié's edition and notes (A 379–480), the Clark Library copies of the first Latin and French editions (Des Cartes 1662, Descartes 1664), and an unpublished translation of *Le Monde* and *L'Homme* by Stephen Gaukroger.

6 The teleology in the relation between the fable's machine world and its real-world counterpart is double. Firstly, God benevolently ensures mapping between material processes and useful outcomes. But, secondly, what counts as useful, what is conducive to life, is given only biologically. This, as Canguilhem points out (1952, 1955/1977: 31–2, 54–6), is not necessarily a lapse from mechanism, since mechanisms have functions (compare A 403, 410, 429; Hatfield 1992: 361). But finality is absent in *L'Homme*: the creator, like the author, disappears behind the fable.

blood and other body fluids, change the spirits, whose influence on cognition in turn gives rise to ongoing changes of state for the body in the world. This is a field of multiple simultaneous interactions, akin to our understanding of dynamical systems in which 'everything is simultaneously affecting everything else': the system's state variables *and* the external parameters which influence their evolution are all changing in various timescales (van Gelder and Port 1995: 9, 23–5; compare Clark 1997: 163–6).

In focusing on the spirits' roles in memory, I bypass the separate 'intellectual memory' until section 3.3 below. A deliberately partial reading makes good sense: both followers and critics fixed only on the neurophilosophical distributed model. Making this model clear poses questions about relations between the two kinds of memory, and about motivations for retreating from the corporeal account. Hall comments (H xxxix) that Descartes 'gives a suggestive model for the hypostasis of memory, wrong in its details but right in its assumption that a physical basis of retention must exist', without saying which details are wrong. Morris (1969: 460), characterising the model only as 'mechanical', mentions Descartes' 'constant retreat away from any commitment to the model as a total explanation of human memory', as he relied increasingly on non-physical intellectual memory. Though Descartes clearly was not satisfied with his corporeal model, understanding of its nature and implications requires a different theoretical framework. One commentator acknowledges the reconstructive nature of memory in Descartes, but wrongly assumes that only incorporeal memory could be reconstructive, on the grounds that corporeal memory must be passive and static (Landormy 1902: 283–7). I deny this.

Corporeal memory in L'Homme
In the section of L'Homme on memory, ideas are explicitly defined as impressions or figures which animal spirits trace on the surface of the pineal gland as they leave it (AT xi.177, H 86–7, CSM 1.106). These idea-impressions derive either directly from sensory impressions or from imagination and several other (internal) causes: contact with reality is possible, but uncertain in any particular case. Whatever their source, traces of these idea-patterns are carried by spirits flowing from the gland and 'imprinted in the internal part of the brain, which is the seat of *Memory*' (AT xi. 177, H 87, CSM 1.106). In the accompanying diagram (Figure 1), the part referred to appears as the large, relatively undifferentiated fibrous mesh of the brain substance. How does this imprinting work?

Declining to comment, as he says he could, on how these traces 'can sometimes even be caused, by certain actions of the mother, to be imprinted on the limbs of the child being formed in her entrails' (AT xi.177, H 87, CSM 1.106; chapter 9 below), Descartes sketches a theory of recall or retrieval. Animal spirits leaving the gland move through the ventricles towards different regions of the brain substance. The spirits pass, Descartes continues,

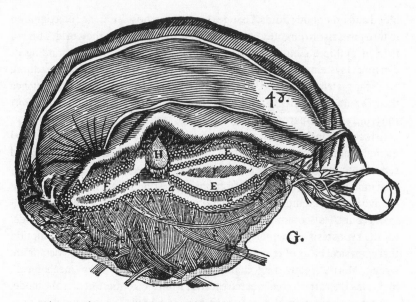

Figure 1 The memory system in Descartes' *L'Homme* (Descartes 1664: 74)

into the pores or intervals that occur between the filaments composing part B [the solid part] of the brain. And [assume] that they are forceful enough to enlarge these intervals somewhat and to bend and rearrange [*plier et disposer diversement*] any filaments they encounter [*en leurs chemins*], according to the differing modes of movement of the spirits themselves and the differing degrees of openness of the tubes into which they pass. *Thus they also trace figures in these gaps, which correspond to those of the objects.* [Assume also] that the first time they accomplish this they do so less easily and effectively here than on gland H, but that they accomplish it increasingly effectively in the measure that their action is stronger, or lasts longer, or is more often repeated. Which is why in such cases these patterns are no longer so easily erased, but are retained there in such a way that by means of them the ideas that existed previously on this gland can be formed again long afterward, without requiring the presence of the objects to which they correspond. And it is in this that *Memory* consists. (AT xi.178, H 87–8, CSM 1.107)[7]

The pattern of the pores, which constrains the patterned flow of spirits, is itself altered over time by the differing motions of the spirits. Note first that patterns are not *stored* faithfully, to endure separately one from another: they are just retained 'in such a way that' they play a part in the (re-)creation of the idea on the surface of the gland. This is representation without resemblance, suggesting a dispositional model: patterns are 'stored' only implicitly, not kept

7 The emphasised sentence (Des Cartes 1662: 83, Descartes 1664: 74) is omitted by Hall, and I use Stoothoff's translation in CSM. The insertions in square brackets are Hall's, except for phrases from the French original which I give to confirm the sense.

in exactly the same form throughout the interval between experience and remembering.

Note too that reconstruction depends only upon physical factors. Spirits fold, enlarge, bend, and arrange the relevant fibres of the brain substance into forms which will in turn filter and sift the spirits' future flows. The critical variables are the degree and pattern of openness of the passageways in the fibrous substance, and the direction and strength of the flow of spirits. The whole scheme operates by contact action alone, and yet patterns, which 'correspond' to absent objects, can be retained as tendencies or dispositions for their reconstruction or re-evocation. The soul may be involved, when it is attached to the machine: but it is not necessary for memory operation.

In this associative mechanism, repetition of recall is one aid to easy recall in the future. Its physical realisation falls out of the model: after spirits have entered the same passageways more and more often, they will tend to find them again more quickly, to enter with greater force, and to remain longer before leaving. Even if particular passageways (through the brain pores) which need to be open for the reconstruction of a particular pattern happen to be closed over, they still 'leave a certain arrangement [disposition] of the filaments composing this part of the brain by which they can be opened more easily later than if they had not been opened before' (AT xi.178, H 89). The microstructure of the brain, altered in the course of experience, makes the spirits' future access to pores easier and quicker.[8]

Descartes gives an analogy with a linen cloth (une toile) which has had 'several needles or engravers' points' repeatedly passed through it (Figure 2). Some holes in the cloth will remain open after the needles have been withdrawn, but even if they close, physical 'traces' left in the cloth will enable them to open again easily (AT xi.178–9, H 89). This mechanism allows total recall on partial input ('the recollection of one thing can be excited by that of another which was imprinted in the memory at the same time'): if only some holes are reopened, this may still suffice for the simultaneous reopening of the others, 'especially if they had all been opened several times together and had not customarily been opened separately' (AT xi.179, H 90). Likewise, 'if I see two eyes with a nose, I at once imagine a forehead and a mouth and all the other parts of a face, because I am unaccustomed to seeing the former without the latter', and seeing a fire I remember heat.[9] An incomplete input can thus generate or prompt a complete

8 As Hall says (H 96, n. 145): 'memory traces . . . consist in residual patterns of openness among the interstices of the filamentous brain substance'.

9 Morris (1969: 454) feels that this is not legitimately mechanical because of the mentalistic content of the term 'accustomed'. But this is merely the phenomenological explanandum, Descartes' common-sense illustration of a phenomenon which his theory explains: the actual theory has already been given, and relies only on a repeated pattern leaving physical effects, the nature of which change over time. Morris is bewitched by 'mechanism', assuming it must exclude all temporal patterning.

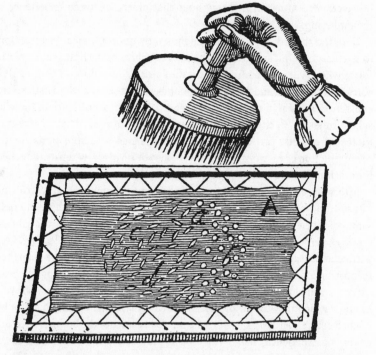

Figure 2 Distributed patterns in a linen cloth as an analogy for associative memory
(Descartes 1664: 76)

memory. Memory representation is a form or associative extension of natural
indication (Mackenzie 1992: 133–41).

In the *Passions of the Soul* (1649), Descartes all but repeats the account (*Passions*
1.42, AT xi.360, CSM 1.344):

> These traces consist simply in the fact that the pores of the brain through
> which the spirits previously made their way owing to the presence of this
> object have thereby become more apt than the others to be opened in the same
> way when the spirits again flow towards them. And so the spirits enter into
> these pores more easily when they come upon them.

But none of this hints at more precise mechanisms for retention and storage
of these traces. What is the state of brain pores and animal spirit motions
during retention, when a particular trace is unactivated, which allows its future
reconstruction?

A distributed model of memory
Descartes had at least an inchoate understanding of *superpositional storage*, the
defining feature of a distributed model (van Gelder 1991b). While the main

evidence that Descartes saw this possibility is in correspondence, there were firm hints in a less familiar part of *L'Homme*. After discussing memory, Descartes describes two corporeal causes of the pineal gland's movements. It can be affected by 'the action of objects that impinge on the senses' (AT xi.185–8, H 96–100). But Descartes gives extended attention to the influence of 'differences among the particles of the spirits that leave' the gland, concluding with an expansion of the theory of memory (AT xi.180–5, H 91–6).

After explaining the internal dynamics of the whole system of gland, brain tubules, animal spirits, nerves, muscles, and limbs, Descartes acknowledges that the pineal gland is often inclined in particular directions by the force of the animal spirits alone, without the involvement of rational soul or external senses. In such cases,

> the ideas that are formed on its [the gland's] surface proceed not only from inequalities in the particles of the spirits causing corresponding differences in temper [*des humeurs*], as mentioned before, but also from the imprints of memory. For if at the region of the brain toward which the gland is inclined, the shape of one particular object is imprinted more distinctly than that of any other, the spirits tending to that region cannot fail to receive an impression thereof. And it is thus that past things sometimes return to thought as if by chance [*comme par hazard*] and without the memory of them being excited by any object impinging on the senses. (AT xi.184, H 96)

This is not the mere automatism of a reflex model, for internal states and processes are maintained and reactivated, and have causal effects, with some autonomy from present sensory stimuli: this is the source of moral danger. The passage implies that there can be more than one trace 'imprinted' in the same 'region' (*endroit*) of the brain. Due to the history of the machine and to the (physical) context, spirits pass through interstitial tubules in one particular pattern, thus reconstructing one distinct trace of all the traces there stored. None of this *requires* a soul: *comme par hazard* means 'without control' as much as 'by chance'. Memory is the scene of a triple displacement of control: neither the non-physical soul, nor the pineal in its role as central executive, nor external reality, *need* inevitably be the cause of ideas. Even when these three putative guarantors of rationality are involved, the decentring forces of superposed memory motions may still influence the context-bound formation of ideas.

Traces are distinct only when reconstructed. But it 'usually happens' (*le plus souvent*) that 'several different figures are traced in this same region of the brain almost equally perfectly': they do not retain independence in this implicit state. When this occurs,

> the spirits will acquire a [combined] impression of them all [*quelque chose de l'impression de chacune*], this happening to a greater or lesser degree according to the ways in which parts of the figures fit together [*selon la diverse rencontre de leurs parties*]. It is thus that chimeras and hypogryphs are formed in the

imaginations of those who daydream, that is to say who let their fancy wander listlessly here and there without external objects diverting it and without the fancy's being directed by reason. (AT xi.185, H 96)[10]

Memories are motions, not bodies, and animal spirits, like other exquisitely small particles, can receive and transmit many different motions at the same time.[11] With traces already mixed, it is all too easy for them to interfere one with another: when spirits acquire combined impressions, the implicit traces' causal effects are holistic, everything in a region making a difference in ongoing processing. There is no fixed *place* for a single 'memory'. As every sensation is, in a sense, many sensations, so every Cartesian memory is many memories: the prejudices of the past are always with us, always to be detected.

Imagination here is the work of memory rather than a separate capacity, a disturbing possibility which haunts the moral physiology of the following century. Although, to stress the moral dangers of brain processes, Descartes uses fantastical examples, suggesting 'the imagination's freedom from natural occurrence, its ability to rearrange wings and legs into new combinations, and . . . [its] eventual capacity to create beyond "need"' (Scarry 1985: 163), the same mechanism operates in ordinary imagining and remembering. There are differences only of degree in the confusion of parts in figures which spirits trace: freedom from melding is either rare or illusory. 'Those who daydream' cannot be securely cordoned off from rational thinkers, who are also subject to the combination and condensation of traces.

In 'Descartes' assimilation of imagination and memory' (Foti 1986b: 636), the direction of explanation is uncertain. Is it that cognitive theory produces a possibility surprising to common sense and to morality, or that a certain part of common-sense psychology drives or suggests the way the cognitive theory is developed? This ambiguity, which recurs in modern relations between cognitive and cultural theory, needs no resolution: scientific and folk conceptions coevolve. Alquié complains (A 453) that, when dealing with associative memory in L'Homme, Descartes transposes to the organic realm ideas which the psychological realm had supplied, and that to this extent, 'he ceases explaining the psychological by the physical' (compare Grosholz 1991: 117–30). But sciences of the organic and the physiological need explananda from somewhere: looking at a few brains is not enough to render salient the key questions for neuroscience. It is not sufficient criticism of the terms of a physiological theory

10 'Combined' is Hall's elucidation. Landormy (1902: 280–1) summarises nicely the role of memory traces in the mechanics: 'les esprits . . . peuvent faire renaître . . . des débris de diverses images autrefois perçues et les combiner en des ensembles imprévus'. In a marvellous, mocking exposition, Krell (1990: 72–3) notes that impressions absorbed 'higgledy-piggledy' are 'prone to moral turpitude, lassitude, lethargy, and benumbment'. These concerns recur in subsequent debates on distributed memory: see chapters 5 and 9.
11 The analogy here is with interference phenomena in the theory of light. See *Le Monde* ch. 14, AT xi.101; Sabra 1967/1981: 17–68; Shea 1991: 212ff.; chapter 4 below.

that they derive from psychological metaphors: only overly pure ideals of science require the two levels connected in reductive explanation to have had no prior metaphorical contact.

Descartes talks of imprinting, of figures and shapes: but it is obvious that these are *not* resembling images of dubious ontological status. 'Figures' are (transient) patterns of openness of brain pores, and the 'parts' of particular figures are the specific tubules which are jointly involved in the reconstruction of the whole figure corresponding to an absent object. But Descartes says no more about what happens to particular traces while unactivated, between their involvement in separate episodes of remembering, until a sequence of letters in 1640.

Impressions preserved in memory, Descartes firstly suggests, are 'not unlike the folds which remain in this paper after it has once been folded' (to Meysonnier, 29 January 1640, AT iii.20, CSM-K 143). Memories are retained in different areas of the brain: impressions are 'received for the most part in the whole substance of the brain', as well as on the gland itself. But this is not yet superposition, for traces extended across wide regions could still be independent of each other (van Gelder 1991b: 48–53).

In the letter which first introduces an intellectual memory, which 'depends on the soul alone' (to Mersenne, 1 April 1640, AT iii.48, CSM-K 146), Descartes is still primarily concerned with specific physical locations for memory impressions, whether in the gland, in the brain, in the nerves and muscles, in the hands of a lute player, or in external aids such as on the pages of a book. The body and the book both support the brain's memory capacity which, because prone to confusion, is fragile. Boundaries blur between 'natural' and artificial memory systems. It is not that brains and books do their recording in the same way, as language of thought theorists think (Fodor 1976): it is that the symbiotic interaction between brains and books is necessary because distinct recording is not common in brains, which thus require certain forms of supplement.

Morris (1969: 455) takes these suggestions about external storage to show that 'Descartes was having trouble finding room in the brain for all the images that his purely physical theory required': he was driven to 'resort to the doctrine of an "intellectual memory"' on finally realising the insufficiency of storage space in the brain. But this is not the correct diagnosis. The problem of finding room in the brain for all of a person's memories was debated in the seventeenth century (MacIntosh 1983). Descartes had worried about it before adopting an animal spirits theory of memory: in the *Regulae*, he identified the phantasy ('a genuine part of the body') with memory in that it 'is large enough to let the different parts of it take on many different figures and generally to retain them for some time' (Rule 12, AT x.415, CSM 1.41–2). Representations had to be independently stamped into the memory wax: this is why the problem of room in the brain arose. But by 1640, Descartes could deflect the problem, since he allowed more than one trace in the same place.

Morris overstates Descartes' concern: in the same letter in which intellectual memory is introduced, Descartes confirms that, despite reference to external aids, it is 'especially the interior parts' of the brain 'which are for the most part utilized in memory' (CSM-K 146). Two months later Descartes elaborates on L'Homme's account of interference between memory traces:

> There is no doubt that the folds of the memory get in each other's way, and that there cannot be an infinite number of such folds in the brain; but there are still quite a number of them there. Moreover, the intellectual memory has its own separate impressions, which do not depend in any way on these folds. So I do not believe that the number of folds is necessarily very large. (To Mersenne, 11 June 1640, AT iii.84–5, CSM-K 148)

Memory impressions are not now like folds in paper: there are real 'plis de mémoire', folds of memory. If traces are in the changing patterns of brain pores which guide spirit motions, these patterns 'get in each other's way' by interfering in the processes of retrieval. But it is *because* different traces are retained in the *same* parts of the system that only a finite number of such parts (the folds) is required.

This is confirmed when Descartes replies to Mersenne's query about the numerical sufficiency of the brain's 'folds' for all our memories: 'I do not think that there has to be a very large number of these folds to supply all the things we remember, because a single fold will do for all the things which resemble each other' (to Mersenne, 6 August 1640, AT iii.143, CSM-K 151).[12] Many memories can be stored superpositionally in the same system. The particular memory elicited from the system at a time depends on the relation between new patterns of animal spirits entering the folds and the existing dispositional states of spirits and brain fibres.

Descartes refers again here to an 'altogether spiritual' memory, which 'is not found in animals', but which 'we mainly use' (CSM-K 151). The fact that intellectual memory is suddenly given a central billing just as Descartes is spelling out more details of the distributed model is obviously significant. I ascribe his increasing need to back up the account of corporeal memory with a catch-all non-physical memory to an awareness that distributed models led to the interference which, in L'Homme, was already pinpointed as a source of daydream, fantasy, and moral slackness. But the new stress on intellectual memory leads

---

12 This notion of 'resemblance' needs spelling out: Descartes does not think traces represent objects by picturing them (chapter 15 below). In the next sentence Descartes wrote of the bodily memory's 'images', but scored this word out in preference for 'impressions', perhaps making clearer the non-resemblance between patterns of motions in the brain and the objects of memory.

Morris (1969: 455–7) to the stronger conclusion that Descartes has *abandoned* the earlier theory by relegating purely physical memory to beasts alone. But, to repeat, Descartes gives the same account of memory in the *Passions of the Soul*, his last published work, as in *L'Homme*. There are detailed parallels between the psychophysiological theories of the two works (as in the account of hatred): but there is no mention in the *Passions* of intellectual memory. Morris has to downplay the later text, making the strange suggestion that 'Descartes was not yet prepared to defend the doctrine [of intellectual memory] in public' (1969: 457). This is implausible, given the doctrine's theological orthodoxy and respectable position in scholastic and Aristotelian philosophy (Kessler 1988: 509–18).

Descartes' references to 'folds' of memory are compatible with the mechanical theory of *L'Homme*. Traces which remain in the brain after images are imprinted dispose the brain 'to move the soul in the same way as it moved it before, and thus to make it remember something. It is rather as the folds in a piece of paper or cloth make it easier to fold again in that way than it would be if it had never been so folded before' (to Mesland, 2 May 1644, AT iv.114, CSM-K 233). Here the metaphor of the folds is used in exactly the same way as that of the holes left by needles in a cloth had been in *L'Homme*, to explain the mechanism of association, whereby repetition of recall renders further recall easier still. So Descartes adumbrated, albeit hesitantly, a distributed model of memory which does not require discrete, independent storage of all memories and their possible combinations, and which was taken up by later supporters and critics.

The model also implies peculiar relations between processing and storage. Strictly speaking, ideas only exist on the surface of the pineal gland. But memory serves to complicate clean divisions between insides and outsides. There are also superpositional memory representations *outside* the pineal, in the folds of memory throughout the internal substance of the brain and in the body too. In fact memory impressions will only be predominantly located on the pineal gland in people whose minds are 'coarse and sluggish': clear thinking requires the continual externalisation or projection of memory traces out from the gland into supplementary storage systems, in brain, nerves, muscles, hands, and on paper (to Meysonnier, AT iii.20, CSM-K 143; to Mersenne, AT iii.48, CSM-K 146). This is, again, not because Descartes is worried about finding enough memory room in the brain, but so that the pineal remains open to the tracing of new figures. This need can never be fully satisfied, since spirits move continually through the gland from the memory folds. Animal spirits are always breaching the resistant memory folds which are in turn modified in a continual play of difference (compare Foti 1986a: 78).[13]

---

13 Foti (1986a: 76) quotes Derrida's (1978b: 200) description of Freud's problematic of 'accounting simultaneously for the permanence of the trace and for the virginity of the receiving substance'. She argues that Descartes is banishing or relegating

It is tempting to assume that even those actions in which the soul is not involved are still driven by a single central executive where 'it all comes together' (Dennett 1991a: 107; Dennett and Kinsbourne 1992). Dennett's sustained attack on the persisting metaphor of the centre is meant to force acceptance that, once dualism is abandoned, it is still necessary to undermine the further intuition that there must be a headquarters inside the brain, an inner sanctum or functional centre where input must terminate and be received, and output be initiated (1991a: 104–8, 144, 257–8, 321–2). No executive nerve centre exists, for cognition and control are 'distributed around the brain' (1991a: 169).

Dennett's choice of Descartes as target here appears natural, for the pineal gland, unique in its unified structure (Passions 1.32, AT xi.352–3, CSM 1.340), seems uniquely to control all processing.[14] But this is not so, and Dennett's label 'Cartesian materialism' in fact applies poorly to Descartes' own views. The kind of 'processing' accomplished by or at the pineal gland is minimal. Ongoing processing actually occurs out in the interactions between input and representations in the folds of memory, in the same system as storage. No entities or independent items are lifted from memory boxes, transported to the gland to influence computation, and then dumped back in their places: that picture of executive control only works for local models with separate fixed items, as I will describe in Hooke (chapter 5). There is space for transcendent central control in the Cartesian philosophy of the brain: but it is very limited in scope and frequency.

confusion, 'errant memory inscription', and difference 'to the outside, beyond the boundaries of presence', to preserve 'the ideal virginity of the present'. But my reading differs, as I do not ascribe to Descartes a belief that memory has a 'proper inscription in the interior parts of the brain' (Foti 1986a: 77–9). In the Cartesian distributed model, as in Derrida's reading of Freud, both desiderata of the problematic are denied: traces are nowhere permanent, and neither pineal gland nor brain is ever clean.

14 Whatever the best interpretation of its role, the discussion of the gland in the Passions is not a joke (Grene 1985: 48) but an edited, matching version of that in L'Homme, and it places the mental firmly in the causal field. On the pineal gland see Lindeboom 1979: 81–3; Krell 1988, 1990: 319–20. There is a suggestive new theory about its (still poorly understood) function: Maestroni and Conti (1991: thanks to Doris McIlwain for this reference) suggest that it has a central role in 'the psycho–neuroendocrine–immune network', in regulating fertility and environmental rhythms (1991: 496), and (for humans) in causing 'affective and psychosomatic diseases, psychiatric and neurological disorders, and cancer' (1991: 496). This role is mediated by the nearest modern analogue to animal spirits, neuropeptides, and if disturbed may cause differential perceptions of and responses to stress (1991: 510–11). Ann Mackenzie (1989: 175) makes the tempting point that the 'general bodily factors' which Descartes accepts as causal factors in cognitive processing include 'some . . . which we would view as importantly hormonal'. Animal spirits, like hormones, were 'primarily conceptualized in relation to notions of control, encapsulating possibilities for both loss of control, through hormonal lack or excess, and (medical) interventions to (re)assert control over multiple and minute elements of life processes' (Harding 1996: 100).

3.3 Objection 1: intellectual memory

Surely I cannot be serious: Descartes the connectionist? No. Yet the concept of distributed memory is independent of the specific technological and computational developments of recent years. Many apparent reasons to resist my interpretation of the Cartesian philosophy of the brain turn out not to hold up. In this and the next three sections I run through a set of objections to my account. In answering them I add more detail to the positive characterisation of the models of memory in which I am interested. Descartes is not always, and never clearly, close to an idealised historical connectionist: I seek the vanishing points in his view of memory, where he holds back from consequences of his own theory. The dialectic in these sections is twofold. I show, in each case, that the objection in question does not unambiguously refute my attribution of a distributed model to Descartes, since resources exist within his account of corporeal memory for dealing with the phenomena in question; and that difficulties in rendering his views consistent result from his uncertainty about exactly what follows from them.

The first objection is this. Descartes cannot have had a distributed model of memory (or any neurophilosophical model), since he believed in an immaterial memory of universals, an intellectual memory more truly human than that of which the mere brain is capable.

Descartes did accept such a memory. But he continually postponed detailed discussion, perhaps well aware of its philosophical limitations.[15] Even if he hoped to integrate theological views on intellectual memory into his overall psychology, his sketchy references to intellectual memory were not taken seriously.

But I take the opportunity to go through four philosophical problems with Descartes' version of an intellectual memory, and in doing so, to develop some positive lines of thought about distributed models of memory. From difficulties about the differences between remembering particulars and universals, we learn something of the relation of exemplars and prototypes in distributed models. From problems about resurrection and the continuity of self, we learn something about personal identity. In correspondence, Descartes resists his own physiological accounts of memory: I look at his difficulties with wonder and with infantile amnesia, and ask why in some contexts he retreated from his speculative neuromechanics. Problems within the intellectual-memory doctrine reveal Descartes' desire for cognitive order, the same desire which sometimes drives him, aware of the fragility of memory, to try to bypass memory altogether.

---

15 'There are many other points to be noted on this topic [intellectual memory] which cannot now be explained in detail' (to Hyperaspistes, August 1641, AT iii.425, K 112; cf. *Principles of Philosophy* 1.74, AT viii(a).38, CSM 1.221). These postponements are enjoyed by Krell (1990: 61).

Universals and particulars

Burman reminds Descartes that even if, in infancy, 'traces are not imprinted on the brain . . . there still exists an intellectual memory, as is undoubtedly the case with angels or disembodied souls' (conversation with Burman, 16 April 1648, CSM-K 336, AT v.150). Descartes stresses that 'I do not refuse to admit intellectual memory: it does exist' (CSM-K 336, AT v.150). What is the function of this 'altogether spiritual' memory, which 'we mainly use' but which 'is not found in animals' (to Mersenne, 6 August 1640, AT iii.143, CSM-K 151), and what wonders can it perform?

This 'entirely intellectual' memory (to Mersenne, 1 April 1640, AT iii.48, CSM-K 146) preserves only abstract knowledge. It 'has universals rather than particulars as its objects, and so it cannot enable us to recall every single thing we have done' (conversation with Burman, CSM-K 337, AT v.150). Intellectual memory may, for Descartes, be one way to access innate ideas (Foti 1986a: 75; Reiss 1996: 600–1). Since the objects of intellectual memory are 'purely intellectual things, memory in the strict sense is not involved' at all, since 'they are thought of just as readily irrespective of whether it is the first or second time that they come to mind' (to Hyperaspistes, August 1641, AT iii.425, CSM-K 190). But memory is in practice often involved, because abstract things can be 'associated with certain names, in which case, since the latter are corporeal, we do indeed remember them'. This seems to imply that incorporeal memory depends on corporeal memory, but Descartes insists that intellectual memory 'has its own separate impressions', independent of the folds of memory in the brain (to Mersenne, 11 June 1640, AT iii.85, CSM-K 148). Memory of intellectual things 'depends on some other traces which remain in the mind itself. But the latter are of a wholly different kind from the former, and I cannot explain them by any illustration drawn from corporeal things without a great deal of qualification' (to Mesland, 2 May 1644, AT iv.114, CSM-K 233).

The inability of corporeal traces to represent universals was stressed in a different way by Gassendi: while there can be 'a trace of a collection, which by their similarities represent many', this will 'only be an aggregate or composite of many, which have a similarity among themselves'. Corporeal memory can retain only exemplars, aggregates of particulars: something non-physical is required to retain prototypic 'universal natures, e.g. humanity, which are precise and distinct from all grades of singulars' (Gassendi, quoted in Michael and Michael 1989: 43).

The assumption here, shared by Descartes and Gassendi, is that corporeal mechanisms can only connect exemplars by juxtaposition, unable to extract or fuse prototypes out of aggregates of particular cases. How could abstract ideas of triangularity, humanity, goodness, and the like, arise by the mere associative recording of instances, isolated nodes in a memory network? Where would the true forms be in the mind?

But it is exactly the ability to generalise to ideals or prototypes that the Cartesian associative memory was set up to have. The network described in L'Homme fills in the rest of a typical face when presented only with a picture of eyes and nose. Automatic generalisation means that the system carries an implicit prototype representation which differs from representations of particular examples (compare McClelland and Rumelhart 1986). Why does Descartes not even address the possibility that his own theory of associative memory might have the resources required? Primarily because the key context to his discussions of intellectual memory is the quite different one of survival and immortality.

Resurrection and personal continuity

In 1642 Descartes comforts the bereaved Huygens with the thought that when, one day, we join the dead in 'a sweeter and more tranquil life than ours . . . we shall still remember the past; for we have, in my view, an intellectual memory which is certainly independent of the body' (to Huygens, 10 October 1642, AT iii.598, CSM-K 216). He protests rather too much the philosophical clarity of this view: the 'very evident natural reasons' for believing it move us more strongly, 'however much we wish to believe', than 'all that religion teaches' (AT iii.599).

One tension in these remarks is pointed out by J. J. MacIntosh (1983; compare Morris 1969: 456). Since all our actions are particulars, and since intellectual memory (which alone survives bodily death) is only of universals, the comfort Huygens should feel in the prospect of eternally remembering the past looks misguided. What is the point of surviving, disembodied, into an afterlife without autobiographical memory of particular experiences in earthly life? What solace will be the recollection of innate ideas, with content which by definition is not tied to the personal history which grief arouses?[16]

MacIntosh's worry can be extended. Eschatology had always been the point of doctrines of intellectual memory. Medieval discussions of the resurrection of the body were consistently materialist, denying that the numerical identity of current and judged individuals could be defended unless their physical parts were reassembled to ensure material continuity: as Caroline Bynum puts it, identity went with the organs (Bynum 1992, 1995b; Davis 1988). But some late scholastics argued, against Aquinas, for a disembodied memory alongside that which depends on corporeal organs, so that the separated soul could recollect the past after death (Kessler 1988: 510; for earlier accounts see Coleman 1992). Separated souls without immaterial memory would be 'crippled for

---

16 Gordon Baker has suggested to me that Descartes perhaps thought of *conscientia*, thought of as reflection on what is *and has been* in the mind, as providing for the mental memory of particulars which is required here. While this seems a possible view, it is not clear that Descartes accepts or emphasises it: see Baker and Morris 1996: 114.

eternity', noted Pomponazzi (1516/1948: 309) (although his conclusion was not that there is such a memory, but that there are no disembodied souls).

In adding a purely intellectual memory to his physiological model, Descartes thus entered an established theological debate with a respectable conservative line. Officially, for Descartes, I am my incorporeal soul, and so the bodily memory to which I am attached in life cannot contribute to my personal identity. He has no further eschatological concern about responsibility: but exactly this point would lead Locke to use memory as a criterion for continuity of self. On Descartes' view, the fact that I will have only (intellectual) memory of universals in the afterlife does not matter, since I will still be myself, my identity given by identity of soul. To later eyes, this seemed grossly unfair: I may be punished by God for sins (particular actions) I no longer remember committing! The alternative state, in which I might be the puzzled recipient of a prize of eternal bliss awarded on the basis of good deeds of which I have no recollection, came to seem almost as unsatisfactory. In one of the weirder seventeenth-century arguments about memory, Henry More claimed that we must in the afterlife retain 'durable traces' of our transactions in this. Only thus could the elect revel in 'peculiar Priviledges of Morality' in the heavenly recollection of their pious lives, while enjoying the spectacle of sinners being punished by amoral officers of justice who torture the unrepentant with 'lascivient cruelty . . . according to the multifarious petulancy of their own unaccountable humours' (IS III.II: 187–92).

Problems about the mechanisms of memory came to be increasingly connected with issues of personal continuity. Philosophers would either have to rely on the unwholesomely materialistic orthodox belief in bodily resurrection, or have to find more secure ways to elucidate intellectual memory. With memory thus embroiled in eschatology, difficulties about secular responsibility would also arise: continuity of memory seems necessary to guarantee that the person praised or punished is the same person who committed the criminal or commendable act. In chapters 7 and 9 below I show just how tricky it was to reconcile this theoretical need for continuity with the ubiquitous idea that memory depended on fleeting animal spirits.

Memory and the physiology of wonder
Descartes comes to use intellectual memory to show how an idea of something past is recognised *as* an idea of something past. He writes in 1648:

> If we are to remember something, it is not sufficient that the thing should previously have been before our mind and left some traces in the brain which give occasion for it to occur in our thought again; it is necessary in addition that we should recognize, when it occurs the second time, that this is happening because it has already been perceived by us earlier. (For Arnauld, 29 July 1648, AT v.220, CSM-K 356)

The running of animal spirits down specific impressed paths through the folds of the brain is not, he now claims, sufficient for memory. The mind has to recognise that traces 'left in the brain by preceding thoughts' have 'not always been present in us, but were at some time newly impressed'. Such mental recognition, argues Descartes, proves that 'when these traces were first made it must have made use of pure intellect to notice that the thing which was then presented to it was new and had not been presented before; for there cannot be any corporeal trace of this novelty' (AT v.220, CSM-K 356). So in ordinary perception the mind must recognise ideas as new, as not past.

The import of these passages, beyond Descartes' increasing willingness in certain contexts to argue for 'two different powers of memory' (for Arnauld, 4 June 1648, AT v.192, CSM-K 354), is not immediately clear. Only through a reflection of the intellect at the time of a first impression can we observe a trace to be new (for Arnauld, 29 July 1648, AT v.220, CSM-K 357). But the claim that there can be no corporeal trace of this novelty is contradicted by Descartes' own later discussion of wonder. I know of no other acknowledgement of the connections between intellectual memory and the treatment of wonder in the *Passions*: although I may be missing something which reconciles them, I will briefly sketch the apparent tension.[17]

Wonder, 'the first of all the passions', occurs 'when our first encounter with some object surprises us and we find it novel' (*Passions* II.53, AT xi.373, CSM I.350). There are two causes of the 'sudden surprise of the soul' in wonder: 'an impression in the brain, which represents the object as something unusual', and 'a movement of the spirits, which the impression disposes both to flow with great force to the place in the brain where it is located so as to strengthen and preserve it there' (*Passions* II.70, AT xi.380–1, CSM I.353).

Wonder fixes a local memory trace, as spirits flow between brain, muscle, and sense organs so as to 'continue to maintain the impression in the way in which they formed it'. Wonder is useful 'in that it makes us learn and retain in our memory things of which we were previously ignorant' (*Passions* II.75, AT xi.384, CSM I.354), and in strengthening and prolonging good thoughts which 'otherwise might easily be erased' (II.74, AT xi.383, CSM I.354). The 'novelty' and the strength of the motions of the spirits (II.72, AT xi.382, CSM I.353–4) conspire to isolate a memory trace and render it, temporarily, independent of others. Wonder is a special case in the cognitive economy, uniquely resulting in the formation of a particular place where an impression is located (II.73, AT xi.382, CSM I.354).

In addition to the interest of these passages in the context of the general

---

17 My reading of Malebranche on wonder and local representation suggested this link: see appendix 2 below. Landormy, Morris, MacIntosh, and Krell say nothing of it. I develop the implications further through a more general discussion of self-control in Sutton 1998.

neurophilosophical model of memory, they imply corporeal traces of novelty. While it can 'perhaps' be through 'an application of our intellect as fixed by our will in a special state of attention and reflection' that the trace of something novel and extraordinary is retained in the memory, 'our idea of it' can also be 'strengthened in our brains by some passion' (*Passions* II.75, AT xi.384, CSM I.355).

In diagnosis of the contradiction, beyond noting that Descartes forgets what the brain can do when wanting to dissociate his theorising from the corporeal, I can only suggest that the deep encoding of a local independent memory trace is, on a distributed model, rare. So, normally, it is difficult for the corporeal mechanism to reveal the novelty of a newly presented object, because new traces are almost always already superposed on a number of other traces in the same fold of the brain. Since a pattern of animal spirit motions through partic-ular brain pores must be reconstructed, it has not always been (explicitly) present, and it is thus hard for the object represented to be recognised as having already been perceived at a particular earlier date. This contrasts with the easy localist account of the perception of duration and of the temporal placement of memories by their location on the coils of memory which critics like Hooke postulated instead (chapter 5 below). Isolated traces may, as the *Passions* sug-gests, occasionally occur in Cartesian neurophilosophy: but they are too unusual, on a distributed model, to form a basis for a complete corporeal account of recognition.

Infantile amnesia

Infants, claims Descartes, have no 'pure acts of understanding', but only con-fused sensations, leaving traces in the brain 'which remain there for life', but which are not alone sufficient for memory. 'For that we would have to observe that the sensations which come to us as adults are like those which we had in our mother's womb; and that in turn would require a certain reflective act of the intellect, or intellectual memory, which was not in use in the womb' (for Arnauld, 4 June 1648, AT v.192–3, CSM-K 354–5).

Memory depends on the act of the mind at the time of encoding in addition to its later recognition of the idea as past. Descartes reasserts this: 'if ever I wrote that the thoughts of children leave no traces in their brain, I meant traces sufficient for memory, that is, traces which at the time of their impression are observed by pure intellect to be new'. The case is supported by an analogy very different from L'Homme's analogies of needles in cloth and folds of paper:

> in a similar way we say that there are no human tracks in the sand if we cannot find any impressions shaped like a human foot, though perhaps there may be many unevennesses made by human feet, which can therefore in another sense be called human tracks. (For Arnauld, 29 July 1648, AT v.220, CSM-K 356–7)

It looks as if Descartes, like Erwin Straus, takes this footprints-in-sand analogy to conflict with all notions of corporeal traces: but perhaps it reveals deeper understanding of the nature of distributed traces. Theorists hostile to the trace (because they assume traces must be crudely held in mental storehouses) see the transformations caused by overlaid foot tracks, when there is no exact match between prints and imprinting or trace and past event, as evidence against the existence of traces, rather than as hints at what reconstructed traces might be (Straus 1962/1966: 83–90; Lyons 1981; Krell 1990: 89–91). But in fact this is a good working metaphor for distributed memory. Obliterated but real tracks, those 'unevennesses made by human feet', are the implicit traces, reconstructible if at all only after transformation, providing only indirect access to the past, reconstructing a past which was never present.

Descartes' overt wish in these letters to distance himself from the corporeal-memory model is, indeed, undermined by an earlier idea of his own. He sketched a different approach to infantile amnesia in one of the 1640 letters, noting that 'it is a mistake to believe that we remember best what we did when we were young; for then we did countless things which we no longer remember at all'. But his explanation differs from that of 1648, and is consistent with the theory of corporeal memory.

> Those we do remember are remembered not only because of the impressions we received when we were young, but mainly because we have done the same things again and renewed the impressions by remembering the events from time to time. (To Mersenne, 6 August 1640, AT iii.143, CSM-K 151)

Infantile amnesia is here caused not by the failure of intellectual reflection at the time of experience, but merely through the lack of repetition of the right combinations of spirit motions and patterns of brain configurations. If actions of infants are not repeated, the spirits will not leave the dispositional traces in the pores of the brain which would render recall easier in the future.

Descartes' intellectual-memory doctrine has met with little modern sympathy (Gaukroger 1995: 392; MacIntosh 1983: 346). Defined only negatively, it is parasitic on corporeal memory (Krell 1990: 62). It suffers all the difficulties of general interactionist dualism with conservation of energy and the means of causation across the substantial rift: in addition, I have suggested specific ways in which the official account is undercut by possibilities that distributed corporeal memory could fulfil its functions. I seek not so much another litany of logical problems in dualism, as insight into the particular dangers of corporeal mechanisms which dualists wanted to avert. It could be just because Descartes' psychophysiology gave the self so little autonomy, such a fragile grip on bodily processes, that he sometimes retreated from his own empirical theories.

3.4 Objection 2: memory, soul, and automatism
Memory in machines

How can a dualist have had a neurological theory of memory? Oliver Sacks (1990) has puzzled over the strange fact that a sizeable number of leading neuroscientists believe in a non-physical mind (Eccles 1994). Descartes too saw no tension between seeking imagination and memory in the brains of animals slaughtered by butchers, and arguing that human flexibility in rational action and linguistic response is only possible if we possess an incorporeal soul. Despite insistence in physiological contexts that God the great artificer has so skilfully moulded inconceivably minute textures of matter that the disposition of the organs they compose gives rise to all the behaviour of living animals, Descartes denies that a completed microbiomechanics will explain these key higher functions: we cannot imagine the requisite complexity of mechanism (*Discourse on the Method*, part v, AT vi.58–9, CSM 1.140–1). So, it seems, nothing in Descartes' physiology could be a model of human memory, whether reconstructive and distributed or not.

The first answer to this objection is that Descartes does not take memory to be a *mental* capacity at all, for it does not require consciousness or soul. Its explanation is embedded among accounts of life functions: God could (and for us has) joined in puzzling mixture a rational soul to *L'Homme*'s living body-machines, but their life processes operate independently of that union. Descartes is clear:

> the effect of Memory which seems to me to be most worthy of consideration here is that, without there being any soul present in this machine, it can naturally be disposed to imitate all the movements that true men – or many other similar machines – will make in its presence. (AT xi.185)

This is not 'memory' in any derivative sense: this just is (corporeal) memory. Only intellectual memory is unique to humans: the celebrated beast-machine doctrine (*Discourse*, part v; to Plempius for Fromondus, 3 October 1637, AT i.413, CSM-K 61–3; to Newcastle, 23 November 1646, AT iv.573–6, CSM-K 302–4; to More, 5 February 1649, AT v.275–9, CSM-K 365–6) does not deny corporeal memory to animals. Soul-less machines or beasts have many capacities which *we* would class as cognitive. Even though Descartes does not so class them, the various phenomena he tries to explain are genuine phenomena of memory, sensation, emotion, imagination, and so on. These are the functions which the strangely powerful spirits and nerves can perform. Knowledge of the physiology here, Descartes thinks, in fact shows us how little our soul is responsible for. So although there can be no Cartesian science of mind, there can and must be a science of memory.

But this answer is unlikely to satisfy. Surely, without a soul, the only 'memory' possible would be reflex action, mere automatism, not the personal memory we care about. Is the fact that Descartes' physiology of memory excludes consciousness not enough for us to dismiss it as unsatisfactory: is it not 'clear that the one thing Descartes was not explaining was the psychological-ity' of what we call psychological events (Richards 1992: 65–6)? It is just because Descartes sees animal action as inflexible, wholly stimulus-driven, that he thinks beasts are automata (Seris 1993). On this view, humans have two modes of response to the world, automatic reflex behaviour, imposed by passive brains soaking up stimuli, and incorporeally-mediated (because con-scious) action, while beasts have only the former.

I address the objection in this form. It assumes falsely that the dichotomy between reflex action and true action derived ultimately from the soul is exhaus-tive, that you are either an automaton or a rational soul. In fact, Descartes accepts an intermediate form of interaction with the environment, a class of responses into which fall many phenomena of great interest to him and to us.[18] To defend this controversial claim, I start with an example of the orthodox interpretation which I dispute.

Reflex action, automata, and beast-machines
Owen Flanagan (1991: 3) describes the impoverished world of the 'Cartesian automaton', restricted, because it is only body, to automatic reflex behaviour in dealing with the world:

> the complete system of wired-in reflex arcs exhausts its behavioral potential. What a particular automaton eventually does, how it in fact behaves, is the inevitable result of the interaction between the environment and the wired-in arcs. Such a system is deterministic in the sense that, barring mechanical failure, there is one and only one response for each stimulus.

This is at best misleading, more probably false. Flanagan implies that automata will always respond in the same way to the same stimulus, and indeed that all (similarly designed) automata will respond likewise.[19] Only initial wiring,

---

18 A related response to the objection, which I do not pursue here, is to accept that Descartes' corporeal memory includes only the forms of memory which psychologists now call 'implicit', with no conscious awareness of remembering (Jacoby 1988). Even if Descartes excludes consciousness (whatever that is) from bodies, implicit memory is vital not only for successful ongoing life processes but also as a central source of explicit subjective remembering in beings like us who also have minds. The effects of implicit memory can feel like 'mental contamination' as we are often unaware of the sources of our remembering (Schacter 1996: 161–91). Descartes' theories of implicit memory are intended to help us in the troublesome task of extending control into the systems which underpin memory-without-awareness, to exchange hard conscious intrusions into associative processes for the common, haunting, intrusive effects of implicit memories on consciousness.

19 Flanagan continues: 'or to put it another way: given any stimulus, it is impossible for the system to do other than it in fact does.' This is a red herring. Descartes probably thought it true even for rational human action that 'given any stimulus, it is impossible for the system to do other than it in fact does.' At least in the Latin Meditations (AT vii.58), he denies that human freedom entails the positive 'two-way' power of determining to do either of two

fixed before the automaton goes out into the world, and immediate present environmental input count: so of course all automata will always react in the same way. The behavioural potential of *some* simple organisms is indeed exhausted by its system of wired-in reflex arcs, with no learning from experience or modification of wiring in new environments. But this is not the case for Cartesian automata (and it is certainly not implied in the very idea of an automaton).

Flanagan, in fact, sets up the issue wrongly by looking at Descartes' philosophy of the body through an 'analogy' Descartes allegedly draws between inorganic automata and the organic human body (1991: 3). The problem is not just that everything artificial is, for Descartes, *also* natural (*Principles of Philosophy* IV.203, AT viii(a).326, CSM 1.288): it is that automata, specifically, *are* organic, self-moving machines which behave as they do because of the disposition of their *organs*. This is not to eliminate the organic (or the cognitive), but to explain it by reduction (Gaukroger 1995: 279, 287–90). The organic nature of living human bodies does not make them, for Descartes, any less automatic (compare Carter 1985/1991: 207–8). Yet the 'disposition' of their organs is not fixed at birth.

The case of memory makes this clear, for in memory processes there is no immediate motor response to stimuli, and if there is a delayed motor output it is not hard-wired (Gaukroger 1995: 280–1). Corporeal memory transmits effects of experience over long temporal gaps, so that they are causally involved in behaviour mediated by complex internal processes. As Descartes notes, it is not necessary for the incorporeal soul always to be implicated in these processes. Yet the determinism involved in these responses is not a simple stimulus/response link, for corporeal causes act holistically, and are not restricted to those immediately current. To put it another way, memory shows that an automaton's physiology changes over time. Automata with different histories, different 'experiences' marking their brains and bodies, will respond differently, and one automaton will respond differently at different times to the same stimulus after new experience has modified the spirits and pores in the folds of its brain.

Conceptual room for this intermediate category between the simply automatic and the incorporeally free can be found at a number of levels in Descartes' texts.[20] I approach it through the neurophilosophy: a schematic outline will help.

contraries, though Michelle Beyssade (1994) suggests that he did accept this incompatibilist Jesuit view of freedom as 'indifference' after 1645 (compare Chappell 1994). So of course Descartes denied free will to automata: but this is not at all equivalent to Flanagan's much stronger claim that an automaton's behaviour is wholly determined *only* by wired-in reflex arcs and current stimulus. Determinism allows greater complexity than that.

20   In the distinctions between three grades of sensory act (replies to the sixth set of objections, AT vii.438, CSM 11.295–6), the first grade is physical and physiological and purely automatic; the second is sensory, in some way the immediate mental result of the mind's union with sense organs; and the third is the grade of judgement. But these distinctions are far from clear, and the intermediate mode of cognitive response which I

Organism/environment interaction: three possible forms

	Hard-wired	Soul	Pineal
1. Simple automatism	Yes	No	No
2. Complex automatism	No	No	Yes
3. True action	No	Yes	Yes

Simple automatism, firstly, is hard-wired, an immediate and invariant response to a sufficient stimulus. Even if Descartes' account of the reflex is 'short on detail about the specifics of neuroplumbing' (Hatfield 1992: 348), the following seems clear (Canguilhem 1955/1977: 27–56; Spillane 1981: 84–9; Clarke 1989: 185; Dennett 1991a: 105, 321–2). Automatic behaviour is mediated, after stimulus information is transmitted from the sense organs, by animal spirits flowing from the brain ventricles into the muscles. It is 'just the same' as the immediate, fixed chains between the passage of air through organ pipes and the particular sounds the organ produces (AT xi.165–6), and this analogy proves that Flanagan's account is appropriate here: 'the organ simply produces the music as a result of an input: it does not represent the notes to itself, in the way that the organist might' (Gaukroger 1995: 280).

Simple automatism does *not* involve the pineal gland: the switch from sensory to motor response occurs when the entrance to a brain pore or tube is opened by the motion of a nerve fibre, and animal spirits from the ventricles enter and are carried through the tube to various muscles (*L'Homme* AT xi.142, H 34–5, CSM I.101–2). Some commentators have been confused into attributing to the pineal gland a role in reflex action by the much reproduced illustration of an automatic response to fire near the foot (Figure 3).[21] But others (such as Jefferson 1949: 699) have understood that the oval form in the brain labelled F is described clearly in the text as 'the cavity F', and thus, in Descartes' vocabulary, can only be the brain ventricle and *not* the pineal gland (Figure 4).

So memory ideas are traced in spirits on the surface of the gland: but the gland is not involved in simple automatism. The difference between reflexes

attribute to Descartes would include both the second grade of sense and some cases of the third, those in which judgements are made on the basis of habits formed in childhood in response to the institutions of nature (rather than the mature judgements of the rational mind). Reed (1982: 736–7) misleads by limiting the third grade to what is 'essentially mental' and not allowing for this division within it. For a better interpretation see Hatfield 1986, 1990: 44–5. All I rely on here is a wider class of responses which do not involve the soul, but which are also not simple automatism.

21 More emphasis can be placed on the textual reference to a cavity than on these pictures, which were not Descartes' (AT xi.vi–vii). But the pineal gland is consistently labelled H (not F). Descartes' later discussion of the different neural effects of placing a hand near moderate and hot fire (AT xi.191, H 102–3) refers only to the differential opening of tubes in the brain mesh and on the internal surface of the ventricular cavities, and not to the gland.

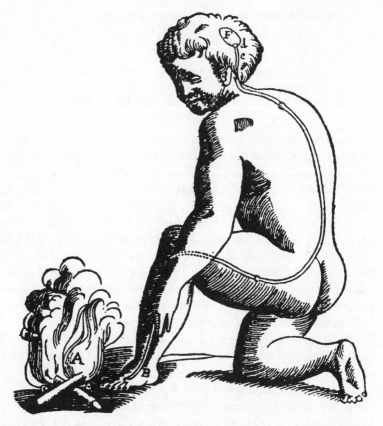

Figure 3 Familiar image of reflex action from *L'Homme* (Descartes 1664: 27), which has encouraged the mistaken identification of 'the cavity F' with the pineal gland

and corporeal memory is that reflex pathways are unalterable, whereas the passage of spirits through the pineal gland drives them into regions of the brain which do change, allowing the plasticity of memory. Therefore there are no ideas or representations, strictly speaking, in simple automatism. This is sensation and immediate response without representation: a primary function of representations, to extend capacity for response over time, is not required.

Actions caused by the soul,[22] at the other extreme, *do* require the mediation of the pineal gland to transmit or direct its action in the physical world. But, and

22 The language of causation here (from mental to physical) seems unchallengeable even by occasionalist interpreters of body to mind relations. John Yolton, who prefers to think of Descartes' physiological events occasioning (rather than causing) sensations, points out (1990a: 72, n. 30) that non-causal occasional or significatory relations apply only in the direction of body to mind, since 'the mind seems able to cause or make the pineal gland move and hence affect the body's physiology'.

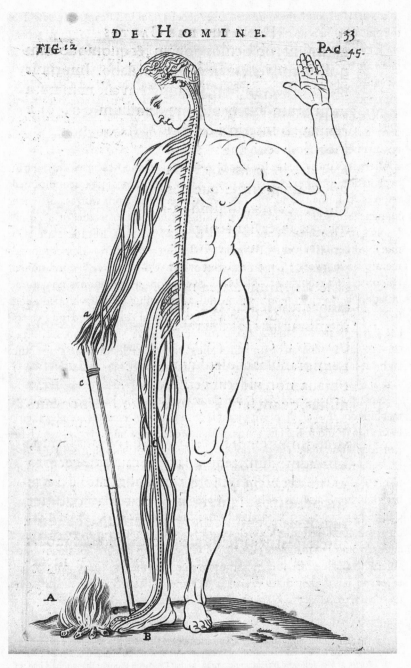

Figure 4 Simple automatism: this strange illustration of a Cartesian automaton, from Schuyl's Latin edition of L'Homme (Descartes 1662: 33), makes it easier to see that 'the cavity F' is the ventricle (Wellcome Institute Library, London)

this is the vital point, there are also cases of behaviour in the causation of which the pineal gland is involved where the soul is not.[23] Thus there are three separate kinds of response. As well as (1) simple automatism and (3) true action, there are intermediate responses (available to organic automata) which could be called (2) complex automatism, 'physical-cognitive', or even 'cognitive-automatic'. Remembering is not *simply* automatic: this is *both* because it involves the pineal gland, and because it can occur over long interrupted periods, longer than the longest kinds of stimulus/response arc. Again, it need not involve the rational soul.

There is extra evidence for this threefold schema in Descartes' attitude to explanation by reflex. He is aware of hardwired immediate unconditioned reflexes in humans and animals, when sheep run from wolves, or when humans throw out their arms when falling 'without the assistance of any soul' (replies to Fourth Objections, AT vii.204, CSM 11.144). But there are also much longer term, yet still wholly physical, responses in which corporeal memory is at work. Some are cases which we would call 'conditioned response', the acquisition of learned associations where there is no natural 'relation' between a representation and its 'meaning'. 'If you whipped a dog five or six times to the sound of a violin, it would begin to howl and run away as soon as it heard that music again' (to Mersenne, 18 March 1630, AT i.134, CSM-K 20). Setters can be trained, against natural inclinations, to stop at the sight of a partridge and run towards it on hearing a gun (AT xi.370, CSM 1.348).

But rather than conceptually isolating these conditioned responses of dog-machines or linking them with simple automatism, Descartes couples them, both in 1630 and in the late 1640s, with more complex human cases which he considers equivalent. The dog howling at the music of whipping is linked with an account of why 'what makes one man want to dance may make another want to cry', when the latter has 'never heard a galliard without some affliction befalling him': he cries 'because it evokes ideas in our memory' (AT i.133-4, CSM-K 20). The case of the trained setter, in the crucial sections of the *Passions* on psychological conflict and self-control, is 'worth noting in order to encourage each one of us to make a point of controlling our passions. For since we are able, with a little effort, to change the movements of the brain in animals devoid of reason, it is evident that we can do so still more effectively in the case of men' (*Passions* 1.50, AT xi.370, CSM 1.348).

---

23 The point of the pineal, then, is not (as caricatures of Cartesianism would have it) simply to buttress metaphysical dualism: animal automata have pineal glands too. Jaynes' claim (1970: 226–7, followed by Harrington 1987: 6) that Descartes thought that animals had no pineal gland is false: Descartes was accustomed to finding it 'without any difficulty in freshly killed animals'. He had more trouble locating the metaphysically crucial gland in human autopsies (to Mersenne, 1 April 1640, AT iii.49, CSM-K 146).

Not everything, then, in humans or in dog-machines, is innately wired in, for 'the movements of the brain' change in the course of experience. Cartesian automata are not the uncanny 'Neurospasts', nimble sprightly puppets which only *seem* to be moved from within, feared by vehement defenders of free will like Cudworth and More (Gabbey 1992: 117). It is just because wholly corporeal long-term conditioning and the long-term workings of associative memory (which Descartes classes together) are flexible in these ways that knowledge of them is so important to those unique beings, ourselves, who do also have souls. The soul's occasional influence on bodily states is its only way of instituting better habits in the wayward dynamics of spirits and brain. Associative memory is the key capacity for us to use in the moral attempt to divert our own internal fluids from running into dangerous traces: we can *learn* 'to separate within ourselves the movements of the blood and spirits from the thoughts to which they are usually joined' (*Passions* III. 211, AT xi.486, CSM 1.403; see also Barnouw 1992: 406–8).

The explananda in *L'Homme*'s soul-less world extend well beyond immediate reactions to stimuli, covering intervening variables like the long-term interactions of corporeal memory traces. There is no incompatibility between all the complexity of the life functions and mechanism (Mackenzie 1989: 168): but the life functions extend well beyond innate reflex arcs. In machines with the right microstructures, the past leaves specific traces in changing motions inside the body. Only physical variables are involved, and yet the notions of experience and individual learning history are applicable. The diverse causal factors involved in registering and integrating information include 'previous brain episodes' and non-neural bodily events as well as current environmental input: 'this is the model of an automaton, to be sure, but not one which operates by reflex' (Mackenzie 1989: 174–5; compare Fearing 1929: 386–7; and Grosholz 1991: 126–7).

This is exactly right: there are response which are 'cognitive' or at least not simple-automatic, which involve the rolling pineal gland, but which do not require the soul. This is enough to correct some unsympathetic criticisms. Marjorie Grene (1985: 47–8) is indignant that Descartes ascribes memory to animals after so foolishly claiming that beasts are machines. But when a conceptual space *between* the automatic and the non-physical is opened, it is no surprise that impressions can be formed in the brains of animals by, among other things, 'the traces of previous impressions left in the memory, or by the agitation of the spirits which come from the heart' (to Princess Elizabeth, 6 October 1645, AT iv.310, CSM-K 270). Generally, contrary to popular views (Williams 1978: 282), Cartesian beast-machines and living automata *can* feel, remember, imagine, sense, and dream (Rodis-Lewis 1978; Gaukroger 1993b, 1995: 287–9, 392–4; Baker and Morris 1996: 91–100).

3.5 Objection 3: mechanism, matter, and active bodies

Inert bodies? In their call for papers, the organisers of an interdisciplinary philosophy conference on 'Body Matters' complained (Burwood and Jagger 1994) that 'The Cartesian legacy has furnished contemporary thinking with a paradigm of the body as an inert, closed, and anonymous object.' A curious consensus in analytic history of philosophy, medical anthropology, feminist theory, and cultural studies at large coalesces around the image of Descartes as anti-magus, stripping nature and the human body of all powers and activity. An earlier enchanted world, criss-crossed by networks of sympathies and antipathies, embracing analogy and suggestion over representation and intervention, traversed by holistic herbalists and natural magicians, coupling earthy bodily realism with organicist ecologism, was sundered and lost with Descartes' blind scientistic drive for the mastery, possession, and penetration of nature. The removal of mind from body is but one symptom, on this view, of multiple damaging Cartesian schisms, dividing philosophy from biology, science from history, power-mongering manipulators of nature from the dead ecology which they exploit, active rational male observers from passive fragmented female bodies, or mechanistic interventionist medicine from a more watchful psychosomatic physic of the whole person (e.g. Toulmin 1990: 107–15).

From this line of thought springs the third objection to my interpretation of Descartes on memory. Distributed memories are always in motion, never faithful in inert cells in a memory palace. Surely, then, the Descartes we all know and love to hate *cannot* have had a dynamic distributed model of memory: his mechanistic natural philosophy notoriously renders the body and its contents, like all extension, purely passive, moved only by the active power of mind or other disembodied intelligence. Specifically, Descartes notoriously reduces (or wishes to reduce) the whole of natural philosophy to mechanics, allowing no dynamics and no active forces: how then could he imagine memory motions superimposed and re-separated in the intuitively non-linear fashion characteristic of distributed models?

I respond by denying the existence of such a clear line in Cartesian natural philosophy between the passive and the active. Despite rhetoric about inert matter, mechanism was (and is) compatible with activity in physical and biological worlds. Immersion in Descartes' neurophilosophy shows that, despite twentieth-century historiography, more 'dynamic' concepts of disposition and pattern have unproblematic mechanistic senses. The human body is a multiply constrained composite, and is not in practice inert: general Cartesian physiology is a dynamics of fluids, a brave attempt to listen to the pulse of the body-machine.

These are large claims, which I overstate to correct easy assumptions of their falsity. I sketch the form of their defence in three directions. I describe the rationale for thinking of Cartesian natural philosophy, and in particular physiology, as (a form of) dynamics. Then I return to the question of machines, arguing that seventeenth-century mechanism was not, as Carolyn Merchant, Otto Mayr, and others in diverse fields claim, intrinsically authoritarian: Cartesian automata are not wholly reliant on external design and direction, but have their own activity, specificity, and causal powers; they lack only the acausal autonomy and authoritarian control over body and brain officially attributed to the soul. Finally, I generalise this point to describe the puzzlingly anti-'modern' nature of the human body in Descartes' neurophilosophy: mechanisation does not eliminate but exacerbates the permeability of the open body.

My motivation here is not to deny the continuing political and intellectual need to undermine the simplifying dichotomies I listed above. They have had real and often damaging effects, structuring thought, feeling, and action, though in many cases later than the seventeenth century. Again, my caricature of fetishised 'false nostalgia' for 'some lost, but recoverable, perfection' in the pre-Cartesian world (compare Reiss 1996: 592–3) is not intended disrespectfully, for the very romance of a pre-modern golden age is the most powerful initial encouragement to seek glimpses of more complex historical differences. But I seek more nuanced understanding both of the target positions and of the space of possible alternatives, through historical dismantling or dissolution of easy stories about their 'origins'. This is not only misplaced scholarly rehabilitation of a maligned metaphysician for a world heavier with grief, anger, and decay than was even his. It is also driven by a desire to test the possibilities and limits of current flirtations with the fragility of memory, by questioning our common visions of the earlier ideas of science and the body which supported and clashed with the image of fluid motions in the folds of memory.

3.5.1 Dynamics, mechanism, and Cartesian physiology

Descartes, judges a historian of physiology, was 'a representative of the baroque, partial to a dynamic interpretation of nature' (Rothschuh 1953/1973: 78; compare Jefferson 1949: 692). This sounds odd to philosophers and historians of science reared on sharp contrasts between the barren world objectified by Cartesian science and the more sympathetic, nested worlds of baroque Leibnizian monads (Deleuze 1993) or Newtonian forces, ethers, and active powers.

Descartes did pursue and extend the anti-secularising project of Mersenne and other Paris mechanists who sought to drain nature of the forces and sympathies of Renaissance Neoplatonists and naturalists, combating above all the atheism implicit in attributing too much autonomy to matter: mechanism was initially attractive, in the 1620s, because of its supernaturalising theological conservatism (Merchant 1980: 196–200; Hutchison 1983; Hine 1984;

Gaukroger 1995: 146–52). But other forms of activity, differently justified and explained, remained in the mechanical cosmos. It is not quite true that in Descartes' work 'all spirits were effectively removed from nature' (Merchant 1980: 204). The survival of paradoxically corporeal animal spirits was not an accidental residue, a pun uneasily transmitted between organicist and mechanistic worlds. Their incessant motion is genuine activity, whether or not it ultimately derives from God: their coalescences, breachings, foldings, and commotions, retaining and transforming patterns over time, can continue quite independent of the individual will.

Historians of science have recently demonstrated the intrinsic roles of activity, sympathy, spirit, and force in later seventeenth-century English 'mechanism' (Henry 1986a; Schaffer 1987; compare Hutchison 1991), and I extend this research in discussing problems of action at a distance in chapter 4. But if pre-Newtonian English mechanism was not just compatible with activity in nature but required it, I can apply a similar strategy in Cartesian historiography, where there is serious difficulty in understanding quite what 'strict mechanism' could have been. Descartes' explanatory ambition did not require the *elimination* of puzzling and complex natural phenomena, as implied by Merchant (1980: 204–5): with strange facts of the organicist world, he sought reduction, *not* elimination. It was not, in many cases, the baffling phenomena (the bleeding of wounds on the approach of the murderer, the weapon salve, sympathies, the maternal imagination imprinting on the foetus) which he rejected, but only certain candidate explanations of them, such as those which attribute thought or free will to corpuscles (*Principles* IV.187, AT viii(a).314, CSM I.278–9; Shea 1991: III–20). These are traditional examples of the activity of matter, and Descartes denies not that they occur, only that it is necessary for matter to have the extremely strong capacity of free rational thought for it to exhibit such behaviour. This is true too for human science: reason, thought, and freedom are unique to immaterial souls, but they are not by any means everything. Passion, dreams, confusion, and long-term reconstructive memory were among the explananda left over for a genuinely dynamic physiology of mind.

Real forces But, in a difficult historiographical debate, some scholars of Cartesian physics claim that Descartes had no dynamics, because he did not admit forces in natural philosophy: force in Descartes' physics is just God, sustaining across discontinuous instants corporeal matter in motion, which has no powers of its own, according to a principle of continuous creation (Hatfield 1979; compare Westfall 1971: 56–98; Gabbey 1980; Gueroult 1980). It is far from clear what this metaphysical doctrine entails in natural philosophy. Stephen Gaukroger argues forcefully for a minimal reading of Descartes' official commitment to inertness, as requiring only 'that matter does not *initiate* any kind of activity': this allows that forces are *sited* in matter although ultimately *derived* from God (Gaukroger 1995: 376–7, my emphasis). In contrast to the popular view (based on the atypically strong claims of the Third Meditation) that Descartes eliminated forces from nature and sought to reduce physics to kinematics (Williams 1978: 261–2), Gaukroger believes that 'force is built into his account at the most fundamental level' as real tendencies to motion (1995: 247, also 70, 83–4, 343–4, 375). Readings which subordinate Descartes' view that bodies have *within* themselves the force to continue to move or to remain at rest (to Mersenne, 28 October 1640, AT iii.213, CSM-K 155) to impose a 'consistent' metaphysics of instantaneous divine action neglect the developmental sequence of Descartes' thought (physics before metaphysics), and ignore his advice to pursue desirable 'physical studies' rather than elaborate metaphysical questions (Conversation with Burman, 16 April 1648, CSM-K 346–7, AT v.165; compare to Princess Elizabeth, 28 June 1643, AT iii.691–5, CSM-K 226–8; see Gaukroger 1995: 10–14, 375).

Many disagree with Gaukroger's claims for forces among the corpuscles. But, just as he cites centrifugal forces in Cartesian cosmology as evidence that 'one could only believe God was the sole site of activity if one concentrated exclusively on Descartes' metaphysics' (1995: 375–6), so my discussion of physiology suggests wider implications of the case for real Cartesian forces. I address Emily Grosholz's critique of *L'Homme*, as a specimen in physiology of the common reading which takes the subordination of physics to metaphysics to be *Descartes'* problem rather than the interpreter's. It is worth touching first on two related (and less controversial) issues in the general natural philosophy: *hydrodynamics* and the *plenum*. Both are given new emphasis in Gaukroger's work, and both support the dynamically tinged Cartesian physiology.

The fluid-filled cosmos While working with the microcorpuscularian theorist, Beeckman, in 1619, Descartes wrote about the behaviour of fluids. His manuscript furnished 'certain concepts and modes of argument . . . which will constitute the essence of Cartesian micro-mechanism in optics, cosmology, physiology, and natural philosophy generally' (Schuster 1977: vol. 1, 94, quoted by Gaukroger 1995: 84; AT x.67–74; Shea 1991: 27–33). The mechanism of the early 1630s remained 'very dependent upon a hydrostatic/hydrodynamic model' (Gaukroger 1995: 225). Solid and fluid bodies are not metaphysically distinct, but on a continuous spectrum, with solids as conglomerations of corpuscles which are closer to rest with respect to one another (*Le Monde*, AT xi.11–15, CSM I.84–5). Descartes illustrates his claim that 'all the motions that occur in the world are in some way circular' with the example of a fish in water, where motion is by displacement (AT xi.19–20). Cartesian astronomy rests on a 'hydrodynamic model of the cosmos, which requires solid bodies, such as planets, to be embedded in a fluid which carries them along in a vortical motion' (Gaukroger 1995: 412, 249–56; AT xi.50–83; compare Rodis-Lewis

1978: 160 on dynamics in mechanism). Descartes' account of planetary motions by the whirling mutual displacements of contiguous vortices subsumes cosmology into hydrodynamics, 'and hence his interest is really in fluids' (Gaukroger 1995: 234, see also p. 247).[24]

The fluid model, this physics of circulation, displacement, and endless motion, is secured by rejecting the void in favour of a plenum (Hesse 1961/1970: 102–8; Heilbron 1982: 22–6). It is natural to think that mechanistic reductionism, whereby all observable bodies are composites of small particles must go (as it did, for example, in Gassendi) with the ancient atomists' ontology of isolable atoms scooting or swerving, alone or in packs, across a void. But this is not so. In 1629 Descartes expressed agreement 'on the whole foundations of Philosophy' with Sebastian Basso, a critic of Aristotle who combined atomism with a neo-Stoic plenum theory (to Mersenne, 8 October 1629, AT i.25).[25] In Le Monde, moving bodies are always surrounded by other bodies. So everything affects everything else, indirectly if not by one of the direct collisions which are the constant fate (or chance) of every conglomeration of material elements (Gaukroger 1995: 230–1, 275).

As Gaukroger points out (1995: 241), it is easy to imagine here the intuitive Lucretian vision of atoms or composites moving for long stretches through a void and only occasionally colliding. But this is where the fish example breaks down, for there is no fluid-free part of the plenum. Cartesian fish are never out of water, since bodies are always colliding and are never out of mutual causal contact. The combination of hydrodynamics and plenum physics has intense intuitive power, in two related respects which I use to bridge the gap between physics and physiology: context-dependence, and causal holism.

Context and complexity In the cartoon version of mechanism which I sketched at the start of this section, the machine metaphor lies behind a deadening inattention to emergent behaviour, to the way wholes act differently from their parts. Mechanism as method is the analysis of complex wholes into

---

24 The tempting thought that this talk of the metaphysical identity of solids and fluids (compare Principles 11.54, AT viii(a).71, CSM 1.245, Description of the Human Body Part III, AT xi.247, CSM 1.319) is in fact a blanket reduction of fluid to solid, to reabsorb fluidity in particulate form, finds support in quite different historiographic traditions (Shapiro 1974; Irigaray 1974/1985b). But I suggest that, in the thoroughly permeable Cartesian cosmos, the diffuse, boundary-blurring, temporally bound fluids seep across all Descartes' natural philosophy.

25 Basso thought that any possible spaces between the smallest particles were filled by a 'universal spirit', something like the Stoic pneuma. This was Descartes' one point of difference: 'I do not explain the ether as he does' (quoted in Gaukroger 1995: 221). His form of 'cosmobiology' did not require the identity of physiological spirits and cosmological matter. Barker and Goldstein (1984) take Descartes' physics as proof that atomism and the plenum were not exclusive options, and trace the transmission of neo-Stoic physics up to and including Basso and Descartes (see also Barker 1991 on the mechanising of Stoic pneuma).

discrete parts, treated in isolation. Critics of mechanism then complain that the nature of bodies, and of events, is correspondingly taken in totalising fashion to be independent of the particular context (physical, social, or temporal) in which they exist or occur (Merchant 1980: 227–35). This context-independence is indeed, crudely, the ideal fiction of atomist kinematics, in which isolated collisions in the void between bits bashing each other model more complex interactions within or between other bodies. But, Gaukroger argues (1995: 241), Descartes' approach is not kinematic but hydrostatic: 'the point seems to be not so much to analyse the behaviour of a body under various kinds of constraint in terms of how it behaves when not under constraint, but rather to account for what happens when a body moves from one system of constraints to another'. In 'body matters', then, Cartesian bodies (human and other) are not isolated or closed: Descartes shows 'almost no interest in unconstrained bodies', but assumes that 'systems of constraint are constitutive' of the phenomena under investigation (Gaukroger 1995: 247–8).[26]

The distributed model of memory sketched above is firmly embedded in this natural philosophy, for in memory too all motions and events are wholly context-dependent. As patterns rise in succession in the folds of memory, their particular cast depends not only on current input from world, body, or soul but also on the contingent dispositional states of the pores in those regions of the brain, and on all the messy factors influencing the state of the animal spirits. Cartesian memories share not only this context-dependence with the physics, but also a second property, that of causal holism. Because different figures are traced implicitly in the same folds of the brain, and because animal spirits can only reconstruct patterns in the present, there is a clear sense in which all (or at least many) traces are causally active in the (re)construction of any one pattern during any memory event.

This is just a special case of the causal holism which, like context-dependence, simply falls out of Descartes' natural philosophy. In the full fluid

26 Merchant (1980: 230–1) quotes *Principles* 11.53 (AT viii(a).70, CSM 1.245), where Descartes says that it is hard to apply his laws of motion 'because each body is simultaneously in contact with many others', and that 'no bodies in the universe can be so isolated from all others'. But this is precisely Descartes' reminder (in a more defensive statement of the laws than that of *Le Monde*) to think of collisions as continuous in a plenum rather than occasional in a void: he is not, as Merchant suggests, unwillingly 'forced to admit' this context-dependence. Jamie Kassler (1997) argues strongly for a sharp contrast between Descartes' and Hobbes' plenum theories, and favours Hobbes' (truly neo-Stoic) picture of tensional forces filling space, including the invisible internal motions of physiological 'endeavour', over Cartesian atomism in which all change of motion in bodies is from the outside by impact and pressure. But Descartes is closer to Kassler's interpretation of Hobbes than she allows. It is not just that 'impact' and 'collision' are inadequate descriptions of the continual circulation of Cartesian bodies in the plenum, but that the example of memory in Cartesian automata proves that changes of motion arise internally, with physiological tendencies to motion maintained over long periods without specific external intervention.

cosmos, any motion anywhere is also necessarily motion elsewhere, for no body is unconnected or unconstrained. As for the Stoics, causation is conserved throughout the integrated cosmic system, with everything holistically linked to everything else (Gaukroger 1995: 242–3). Memory motions, like all material interactions, are embedded in multiple conspiracies of causes.

Real patterns Psychophysiological dynamics are of a piece with the complex interconnected meshings of forces throughout the Cartesian universe. But critics claim that the dynamic elements which causal holism imports into Descartes' physiology are somehow illegitimate, 'smuggled goods' or tacit annexations which enrich with forces and thus violate a basically pure official static mechanism (Rodis-Lewis 1978: 152–4). In a well-constructed critique which opens up a set of difficult issues, Emily Grosholz (1991: 118–19, 127–8) complains at Descartes' invocation of non-linear feedback systems which are hardly analogous to the simple impact machines on which his physics was meant to be based. She is, perhaps, too carping in blaming Descartes for theorising non-linear systems which are not quantifiable 'by means of the mathematics he knows' (1991: 128). When, as I do, one has independent motivations for interest in deterministic but non-linear dynamic models of memory, there is ample cause to seek keenly their perceived implications.

Grosholz follows, with modifications, the tack of interpreting all Cartesian texts by the methodological standards of the *Meditations*. Despite Descartes' point that theories in natural philosophy are not uniquely constrained by metaphysical principles (Hatfield 1985), she attributes to him the desire always to move in physics back from complex bodies and phenomena to the sparse set of simple natures and elements justified in metaphysical reflection. His 'unexamined faith' in reductive analyses, argues Grosholz, leaves Descartes unable to explain complex entities and processes, imposing unnatural homogeneity on diverse phenomena, impoverishing domains in which the action of complex unified wholes is irreducible to the dull mechanical interaction of their isolated parts.

Physiological and cognitive phenomena are subject to one unnatural reduction of natural complexity imposed by this Cartesian 'method at odds with itself' (Grosholz 1991: 118). Not only is Descartes' use of 'animal spirit' suspiciously unmechanistic in spiritualising subtle matter (1991: 122): he further invokes as analogies, unfairly, not simple machines but feedback mechanisms to suggest that cognition, like respiration, is 'really a highly sophisticated feedback mechanism' (1991: 126). This applies notably to the idea of corporeal memory as diverse or patterned motions, and to Descartes' use of the pineal gland as 'a locus for complex algorithms which convert perceptual patterns into patterns inducing movement' (1991: 126–7).

This key concept of the 'pattern' is essential for the neurophilosophy to get off the ground. 'Pattern' and the related term 'disposition' are something like second-order physical properties, properties which supervene on first-order physical properties like size, shape, rotation, and so on.[27] But Grosholz argues that, given his officially meagre mechanical ontology, there is in fact 'no room ... for the notion of pattern which is so central to Descartes' cognitive physiology' (1991: 127). The need for 'more or less permanent configurations in the fibres' to ground his theory of memory forces Descartes to 'either revise or short-circuit his original conception of causal interaction' (1991: 126-7).

The problem here is not only that Grosholz overemphasises the permanence of patterns in the spirits moving through folds of memory, nor that she just rejects the reality of forces sited in matter, though I have suggested reasons for differing on these points. More specifically, I think that Grosholz's case *assumes* the central point at issue: she simply *denies* that animal spirits which are merely bits of matter in motion could *also* be 'active and patterned, conveying information' (1991: 129). But the contention of the cognitive scientist (Cartesian or connectionist) is that items which interact *only* in virtue of their physical properties *can* also maintain *some* regularity of pattern through the course of such interactions. Patterns do *not* have to be transmitted '*qua* patterns' in order to have causal effects (as Grosholz says they would), because they can be transmitted by ordinary physical-causal means.

Grosholz makes the strong contrasting claim that 'for a pattern to be [causally] consequential it must be recognized as such, interpreted, cognitively grasped, by a consciousness' (1991: 129). This view is partly backed by her invocation of Gibson's psychology (for which, in the context of memory, see chapter 15 below), and is intended as a critique not only of Descartes' mistakes but also of those which 'permeate contemporary materialist accounts in epistemology and cognitive psychology' (1991: 130):[28] but it entails that there could

27 On 'second-order physical properties' in a similar context see Fodor 1985b/1991: 41–2. Fodor is talking of 'syntax' but patterns and dispositions fit too. Richard Carter's insightful account of three uses of the concept of disposition in Descartes includes the interrelation of parts (1983: 99–103; see also Krell 1990: 320–1, n.13). The related notions of texture and power also played important parts in subsequent developments, especially in Locke: see chapter 7 below. Dennett (1991b) defends (a form of) realism about patterns and the legitimacy of invoking them in ontology and cognitive psychology.

28 Earlier Grosholz singles out the Churchlands and Quine as representatives of those modern philosophies which bear 'the traces of Descartes' reductive method' and which support a 'hegemony of the notion of theory' which she vehemently opposes (1991: 10). But neither reduction nor theory entails, as she assumes, the ruling out of complexity of the 'multifarious' and 'prodigal' kind (1991: 81, 9–10) which she wants to defend. Reductionism is not eliminativism, and does not require the denial of the multiplicity of levels of description (1991: 127). Where Grosholz convicts Descartes of illegitimately violating his own order of reasons by bringing 'complexity in by the back door' (1991: 72), I see mechanistic openness to complexity as the way to imagine, feel, and understand it from underneath, distrusting assumptions that real complexity at a level requires that level to be irreducible to or autonomous of other physical processes. For a reply to similar criticisms see Paul Churchland 1989b.

be no patterns in nature without consciousnesses to grasp and interpret them. This is one interpretation of the Gibsonian stress on the existence of environmental regularities only as affordances for the active organism: but it seems an unnecessary slide away from realism about the independent existence of patterns. The fact that the animal spirits, 'almost always differing among themselves in some way' (AT xi.180, H 91; see Foti 1986a: 77–8 and Krell 1990: 65–8 on the uses of 'difference' in L'Homme), actualise or embody patterns of motions and thus mediate in intelligent processing, does not entail that they are themselves required to be intelligent.

3.5.2 Animated statues, liberty, and psychological control

If I am right, how pure or strict can Cartesian mechanism ever have been? Were the machines taken as models for natural bodies not then passive and static? There are different forms of this question, which I seek to clarify in this section by showing how the active/passive boundary shifts (compare Lloyd 1993a: 78–82). Cartesian automata and body-machines did, contrary to common views, have their own 'activity', in a certain (deterministic and temporary) independence from external control. They did not, however, have the acausal autonomy attributed to souls which will and act freely, and judge rationally. From the metaphysical perspective in which only the immaterial can be truly active, of course body-machines are passive. But it is appropriate still to use 'activity' of them in a Cartesian world, because of their resistance to the commands of the will, the inability of the rational soul perfectly to control and order their movements or clearly to understand their state.

Again, I take as stalking-horse a firm, representative statement of an interpretation different from my own. Otto Mayr (1986: xviii) aligns Descartes with the 'growing commitment on the Continent to the value of authority' against an opposing commitment 'in England, to its antithesis, liberty'. The mechanical philosophers relied on the metaphor of the clock for natural philosophy because of its obvious reliance on external regulation (1986: 28–121; compare Merchant 1980: 217–27). Only slowly did English theorists question the authoritarian implications of mechanism and look to the coincident development of feedback systems in technology for alternative models of balance, harmony, and self-regulation (without external control) which better suited a more democratic 'liberal conception of order' (Mayr 1980, 1986: 122–99). Mayr's account is much more nuanced than this: but even if his strict dichotomy between authority and liberty could be maintained, his scheme is the wrong way round. In chapters 5 and 9 I argue that English natural philosophers rejected the Cartesian philosophy of the brain not because of its authoritarian nature but because it was not authoritarian enough: too much liberty was given by Descartes to the confusing animal spirits, which had to be stabilised, neutralised, and finally eliminated in the search for some control over memory and the past.

On the 'Continental' side, Mayr says that the physiological scheme of L'Homme assumes an analogously hierarchical organisation in simple machines and in organisms, in which a 'single supreme organ' has sovereign power over the system (1986: 62–7). In humans the incorporeal soul rules and regulates, but

> in animals it was the brain that, consisting entirely of memory and therefore capable only of initiating preprogrammed action, corresponded closely to the mechanical program controlling automata. Between the different levels of the hierarchy, organs were connected in linear, unidirectional, cause-and-effect, or command chains. (Mayr 1986: 66)

There are insights in this misreading. In a sense Cartesian brains do consist entirely of memory (except for the pineal gland which has to be kept clear of memory motions); and there is a central executive organ, independent in body-machines of the soul (though it is the pineal gland rather than the entire brain). But, as I argued against Flanagan above, brains (or other machines) 'consisting of' memory are *not* thereby restricted to pre-programmed action. Memory goes with *learning*. It is precisely memory which, carrying particular contingent experience in its folds, guarantees the specificity of the organism's behaviour and cognition in a context. Corporeal memory provides for the machine a flexibility or an independence from the arbitrariness of current stimuli, not in the sense of spontaneity or indifference, but in the sense that the constraints which act on the body, the ties that bind, are constraints and ties to that particular body, to that particular past.

Indeed Mayr's own more detailed analysis undermines his meta-narrative. In his official view, mechanism is a system with a 'single central cause' (whether God, king, soul, or brain), where this centre has command of all information, memory, judgement, decision, and spontaneous action (1986: 117–18). But this does not in fact apply, as his story requires it must, either to Descartes or to clocks. Mayr is puzzled that the program function imposed to guide 'program-controlled' Cartesian automata was 'not located in a single, easily-identifiable element but was distributed throughout the mechanism', in, for example, 'the disposition of the organs' (1986: 66): he is forced to complain in a note (1986: 219–20, n. 61) that Descartes does not exploit his own hints about cooperative interaction between systems which could allow for unprogrammed responses to unrehearsed situations. But in fact Descartes, like other mechanistic physiologists, is fully aware of the importance of feedback and cooperation in the bodily 'maintenance system': digestive, respiratory, and circulatory homeostasis is necessary for the reliable operation of the cognitive-informational system (Rorty 1992:

377–80).[29] Memory is not located (wholly) at the centre but is distributed across the brain surfaces and out on the independent bodily periphery. So body-machines are not narrow, specialised slaves as Mayr claims: they lack the soul's freedom, but they do not lack flexibility, a degree of self-maintenance, and adaptiveness to new environments.

In turn, the clock metaphor, meant to carry the case that mechanism and authoritarianism are intimate, is more complicated. Mayr's mechanists took clocks, like mechanical organisms, to have a single central origin governing ordered passive parts in a hierarchy. But he acknowledges that there was no consensus about what the central executive was: the original designer, the energy source, the regulator, the memory-analogue, or what (1986: 42, 117)? Georges Canguilhem, in contrast, used Descartes' Description of the Human Body (AT xi.225, CSM I.315) to reject the simple authoritarian interpretation. The body is not commanded by a sovereign soul:

> Envisioning the body in terms of a clockwork mechanism, Descartes saw the various organs as controlling one another in much the same way as the gears of a clock. Descartes thus replaced a political image of command and a magical type of causality (involving words or signs) with a technological image of 'control' and a positive type of causality involving a mechanical meshing or linkage. (Canguilhem 1952/1994: 231)

Two different strains of properties are being attributed to machines and thence to mechanism (as seen also by Baker and Morris 1996: 91–4, who develop the point differently). Mayr's official line stresses only machines' dull mechanical nature: they are passive, entirely predictable, unable to give rise to complexity. But as well as dullness and passivity, machines seem unreliable, dangerous, uncertain, likely to escape the control of their designers. This is not an invention of modern science fiction: the uncanny capacity of imagined and dreamed machines to mimic and then exceed human possibility is a recurrent theme in historical fantasies of automata between technology and natural magic. Mayr knows this, detailing not only traditional tales of quasi-demonic automata (1986: 24–6; compare de Solla Price 1964: 10–12; and Bedini 1964), but also early modern references to the fragility and untrustworthiness of machines (1986: 42–53, 124). But because he attributes only to the English a 'rejection of the clock metaphor in the name of liberty' (1986: 122), Mayr fails to see that such concerns about the complexity and unreliability of mechanisms

---

29 Amelie Rorty in this fine paper demonstrates just how intertwined epistemology and physiological homeostasis are in Descartes' approach to 'thinking with the body'. My only query is whether it is possible to divide informational and maintenance systems even to the extent she does. She does not address the importance of the specific point that animal spirits, the bearers of distorted or accurate information, are themselves generated in and marked by non-cognitive bodily processes. See below (section 3.5.3) on the permeable body.

spring from genuine dynamic properties of the (Continental) mechanical models themselves.

If machines and mechanical models had only the properties of dullness and passivity, their subordination to external authority (God and soul) and the predictability of their behaviour would not have been questioned. There would seem no risks of confusion and danger. The fact that both proponents and critics of mechanism were in fact all too aware of the threat of ataxy and disorder which machines could bring suggests that there may have been some theoretical basis for the perceived, problematic activity. The dynamic elements in mechanical models made it seem possible that machines might not be wholly and obediently subject to the demands and commands of external authority. In body-machines, the psychological control which (many different) official views of soul, will, and reason required seemed menaced by the ongoing physical processes by which fibres, pores, spirits, and internal organs 'ticked' or flowed on, often inaccessible to consciousness and thus unpredictable.

Carolyn Merchant usefully separates two aspects of the 'reordering of reality' achieved by mechanism. 'Autonomous' machines like clocks symbolised order, while non-autonomous technology like windmills and pumps symbolised human power: 'Order was attained through an emphasis on the motion of indivisible parts subject to mathematical laws and the rejection of unpredictable animistic sources of change. Power was achieved through immediate active intervention in a secularized world' (Merchant 1980: 216–17). Different emphases on order or power depended partly on a position about God, whether intellectualist (God's ordered rational intellect over His will) or voluntarist (God's supremely free power of the will, unbound by logic or law: see Ayers 1993). Merchant's 'order' pole corresponds to my category of dull passive mechanical machines. But her 'power' pole needs to be further divided. Of course machines were meant to reveal the operative power of God and of the soul, the teleological need for a designer and for external governance of predictable, ordered nature and the passive body. But in practice, menacing the rhetoric of control, machines were often invoked in language or in contexts where it is their power, and their threat to incorporeal power, which seems central.

Writing in the late sixteenth century, Thomas Nashe, in The Unfortunate Traveller, describes fictional songbird-automata ('sweet resembled substances without sense') which produce wondrous harmonies due to fluid flows through the 'many edged unsundered writhings & crankled wanderings aside' in 'long silver pipes enrinded in the entrails of the boughs whereon they sat' (in Knoespel 1992: 113). There is nothing straightforward in the way even simple animal-machines are seen, no easy relegation to the passive. Charged metaphorical descriptions of machines which really are pre-programmed, which have no capacity for learning and memory, suggest some of the cultural weight imbued in the more complex, more dangerous cyborgs.

This suggests just how appropriate was the strange machine analogy used by Descartes to illuminate his account of the body-machine: he compares the animated statues of his fable in L'Homme to finely wrought devices in 'the gardens of our kings'.

> External objects which merely by their presence act on the organs of sense and by this means force them to move in several different ways, depending on how the parts of the brain are arranged, are like strangers who, entering some of the grottoes of these fountains, unwittingly cause the movements that then occur, since they cannot enter without stepping on certain tiles so arranged that, for example, if they approach a Diana bathing they will cause her to hide in the reeds; and if they pass farther to pursue her they will cause a Neptune to advance and menace them with his trident; or if they go in another direction they will make a marine monster come out and spew water in their faces, or other such things according to the whims of the engineers who made them. (AT xi.130–2, H 21–2)

The drama of the royal garden grotto (de Caus 1659; Jaynes 1970), argue critics of mechanism, has nothing to do with the simple hydraulic mechanism beneath the disguise. Wells (1985: 80) complains, for example, at the subtle suggestion that L'Homme's austere explanatory apparatus of spirits, fluids, and nerves could, when scaled up, give rise to such affective complexity. But the analogy has a certain strangeness in its detail.

Most of the analogical elements are easy enough to apply to L'Homme's animated statues. The nerves are the fountains' tubes for carrying water, the ventricles are the water main, muscles and tendons are the 'engines and springs', and so on (animal spirits as water, heart as water source, God as engineer). But the analogy vanishes at a key point. There is no obvious analogue for Diana and her marine defenders Neptune and the monster. They can only be equivalent to particular internal parts of the body: violent reprisal is potentially internal in origin, as the body carries destructive capacities.[30] This motivates the Cartesian ethics of knowledge of, and control over, physiology. Philosophers' alleged subduing, murder, and forgetting of the human body, their neglect of the microprocesses of human nature, was not a significant seventeenth-century phenomenon. There was continual awareness of and vigilance towards the violent, excessive body, which through early modern philosophy was always being urgently rethought.

---

30 Erica Harth (1992: 95–8) quotes an intriguing poem of the 1690s by Catherine Descartes, the philosopher's niece, which reinterprets Diana as an angry Nature turning on the dying Descartes. Harth sees Catherine (re)infusing Nature with life and soul, seeking to reverse the mechanists' murder of nature, who 'kills Descartes' discourse by feminising it' (1992: 98). But she does not note the additional direct parodic echo of L'Homme in Catherine's verse: Descartes dying in Sweden is the peeping Actaeon being turned on by his own body-monsters. (Renaissance interpretations of the Actaeon myth took Actaeon's hounds to represent his own thoughts and desires (Barkan 1980; Vickers 1982).)

As in Descartes' other flirtations with automata (de Solla Price 1964: 22–3; Rodis-Lewis 1978: 154–9; Shea 1991: 107–9; Gaukroger 1995: 1–3, 63–4), the emotive blurring of myth, magic, and mechanism in the Diana analogy reveals the need for both technology and theory to retain contact with 'the exigencies of life . . . since we cannot make ourselves a new body, we must augment our internal organs with external organs and supplement our natural ones with artificial ones' (Canguilhem 1937/1994: 225). It is just because body-machines are weak and exist in history, because hair turns white (AT i.435), that medicine is central to Cartesian philosophy. The myth of the pre-programmed machine dully reproducing its hardwired fate, eternally churning out fixed action patterns, does not apply to the animated statues of organic nature. The intermediate level of response, neither simple reflex nor incorporeally derived action, opens up Cartesian bodies to memory and history, with all the sadness, resistance, and complexity which the matter of the past brings along.

3.5.3 The permeable body
A damaging aspect of the 'the submergence of the organism by the machine' (Merchant 1980: 193), which many attribute to Descartes and his ilk, was the closing off of the human body from the world, rendering it a possession of the individual soul. Descartes is an easy villain in New Age psychosomatics and 'liberatory eco-holism' (see Brown 1985). Similarly, historians caught up by Descartes' metaphysics of free active mind gesture at critical mistakes made in the scientistic physiological construction of the passive body. Descartes sought to reduce all bodies to sameness, to fit a single micromechanical model, imagining them as automata 'endlessly repeatable, and by definition not particular, not the subjects of a specific history' (Reiss 1996: 604): they can be manipulated by the interventionist scientist just as they are by the immaterial soul, and are distant from the rational mastery exercised by this immaterial governor. Bodily events, including death, occur as if to another: 'the true self cannot be threatened by the demise of that which from the start was mere mechanism . . . The corporeal threat is, as far as possible, subdued' (Leder 1990: 148).

I hope it is now obvious that this picture is misleading. It is not only that the body's homeostatic 'maintenance system' must remain healthy to ground reliable information processing (Rorty 1992; Mackenzie 1989: 173–5). In fact, the Cartesian 'body, with its interactive openness', far from being inevitably moulded to one hardwired model, is the means by which difference is introduced into the human compound (Foti 1986a: 76; Reiss 1996). Particular experience teaches through the mixed dispositional traces enfolded in brain and body which, when actualised, cause action in a specific context.

In the ancient and Renaissance physiologies of humours and spirits, across boundaries between Aristotelian and Hippocratic/Galenic systems, the body was by nature open, the internal environment always in dynamic interrelation with the external environment (chapter 2 above). Its state depended on the non-naturals, on regulation of temperature, and on the maintenance of fragile fluid balances in the internal media. Certain proper mean states could maintain its normal capacities to resist the immediate stimuli and to avoid surrendering its health/balance in temporary environmental upheavals. Urgent steps could be taken to close off its vents and windows, barring the orifices by which external dangers could intrude. But this seasonal body was always vulnerable to climatic effects, and permeated by the environment right through to its cognitive capacities.

Almost all of this survives in Descartes' 'corpuscularized Galenism' (Grosholz 1991: 120), transformed into principles of fluid mechanics by which inner and outer continually interact. A long passage in L'Homme (AT xi.167–70, H 73–5) ends: 'in sum, whatever can cause any change in the blood can also cause change in the spirits'. Here the animal spirits, as ever, are the medium of interplay between body and world. Descartes retains the central role given to blood in traditional physiology, and examines the internal and external variables affecting the spirits derived from the blood, including food and digestion (the body's nimbleness and quickness depends on the qualities of food), respiration and climate, and the states of liver, gall bladder, spleen, and heart. There are lines of causal influence straight from the non-naturals through blood and spirits to the quality and context-specific nature of cognitive functions (given that, as I have argued, animals and other 'machines' have such functions even without a soul).

The model for these processes is a kind of circulation or antiperistasis, obvious when the body exists in a plenum, and giving further content to the notion of holism in Descartes' physiology: everything affects everything else, in the body as in the cosmos (Carter 1983, 1985/1991). The causal factors affecting the animal spirits and thus all psychophysiological processes are numerous, and certainly do not stop at the limits of the skin. As Malebranche would state bluntly, introducing his account of the passions, the Cartesian view of the body implies that 'we are to some extent joined to the entire universe': because of the nature of animal spirits, culture and cosmos permeate the innards, for everyone is joined 'through his body to his relatives, friends, city, prince, country, clothes, house, land, horse, dog, to the entire earth, the sun, the stars, to all the heavens' (Malebranche, LO 342, v.2; compare Sutton 1998). Medical knowledge and power will be prescriptions for a regimen to cope with environmental shifts, seeking to ensure that the body can again be appropriately coupled to its physical and social surroundings.

In spelling out optimistically the explanatory scope of spirits theory, Descartes uses the language of humours (L'Homme AT xi.166–7, H 72–3). The mechanisation of physiology is a reduction of Galenic humoralism rather than an elimination (compare A 438). Further, there are even echoes of the

Renaissance assumption that body fluids are all in principle interconvertible. Blood, milk, fat, sperm, spirits, humours, sweat, tears, and so on, were all versions of the same set of fluids, all subject to the same principles of fluid mechanics (Laqueur 1990: 35–43, 103–8). Only in this light does Descartes' insistence on the common source of animal spirits and generative seed make sense (AT xi.128, H 18; chapter 9 below).

It is not that Descartes' mechanisation in these domains is incomplete, but that a physiology modelled on hydrodynamics explicitly theorises an active, runny, permeable body, set in a full fluid universe. Descartes' moral advice on psychological control is a set of maxims for trying to bind this open body, to stabilise the flux. The strangeness of this demand is worth pausing on. It should complicate further the difficult attempt to document multifaceted conceptual and phenomenological shifts from grotesque and open to classical and closed bodies, from spectacular to docile bodies, or from public to private bodies (Bakhtin 1965/1984: Foucault 1977: 16–31; Barker 1984). Theory which itself is alien to us imposes puzzling requirements for self-control, in which the part of nature that it is most important to master is the part we might have thought we already possessed, our own fluid spirits and the unpredictable body bits through which they pass.

3.6 Objection 4: memory, method, and metaphysics

A final objection to my interpretation of Descartes' remarks on memory lurks in the puzzling connections between the physiology of memory and Cartesian metaphysics. The destruction of opinion is, notoriously, the prerequisite of Cartesian method. A new foundation for thought is possible once the house of belief has been rased. The natural light of reason will suffice as origin for a new structure. It seems as if the method, then, requires the total forgetting of everything learned and taken on trust, the effacing of book 'knowledge' from the mind. We must, as Andrew Benjamin (1993: 42) puts it, refuse the gift of the given, closing off the possibility of repetition in order, like Descartes, to take up our subject-matter as if for the first time (compare Schouls 1989: 144–5 on Descartes' distrust of the past).

This demand that all opinion be erased is provocatively discussed in the context of Descartes' theories of memory by Benjamin and by Tim Reiss. The difficulty is that the idea of *deciding* to forget is not obviously coherent. Reiss (1996: 595) quotes Gassendi's complaint that 'memory . . . cannot be erased at will'. Even if it could, a regress of forgetting looms: the memory of the act of erasure would itself conceal the old opinion, and would thus itself have to be forgotten, *ad infinitum* (Benjamin 1993: 50–1).

Benjamin leaves the dilemma in place in characterising the 'inherent instability' of forgetting: either the regress ensues, or the old opinion remains traced in the memory alongside the new, when the inadvertent intrusion of unwanted traces into the new rational thought will always remain a threat. But Reiss thinks that Descartes answered Gassendi's challenge: the emptying of memory is not, in fact, required. After subjecting beliefs to rational examination, one will know by the natural light which candidate beliefs to assent to: but even after such rational rejection of old ideas, 'one does not fail, for all that, to retain the same notions in one's memory' (to Clerselier, 12 January 1646, AT ix.204, in Reiss 1996: 596). The positive procedure for evaluating beliefs is to balance old ideas against new, by multiplying contrary traces: critics like Gassendi missed this precise project of avoiding

> those many divers traces always already imprinted on, bored through, folded into the brain. They did not grasp that it was never a question of making these vestiges disappear. Descartes agreed that such a project would have been time wasted, because impossible. The body's marks were indelible. What he sought, rather, was to render this physical history inoperative. (Reiss 1996: 601)

Reiss' claim that Descartes did not, ludicrously, believe in the self's perfect control over memory is exactly right. It is rare for us really to have a hand in our forgetting. But if Reiss is correct about Descartes' reasons for denying this freedom to forget, then my account of distributed memory in Descartes cannot be right. Reiss (1996: 597–9) analyses Descartes' descriptions of the physiology of memory, from the impressions in wax of the Regulae, through the stories in L'Homme of nervous spirits ('what we would now describe as neuro-electrical impulses') opening holes in the tissue of the brain, to the discussions of memory folds in the correspondence. In all these models of memory traces, 'one thing was sure. Whether imprint, hole, or fold, the impressed mark was permanent. It was there, once and for all' (Reiss 1996: 599–600).

By contrast, according to my interpretation, no marks are permanent (save perhaps the rare traces deeply graven in excessive wonder): dispositional traces continually act together, and are not even easily isolable. Permanence, possible only if memory representations remain explicit throughout the storage period, is impossible if many traces are stored in the same physical system: if remembering requires the reconstruction and re-separation of memory motions in the animal spirits, then interference effects make it unlikely that traces of old opinions will be formed perfectly identical to those at the time of initial learning.

Descartes does not state that traces are permanent and unchanging. When he writes to Clerselier that after rational examination of an old and acceptance of a new belief, one retains the same notions in one's memory, this does not, I suggest, mean that items in memory never change: it means, rather, that they do not disappear at will, that the act of rational examination may not itself change them.

Reiss' central contention about our lack of control over memory can be maintained without committing Descartes, implausibly, to the permanence of items in memory. The threat of continuous mixture in memory was more worrying than any model which guaranteed permanence, and this is one reason why Descartes is so concerned, when thinking about method, to finds ways of bypassing memory entirely.[31] How can truth be preserved in thinking when memories are superpositionally stored in the folds of the brain, blended or confused one with another? Reiss also suggests that Descartes was concerned that memory is unreliable, weak, and unstable (Reiss 1996: 600), always bringing obscure and confused ideas to mind, mixing impressions derived from different sources, adding prejudice to perception. Although either permanence or unreliability would explain why memory and forgetting are beyond conscious control and free decision, it seems unlikely that memory traces are both unstable and permanent. I suggest that the tension here can be resolved by accepting that the unreliability, not the permanence, was Descartes' worry. It is not that traces are too static, mechanical, and dully permanent, but that they are too fickle, fleeting, and fragile.[32]

Both Benjamin and Reiss note the irredeemably bodily nature of the constraints which memory imposes on Cartesian method. The soul never has absolute power over corporeal things. But bodies are in motion incessantly, not forever fixed.

3.7 Control and self-mastery

The four objections do not succeed in refuting the idea that Descartes had an inchoate distributed model of memory. But there is still good reason to classify his theory of memory as not just historically but also conceptually distinct from the modern connectionist picture. Descartes did acknowledge that non-conscious memory processing occurs out in the folds of the brain, or elsewhere in the body: this looks, as I have suggested, not unlike the

31 This is most explicit in the *Regulae*, where the intellect relies on memory to connect the steps in a reasoning process. But the instability of memory means that the task of reason is to run over all the steps of an argument until 'memory is left with practically no role to play' because intuition can encompass the whole (Rule 11, AT x.409, CSM 1.38). This relieves our memory and enlarges intellectual capacity (Rule 7, AT x.387–8, CSM 1.35).

32 One of Tim Reiss' suggestions in correspondence is that Descartes' problem about memory and method is not so much about how to neutralise fixed memory traces, but about how to render them dynamic, and thus open to rational re-evaluation. As Reiss puts it, 'that memories need reconstructing does not contradict the fact that they can't be erased': but he wonders whether, on my interpretation 'reconstruction can be the right term, for, if so, we're surely no longer talking with any security about *memory*? Are we not, then, in the realm of either imagination or judgment?' (personal communication). This exactly is Descartes' worry, for, on my interpretation, traces already are dynamic, but tending more in the direction of imagination, beyond the pale of reason and will, than of judgement.

connectionist urge to collapse storage and processing so that computation is incessant rather than occasional. But Descartes retains a gap between storage and processing to the extent that he still postulates a central executive mechanism located at the pineal gland, which must be kept clean for vigorous ongoing processing of input and computation. Not only beings with rational souls, but also Cartesian automata, have this singular control engine through which animal spirits must be filtered and across which corporeal ideas play.

We could ascribe the role of this control centre entirely to Descartes' metaphysical dualism, and then stress the highly restricted scope of the incorporeal in the physical world. Yet however minimal the dualism, Descartes still imposes a single centre which receives input from body and world and, in its swivelling and jiggling, orients the organism's responses (Dennett 1991a). Descartes' worries about control are directly connected with memory. In conversation with Burman, Descartes said that 'the difference between sense-perception and imagination is thus really just this, that in sense-perception the images are imprinted by external objects which are actually present, whilst in imagination the images are imprinted by the mind without any external objects and with the windows shut, as it were' (AT v.162–3, CSM-K 145). Memory, significantly, just does not fit this scheme, for it bridges the distinction between untrustworthy constructive imagination and passive input-driven perception. In memory, objects or events are absent, for they are in the past. But memory, imagination, and sensation are all available to non-human animals and to humans when their minds are elsewhere. So the 'painting' of representations in the spirits can go on without being done by the mind, and without being directed by the objective external world. Who, or what, is in charge? There is only the folding, sieving, and commotion of the physiological fluids and fibres.

It is for this reason that Descartes and, more explicitly, Malebranche (chapter 9 below) construct strategies of evasion, ways of reasserting control over the wayward body. Longing for inner discipline springs, in part, from awareness of the dangers of distributed memory: and the fragile authority of a central executive, whether the incorporeal intellectual memory or the rolling pineal gland, is the only security.

Some seventeenth-century memory theorists, like Digby and Hooke (chapter 5), favoured local models of memory just because they required a simple picture of strong central control of cognition, with passive items needing active manipulation. But distributed models, which take traces to be in, or to be, the interrelations of physical parts, do not sit so easily with this ideal of global control, of an executive with access to and control over what is going on everywhere in the system. On a distributed model, memories actively alter all the time.

Where then does Descartes slot in? The history looks paradoxical. I have argued that Descartes had at least a partial understanding of distributed models: but, notoriously, Descartes posits a central executive, both for dualist purposes and as a control mechanism. Something must give: either Descartes really does not have a distributed model, or distributed models can in fact coexist with a central executive, or Descartes does not have a central executive. This is the key historical crux in Descartes, the point at which coherence gives out. There is much to be said for the second option, that distributed memories can be made compatible with central control, for the local versus distributed distinction is technically independent of issues of cognitive control. But in Cartesian terms, with regard to the work of psychological explanation, Descartes does not in effect have much of an executive, the pineal's control and anchoring functions being swamped by the physiological dynamics: his theory is under terrible internal pressure.

The wishful executive does not have access to the whole system, to all the information passing through the pores, for the continually shifting fluids which ground memory capacities cannot always all be tracing their figures on the surface of the gland. They whoosh round in patterns through brain and body, causing all sorts of motions of which the executive has no inkling. The pineal gland is buffeted on all sides, beset around by the winds and flames of the animal spirits. Hence Descartes' increasing attention to psychological conflict, and hence his recurring desire to distance himself from his own theories of physical-cognitive processes like remembering by mentioning piously the importance of intellectual memory, or by seeking to bypass and eliminate memory from the life of the rational agent. Executive control is either illusory, or, at best, fragile.

Yet there is a further, positive picture of self-mastery, which holds both control and memory activity together, just visible in Descartes' later work and in Malebranche. The plasticity of corporeal memory is indeed dangerous: but it is, also, the soul's only hope. Moral neurology was not the old dualist diatribe against the body, but the knowing use of habit and association to encourage the sources of passion in brain and body to shift into morally sanctioned paths. The *Passions'* recommendation to understand physiology in order to live better is not just scientistic raving, requiring direct introspection of our brain states. It involves provisional maxims, applicable differently in each individual, for applying intelligence to the reflexes, and (fallibly, interminably) re-colonising the body.[33]

Though I cannot expand on this suggestion here, it is worth pointing out that the much maligned Cartesian gap between self and body starts to look better

---

33 Thanks to Doris McIlwain for suggesting this way of formulating my interpretation. It is developed a little further in Sutton 1998: compare Morgan 1994: 154.

motivated from this perspective. John Cook (1969: 118–21) complained that Descartes 'failed to realize that he was introducing an extraordinary sense of the word "body"', in which a 'distinction between *himself* and his body' makes sense (where it allegedly does not in ordinary language). But the programme of extended autopersuasion which Descartes advised for Princess Elizabeth allowed the active mind to mould associative responses, gradually becoming an architect of one's own passions and (correspondingly) of the landscape of pores and fibres which the spirits sculpt. Against the immediate dictates of the preservation of the body, the task is to work towards the permeation of body and brain by intellect and will, a permeation directly parallel with, and often contrary to, that already enacted by the physical world on the body. As thinking beings embedded in living body-machines, we must often correct for the hasty norms appropriate for those machines as biological beings alone. Only thus might the compound creature which thinks and eats, reasons and dreams in such a marked, particular body ever become more truly what, as a unified whole, it is.

Appendix 1: nerves, spirits, and traces in Descartes

I have suggested a new interpretation of Descartes' views on corporeal memory, and shown how it was embedded in his general physiology and natural philosophy. In this appendix, to set memory even more firmly in Cartesian nature, I provide further background to the theoretical framework of *L'Homme* and Cartesian physiology for readers unfamiliar with it (Kemp Smith 1952: ch. 5; Riese 1958; Hall 1969, 1970; Krell 1990: 62–73; Grosholz 1991: ch. 6; Shea 1991: 182–9; Gaukroger 1995: 269–90). The structure of *L'Homme* repays close attention: it is a complex weave of postponements, repetitions, promises, and reconstructions which often comes at the same topics from a number of different angles.[34]

The machine Descartes describes 'can be moved in all the ways that our body can, solely by the force of the animal spirits which flow from the brain into the nerves' (*L'Homme*, AT xi.137, H 29). He departs from neurological tradition only in placing sensory and motor functions in the same nerve, in opposition to both Galen and Vesalius (AT xi.133–5, H 22–6 and notes). The nerves are hollow tubules or pipes enclosed in a double membrane continuous with the brain's *pia mater* and *dura mater* (AT xi.133, H 23; on hollow nerves see Clarke 1968; Clarke and Jacyna 1987: 160f.). They contain threads or tiny fibres in a central marrow running between the brain and the periphery; the fibres are sur-

---

34 Hall's judgement that *L'Homme* is 'topically unbalanced' presupposes that it was intended as a general physiological primer, with completeness as a goal: he is closer in describing it as 'an essay in physiological psychology with supportive – but subordinate – sections on other physiological topics' (H xxxvii).

rounded and protected by animal spirits (AT xi.134, H 24; AT xi.141–3, H 33–6, CSM I.101–2).[35]

Theories of sensation and neuromuscular action follow. In sensation, stimuli displace the peripheral and thus, simultaneously, the central ends of the nerve fibres, instantaneously and mechanically transmitting to the brain some kind of structural isomorph of the impression made on the sense organ (AT xi.141–5, H 33–40 and notes, CSM I.101–3; *Passions* I.12–14, AT xi.337–9, CSM I.332–4; Brazier 1984: 18–29; Clarke 1989: 27f.).[36] The mechanisms by which different sense organs transmit patterns to the brain are discussed at length. Blows on the tympanic membrane from the outside air, for instance, pass to the brain by the nerves, and the soul conceives the idea of different sounds depending on the frequency, and on various relations between the blows. Quantitative differences between patterns of blows result in qualitatively different sensations of hearing (AT xi.149–51, H 45–8; on music, hearing, and harmony see Shea 1991: 69–92; Gaukroger 1995: 74–80, 286–7; Kassler 1995: 43–8). The isomorph, which is a set of physical states of the brain resulting from the transmission of motions from the organs, somehow makes the soul have different sensations (AT xi.143–4, H 36–40, CSM I.102–3). Resultant changes in the patterns of motions of spirit particles in the brain in turn cause differential outflows of the spirits into the nerves (AT. xi.159–60, 171, H 59–60, 77–8), causing muscular motion by inflation (Nayler 1993: 38–89).

Descartes eliminates the traditional 'vital' spirits:[37] animal spirits pre-exist as the finest, most subtle, and fastest moving vigorous parts of the blood. These are 'extremely small bodies which move very quickly, like the jets of flame that come from a torch. They never stop in any place' (*Passions* I.10, AT xi.335, CSM

35 At *Dioptrics* IV (AT vi.109–12) Descartes reiterates the three components of the nerves: enclosing membranes, internal threads, and animal spirits. Although 'the anatomists and doctors have adequately demonstrated that these three things are in the nerves . . . no one among them has adequately distinguished their uses'.

36 The internal nerve marrow is involved in this sensory process only, and has no motor function. The animal spirits transmit only motor impulses all the way between brain and periphery. But they are still necessary for sensation. It is not only that their function in inflating the nerve tubes ensures that the small fibres which run from periphery to brain 'do not crowd or impede each other in any way' (*Dioptrics* IV, AT vi.110); they also, crucially, must receive in their patterned motions through the brain, a sensory representation of the cause of the sensory input. This is why disruptions in the state of the spirits, a proneness to turbulence or stagnation, can threaten confidence in the subject's comprehension of, as well as interaction with, the world. Starobinski (1966: 176–7) takes a different view, that Descartes privileges muscular motion over sensation.

37 Descartes accepts the existence of particles drawn out of food which others call natural spirits and of particles heated by the heart and separated from other parts of the blood, 'which the medical men call "vital spirits"'. But 'there is virtually no difference' between these two, and they are unlike the 'pure' animal spirits in not being separated from the blood (to Vorstius, 19 June 1643, AT iii.688–9, CSM-K 225–6). As Hall says (H 21, n. 43), Descartes gives these traditional spirits no role of their own, and discards them from actual physiological explanation.

1.331–2). After their separation from the blood and passage through the pineal gland, they enter the brain and its unstable economy of spirits. They flow through the pores of the brain, to which Descartes assigns a central explanatory role. These are 'no different from the spaces that occur between the threads of some tissue; because, in effect, the whole brain is nothing but a tissue constituted in a particular way' (L'Homme, AT xi.170, H 77: on the term 'tissue' see Hall's note 123 (H 77) and Rather 1982: 138–40).

The brain is 'a rather dense and compact net or mesh' linked by 'conduits' which receive the animal spirits as they leave the pineal gland via the ventricles (AT xi.171, H 77–8). Threads arise from this net and extend to the rest of the body as the bundles of filaments enclosed within nerve membranes. These are channels, as Hall puts it, which conduct animal spirits into the nerves with which they are continuous (AT xi.171, H 78, n. 124).

The whole brain mesh, composed of filaments with pores between them, is affected by the particular motions of the animal spirits in three ways. The pores can be 'diversely enlarged or constricted by the force of the spirits that enter them'. Secondly, the filaments themselves 'can be flexed rather easily' by the same force as the spirits. Thirdly, and of importance for Descartes' account of memory, the filaments 'can retain, as if made of lead or wax, the flexure last received until something exerts a contrary pressure upon them' (AT xi.171, H 79).[38]

In thus describing the pores of the brain Descartes, at this point in L'Homme, is outlining 'in proper order' the second of three factors on which alone life functions depend (AT xi.166, H 72, CSM 1.104). Having earlier postponed a full account of the spirits and the functions they support (AT xi.133, H 23), and moved on to deal with muscular motion, respiration, and the various external and internal senses, Descartes finally agrees to 'commence to explain to you how the animal spirits pursue their course in the cavities and pores of its [the machine's] brain, and what functions depend on them' (AT xi.165, H 71, CSM 1.103). Just as the harmonies of a church organ depend not just on the structure of its parts, but on the supply and distribution of air through its pipes, so the harmonious functioning of the body-machine depends not on gross structural anatomy but on (a) the animal spirits; (b) 'the pores of the brain through which they pass'; and (c) 'the way in which these spirits are distributed to these pores' (AT xi.165–6, H 71–2, CSM 1.103–4). This third factor in fact marks the break-

38 Landormy (1902: 271, 265) took this to imply that the facility of brain fibres for the retention of images is just a consequence of Descartes' general principle of inertia, whereby it is a universal property of extended matter to retain a modification once applied to it. But more is required for the preservation of memory motions in the brain over longer periods of time: the problem will be to explain the possibility of reconstructing a 'flexure' after many different contrary pressures have been received, and this is what Descartes tries to do later. The idea that there is some physical constancy in the brain tissue is simply a first step.

down of the organ analogy, since it explains why organic automata are not restricted by their hardwiring to reflex responses to immediate stimuli alone.

The distribution of fluids through the brain is unceasing, since the spirits are in incessant motion (AT xi.172, H 79). They continually flow out from the pineal gland through the brain cavities, and some enter particular brain tubules.[39] Entering interstices in the fibrous mesh of brain substance, and tracing patterns by their motions through these pores, the spirits 'tend where the arrangement of the brain at the time impels them, not necessarily to regions that face them rectilineally' (AT xi.173, H 81). The specificity of patterns at a given time is important here, for this is how current context, in the form of incoming patterns of motions from the environment and from elsewhere in the body, will meet and interact with current context in the form of the existing dispositional states of the brain. Only physical variables are involved, and yet experience and individual learning history can encounter present environmental factors. The operative principles are to do with differences in motions: perceptible differences in objects are in some as yet unexplained way perceived by means of various differences in the spatiotemporal paths traced by the animal spirits in the brain.

Descartes talks of 'traces' and 'figures' as these explicit, specific patterns in the spirits at a given time.[40] The spirits flowing around the neural system keep the filaments of nerves and brain 'so tense' that patterns of motions are easily transmitted (AT xi.175, H 84). This is how 'ideas of objects that impinge on the senses' are formed: just as a figure 'corresponding to that of [the] object' is traced at the back of the eye, so 'the different ways in which tubes 2, 4, and 6 are opened trace on the internal surface of the brain a figure corresponding to that of [the object]' (AT xi.175–6, H 84–5).[41] Likewise, the pattern of motions of spirits as they leave the pineal gland traces the same figure on the gland's surface. 'Figure' here, says Descartes, refers to everything which can cause any sensations, not just to 'things that somehow represent the position of the edges and surfaces of objects' (AT xi.176, H 85). The role of 'figures' as

---

39 Those without sufficient strength to do so, or which are blocked by closed tubules, can pass into the nostrils and cause sneezing or be turned back on to the internal surface of the brain, causing dizziness or vertigo (H 79–80).

40 In fact, Descartes' use of these terms is more ambiguous. Such terms sometimes refer to transient patterns in or of the spirits, and sometimes to enduring changes in the brain pores. The ambiguity is not necessarily problematic, but it does invite further conceptual clarification: in chapter 6 below, I distinguish between (transient) explicit representations and (enduring) implicit representations. The distinction applies as clearly in Descartes' account of memory as in modern connectionist models.

41 Hall's note to this passage (H 85, n. 132) acknowledges that, while 'later physiologists were to repudiate animal spirits and substitute neuronal pathways within the brain for the currents envisioned by Descartes', the idea of 'a correspondence between retinal and cerebral patterns . . . was ultimately to become a stable part of the theory of visual perception'.

representations, in other words, is *not* to resemble all qualities of the object represented, but simply to vary with the perceptible qualities. Representation can operate without simple resemblance, as he stresses elsewhere (chapter 15 below).

This account provides sufficient physiological background for us to interpret the distributed model of memory which I described in section 3.2 above. Physical 'patterns' of spirit motions are the key, flowing across fibres which can retain certain flexures: in memory, certain of the superposed patterns can be formed again 'long afterward', because of the dispositional traces, in the form of physical alterations to the connectivity of pores in the brain folds.

Appendix 2: Malebranche on memory

The spread of the distributed model of memory based on patterns of motions of the animal spirits through the pores of the brain was initially due to Descartes' *Passions of the Soul* and, when published, his *L'Homme*. In chapter 5 I look at some English responses to and criticisms of these expositions. But I want to buttress the plausibility of my interpretation of Descartes through a brief consideration of the account of memory in the work of his follower Nicolas Malebranche. Malebranche's model is, I think, more explicit in its commitment to the twin requirements for distribution, the *extendedness* of a memory trace, and the *superpositional* storage of traces in the same physical system.[42]

Even more so than in Descartes' case, historical attention to Malebranche is restricted to metaphysics. There is only one reference in the *Bibliographia Malebranchiana* to memory (Easton, Lennon, and Sebba 1992: 80), namely to an Italian article of 1893 which reportedly criticises his mechanical psychophysiology of memory as incompatible with his occasionalist metaphysics, whereby there should be no continuity in the physical world. So I make no apologies for taking Malebranche's psychophysiology both seriously and out of context. Much English-language Malebranche scholarship has focused on occasionalism, on his representational theory of ideas by which we see all things in God, and on his disputes about ideas with Arnauld (Radner 1978; Nadler 1992). Yet neurophilosophy takes up a huge amount of his writing, and

---

42 In one of the few brief references to Malebranche's physiology by Anglophone scholars, McCracken (1983: 35), unwilling to be detained by the details of Cartesian spirits theory, wrongly takes Malebranche's views of the retentive powers of imagination to depend 'wholly on the capacity of the brain to serve as a storehouse'. Only awareness of the nature of distributed models of memory reveals just how important it was to Descartes and Malebranche that the brain was not in any obvious sense a storehouse. More general examination of 'seventeenth-century French connectionism' (Diamond 1969) will require greater attention to the psychophysiological writings of La Forge and other early Cartesians than Anglophone scholarship has yet given.

a sizeable proportion of the 5,598 uses of the word *esprit* in his major work are in the plural, referring to the *esprits animaux* (Robinet 1984).[43]

In fact, reactions to 'the Cartesian philosophy of the brain' owed as much to Malebranche's as to Descartes' version. John Wright has demonstrated, in particular, the extensive use made of Malebranche's psychophysiology by Hume (Wright 1983: 70–4, 212–15, 224–6). Six editions of Malebranche's *De la recherche de la vérité* appeared between 1674–5 and 1712, and two English translations of the fourth edition (1678) appeared during the 1690s.[44] John Yolton (1984b: 186) notes later judgements by both La Mettrie and Joseph Priestley that Malebranche was 'said to have been the first who brought into vogue the doctrine of *animal spirits*'. Malebranche received lavish praise from later psychologist-historians of theories of memory. Burnham in 1888, after lamenting Descartes' 'crude physiology' and 'dogmatism', dubbed Malebranche, for his account of brain traces and memory, 'a true pioneer in the field of physiological psychology' (1888: 66–8). Gomulicki (1953: 4), while regretting that Malebranche agreed with his contemporaries 'in still accepting such concepts as that of "animal spirits"', praises his terminology for the physiological basis of memory on the grounds that it 'might almost be modern'. As well as confirming and illustrating the Cartesian model, a brief discussion here serves as background for my use of Malebranche in chapter 9 on the relation between distributed animal spirits and views of the self.

Malebranche explicitly links his views on animal spirits and 'the structure of the brain' to the 'hypotheses or suppositions' of Descartes' *L'Homme*, suggesting that attention to it will satisfy the reader 'on all these questions because of the method he provides for their resolution' (LO 93, II.1.2.iii). Malebranche's chance reading of *L'Homme* in 1664, he related, made his heart palpitate with excitement (Heilbron 1982: 31; Gaukroger 1990: 41). But in his own exposition of the mechanical physiology of nerves and spirits, Malebranche displays a caution which is surprising within the allegedly wild rationalistic speculations allowed by Cartesian method: he reflects that proofs of his account would require 'a general survey of physics and then a very precise account of the human body' (LO 355, V.3). He is sanguine in allowing that these sciences are as yet too imprecise.

In book 1, on the senses, Malebranche's 'explanation of the sense organs' is a description of their anatomy and of the physiology of sense perception. The nerve filaments running between sense organs and 'the middle of the brain' are 'hollow like little canals and are completely filled with animal spirits' which make them taut (LO 49, I.10.ii). He remains neutral over whether sensation is

---

43 '. . . chez lui comme chez Descartes, les conseils de méthode sont inseparables d'une conception physiologique de la mémoire, de l'imagination, et de l'association des idées' (Alquié 1974: 30).

44 By Thomas Taylor in 1694 (2nd edn, 1700), and by Richard Sault in 1694–5.

due to vibrations of the animal spirits or to 'the continuous displacement of the filaments right up to the brain' (LO 50, 1.10.ii). Book II, on the imagination, is founded on the possibility of explaining 'all the different characters encountered among the minds of men' by reference to differences in the same physical variables on which Descartes relied (LO 89, II.1.1.iii). The brain fibres can be delicate or coarse, moist or dry, malleable or rigid, while the animal spirits can be abundant or scarce, rapidly or slowly agitated, dense or light, and vary in 'pressure', causing differences in 'the depth and clarity of the traces in the imagination'.[45] The variables of animal spirits and brain fibres are, almost, explanatorily exhaustive: 'it is the variety found in these two things that constitutes nearly all the great diversity observed among minds' (LO 89, II.1.1.iii).

On top of this basic explanatory apparatus,[46] Malebranche gives a mechanism for the lasting effects of experience on the brain. This, indeed, is central to the whole project of The Search after Truth, which is to expose and explain 'all the errors of men and their causes', to try then 'to relieve the mind of the errors to which it is subject', and to give a 'general method for conducting the search after truth' (LO 17–18, 1.4.ii–iii). The first source of error, and the subject of book I, is sense perception. Ordinary perception is when the impression made by objects on the external organs is communicated to the brain: but when 'the flow of animal spirits makes a similar impression in the brain', the soul can perceive even absent objects as represented by the imagination in the brain (LO 17, 1.4.ii). Vestiges of past impressions, then, can survive. The difference between sensing and imagining is only one of degree, since the agitation of fibres in the brain is sufficient for the soul to perceive something, and such agitation can originate in internal disturbances in the flow of animal spirits as well as in impressions made by objects (LO 87–8, II.1.1.i; Wright 1983: 213;

---

45 The animal spirits are corporeal, we are told at LO 91 (II.1.2.i), 'merely the most refined and agitated parts of the blood', which are separated from the blood in the brain. This chapter gives the Cartesian account of the origin and formation of spirits, and II.1.3 allows for environmental effects on their nature by way of differences in the air breathed. Malebranche gives details (II.1.2.i) of the different kinds of fermentation or refinement of the blood which can affect the spirits, making them, for example, too agitated or too inactive: in addition, 'depending on the stability of the blood particles, the animal spirits will be more or less stable themselves'. In the 'examples and indisputable experiments' which Malebranche here promises to give us, this potential instability of the animal spirits is often the source of moral and psychological danger and imbalance.

46 Malebranche also accepts Descartes' hydraulic account of muscular motion, stressing that the effusion of animal spirits into muscles can be swift enough. 'The whole question', he says, 'regarding voluntary movement can be reduced to knowing how the small quantity of animal spirits contained in an arm can suddenly swell its muscles according to the orders of the will with sufficient force to lift a load of a hundred pounds and more'. Convulsive movements in turn are due to irregularities in nerves or spirits, when, for instance, the nerves are 'plugged by some humor' (LO 502–3 and 508, VI.11.8). For a discussion of Malebranche's views on action and muscular motion in the context of his occasionalist metaphysics see Yolton 1984b: 128–31 (also pp. 160–2 on Malebranche's accounts of animal spirits and brain traces).

Yolton 1984b: 160). Malebranche uses the word 'trace' for what survives in the imagination after the spirits have traced patterns in perception (LO 88–9, II.1.1.ii–iii).[47]

After a long explanation of the possible internal and external causes of changes in the animal spirits 'and as a result in the imagination' (LO 99, II.1.4.iii), Malebranche goes on in the dense chapter 5 of part I of book II to examine 'the connection between our thoughts and the brain traces, and the reciprocal connection of these traces'. This involves the same dispositional account of memory traces and of associative mechanisms for reconstructive remembering which was central to Descartes' model. The mutual connection of traces, says Malebranche, 'consists in the fact that the brain traces are so well tied to one another that none can be aroused without all those which were imprinted at the same time being aroused' (LO 105, II.1.5.ii). This is what allows for the use of names and other marks as memorial aids. Some connections between traces, like the association between 'the trace of a great elevation one sees below oneself, and from which one is in danger of falling' and the trace 'that represents death to us', are natural and 'necessary to preservation of life': such a tie between traces cannot be broken, for 'it consists in a disposition of the brain fibres that we have from birth' (LO 106, II.1.5.ii). Other connections, those which Malebranche will address at length as the source of our errors, are acquired and fortuitous, depending, for instance, on

> the identity of times at which they were imprinted on the brain. For it is enough that many traces were produced at the same time for them all to rise again together. This is because the animal spirits, finding the path of all the traces made at the same time half open, continue on them since it is easier for them to travel those paths than through other parts of the brain. This is the cause of memory and of the bodily habits we share with the beasts. (LO 106, II.1.5.ii)[48]

47 The patterns originally traced are usually called 'images' of objects by Malebranche, but in his first introduction of the survival of traces of absent objects, in 1.4.ii, he adds the reservation that what are formed are only 'images of them [objects], *as it were*, in the brain' (LO 17, my emphasis). There is no need to assume that Malebranche is requiring simple resemblance: the relation between trace and object is psychophysiological, at the level of isomorphism of pattern of animal spirit motions from the time of experience to the time of remembering or imagining. This too is consistent with Descartes, for whose attacks on representation as resemblance see chapter 15 below. Malebranche confirms this interpretation later when he finds it 'absolutely necessary' to remind us that 'these images are nothing other than the traces the animal spirits make in the brain' which vary in depth and clarity according only to the ease or facility with which the spirits can re-enter their paths or patterns of motions (LO 134, II.11.2). Nadler (1992: 46) stresses that 'there is not a single Cartesian in the seventeenth century who opts for the resemblance view of representation'.

48 On the distinction between natural and acquired connections see also Wright 1983: 227f.; Yolton 1984b: 162; and chapter 9 below on natural associations. The importance of Malebranche's references to what is necessary for the preservation of life is well brought out in Gaukroger 1990: 26–34.

The distributed nature of Malebranche's model appears here in that the traces do not remain, or are not conserved, explicitly from experience to retrieval. They have to 'rise again': and they can change over time as a result of continuing processing, for 'not always being necessary for the preservation of life, they need not always be the same' (LO 106, II.1.5.ii). It is in these acquired connections between traces, traces which exist only as dispositions for the animal spirits to find more easily old patterns of motion, that plasticity of mind enters Malebranche's neurophilosophy.

'The nature of memory' falls easily out of this model. It is a dispositional account in terms of the retention of a facility for the reconstruction of certain patterns of motions of spirits in fibres:

> just as the branches of a tree that have remained bent in a certain way for some time preserve a certain facility for being bent anew in the same way, so too our brain fibers, having once received certain impressions through the flow of the animal spirits and by the action of objects, retain some facility for receiving these same dispositions for some time. Now, memory consists only in this facility, since one thinks of the same things when the brain receives the same impressions. (LO 106, II.1.5.iii)[49]

The preservation of traces, then, is not a straightforward conservation of unchanging items passively stored: it consists rather in physical dispositions for the reconstruction of particular episodes of processing. The usual ambiguity within distributed models over the individuation of traces is present in this passage, most clearly in the somewhat paradoxical analogy with branches which 'preserve a certain facility for being bent anew in the same way': a distributed memory trace too is constructed anew, but in the same way as an earlier trace. Malebranche is able simply to dismiss 'the prejudice that our brain is much too small to be able to preserve such large numbers of traces and impressions' (LO 107, II.1.5.iii), for the traces do not all have to be simultaneously active: they are 'stored' only superpositionally, in 'the changes occurring in the fibers of the principal part of the brain' (LO 106, II.1.5.iii).[50]

The ease with which spirits cause associated traces to rise again together is a principal cause of the 'disorder of men's imagination' (LO 130, II.11.1), and, it becomes clear, even more so of women's. We often fail to 'judge things soundly' because 'the animal spirits ordinarily flow in the traces of the ideas most familiar to us' (LO 134, II.11.2). Because traces are distributed and super-

---

49 Malebranche goes on to explain 'why we do not recall all the things we have perceived equally well', and to suggest that each reader go on to work out 'the cause of all [the] surprising effects of the memory'.

50 Malebranche's confidence that finding room in the brain is no serious problem for his theory strongly confirms that it is a distributed model, and also supports my suggestion above that Descartes' view of memory did not lead him to despair of finding storage space in the brain.

posed, interference between them is inevitable: brain traces can become 'confused with each other, because there are so many of them, and reason has not arranged them in order . . . When the mind wants to open certain traces but encounters other more familiar ones crossing them, it is misled' (LO 141, II.11.4). The 'crossing' of traces in the same system is superposition: the capacity of such a system in the brain not being infinite, it is, says Malebranche, 'nearly impossible for so many traces, formed without order, to avoid becoming mixed up and bringing confusion into the ideas'. This is why remembering many things is often incompatible with ordered reason and judgement (LO 141, II.11.4).[51] The preservation of original order, then, is not a natural property of distributed memory. It is an achievement to avoid confusion, for confusion is the primitive mechanism by which remembering operates. Since memories are not stored explicitly at separate memory addresses independent of each other, generalisation, blending, and mixing are all but automatic. Traces are, as Malebranche says, 'formed without order'.

Misassociation is an ever-present danger because of this dangerous plasticity in memory. Malebranche gives a variety of 'very obvious and intuitive examples' of what can happen when 'the animal spirits, finding some resistance in the parts of the brain whence they should pass, and being easily detoured crowd into the deep traces of the ideas that are more familiar to us' (LO 135, II.11.2). We see a face or a man on horseback in the moon, we see chariots, men, or lions in the clouds, we mistake all diseases for the familiar scurvy, we dream of objects we have seen during the day, we see heads on walls which have 'many irregular colored patches', or we take everything to be connected with the subject of our continual study. Spirits of wine (which Malebranche has earlier told us are 'almost fully formed animal spirits, but libertine spirits, which do not voluntarily submit to the commands of the will' (LO 92, II.1.2.iii)) can enter easily into familiar traces and thus, without the involvement of the will, 'cause the most important secrets to be revealed' (LO 135, II.11.2).[52]

Confusions between traces, and the misassociations involved in disorders of the imagination, require much vigilance and continual efforts to assert control over the potentially libertine animal spirits. I discuss these topics in relation to the psychophysiology of self in chapter 9. Here I note remarks from later in Malebranche's work which echo Descartes on the psychophysiology of wonder, and again reveal Cartesian hesitancy about accepting the implications of the distributed model.

---

51 Compare the discussion of the utility of forgetting and of Montaigne's alleged excellence in forgetfulness at LO 187–8, II.III.5.

52 Wright (1983: 70) also discusses the moon example. It is, in a sense, just an extension of Descartes' example, in the original exposition in L'Homme of total recall on partial input, of adding all the elements of a face when we see some of them. Veridical remembering and imagining differ psychologically only in degree.

Because error is so easy on a distributed model, the kind of safe, clear, and distinct cognitions which the pure seventeenth-century moral physiologists desire are an achievement, to be worked at and valued.[53] In book v of *The Search After Truth*, on the sources of error in the passions, Malebranche takes up large parts of two chapters to discuss the ill and the good effects of wonder, of what happens 'when the brain is struck in places in which it has never been struck before, or when it is struck in an entirely new way' (LO 375, v.7). Wonder can work ill effects through the dangerous traces formed by violent and unruly animal spirits (chapter 9 below; Sutton 1998). But Malebranche does spend a little time acknowledging that, of the passions, only wonder 'illumines the mind', making it alone potentially 'useful to the sciences' (LO 385, v.8). This is because 'In wonder, the animal spirits are forced toward those parts of the brain representing the new object as it is in itself; there they make distinct traces that are deep enough to be preserved a long time. Consequently, the mind has a sufficiently clear idea of the object and easily remembers it' (LO 385, v.8). Where other passions move the spirits so that 'they represent objects only according to their relation to us and not as they are in themselves', wonder seems, sometimes, to allow acontextual remembering.

It looks, then, as if Malebranche thinks that clear and distinct remembering requires the difficult isolation or localising of each memory trace from others. Wonder might be the limiting case in which this happens, when one trace is distinct, deep, and independent enough to be preserved explicitly for a long time.[54] This contrasts with the normal case on a distributed model, which is the superposition of traces in one system whereby each particular trace is not itself explicitly preserved a long time. It is very hard, Malebranche says, to apply oneself to something which fails to excite wonder, 'since then the animal spirits are not so easily led into those parts of the brain necessary to represent it' (LO 385, v.8). This is a sign of some wish or hope for local representation, a desire that distributed memory not be all that we have.

It is worth just mentioning again that, beyond the general institutional

---

53 Medieval memory education, Mary Carruthers argues (1990: 7–12 and *passim*), had been a moral education, aimed at avoiding the murky forests of confused memories by institutionalising to-be-remembered material in rigid random-access cognitive formats, thus encouraging prudence, piety, and good citizenship. The source material which Carruthers analyses primarily in terms only of spatial metaphors for memory reveals the differing moral implications of local and distributed models of memory. I address wider implications of these moral memory systems in Sutton 1997.

54 Explicit representation seems to guarantee immunity from melding. This is clear on a generally localist model, which is set up to exclude interference (see on Hooke, chapter 5 below). But it is also true of a predominantly distributed model: when (very rarely, as in wonder) a single pattern of activation is explicit over the parts of a physical system in which other traces are also stored, this means that there have been insufficient changes to the patterns and interrelations of the physical parts which store all these traces to cause the explicit representation's degeneration, transformation, or condensation.

strength of Cartesian natural philosophy in general (Heilbron 1982: 26–38) and physiology in particular (Sloan 1977), the animal spirits theory of memory gained immense popularity over the late seventeenth and early eighteenth centuries. From Descartes until, roughly, the 1740s, remembering was the motion of animal spirits through the pores of the brain (Yolton 1984b: ch. 8). The rife associationism of the eighteenth century, in fields from aesthetics and ethics to psychology and physiology, derived much of its plausibility from such earlier distributed models. Even if Hume was right to identify a neurophilosophy as specifically Cartesian, it was soon taken up by writers of differing metaphysical persuasions. Malebranche's strong affirmation of the centrality of the spirits for psychological explanation set the tone: 'all the changes occurring in the imagination and the mind are only the consequences of those encountered in the animal spirits and the [brain] fibres' (LO 134, II.11.2). The animal spirits had the entire realm of mental processes in their wriggling power.

PART II

Inner discipline

The history of inhibition is a dialogue between the desire to exercise moral
control and the description of natural control . . . Scientific theory, to be
intelligible, had to show how the workings of nature made possible normative
controlling actions in the lives of human subjects.   (Roger Smith 1992: 10, 231)

> To flee from memory
> Had we the Wings
> Many would fly
> Inured to slower things
> Birds with surprise
> Would scan the cowering Van
> Of men escaping
> From the mind of man   (Emily Dickinson (c. 1872), 1968: 56)

. . . we can assume a complete dominance of the brain by the self . . .
                                   (Sir John Eccles 1994: 168)

Introduction

It is sometimes difficult to see how 'sciences of mind' could have got off the ground in the wake of the 'scientific revolution'. Dualism in theology and metaphysics required the cordoning off of will from science (Burtt 1932: 318–19; Young 1970: 1–3; Daston 1982): along methodological divisions driven by the programmatic rhetoric of supernaturalist mechanism, philosophy took up abstract concerns about understanding, soul, and reason, while physics and biology studied inert bodies. But, of course, many phenomena between metaphysics and physiology were still studied, in joint philosophical and physiological theorising of memory, dreams, imagination, perception, and the passions.

Part II follows the linked fates of animal spirits and of neurophilosophical models of memory through the century after Descartes. Theories of memory as the brain's folding of the past excited cultural concern at psychophysiological fluidity and loss of control. The seductions of animal spirits theory, particularly in England, often lay outside the strictly physiological, in the attractive fluidity of the anxious discourses which medical psychology employed around it (compare Rousseau 1989: 38–44). Chapters 4, 6, 8, and 10 embed animal spirits in early modern natural philosophy, and develop the metaphysics of memory which they supported. I set up mysteries about why the fleeting hypothetical entities survived well into the Enlightenment despite experimental evidence against them, and about why they did eventually disappear in the eighteenth century before the development of a coherent replacement theory of neural transmission.

The other strand of part II, in the longer odd-numbered chapters, tentatively responds to these puzzles by showing how animal spirits and memory were, especially in England, implicated in larger cultural and philosophical debates about order and confusion in cognition; about the proper handling of the past; and about control of one's own physiology, the learned ability of self or soul to impose its ruling will on swirling animal spirits. Chapter 5 examines four English critics of the Cartesian approach. In chapter 7, I connect physiological theories of memory with early modern views about the continuity of personal identity over time. Chapter 9 looks at stratagems of evasion devised to ward off the seductions of the transient spirits, with their unwholesome associations.

This is still, in a sense, a story of disenchantment, another nostalgic fable of the disappearance of spirits. But it differs from other grand narratives of shifts from sympathy and resemblance to representation and correspondence, from fluids to solids, from earthy organs to bloodless machines, or from timely local wisdom to context-free and universalisable knowledge. Crudely, I ascribe the narrowing and immobilising of presumed physiological forces not to seventeenth-century Cartesian mechanism but to eighteenth-century moralism, not to scientific authority but to changing social formations of personal identity. The soul imprisons the body not on publication of the *Meditations* but as control of truth in memory assumes deeper ethical urgency: the dominance of the brain by the self becomes not a slow immersion in embodiment, as in the Cartesian application of intelligence to the reflexes, but a social responsibility.

The historiographic picture I question is exemplified in two recent discussions of mechanism and the body. A medical historian, carefully delineating relations between late seventeenth-century theory and practice, notes how hard it was to reduce 'the complexity and apparent vitality of the body' to analogy or identity with 'the crude machines of the time' (Wear 1995: 359). He comments on the introduction of a concept of irritability in biological matter by an English physiologist, Francis Glisson (Wear 1995: 344): 'This deeply felt need to prevent the world from being reduced to complete lifelessness indicates the anxieties that might be aroused by too rigid an application of the mechanical philosophy.' Jonathan Sawday, in a marvellous multidisciplinary history of 'vivid dreams of punishment and partition' in Renaissance 'cultures of dissection', similarly argues that the triumph of 'the colder eye of science' silenced the body, newly 'divested of its latent capriciousness' (1995: 53, 22, 37; Sutton 1996). Epistemological ruptures as 'a world of affinity was collapsing' left the fearful self at odds with dead nature, for everything was 'falling into a collapsed and fragmentary rubble of displaced body parts and Cartesian doubt' (Sawday 1995: 234, 128).

But in fact the mechanists' world was not lifeless, and Cartesian bodies and brains were still capricious. As Catherine Wilson argues, 'there is no sudden impoverishment' in corpuscularian natural philosophy, and rhetoric of detachment and mastery long coexisted with receptive engagement with nature and living bodies (1995: 21–2, 38). Anxiety comes elsewhere, in conflict between the fragile control of memory and body which both old theory and phenomenology suggested, and more locally imposed norms of voluntary cognitive propriety.

4
Spirit sciences, memory motions

... there must be in the brain and its *appendix* the *cerebellum*, far more of mechanism
than is obvious to a vulgar eye, or even to that of a dissector. For though this
seemingly rude lump of soft matter does for colour and consistence look almost like
so much custard; yet there are strange things performed partly in it, and partly by the
animal spirits that it produces ...

(Boyle, *The Christian Virtuoso* (1772/1965: vol. VI: 741))[1]

Ontologies of the invisible

Why should we believe in what we cannot see? Our innards pose epistemologically peculiar difficulties. In health, or 'life lived in the silence of the organs'
(René Leriche, in Canguilhem 1966/1989: 91), body parts are phenomenologically absent, churning on in normal function 'below' or 'outside' conscious
awareness (the hopeless metaphors are one reason to query common-sense
notions of consciousness). We have quite false pictures of what a brain, for
instance, looks like (Mundy and Gorman 1969). Organs come to notice only
when something goes wrong, in what Drew Leder calls 'dys-appearance'
(1990: 69–106): turbulence or stagnation is sensed, technologies invade or
scan, and medical art conspires with folklore and imagination to produce vivid
images of dysfunction, seeking to dispel helpless incomprehension by picturing the unseen.

But we are unused to *sensing* disruption in the nervous system, and the brain
is for us pre-eminently insensible (Leder 1990: 111–14): even when its physical
presence evokes powerful emotions, as Eliseo Subiela's film *Man Facing South-
East* (1986), the poignancy arises from perceived distance between the lumpen
wetware and the complexity of cognition and personality, not from direct
recognition of a brain's sad particularity. Popular AI, cyberpunk, and virtual
reality in different ways can function to reinforce hopes that neural matter
could be substituted, detached, or dispensed with: in the 1995 film *Johnny
Mnemonic*, 'synaptic seepage' is the interference of an artificial memory implant
with the 'natural', nostalgic childhood memories it was meant to supplant. But
memory and brain were once part of an odder phenomenology, a direct experience of neurophysiological process. Historical use of analogies from the
natural world does not entail that only 'homely views were entertained of the

---

1 Thanks to Peter Anstey for this reference.

insides' (Porter 1995: 441). Our vestigial metaphors (minds in a whirl, memories being rummaged, brains scraped) barely hint at the baffling neural dramas which 'pre-' and early modern people seem to have sensed as spirits and fluids flowed, melded, clashed, and fought: historians have had to work hard to allow us even to glimpse more recent cultural brain-fears (Rousseau 1991; Oppenheim 1991).

In trudging through early modern texts, one can feel sudden jets of bewilderment about how people could have believed in the animal spirits. Was it not *obvious* that they were fantastical, theoretical wastrels which could not explain real complex functions? How can we relate to human sense the invisible exploits of warring spirits? Although there is no chance of reconstructing what it might have felt like to believe in animal spirits, and although I can offer only more skating among representations in lieu of historical phenomenology, it is possible indirectly to address some of the aura of alien inconceivability from these weirdly bodily mentalities.

Firstly, diverse 'histories of the invisible' reveal to us many forms of past trust in unseen causal powers and processes, supernatural, emotional, and scientific (Duden 1993: 8–10). Secondly, the imperative of visualisation, the demand that something be *seen* before it is believed in, had itself to be constructed, developing alongside new techniques for searching, sensing, and imaging the unseen in the cosmos and the body (Stafford 1991: 1–83, 401–63). Angels, ancestors, and attractions, saints, souls, and sympathies, ghosts, gods, and forces, provided cognitive frameworks for the possibility of coursing microfluids. What then was taken to be specifically at stake in including or excluding bodily spirits from an ontology? What criteria were deemed relevant? How strange, compared both to surrounding sciences and to social expectations, was the account of memory which spirits theory provided?

Because animal spirits were insensible, their ontological status was always open to question: critics could just deny their existence on the grounds that they could not be observed.[2] But it is historically naive to claim that 'as a scientific theory medical spirits have one obvious defect from a modern point of view: it would be very difficult to disprove them empirically, since they are invisible and dissipated at death' (Walker 1953/1985: 125). Excessive profligacy and unnecessary prudery in the postulation of hypothetical constructs are both dangers. But rather than entering relevant general disputes on realism (Hacking 1983: 21–52), I focus on actual historical debates about the existence of these particular delightfully mobile theoretical entities.

---

2 After long searching in vain for an early modern visual representation of animal spirits, I have finally seen them pictured in flow. In an animated account of Cartesian physiology which forms part of a CD-ROM presentation on Descartes (*René Descartes: vie, philosophie, et oeuvre* (1996)), the spirits are shown roaming up into the brain and spreading across its pores. They are blue and yellow, rather like worms or Miro creatures.

Historically, there were analogous disputes about early modern ontologies of the invisible across different parts of the spirit realm. The all but ubiquitous belief among natural philosophers in supernatural and supra-mechanical causes had considerable methodological importance, since observability could not be the sole criterion for reality. Remember that animal spirits functioned as analogue angels, ferrying messages between soul and body, brain and organs (chapter 2 above): the place of angelology as respectable philosophy (not just theology) was secure through to the early eighteenth century (West 1955; Heilbron 1982: 3). Even if Locke, as Catherine Wilson (1995: 239) argues, was 'edging away from the vision of a world in which angels and animalcula could occupy the same referential space, being merely invisible in different ways', invisible and subvisible spirits long remained associated. Angel-discourses, like talk of animal spirits, did not simply stop with the 'scientific revolution', or even become stuck among marginalised groups. Animal spirits were useful tools for thinking about memory, self, and body, just as talk of angels fulfilled a number of important functions beyond the basic issue of their existence, opening space for debates about impenetrability and individual boundaries, about the perfectibility of cognitive capacities, about psychology and purity (Sutton 1994a).

Matter, memory, morality

Many natural philosophers in the seventeenth century took it for granted that theories of cognitive functions like memory and perception would be constrained by, and part of, their wider picture of the physical world. Sciences of matter and of memory were mutually relevant. The explanatory and ontological connections across domains may now seem too swift: but for those concerned with relations between the psychology of memory, society, and neurobiology, the distaste of English Restoration philosophers for Descartes' model of memory exemplifies discourses in which later firm lines between the moral, the cognitive, and the physical are lacking. Critics of distributed memory display aggrieved reactions to a perceived 'transgression and confusion of boundaries that it is important to restore to their proper order' (Irigaray 1974/1985b: 106): their localist theories sought to guarantee memories an ordered immunity to melding, with the diffuse spirits eventually being dismissed from science.

Historians of distributed representation have extra cause for interest in early modern interdisciplinarity. Neural nets are promising potential models for human memory partly because they offer a bridge between the brain, which must somehow support the persistence of memory in a changing physical system, and other, more easily studied, dynamic systems. Holograms, Hopfield nets, and spin glasses offer different models for the distributed storage of many patterns (Pribram 1971: 152–66; Cowan and Sharp 1988;

Metcalfe 1989; Churchland and Sejnowski 1992: 82–96). Similarities between neuroanatomy, experimental psychology, image processing, and optics justify the use of the term 'distributed' for connectionist representations (van Gelder 1991b: 33–5). The concept of distributed representation, then, does not, as is sometimes alleged, depend on any one fashionable new technology, but describes a set of related dynamical systems. Whether implemented in animal spirits, in Newtonian vibrations, in brains, or in artificial nets, it provides a peculiar and fragile form of representational stability over time.

Mechanism and magic
Ongoing concern with the mechanics of imaginary fluids does not, then, reveal pockets of traditional supernatural belief surviving even among leading mechanical philosophers, great but divided men who bridged the worlds of magic and science, religion and rationalism. Animal spirits were wholly compatible with the new corpuscularian philosophies of the seventeenth century, and in this section I show that early modern memory theories too were part of, and had to be compatible with, broader mechanical views. Mechanism, as historians of science have demonstrated, was neither a secularising nor a 'progressive' force in any obvious sense. The old spirits and the chaotic mix of transmitted theories were not just eliminated. To the extent that new natural-ising explanations did gain ground, for instance as reference to medical causes displaced possession (Schwartz 1978; Macdonald 1981; Walker 1981), this is hard to interpret simply as new explanation of the unknown by reference to the known. Many active principles and invisible entities, occult qualities and sym-pathetic forces, were incorporated into the new mechanistic mainstream (Hutchison 1982, 1991: Henry 1986a, 1989a; Schaffer 1987; Brooke 1991: 117–51). Wilson (1995: 40–1) argues that, in the 'recalibration of human knowl-edge with respect to the very small', a 'materialization of hidden resident spirits' was more influential in the rise of mechanism than any intrinsic con-ceptual virtues. In England in particular, the spread of mechanism saw philoso-phers 'capture rather than discard the domain of spirits' (Brooke 1991: 135). This was necessary to preserve the supernatural and the idea of free will against naturalists, magicians, and Hobbist atheists who threatened to explain every-thing by the mere jumbling together, 'rumblement', and confused causal motions of matter (Gabbey 1982: 200, 1990: 26; Jacob 1978; Jacob and Jacob 1980; Hutchison 1983).

Specifically, the insensibility of animal spirits was no bar to their intelligibil-ity within the new philosophy. Aristotelian scholastics, broadly, had assumed that what is unobservable must be either incorporeal or inaccessible to natural philosophy, in a realm of occult (as opposed to manifest) powers specific to particular natural agents. In the new philosophy, by contrast, the basic mecha-nisms cited to explain ordinary corporeal interactions were micromechanisms, and thus unobservable (Hutchison 1982). Further, entities and processes which *are* observable are not thereby guaranteed intelligibility: the multiple mediations involved in perception entail that perceptual 'data' must be interpreted, and do not simply offer up reality. Mechanists, far from eliminating occult qualities, rendered all properties of objects equally 'occult' or equally intelligible: accessibility to the senses was no longer a privileged criterion in ontology (Hutchison 1982; Wilson 1995: 51–7).

These historical accounts of mechanism chime well with the defence of a form of scientific realism offered by Paul Churchland (1985) in rejecting anti-realism about theoretical entities. Global excellence of theory is the best measure of ontology, and 'superempirical' virtues such as simplicity and reductive potential should be more powerful criteria than observability: understanding the idiosyncrasies of our perceptual and cognitive mechanisms will, Churchland argues, undermine the temptation to privilege perception and the middle-sized objects it prefers. Churchland focuses on criteria for the success of a theory which are 'internal' to the science of a time, although in recent work (1993, 1995) he is increasingly aware of the place of cultural and historical factors among the 'superempirical' influences on acceptance or rejection of theoretical entities.

No account of the 'real' criteria used in debates about hypothetical entities can bypass close attention to the specific locations in which such debates occurred. Simon Schaffer has undertaken just such a study of the sciences of spirits in English natural philosophy of the 1670s. Though he does not deal with animal spirits or physiology in particular, Schaffer's results provide a framework for my analysis of mechanism and English theories of memory in this chapter and the next. Through the stages of 'the experimental naturalization of spirit' (Schaffer 1987: 77) by Restoration natural philosophers, theorists retained an inherently ambivalent attitude to the mechanical principles with which they justified and defended their postulation of various active principles. Mainstream Royal Society scientists like Boyle, Hooke, and Mayow, as well as the increasingly marginalised Henry More (Gabbey 1982), were aware of the dangers of explaining too much, attributing powers too complex to confused matter.

Restoration *pneuma* theory, then, had to simultaneously produce and control knowledge of spirits, both extending and limiting their domains (Schaffer 1987: 55–8). Seeking a political psychology of the incorporeal, Schaffer identifies collective methods for ensuring the safety of pneumatological inquiry. Safe laboratory spaces, sites of discipline and technology, were created and claimed as necessary for producing secure testimony from reliable witnesses, as Boyle and Hooke distanced themselves from wonder-mongering stories about spirits and apparitions collected by More and Glanvill from around the country (Easlea 1980: 201–7; Jobe 1981; Shapin and Schaffer 1985:

314–17; Sutton 1994a). Enthusiastic anecdotes were to be controlled by attention to the status of the teller, and nature's activity was to be controlled within the experimental space. The ultimate derivation from God of all activity in nature was supplemented by a range of intermediate 'supra-mechanical' active principles and subtle fluids which were neither part of the realm of blockish inert matter nor challenges to the authority of the supernatural (Henry 1986a). The explanatory utility of any candidate entity was partly judged by its politico-juridical and theological standing. Boundaries between natural and super-natural realms in various research programmes were increasingly policed, with active spirits and agile invisible fluids both necessary to and dangerous for the natural philosophers' enterprise.

It is important not to overestimate the success of the mechanists' super-naturalism (Hutchison 1983), or of the more general Christianising of European culture in the seventeenth century (Gaukroger 1995: 24–8). Repeated and conflicting attempts to tidy and reinforce boundaries between matter, spirits, and the supernatural may just as easily have blurred as clarified them, and certainly did not necessarily enforce acceptance and obedience to any particular way of drawing the lines. But there was at least pressure, in every domain of natural philosophy, to align the account of theoretical entities in that domain with a complex and shifting set of constraints ranging from the need to be consistent with other sciences to the necessity of distancing reliable knowledge from (what were perceived as) dangerous claims made by others.

Memory and action at a distance

The mechanical philosophers in particular needed a good theory of memory. Their commitment to contact action as the means of change in the natural world,[3] and their rejection of allegedly occult action at a distance, encouraged them to posit specific mechanisms by which to bridge the temporal gulf between experience and remembering.[4] If past events in some sense 'become present' in remembering, the apparent action at a temporal distance called for mechanical explanation just as much as did stranger phenomena like

---

3 'The next thing to be consider'd, is how *Bodies* produce *Ideas* in us, and that is manifestly *by impulse*, the only way which we can conceive Bodies operate in' (Locke *Essay* II.8.11). For Henry More, matter communicates not at a distance but 'by jogging or crouding the parts interjacent' (IS preface, p. 6). Compare the list of overlapping principles under the umbrella of 'mechanism' in McGuire 1972: 523, n. 2.

4 In the more familiar context of perceptual theory, it is well known that many early modern philosophers accepted a principle of 'no cognition at a distance' (Yolton 1984a: 12–13, 1996: 84–100). I know of no extension of this point in the secondary literature to the case of memory. Yolton is sceptical about the plausibility of the requirement of no cognition at a distance, since he argues that we have a form of direct acquaintance with distant objects. But the principle seems even more plausible in the case of remembering: only a feeling that there is something mysterious about the existence of causal processes connecting past and present could encourage its rejection.

magnetism, ship-stopping fish, and the marine torpedo which 'suddenly benumbs the hand that touches it, even at a distance through a rod'.[5] Tales of prodigious memory were often repeated in the place-memory tradition from Pliny's *Natural History* (1962: 86–7). Early mechanists found them as unpalatable as they did the other occult happenings dear to Renaissance natural magicians, and sought reductive explanations of how physical continuity is in fact maintained between experience and remembering.[6]

This is a general motivation in the sciences of memory: causal processes in physical media, it is argued, preserve some trace of an experience or event (Warnock 1987: 43–52). It is by way of this trace that the original experience may be operative in partly causing (not determining) an episode of remembering (Martin and Deutscher 1966). Historically, it is clear that this need was at work in early modern theories.

We have returned, by a different path, to the point at which part I ended. The mechanists' need for causal processes as mechanisms of continuity imposed one of the two possible views deriving from the medical philosophies sketched in chapter 2. Memory is either a body or a motion, either an atom or a pattern. Either actual bits of matter are transferred from object to brain and kept there, or (patterns of) motion are transmitted through different material media from object to brain[7] and are somehow later recreated. The general requirement of causal continuity was shared by Cartesians and scholastics: information somehow transmitted from object to brain has then to be stored. I showed in chapter 3 that Descartes made the medium of storage the motions of animal spirits through the pores of the brain, rather than things (whether dedicated in the brain or arriving from the object). Chapters 5 and 6 address historical and conceptual implications of this approach: but first I demonstrate that neighbouring domains in natural philosophy provided rich sources of comparison in decisions between these differing theories of memory.

---

5 Ficino, *De vita coelitus comparanda* (1489), quoted in Copenhaver 1990: 275. On action at a distance and magical explanation see also Henry 1988, 1990. Mary Hesse (1961/1970: 112–21) shows how the commitment to contact action in seventeenth-century mechanism was shared by both corpuscularian and medium theorists.

6 For the hostility of early mechanical philosophers to Renaissance naturalism see Heilbron 1982: 11–22; Hine 1984; Gaukroger 1995: 146–52. Copenhaver (1990, 1991) gives a wonderful account of the history of explanations (through to Gassendi, Boyle, and Borelli) of the torpedo (the electric ray) and the 'ship-holder' or *echeneis* fish. The torpedo/ray was 'disenchanted' only when John Walsh in 1773 showed conclusively that its effects were electrical. Copenhaver comments (1990: 279) that this 'ended the ray's career as a magical object . . . except insofar as eighteenth-century conceptions of "electrical fluid" resembled the *spiritus* and *pneumata* long counted among the arcana of the magus'.

7 Most historians of these theories have discussed perception. The importance of changes in optical theory for early modern theories of cognition as a whole has often been noted: recent work includes Hatfield and Epstein 1979; MacIntosh 1983; Straker 1985: 264ff.; Meyering 1989: chs. 2, 5, 6. Only MacIntosh makes the link with theories of memory.

Superposition and interference: optics and memory

Because the mechanists' memory theory required the internal preservation of motions, it was inevitably caught up with continuing developments in matter theory. Superposition, the key mechanism for 'storing' many traces in the same region of the brain, was a physical principle, clarified by Galileo, which describes situations 'in which one motion is a result of combining two different components' (Prudovsky 1989: 455). The desirability of superposition became a controversial topic in early modern disputes about light and sound, which inevitably became entangled with the neighbouring sciences of memory and brain. This analogy between memory and light explains how mechanists, who believed all material bodies to be composed only of atoms or corpuscles in motion, could still accept that two memories could, in a sense, overlap or be in the same place without violating principles of impenetrability. In the case of light, I suggest, most believed that 'interference is a direct consequence of the principle of superposition' (Kassler 1995: 112), that the motions overlaid would not be re-separable, and that this was good reason for resisting the application of superposition to key physical or cognitive domains.

In the Cartesian plenum, light is a motion or a tendency to motion, and is the transmission of energy not of a body: Descartes hoped that there would be no interference between light rays if they are only lines of tendency rather than actual motions (Sabra 1967/1981: 11, 59). Before the success of Newton's optics (Hakfoort 1988), many were attracted to continuum ('wave') theories over emission ('corpuscular') theories (Shapiro 1973: 136, n. 5): Robert Hooke, whose memory theory I examine in chapter 5, worked closely on the different continuum theories of Descartes and Hobbes (Shapiro 1973: 134–43, 189–202; Sabra 1967/1981: 186–95, 251–64; Westfall 1971: 206–13).[8] At a gross conceptual level, interference is not a pressing concern if light (or sound, or memory) is a body, for the identity of the individual atoms which are the ingredients in any compound is never in doubt: in principle the component bodies can always be re-separated. But if light (or sound, or memory) is thought of as a compound of motions (or of dispositions to motion), questions about interference and confusion between the motions immediately arise. It becomes much harder to see how the elements of the composite can retain their own identity: ingredients seem irretrievably altered in the process of mixture (compare Shapiro 1973: 188, 1994 on colour mixing).

In early 1672, Hooke considered but rejected (as 'unnecessary') the idea of

---

8 Shapiro argues (1973: 136–7) that 'study of the dynamics of wave propagation' did not begin until the end of the seventeenth century and so is really part of eighteenth-century rational mechanics. Although quantitative and experimental approaches to dynamics did take some time, it is clear that the entirely qualitative animal spirits physiology had an intuitively dynamic tinge. Psychophysiology here was out of reach of the mathematical and physical concepts on which it was meant officially to be based.

the original heterogeneity of light, by which in white light various vibrations coalesce and destroy each other, just as many vibrations are 'dormant' as a 'coalition' in a musical string: Sabra sees Hooke here as 'the first to conceive of the principle of the superposition of waves as applied to light' (1967/1981: 259–60, 295). Newton responded to Hooke in part by developing this discarded suggestion, but continued to state his own conviction that white light was originally heterogeneous (Shapiro 1973: 189). He thought that a condition of success for a continuum theory, in which the waves composing white light might cross one another, was that they must not 'combine, or alter one another; they must exist as differentiated elements of a *heterogeneous* mixture' (Sabra 1967/1981: 279). Newton could not see the possibility of the pulse motion suggested by Hooke in which the components have lost their identity:

> though I can easily imagin [sic] how unlike motions may crosse one another, yet I cannot well conceive how they should coalesce into one *uniforme* motion [the pulse], & then part again [by refraction] & recover their former unlikenesse; notwithstanding that I conjecture the ways by wch Mr Hook may endeavour to explain it.[9]

So Newton takes the impossibility of re-separating out individual components from a coalescence or superposition of waves to be evidence against the wave theory of light. For a wave theory to work, superposed rays would have to preserve 'their separate existence and identity unaltered within the compound' (Whittaker 1951: 17, in Sabra 1967/1981: 282). But, for Newton, this is not possible: there can be no mixture, he thinks, without confusion. By late 1675, Newton claimed that Hooke had abandoned his own view and adopted Newton's idea of 'colours, like sounds, being various, according to the various bignesse of the Pulses' (Sabra 1967/1981: 327–8; Shapiro 1973: 201–2; 'bignesse' is related to the later concept of 'wavelength'). Hooke's position, however, remained in flux: in the early 1680s he wrote favourably of Descartes' theory of light as motion (Hooke LL 4.3: 113).

In these considerations about superposition in optics and acoustics, then, the decisive issue is confusion. By 1675, it seemed that light could not be motion, since if it was, motions would cross and destroy each other in a manner inconsistent with the observed results of prismatic refraction: it would be impossible for individual motions to be extracted or re-separated, for they would have blended irretrievably into the mix of motions. Seven years later, when Hooke lectured to the Royal Society on memory, he was all too well aware

---

9 Newton's *Correspondence*, in Sabra 1967/1981: 281. Sabra comments that Newton's objection 'derives its apparent plausibility only from interpreting the change produced by refraction as a disturbance (or confusion) rather than a regularization'. Newton had been impressed by More's argument (chapter 5 below) that we could not determine our own recollections if remembering was merely matter in motion (Iliffe 1995: 442).

of the parallel problems about confusion and mixture in the theory of light. So he knew well the difficulties likely to arise from thinking of memory as motion. If memories were just motions of animal spirits in the folds of the brain, we would never be able to isolate any past event, to re-separate one memory trace from all the other trace motions superpositionally stored, as dispositions or tendencies, with it. The problem with all sorts of spirits is that, as Milton's Raphael confessed, 'if Spirits embrace / Total they mix'. Only confusion and inadvertent productivity could result, and disorder is as dangerous in the cognitive as in the political realm.

5
Cognition, chaos, and control in English responses to Descartes' theory of memory

MEMORIE
A comon Inne all comers to reteyne.
A sive where good run out and bad remayne.
A burrow with a thousand vermin hylles.
A den where nothing that is good abides.

> (Thomas Jenner, c. 1650. Appended to an engraving entitled 'A Man Writing,
> Representing the Facultie of Memorie')

that is to be judged *knowledge*, as I see it, which does not disquiet the mind, but
settles it   (Henry Oldenburg to Thomas Coxe, 1657, in Shapin and Schaffer 1985: 299)

The tranquillity which I now enjoyed did not endure. Memory brought madness
with it . . .   (Mary Shelley, *Frankenstein* (1818/1974: 187))

And then we acknowledging Man to dwell as it were in the borders of the Spiritual
and Material world . . . we shall not wonder that there is such tugging and pulling
this way and that way, upward and downward, and such broken disorder of things;
those that dwell in the confines of two Kingdoms being most subject to disquiet
and confusion.   (Henry More, AAA II.12.16)

5.1 'A great deal of preposterous confusion'

The Cartesian animal spirits theory of memory was loathsome and morally
abhorrent in the eyes of English critics. The idea that memories are just patterned motions of spirits through brain pores denies the systematicity, stability, and structure characteristic of true thinking, reducing all cognition to mere
association and the chance fusion of jumbling motions.

Henry More complained that such an idea would 'force a great deal of pre-
posterous confusion' on memory and mind (IS II.2.7: 68). Memory traces
which naturally interfere and blend were too irregular, too disordered. Animal
spirits models of memory were linked in the minds of their opponents not only
with materialism and atheism, but also with a dangerously irrational picture of
remembering and cognition. Many, like Lucy Hutchinson (Jones 1989: 195–6),
did decry the men 'reviving the foppish casual dance of atoms': but resistance
to materialism, though strong (Mintz 1962), was less significant than fear of
the loss of sovereign control of one's own psychophysiology. How could the
soul direct the fleeting animal spirits in the secret channels of the brain?
Glanvill could not see how the spirits 'should not lose their way in such a
wilderness': the soul's authoritarian task seems too hard if memory is just

motion, since it is 'as inconceivable how it should direct such intricate Motions, as that one that was born blind should manage a Game at Chess, or marshal an Army' (EACP: 5).[1]

Approval of a theory of mind and memory thus depended in part on whether it allowed the requisite inner discipline in cognition, the imposition of central psychological control over spirituous anarchy. Various ways of theoretically reintroducing control of the processes of remembering were offered as alternatives. Cognitive discipline had to be imposed over the mere babble of Cartesian automata. Memories could be disciplined in both personal and theoretical contexts, in the intimacy with which the self dealt with its unruly brain, or in the public ridicule and denigration of theories which overemphasised that unruliness. Discipline, in other words, was as much prescription and wish as description and observation. While angels needed no memory (Locke, Essay II.10; Sutton 1994a), human confinement in sequential time required ongoing struggles to order and tame the personal past.

The force of these English critiques is obviously limited: they assume just those facts about order in memory for which they needed to argue. But their complaints reveal both the perceived implications of the animal spirits theory of memory, and the coherence of the set of concerns about control over mental contents which seemed threatened. The detailed examination in this chapter of four critical responses to Descartes will demonstrate the connection between localist models of memory and strong views of executive control over physiological processes, and show why distributed models seemed to lead to distasteful psychological chaos. Chapter 6 will then aid historical clarification of the distinction between local and distributed representation.

In a selective rather than exhaustive survey of early responses to Descartes, I focus on Digby, More, Glanvill, and Hooke. Philosophers on the Continent found more sympathy with memory as patterns of spirit motions (Diamond 1969; Clarke 1989: 183–6). I concentrate on specifically English changes in views of subjectivity and rationality in the later seventeenth century. The English reaction to the Cartesian physiology of memory was not part of a democratic revolt of free spirits against the authoritarian implications of mechanical models of mind (Mayr 1986: 122–36). It was, rather, a gradual realisation that Descartes' account left authority much too fragile, vulnerable to fluid material processes which are unconstrained by the soul. Mayr lists imagery of balance, equilibrium, feedback, and self-regulation in English culture and philosophy which (he thinks) proves the value placed on liberty in the English Enlightenment (1986: 139–89): but, significantly, his examples cover political, physical, and economic discourses, with nothing from philosophy of mind or

---

1 Both SS and EACP are revised versions of VOD: see Willey 1934/1962: 158–75; Medcalf 1970; Vickers 1987: 212–17.

neurophysiology. In fact, Cartesian mind/brain theory was not authoritarian *enough* for the English. Immanent order in mixtures of memory motions never seemed possible, and order had to imposed from outside.

Even in England, there were many more approaches to memory than I discuss. I omit Willis' puzzling psychophysiology (Frank 1990; Kassler 1998), and concentrate on responses to Descartes rather than the reception of Hobbes' ideas about memory (Kassler 1991, 1995: 110–18, 1997). More and Glanvill in particular criticise Hobbes as well as Descartes for not ruling out unacceptable confusion in memory: the points made against the two are not always clearly distinguishable, and I will, with caution, use some of them interchangeably.

The texts I do deal with are a series of snapshots spanning the period from 1644 to 1682, a time of intense struggles in English natural philosophy. Treating them together risks neglecting the context in which each was written, and the analysis needs integration with historians' increasingly nuanced accounts of Restoration science and society, and of the reception and cleansing of Cartesian mechanism. But there are conceptual connections across these texts which a focus on memory renders apparent, and as excuse I plead the neglect in previous research of this domain between physiology and cognition.[2]

Kenelm Digby, Henry More, Joseph Glanvill, and Robert Hooke knew Descartes' work and each other's. Glanvill, for example, knew Digby, had meals and coffee with Hooke, and was a long-term ally of More in a joint campaign to prove the ubiquity of spirits: More told Anne Conway in 1671 that he was 'well assured of his [Glanvill's] virtue' (Cope 1956: 33, 38–9, 60, 87–103, 123; Hall 1990: 175–8). Hooke owned an impressive collection of books on medicine, physiology, and philosophy (Rostenberg 1989).

Although Descartes' *L'Homme* was published only in the 1660s, when it was immediately sought by natural philosophers from England to Italy (Brown 1968/1982: 80–4), there were sufficient clues in the work published in

2 General treatments of the reception of Cartesianism in England (Lamprecht 1935; Heilbron 1982: 26–35; and Rogers 1985) say little on physiology. There are outstanding microstudies of the development of English physiology on both sides of the Restoration by T.M. Brown (1968/1982, 1977) and Bob Frank (1980), but both authors explicitly steer clear of many problems which their subjects addressed about the relations between physiology and the philosophy of mind. Heilbron (1982: 30) outlines a chronological scheme of initial uncritical acceptance of Descartes by the English followed by increasingly wary revision, according to which 'Descartes' day in England was brief . . . the British had shivered before the materialist consequences of Cartesianism and drawn back' (compare Gabbey 1982, 1992). This may fit the special case of cardiology, in which defence of Harvey against Descartes was paramount (Anstey forthcoming), but it is not easy to apply to the general history of physiology: Brown (1977: 26,54) argues that initial ambivalence towards mechanistic physiology before 1660 changed 'to a fuller, less qualified enthusiasm' and 'would remain entrenched for at least 60 years'. Attention to issues of control, rather than materialism, in the sciences of mind may help work this out.

Descartes' lifetime to make the tendency of his spirits physiology clear. Indeed, these texts clearly confirm that something like what I have called a 'distributed' model of memory (involving superposition and interference) was the subject of considerable debate, and that it was located by critics in Descartes' neurophilosophy. Descartes' doctrine of the intellectual memory, on the other hand, is not mentioned. Digby, More, and Glanvill specifically criticise Descartes' theory of memory; Digby, More, and Hooke construct their own accounts; Glanvill, trying to discredit existing psychological theory, has a purely critical focus.

There is a fair amount of work on More, Glanvill, and Hooke, but Digby is less well known.[3] He was an early English mechanist of an idiosyncratic sort (Petersson 1956; Henry 1982), attending more (though critically) to Descartes' natural philosophy than to his metaphysics. Digby believed in continually emanating 'spirits or little bodies', and is better known for his quasi-mechanistic accounts of 'occult' phenomena like the weapon salve and alchemical transmutation (Dobbs 1971–4). Of his *Two Treatises*, the first (on body) is three times longer than the second (on soul), and his eclectic engagement with contemporary problems in physics and physiology was intense. Each of these four writers' accounts of memory meshed with the rest of their natural philosophy. But here I stick to memory and brain, my historical purposes being as much polemical as exegetical.

It is not surprising that memory should have increasingly preoccupied English philosophers through the seventeenth century. The obsession with order after the Civil War, and after the Interregnum's uncontrolled multiplicity of opinion, produced not only impositions of unity in worship, dress, and conduct, but also attempts to keep the past in place. Both collective and cognitive memory had to display unity and concord, even at the cost of imposing false continuities on the political and personal past, by developing clear narrative structures to organise uncertain events. A fixation on sameness required external discipline to be applied as much to internal, potentially anarchic, psychophysiological flux as to unruly social forces (compare Martensen 1992 on relations between social order and Willis' 'physiology of reason'). Many descriptions of memory did not encourage confidence in its stability or accuracy: Margaret Cavendish in 1656 described memory as 'Atomes in the Brain set on fire' (in Singer 1976: 126). So Royal Society members, pursuing Bacon's desire to pry into the 'secret motions of things', sought control over research in the body as in the cosmos: in 1667 Secretary Oldenburg asked a correspondent in Connecticut 'to remember, that we have taken to taske the whole Universe' (Hunter 1981: 13, 37). The fact that

---

3 Digby, Glanvill, and Hooke are treated together by Jamie Kassler in *Inner Music* (1995: 108–47), and I am much indebted to her work (also Kassler 1984), although our evaluations of seventeenth-century theories of memory are quite different. I am grateful to Kassler, James Jacob, and Mark Pallas for helpful conversations about this chapter.

English philosophers were disappointed in their desire to play wider roles in running the country (Hunter 1981: 136, 1994: 35–54) makes cognitive theory, the vision of what mind and memory are and ought to be, as good a case as any for teasing out their assumptions, fears, and wishes.

I take an issue-based approach to the writings on memory of Digby, Glanvill, and Hooke, and follow with an overview of More's position which confirms and extends the same points.

5.2 Distributed representation and the preservation of motions

An 'insuperable' problem for Descartes' physiological psychology of animal spirits, says Digby, is its inability to explain 'how thinges are conserved in the memory' (TT 32: 282). Memory seems impossible on Descartes' assumption that 'nothing but motions do come into the braine. For it is impossible, that in so divisible a subject as the spirits, motion should be conserved any long time as we evidently see in the ayre' (TT 32: 282).[4] Only dry, hard bodies can conserve motion, and even they cannot 'conserve it very long, after the cause which made it, ceaseth from its operation'. Long-term storage, vital for 'the use and service of a man', would be impossible if memory is, or contains, only 'a multitude of pure motions' and fleeting spirit patterns (TT 32: 283).

Descartes, of course, did not think that every memory motion was always actually (explicitly) conserved: the enduring changes were not in spirits but in brain pores. Digby refers briefly to this idea that only dispositions for the re-evocation of explicit patterns are 'stored'. Descartes, he notes, could reply to his complaint by saying 'that it is not necessary the motions themselves should always be conserved in actual being; but that it is sufficient, there be certain causes kept on foote in our heades, which are apt to reduce these motions into act, whensoever there is occasion of them' (TT 32: 283). But Digby complains that this is ad hoc, 'meerely a voluntary position' lacking any supporting evidence.

Descartes was vulnerable to problems about the preservation of motion. The laws of nature, for him, depend 'on God's preserving each thing by a continuous action, and consequently on his preserving it not as it may have been some time earlier but precisely as it is at the very instant that he preserves it' (Le Monde ch. 7, AT xi.44, CSM 1.96). This is the occasionalist strand in Descartes: the

---

4 To replace Descartes' view of sensation as 'a pure driving of the animal spirits' upon the brain, Digby postulated 'the driving thither of solid material bodies (exceeding litle [sic] ones) that come from the objects themselves' (TT 33: 284). Actual particles from objects enter the body and are 'removed' by 'locall change . . . within our body from one place to another' by the animal spirits, 'the porters of all newes to the braine' (TT 32: 276). So spirits are only the 'instruments of this conveyance' (TT 32: 277), rather than the active representations themselves.

only continuity across instants of time is provided by God's incessant intervention to preserve the world as it is. This seems to be in tension with the account of
memory as distributed patterns of activation, thus justifying Digby's worry. But
even if Stephen Gaukroger's defence of real forces in Descartes' *general* metaphysics (chapter 3 above) fails, it is safe to bracket the problem in discussing
particular physical problems: God's action has to be assumed or ignored in
dealing with ordinary natural phenomena (Gaukroger 1995: 375). Descartes'
reliance on God is in no way a *special* difficulty for the theory of memory as the
preservation of motions: it applies to all physical continuity and cannot be
raised *only* in this psychophysiological context. Digby, indeed, is arguing *within*
the physiological framework rather than metaphysically. What remains to be
debated is how, within a world in which some things do endure across time,
patterns of animal spirits in the brain can be among them.

Digby thought they could not be: no dispositional account will explain how
animal spirit motions could remain constant 'for so long a time as [a man's]
memory is able to extend unto' (TT 32: 283). Glanvill, pertinently, queried the
preservation not only of motions of the spirits, but of the changes in the pores
of the brain which are meant to ground the relevant dispositions. The brain is
so 'pervious' and 'of such a clammy consistence' (VOD: 35, 38) that

> it's difficult to apprehend, but that these *avennues* should in a very short time be
> stopped up by the pressure of other parts of the matter, through its natural
> *gravity*, or other alterations made in the Brain; And the opening of other *vicine*
> *passages* might quickly obliterate any tracks of these; as the making of one hole
> in the yeelding mud, defaces the print of another near it. (VOD: 35)[5]

Glanvill cannot see how spirits should be determined to pass through one
passage rather than another: or how diverse superpositionally stored items can
be distinct from each other when recalled if their 'Images without doubt pass
through the same *apertures* [in the brain substance]' (VOD: 34).[6]

Hooke, significantly, does not stress this difficulty in his 1682 Royal Society
lecture on memory.[7] While his model of memory is very different from
Descartes', he shares Descartes' confidence that, as theories of matter and
motion in other domains of natural philosophy were suggesting, matter in

---

5 This charged passage was toned down, and its second part (from 'And the opening...')
cut, in the 1676 version.
6 Mintz (1962: 76) compares Thomas Tenison's 1670 *The Creed of Mr Hobbes Examined*.
Tenison accepts that a quivering or trembling in the brain can remain after an object of
sight is removed, but asserts that in a machine such motion will soon vanish: whereas,
'the Re-action must remain extremely long, in such Men (for Instance), who at the
seventieth year remember most perfectly, and will repeat with pleasure, the passages of
their School-play, even those who retain not the things more newly passed'. Mintz quotes
the Glanvill passages only from the 1676 version (EACP), and claims that Glanvill has
repeated Tenison's argument. The priority is in fact the reverse.
7 On the occasion of this lecture see Singer 1976: 115–21; Oldroyd 1980.

certain arrangements may be specifically 'adapted' for the retention and 'containing' of particular inputs.[8] The 'Repository' of memory 'is continually supplied' with the relevant 'kinds of Substances' fitted to 'imbibe' and retain various impressions (LL 7.3: 142). As I suggested in discussing theories of light (chapter 4 above), Hooke's optical and acoustical analogies for brain matter set his psychophysiology in the wider contexts of theories of vibration, elasticity, and resonance (Gouk 1980: 585–91; Kassler and Oldroyd 1983: 574–89; Kassler 1995: 129–39), and of that variety of mechanical philosophy which allowed intelligible active powers, including the power to preserve motions, to specific organisations of matter (Henry 1986a, 1989a). The differences between Hooke and Descartes relevant here, then, are not over continuity of motion in matter. Nor are they over mind/body dualism, on which Hooke's position is far from clear. Instead they lie on the axis between distributed and local representation, where Hooke is closer to Digby and the anti-Cartesian tradition.[9]

5.3 Local representation, order, and fidelity

For memory to conserve anything on Descartes' assumption that 'nothing but motions do come into the braine', says Digby, it would have to be the case that 'the impressions upon the common sense . . . must be actually conserved, always actually moving in our head, to the end they be immediately produced, whensoever it pleaseth our will to call for them' (TT 32: 282–3). This is, he thinks, as implausible as that 'a lessen played upon the lute or virginals' could be conserved 'ever continually playing'. Note the requirement Digby is placing

---

8 Hooke describes how impressions of each sense might be retained, comparing 'Bononian [Bologna] Stone' which can (albeit briefly) retain impressions of light; for impressions of sound he compares bells, vases, and strings (LL 7.3: 141–2). Commentators variously compare memory models like Pribram's 'laser-produced holograms' (Singer 1976: 129) and radar (Oldroyd 1980: 22). Colville-Stewart (1975: 117–97, 120–1 on Hooke) has a more principled treatment of historical analogies between memory and various physical and chemical phenomena which display the influence of past on present events over a temporal gap. For a provocative account of the relation between Hooke's studies of bells and his theory of memory see Kassler 1995: 143–59.

9 Although Hooke does not explicitly attack Descartes' theory (which he knew from his edition of L'Homme), and although he shares Descartes' commitment to physical continuity in the brain between past and present, my analysis below shows how antithetical the two approaches are on the key issue of *how* this continuity is realised. These differences have been missed by previous commentators, with Hooke's theory characterised as everything from 'thoroughly materialist' (Richards 1992: 69) to 'a basically sympathetic extension and reformulation of easily identifiable Cartesian notions' (Brown 1971: 5) or 'essentially a form of Cartesian dualism' (Oldroyd 1980: 21). The correct diagnosis is that Hooke and Descartes differ not so much about the relation of soul to mental representations (although the ontological status of soul in Hooke is unclear (Henry 1989a: 153), and although his use of concepts like radiation, attraction, and vibration is an attempt to sidestep the problems of interaction), but, crucially, about whether the memory representations themselves are local or distributed.

on a theory of memory: stored items, whatever they may be, must always be actually present, available for inspection by the will at any moment. Digby is led from here to formulate his own theory of memory. The demand that memories be always explicitly represented requires the discrete storage of every memory at a separate location.

The 'exceeding litle' bodies from objects which are driven against the brain, according to Digby, 'must rebound . . . upon other partes of the braine; where at length, they find some vacant cell, in which they keepe their rankes and files, in great quiett and order; all such sticking together, and keeping company with one an other, that entered in together: and there they lye still and are at rest, untill they be stirred up' whether by appetite, chance, or the will (TT 33: 284–5). Any of these three causes 'rayseth them up, and giveth them the motion that is proper to them; which is the same with that, whereby they came in at the first'. Referring to Galileo's teachings on the proper motions of undisturbed bodies, Digby describes how, after memories 'slide successively through the fantasie' in their original order, they 'return gently to their quiett habitation in some other part of the braine, from whence they were called and summoned by the fantasies messengers, the spirits' (TT 33: 285).

The important point here is that the bodies resting in the memory do not change as processing continues elsewhere in the system. Storage is separate from processing, so that the original order of memories is preserved intact: each individual memory in its once vacant cell keeps company with the other memory corpuscles with which it is associated. Even after a processing episode, when a group of memories is called out of storage by the executive will, no change normally occurs: each conveniently returns to its storage location, untouched by the context of retrieval. Not motions but bodies themselves are preserved over time.

Digby's picture gives us the flavour of local memory representation. There is no obvious place for the blending or reconstructive patching up of memories in different contexts which others take to be characteristic of human remembering. Connections between the individual elements of memory occur not by overlap or fusion but by the juxtaposition of their 'cell' addresses. This makes it hard to see, for instance, how a change in knowledge which affects one memory can affect other memories (without some explicit updating by soul, will, or other executive). Localist models of memory do not easily catch relevance and context, or allow experience automatically to influence background knowledge.

Digby's idea of the physical transfer of material atoms from objects to sense organs and into memory cells received little support. But the general notion of local storage recurred in Hooke's model. Memory, which is 'really Organical', is 'nothing else but a Repository of Ideas' (LL 7.1: 140) seated in the 'spirals' of the brain. David Oldroyd (1980: 22) describes this as a typically mechanist vision: the brain is like a 'butter factory, storing various pats of butter in a bizarre helical warehouse'. But the brain according to Hooke maintains much greater stability than do the incessantly shifting and refolding flows of Descartes' L'Homme. For Hooke, corporeal ideas, formed from the material of the brain substance, are throughout the course of one's life incessantly laid down in 'a continued Chain of Ideas coyled up in the Repository of the Brain, the first end of which is farthest removed from the Center or Seat of the Soul where the Ideas are formed, which is always the Moment present when considered'. It is by way of this spatial layout of ideas in the coils of memory that the soul becomes 'apprehensive of the Time interposed' (LL 7.2: 140). The price of an explanation of time perception is a theory of local representation.

Describing ideas emitted from 'the Center' (of which more below), Hooke outlines the features of local memory traces:

> These Ideas I will suppose to be material and bulky, that is, to be certain Bodies of determinate Bigness, and impregnated with determinate Motions, and to be in themselves distinct; and therefore that not two of them can be in the same space, but that they are actually different and separate one from another; and as they have their distinct Figures, so have they each of them their distinct Qualifications of Motions and Constitutions. (LL 7.4: 142)[10]

This is clear. Ideas in the memory which are 'in themselves distinct' are local memory representations, whereas distributed traces can, in contrast, be two partly in the same space, in overlapping superpositional storage.

Hooke's defence of a localist theory is illuminated further by Lotte Mulligan's work on Hooke's other writings on memory and natural history, suggesting sources of his theoretical desire for ordered and distinct memories. Aubrey (1949: 243) thought Hooke's own memory was poor. His 'inveterate list-making', in recording the weather, his health, and his sexual encounters, as well as in collating and organising data for the Royal Society, was meant to guard against 'the Frailty of the Memory' (Mulligan 1992: 58, 60). This frailty, invoked by Hooke in the preface to Micrographia and elsewhere, is a barrier to scientific progress: it is because 'man's memory seems very shallow and infirm, and so is very prone to forget Circumstances', that the understanding is 'more apt to be sway'd' erroneously, 'very apt to be seduc'd' into false opinions (Hooke, in Mulligan 1992: 49). Diaries, lists, memory aids, and the right sort of

---

10　Boyle also assumed the independence of items in memory, being amazed that 'in so small a portion of matter as the memory is seated in, there should be so many thousands or myriads of distinct traces, footsteps, impressions, or whatever you please to call them, [which] lie not only unconfounded, but so distinct, that at the bare will and pleasure of the learned man' any set of items will spring up 'in the right order': he is persuaded that the brain contains 'an amazing structure' which 'in a little room can afford distinct traces or cells' (Boyle 1772/1965: VI:742; compare IV:454). Peter Anstey, to whom I am grateful for these references, confirms that this localist theory appears to be Boyle's only account of memory (see Anstey 1996: ch. 3).

theory of memory could reassure, and prompt the self toward the requisite regularity. This fear of seduction by the shallow memory is a common theme in early modern memory theorists, who are driven towards imposing order on memory. This is done in two ways: by stressing the role of external systems and aids, and by favouring local models of memory, which alone gratify the wish for order and defend against the fear that distributed models will leave the understanding unprotected.

Firstly, as Mulligan has documented (1992: 61), Hooke obsessively constructed external aids to memory, using systems of recording as 'well-honed epistemological tools' in warding off confusion and forgetfulness.[11] Sprat portrayed Royal Society members as plain, diligent, and laborious observers (Hunter 1981: 8–31), seeking a 'strict purity of procedure' ('Espinasse 1956: 28). Hooke thought that lists and 'a proper History' would aid the storage of 'plain, simple, clear, and uncompounded representation[s]' (in Mulligan 1992: 58, 57). When the intellect, 'like a skilful Architect', is collating such a history, 'those materials are to be carefully sought for and collected and safely laid up in so convenient an Order that they may not be far to seek when they are wanting . . . and cleansed . . . so as not to perplex the User' (Hooke, in Mulligan 1992: 58).

This points towards the second, less explicit tactic for supporting the frail memory. The processes of purification of memories and of laying them up in convenient order do not occur only in Hooke's Baconian sorting techniques. It is also, perhaps, at the level of psychological theory that the materials of memory are 'cleansed'. In imposing on memory theory, hypothetically as it may be, stored ideas which are 'in themselves distinct . . . [and] actually different and separate one from another', Hooke expresses a specific view about what counts as, respectively, 'the Perfections and Imperfections of Humane Nature' (Hooke, in Mulligan 1992: 48). I pursue this theme by examining remarks in Digby and Glanvill which suggest *why* they are so hostile to distributed models of memory.

5.4 'Borrow'd from midnight': interference and the fear of chaos

Glanvill sees no major difference between Descartes' and Digby's accounts of memory: both, though 'ingenious attempts', are not only false but unintelligible, 'sad evidence of the infirmities of laps'd humanity' (VOD: 33–4).[12]

---

11   Mulligan also refers (1992: 53) to his schemes for improving the conduction of ideas along the coils of memory by taking silver filings, mercury, and gold. On Hooke's strange medical practices see Beier 1989.

12   Glanvill's initial praise of Descartes' progress in natural philosophy, like More's, was strongly toned down in later versions (Medcalf 1970), but it had never extended to Cartesian memory theory: in SS: 24–30 (1665) he reorganises the chapter on memory to

Glanvill equates Digby's travelling particles ('arbitrary precarious Creatures') with Descartes' patterns of animal spirits roaming through the pores of the brain: he does not understand the difference between local and distributed models. He criticises Digby's theory for being as incapable as is Descartes' of preserving memories faithfully and separately from each other: the expression of this complaint reveals a rhetorical division between order and chaos constructed to match the distinction between faithful local storage and reconstructive distributed memory.

Even if each of Digby's active particles, 'which have no *cement* to unite them, nothing to keep them in the order they were set', has a distinct and separate cell allotted to it, Glanvill fears for the preservation of that order:

> And how is it conceivable, but that carelessly turning over the Idea's [sic] of our mind to recover something we would remember, we should put all the other Images into a disorderly floating, and so raise a little *Chaos* of confusion, where Nature requires the exactest order. According to this account, I cannot see, but that our *Memories* would be more confused then our Mid-night compositions. (VOD: 35–6)[13]

It is, for Glanvill, an indispensable requirement that a theory of memory allow its traces to be 'capable of Regularity', a regularity which, he thinks, is present in nature. The opposition of chaos to order sets the 'tumultuary agitations' of the liquid brain against the 'uniformity in motion' which memories *ought* to have. The reader is made complicitous in accepting that human remembering in no way resembles 'a disorderly floating': and, especially, in seeing psychological anarchy as the only alternative to the strict regimenting of memories, which 'should so orderly keep their Cells without any alteration of their site or posture, which at first was allotted them' (VOD: 36).

On similar grounds, Digby had qualms about Descartes' animal spirit motions as the medium of memory. Querying the possibility of the preservation of motions, Digby's doubt had been that all the motions could 'be kept on foote in [man's] braine, without confusion' (TT 32: 283). In Descartes' model interference between traces is inevitable, and increases as more traces are added into the system. It is the idea of such interference that is met with hostility by the critics, whose language becomes coloured with moral force. Digby, though looking forward to explication in an unpublished work of Descartes,[14] cannot

---

stress that there is 'no security neither' in Descartes' account, and cuts Descartes and Gassendi from VOD's list (VOD: 240) of 'illustrious Heroes', replacing them with 'the Royal Society'. Glanvill's sceptical destruction of existing theories leaves memory 'obscure' (VOD: 32), as Reid's attack on Hartley's model would leave it unaccountable (chapter 14 below).

13 In 1676, the metaphoric critique is altered: 'I cannot see but that our Memories would be more confused than our Dreams, and I can as easily conceive how a heap of Ants can be kept to regular and uniform Motions' (EACP: 8–9).

14 I have no confirmation, but assume that this 'worke of his, which the world of learned men so much longeth for' is *L'Homme*.

understand how 'any determinate motion should long be preserved untaynted in the braine; where there must be such a multitude of other motions in the way, to mingle with it, and bring all into confusion' (TT 33: 284).

The promiscuous distributed traces are the source, then, of confusion, disorder, and cognitive chaos: the infection lies within. This is a repeated theme in writers reacting to the distributed animal spirits model of memory. There was a basis in Descartes for concerns about the tainting by physiology and matter of pure intellect and divinely given motion. In *Le Monde* he runs an analogy between, on the one hand, that theodicy which gives the human will responsibility only for evil action while making God the author of all good action, and, on the other, the relation between rectilinear motions, of which God alone is author, and 'the various dispositions of matter which render [motions] irregular and curved' (AT xi.46, CSM 1.97). Then in the *Passions of the Soul* (written after Digby's *Two Treatises*) Descartes, in an extended discussion of psychological conflict, converts all alleged conflict between different parts of the soul into oppositions between the movements of the animal spirits in the body and the movements or tendencies produced by the soul 'by means of its will'. The spirits and the soul fight for control of the motions of the pineal gland (*Passions* 1.47, AT xi.364–5, CSM 1.345–6). This theme, of a physiological site for epic conflict between soul or will and mischievous corporeal spirits, has an enormous subsequent literature from morality to medicine. Here just note the immediate effect on theories of memory. The interference characteristic of distributed models of memory is perceived as a threat not merely to the regularity of remembering, but to a moral order which depends on excluding chaos from the psychological realm.

The dangers of distributed memory are even more explicit in Glanvill's related critique of Hobbes' theory of memory as 'a *Mixing of Parts in an Object*' (VOD: 37–9). After voicing the usual concern about the conservation of motions in the '*Quagmire*' of the brain and the fluid spirits, Glanvill says that even if a motion were preserved, 'it would be quickly deadned even to an utter cessation, by *counter-motions*; and we should not remember any thing, but till the next impression'. Catastrophic interference, Glanvill is suggesting, would dampen away all distinct memories. It is inconceivable 'how such an abundance of *motions* should orderly succeed one another, as things do in our *memories*'. Glanvill continues instructively:

> And to remember a *song* or *tune*, it will be required, that our Souls be an *Harmony* more then in a *Metaphor*, continually running over in a silent whisper those *Musical Accents* which our retentive faculty is preserver of. Which could we suppose in a single Instance; yet a multitude of *Musical Consonancies* would be as impossible, as to play a thousand tunes on a *Lute* at once. One motion would cross and destroy another; all would be clashing and discord: And the *Musicians* Soul would be the most *disharmonious*: For according to the tenour of

this opinion, our *memories* will be stored with infinite variety of divers, yea contrary motions, which must needs interfere, thwart, and obstruct on another: and there would be nothing within us, but Ataxy and disorder. (VOD: 39)

In this passage Glanvill first requires the continual *explicit* representation of memory traces (the soul must *continually* run over what the memory preserves). Announcing, rightly, that the models he is attacking do not have such explicit representations, he disparages the results of such models and the interference they encourage as leaving only ataxy and chaos inside us. But Glanvill's belief that human remembering is *not* a matter of confused, disordered, chaotic motions is not simply a description of indisputable explananda. It can be read, rather, as a normative or perhaps nostalgic wish for how our memories *should* orderly succeed one another.

A clue to this reading is given by Glanvill's reference to the disharmonious nature of the musician's soul on the distributed-memory hypothesis. He might wish that motions should not cross and destroy each other, and that there should be less clashing and discord. For the context of the chapter on sensation and memory in *The Vanity of Dogmatizing* is one of lament for the loss of human perfection, the deprivation of which has left us unable to understand the least part of the creation or of ourselves. Mysteries and ignorance are our lot after the Fall (VOD: 1–16; Medcalf 1970). Memory was not obscure in the beginning, for 'Adam needed no Spectacles' (VOD: 5) or other imperfect aids to his understanding (aids of the kind Hooke was so to exert himself in perfecting). Whence then does disharmony arise? From the fall of man: 'Man was never at odds with himself, till he was at odds with the commands of his Maker. There was no jarring or disharmony in the faculties, till sin untun'd them' (VOD: 4).

This wistfulness at the clashing discord of our post-lapsarian faculties echoes in Glanvill's complaints against distributed memory. He cannot even raise the possibility that the truth about fallen humanity, and thus about the explananda for a scientific psychology, could be closer to the ataxy and disorder of distributed memory traces than to the localist vision of distinct items which quietly keep their rank and file until called on by the will.

5.5 The soul and the centre

There is a final set of connections to be made through this set of texts. Glanvill's worry about clashing and discord in the musician's soul points the way. What implications have local and distributed models of memory respectively for views about the origin of action, the relations between personal-level psychology and subpersonal or subcognitive parts, and, generally, for ways of thinking about control, mind, and self?

In distributed models, storage is not separate from ongoing processing, whereas local models need some means by which passive memories can be fetched from a repository or memory bank by some executive mechanism. This means that local models all but require a central executive of some sort, whether an immaterial soul or a central processing unit in a computer. These links between local memory traces and strong conceptions of a powerful central executive, often identified with the will or the soul, are apparent in both Digby and Hooke.

Digby needs an account of what happens when the fancy calls for things conserved in the memory, of how, for example, the will can raise 'the litle [sic] similitudes, which are in the caves of the braine wheeling and swimming about' (TT 33: 285). How is control imposed and maintained over the atomic memories? The 'tribunall of the braine' has to 'judge' the bodies that rebound 'to the circle of the memory' (TT 32: 282, 34: 293).

> Now as soone as the braine hath lighted on any of those it seeketh for, it putteth as it were a stoppe upon the motion of that; or at the least, it moveth it so, that it goeth not farre away, and is revocable at will. (TT 33: 285)

This even allows some mutual inhibition of unrelated ideas to help in avoiding misassociation, for this process

> by this means hindereth other objects, not pertinent to the worke the fansie hath in hand, from offering themselves unseasonably in the multitudes that otherwise they would do. But if the fansie should have mistaken one object for an other, by reason of some resemblance they have betweene themselves; then it shaketh againe the liquid medium they all floate in, and rooseth every species lurking in remotest corners, and runneth over the whole beaderoule of them; and continueth this inquisition and motion, till eyther it be satisfyed with retriving at length what it required, or that it be grown weary with tossing about the multitude of litle inhabitants in its numerous empire, and so giveth over the search, unwillingly and displeasedly. (TT 33: 285–6)

In these wonderful passages, Digby refers to the agent as the brain as a whole, as the will, and as the fancy.[15] The agent, whatever it be called, has the power to halt, rein in, and control the physical whereabouts of the locally stored memories at a 'common rendez-vous' (TT 33: 287). Scanning its liquid empire, it engages in a systematic search, running over its whole dominion of inhabitant traces, prone even to boredom and petulance when unsuccessful. The important point here is the necessity, on the assumption of passively stored independent memories, for exhaustive search by some such all-powerful intra-

---

15 Of the three causes which Digby says (TT: 285) can 'raise these bodies that rest in the memory', he dismisses chance (because 'the principles that governe it, are uncertaine ones'), and allows that appetite and will 'have a power . . . of moving the braine and the nerves depending of it, conveniently and agreably to their disposition'. Yet in the other passages quoted in the text above both brain and fancy are also used as the subject doing the seeking, shaking, and inquiring. It is far from clear that the principles governing the operations of appetite and will are much less uncertain than those of chance.

cognitive agent. There can be no automatic activation of a relevant memory in the course of processing, as in the content-addressable memories characteristic of distributed models. Because the agent of processing is itself active and wholly distinct from the stored things it processes, its laborious search into the remotest recesses of the storage system becomes necessary.

Hooke has a more developed account of the accessing mechanisms for a local memory system. He sees the intimate connection of the problem with the explanation of attention, and refuses any possibility of cognitive functioning, for instance in the laying down or encoding of memories, without the explicit intervention of the central executive, which he is happy to identify with the soul: 'no Idea can really be formed or stored up in this Repository without the Directive and Architectonical Power of the Soul' (LL 7.1: 140). It is at the primary (physical) location of this directive power that any new impressions are formed by the soul into ideas to be laid down in the memory. This process follows the strict order of input, as 'the present always pushes those that were formed before it further into the Repository' (LL 7.4: 144), where they take their ordered places in the coils of memory. New ideas continually intrude, filling out the encircling Orbs which spiral out from the centre in the same way that planets circle the sun, to which Hooke compares 'the Soul in the Center of the Repository' (LL 7.5: 147). This is not a relic of outdated sun-worship, but a strict analogy: the soul, like the sun, has an attractive power over the bodies which it regulates and governs in their motions.[16] While it may have effects elsewhere in the body, it has 'a more than ordinary and commanding Power over all the Ideas placed within its Repository' (LL 7.5: 147).

Hooke, then, embraces a central executive with a vengeance. Human memory is not only a passive faculty, receiving stamps from the world, but also an active faculty, 'in the most secret parts and passages of the body', which can regulate defective impressions and spot the disfiguring of true figures (Hooke, 'Philosophicall Scribbles' MS [1681/2], in Oldroyd 1980: 17–20). The will even has the power of 'fixing or darting its Radiation more powerfully upon this or that Idea' (LL 7.4: 145). Resonance and irradiation are not, however, symmetrical forces between cognitive centre and mnemonic periphery, for in normal function only the central soul genuinely acts on the items it holds captive in the memory coils, snatched from the past for future use. Hooke explicitly baptises the soul's prime location, whence it exercises its power over the ideas of the memory, mentioning 'this place, which I will henceforward call the Center', surrounded with a sphere of memory (LL 7.4: 142). Even though the soul is not always only at this 'Center' as it darts its radia-

16 On the analogy of light and soul see also Henry 1989a: 151–7. Compare a looser use of the same image by Richard Burthogge (1694/1976: 242), who says that the soul puts congealed spirits in motion, as the sun communicates required motions to the planets.

tion round the memory spirals, the hierarchical implications of Hooke's model are clear. Hooke finds that this powerful, imperious 'Center' fits well with his hypothesis of order in memory by way of the passive local storage of memory ideas in ever increasing coils.

When the executive processing is divided from the storage system in this way, the moral undertones of support for local models become more apparent, as did those of hostility towards anarchic distributed models. Local-memory systems not only allow the strict isolation of the ruling will from the passive storers of information, but also open up a gap between the locus of control in the soul or self and the locus of potential disorder, the memories, which are outside the true self in the passive storage circuits of the brain. Thus late seventeenth- and early eighteenth-century moral physiologists were able to construct moral principles out of the need for control to be imposed by the soul over what John Smith called 'the undisciplin'd petulancy of our Animal Spirits' (1660/1979: 119). Psychological conflict is located in a psychophysiological interior space, not all of which is really owned by the supposed unified subject in its perpetual struggle with physiology. Worries about virtue, soul, and self easily entwined with the disputes over local and distributed memory traces.

5.6 More on memory

As an appendix to this issue-based analysis of responses and alternatives to the distributed model, this is a brief examination of the way the same problems surface in the work of the Platonist Henry More. Good philosophy of mind, for More, helps to render us 'safe from all seduction', to 'rectifie what is perverse' (IS preface, p.2), and to evoke repugnance at those 'that are so sunk into the dull sense of their Bodies' as to deny the incorporeal realm (quoted in Hall 1990: 140), who reduce all change to 'the result of an Eternal Scuffle of coordinate Causes, bearing up as well as they can' (AA 1.9.2).

More's early *Platonical Song of the Soul* sought to prove the existence of 'memorie after death' (compare IS III.11: 187–92). Memory is 'the very bond of life'. This 'very intimate' faculty, 'the watchman of the soul, lest she should flie / Or steal from her own self', must have 'a sure fixation' independent of the body, and win 'her deep'st desire' in heaven (1647/1969: 292–5). But the dangers of memory are also evident, as More imagines what would be the case if, impossibly, remembrance should 'spill'.

> If it were cut away
> Our being truly then you might contrive
> Into a point of time. The former day
> Were nought at all to us: when once we lay
> Our selves to sleep, we should not know at morn

That e're we were before; nor could we say
A whit of sense: so soon as off we turn
One word, that's quite forgot. Coherence thus is torn.

(1647/1969: Stanza 33)

A dynamic sense of temporal continuity is necessary for human coherence: on memory depends 'the very selfnesse of the soul' (1647/1969: 295) and the continuity of personal identity on which morality depends. But it must be imposed from outside: More's hatred of immanence makes memory dangerous, for while our souls 'tumble and wallow in matter' (AAA 3.1: 149), memory operates 'onely by virtue of a fit tenour of Spirits and due temper of Brain', so that everyone's memory is different (IS preface, p. 10). In life, animal spirits are a 'necessary instrument' of memory, which will be 'more perfect after death' (IS III.11.1: 187). But in this coarse life they bring only temptation, when even 'the sweet motions of the animal spirits' in love 'can hardly be commanded from bordering' on shameful lust (in West 1955).

Like Digby and Glanvill, More is sceptical about any long-term preservation of memory motions in the brain. Arguing in his Antidote against Atheism that the soul cannot be a modification of the body, More claims that it is impossible for the animal spirits themselves to have 'Animadversion, Memory and Reason': the spirits (being 'nothing else but matter very thin and liquid') are capable of nothing but motion, and 'being loose from one another, fridge and play up and down according to the measure and manner of agitation in them' (AA 1.11.2: 33). These ill-disciplined spirits are clearly 'utterly uncapable of Memory ... it is as impossible to conceive Memory competible to such a Subject, as it is how to write Characters in the water or the wind' (AA 1.11.3: 33). The brain, through which Descartes thought the spirits pass in leaving reconstructable traces, is just a 'loose Pulp' of 'a laxe consistence', which is pervious to much grosser juices than the animal spirits: it is no more likely to perform our noble cognitive operations than is 'a Cake of Sewet or a Bowl of Curds' (AA 1.11.5: 34). The irrelevance of the brain is proved by the survival of some people without brains (AA 1.11.7: 35).[17]

More too was attracted to the idea of local representation and the freedom it allows the unified soul, expressing distaste for the potential chaos of distributed models. The central context of the treatments of memory in the Antidote against Atheism and The Immortality of the Soul is the rejection of various possibilities for a material seat for the soul and its faculties. He considers stomach, heart, animal spirits, brain, and the pineal gland, which in 1668 he mocked for

17 More is still rejecting the preservation of memories in brain matter in his Enchiridion metaphysicum of 1671: 'for if it is fluid, the images will suddenly disappear ... if the matter is hard or viscid, the vibration will cease suddenly and memory will immediately perish' (in Singer 1976: 128). This is more sceptical about memory in hard dry bodies than was Digby (TT 32: 283).

its 'ridiculous Noddings and Joggings . . . encountered by the animal Spirits rudely flurting against it' (in Gabbey 1982: 243).

After ridiculing those who locate memory and reason in any particular 'part or parcel', any 'knot, loop or interval' of the brain, More remarks:

> And if you will say in all together, you must say that the whole Brain is figured into this or that representation, which would cancell Memory, and take away all capacity of there being any distinct Notes and places for the several Species of things there represented. (AA 1.11.5: 34)

For More too, memory requires distinct, independent representations. The difficulty he sees in any alternative is that, unless individual items are explicitly represented continually, newly activated representations in the same system will erase all the old. This applies both to the brain as a whole and to Descartes' pineal gland theory. If different parts of a representation are superimposed on each other 'upon every part of the Conarion [pineal gland] wherein the Image is, it will be utterly impossible but that the whole Image will be confused' (AAA 10.2: 169). Memory in turn cannot be located in the pineal, ridiculed as 'a mere pulpous protuberant knob' (AAA 10.6: 170), because memory is 'the standing seal or impression of external Objects': for if impressions did 'stand' (if they were explicitly present), 'it would spoil the representation of things present, or rather after-Objects would be sure to deface all former impressions whatsoever'. Continuing perception is incompatible with anything other than a local model of memory, for otherwise memory impressions will always be obliterated by new impressions 'which must needs displace them' (AAA 10.3: 169). More is denying not that the brain is 'the seat of Memory', but that any 'impression once wiped out' could ever be reconstructed or recognised by the soul as having been previously encountered (AAA 10.3–4: 170).

The only kind of memory traces possible, then, are local representations with their distinct notes and places. To be 'compleat', a representation must be 'intirely in the same circumstances' as in its original encoding (IS II.10.9: 105). The need for such 'distinct and perfect representations of things' (IS II.7.16: 93) is in fact what proves to More that matter is not sufficient for memory. If 'the bare laws of matter' were responsible for the impressing and retention of representations, they would become 'strangely depraved, if not obliterated' (IS II.10.9: 105; More uses 'depraved' twice on this page for the effects of matter on images).

Earlier in The Immortality of the Soul, More analyses Descartes' Passions of the Soul and confirms that it is the dispositional account of memory in the distributed model which he is attacking. For Descartes, the openings by the animal spirits of 'such and such Pores of the Brain'

> remain as tracts or footsteps of the presence of these Objects after they are removed. Which tracts, or signatures, consist mainly in this, that the Spirits

will have an easier passage through these Pores then other parts of the Brain. And hence arises Memory, when the Spirits be determined, by the inclining of the Conarion, to that part of the Brain where these tracts are found. (IS II.5.1: 80)

More argues that these 'mere Mechanical reasons' do not include sufficient variables to explain the memory of colours. Perception of colours, for Descartes, depends on the varying speeds of particles moving into and through the brain: More thinks, for unspecified reasons, that these differences in speed could not be encoded in the distributed model (IS II.5.7: 82–3).[18] 'Mere matter', says More in a more revealing criticism, could not allow for the 'distinct remembrance' or 'distinct memory' of every one of many simultaneously presented items: without the soul, 'there would be a necessary confusion of all' (IS II.5.7: 83).[19]

More further takes the incompatibility of distributed models with strong assumptions about the unity of the soul and about the nature of its control to be evidence *against* such models. The soul, an indivisible immaterial substance distinct from the body (AA 1.11.11: 36; AAA 10.9: 172–3), is like the 'radiant Center' of a sphere or orb of light: when its 'exterior parts' are 'affected by the parts of the Object with such circumstances as they are in, the inward Center receives all so circumstantiated, that it has necessarily the intire and uncon-fused images of things without' (AAA 10.10: 173). Only such a spiritual 'inward Center' could receive 'multitudes of particular figurations' while keeping them 'yet distinctly represented' (AAA 10.10: 173).[20]

In some difficult pages, which also include analyses of forgetting and of the causes of prompt or slow recall, More does provide a positive account of memory, 'a Faculty of a more peculiar consideration' than reason or imagina-tion (IS II.11.4: 106). The thinking is that only a local model of memory can work, but that, since the spirits and brain are too unstable to support local

---

18 Henry (1989b: 103) seems to endorse this criticism. But the variables listed in L'Homme included differences in the agitation of the spirits and in their uniformity of motions as well as in the nature of the 'easy aperture of the same Pores' (IS II.5.7: 82). There seems no obvious reason to suppose that colours would be particularly difficult to remember: and even if there was some special problem, the theory of colour perception could be rejected while maintaining the distributed model of memory.

19 That the unsuitability for human cognition of matter is due to the body's endemic irregularity is clear too in his rejection of the view that the heart is the seat of the soul. The control of 'Free and Spontaneous progressions [actions]' and 'Perceptions also would be horribly disturbed by its squeezing of it self, and then flagging again by vicissitudes' (IS II.7.8: 91). Stability and order, for More, must be a cognitive given, unchanging and pure rather than rhythmic or cyclic. The 'foulness and coursness of Matter' is the only threat to the exquisiteness of the living creation, which therefore could not have arisen out of 'the tumbling of Atomes' (IS II.10.2: 102).

20 At IS II.7.2: 79, the soul is compared to the centre of a circle on the circumference of which are the external senses. More also defends intriguing and unorthodox views of the peculiarly intimate connections between the soul and the animal spirits (IS II.8–11): see chapter 9 below.

representations, the soul must be involved in all remembering. More accepts that 'the Pith of the Brain' is especially important for memory. 'But that the Brain should be stored with distinct images (whether they consist of the Flexures of the supposed Fibrillae, or the orderly puncture of Pores, or in a continued modified Motion of the parts thereof, some in this manner, and others in that)' has been proved impossible (IS II.11.4: 106–7). What then is the role of the brain in memory? Although only the soul 'her self' can retain the requisite local and distinct representations,

> it were admitted that she might make an occasional use of some private marks she impresses in the Brain; which haply may be nothing at all like the things it would remember, nor of any considerable magnitude nor proportion to them. (IS II.7.16: 93)

Representation operates without resemblance, but only with the (homuncular) soul there to code and interpret. These marks, More tells us in an intriguing passage,

> must be a kind of Brachygraphie, some small dots here and there standing for the recovering to Memory a series of things that would fill, it may be, many sheets of paper to write them at large. (IS II.11.4: 107)

Hooke too wondered if cryptography, hieroglyphics, shorthand, and brachygraphy might more securely perpetuate truth through brevity (Cope 1956: 150–3).

Wittgenstein (1967: sect. 612) imagines 'jottings', marks on paper which are necessary for someone to reproduce a passage of text, and yet which are not a rendering, translation, or storage of the text. Like Wittgenstein, More thinks that the rejection of straightforward resemblance between the hypothetical memory trace and the object of memory implies that nothing is stored. Again like Wittgenstein, More takes this to entail the falsity of any mechanical account of memory: he concludes from this discussion of 'brachygraphie' that 'it is plain that the Memory is in the Soul, and not in the Brain' (IS II.11.4: 107; compare Sutton 1997: sect. 3). But there are still patterns in compressed and transformed jottings: strangely condensing their contents, private marks or dots in the brain may yet be constrained, complex and mechanical at once.

6
Local and distributed representations

The distinction

What use is all this history? My accounts of writers who did not have available the explicit categories of local and distributed representation should fulfil two demands. Already some otherwise invisible disputes and controversies in historical theories of memory have been brought to the surface. But further, the metaphysical and scientific utility of the local/distributed distinction itself should be illuminated by these old ideas. In this chapter, then, the focus shifts briefly from historical responses to the animal spirits model of memory to conceptual evaluation of its implications. I introduce the key distinction within distributed models between explicit and implicit representation, and conclude with a speculative mapping of the analogy between animal spirits and connectionist versions of distributed representation.

It is not obvious that dividing distributed from local models of memory is, even now, a sensible thing to do. Even if there is a genuine distinction, it cross-classifies ideological divisions between connectionist and classical cognitive science: not all connectionist models are distributed. More importantly, the distinction seems to be only perspectival, describing the ends of a spectrum of possible models rather than well-defined alternatives (Clark 1989: 95). As Churchland and Sejnowski remark, 'On the face of it, the difference between local and distributed representations . . . falls rather short of spine-tingling, barn-burning stuff' (1992: 163). Like them, however, I think that the utility of the distinction can be shown (see also Lloyd 1989: 102–16). I test it in historical practice, by setting up possible applications and arguing for my own.

Hooke's view that memories are 'in themselves distinct', I suggested, is characteristic of localist approaches to memory, in which one unit codes one item. But Jamie Kassler, surveying seventeenth-century theories (1995: 129–39), takes Hooke to have a partly *non-localised* theory of memory. This reveals alternative ways of drawing the local versus distributed distinction, through alternative meanings of the term 'local'. Kassler (1995: 113–15) sees the distinction as marking the *amount* of body and brain substance involved in storage. This brings the issue close to the traditional problem of whether the soul is coextensive with and spread (distributed) throughout the body, or is localised at a particular seat (French 1969). Because Descartes has the soul interacting with the body only at the pineal gland, this scheme assigns him a *local* model of memory. There would be no *special* difference between local and distributed memory separate from questions about the manner of psychosomatic interaction. On Kassler's account, the opposite of 'local' is not 'distributed' but 'outside the brain'.[1] Descartes' statement that memory impressions are 'mainly located in the whole substance of the brain', and his explicit denial that they are exclusively located in the pineal gland would not mitigate his localism.

I distinguish local from distributed models quite differently. I defend my distinction not only because it is more in line with other uses of the distinction in new connectionism and the cognitive sciences, but because it makes more sense of the historical theories. The distinction as I use it, relates to the nature of the storage involved *wherever* memories are stored: it is about the discreteness or independence of memories one from another. In any model, do memories remain separate, or do they naturally combine?

The question of whether the soul had a particular seat or was dispersed through the body is not, in my view, at issue in the specific case of memory. Accepting, as Descartes did, that memory can be in the hands, say, or that other parts of the body, like the heart, can *influence* remembering is not directly relevant. *Everyone* agreed that relations between brain and the rest of the body explain peculiarities or abnormal cognitive and behavioural functioning. For Descartes, as I showed in chapter 3, the nature of the animal spirits arriving from the heart is a vital factor in ongoing cognitive processes, and their nature is affected in all kinds of ways by a wide variety of bodily states and processes, such as stomach juices, the air taken in in respiration, and the states of the liver, gall bladder, and spleen (*L'Homme* AT xi.168–9, H 74–5). Nobody saw the brain as an isolated, independent unit. But the mere influence of the rest of the body on remembering is not enough to make a theory non-localist: indeed only local memories (in my sense) remain carefully bounded in their memory places.

The distinction is not to do, in turn, with the *amount* of brain substance involved in memory storage. Distributed traces are compatible with macroscopic localisation of function in the brain. Localisation in the latter sense does not get neurophilosophy very far: 'knowing roughly where a process takes place in the brain typically tells us very little or nothing about the . . . mechanics of the process' (Hatfield 1988a: 727). There may be extensive systems of relatively independent localised modules, devoted say to mental images or to parsing sentence structure, some or all of which still employ distributed representations. As Hinton, McClelland, and Rumelhart say (1986: 79), 'The distributed representations occur within these localised modules . . . the representations . . . are local at a global scale but global at a local scale.' It is globality at the local

---

1 Hobbes is seen as a non-localist because he takes remembrance to be extended through the body and recollection to result, partly, from motions transferred from the heart by the *pia mater* to the brain.

scale which makes them distributed. Again, there is a real issue here about whether memory is separate from any 'executive', or whether storage is separate from processing. But this is not the local versus distributed distinction, although it is connected (as in Hooke's preference for a strong division between an executive 'center' and locally stored memory ideas).

When Descartes says that the 'folds of memory' are 'mainly located in the whole substance of the brain', this is not *sufficient* to prove his model to be distributed, though it is suggestive. But there could be local representation occurring in every part of the brain: and this indeed is the case in Hooke's theory. What more then is required for distribution? Memories must be superpositionally stored (van Gelder 1991b: 36–45, 53–4), many in the same place. The right sense of 'local' to contrast with 'distributed' is where local means 'discrete, separated or nonoverlapping' rather than a sense of restriction in extent (van Gelder 1991b: 42).

Room in the brain

This catches what is distinctive in the Cartesian view: Descartes bypassed, and Malebranche dismissed, the problem of finding room in the brain for every memory, by suggesting that a single fold of the brain holds many traces. John Hawthorne (1989: 9) argues that the room-in-the-brain argument favours contemporary connectionism over local models, which entail that I can only entertain as many propositions as there are neurons in my head. Does Hooke's local model bypass this difficulty?

Boyle roughly calculated the number of distinct words and things an aged learned man might remember, to understand 'how in so narrow a compass, as part of a Human Brain there should be so many distinct Cells or Impressions as are requisite...' (1772/1965: VI: 742). The problem arises with force only on the assumption that impressions *must* be distinct. When Hooke outlined his view of memory, he worked out in more detail how many ideas one person might store in a whole life. He started working on one idea per 'moment', but revised this frightening calculation down markedly to end with a figure of 1,826,200 ideas over 50 years (compare Rose 1993: 90–1 on modern versions of this peculiar quest for the total number of separate items an individual memory might retain). But even if we could 'remember 100 Millions [of distinct things], and consequently must have as many distinct Ideas', Hooke thinks that this number may 'actually be contained within the Sphere of Activity of the Soul acting in the Center' (LL 7.4: 143), and simply concludes that 'we shall not need to fear any Impossibility to find out room in the Brain where this Sphere may be placed, and yet find room enough for all other Uses' (LL 7.4: 144).

MacIntosh and Kassler explain Hooke's optimism here by referring to the previous lecture 6 of the *Lectures of Light*, in which, impressed by his microscopic observations of innumerable infinitesimally small organisms, Hooke suggests that there might be no limit to the smallness of a piece of matter which could yet contain enormous numbers of distinct things:

> there are in every *sensible* Point of Matter a sufficient number of distinct Particles to convey every one of those Motions distinct, without interfering one with another: For as there may be Millions of Motions communicated to a *sensible* Point, so there may be as many Millions of distinct Particles to receive each of them distinctly. (LL 6.5: 134; compare MacIntosh 1983: 347–8)

Interference in local models

Hooke's later statement in the lecture on memory that the 'material and bulky' ideas of memory must be 'in themselves distinct . . . actually different and separate one from another' echoes this passage. Hooke rules out of his theory of memory the interference which Descartes and Malebranche expected as a consequence, albeit a potentially dangerous one, of their distributed model. Hooke does not even canvass the possibility of non-local representation (in my sense): memory ideas just cannot ever be 'two . . . in the same space' (LL 7.4: 142). All Hooke's memories are always explicit, lurking in the coils of the brain. The only difference possible in their state is when the soul in its circular course from 'the Center' finds and uses one of them in its processing or reasoning before returning it unchanged to its own memory spiral.

But a further look at Hooke's account may suggest that my analysis is mistaken. Hooke, in fact, *does* think that his model allows for interference. Kassler, using her own local versus distributed distinction, accordingly credits him with a successful account of non-catastrophic interference which avoids the terrible disorder and confusion which so concerned Glanvill and More (Kassler 1995: 135–6). But Hooke's claim is misleading, for his is not genuine interference. He needs to account for various phenomena of which one with such a sense of the fragility of memory was well aware: forgetting, for instance, occurs when material ideas decay in the very furthest orbs of the memory coils. Ideas are material and so subject to change: those which, 'shifting and changing place in the Repository', get 'closer and closer stuffed and crouded together' can 'be in time alter'd, and sometimes quite lost' (LL 7.4: 144). This alteration of memory ideas may look like interference, and might be used to account for the blending and generalising tendencies of human remembering. But Hooke's continuing exposition shows that his localism carries more weight than the phenomena of interference.

Other memory ideas, says Hooke, interpose between the memory sought and the centre which seeks, as a physical 'Impediment to this Radiation of the Soul' in remembering. He compares 'the manner as the Earth interposing between the Moon and the Sun, hinders the Sun from radiation upon the Moon' (LL 7.4: 144). This echoes Hobbes' notorious account of 'decaying sense': 'this "decaying" must actually be seen as an ellipsing' or occluding, since bodies keep moving until hindered (Pye 1988: 289–90; compare Hobbes 1651/1968: 88–9, 657–8). There is no fusion of memory motions here, only a particular spatial juxtaposition of bodies, which, from the point of view of an assumed inner viewer, obscures one of them.[2] Executive access to a bit of memory information is blocked by the interposition of a new or another memory.

Hooke denied that his kind of 'interference' would be catastrophic on the grounds that the parts of the brain involved in memory are so incomprehensibly small that there is room in the brain for all of them to be separately stored. He accepts that sometimes ideas which have not 'kept the same Order in which they were made' can 'intrude and thrust in themselves between . . . so as often to interrupt and break the Chain or Order of Insertion' (LL 7.4: 144). But even such 'reaction and repercussion', such violation of order, is done in an orderly manner: the ideas never lose their own identity, but remain always, even in intrusive insertion, 'in themselves distinct'. What he calls 'the Interposition of other Ideas between the Center and the Idea sought' (LL 7.4: 144) still operates by local representation, and cannot provide for any genuine mingling of memories to the extent that they might lose their original identity. Hooke's memories remain independent of each other, with their own distinct constitutions and motions.

Implicit and explicit representation

Thinking of memory as a motion in the nimble spirits rather than a body meant that remembered items could not all be continually represented in explicit formation. At any time most memory patterns will not, in one sense, actually be present: all that is there are physical dispositions for them to be recreated, just as the linen cloth which has had many patterns of holes traced through it has dispositions for the easy reopening of particular patterns. The ontological status of the memory patterns which are not actually present at a time may seem unclear: and yet the dispositions are real, for brains or cloths with different histories will not recreate the same patterns.

One way to spell out the strange metaphysics of the distributed memory trace is to invoke a distinction between *explicit* and *implicit* representations. Though developed for new connectionist models (O'Brien 1993; compare Hatfield 1991: 95–6; and Churchland and Sejnowski 1992: 165–70), this distinction is also fruitful when applied in historical cases: in chapter 7 I will show that Locke

---

2 Digby, likewise, wants to incorporate an account of forgetting by fusion and loss of memories (rather than their mere obstruction from executive view) into his localist model. But fusion is impossible if memories are bodies: the closest they can come is 'coupling'. Despite rhetoric of mouldering and defacing ideas in memory, Digby is consistent in not allowing genuine interference: bodies only take on 'a maimed and confused shape in the memory' when shocked by collisions with other bodies (TT 33: 287).

clearly understood it. Local models have no implicit representations, and must get by with enduring static explicit representations. In contrast, explicit representations in distributed models are passing patterns of activity, evoked across neuronal units or animal spirit motions by the combination of previous activity pattern, patterns of connectivity and connection weights, and present input. Any one system can only be in one state at a time, and cannot simultaneously display multiple patterns of activity.[3]

So when I describe philosophers thinking of memories as motions, I mean that they take the explicit tokening of a pattern of activity to be, or to be correlated with, the occurrent remembering. Remembering the analogy with light (chapter 4), however, we might prefer to see memories as tendencies to motion. It is in this latter sense that there can be many memories overlapping in the same place, as implicit representations which can all potentially be rendered explicit or actualised.

Where explicit representations are transient, implicit representations endure. They are dispositions which allow for or ground the recreation of the explicit patterns, the changes in the connection weights or brain pores without which such reconstruction would be impossible (McClelland and Rumelhart 1986). Of course there is only one set of values in the weights at any one time: so to be precise some speak of many representations in one 'representing' (van Gelder 1991b). Indeed, on some views, only implicit representations are strictly distributed: explicit representations, some argue, are 'functionally discrete' just because there is only one at a time in a system (O'Brien 1991, against Ramsey, Stich, and Garon 1991). I do not pursue this debate because the difficult consequences of superposition arise even when attention is restricted to implicit traces, multiply coexisting in the same space at the same time.

What is at one time explicit may in future processing become implicit. Information represented implicitly is tacit, 'in the weights', only potentially active. This is the way in which, most of the time, we 'store' our telephone numbers: but on request, it comes to be explicitly represented. In turn, what I have been calling 'reconstruction' is the change in state from implicit to explicit, the actualising of a disposition. As the example of the phone number shows, confusion does not inevitably result: I usually remember where in the car park I will find my car without confusing today's location with every

---

3 This does not rule out the 'explicit' remembering of many things at once, for one organism or machine may have many systems. Further, there may be inconceivable rapidity of change in the patterns of activity within one system as one explicit trace shades or shifts into another or between many: temporal dynamics account for many of the phenomenological effects of association. However, it is not easy to spell out just what 'explicitness' requires here, or in particular how it relates to consciousness. I avoid this issue: for speculation see O'Brien and Opie forthcoming. My interest in this book is primarily in implicit traces.

previous day. The question is whether these examples tell us much about more complex autobiographical remembering.

Burdens of explanation

So distributed models must allow the occasional retrieval of distinct memories: local models must allow occasional fusion between, or generalisation across, memories. Local models take the distinctness of the 'figures', 'motions and constitutions' of memory traces as primitive, whereas a distributed model takes as primitive the particular way superpositional storage occurs in the physical substrate. Can distributed representations effectively avoid catastrophic interference so as to approximate the faithful recall which we sometimes achieve? Can local representations gerrymander blending and context effects by adding extra twists or mechanisms of the kind we found in Hooke?

Our intuitions about local representation fit ordinary digital computers. When each memory is discretely stored, unchanged in its location until recalled by the central executive, information is faithfully reproduced, unaffected by intermediate experience. The memory brought out of storage into working memory or a temporary buffer is a duplicate of that which was originally encoded.[4]

Disputes between the models can also address the nature of the alleged phenomena of remembering which they seek to explain. If humans almost *never* claimed to be remembering when in fact confabulating or spuriously reconstructing, then the local model of memory would look much more attractive. The human mind/brain would be much more like other storage mechanisms, external means of recording and keeping information safely. It is vital, *for us*, that our word processors store discrete, independent files in identical form overnight: any interference, blending, or mutual contextual changes of different files stored on the same disk would be disastrous. Much writing on these subjects, whether it acknowledges this or not, has been trying to characterise the explananda suitably and convince others that some phenomena are more theoretically important than others. Should cognitive theory *impose* order, or allow order to emerge?

Animal spirits and neural nets

To sum up with irresponsible anachronism, I conclude by fitting animal spirits into the conceptual framework also exemplified by connectionist models

---

4 Advocates of distributed memory can argue that the decision to call the localist storage system of the digital computer a 'memory' was little more than an unfortunate bad pun. Babbage called his recording device a 'store', and the storage system of the American wartime computing project was not called a 'memory' until John von Neumann introduced the term as part of an explicit, forced analogy between computers and human brains (Bolles 1988: 166–8).

(O'Brien 1993). Distributed representation operates at a level of abstraction from specific neural matter.

Abstract feature	Parallel distributed processing	Spirits
ARCHITECTURE		
Processing units	'Neurons'	Brain pores
Activation value	Spiking frequency	——
Range of inputs	——	Spirit flow
Output	——	Spirit flow
Networks of units	Neural nets	Regions of brain
Pattern of connectivity	——	Structure of pores
Mechanism for plasticity	Connection weights	Microstructure
(DISTRIBUTED) REPRESENTATION (Information is encoded through plasticity)		
Explicit representations ('traces'?)		
Transient	Patterns of activity	'Figures traced in gaps'
Extended	Vectors	(Implicit in sensory isomorph)
Implicit representations (= traces)		
Enduring	Modifiable connection weights	Altered pores
Superpositional	Single weight matrix	Many in same region

PROCESSING/COMPUTATION

Method of computation depends on architecture

Processing in both cases is analog: 'rules' for computation are physical causal laws; thus changes in operation are changes in the substrate

Both models exhibit causal holism by which all superposed traces influence product of any processing

7

John Locke and the neurophilosophy of self

... the memory, a no very sure repository   (John Locke, *Essay* IV.21.4)

Consistent with the spirit of Locke and Lashley, current connectionist models may argue for a memory as not existing locally, and as being realised only on retrieval.

(Herbert F. Crovitz 1990: 174)

DIDEROT: Could you tell me what the existence of a
    sentient being means to that being himself?
D'ALEMBERT: Consciousness of having been himself
    from the first instant he reflected until the
    present moment.
DIDEROT: But what is this consciousness founded on?
D'ALEMBERT: The memory of his own actions.
DIDEROT: And without that memory?
D'ALEMBERT: Without that memory there would be no
    'he', because, if he only felt his existence at
    the moment of receiving an impression, he would
    have no connected story of his life. His life
    would be a broken sequence of isolated
    sensations.
DIDEROT: All right. Now what is memory? Where does
    that come from?
D'ALEMBERT: From something organic which waxes and
    wanes, and sometimes disappears altogether.

(Denis Diderot, 'D'Alembert's Dream' (1769/1964: 155–6))

Introduction

Responses to Descartes' distributed model revealed perceived connections between theories of memory and wider views about human nature: how ordered or chaotic were cognitive processes thought or desired to be? This chapter explores more explicit relations between the animal spirits model of memory and concerns about psychological unity and order, through philosophical discussions of the continuity of personal identity. How likely were the fleeting spirits to preserve sameness of personhood over time?

For John Locke, a hierarchy of dependence ran from religion and morality through personal identity, by way of consciousness as extended by memory, which rested in turn on fleeting animal spirits. The vulnerability of his scheme became increasingly obvious. Locke's critics complained that he reduces a person to a club of jostling spirits in the brain: since true memory is agreed by all to be impossible in fleeting matter, worried Samuel Clarke, Locke's anchoring of self in memory means that we are all 'unavoidably we know not who, and do but fancy and dream ourselves to be the Persons we think we are' (in Fox 1988: 54–5, 144–5).

In chapter 9 I further adumbrate the perceived immorality of the animal spirits by looking at their unwholesome associations with contagions of the imagination, seductive and garish images, demonic action, and male sexual insecurity. Conservative critics of Locke questioned the reductive flow from morality through memory to inconstant spirits at the first hurdle, by denying the link between the thinking substance of the self and any psychological (let alone physiological) process. But Locke's refusal to rest the great questions of responsibility and accountability for action on obscure theological ontology was influential. Immaterial substance no longer being certain, the person might be but 'a system of floating ideas'. In the Lockean world of the eighteenth century, that hierarchy of dependence was harder to resist, and 'moral Man' would be saved only by the introduction of greater stability and continuity into physiology by eliminating the animal spirits (chapter 10).

7.1 Memory and personhood: a physiological puzzle
The puzzle

Theories of distributed memory afford an unusual perspective on Locke's views of personal identity. Even if we do not accept G.S. Rousseau's claim (1969/1991: 4) that Locke's 'deepest questions are ultimately physiological', neurophilosophical themes are at work in more of his discussions of psychological phenomena than commentators generally admit. It is possible, in particular, to come to grips with a strange physiological puzzle in Locke's account of the self, the first major treatment of the modern 'problem' of personal identity.

Locke's new theory of personal identity, summarised with the maxim 'consciousness alone makes self' (*Essay* II.27, heading to 23–5), fuelled immediate controversy (Fox 1988) and is still often taken as a basis for the construction of philosophical theories of self (Shoemaker 1963; Wiggins 1976; Parfit 1984: 205ff.; Wilkes 1988a). Yet there is a neglected oddity towards the end of the long chapter on personal identity added to the second edition (1694), when Locke reflects on 'some suppositions that will look strange to some readers' (*Essay* II.27.27). In line with his general hostility to essentialist views of identity which located selves in non-physical souls (Allison 1966/1977), Locke remarks again on our 'ignorance of that thinking thing, that is in us, and which we look on as our *selves*'. He continues with this worry:

> Did we know what it [that thinking thing] was, or how it was tied to a certain System of fleeting Animal Spirits; or whether it could, or could not perform its Operations of Thinking and Memory out of a Body organized as ours is; and

whether it has pleased God, that no one such Spirit shall ever be united to any but one such body, upon the right Constitution of whose Organs its Memory should depend, we might see the Absurdity of some of these Suppositions I have made. (Essay II.27.27)

I do not know of any extended discussion of this passage by commentators:[1] but this is a strange, strong disclaimer. If we knew more about 'a certain System of fleeting Animal Spirits' and about the right constitution of the bodily organs on which memory depends, Locke's new account of the person might look absurd! Why this tension?

It is hard to locate the source of Locke's worry in this paragraph. One concern, as earlier in the chapter (II.27.13–15), is with 'strange Suppositions' about transmigration: can God's goodness be relied on to prevent the existence of many persons in one body or the same person in many bodies, for which Locke's theory seems to allow (Curley 1982: 305–6, 310–14)? Since the 'Spirit' about which Locke wonders must be immaterial substance, he is also reiterating doubts about the utility of reference to such thinking things in this context, on the grounds that it will be impossible to individuate persons by reference to something of which we are 'in the dark' (II.27.27).[2] But why are these more familiar points raised here in the context of possible connections between thinking substance, animal spirits, and the bodily organs of memory?[3]

1 Along with most other references to physiological psychology, it is omitted from A.D. Woozley's abridgement of the Essay (chapter 1 above; on abridgements compare Alexander 1985: 2–3). Yolton (1984b: 158–9) notes the mentions of animal spirits here and at II.27.13 (see below), without examining the suggested threat to Locke's suppositions. He argues rightly that Locke resists the identification of thought with matter which others would ascribe to him. But Locke's language here is looser than that of identity: thought could be 'tied to' matter in many ways without being matter. I suggest that only material constraints on cognition are necessary to raise trouble for Locke here, and that Locke accepted that there were such constraints.

2 Immortality is the central context for all early modern debates about personal continuity. Responsibility at time of Judgement seemed to require a strong form of identity between the sinning agent and the judged sinner. For the complexity of orthodox views on the resurrection of the body see Davis 1988; Bynum 1992, 1995b.

3 Michael Ayers, to whom I am extremely grateful for helpful conversation and correspondence, disagrees with my reading of the puzzle. Ayers takes the 'suppositions' which conflict with physiology to be not Locke's own views about personal identity, but the set of thought experiments used to demonstrate the irrelevance of immaterial substance to problems of individuation and accountability. The reference of 'suppositions' is not clear. Certainly, Locke's readers did not need to refer to a particular physiological theory to criticise the structure of his views, which seemed wrong-headed in basing personal identity in a 'mode' like consciousness, since modes are by nature fleeting, rather than in immaterial substance. But my suggestion is that both Locke and some critics did at times recognise specific problems arising, for his own views, from those theories of memory and its physiology which did not allow items to be stored and recalled independently one from another. Ayers accepts the general threat posed by animal spirits accounts of memory to personal identity. His own clear account of Locke's theory and its contemporary critics is in Ayers 1988: vol.II, 260–77.

I approach this question in roundabout fashion, looking at its historical and philosophical aspects. I show how Locke's treatment of memory responds to theoretical issues about local and distributed representation, and for this reason plays an ambiguous role in his account of the person. Firstly, though, I need to set out briefly the relevant aspects of the influential chapter on identity.

Memory, consciousness, and self

Though the details are hard to work out, memory plays some central role in Locke's account of personal identity. For Locke, consciousness, both in the present and as it extends backwards in time, is the sole criterion for sameness of personal identity. Personal identity thus depends not only on 'that consciousness which is inseparable from thinking and, as it seems to me, essential to it' (II.27.9) but also on memory.

> For since consciousness always accompanies thinking, and it is that that makes everyone to be what he calls Self, and thereby distinguishes himself from all other thinking beings: in this alone consists Personal Identity, i.e. the sameness of a rational being. And as far as this consciousness can be extended backwards to any past action or thought, so far reaches the identity of that Person: it is the same Self now it was then, and it is by the same Self with this present one that now reflects on it, that that action was done. (II.27.9)

There is much dispute on the extent to which Locke makes continuity of self dependent on memory. Although eighteenth-century reactions to his theory assumed that Locke identified consciousness with memory, or made memory a sufficient condition for identity over time, this is by no means an inevitable interpretation (see the appendix to this chapter). It is simply that memory is, for Locke, at least one important form of the necessary kind of psychological continuity.

Locke uses his psychological criteria for personal identity to buttress the social functions played by the concept of a person. There are thus two strands in Locke's treatment, one ontological and psychological, the other normative and 'forensic'. The importance of the latter strand lies in its links to moral, legal, and social institutions and practices. The relation between the two strands is not entirely clear in Locke, and he has been criticised for confusion between them.[4] Tensions between the ontology of the self and

---

4 Tennant (1982: 74) laments Locke's 'linguistic errors in bringing together the ontological and the forensic' and the way in which he 'inextricably links and confuses the two issues'. Mary Douglas (1992: 46–9) argues that Locke's new vision is driven only by 'fit with legal and economic institutions', implausibly grounded in theological necessity: 'a unitary, responsible self-agent must be supposed to exist because it is intellectually, juridically and morally necessary' (1992: 49). See also Mackie 1976: 183. Ross Poole and Catriona Mackenzie tell me that criticism of Locke for confusion on this point has been a common theme in discussions of personhood in applied ethics and social philosophy, especially when critics take the social strand to be in fact primary and consider the ontological and psychological strand dispensable. Compare Poole 1992, 1996.

consideration of what Locke called the *'moral Man'* who is a 'corporeal rational Creature' (III.11.16; Behan 1979: 61–3) fuel the remainder of this chapter.

'Moral Man'

What are the elements of this strong conception of self? In looking at responses to Descartes in chapter 5 I showed the tension between distributed models of memory and certain strong conceptions of psychological order and control. Through Locke, tensions with interpersonal and with social/institutional requirements can be added. 'Person', for Locke, is 'a Forensick Term, appropriating Actions and their Merit; and so belongs only to intelligent Agents capable of a Law, and Happiness and Misery' (II.27.26).

This normative concept is the basis of moral responsibility, and is the ultimate source of 'all the Right and Justice of Reward and Punishment' (II.27.18; Allison 1966/1977: 109). A person will 'extend it *self* beyond present Existence to what is past' through concerned consciousness, consciousness 'founded in a concern for Happiness' (II.27.26). Only in appropriating past actions as one's own, or by reconciling a present self to them, are persons accountable. The juridical system requires such accountability, for punishment is 'annexed to personality, and personality to consciousness' (II.27.22). Rationality is a further condition for these ethical, legal, and social norms: personal identity, 'the sameness of a rational being' holds only for 'a thinking intelligent Being, that has reason and reflection' (II.27.9). The absence of either rationality or concern for actions is taken, in Locke's thought experiments, to be just as strong evidence against a being's personhood as is total amnesia. The forensic nature of the concept of person implies that not all humans will be persons. Some will be excluded as not meeting the required standards which only 'intelligent Agents capable of a Law' meet.[5]

This idealised concept of person, then, must bear a lot of weight. It is persons who are truly free rational agents, who are the loci of moral responsibility, who are the individual units in a just political society. And, although consciousness can also extend forwards, memory is one important means for the extension backwards of concerned consciousness to past actions or thoughts.

---

5 Locke takes the gap between human and person to be a strength of his theory: while we have to ascribe responsibility and agency to a 'rational Parrot' (II.27.8), we need a separate set of (biological) criteria for the identity of a human (II.27.1–7) which do not presuppose intelligence and capacity for a law. The talking parrot was denounced as 'devilry' by Richard Burthogge (1694/1976: 13–22).

7.2 The spirits and the soul

The 'problem' of the self

It is far from obvious on 'internal' grounds alone why the concept of person should have come to concern Locke relatively late in his philosophical thinking.[6] The philosophical 'problem' of personal identity, in the form of a search for conditions or criteria for identity of self across time, was not a traditional one, but came to exercise philosophers rather suddenly: Hume, depressed by his own failure to catch his 'self', reflects within fifty years of Locke's *Essay* that the question of personal identity 'has become so great a question in philosophy, especially of late years in England, where all the abstruser sciences are study'd with a peculiar ardour and application' (*Treatise* I.iv. 6: 259).

The causes of the peculiarly English concern with personhood from the late seventeenth century are obscure and various. Relevant factors include dissatisfaction with Cartesian and theological essentialisms, new concern to justify the location of basic political and economic rights and responsibilities in the individual, the imposition of order and unity in religious contexts, and a parallel concern in political ideology with affirming national identity through national history. If sameness of nationhood over time is guaranteed and extended backwards by historical continuities, then memory will function to provide analogous access to continuities in the individual past.[7] Changing usage in the seventeenth century of words like 'individual' (Williams 1976: 162–3) and 'consciousness' (Wilkes 1984, 1988b; Hagstrum 1987; Thiel 1991), as well as 'person', mark the conceptual shifts, although recent cautions about the arbitrariness and futility of generalised searches for origins in the history of the self (Tomaselli 1984a; Skinner 1991; Reiss 1996) warn us against taking etymology as more than suggestion. Without here trying to unravel these larger changes, I want to approach the historical aspect of Locke's physiological puzzle. Why, firstly, would anyone think that the self or soul was 'tied to a certain System of fleeting Animal Spirits'?

Her invisible self

It had been common in ancient and Renaissance physiology to see the spirits as the immediate instruments of the soul (chapter 2 above). But in the seventeenth

---

6 As Fox argues (1988: 28, 140), concerns with Descartes' *cogito* and problems about thinking substance, which had worried Locke at least since 1682, were part of the motivation. I discuss below one earlier remark of Locke's on personhood and corporeal spirits.

7 So Hume (*Treatise* I.iv.6, p. 261) compares the soul to a commonwealth, remaining identical through total changes of its laws and members; this is evidence that memory produces, rather than discovers, (the fiction of) personal identity, as history produces national identity. On the production of group history as national memory by the English, constructing themselves as the new Protestant elect and Anglicanism as the true faith lost behind the corruptions of religious history, see Trevor-Roper 1989: 120–65; compare Pocock 1971; Rattansi 1988.

century, some began to think specifically that the animal spirits might provide some privileged kind of access, unavailable in any other way, to the innermost interiority of the soul. The topic is addressed in detail by Henry More.

Though hostile to Cartesian uses of animal spirits in distributed models of memory (chapter 5 above), More argues, in defending The Immortality of the Soul, that corporeal animal spirits are 'the immediate engine of the Soul in all her operations' (IS II.8.3: 95; on More's version of animal spirits theory, see Iliffe 1995: 437–9). Because the spirits are found 'in their greatest purity and plenty' in the fourth ventricle, this is where 'that precious and choice part of the Soul which we call the Centre of Perception is to be placed': the fourth ventricle, whence the soul can command the spirits, is suitably called 'the Root of the Soul' or 'the Eye of the Soul' (IS II.8.2: 95; II.11.10: 109).[8] The intimate connection between spirits and soul explains the instantaneous effects of the soul's commands, for the spirits' 'Swiftness of Motion is much like that of Light, which is a Body as well as they' (IS II.9.4: 100).[9] The soul, which cannot move matter but only determine it in motion, is in immediate contact with the spirits as they are 'playing about and hitting against the sides of the Caverns they are in', and in voluntary motion 'she, when they are playing onely and gently toying amongst themselves, sends [them] forth into the exteriour members' (IS II.8.10: 97; II.9.3 100). Arguing against those who believe that something other than animal spirit is the immediate seat of the soul, More tries metaphorically to ward off any danger arising from the spirits. But he has to accept their potentially harmful effects on the soul:

> And it is no wonder, if the continuation and natural composure of the Spirits be Rest and Ease to the Soul, that a violent disjoyning and bruising of them, and baring the Soul of them, as I may so speak, should cause a very harsh and torturous sense in the Centre of Perception. (IS II.10.8: 104)

More, then, advises us to 'contain our selves within the capacities of the Spirits': the frequency, vividity, or novelty of an impression can, through the action of these spirits, 'pierce the Soul', sometimes 'with an extraordinary resentment' (IS II.11.5: 107). He hopes to support a substantialist view of the self, by showing the ontological gulf between the corporeal spirits and that to which they had access. It is important, he reminds us, 'that the spirits are not

---

8 The only important function of the entire brain is to act, with the nerves, as 'one continued Receptacle or Case of that immediate Instrument of the sensiferous motions of the Soul, the Animal Spirits', and thus protecting the 'chief seat and Acropolis of the Soul' in the fourth ventricle (IS II.8.13: 98).

9 This is to answer the 'frivolous objection' of 'simple and careless . . . Opposers of this ancient and solid Opinion', that corporeal motion could not be quick enough (IS II.9.4: 100, and II.9.1: 99). More does not think it 'so hard a business that these Spirits should be commanded downwards into the Nerves'. The effects of different atmospheric conditions on the spirits too explains why our thoughts are clear in clear air 'and in cloudy more obscure and dull' (II.8.4: 95).

sufficient of themselves for these Functions; nor the Soul of her self, without the assistance of the Spirits' (IS II.11.1: 106). But, as Henry (1986b) argues, emphasising the containment of the self within the capacities of the spirits could also lead towards materialism: if the spirits can do so much of the soul's work, the need for reference to the soul could drop out. One possibility, then, is that since Locke had little sympathy either for substantialist views of self or for materialism, he could not be expected to approve of talk of the spirits' access to an invisible soul.

The idea of special intimacy between soul and animal spirits continued to fascinate. In a dialogue on the 'Volatil Oeconomy of the Brain' which synthesises early eighteenth-century theory, Mandeville's mouthpiece Philopirio praises

> the transcendent subtilty of those airy velocious Agents, the chief and immediate Ministers of Thought; that officiating between the Soul and the grosser Spirits of the Senses have always access to her invisible self. (Mandeville 1711/1976: 131)[10]

Strange consequences follow from this intimacy, for the spirits are intimately connected not only to the soul but also to grosser functions from which moral philosophers officially wanted to keep the self clear (chapter 9 below). Locke's new psychological criterion for sameness of personhood combines with the peculiarly modern attempt to penetrate the recesses of the (female) soul, inviting heroic quests into the mysterious interior (Tomaselli 1984a: 198–201; compare Dollimore 1984/1989: chs. 1, 5, 10, 16; Barker 1984; Belsey 1985: ch. 2; Sutton 1990). But to my knowledge the link between his theory of personal identity and the seventeenth century's 'shadow of physiology'[11] in the form of the animal spirits has not yet been noticed.

Sydenham on self

Firstly, it is worth pointing out who Locke is answering. The phrase used by Locke in the passage from the Essay which set our puzzle was 'a certain System of fleeting Animal Spirits'. The phrase echoes the following intriguing passage from a 1682 discussion of hysteria by Locke's medical friend, mentor, and colleague Thomas Sydenham:

> Beyond what we may call the exterior man, who is composed of parts which are visible to the senses, there is an interior man formed of a system of animal

---

10 Also quoted by Monro 1975: 62. Mandeville changes his name for Philipirio (1711/1976: xi). Despite official caution about hypotheses, Mandeville/Philopirio devotes long tracts of this second dialogue (1711/1976: 121–48) to speculation on internal mixtures, to give the hypochondriacal Misomedon 'a clear Idea of the broken contexture of [his] Spirits' (Mandeville 1711/1976: 148).

11 The phrase, for those intrusions of physiology which irk the dualist, is Keith Campbell's (1970: 51–5).

spirits, a man who can be seen only with the eyes of the mind. This latter man, closely joined and so to speak united with the corporeal constitution, is more or less deranged from his state to the degree that the principles which form the machine have a natural firmness. That is why this disease attacks women more than men, because they have a more delicate, less firm constitution, because they lead a softer life, and because they are accustomed to the luxuries and commodities of life and not to suffering.[12]

Sydenham's links with Locke have been well documented (Niebyl 1973: 369–72; Romanell 1984: ch. 4; Sanchez-Gonzalez 1990).[13] Locke's papers often mention Sydenham's reliance on animal spirits in therapeutic practice. In 1679 he records that Sydenham informed a Mrs Duke that her false conceptions proceeded 'from want of spirits and coldnesse in the habit and womb' (in Dewhurst 1963: 177). In 1680 Sydenham told Locke that he had cured the Earl of Salisbury of a 'total suppression of urine' which was 'from a disorder of the spirits' (in Dewhurst 1963: 193). These examples remind us of a practical dimension of seventeenth-century medicine in which spirits, humours, and fluids continued to drive treatment. The theoretical role of spirits made this inevitable.[14] Sydenham writes to Cole that 'the strength and constancy of the mind, so long as it lies in this our bodily crust of clay, depends most especially upon the strength and constancy of the spirits that lodge along with it' (1682/1685: 134).[15]

Both mental and physical symptoms of hysteria 'proceed from a Confusion

---

12 Sydenham's *Epistolary Dissertation to Dr Cole* (1682). This dramatic, free translation is by Richard Howard, from a 1784 French translation quoted by Foucault 1965: 149. The original Latin is in Sydenham 1682/1685: 133–4, and there are different English versions in Sydenham 1697: 416 and 1850: sect. 80. I am not sure how widespread this notion of a second interior person was: compare Cudworth 1678/1743: 806, on our twofold body, the interior spirituous one being 'the soul's immediate instrument of sense and motion'. Foucault uses the Sydenham passage in a powerful meditation on the replacement of the 'dynamics of corporeal space' by 'a morality of sensibility': see chapter 10 below.

13 Authorship of two medical essays of the late 1660s is disputed between the two (Dewhurst 1966: 73). In 'Anatomie' (1668) the author (Sydenham or Locke) argued that diseases can be caused by 'the invisible and insensible spirits that govern preserve and disorder the oeconomie of the body' (Dewhurst 1966: 91–2). Dewhurst rejects the myth of Sydenham as a pure empiricist free of pre-observational opinion: 'like many practical men, Sydenham deluded himself into believing that he had completely discarded theory' (p. 60; compare King 1970: 129–30). Contrast G.S. Rousseau's praise (1993: 138–45) of Sydenham's medical anthropology of hysteria-as-imitation.

14 It is misleading, then, to think of new 'mechanistic' neurophysiology as incompatible with traditional theories of humours or spirits and practices based on such theories. I find it less surprising than does Mark Micale (1995: 121–2) that Katherine Williams' (1990) study of treatments of 'hysteria' reveals that 'despite the new and widely publicized theories of the neurophysiological nature of hysteria of the 1670s and 1680s . . . professional contemporaries of Willis and Sydenham clung tenaciously to Hippocratic and Galenic conceptualizations of the disorder'. The example of animal spirits shows that neither old and new, nor practice and theory, can be so easily disentangled.

15 Also quoted by John Wright (1980: 241–2), who stresses similarities between Sydenham's thought and the Cartesian neurophilosophy.

[*ataxia*] of the Spirits' in various kinds of 'unequal Distribution, which is altogether contrary to the Oeconomy of Nature'. Ataxy and disorder in the spirits occur when 'too many of them in a Croud, contrary to proportion, are hurried violently upon this or that part', perverting organ functions: this explains too hysteria's characteristic protean adaptability to the peculiar symptoms of different body parts (Sydenham 1682/1685: 132–3). An offence to corporeal harmony, the contrary spirits seem by nature compelled to interfere, thwart, and obstruct proper order in memory and body (Glanvill, *VOD*: 39; chapter 5 above).

I return in chapter 9 to the threat to sanity posed by the animal spirits theory of memory. But already there is reason to think that the puzzling passage in Locke's essay is aimed in part at the way Sydenham tied an 'interior man' to a system of animal spirits. It was, indeed, in 1683 that Locke first articulated his unusual view of sameness of personhood over time:

> Identity of persons lies not in having the same numericall body made up of the same particles, nor if the minde consist of corporeal spirits in their being the same, but in the memory and knowledg of ones past self and actions continued on under the consciousness of being the same person wherby every man ownes himself.[16]

Even if matter, in the form of corporeal animal spirits, *could* think, only psychological continuities of memory and consciousness could guarantee sameness of personhood. Animal spirits, like all material particles, do not remain stable or constant over time, and so personal identity is to be sought not in physiological identities across time but in the extension backwards, through memory, of consciousness and in the appropriation of one's past self and actions. Yet by the time he writes *Essay* II.27.27, even after expanding these suggestions about psychological continuities and examining their implications for puzzle cases, Locke feels residual tension between the animal spirits psychophysiology and the important role he has given to memory in discovering sameness of consciousness over time. I suggest this is because he has also been thinking more about memory, and has found little to ground confidence in the kind of continuity which persons must have if the forensic functions of the concept are to be fulfilled.

7.3 Amnesia and identity: the fragility of memory

With some historical background to Locke's puzzle in place, I return to the philosophical issue. Why does Locke fear the collapse into 'absurdity' of his account of self if memory depends on 'the right Constitution' of certain bodily

16   Locke's journal, Tuesday 5 June 1683 (British Library MS Locke, fo. 7, p. 107), in Dewhurst 1963: 222. I am grateful to Udo Thiel for bringing this note to my attention.

organs and 'a certain System of fleeting Animal Spirits'? The answer is in the detail of his views on the psychophysiology of memory.

Locke on memory

Locke is officially unwilling to 'meddle with the physical consideration of the mind' (Essay I.1.2). But he does assume his readers' familiarity with the ubiquitous late seventeenth-century animal spirits physiology (compare Wieand 1980: 69–70). He is as sympathetic to it as to the other ideas in natural philosophy which were being put forward by such as Boyle, Sydenham, Huygens, and Newton, the four 'master-builders' of the commonwealth of learning for whom Locke claims to be a philosophical under-labourer (Essay, 'The Epistle to the Reader', pp. 9–10).[17]

In the chapter on retention, Locke is reluctant to enquire into the extent to which memory might depend on 'the Constitution of our Bodies', 'the Temper of the Brain', and 'the make of our animal Spirits' (Essay II.10.5).[18] But he admits that it seems 'probable' that 'the Constitution of the Body does sometimes influence the Memory'. He cites examples of how diseases and fevers can 'calcine all those Images to dust and confusion, which seem'd to be as lasting, as if graved in Marble' (Essay II.10.5). Ordinary remembering and forgetting, he accepts, are probably influenced by multiple corporeal factors even in health.

In the first edition of the Essay Locke writes that 'Memory . . . is as it were the Store-house of our Ideas', the 'Repository' where ideas are laid up (Essay II.10.2). This seems a straightforward localist storehouse theory like Hooke's, by which ideas are statically 'lodg'd in the Memory' (Essay II.10.7). But in the second edition, responding to criticism from Norris,[19] Locke adds the claim, or disclaimer, that

> this laying up of our Ideas in the Repository of the Memory, signifies no more but this, that the Mind has a Power, in many cases, to revive Perceptions, which

---

17 Locke's library (Harrison and Laslett 1971) included works by many authors in the spirits tradition, including Descartes, Digby, La Forge, Malebranche, More, and Willis. On Locke's uses of Willis' physiology see Wright 1991a.

18 The phrase 'and the make of our animal Spirits' was not added until the fourth edition of 1700. But this does not mean that he did not accept their particular relevance earlier: motions of animal spirits in birds, he notes in the first edition, can mechanically 'leave traces in their Brains' (II.10.10). Other mentions of animal spirits (II.1.15, II.8.4, II.8.12, and II.8.21) refer to their role in perception. Compare references at IV.10.19 (2nd edn) and II.33.6 (4th edn), and Yolton 1993: 11–12. One earlier connection between memory and corporeal spirits is in Locke's journal for Thursday 1 July 1677, while in France: 'for the memory they take the dried flowers of sage and rosemary infused in the spirits of wine which they use' (Dewhurst 1963: 83). Compare Hooke's more grating schemes for improving memory by the intake of various metals (chapter 5 above).

19 Norris pointed out that ideas could not, on Locke's view, really be stored or 'as it were laid aside out of Sight' (Essay II.10.2), because all ideas, for Locke, must be currently perceived (Essay I.2.5). The relevant passage in Norris is quoted by Wieand (1980: 65–6). On Norris' critique see Yolton 1956: 65–7, 91–5; Whyte 1962: 96.

it has once had . . . in this Sense it is, that our *Ideas* are said to be in our Memories, when indeed, they are actually no where, but only there is an ability in the Mind, when it will, to revive them again. (II.10.2)

Stressing again his conviction that ideas, as 'actual Perceptions in the Mind', must 'cease to be any thing, when there is no perception of them' (II.10.2, added in the second edition), Locke says that it is only metaphorically that we talk of ideas being (stored) in our memories.

Critics of trace theories from Reid to Norman Malcolm (1977: 195–7) have taken Locke to be confused or unclear in his attitude to the storehouse metaphor or model over the two editions. Yet inconsistency disappears if Locke is seen as moving towards the Cartesian theory of memory. Ideas do not remain explicitly in memory over the period from experience to remembering. What is 'stored' is not the idea itself, as in Hooke's localist model: in one sense nothing at all is stored,[20] for all that happens in 'laying down' a memory is that a change occurs in the 'temper of the brain' after which a physical disposition exists by which an idea can in certain circumstances be 'revived' or reconstructed. In a distributed model of memory,

> patterns which are not active do not exist anywhere. They can be re-created because the connection strengths between units have been changed appropriately, but each connection strength is involved in storing many patterns, so it is impossible to point to a particular place where the memory for a particular item is stored. (Hinton, McClelland, and Rumelhart 1986: 80)[21]

It is, then, plausible to identify a memory trace not with a specific explicit pattern of activity in the motions of spirits, but rather with an implicit disposition for the evocation of the explicit pattern. As Locke claimed, we say that our ideas are (dispositionally) in our memories, when indeed they are actually (explicitly) nowhere.[22] This distinction between explicit and implicit repre-

---

20 Wieand (1980: 72–3) says that Locke must be understood as taking *impressions* of the senses to be stored, impressions 'from which we are able to generate (if we remember correctly) an idea which is numerically distinct from, but in certain respects descriptively the same as, the idea originally generated by the impression'. But this does not seem quite right, since impressions are fleeting: only dispositions endure.

21 This feature of distributed representation is 'the main difference from a conventional computer memory': it is certainly not a storehouse in which sacks of grain lie passive and unchanging save for a little decay until hauled out again. Where Aaron (1955: 138) wonders if Locke has completely given up the repository theory, Wieand (1980: 67) remarks that 'there is good reason to suppose that Locke never held the storehouse theory'.

22 It remains unclear what sort of similarity exists between the original memory and that which is revived. Distributed memory traces, with their tendencies towards interference, can easily lose their identity. David Krell (1990: 76–7) grants, on the basis of this passage, that for Locke 'memory is more construction than conservation', but goes on to question whether his voluntaristic assurance in the ability of the mind to revive ideas 'when it will' is justified by his own views on forgetting and decay. This parallels my strategy of eroding confidence in the comforts which memory holds for the self: see below on control.

sentations requires a mechanism for causal continuity between experience and remembering without simple storage: only a physiological basis for the future revival of a trace can remain over time.[23]

Locke's references to powers for the re-evocation of memories imply a metaphysics of physical dispositions, patterns, or textures. The patterns can come originally from the external world: in a sentence of Draft B of the Essay which did not find its way into the final version, Locke says that one way 'of reteineing of Ideas'

> is the power to revive again in our mindes those imaginations which the objects from whence they came first caused in us when they affected our senses whether by motion or otherwise it matters not here to consider. (Draft B, Locke 1990: sect. 23, p. 134)

Peter Alexander (1985) has shown how the view that patterns can be transmitted from the 'textures' of objects to the 'textured' motions of animal spirits in the brain runs through the corpuscularian philosophy which Locke shared with Boyle.[24] Different 'particular Textures of Matter' receive impulses differently (Burthogge 1694/1976: 158). These patterned motions are the basis for all remembering.

But this psychophysiology is in two kinds of tension with the need for memory to discover and to ground, in part, the continuity of personal identity over time. Even if memory can sometimes extend a self backwards in time to past consciousness and actions, it is threatened by both intrusions and interruptions. Firstly, the causes of present motions may not always be simply the original patterns from objects. This leads to problems in distinguishing memory from imagination and in controlling what is associated in memory. The intrusions of inappropriate ideas into the memory of 'moral Man' are my topic in chapter 9. The second threat to the Lockean self derives from the impossibility, on the model of implicit memory traces which he accepts, of the perfect preservation of motions and thus of memories. Locke laments that 'the Ideas, as well as Children, of our Youth, often die before us' (Essay II.10.5). The defects of memory mean, then, that prospects are poor, on Locke's theory, for perfect continuity of personhood between youth and maturity.[25]

23　Locke's belief in the physiology of animal spirits leads him to say that it is 'impossible' to refuse to grant memory to 'several other Animals'. The sounds birds hear make traces which 'by their after-endeavours' allow the production of similar sounds (Essay II.10.10). The ascription of memory and perception to animals is not anti-Cartesian, as Wright (1991a: 255) claims: Descartes' beast-machines too dream, feel, and remember (chapter 3 above).

24　See especially Alexander's chapter 4 on ideas, chapter 7 on powers, and chapter 10 on patterns, with a discussion of the animal spirits theory of memory on pp. 192–3. Alexander's reading depends on taking Locke's corpuscularian scientific realism seriously. I cannot defend this here, but a classic statement of the case is Mandelbaum 1964.

25　This would push Locke's account of personal identity into a familiar circularity if memory was the only kind of psychological continuity which he allowed as a criterion. But if other

Locke on forgetting, physiology, and self
In paragraphs on forgetting and other failures of memory, Locke refers frequently to psychophysiological factors. This is more than religious degradation of the body and attribution of human failings to the corporeal: there is specific reason for memory's inability to reproduce the past in all its desired presence within the theory of memory.

Sections 4 and 5 of *Essay* II.10 describe how '*ideas* fade in the memory'. At times Locke talks conventionally of how deep an imprint needs to be, of the mind's regular failure to set 'the stamp deep into it self' (*Essay* II.10.4). Mixing metaphors, he describes regretfully the wearing out of the print and the fading colours of 'the pictures drawn in our Minds', even of 'those which are struck deepest'. Ideas can vanish, even from 'Minds the most retentive', 'leaving no more footsteps of remaining Characters of themselves, than Shadows do flying over Fields of Corn' (*Essay* II.10.4–5). Even conscious attempts at careful remembering are vulnerable to weakness in memory 'either through the temper of the Body, or some other default' (II.10.4). Without the requisite repetition of recall which (as Descartes' *L'Homme* had suggested) would refresh the memory, the fading ideas of the memory will 'vanish and disappear'. It is at this point that Locke is forced back to physiology:

> How much the Constitution of our Bodies, and the make of our Animal Spirits, are concerned in this; and whether the Temper of the Brain make this difference . . . I shall not here enquire, though it may seem probable, that the Constitution of the Body does sometimes influence the Memory. (II.10.5)

Forgetting, then, falls naturally out of the psychophysiological theory, as patterns traced in the animal spirits fail to stick, fade, or disappear entirely.

Locke's reluctance to enquire further into differences made by body, brain, and spirits is not so surprising. Memory, according to Locke, is, for 'an intellectual Creature' like a man, 'of so great moment that, where it is wanting, all the rest of our faculties are in a great measure useless' (II.10.8). But if memory depends on the dispositions and motions of the fleeting animal spirits, and personal identity depends on memory, and morality depends on identity, then the purpose of the whole *Essay*, the preservation of the 'great Ends of Morality and Religion' (IV.3.6), may be thwarted at the outset by the rare and subtle corporeal particles. Ontological caution is a necessary, prudent defence.

That this is the right direction for interpreting Locke's puzzle is perhaps confirmed by another reference to the animal spirits earlier in the chapter on identity which shows that Locke is alive to the kind of threat they pose. Noticing (in a perplexing passage) that his theory requires God benevolently to have

continuities, like the connections between intentions and actions, or emotional
continuities, can discover sameness of personhood over time for the adult, then there can
be genuine questions about what kind of history this adult has.

ensured that the same memories and consciousness belong, as a matter of fact, to only one human, Locke remarks: 'How far this may be an argument against those who would place thinking in a system of fleeting animal spirits, I leave to be considered' (II.27.13). Even though it is only a few pages further on that Locke complains about absurdity in his own account if knowledge of the fleeting spirits were more advanced, it seems here that it is the animal spirits physiology which might not survive a proof of its incompatibility with the new theory of the person.[26] Any tension between animal spirits and the forensic concept of a person might in time encourage revision of the psychophysiology in order to retain the normative notion.

Hume on forgetting, physiology, and self

I quoted at the start of chapter 3 Hume's approval of 'the Cartesian philosophy of the brain' in explaining an odd case of amnesia (in Hume 1948: 502, also in Wright 1983: 84 and Yolton 1984b: 188). Descartes' neurophilosophy provides a framework for understanding how connections with the personal past could be severed: might it also lie behind Hume's criticisms of the way Locke makes personal identity dependent on memory, and his own failed attempts to catch the self? For Hume the formation of our (fictional) idea of a unified self depends upon associative 'easy transitions' from one past perception to another in acts of memory (Treatise 1.iv.6: 262).[27] The associative relations of resemblance and causation on which 'identity depends', and which associate 'the whole train of perceptions' in the imagination, are both mechanisms of memory. Memory is 'to be consider'd . . . as the source of personal identity'

---

26 I am very unsure about the import of this whole passage at II.27.13. God, caring about the 'Happiness or Misery' of 'his sensible Creatures', will not, says Locke, 'by a fatal Error of theirs transfer from one to another that consciousness, which draws Reward and Punishment with it'. I understand neither why this would be an error made by the creatures, nor what exactly it is which Locke thinks might be an argument against those who place thinking in the system of fleeting animal spirits. Nothing I have read on the passage throws any light on these questions. Flew (1951: 164), Mackie (1976: 184–5), and Taylor (1989: 543–4) are all preoccupied with convicting Locke of circularity, and argue that there would not be any error here in the first place because the transfer of consciousness would by definition also transfer identity. But, as I have suggested, psychological continuity does not only extend into the past, and so there are other criteria than memory for sameness of personhood. Alston and Bennett (1988: 42) and Wedeking (1990: 177–9) take the error to be in the unfairness done to the substance, not to the person, who (which?) is punished. But no one discusses the use of these considerations against those who place thinking in the animal spirits. As Wedeking says (1990: 178), it may be that this passage of Locke's 'will forever defeat any attempt to read the section as a coherent argument or line of thought'. Michael Ayers (personal communication) thinks that those who place thinking in animal spirits are not materialists, but dualists for whom the soul is meant to use spirits as instrument (when 'transfer' of one soul to another physical system would seem possible).

27 I cannot here go into detail on the interpretation of this chapter or the remarks on personal identity in the 'appendix'. Good expositions are Flage 1990: ch. 7 and Pears 1990: chs. 8–9; for a survey of views, with original interpretations, see Fogelin 1985: ch. 8.

because it 'alone acquaints us with the continuance and extent of this succession of perceptions' which we thus naturally tend to think of as really bound
together (1.iv.6, 259–61).

But although the fact is not explicitly mentioned at this point in Hume's
'accurate anatomy of human nature' (1.iv.6: 263), we have already been told
that associative memory is psychophysiological. While Hume is reluctant to
examine the causes of associative principles, he does have a view, 'specious and
plausible', on the subject:

> 'Twou'd have been easy to have made an imaginary dissection of the brain, and
> have shewn, why upon our conception of any idea, the animal spirits run into
> all the contiguous traces, and rouze up the other ideas, that are related to it.
> (1.ii.5: 60)

But the unruly spirits are by nature unreliable: it is true that they

> always excite the idea, when they run precisely into the proper traces, and
> rummage that cell, which belongs to the idea. But as their motion is seldom
> direct, and naturally turns a little to the one side or the other; for this reason
> the animal spirits, falling into the contiguous traces, present other related
> ideas, in lieu of that which the mind desir'd at first to survey. (1.ii.5: 61)

Because we are not always sensible of this change in the ideas presented by
the spirits, their erratic motions are 'the cause of many mistakes and sophisms
in philosophy' (1.ii.5: 61).[28] The spirits escape conscious notice, exceeding the
will.

Memory and psychological control

I return to the special dangers of misassociation in chapter 9: but Hume's
pessimism about personal identity will not be allayed by looking for any constancy in the spirits' role in the processes of memory and association. Yet so
far I have given little weight to the voluntaristic talk which both Locke and
Hume keep up in describing the relations between self and psychophysiolog-

---

28 See the clear discussion of Hume's psychophysiology of error in Wright 1983: 68–9,
71–4. Wright demonstrates Hume's proximity to Malebranche on these issues, and
suggests (1983: 73) that understanding the ties which philosophers 'believed to exist
between the continuous motion of fluids in the brain and the dynamics of our mental
lives' will aid insight into Hume's view of the self as 'no more than a continuous series
of perceptions related in certain ways'. There is, however, considerable debate (which
I cannot go into here) over whether or not natural relations among ideas are for
Hume, as Wright says (1983: 74), 'really neural in character'. This reading relies,
plausibly in my view, on a physical reading of Hume's talk of dispositions and natural
transitions in his chapter (1.iii.8) on 'the causes of belief' (e.g. *Treatise* p. 99). Wright
defends this fully in his chapter 5, especially pp.214–19. See also Anderson 1966:
118–24 and ch. 13; Anderson 1976; Wright 1991b: 150. For different views see
McCracken 1983: 278–9; Yolton 1984a: ch. 10. Ross (1991: 344) compares Hume
and connectionism.

ical processes. Will the mental origin of activities of recollection not suffice to guarantee sufficient continuity over time for the normative conception of the person as a rational, free, responsible moral agent to remain in place despite the obvious empirical frailties of human memory? Locke's view, after all, was that 'the Mind has a Power' to revive ideas 'when it will': and, even with physiology in focus, Hume says 'that as the mind is endow'd with a power of exciting any idea it pleases; whenever it dispatches the spirits into that region of the brain, in which the idea is plac'd' (1.ii.5: 60–1) the various consequences described above follow. In both cases it looks as if the mind is meant to be genuinely 'active' in directing and controlling brain processes. But, not surprisingly, the details of this control over the corporeal continually slip away in the texts.[29] The idea of dominating one's own body is little more than a wish, always already enveloped in the stronger seductions of surrender.

Locke announces that, in remembering,

> the Mind is oftentimes more than barely passive, the appearance of those dormant Pictures, depending sometimes on the Will. The Mind very often sets it self on work in search of some hidden Idea, and turns, as it were, the Eye of the Soul upon it. (Essay II.10.7)

It is in passages like these that Locke seems most vulnerable to attacks on the kind of homuncular scanning, interpretation, or 'viewing' of inner ideas which critics of trace theories often denounce as incoherent. But the real difficulty with this talk is not in the assumption of memory traces but in the postulation of an active subject behind the traces which reviews and manipulates them as they lie passive in a memory store. In these passages, which date back to the early 1670s (Locke 1990: 135), Locke's view of memory does seem to be a localist, storehouse one. But he is already aware, too, of the other phenomena which a distributed model takes seriously, and which threaten to undermine the desired executive control:

> sometimes too they [memory ideas] start up in our Minds of their own accord, and offer themselves to the Understanding; and very often are rouzed and tumbled out of their dark Cells, into open Day-light, by some turbulent and tempestuous Passion; our Affections bringing Ideas to our Memory, which had otherwise lain quiet and unregarded. (II.10.7; also in Draft B, Locke 1990: 135)

This passage, acknowledging the effects of emotion on memory and the potential for unbidden activity among memory traces (which are after all dispositions in the pores of the brain and the continually flowing patterns of

29 This paragraph and the next are indebted to Krell 1990: 77–80. But Krell's intention is to complain that 'active reminiscence is given short shrift in Locke's account' (1990: 79), for Krell's own view of memory requires a truly active subject to account for 'mnemic output' (1990: 89).

motions of the animal spirits),[30] anticipates the chapter on association of ideas which Locke added to the fourth edition of the *Essay* in 1700 (chapter 9 below). Together with forgetting and the other defects of 'oblivion and slowness' in memory, such tumbling and confusion among memories suggests that the putative self, which needs the assistance of memory to 'proceed beyond present Objects' (II.10.8), has a severely curtailed or shrunken domain of untainted influence.

Development of my intrigue at this combination, at the coupling of official stress on the possibility of 'moral Man's' control over his own physiology with repeated examples of the intrusion and spillage of the corporeal into his most exalted powers and activities, requires a foray into other metaphorical fields in which the quick and nimble spirits rummaged. Having suggested the intimacy between the animal spirits which form memory traces and the self, I can, in chapter 9, broaden the scope to include applications of the spirits theory to other mental, physical, and social phenomena. But first I return to the problematic search for the troublesome spirits.

Appendix: memory and self in *Essay* II.27

Until recently, some commentators assumed that Locke held a simple 'memory theory' of personal identity: passages like II.27.9, quoted in the text above (p. 160), were thought to imply that remembering doing something was both necessary and sufficient for being the same person as the person who did it. This view however seemed open to a barrage of criticisms. Sergeant, Butler, and, influentially, Reid complained that memory could not constitute personal identity, since memory *presupposes* personal identity: Locke's theory thus seems circular, for nothing counts as remembering unless sameness of person between past and present is already assumed.[31] Reid's charge (1785/1849: 352) that Locke has confounded consciousness with memory was supported by modern critics from Flew

---

30 Compare, from Locke's posthumously published 1692 reply to Norris: 'ideas may be real beings, though not substances; as motion is a real being, though not a substance; and it seems probable that, in us, ideas depend on, and are some way or other the effect of motion; since they are so fleeting . . .' (quoted by Winkler 1991: 218). The word 'fleeting' was associated for Locke both with 'ideas' and with 'animal spirits'.

31 For these criticisms see especially Behan 1979. Locke's own reply, taken from marginal notes in his copy of John Sergeant's *Solid Philosophy Asserted . . .* (1697), is discussed by Thiel (1981). Both Behan and Thiel plausibly deny the force of the circularity objection, on the grounds that, for Locke, only the (natural) human is presupposed by remembering, not the (forensic concept of) person. Parfit (1984: 219–23) amends Locke by introducing a kind of memory, quasi-memory, defined so as not to presuppose the identity of the person who remembers, for example, having an experience with the person who had the experience.

(1951/1968) on. The notion, especially, that remembering having done something should be *sufficient* for having done it seemed, as Reid said, to conflate personal identity with our *evidence* for sameness of personhood: how could my suddenly remembering having done something suddenly *make it true* that I did it?

More recent scholars, then, querying the Reid/Flew strategy of interpreting Locke as exclusively a 'memory theorist' only to attack 'memory theory', have denied that Locke identifies consciousness with memory. The continuity provided by memory need not be the *only* kind of psychological continuity which a Lockean relies on: the same consciousness, indeed, 'can extend to Actions past *or to come*' (*Essay* II.27.10, my emphasis), so that continuity between, for instance, intentions and future actions too can be seen as important for sameness of personhood (and in turn actual disruptions to the links between action and intention will threaten continuity). A 'functional distinction' can be accepted between memory and the relevant kind of consciousness (Behan 1979: 66): for Edwin McCann (1987), 'memory has its special role to play in personal identity only because of its connections with sameness of consciousness', where 'sameness of consciousness is the basic relation making for personal identity'. This explains why Locke uses the word 'consciousness' throughout the chapter while only referring explicitly to memory on a few occasions:[32] yet memory is still left with a central role (Wiggins 1976: 150–1; Parfit 1984: 205; Schechtman 1994: 4–7). Memory is our main access to the past: for Locke, 'memory is necessary if a person is to have a history' (Behan 1979: 66). The ability to remember, in the present, having been an agent or having had certain experiences in the past is still something like a necessary condition, even if not a sufficient one, for being now the same person as the past person who acted or experienced.

The strongest point in favour of retaining memory as one central kind of psychological continuity even if it is not equivalent to consciousness is that Locke explicitly says that total amnesia rules out continuing personal identity. A being, whether material or spiritual, which has been 'wholly stripp'd of all

---

32 Much weight is placed on this point in one strong attack on the centrality of memory to Locke's theory. Margaret Atherton denies (1983: 279) that 'Locke's construal of personal identity was a notion compatible with diversity'. She believes that 'what is distinctive about each person is that each is a consciousness constituting an individuating center of consciousness'. This forces her, as it did Hooke, to make a sharp distinction between the executive self which possesses and processes memories and the passive memories themselves: 'we can imagine all too readily having memories other than our actual ones, or even having some other person's memories, but we would expect them to be incorporated into and had by our own individuating consciousness' (1983: 284). Her view (1983: 287) that 'our mental powers are all powers of some single cause' and produce 'a thoroughly integrated set of mental operations or behavior', makes Locke's view very similar to those traditional substantialist views of self which he is usually taken to have been attacking (but compare Winkler 1991: 222–3).

the consciousness of its past Existence', when such consciousness is lost 'beyond the power of ever retrieving again', may retain some other form of identity, such as identity of substance or identity of natural hu/man, but is not the same *person* as the earlier being (II.27.14; cf. II.27.20).[33]

33 Atherton (1983: 284–5), denying the importance of memory, has to interpret this in a very forced fashion. She argues that, 'when Locke is talking about amnesia', he is thinking not of things which you thought or did but cannot now remember, but of 'things you never thought or did and hence cannot remember' and which are not 'a part of you' because you could *never* have remembered them. There seems no independent reason to believe this, and the way in which Locke sets up his second description of the case (II.27.20), specifically asking us to 'suppose I wholly lose the memory of some parts of my Life, beyond a possibility of retrieving them', looks *prima facie* to confirm that the relevant actions or experiences have actually been forgotten (have once been available to memory, but are no longer).

8

The puzzle of survival

Introduction

John Locke chose neural spirits as an example ('remarquable sur cela', added his French translator Coste) of the 'imperfection of words', of how 'doubtful and uncertain in their significations' many of them are (Locke, *Essay* III.9.1). He told of a 'Question, whether any Liquor passed through the Filaments of the Nerves', which had arisen 'by chance' at a meeting he once attended of 'very Learned and ingenious Physicians' (III.9.16).

The historical, plain Locke, aware that many words 'may serve for Civil, but not for Philosophical use' (*Essay*, heading to III.9.15), required his colleagues to establish 'what the word Liquor signified' before they continue their debate. The philosopher-narrator achieves his aim of proving the signification 'not so settled and certain, as they had all imagined', since 'each of them made it a sign of a different complex *Idea*'. But his own wry judgement that 'liquor' is not one 'of the most perplexed names of Substances' is vindicated, for, after Locke has kindly helped them clear away the verbal undergrowth obscuring their ideas, it turns out that the physicians 'differed very little in their Opinions, concerning some fluid and subtile Matter, passing through the Conduits of the Nerves; though it was not so easy to agree whether it was to be called Liquor, or no, a thing which when each considered, he thought it not worth the contending about' (*Essay* III.9.16).

Locke plays down ontological commitment in favour of linguistic purity: but his story confirms widespread belief in spirituous yet material nervous transmission. I described in chapter 7 Locke's own uses of the animal spirits theory of memory: here I return directly to the ontology of spirits and to the problems about theoretical change I set up in chapter 2. Why did philosophers and others believe that nimble spirits flow incessantly through those 'hydraulicopneumatical engines we call human bodies' (Robert Boyle, in Rather 1965: 3)? What should historians of science do with 'spirits no one had seen but which all were certain existed' (Rousseau 1991: 218)? How could such a fantastical theory have survived so long into the rational and empirical modern age?

The puzzle intensifies: how, we wonder, could Locke's medical contemporaries accept nervous fluids, when we find that William Harvey, renowned as the first great modern physiologist, was a mocking sceptic about the fleeting spirits?[1] As is well known, Harvey had sought to disprove the existence of spirit familiars and thus of witches by dissecting a toad. He complained that spirits are multiplied needlessly by bad philosophers. Animal spirits are brought, like gods in machines, on to the stage of the body, to unravel the plot and to bring the catastrophe (Harvey 1649/1990: 115–20). In fact, from at least as early as 1616, Harvey had believed there to be no neural spirits, good or bad, or causing diseases as the 'schoolmen' think: 'spirits' only exist in the blood (1649/1990: 118; Frank 1980: 1–16, 38–42). Historians of Harvey's work have often assumed that his attack must have been successful. We hear of 'Harvey's refutation of the spirits' (Temkin 1973: 158), or that 'the theory of *pneuma* lost its sense and relevance' (Brown 1968/1982: 46; compare Goodfield 1960: 18–20). But, as I have shown, the drama of the spirits continued long after Harvey's death, and only took more intricate turns with the new philosophies. Why?

Two puzzles

I divide the question into two more specific puzzles, about the survival of the spirits, and about their eventual disappearance. I complained in chapter 2 about historians' tendency simply to assume that the theoretical replacement of primitive spirits by more scientific concepts was inevitable. Such a view, I suggested, fails to explain when, why, or how theory-change occurred, and to account for the attractions of the tenacious spirits.

So the first puzzle, which I address in this chapter, concerns the spirits' survival in the face of apparent empirical refutation. The oddity has been noted before: Jackson (1970: 403) wondered why 'the continuing failure to demonstrate an actual [nerve] fluid only very gradually turned people away from the use of this term'. But no explanation is at hand. John Wright (1980: 246), puzzled that even empiricists employed and argued for animal spirits, suggests one possible answer: 'perhaps the real explanation of [spirits theory's] resilience to experimental refutation lay in the need, felt by the leading thinkers of this time, to assign psychological functions to physiological processes'. This sensible answer is also given by L.S. Jacyna in an important recent survey of 'animal spirits and eighteenth-century British medicine' (1995: 157–8). But,

---

1 For a full, nuanced account of the motivations behind Harvey's attacks on Renaissance theories of medical spirits, see Bono 1995: 85–122.

as both Wright and Jacyna are aware, it is far from enough.[2] Leading critics of animal spirits were not necessarily hostile to physiology, and nothing dictated that, of all possible physiological entities, animal spirits in particular should be the key.

Although I raise below some other possible answers to the puzzle of the spirits' survival, none is fully satisfactory. This means that wider neuro-philosophical concerns about the spirits' role in preserving continuity of personal identity must be taken into account. The spirits had roles to play outside physiology, in debates about personal identity. In chapter 9 I show that their central place in accounts of moral control of one's own body, and in explaining tensions between physiology and morality, made them a ubiquitous theoretical foil in ongoing battles against confusion. The criteria for excellence of theory extended widely, well beyond the confines of what now look like 'internal' grounds.[3] Theory in physiology had practical and personal implications: knowing brain and body was a moral as well as a medical task.

The second puzzle, addressed in chapter 10 below, is this. Why did the eventual elimination of the spirits from neuroscientific ontology, from the 1740s on, occur *before* the advent of a clear alternative theory? This process was not an inevitable sloughing off of ancient neuromyths by scientists finally confident enough to jettison the venerable spirits before constructing a new, truly experimental theory of neural electricity. If this theory-change was indeed elimination, rather than reduction, its timing was due as much to changing moral and social ideals, the shifting normative expectations which neurophilosophy was meant to uphold, as to renewed attention to empirical doubts.

2 In his important survey, which I found too late for more extensive use in this book, Jacyna outlines a further candidate answer to the puzzle of survival. Like me, Jacyna thinks that the debate about nervous fluids 'did not . . . occur in a purely theoretical context' (1995: 149). He argues for the importance of practical medicine, suggesting that the traditions of talking about order, calm, and regularity in the spirits when diagnosing pathology and prescribing therapeutic remedies, made physicians comfortable in retaining spirits as theoretical entities (1995: 149–56): 'the doctrine of animal spirits readily accommodated key features of the system of "Bedside" medicine that was definitive of eighteenth-century practice' (1995: 158). There is no doubt about the importance to this problem of the social history of eighteenth-century medicine, and my brief remarks in chapter 9 about sensibility are, I think, compatible with Jacyna's suggestion. Yet neither of us has more than a hunch about what changes in medical practice might have contributed to the spirits' eventual elimination. In this short paper, Jacyna does not deal at all with the place of spirits in debates on the ontological status of hypothetical entities, or with the broader rhetorical roles of spirits in talk about the body and the self.

3 Reviewing the 'externalism/internalism' debate in the history of science, Shapin (1992) calls for attention to the boundaries constructed by historical actors between central, peripheral, and irrelevant concepts and issues. In this case, writers both for and against animal spirits threw the theoretical net wider than would later neurophysiologists; no clear line excluded moral implications from the justification conditions for physiological concepts.

Spirits: the case against

By the late seventeenth century, believers in spirits theory had a range of considerable obstacles to overcome. Despite its popularity, the theory of spirits and nervous fluids 'never enjoyed an unquestioned, unanimous support' (Pera 1992: 56). I examine a battery of objections to it, both logical and empirical. Some denied that nerves were hollow, as required for spirits to flow through; others complained that physical fluid spirits would be too inert to carry the commands of the will to the body's periphery as swiftly as action seems to follow from thought; a few experimentalists vainly sought indirect laboratory evidence for the spirits theory of muscular motion; and a number of natural philosophers questioned the theoretical need to postulate such problematic entities. I rely heavily on the work of modern historians of medicine to show that the many supporters of animal spirits must have had strong motivations for maintaining their beliefs (compare Jacyna 1995: 141–3 for another survey of challenges to the doctrine of spirits).

Hollow nerves

Despite their official invisibility, later seventeenth-century experimental neurophysiologists did embark on searches for the spirits. One strand was the search for nerve canals down which spirits were meant to flow (Flemyng 1751: 1–11). Antoni van Leeuwenhoek wrote to Oldenburg, in a letter published in the Royal Society's *Philosophical Transactions* of 1674, that he 'could find no hollowness' in the optic nerves of cows (in Brazier 1984: 35). But within a year he claimed to have seen 'a little pit' appear around the middle of the nerve, which pit, he imagines, 'Galen took for a cavity' (Brazier 1984: 35). By 1716, Leeuwenhoek claimed to have observed nerve canals 'often, and not without delight', but had 'been unable to display these cavities to anyone, for no sooner did I move them to my eyes for examination than almost immediately, in less than a minute, they dried out and contracted so that this astonishing sight wholly vanished beyond recall' (in Brazier 1984: 36).

This was received with some scepticism (E. Clarke 1968: 135–7), and most writers agreed with George Cheyne that the 'nervous Fluid has never been discovered in live animals by the Senses however assisted' (Cheyne 1705/1715: 306, in Yolton 1984b: 164). Doubts about hollow nerves led to doubts about their spirituous contents.

> How do you know that there are Animal Spirits at all? The Nerves, through which they are supposed to flow, are not hollow, made like Pipes, as Arteries, Veins, Lympheducts, Lacteals, and other Vessels, that are contriv'd to convey Liquids: They are solid Bodies like Strings, or Cords made up of many lesser Strings: No Liquid is found in them, nor have they any Cavity to contain it. Therefore this Business of the Animal Spirits is only a Dream. (Mandeville, *Treatise*, 3rd edn (1730), in Yolton 1984b: 168)

Disagreement over the hollowness of nerves became a popular feature of eighteenth-century neuroscience, as attention in general natural philosophy shifted from fluids to solids. But animal spirits did not stand or fall with hollow nerves alone. Solid-nerve theories did allow the application of forces by vibration, resonance, and impact without the use of fluids (chapter 10 below): but for Cheyne, for example, the solid-nerve hypothesis would alter our view not about the existence but simply about the nature of animal spirits. We would know them to be an 'infinitely subtle Spirit' which could pervade solid fibres 'with as much Facility as it would the most *pervious* Tubes' (Cheyne 1705/1715: 306, in Yolton 1984b: 164). Spirits could always be saved by turning them into even subtler matter. But in any case, as Clarke's survey shows (E. Clarke 1968: 137–9, 1978: 303), belief in hollow nerves survived far into the nineteenth century, well after animal spirits were either reduced or eliminated: so this could not have been a decisive objection.

The speed of thought

A second and related objection to the animal spirits theory of muscular motion was raised with increasing frequency during the eighteenth century. It started from the phenomenological absence of any temporal gap between willing and acting. Malcolm Flemyng, defending the nervous fluid, complained at the 'bugbear' of critics' harping on the celerity of the will (1751: 37). If I just decide to pick up my watch, the communication between soul and hand or centre and periphery seems to be almost instantaneous. How could particular spirit particles move from one end of a nerve to the other instantaneously if the nerves are fluid-filled? Even in cognitive activity, when the will wants something, its 'Volatile Messengers . . . are sent with unconceivable swiftness to penetrate every cranny of the Brain' (Mandeville 1711/1976: 158–9). Some thought that the vital messages of the will would not be carried to muscles or brain nooks fast enough, and calculated the velocity required of a nervous fluid (Brazier 1958: 206–7). It was, further, impossible to locate sensory and motor functions in the same hollow nerve, since fluids sent out from the brain would collide with spirits bringing news from the sensory periphery (Carlson and Simpson 1969: 103–4).

But these objections too were indecisive. Many were happy to separate sensory and motor neural functions. Flemyng grumbled that he had a right not to answer the objection from the metaphysics of the will, but went on to point out that the instantaneity of voluntary motion is only apparent, and that spirits theory did not require the *same* particular bit of fluid to travel all the way from brain to organ (1751: 26, 32, 34). Sound operates by waves, and the quickest voluntary motion is slower than sound (1751: 37). In 1783 Alexander Monro, whose father had, in 1729, listed objections to nervous fluids (Brazier 1958:

205–6), argued that the apparent inertness of neural spirits was no reason to deny that they serve 'the offices performed by the nerves'. His analogy was with the production of complexity from simplicity in reproductive physiology: 'the secretion and mixture of the fluids of the testes and ovaria' produces even more incomprehensible effects, so simple fluids in nerve ducts can give rise to flexible action (Monro 1783: 74–6).

Experiments in inflation

The inaccessibility of animal spirits to empirical investigation was not, however, universally accepted. Indeed there seems to have existed experimental evidence against them from the 1660s or 1670s (Mazzolini 1991: 81). English physiologists like Charleton had expressed doubts about the idea (common to Descartes and traditional spirits theorists) that muscular motion results from the inflation of a muscle by an influx of nervous fluid, and experiments in the late 1660s by Goddard and Glisson failed to find any increased volume in arm muscles on contraction (Brazier 1984: 55–9; Nayler 1993: 322–34). Glisson was sympathetic to a chemical interpretation of active spirits (Clericuzio 1994: 59–60), but developed an account of muscular motion, without reference to the spirits, which required nerves to learn the brain's commands directly (Henry 1987).

Jan Swammerdam, who had studied under Sylvius at Leiden and knew Cartesian physiology well, followed Descartes in interpreting 'the old animal spirit, passing from nerves into muscle, as a very subtle but material fluid' (Winsor 1976: 170). In an experiment which became classic only later, he tested the Cartesian idea that spirits flow into a muscle during contraction. While the enclosed nerve muscle on which Swammerdam stimulated contraction changed its shape, there was no increase in its volume. So whatever the 'supposed animal spirits' were that caused contraction, they do not inflate the muscle. Swammerdam claimed that 'no matter of sensible or comprehensible bulk flows through the nerves into the muscles' (Brazier 1984: 42–4 includes Swammerdam's illustration). The only possible empirical test for spirits resulted unambiguously in failure.

Against hypothetical constructs

Swammerdam's experimental critique supported a theoretical challenge to animal spirits by his intimate friend, the future bishop, Nicolaus Steno, who would discover the principle of superposition in geology (Gould 1983/1990). Steno questioned the excesses of Cartesian physiological speculation in a 1665 Paris lecture (Steno 1669/1965; Rome 1956; Brazier 1958: 204; Scherz 1965, 1976; Nayler 1993: 226–87). The ontological status of spirits is unclear, for nothing is known of similarities and differences between fluids in anatomically distinct parts of the body.

Nor is it known whether any of these fluids are really like any one of the fluids so far known to us. Animal spirits, the more subtle part of the blood, the vapour of blood, and the juice of the nerves, these are names used by many, but they are mere words, meaning nothing. (In Brazier 1984: 50; compare Djørup 1968)

Steno sought a purer form of mechanism, purged of ambiguous spirits. His own theory of muscular motion, published in 1667, was geometrical in form and did not rely on uncertain inflation: good physiology would agree with Descartes in principle and Swammerdam in fact (Brown 1968/1982: 91–9; Kardel 1994a).

Descartes had defended the postulation of theoretical constructs in physiology by relying on analogies between the insensible parts of the body-machine and the larger parts of artificial machines. Parts which 'because of their smallness are invisible' can be made known through 'the movements which depend on them' (Descartes, L'Homme, AT xi.121, H 4, CSM 1.99). French Cartesians responded to general attacks on micromechanical speculation by emphasising the hypothetical nature of their claims (D. Clarke 1989: 152–6, 162–3, 186).[4] But the critics were accepting Descartes' terms, not simply rejecting the intelligibility of insensible entities. Swammerdam and Steno did not expect to be able to see the spirits, even with the aid of a microscope. Swammerdam looked for indirect confirmation of the theory in Cartesian fashion, seeking facts about small parts by examining the movements which allegedly depend on them, while Steno found no place for animal spirits in the range of existing sciences of fluids. Did these considerations not conclusively end the spirits' career?

Theoretical retention

Marielene Putscher, in an impressive survey of ancient and Renaissance theories of spiritus and pneuma, refers to 'the end of the pneuma-doctrine in the 17th century' (1973: 77, 94–6). Her list of relevant works includes only three books published between 1680 and 1700, and only three after 1700 (1973: 209–33). This might suggest the rejection of animal spirits in a new scientific age. But, as I have indicated, the impression is misleading, and is an artefact of Putscher's expertise in earlier periods rather than a reflection of the historical disappearance of the spirits. In fact, 'the doctrine of animal spirits did not succumb to the attacks made upon it' (Jacyna 1995: 143), and eighteenth-century physiologists, as other surveys make clear, were, if anything, even more occupied with problems about nervous fluids and spirits than their predecessors (Rothschuh

---

4 Rohault, in a textbook which remained influential among eighteenth-century Newtonians, agreed that Descartes' account of the formation of the spirits from blood involves untestable assumptions, postulating as it does 'yet another Sort of Matter not to be perceived by the Senses': but 'that there are such [spirits] cannot be doubted' (1723/1969: 271; compare D. Clarke 1989: 156). Thanks to Trevor McClaughlin for help here.

1958: 2963–8; Foucault 1972: 226–316, (trans. 1965: 85–158); Rousseau 1976, 1989). The century's most celebrated physiologists, Boerhaave and von Haller, strongly defended nervous fluids, Haller undertaking an extensive history of the doctrine before arguing for the existence of spirits as mobile, subtle, and invisible rapidly flowing fluids (Hoff 1936: 163–8; Lindeboom 1974; Pera 1992: 55–9). The Encyclopédie article 'nerf', by Jaucourt, retained nervous juices in preference to vibrations (Starobinski 1966: 177–80). William Cullen's physiology, towards the end of the eighteenth century, was based more on solids, but still retained a central role for neural fluid (Riese 1959: 52–8; Jackson 1986: 124–8; Wright 1990: 292–301).

So despite all complaints about the unsuitability of spirits, and despite various alternative forces, vibrations, and ethers, the spirits hung on in. Why? Marcello Pera (1992: 56) complains that the defence of spirits in both Boerhaave and Haller is obviously unsatisfactory, 'regressive reasoning' which seeks to establish the properties of spirits on the assumption that some such fluid must exist: their 'regressive method . . . took as its starting point the very phenomena it should have explained'. If Swammerdam's experiments 'refuted' and 'destroyed' theories of nervous fluids (Singer and Underwood 1962: 134, 140), why do we find rational physiologists continuing to succumb to the seductions of the spirits?

It is not, as I initially thought, that the attacks failed to reach their audience.[5] Swammerdam's experiment was only published by Boerhaave in the 1730s and translated into English in 1758, and the dissemination of his ideas is hard to trace (Schulte 1968). But it seems likely that Locke, for instance, was aware of his work: Locke owned four of Swammerdam's published works (as well as four of Steno's), was a member of the Amsterdam College to which Swammerdam had belonged, and visited Swammerdam's museum in 1684, four years after Swammerdam's death (Harrison and Laslett 1971: 239, 242; Colie 1960/1990; Rupp 1990: 276; Dewhurst 1963).[6] Steno was active in European physiological correspondence: his research was praised by Oldenburg in the Royal Society Philosophical Transactions of the late 1660s, and Hooke as curator of experiments was asked to replicate some of Steno's methods (Brown 1968/1982: 104–21). The September 1669 Transactions recommends Steno's Discours sur l'anatomie de cerveau, the newly published version of his 1665 attack on Descartes' nerve fluids (Rome 1956: 260–1). Borelli tried to

---

5 Although Franklin Fearing (1929: 384) was unfair in complaining that (in addition to 'an anatomy the details of which were largely imaginary') Descartes's 'major error' in retaining animal spirits was due to his 'ignorance of the work of his contemporary [sic], the Dutch naturalist, Jan Swammerdam'. Swammerdam was born in 1637, only thirteen years before Descartes' death.

6 In 1686, Locke did meet Leeuwenhoek, who showed him 'some red blood cells, a human tooth, and the spermatozoa of a dog' (in Dewhurst 1963: 229).

bypass the negative results of the inflation experiments with new geometrical models in which inflation occurs only within a complex structure of massed chains of rhombs in muscle fibre:[7] so when Steno visited Italy in 1666–7, his disagreements over nervous spirits with Borelli and Bellini were eagerly followed. William Croone had met Steno in Montpellier in 1665, and they corresponded: Steno's 1667 work on muscular motion halted Croone's revision of his own 1664 book (Rome 1956: 245–53; Wilson 1961: 164–5; Kardel 1994a: 23–37).[8] Hooke addressed Steno's work in both geology and muscle physiology (Brown 1971). So English as well as Continental theorists, it seems, should have been further swayed by the critics.[9]

The invisible world

An answer about the puzzle of spirits' survival can start with two thoughts about the Swammerdam/Steno critique, to do with observability and with explanatory ambition. Firstly, Swammerdam himself did not interpret his own experiments as proving that there are no animal spirits: instead he argued that, if matter does flow through the nerves, it must be *completely* insensible, its effects below the threshold of measurement (Winsor 1976: 170). Neither experiment nor the new microscopy could resolve decisively the ontological issue (Brazier 1958: 202). Nayler concludes her vast analysis of theories of muscular motion by denying the possibility of a crucial experiment on the inflation hypothesis and the existence of animal spirits (1993: 579); Kardel (1994a: 47–57) believes that only new computer-modelling techniques allow full appreciation of Steno's detailed theories.

The problem was not just that spirits dissipate on removal from the living nerve, or that Hooke's advice in Observation 43 of *Micrographia* to avoid putting Nature into disorder by experimental violence, and instead to 'quietly peep in at the window, without frighting her out of her usual byas' ('Espinasse 1956: 58; Guerrini 1989) could hardly be applied to animal spirits. It was still open to corpuscularian spirits theorists to argue that the wonderful invisible world

---

7 Borelli had been disappointed at *L'Homme* on its publication in 1662, considering that he had already taken mechanistic physiology further than Descartes by attempting geometrical models which would aid quantification (Brown 1968/1982: 82–91).

8 Wilson (1961: 164) claims that Croone 'altered the concepts of spirit from that of a vague and ethereal wind to that of a definite physical juice and thereby made them susceptible to observation and reason': however, there does not seem to be any evidence that Croone became the only person ever to see animal spirits.

9 An early response to Steno was John Mayow's attempt to render animal spirits static, and attribute the turbulence which causes physiological and psychological disorder instead to other bodily substances. Responding to Steno's denial of inflation, Mayow argued that animal spirits never change, but that they are affected by the volatile 'nitro-aerial spirit' which can 'penetrate deep into the brain and perturb the animal spirits' (Mayow 1674/1957: 233, 251, 280). Mayow renders animal spirits so 'ethereal' that he rules out a theory of memory, for they are 'so slender that they are at once dissipated and leave no vestige of themselves' (p. 252). On nitro-aerial spirit see Frank 1980; Clericuzio 1994.

recently opened up by microscopes concealed yet further depths. The young Robert Boyle spent more time on anatomy, 'conversing with dead and stinking Carkases', than he would later. He thought that the hairs on a mite's leg must themselves be composed of 'unimaginably little' parts, and asked 'how much more subtle must be the animal spirits that run to and from in nerves suitable to such little legs?' ('Of Atoms' (1650), quoted by Frank 1980: 95).[10] Henry Power in 1664 likewise wrote of subtle animal spirits running to and fro in the 'prodigiously little spindle-shank'd leggs' of mites in cheese (*Experimental Philosophy*, in Vickers 1987: 92). As in debates about the preformation of embryos (Roe 1981: 45–88), inability to see or measure postulated entities could always be deflected by reference to human sensory limitation.

Without the spirits . . .

There may be a second reason for the spirits' survival beyond the Swammerdam/Steno critique. Steno's antipathy to theoretical entities and hypothesising left certain areas of physiology and neurophilosophy all but inaccessible. K.D. Keele (1967: 199) comments on Steno's rational critique of Thomas Willis' rash speculations on cerebral spirits: 'Steno was right: so right indeed that he himself made no other contribution to cerebral physiology. He abandoned the physiology of the brain as a mystery known only to God.'[11] Despite their commitment to mechanism in muscle physiology, neither Steno nor Swammerdam wanted to pursue mechanistic accounts of cognitive function: they turned, respectively, to Catholicism and to Antoinette Bourignon's charismatic religion.[12] Spirits theory had never been restricted in domain to muscle physiology, and the realms of cognition, perception, memory, emotion, and so on, remained irresistible to natural philosophers of other persuasions.

It is not quite the case that those who rejected animal spirits were thereby restricted to theorising muscular motion alone: Hartley would employ Newtonian vibrations (rather than spirits) in sophisticated accounts of memory and other cognitive functions. But animal spirits did encourage flirtation with suggestive metaphors which were unavailable to critics. This raises

---

10 On Boyle's uses of animal spirits see MacIntosh (1983: 332), who quotes a reference in Boyle's *Languid and Unheeded Motion* (1685), to 'minute' and 'invisible' animal spirits of which 'prying Anatomists have not been able in dissected Nerves to discern so much as the channels, through which they pass' (Boyle 1772/1968: IV: 34).

11 The point that Steno's discourse had a 'shattering effect' on European neuroscience was made by Max Neuburger: see Meyer and Hierons 1965: 147. On Willis and Steno, compare Bynum 1973: 458.

12 I do not intend here to make the psychological claim, for either of the two men, that there were direct causal connections between their attitudes to religion, to metaphysics, and to theoretical entities in physiology. But at least nothing in two outstanding recent studies rules out such connections: see Kardel 1994b on Steno, and Ruestow 1996: 105–45 on Swammerdam.

an irksomely evaluative question for the historian of neurophilosophy, which forces an attitude towards our current mind/brain sciences. Was this retreat from neurocognitive explanatory ambition a necessary theoretical purification, the abandonment of metaphorical language which could only be 'a deterrent to the development of a more scientific hypothesis of nervous action' (Brazier 1958: 203)? Or was the establishment of a more insulated and isolated neuroscientific discourse an unnecessary prudery, the cowardly refusal to countenance microstructures of cognition?

'Newtonian' physiology is a useful test case. Newton's authority buttressed scepticism about spirits by enforcing positivist caution about hypothetical entities: Mary Brazier (1958: 204) tells us that Newton, 'the greatest scientist of his time', found animal spirits theory to be 'not acceptable'. Newton's early interest in memory and imagination was coupled with doubts about the evidence for animal spirits (McGuire and Tamny 1983: 487–8; Newton to Oldenburg 1675, in Turnbull 1959: 366–70): he retreated, like Steno, from cognitive theory, and later reinterpreted animal spirits in line with his changing views on ethers (Iliffe 1995: 445–51). The views on spirits of eighteenth-century followers of Newton are hard to interpret, but it is clear that many were aware of the potential threat which uncontrolled mechanical neural processes posed to reason, and constructed their physiology to suit what Iliffe calls a 'theological politics of self' (1995: 453–8). Some rejected the 'received Opinion' about spirit's role in muscular motion, complaining that 'such a Fluid is altogether unfit for such work' and preferring vibrations, since 'Sir Isaac Newton is of [that] opinion' (Bryan Robinson, in Hoff 1936: 165): others retained nerve fluids reconstrued as non-mechanical active principles; for example, during the 1740s, Richard Mead saw melancholy as 'alterations . . . in that active liquor, by which the mind governs the body' (Jackson 1986: 123–4). Just as Newtonian cosmologists denied the need for Cartesian vortices and other hidden causes simply to cover apparent gravitational action at a distance, preferring just to describe observed phenomena (Hesse 1961/1970: chs. 6–7), so the tendency of Newtonian physiology was to deny, or at least neglect, theoretical need for hidden neural processes to fill the temporal distance between past and present which memory bridges.

The institutional and rhetorical success of Newton's disciples in many fields (Schaffer 1980: 58–71, 1990; Shapin 1980) did not extend to physiology, where the desired mix of mathematical analysis and experimental manipulation failed. Attempts to quantify by transporting physical formulae to the life and cognitive sciences had limited application: James Keill and Stephen Hales integrated experiment and number in limited domains, but Thomas Morgan's 1725 description of imagination (force) as the product of nerves (mass) and animal spirits (acceleration) was wishful (Rousseau 1969/1991: 11). Pitcairne's programme for establishing the 'Laws and Properties of the Fluids and Canals of Human Bodies' was meant to purge physiology of the 'uncertain wandering' of multiple bodily fluids and other poetic fictions, but foundered on the difficulty of quantification, remaining 'more Cartesian than "Newtonian" (Brown 1968/1982: 192–237; Guerrini 1987). The 'Newtonianism' in Richard Mead's physiology was, likewise, 'spurious' (Coleman 1970: 328). Brown's history of the movement (1968/1982: 308–53, 1987) ends with a loss of direction and 'sudden demise of Newtonian physiology' in the 1730s.

We can, then, construct from the Newtonian case a bare hint of an answer to the puzzle of the spirits' survival. Those who remained true to the ideal of freedom from hypothesis and cared little for invisible body fluids found theorising beyond muscular motion all but impossible. Perhaps, despite the experimental and conceptual objections to animal spirits, the theory survived because of the possibilities it opened, in physiology and culture, for connecting domains that more sober approaches just could not reach. The very linguistic and conceptual confusions and conflations at which cautious critics carped were the sources of the enabling discursive power of spirits talk. Such talk permitted theorists to approach cognition without dreaming of a language purged of body, culture, and context, and immediately raised important, difficult, and resistant questions about order and chaos in self, memory, and mind.

If there is anything in this diagnosis, and animal spirits survived in part because of their rhetorical uses, it should be the case that change in the cultural image of the cognitive functions they were meant to underpin would affect their fate. Chapter 10 below suggests that the timing of the spirits' decline depended in part on increased awareness that they could not play the required extraphysiological roles. Eighteenth-century assumptions and ideals about memory and personal identity would sit less and less well with animal spirits, beating and ferreting around the brain with rare and random violence. Before returning to the ontological narrative, I attempt a final sketch of the wider cultural setting.

9
Spirits, body, and self

If we want to know what the eighteenth century most profoundly valued or despised in all aspects of culture, then we must examine its fearful disdain of mixtures.

(Barbara Maria Stafford 1991: 211)

This I thinke that haveing often recourse to ones memory and tieing downe the minde strictly to the recollecting things past precisely as they were may be a meanes to check those extravagant or turning flights of the imagination.

(John Locke's journal, 22 January 1678, in Dewhurst 1963: 101)

We have to do with men for the most part whose soul is the great object of their regard; but let them not forget they have a body.

(John Hill 1766/1969: 33, in Deutsch 1994: 26)

9.1 Introduction: the hurry of the spirits

Joseph Glanvill (chapter 5 above) feared that overdependence on hurried spirits in normal cognition would condemn memory to be more confused 'than our Mid-night Compositions'. The imposition of ill-sorted ideas on the mind internalises the uncanny, but by physiological means. The supernaturalising of the mind in which Romantics would revel (Castle 1988: 52) already occurred in disruptions of 'natural' order among ideas to which ill-disciplined neural fluids were prone. Historians of early eighteenth-century literature describe the peculiar amalgam of disgust and desire with which satirists treated their innards: transgressive internal processes were indulgently deployed while poets preached probity and rejected disorder, only to rediscover in themselves the shock of grotesque and motley spirits (Stallybrass and White 1986: 103–8, 113).

During a long illness in 1712 and 1713, Isaac Watts composed a sequence on sickness and recovery, including a poem on 'the Hurry of the Spirits, in a Fever and Nervous Disorders'.[1] Suffering 'the disorderly Ferments of natural Spirits' (1734: 172), he finds that 'this Flesh, this circling Blood' and all his bodily

---

1 After a prose introduction, which was apparently written when preparing 'Sickness and Recovery' for publication some twenty years later, the sequence comprises the following poems: 'The Hurry of the Spirits, in a Fever and Nervous Disorders' (Watts 1734: 172–4); 'Peace of Conscience and Prayer for Health' (1734: 174–7); 'Encourag'd to Hope for Health in May' (1734: 177–9); 'The Wearisome Weeks of Sickness. 1712, or 1713' (1734: 180–1); and 'A Hymn of Praise for Recovery' (1734: 181–3). For a general discussion of Watts' writings and philosophy see Hoyles 1971: 141–250.

powers easily 'turn Rebels to the Mind' (1734: 173). 'Strange Images' rise upon him physiologically induced:

> The Engine rules the Man.
> Unhappy Change! When Nature's meaner Springs
> Fir'd to impetuous Ferments break all Order;
> When little restless Atomes rise and reign
> Tyrants in Sovereign Uproar, and impose
> Ideas on the Mind; confus'd Ideas
> Of Non-existents and Impossibles,
> Who can describe them? Fragments of old Dreams,
> Borrow'd from Midnight, torn from Fairy Fields
> And Fairy Skies, and Regions of the Dead,
> Abrupt, ill-sorted. O 'tis all Confusion!
>
> (1734: 173)

Watts officially deplores the 'strange wild convulsive Force' which overtakes him while 'all the poor Machine / lies fluttering' (1734: 177–8). Like Cartesian cyborgs, this fluttering pulsing engine is an unusual machine. The noted hymnographer thanks God that 'amidst all the Violence of my Distemper . . . I never lost Sight of Reason or Religion' (1734: 172), and takes the opportunity of illness to seek out sins in 'the Plies, the Folds, / And hollow winding Caverns of the Heart' (1734: 182). Meanders of a moralised heart are safer than the folds of the brain: its scene is distantly eschatological, whereas spirits and nerves play with abrupt ideas in the present. He reassured himself, a 'creeping Worm' under the sway of 'each noxious Juice' in his 'vital Humours' (1734: 175), with the (odd) knowledge that God's

> Eyelids mark'd my painful Toil,
> The wild Confusions of my shatter'd Powers,
> And broken fluttering Thoughts.
>
> (1734: 176)

Watts elsewhere defends the substantial immaterial soul against Locke's 'shifting and changeable principle' of memory (Fox 1988: 57–66). For him, in the end, the 'tottering Body' is subject only to the 'Divine Physician' (Watts 1734: 182); meanwhile he is

> bound to bear the Agonies and Woes
> That sickly Flesh and shatter'd Nerves impose.
>
> (1734: 181)

But in this chapter I show that problems about the interdependence of self, memory, and spirits were common to Lockeans and anti-Lockean substantialists alike. In any bodily context, with health, passions, diet, or brain at issue, even the essentialists' thinking substance required unlikely docility from its fluid vehicles.

The wistful dreamy violence in Watts' descriptions of fevered altered states acknowledges certain seductions of the wild confusions caused by disordered spirits. The written memory of his broken thoughts, distanced in publication twenty years later among other 'miscellaneous thoughts . . . written chiefly in Younger Years' (1734: title page), is in part nostalgia for brief psychophysiological chaos. The unexceptional poem catches a historical crux in attitudes to physiology. It falters between moralistic exhortation 'to calm the Tumult and command my Thoughts' and fascination with the 'strange Commotion' in his 'inmost Centre', the 'endless Medley' of images which

> rush upon the Stage,
> And dance and riot wild in Reason's Court
> Above control.

(1734: 173)

The eighteenth-century neurophilosophical writer will be caught between the desire to be violated by the excesses of his own body, to be 'caught up into the Storm, and ride the Wind', and the fear of being left 'helpless' and 'beyond the Ken of Shore' as restless atoms break all order and 'the throne of reason shakes' (1734: 173–4).

It is pleasurable, in a world where rationality and morality are hard to maintain, to surrender to images 'above control' (1734: 173). Associated ideas will 'follow one another . . . without any care or attention' (Locke, Essay II.33.6): in despair at the failures of reason, Hume would find, wonderfully inverting Locke's nervous point, that 'carelessness and in-attention alone can afford us any remedy. For this reason I rely entirely on them' (Hume, Treatise I.iv.2: 218).

But the orthodox philosopher and poet Watts, in contrast, keeps an eye on reason and religion even in fever. The claim to be doing so licenses ongoing flirtation with loss of control over his own brain and memories. In this chapter I examine various unwholesome but enticing associations of the animal spirits, which helped to keep them in theoretical circulation. The topic is a series of internal tensions in models of psychophysiological self-control. Eighteenth-century men, in England at least, increasingly sought to escape their own minds, to flee from memory and animal spirits. G.S. Rousseau argues (1969/1991: 10) that it was neurophysiology that unseated eighteenth-century ideology from traditions of order: I flesh out this claim by widening the philosophical and cultural domains of reference of the petulant spirits. They work incessantly to level optimistically rigid distinctions between rational mental discipline and sex, madness, or unreason, suggesting that, if there is to be fragile order in cognition, it must arise as much from body, belly, and brain as from mind and will.

'The Hurry of the Spirits', significantly, ends with rhythmic and moralistic weightiness. The final two lines destroy the ambiguity, denying the incitements of confusion in a wishful imposition of discipline. There is to be no doubt that, in the normal, sound state, God is on the side of the ruling mind.

> Ah, when will these tumultuous Scenes be gone?
> When shall this weary Spirit, tossed with Tempests,
> Harrassed and broken, reach the Port of Rest,
> And hold it firm? When shall this wayward Flesh
> With all th'irregular Springs of vital Movement
> Ungovernable, return to sacred Order,
> And pay their Duties to the ruling Mind?
>
> (1734: 174)

In subsequent chapters, I trace the course of various attempts, historical and modern, theoretically to return the wayward flesh to order and impose the rule of mind on the hurry of distributed memory traces. But first I sketch failures in both Cartesian and Lockean attempts to mould memory and brain to the safe maintenance of moral identity.[2] The recurrent problem is uncertainty over the control and causation of motions of animal spirits, and of the ideas which accompany them. How is 'moral Man' to know if his ideas proceed from appropriate causes, if his true Self is the unique originating cause of thought and action, or if his cognition is riddled with physiological and cultural influences beyond his ken? Theory is moulded, in part, by social and personal desires not to be certain sorts of persons, to keep a safe distance from those (women, enthusiasts, fanatics, sectarians, dreamers) who give in to roaming animal spirits, to charismatic religion, to libidinal excess, who fail to impose the rule of mind on rioting spirits and to trample bodily commotions.

9.2 Contagions of the imagination

Cognition meets culture in late seventeenth- and early eighteenth-century attitudes to animal spirits theories of memory and mental life. Some, like the 'French prophets' studied by Hillel Schwartz (1978: 73–4), found that, in their ecstatic transports and creative remembering, they could 'glory in confusion'. Their critics, on the other hand, 'viewed memory as conservative; memory maintained the proper distance between events, and their proper sequence' (1978: 75). This rhetorical distinction between chaos and order was often invoked in debates on the fringes of physiological philosophy: norms of social and individual behaviour and thought came to be seen as threatened by invidious neurophilosophy. The fear is that irregular motions of ruffled animal

---

2 Lockeans who made memory central to personal identity were not so distinct in practice from Cartesians and other substantialists (compare Coleridge 1801/1990: 261, 266–7): both camps saw defects of memory and physiology as cause for moral concern. Even anti-Lockeans who denied the relevance of memory for deciding personal identity at the Resurrection needed secular links between present and past.

spirits will cut off the transparent past, renewing only 'many confus'd Ideas of things past' in the 'Emporium of the Brain' (Purcell, A Treatise on Vapours (1702), in DePorte 1974: 8).

The stakes were high. By the late eighteenth century, Scots 'common-sense' philosophers would need to assert heavily the stability and dependability of memory, and the unity and continuity of personal identity. They make the social and moral importance of psychological questions manifest. James Beattie in 1770 writes that: 'to a man who doubts the individuality or identity of his own mind, virtue, truth, religion, good and evil, hope and fear, are absolutely nothing' (in Cox 1980: 21). Thomas Reid in turn denies that any 'sound' man can confuse memory and imagination, since belief accompanies only the former. Truth just goes along with, and only with, the phenomenological experience of remembering:

> Perhaps in infancy, or in a disorder of mind, things remembered may be confounded with those which are merely imagined, but in mature years, and in a sound state of mind, every man feels that he must believe what he distinctly remembers, though he can give no other reason of his belief, but that he remembers the thing distinctly; whereas, when he merely imagines a thing ever so distinctly, he has no belief of it upon that account. (Reid, Essays III.1: 340)

I look at Reid's attacks on neurophilosophy in chapter 14: but it is already clear why these philosophers would want to distance memory from physiology, and to distance personal identity from memory. Stability in memory or in identity was an achievement, gained at the cost of abandoning the fleeting animal spirits over the course of the eighteenth century. Patricia Meyer Spacks (1976: 4) takes this passage from Reid at face value as representative of a 'general faith in memory' in eighteenth-century philosophy.[3] But attention to discussions of memory, imagination, and association reveals that, while others might have liked to share Reid's confidence, their empirical views made it desperately difficult to do so.

Memory and imagination
Beyond the absurdity with which animal spirits threatened to taint Locke's account of the person, there is a further tension in any attempt to found on memory a forensic concept of personal identity. If the rational agent is to rely in

---

3 Spacks rightly notes a dichotomy in philosophic texts between 'the undependability of imagination' and 'the solidity of memory' (1976: 4), but does not see that confidence in the latter was undermined in philosophy as well as literature. Her judgement that 'eighteenth century philosophers . . . strikingly concur in their reluctance to wonder seriously about the reliability of memory' (1976: 3) is hasty, forcing her to ask 'did they ignore their own experience of fallibility? or was it different from ours?' In fact it was not only in autobiographical and fictional texts that memory's reliability was challenged: the physiological theories which underpinned philosophical psychology did the job too.

action on his consciousness as it extends backwards into the past (*Essay* II.27.9), he needs some principled way to distinguish genuine, veridical memory (of what really happened) from mere confabulation or spurious reconstruction.

This is one source of obsessive philosophical attempts to find some internal, phenomenological criterion to demarcate memory from imagination. Hume tried to do it by attaching special feelings of vivacity and liveliness to the uniquely ordered ideas of the memory (*Treatise* I.i.3: 8–10; I.iii.5: 84–6; appendix, pp. 627–8).[4] Memory is 'ty'd down' to preserving the original 'order and position' of ideas: any failure to do so is a 'defect or imperfection in that faculty', whereas imagination has a liberty 'to transpose and change its ideas' (*Treatise* I.i.3: 9–10; I.iii.5: 85). In imagination, as evidenced by fables, poems, and romances, 'nature . . . is totally confounded, and nothing mentioned but winged horses, fiery dragons, and monstrous giants' (I.i.3: 10). The fluttering contents of Hume's baroque imagination, torn, like Watts', 'from Fairy Fields', echo Descartes' *L'Homme*. Descartes' *unified* account of memory and imagination explains (i) the reconstruction of traces which have previously been formed, (ii) the return of past things to thought 'as if by chance', and (iii) the formation of 'chimeras and hypogryphs' in the imaginations of those 'who let their fancy wander listlessly' (AT xi. 178, 184, H 87–8, 96).

Hume recognises that the preservation of order in ideas cannot distinguish memory from imagination, for we have no independent, non-circular, recall of past impressions to check whether the arrangement and sorting of the present impressions 'be exactly similar'. So he retreats to a second criterion, based on the 'superior force and vivacity' of memory ideas (*Treatise* I.iii.5: 85). Ideas in memory are lively, strong, and forcible, where ideas in imagination are faint, languid, 'and cannot without difficulty be preserv'd long by the mind steddy and uniform for any considerable time' (I.i.3: 9). But although this distinction is reiterated with some confidence in the appendix (p. 628), Hume undermines its plausibility himself. He acknowledges that 'we are frequently in doubt concerning the ideas of the memory, as they become very weak and feeble; and are at a loss to determine whether any image proceeds from the fancy or the memory' (I.iii.5: 85). I may be imagining when I think I am remembering, and remembering when I think I am imagining, since force and vivacity are not uniquely attached to memory ideas. The fact that vivid ideas bring with them belief or assent cannot *guarantee* their veridicality (I.iii.5: 85–6).

This is not surprising in the perspective of distributed models of memory. Hinton, McClelland, and Rumelhart note

---

4   For criticism and analysis see Flage 1985a, 1985b; Traiger 1985; Johnson 1987. Traiger
    alone thinks that Hume may not have needed a sharp distinction. None of these writers
    mentions the physiological bases of memory.

there is no sharp distinction between genuine memory and plausible reconstruction. A genuine memory is a pattern that is stable because the inference rules were modified when it occurred before. A 'confabulation' is a pattern that is stable because of the way the inference rules have been modified to store several different previous patterns. So far as the subject is concerned, this may be indistinguishable from the real thing. (1986: 81)

We all know that 'a subjective experience of remembering can be simultaneously compelling and dead wrong' (Schacter 1996: 129). Yet Russell, in turn, would try to engineer a clear distinction by attaching to memory ideas implausible feelings of familiarity and pastness (1921: 157–87). Subsequent concern in analytic philosophy about justifying knowledge of the past against sceptical challenges is a further consequence of the perceived need for such a distinction. But there may not be *subjective* criteria to tell veridical remembering from confabulation.

Imagination, then, can confound and deceive, upsetting the order of past events, and sometimes presenting 'ill-sorted' ideas as forcibly as does memory. The vigorous spirits, unfortunately for the moral philosopher, threaten to pull physiology and self apart by inciting plausible but improper and irrational imaginings. Without a way to keep memory distinct from imagination, the peculiar sanctity of memory's access to a real past seems reduced to mere confabulation. Descartes had already raised the alarm about morally damaging effects of physiological preservation of those traces which correspond to thoughts 'on which it is not good to dwell' (*Passions* II.74, AT xi.383, CSM I. 354). Fears about the perversions of reason which can arise from various corporeal sources come to occur in both Cartesian and empiricist traditions.[5] The concerns are intimately at once about the lure of factual errors, and the seductions of morally impure ideas and memories.

Techniques for controlling the brain: purity and danger

I have already discussed the extension of Descartes' distributed model of memory by Malebranche, who was Locke and Hume's source (chapter 3, appendix 2). Before treating memory directly, Malebranche tried to explain the distinction between veridical perception and imagination. Agitation by the spirits of the fibres leading to the brain is sufficient for the soul to have perceptions. Imagining occurs when the flow of animal spirits disturbs the fibres *without* the presence of the object. But this was the definition of *memory*, not imagination, given by Descartes in *L'Homme* (AT xi.178, H 87–8, CSM I.107). The shock of neurophilosophical models of memory is that they make memory the *work* or production of imagination.[6] Remembering too is both creation and loss.

---

5 For a general discussion of the relation between error and physiology in early modern philosophy see Ayers 1994: sect. 2.
6 'No imagination without memory; no memory without imagination' (Diderot, in Huet 1993: 103).

Fortunately, Malebranche retorts, it usually happens that the fibres 'are agitated much more by the impressions of objects than by the flow of spirits' (LO 88, II.1.1.i), and we can thereby distinguish perception from imagination. As Hume would, Malebranche hopes that the agitation of fibres is stronger in genuine cases of remembering. But the prospects are not good. Malebranche continues:

> However it sometimes happens that persons whose animal spirits are highly agitated by fasting, vigils, a high fever, or some violent passion have the internal fibers of their brain set in motion as forcefully as by external objects. Because of this such people *sense* what they should only *imagine*, and they think they see objects before their eyes, which are only in their imaginations. (LO 88, II.1.1.i)

The list of contextual factors which can disrupt the spirits and confuse the mind is growing. As well as disease and fever (for Malebranche in theory as for Watts in practice), oddities of diet, of religious behaviour and feeling, and of emotional extremity can all cause unnatural internal turbulence and consequent error. We can add diseased or contagious imagination, and also fright or shock, after which, wrote Richard Blackmore (1725: 31), animal spirits are 'impelled into confused Motions, and their Ranks and Connexion broken or ruffled'. Animal spirits flow, after so many years, in bodies still as embedded in material and social worlds, still as open and vulnerable to environment and culture, as the bodies described by earlier medical theories in the language of the non-naturals (chapter 2 above). What contexts, we may wonder, are safe? Whence cognitive purity, among so many forms of danger?

Malebranche warns against the seduction of youth by the wonders of poetry and science. The young man (*sic*) 'must always guard the purity of his imagination, i.e., he must prevent those dangerous traces that corrupt the heart and mind from being formed in the brain' (LO 388, v.8). The animal spirits, which receive 'many secret directives from the passions' and 'are easily diverted from the new and difficult channels into which the will would lead them' (LO 386, v.8), must be controlled. How? The will, which we often find 'exhausting itself in controlling the unruly spirits' (LO 386, v.8), is not sufficient itself; it must trick the imagination 'in order to stir the spirits' by using 'cleverness' and 'stratagems to deceive an enemy that attacks only by surprise'. Suggested techniques include thinking of things opposed to the objects of the dominating desire in order to produce revulsion, and, as a very last resort, adding 'the thought of eternity, or some other solid thought' (LO 388–9, v.8). This is a remarkable line of attack on one's own innards: fixity is to be imposed on the fleeting spirits.[7] Yet not even 'this sort of defense' can render us 'impregnable':

---

7 The stasis which the will must encourage, however, is a distant dream, given Malebranche's acceptance of transience in body and nature. 'Briefly, man's life consists only in the circulation of the blood, and in another circulation of his thoughts and desires' (LO 90, II.1.iii). I discuss Malebranche on passion, wonder, and fixity in male cognition further in Sutton 1998.

sometimes the 'motion of the spirits can be so violent that they occupy the soul's entire capacity' (LO 389, v.8).

Malebranche's concentration on relations between men's thoughts and bodies exemplifies the continuing concern for control which went along with porous memories. With women figured in such discourse as naturally grotesque, susceptible because of their delicate brain fibres to distraction by 'only the surface of things' (LO 130–3, II.II.I.i–ii), men's supposed access to depth is a curse. When 'man is naturally whole, close, opaque, self-contained', in contrast to 'open, permeable, effluent, leaky' woman (Paster 1993: 92), the fact that men's bodies and memories, too, fail to keep their proper boundaries becomes shameful, horrifying.

The poor oppressed male soul, its power dependent on unlikely 'obedience rendered to it by the animal spirits' (LO 88, II.I.I.ii), buffeted by their every new distribution and their every heavy flood, is blindly ignorant of the body's activities (LO 350–2, v.3).[8] Sources of evil and danger are internal. Body fluids are not self, not good, not true, not pure. Despite the necessary rhetoric of control, the mind ends up merely sitting in the brain,[9] watching 'while Spirits thro' the wandring Channels wind' (Henry Brooke, Universal Beauty, a Poem (1735), in Rousseau 1969/1991: 21).

Misassociation

The corporeal associative mechanisms of imagination and memory, then, introduce troublesome disorder, turning the mind away from contemplation of truth and reality (whether of religious and moral truths or simply of the external world and the real past) into dangerous realms of images unfettered by goodness. Crudely, three trends in eighteenth-century natural and social philosophy reveal reactions to the encroaching of physiology on morality and rationality. Firstly, the animal spirits, which would not stay put, were too dangerous to be left untamed, and had to be eliminated (chapter 10 below). Secondly, new (cultural, medical, and philosophical) attitudes to imagination emerged. The failure of attempts like Malebranche's and Hume's to distinguish memory from imagination were rendered less threatening, as Enlightenment aestheticians and moralists tamed the imagination, making it

---

8 This passage also discusses body mechanism, drawing on Descartes' accounts of our natural error in thinking that the soul is the cause of what are really mechanical effects (e.g. Description of the Human Body, part I, AT xi.223–7, CSM I.314–16). Malebranche notes that we wrongly but 'naturally humanize all causes' (LO 352, v.3): only acquired theoretical knowledge of such physiological processes as the formation of brain traces and the motions of animal spirits will help us practically in learning to avoid error.

9 Compare Croone 1664: 161: 'we shall consider the living body to be nothing else but a kind of machine or automaton and the Mind, which is in us, we may move meanwhile by its own thought, or at least we may arrange to sit in the brain merely as a spectator of this play which is acted out in the scene of the body'.

an indispensable tool in the poetic armoury of the man of feeling. I make some brief remarks about this complex topic below.

The third means of warding off unwelcome bodily intrusions into the moral self was to rethink the nature and scope of association. Theories of associative mechanisms were extended to cover all mental sequences, not just disordered and dangerous ones. Hume's three relations of association and Hartley's comprehensive applications of association in the 1740s are a far cry from Locke's warnings about the dangers of misassociation. There are no inevitable cultural implications of associationism: but then, as now, it focused urgent debates about the sources, justification, order, and integrity of cognitive processes. Sceptical readings of Hume, then and now, see his application of association to 'normal' thought as an exposé, in an inversion of Locke, of 'the sordid background of reason itself' (Wright 1987: 116). Although, as John Wright argues (1987: 120), Hume was not quite in the business of 'reducing all reasoning to association', the possibility of exhaustive accounts of cognition in terms of association is alive again in the late twentieth century, and worries about its implications for rationality and self are again alive. Here I sketch why association seemed a threat by detailing its effects and physiological bases in Locke, whose eloquent account of misassociation was one of the most influential aspects of his thought (Aarsleff 1994: 268–71), and haunted even those who sought to sentimentalise or tame its effects.

In chapter 7, I mentioned Locke's early concerns about the way memories can offer themselves up unbidden, of their own accord, out of the dark cells of the mind/brain. After reading Malebranche, Locke added a discussion of association to the fourth edition of the *Essay* in 1700, explaining why there is 'something unreasonable in most Men'.[10] But he did not subsume rational thinking under the mechanisms of association (II.33.1).[11] Our 'degree of Madness' comes from 'a Wrong Connexion of Ideas' (II.33.4–5). To explain particular combinations of ideas which are not in themselves 'at all of kin' (II.33.5), we must understand the social setting of such ideas, different men's 'different Inclinations, Educations, Interests, etc.': but the habits of thinking,

10 Locke told Molyneux that he would add material on association and on enthusiasm (see section 9.3 below) in April 1695, as he was reading Malebranche (Locke 1979: 350–3; Wright 1987: 111–14). Wright stresses the importance of the chapter on association for Locke's campaign against error, and discusses the tension between its deterministic tone and Locke's official view that error is, at times, voluntary. McCracken's discussion of Locke's responses to Malebranche (1983: 119–55) does not cover association or physiology.

11 Reason's 'Office and Excellency' is to 'trace' those ideas which have 'a natural Correspondence and Connexion one with another', whereas associative connections are 'wholly owing to Chance or Custom' (*Essay* II.33.5). In terms of the Cartesian distinction between natural and acquired connections between ideas, Locke thinks that only acquired connections require associationist explanation. Wright (1987) separates the two meanings of 'natural' as 'innate' and as 'objective' or 'rational'.

willing, and moving which are instituted by custom all have proximate physiological causes. Society and culture act on and through the individual by way of
the brain. Every such result of custom, says Locke, 'seems to be but Trains of
Motions in the Animal Spirits, which once set a going continue on in the same
steps they have been used to, which by often treading are worn into a smooth
path, and the Motion in it becomes easy and as it were Natural' (II.33.6).[12]

The misassociating spillage of the spirits is blamed for a range of socially
undesirable effects. Ideas which ought to be 'loose and independent one of
another' connect wrongly, and 'set us Awry in our Actions, as well Moral as
Natural'. Misassociation can cause psychogenic antipathies to particular
foods; nightmares and irrational fears of darkness; lasting personal hatreds
resulting only from 'slight and almost innocent Occasions'; unhappiness at
school and aversion to books; conditioned responses;[13] and a whole range of
'intellectual habits and defects' (II.33.9, 7, 10–11, 15, 16, 17). Locke was apparently thinking along the same lines, linking association explicitly with spirits,
when discussing childhood fears in Some Thoughts Concerning Education. Fearful
apprehension or terrible objects 'often so shatter and discompose the spirits
that they never recover . . . Whether this be from an habitual motion of the
animal spirits, introduced by the first strong impression, or from the alteration
of the constitution by some more unaccountable way, this is certain, that so it
is' (Romanell 1984: 124–5; compare Myer 1984: 101).

Locke's picture of the cognitive and social phenomena on which a psychological theory should bear is broad, realistic, and sad, and worth contrasting
with Hooke's reluctance to accept blending and interference in memory as
central explananda (chapters 5 and 6 above). Hooke's awareness of the weaknesses of memory led him to theorise, wishfully, that items in the coils of
memory must be, by nature, distinct and independent. Locke, driven by the
spirits physiology of memory as motion, and acknowledging the social importance of cognitive mixture, implicitly confirms the difficulty of the task faced by
'moral Man' in dominating his own mind and brain.

It is far from clear whether eighteenth-century extensions of association
were, in motivation or effect, a taming of this confusion. The application of
associative principles to aesthetics and to literary composition and criticism
(Kallich 1970; Christensen 1981) did not conceal problems about the uncertain
control of association by the creative or moral agent. Officially the rummaging

---

12 This passage is used by Sterne in the first chapter of The Life and Opinions of Tristram Shandy
    (section 9.4 below). Locke goes on both to disclaim interest in physiological causes and to
    admit that the instances he gives make it 'probable' that 'the natural cause' of a man's
    associated ideas is 'the Motion of his Animal Spirits' (Essay 11.33.6).

13 In an echo of Descartes' case of association in which hearing a galliard is always paired
    with 'some affliction', Locke reports that a man who learnt to dance in a room with an old
    trunk in it could only ever dance well with the trunk present.

motions of nervous fluids were meant to be at the service of the (male) artist. But it was and is uncertain whether this required a rigid distinction between agent or artist and the cognitive and neural processes he uses, or instead invited a more dangerous surrender to, or identification with, those psychophysical processes. The latter is hinted at, for instance, by some readings of later eighteenth-century aestheticised landscapes, in which 'the human figure functions like the animal spirits, moving up and down the tracks and defiles and generating new images and sensations at every turn' (Lamb 1989: 62). Similar historiographic difficulties arise in relation to imagination, to which I briefly return, sketching possible directions on problems which are parallel to those I am concerned with here.

Imagination, sensibility, and autobiographical memory
The difficulty of distinguishing veridical memory from vivid confabulation within the psychophysiology of animal spirits could only fuel concern over the moral dangers and contagions of the distempered imagination. The 'integration of ethics and physiology' characteristic of eighteenth-century thought was never easy, for physiology could all too readily unbalance the precarious harmony of the moral man of feeling (Mackenzie 1771/1987; Rousseau 1976). Conceptual transfer and feedback between physiological and moral uses of 'sensibility' and 'sympathy' allowed aestheticised physiological concepts to be incorporated into, rather than seen as threats to, the 'sensitive' social life (Figlio 1975; Lawrence 1979; Cox 1980: chs. 1–2).

Many historians agree that eighteenth-century cultures of sensibility involved the dematerialising and moralising of imagination.[14] No longer the deforming corporeal enemy of reason and religion vulnerable to incursions into an open body, imagination was moulded by the time of the early Romantics into a creative and constructive spirit of unity contained in a newly sealed and internally differentiated body (Schulte-Sasse 1995).[15] Was this conceptual

---

14 Beverly Southgate (1992) argues that this was already the case in seventeenth-century philosophy. Southgate takes any mention of the 'wild imagination' as 'shorthand' for causal factors 'outside the pale of real science' (1992: 281, 287). But this ignores the project, in psychological medicine and physiological philosophy, of incorporating the imagination as a corporeal cause. Evidence for belief in the psychological causation of behaviour, which Southgate cites, is less surprising when one realises the ubiquity of seventeenth-century belief in the physiological dependence of psychological states. Southgate is motivated by a view that non-physical psychological factors, displaced in the mechanistic revolution, are again coming to be accepted in the late twentieth century (1992: 291–2). But acknowledgement of 'wildness' or unruliness in cognition does not, and did not in the seventeenth century, require the abandonment of explanation or science.

15 Recent writers on the maternal imagination (the view that a mother's thoughts can be imprinted, by resemblance and through spirits and fluids, on the skin of the foetus) have carefully contextualised the theory from the Greeks to Malebranche and Turner, showing the gaps in progressive histories which take its displacement in the eighteenth century as

transformation the secularising production of a new organicist view of subjectivity, an escape from 'imagination's despotism' (Porter 1987: 60),[16] or a more rigid imposition of moralised dualisms whereby access (for some) to a creative imagination requires transcendence of the merely natural capacities to which others are restricted? The delicate sensibility (of nervous tissue and moral sense) of the new imaginative agent was available only to those sympathetic souls in the right social bracket (Porter 1987: 81–7; Rousseau 1989: 40–4, 1991: 225–45). The class-specificity of nervous disease was accompanied by a difficult and incomplete imitation and absorption, by men of feeling, of trembling femininity: as Helen Deutsch puts it (1994: 35, 9), 'an imagined female sympathy that must remain silent' was incorporated in the production of 'a disembodied creative masculinity' (compare Jordanova 1989: 27ff.; van Sant 1993: 104–7). Even when, in the earlier stages of the sensibility cult, excessive or depressed feeling was still located in the body (van Sant 1993: 98–115), the point was that, in its creative manifestations, imagination could and should be an instrument of cognitive control, a voluntary imposition of artistic or moral discipline on, and over, recalcitrant matter (Porter 1987: 100–3).

The difficulty for such idealised images of agency and control in acknowledging disorder or internal strangeness leaves marks through eighteenth-century literature. When Edward Young in 1759 advised the aspiring writer to 'contract full intimacy with the Stranger within thee' and to think well on the 'naked self' (Cox 1980: 3), many were already suspicious that the quest was doomed, for explicit models and theories of self and agency were increasingly stressing unity and autonomy over complexity. Here there is a need for work between history of science and the abundant scholarship on the literature of sensibility (on the historiography, see Rousseau 1980). Uncertainty about rhetoric of autonomous subjectivity can be teased out in analyses of literary strategies of evasion, in autobiography and the novel (Flynn 1990), and in changing ways of writing philosophy.

Self-creation in and through words, and the ways words do things to and with us, are processes much discussed by modern theorists of personal identity who see the self, with Daniel Dennett, as 'a centre of narrative gravity' (Dennett 1991a: 410; see also 1991a: 227–52, 412–30; compare Glover 1988; and Rorty

---

the victory of newly scientific approaches (King 1978: 153–81; Stafford 1991: ch. 2; Wilson 1992; Huet 1993: chs. 1–3; Schulte-Sasse 1995). But it remains true that the context in which the attribution of such powers to maternal imagination made sense (that of an embedded body and mind traversed by physical and cultural forces) did evaporate: not with dualism and mechanistic physiology (Descartes and Malebranche accept the old stories: see footnote 24 below), but with new stress on the independence of closed bodies from their environments and on the autonomy of cognitive powers. I address the survival of parallel theories, equally strange to us, about relations between cognitive and reproductive systems and energies in men in section 9.4 below.

16 My thanks to Jochen Schulte-Sasse, whose view this is, for discussion on these topics. Compare Schulte-Sasse 1987.

1989). This philosophical work, as well as the experimental psychology of autobiographical memory, needs additional historical dimensions, for different kinds of writing mediate, reflect, and help to produce different kinds of selves and different norms of remembering. The functions of spinning a self in language are context-dependent and socially mediated: Hume's own auto-biography (Hume 1776/1993b) creates one fictitious past self for specific audiences (Bell 1975; compare Lloyd 1993b: 61–77). 'Putting a life into words', as Spacks notes (1976: 21), 'rescues it from confusion, even where the words declare the omnipresence of confusion, since the act of declaring implies dominance.' Story-telling, in fiction or in autobiography, permits many differing forms of coherence: but eighteenth-century life narratives which employed 'autobiography as prosthesis' (Mascuch 1997) imposed increasingly dichotomous ideals of control over messy pasts and unreliable bodies. Herder would celebrate the new order:

> One can witness in the history of humanity what narrative fiction . . . has achieved in helping tame and order the phantasy, in giving all forces and inclinations of human nature direction . . . It has forced the unleashed and infinitely roaming phantasy of ignorant beings into a framework of laws and limits. (In Schulte-Sasse 1995: 23)

This is one perspective on the result of eighteenth-century philosophical debates around the edges of issues of personal identity. Through new defences of free will, strong new visions of agency and autonomy, through moral-sense theories, new ways of thinking of gender difference, new social and political ideas about the ontological independence of individual political and economic agents one from another, it had become possible for the male theorist to believe, in certain moods at least, that the inarticulable, 'infinitely roaming' forces of dangerous cognitive and corporeal confusion had been or could yet be definitively disciplined, producing only pure thoughts and memories unmixed with baser matter, under the sway of a unified subjectivity.

Yet the memory of physiology would stalk and trouble this tenuous dominance. If eighteenth-century optimism relied on 'the reassurances of stability' (Spacks 1976: 9), then the awful gap between the inner self and those internal processes of which it was not aware, and over which its control was evanescent, had to be narrowed. The internalisation of a quest for authorisation, the location in the self of what Camus (1942/1975: 38) called 'nostalgia for the absolute', required, as Rousseau (1976: 157) argues, 'a specific neurological legacy'.

9.3 The Devil, the rational will, and the animal spirits

Animal spirits physiology, in which patterned motions lack obvious boundaries left a series of puzzles about the causation of thought and of action. From the inside at least, it was impossible under these theories to know whether current cognitions and actions were caused by reason or madness, by genuine religious inspiration or enthusiastic fanaticism, by the Holy Spirit or by evil spirits, by the Devil or the will.

These worries spring from perceived distance between self and memories, or self and body, which requires efforts at closure through odd procedures for the mastery of (the less acceptable aspects of) the self by the (true, intimate) self. John Smith, the Cambridge Platonist, describing the animal spirits physiology of 'a late sagacious Philosopher', looks for the physical causes of 'all the imperfect motions of our Wills'. It might not, he warns, only be the soul (which 'sits enthroned, in some mysterious way' in the brain) that is 'apt to stir those quick and nimble animal spirits'. Smith announces that the mark of a rational soul is 'by the exercise of true Vertue [to get] dominion over them' and control the spirits' potentially 'disorderly and confus'd' motions (Smith 1660/1979: 116–17). 'Moral man' is under heaviest pressure if the body is itself active rather than passive, if the forces of 'not-self' are already on the march, besieging the inner citadel where self sits obscurely enthroned.[17] This partly explains the way early modern moral exhortation on the disciplining of self by self often took the form of wishful surveillance of the animal spirits.

Memory, madness, and enthusiasm

Malebranche finds, throughout books II and III of The Search after Truth, 'the moral causes of error' in the delicacy of brain fibres (LO 130–1, II.11.1.i). Such delicacy is 'usually found in women', who 'consider only the surface of things'. Men, before fashions of delicate nervous sensibility, are ascribed internal solidity and access to depth: yet Malebranche still thinks that his stategems need to be addressed primarily to men. A neurophilosophical definition of mental soundness follows: 'strength of mind consists in a certain constitution of the volume and agitation of the animal spirits with the brain fibers' (LO 130, II.11.1.i). Without defence against violent passions, error will inevitably follow through the confusions of brain traces (LO 131, II.11.1.i–ii; 141, II.11.4). Fixations and obsessions result. If one passion dominates, then as some animal spirits 'violently descend' in unnatural motions to the periphery of the body, others, 'swirling irregularly in the brain, stir up so many traces' that the soul, which is 'continually constrained to have the thoughts tied to these traces', 'becomes, as it were, enslaved to them'. Vigilance must, therefore, be unceasing (LO 349, v.3; 203, III.1.2.i; 151, II.11.6). Malebranche is worried here, not about fixity in itself (as we've seen, stasis is to be willed), but about loss of control.

Malebranche's concern about the dangers of fixation and obsession is one sign of fears about the way brain traces could suck one towards insanity. When

---

17 Compare Haraway 1989/1991 and Waldby 1992 on modern immunological discourses about the repulsion of alien intruders from carefully patrolled internal boundaries.

one criterion for sanity was the ability to separate impulses of internal from those of external origin (DePorte 1974: 25–30), the memory/imagination blur was ominous. A century after Malebranche, Cullen would analyse delirium as dependent on inequalities in the brain which disrupt the 'orderly and exact recollection or memory of associated ideas' (Porter 1987: 179). Memory was a talisman against madness. Locke, in a journal note, hoped that having recourse to memory, to rendering present 'things past precisely as they were', will ward off extravagant flights of imagination. He diagnosed madness as a failure to use memory sufficiently:

> I guesse that those who are about madmen will finde that they make very little use of their memory which is to recollect particulars past with their circumstances but haveing any partiall Idea suggested by their memorys phansy dresses it up after its own fashion without regard to the original.[18]

Early modern physiologies of madness have neurological roots in spirits theory (for general accounts in which unruly physiological entities loom large see DePorte 1974: 3–53; Porter 1987: 169–84). Newton had noted that 'commotions of ye spirits', in physiological excess or deficiency, disrupted the proper operations of imagination (McGuire and Tamny 1983: 394–6). The exercise of memory was a discipline of fixity, meant to re-present a transparent past, evading, by repetition of original order, the wild associative jumbling of the mad. Worries over excessive individual difference also confronted physiology: needs for social regulation and consensus in representation seemed incompatible with the transformations inevitably imposed upon perceptual input by animal spirits which were rarely likely to mirror or resemble their causes. Trust in the freedom from error of other perceiving and remembering subjects required a neurophysiological counterpart to sound social status: everyone, Shaftesbury advised in his *Letter Concerning Enthusiasm* (1708), must 'prove the Validity of his Testimony by the Solidity of their Brain' (DePorte 1974: 43–4). The hopelessness of this demand was clear: everyone knew that brains are just loose pulp. Association and memory, when tied to fleeting spirits, make the variety of effects of history and context on individuals glaring: every brain-machine is different.

This was marked, for example, in debates over the propriety of unusual individual and social religious responses. The only chapter other than that on

---

18 Locke's journal, Saturday 22 January 1678, in Dewhurst 1963: 101. But since *everyone* in trying 'to retaine only the traces of the patterne [is] looseing by degrees a great part of them', the proper 'regard to the original', to the full plenitude of the past, is impossible: 'the Ideas of memory like painting after the life come always short, i.e. want something of the original' (in Dewhurst 1963: 100–1). This early thought chimes with the *Essay*'s claim (II.II.13) that the 'disorderly jumbling ideas together', which characterises the mad and proceeds from 'the violence of their Imaginations' differs only in degree from ordinary (mis)association.

association which Locke added to the *Essay* in 1700 was on enthusiasm. Following Henry More (Wright 1987: 114–15), Locke defines what is 'properly Enthusiasm' by its difference from both reason and true divine revelation. Enthusiasm rises only 'from the Conceits of a warmed or over-weening Brain' (*Essay* IV.19.7).

The fight for control of the quick spirits was not only in individuals' dualistic battles between reason and passion. Remember Malebranche's exhortation to think of eternity as the last internal bastion against the corrupting effects of the unruly spirits (section 9.2 above). In popular conceptions of animal spirits theory at least, physiology had a directly theological dimension, old associations across the spirit realm remaining strong through the seventeenth century. Evil spirits lurk within, in extremity operating as animals, ghostly or monstrous inhabitants of possessed innards (Ginzburg 1966/1983: 19–20; Macdonald 1981: 203). The animal spirits of the victim are physically invaded, thought More (one theorist of the last great panic witch-scare in England in the 1660s), the imagination being directly interfered with through physiological channels (Crocker 1990: 139).[19] One could be assuredly free of such deviant causal sources of cognition and action when operating by socially sanctioned norms of religious expression: but as long as grand eschatological concerns lingered within religious orthodoxies, it could not be officially denied that the pores of the brain and their fluid contents might be the site of the ultimate struggle.

The Devil and the will: rational and irrational choice
In book IV of *Paradise Lost*, Gabriel's ministering angels go to check on Satan's doings in the Garden:

> him there they found
> Squat like a Toad, close at the ear of Eve;
> Assaying by his Devilish art to reach
> The Organs of her Fancie, and with them forge
> Illusions as he list, Fantasms and Dreams,
> Or if, inspiring venom, he might taint
> Th'animal spirits that from pure blood arise
> Like gentle breaths from Rivers pure, thence raise
> At least distemperd, discontented thoughts,
> Vain hopes, vain aims, inordinate desires
> Blown up with high conceits ingendring pride.
>   (Milton 1667, book IV, ll. 799–809)

---

19 Crocker quotes a letter to Hartlib, possibly of 1652. I am indebted to Doris McIlwain's unpublished work on enthusiasm. The best survey is Heyd 1981, especially pp. 271–80 on medicine and culture; see also Schwartz 1978: 50–2. On Restoration witch theory see Easlea 1980: ch. 5; Jobe 1981. Walker (1981) examines case studies in possession.

One persuasive, toadying spirit infiltrates the female defences to pervert the 'natural' course of other spirits, producing all the worst sorts of thoughts. The failure of discipline in Eve's animal spirits is the Fall.

Cognitive distempers, vanity, and pride were also infused by the Devil into the animal spirits of the 'French prophets': or so said their critics. While orthodox Anglican divines and scholars laboured at exact biblical chronology, at putting the past in its proper order, the prophets themselves claimed inspirational causation: their bodily agitation, garbled pronouncements, and disorders of memory (which sometimes prevented later recall of what they said and did in prophetic trance) were caused by the action of the Holy Spirit on its metaphysical messengers and kin, the animal spirits (Schwartz 1978: 71–81). The prophets deny themselves status as the origin of their own action, surrendering autonomy to prior causal force.

Hume had these prophets in mind when, in a letter of 1734 to a doctor (Cheyne or Arbuthnot), he eloquently described his history of nervous disorders, wasted spirits, and courses of 'Anti-hysteric Pills'. He spied a 'pretty parralel' between his case and that of 'the French Mysticks, and . . . our Fanatics here'. Since their 'kind of Devotion depends entirely on the Force of Passion, & consequently of the Animal Spirits', Hume conjectures that 'their rapturous Admirations might discompose the Fabric of the Nerves & Brain, as much as profound Reflections, & that warmth or Enthusiasm which is inseperable from them' (Hume 1734/1993a: 349). Author of his own case history, promoting himself to 'the Disease of the Learned' within a community of sympathetic readers (compare Deutsch 1994: 10–17), Hume here also betrays an ambiguity between philosophy and possession which haunts the eighteenth-century scholar. Isolated reason in excess springs from rapture and desire just as does cult behaviour. 'Profound Reflections' tax nerves, brain, and animal spirits in a bodily economy with limited resources, in which the 'pretty parralel' with the action of disreputable religious forces brings no security to the sensitive suffering reasoner.

But the point is not just that the varieties of spirit remained metaphysically proximate into the eighteenth century. New ambition in physiological psychology now placed individual reason or will, depending on the metaphysical scheme, alongside all the other possible causes of spirit motions. No matter what the ontological status of soul and volition, rational choice had to operate through the animal spirits just as God and the Holy Spirit had always been meant to. Extra strain on the individual as the origin of action left it difficult safely to distinguish reason from its shadows. In illustration of this I take a minor medical writer carefully studied by Lester King.

Friedrich Hoffmann writes in his popular *Fundamenta medicinae* of finely particulate animal spirits which control all tissues and organs (Hoffmann 1695/1971). Even if Hoffmann's vaunted mechanism disguises belief in Neoplatonic hierarchies of souls, he tries to use animal spirits in a number of naturalistic explanations (King 1970: 181–204, 1978: 36–9). But in a wonder-fully titled later work, De potentia diaboli in corpore, Hoffmann lists the ways in which the Devil can act through his intermediaries, the animal spirits (which thus become evil spirits), to produce such undesirable effects as convulsive disorders (when the spirits are agitated), and, when Satan diminishes the spirits' force, melancholy, impotence, and 'slack tonus' (in King 1978: 203–7).

As King notes, the fact that the same disorders of animal spirits which cause disease could themselves spring either from supernatural demonic malevolence or from an 'involuntary internal cause' which is natural raised severe diagnostic difficulties.[20] The philosophico-moral difficulty is related, for diabolic action on animal spirits works in exactly the same way as the action of the rational soul on the spirits is meant to in ordinary decision-making (King 1978: 205). It had always been hard, in fraught contexts, to tell who is 'strangely deluded by some cogging divell' (Babb 1951: 47), to know which 'memories' are false.

Spirits theorists easily project on to the Devil what was feared about the violence and randomness of the spirits' passages in ordinary cognition. Rational choice is mechanically and phenomenologically indistinguishable from less acceptable procedures, with only social norms capable of arbitrating. The beneficent balance of the spirits is threatened and displaced by 'distemperd, discontented thoughts'. Hillel Schwartz draws these themes together in outlining a gradual early eighteenth-century shift towards naturalising explanations of mental disorder, in a slow movement 'from evil spirits to animal spirits' (Schwartz 1978: 43). A blur between natural and supernatural was convenient for many social groups, who could talk equally of brain agitations and demonic possession, 'as if medical terms were but euphemisms for the wiles of the devil' (1978: 47). Inability to maintain proper cognitive discipline could be both symptom and source of awful internal anarchies, as victims of physiological turmoil or frailty slipped from order into interior chaos.

The construction and fortification of the moral agent, then, required vigilance against the mischievous spirits' roles in misassociation and imagination: the ordered action of the soul on the spirits, rendering them its obedient messengers, constitutes the agent's rationality. Memory, rationality, and personal identity are interdependent, and all rest on fleeting animal spirits.

9.4 The scholar's fragile virility
Ruffled spirits

Tristram Shandy, assuming that 'you have all, I dare say, heard of the animal spirits', begs us at the outset of his tale to take his word that 'nine parts in ten of a man's sense or his nonsense, his successes and miscarriages in this world

---

20 King (1978: 206–7) discusses seven unconvincing criteria for cases of demonic influence suggested by Hoffmann.

depend upon their motions and activity, and the different tracks and trains you put them into' (*Tristram Shandy* 1.1: 5). Sterne is even less sanguine than Locke about our chances of voluntarily putting the fleeting spirits anywhere. Tristram's manliness is always in question, for the animal spirits of his wriggling embryonic homunculus have been 'ruffled beyond description' (1.2: 6): Mrs Shandy's untimely question to Tristram's father Walter about the winding of the connubial clock resulted in involuntary emission and a horrible disordering of the paternal animal spirits. It does not take much disruption in initial conditions for a whole life to be 'ruffled': small differences in Shandean causes (like Slawkenbergius' nose) have large effects (Berthoud 1984: 27–8).

Sterne's play here is one of his serious parodies of philosophical theories borrowed through Locke from Descartes.[21] He catches the feel of theories of associative memory in the Cartesian-empiricist philosophy of the brain: when, Tristram declares (still on the opening page), the spirits

> are once set a-going, whether right or wrong, 'tis not a halfpenny matter, – away they go cluttering like hey-go-mad; and by treading the same steps over and over again, they presently make a road of it, as plain and smooth as a garden-walk, which, when they are once used to, the Devil himself sometimes shall not be able to drive them off it. (I.1: 5)

A century after Milton, the manic spirits are even more powerful than Satan (though, as we shall see, the Devil gets them in the end). In what Sterne refers to as Locke's 'history-book', he finds among the causes of 'obscurity and confusion, in the mind of man' certain defects of memory, 'a memory like unto a sieve, not able to retain what is received' (II.2: 70–1).[22] I return below to the comic arguments which Sterne, revelling in the polysemy of medico-moral terms (Porter 1984: 87), uses to undermine cognitive discipline in memory theory. But first it is worth tracing back to the mainstream Cartesian tradition the Shandean suggestion that overuse of the animal spirits in the brain, in study or contemplation, may render the scholar 'less suitable for procreation'.

The expense of spirits
The 'Cartesian philosophy of the Brain' describes how, in the differing motions of blood away from the heart, its 'liveliest, strongest, and most subtle' parts

---

21 For background on Sterne's uses of Locke see Tuveson 1962; Day 1984; Hawley 1993. Lamb (1989: 56–82) looks at Sterne's use of Hartley and other associationists. On physiology in Sterne, see DePorte 1974: 107–35; Myer 1984. Sterne is working closely with the entwined Cartesian/Lockean animal spirits theory. Myer's paper is one of the few extended discussions of animal spirits theory of which I know, and it suggested the title of this section.

22 The narrator undertakes, in a little home experiment, to make this matter so plain to 'Dolly your chambermaid' that she 'should understand it as well as Malebranch' (p. 71). The Cartesian heritage of Lockean psychophysiology is clear, Sterne's uses proving that this network of ideas was at once mechanistic and psychosomatic (Porter 1984: 91).

pass out by the straightest line (according to Descartes' physics of motion), the 'direct route' via the carotid artery to the brain. There animal spirit particles are separated out further, to play the roles I have sketched in sensation, memory, and muscular motion. But those particles which are next in strength and liveliness, which cannot reach the brain because of the narrowness of the carotid artery, are drawn instead 'to the organs designed for generation' (Descartes, *L'Homme*, AT xi.128, H 18; Figure 5).[23]

In a note to this passage, on the verge of Descartes' full treatment of memory, his editor, the physician and physiologist, Louis de La Forge appended the following observations:

> one can confirm this dependence and communication which obtains between the spirits of the brain and those of the testicles by experience, which shows that those who are dedicated to study and who exercise their imaginations and their brains a lot, are not ordinarily very suitable for procreative functions . . . since most of those parts of the blood which have greater strength and motion have gone to their brains, there are hardly any of them left for procreation. By contrast, those who are given to debauching women are not very suitable for serious application to study. (La Forge 1664: 210)[24]

The idea of a peculiarly intimate connection between psychological and generative functions is ancient (chapter 2 above). But in the late seventeenth century, as Desmond Clarke shows (1989: 154), the specific hypothesis of a link between study and decreased male fertility suddenly came to be treated as established empirical fact. Clarke quotes the Cartesian Claude Gadroys: 'there is an infinity of examples which prove this communication. Those who weary their imaginations by study are less suitable for procreation, while those who, on the contrary, dissipate their minds in debauching women are not as suitable for study.' The idea spawned research programmes: the Oxford physiologist Richard Lower (an acquaintance of Locke's) tested the theory that spirits are

23 Although here Descartes does 'not wish to enter further into this matter', he does refer to similar views in the *Description of the Human Body* and *First Thoughts on the Generation of Animals*.

24 Translated by Desmond Clarke (1989: 154), to whose account I am indebted. Whether or not there is a parallel story for women's animal spirits is unclear: Descartes only refers, cryptically declining to expand, to the way in which traces 'can sometimes even be caused, by certain actions of the mother, to be imprinted on the limbs of the child being formed in her entrails' (*L'Homme*, AT xi.177, H 87, CSM 1.106). Malebranche's discussion of 'the communication between the brain of a mother and that of her child' (LO 112–24, II.1.7) is an attempt to link the detailed psychophysiology of animal spirits and memory traces in the first chapters of book II with tentative developmental and educational theory and advice in II.1.8 (LO 125–30; contrast Huet 1993: 45–55). See footnote 15 above on maternal imagination. But it is important in this context, where historians have puzzled over the way women's bodies were constructed in the eighteenth century as too intimate with themselves (Foucault 1965/1988; Rousseau 1993), to stress that the problematic male economies of fluids which I discuss in the text rendered obvious the incompleteness of conceptual desires to seal the male body and guarantee its self-sufficiency.

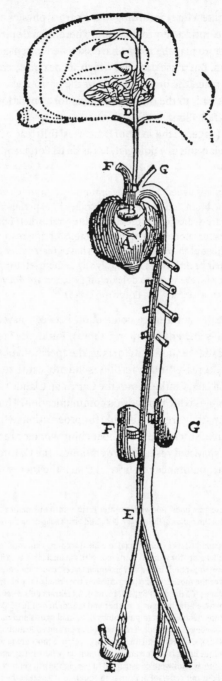

Figure 5 Channels of communication between spirits of the brain and of the
testicles (Descartes 1664: 18).

the origin of sperm by looking (unsuccessfully) for channels through which spirits might flow in the testicles of a boar (Brazier 1984: 69). Mandeville describes the 'extraordinary commerce' between the soul and both genitals and stomach, and the concomitant dangers to the intellect of squandering away the spirits in venereal pleasures (Mandeville 1711/1976: 132–3, 144–5; Monro 1975: 62–5). So Sterne's readers would have known, as he expected them to, of how the animal spirits are 'transfused from father to son, &c. &c. – and a great deal to that purpose' (Tristram Shandy 1.1: 5).

What can historians make of all this? T.S. Hall, referring only to Descartes' suggested links between the spirits of the brain and those of 'the organs designed for generation', laments that his 'whole picture is speculative and deductive and exhibits the sometimes disastrous consequences of his incautious dependence on reason divorced from adequate observation' (H 18–19, n. 39).[25] This is too quick a dismissal. It would make sense, even within a Whiggish history of science, only if we were entirely confident in dismissing the theory as an explanation of a wholly chimerical set of explananda. But it is at least controversial for us to deny that an important source of energy for psychological function is libidinal. Mandeville, one of many theorists explaining the peculiar female susceptibility to hysteria, has one character remark that 'one hour's intense thinking wastes the spirits more in a Woman, than six in a Man' (in Porter 1987: 105; compare Monro 1975: 66–7). So at the very least, social constructions of both intellectual and sexual gender characteristics which relied on such a connection have to be explained.[26] While philosophers of consciousness might always have liked to restrict the scope and effects of 'the naughty and nasty bits ... the seamier side of one's mental life' (Churchland 1983: 81),[27] perhaps early modern neurophilosophers had more of a sneaky awareness than they have been credited with that the sexual instincts and their vicissitudes might permeate even the loftiest and most sublime realms of scholarly activity.

25 Clarke's concern (1989: 131–63) is to defend Cartesian hypothesis-formation, in line with Descartes' view that the natural philosopher is free to make any assumption provided 'that all the consequences ... agree with our experience' (Principles III.46, AT viii(a). 101, CSM 1.256–7): but in this specific context, while he thinks the research programme is not a 'complete methodological aberration', Clarke rejects Descartes' particular account as 'mere speculation, with none of the redeeming qualities required to save it from being "purely arbitrary"' (1989: 153–5). The very prevalence of the idea in traditions both before and after Descartes should suggest that, even if false, it is not purely arbitrary.

26 In Unstable Ideas, Jerome Kagan (1989: 116–17) looks briefly at one strand of the subsequent history of the idea. Gradually it became useful to those seeking reasons to debar women from higher education. Since women require more energy for reproductive functions, they have less energy to spare for thought, and so must be freed from troubling studies. Thanks to Doris McIlwain for this reference. I do not know how those male scholars in subsequent periods who still accepted the theory thought of their own suitability for procreation.

27 Churchland, of course, is arguing that, in fact, much more than the naughty bits escapes our introspective awareness.

Tristram Shandy's disordered narrative and life resulted from the disorder of animal spirits caused by his father Walter's lack of control. Both Walter's obsessively tangled rationality and Tristram's own impotence (*Tristram Shandy* VII.29: 415) derive from the tricks played on them by the quick and nimble animal spirits.[28] Binding the scholar to the limitations of his body, spilling into every enclosure of brain and nervous system, fickly unable to keep to their proper traces, the miraculous, volatile animal spirits are no fit vessels to bear the weight of the self-conscious male moral agent. As the fluid medium of memory, they threaten at every turn to upset the Lockean person's confidence in the continuity of his identity over time. Memory is no bulwark against irrationality, atheism, and immorality because it renders 'moral Man', in a sense, hostage to the animal spirits: if they cannot be controlled, kept from undesirable associations in the dark caverns of the mind/brain, the whole fragile construction may collapse into absurdity.

Myer suggests (1984: 109–10) that Walter Shandy, with his rambling discourses 'held together only by random links of memory and leading nowhere', is a 'victim of the association of ideas, a severed head', whose distrust of the body and privileging of the intellect holds lessons for us all. She quotes Walter's 'lamentation' for the 'embryotic evils' of Tristram's conception, when, according to Walter, 'the few animal spirits I was worth in the world, and with which memory, fancy, and quick parts should have been convey'd, – were all dispersed, confused, confounded, scattered and sent to the devil' (IV.19: 236). Satan is victorious, the best-laid plans of the rational agent foiled again, unmanned by confusion of the animal spirits. The regularity which theorists who privilege cognitive discipline wish to find in human psychology is internally fragmented into fluttering thoughts, satirised while sought by Sterne's characters in their comical and tragic attempts to live like the Pythagoreans by 'getting out of the body, in order to think well' since 'no man thinks right whilst he is in it' (Flynn 1990). Shandeism is intended as tonic, full of digressions and fractured narratives to force the blood 'and other vital fluids of the body to run freely' (Porter 1984: 90). But the animal spirits which subserve and drive memory, imagination, and action do not inevitably provide extra therapeutic security when running their anxious paths.

In one of Toby's disputes with Walter, association just *is* confusion in a

---

28 When Phutatorius ('the copulator') was struck by a hot chestnut through an unfortunate 'hiatus in [his] breeches', even his soul, together with his imagination, memory, and all other mental capacities, 'with ten batallions of animal spirits, all tumultuously crouded down, through different defiles and circuits, to the place in danger' (*Tristram Shandy* IV.27: 257; Myer 1984: 106). In a crisis of virility, the organs designed for generation dominate mind and soul, the animal spirits' passage 'leaving all his upper regions, as you may imagine, as empty as my purse' (IV.27: 257).

context-dependent machine. Cognitive processes and theories of cognitive processes change over time as history, technology, and culture change.

> Now, whether we observe it or no, continued my father, in every sound man's head, there is a regular succession of ideas of one sort or another, which follow each other in train just like – A train of artillery? said my uncle Toby. – A train of a fiddle stick! – quoth my father, – which follow and succeed one another in our minds at certain distances, just like the images in the inside of a lanthorn turned round by the heat of a candle. – I declare, quoth my uncle Toby, mine are more like a smoak-jack.[29] – Then, brother Toby, I have nothing more to say to you upon the subject, said my father. (III.18: 151)

What, then, is the 'sound man' to do? Confusion has its seductions too, and Walter cannot get Toby's smoak-jack out of his head, for 'there was something in the comparison at the bottom, which hit his fancy'. His wishful Lockean point about the regularity of associative trains is left unmade: with Walter's 'spirits being wore out with the fatigues of investigating new tracts . . . the idea of the smoak-jack soon turned all his ideas upside down, – so that he fell asleep almost before he knew what he was about' (III.20: 152). But a more lasting and more secure response than sleep or exasperated silence was already being made, as moral physiologists tried to strike at the heart of the cause of the confusion, and eliminated the animal spirits.

29 A 'smoak-jack' is 'a machine for turning a roasting-spit by use of currents of hot air in a chimney'.

10

The puzzle of elimination

... the Human Body is a Machin of an infinite Number and Variety of different
Channels and Pipes, filled with various and different Liquors and Fluids, perpetually
running, gliding, or creeping forward, or returning back ...

(George Cheyne 1733/1976: 3–4)

Introduction

Remember Locke: the way a single human can, through continuous consciousness, incorporate past and present memories may be 'an argument *against*
those who would place thinking in a system of fleeting animal spirits' (*Essay*
II.27.13, my emphasis). It comes as no surprise to find the animal spirits which
threaten such continuity disappearing as theoretical entities from roughly the
1740s onwards. The properties of spirits theory which were discarded in the
conceptual change were, I suggested in chapter 8, as much metaphorical as
physiological.

Making sense of the eventual rejection of spirits theory is a difficult task,
which becomes visible only after dropping the assumption that animal spirits
just obstructed neuroscientific progress. The spirits survived long into the
Enlightenment, in the face of powerful objections from at least the 1660s
onwards. What changed in the second quarter of the eighteenth century to
make their elimination possible? Answers are hard to find, and mine are still
badly formed. I consider five hypotheses: (1) that the elimination of animal
spirits was inevitable; (2) that alternative theories displaced them; (3) that they
were not eliminated but reduced (to nervous electricity); (4) that they were
moralised out of existence as a function of the end of the dynamic aesthetic of
the Baroque; and (5) that they became unable to support increasingly narrow
conceptions of personal identity. Except for the first, these hypotheses are not
mutually exclusive. This is all speculative, dealing as much with historiographical patterns as with historical truth, for there is a huge amount of source
material still to survey.[1] I demonstrate the existence of the puzzle without conclusively solving it.

A couple of cautious quotations set the scene. Verbeke notes (1945: 506), at
the end of a classic survey of ancient *pneuma* theories, that the doctrine of

---

1 For orientation in primary texts see Rousseau 1969/1991, 1989; Clarke 1978; Yolton
1984b: ch. 8.

spirits, 'remaining vigorous until the seventeenth century, was gradually undermined by the experiments of Swammerdam, Galvani, and Volta' (compare Oppenheim 1991: 79). Vivian Nutton remarks (1981: 331) that the 'doctrine of animal spirits survived Vesalius' demonstration of the absence of the rete mirabile in man, and was not wholly replaced as a physiological explanation for sensation and action by Galvani's theory of animal electricity'. Verbeke and Nutton are more careful than those who assume that spirits were simply eliminated as neurophysiology at last became truly scientific. But their guarded statements reveal the magnitude of the historical problem. If animal spirits theory was 'not wholly replaced' by animal electricity, what did happen to it? If experimental evidence 'gradually undermined' nervous fluids and spirits, why did they succumb only when they did?

Hypothesis 1: inevitable elimination

In chapter 2, I quoted historians who wish the spirits had never retarded physiological theory: neuroscientists had to drop untestable hypotheses before their science could reach maturity. Brazier (1958: 198) complains that Galen's paralysing authority left spirits theory so sacrosanct that 'no one seems to have tested [it]' before the late seventeenth century: the picture of animal spirits and hollow nerves 'had to be dislodged' before electricity could be recognised as a factor in the transmission of nervous activity. But this last claim in fact points to a historical problem with the teleology which such language of inevitability implies.

The disappearance or fading of animal spirits from physiology occurred well before the development of a clear replacement. There was no consensual alternative for the radical young to rally round, pushing through a paradigm shift by dropping woolly old spirits. Electrical neurophysiology was little more than the dream of a theory at the time that theorists started to desert the spirits, as recent historians of animal electricity agree. The analogy between electricity and the nervous fluid was not a promising research subject before Galvani's experiments in the 1780s (Kipnis 1987: 111): Marcello Pera claims in The Ambiguous Frog (1992: 62) that the theory of neural electricity before Galvani was 'no more than a feebly substantiated conjecture'.

The disappearance of animal spirits was not inevitable: it was caused neither by the powerful objections to them, which had existed for many years, nor by the rapid development of a replacement, for the successor theory was uncertain.

Hypothesis 2: alternative theories

Even if need for a replacement theory was felt, most candidates were just as mysterious as spirits (Mazzolini 1991: 81–2). To say that animal spirits were replaced by nervous fluids (Clarke and Dewhurst 1973: 85) or abandoned in favour of nervous ether (Carlson and Simpson 1969: 108) is not enough without specifying the relevant new theoretical framework more fully. This hypothesis is that animal spirits were superseded by theoretical entities deriving from newly attractive alternative physiologies, 'Newtonian' and 'vitalist'. But neither alternative was intrinsically more advanced, nor did they immediately open up new experimental domains.

Hartley and other 'Newtonian' physiologists shifted away from spirits towards ether and vibrations during this key period.[2] Cheyne retained animal spirits in 1715 but in 1740 rejected them and all kinds of subtle matter in favour of an elastic self-moving nervous mechanism described in terms of undulations and tremors (Yolton 1984b: 179). Browne Langrish, too, accepted animal spirits in 1733, while acknowledging that their unobservability raised doubts: but in 1747 he decided against nervous fluid, since ethereal nervous matter is moved by vibrations caused by an immaterial mind (Yolton 1984b: 174, 180). David Kinneir (1739: 11–19) explicitly set out to metaphorise usage of the term: any reference to a lively person's good spirits is really 'saying no more, than that such a one enjoys a good state of health' (1739: 11–12). But there was insufficient positive momentum to 'Newtonian' physiology, and its faltering progress in the 1730s (Brown 1968/1982: 308–53, 1987: 644–6; Suzuki 1992: 73–121) makes it hard to construe as a powerful research programme. Easy transfer from physics, not a coherent Newtonian alternative in physiology, partly motivated these changes of mind.

Another candidate alternative framework, which I can only mention, was the set of physiological beliefs which gained ground in a mid-century shift 'from mechanism to vitalism' (Brown 1974; compare Schofield 1970: 191–209; Roger 1980: 270–8; Shapin 1980: sect. 5; Wright 1985; Taylor 1988: 66, 80–1). Animal spirits were not necessarily incompatible with the reintroduction of soul into physiology, but they were often associated with Cartesian mechanism which denied the relevance of soul to life functions. Forms of 'vitalism' were motivated by desires to ward off the reductionist materialism implicit in Cartesianism, and to refute the atheistical identification of soul with animal spirits which materialists defended (Vartanian 1953: 216–41; Yolton 1991a). But there is no reason to believe that this forced the end of spirits theory, which had been accepted for centuries by many who were not materialists. The problematic capacities of the spirits, which seem sometimes to require intelligence of their own, were in no way intrinsically unusable by vitalists.

Hypothesis 3: reduction

One reason to query confidence in these explanations of the spirits' demise is that it is not clear that they really did disappear. Some historians of the spirits

---

2 In the late 1740s, Hartley claimed to accommodate all hypotheses about animal spirits into his 'Newtonian Hypothesis of Vibrations' (OM 21, 1.i.1, prop. 5; chapter 13 below).

fail to distinguish between two possibilities on the spectrum of theory-changes. Animal spirits might have been *eliminated*, as misplaced composites useless to a better successor theory (Cussins 1993), unrelated to the hypothetical constructs of that better theory. Alternatively, animal spirits might have been *reduced* (and not eliminated), in which case they would (have been decided to) be *identical* or closely related to the new theoretical entities. So when historians say loosely either that spirits just *are* nervous or neuro-electrical impulses (Jefferson 1949: 699; O'Neil 1974: 65; Monro 1975: 61; Schwartz 1978: 32; Reiss 1996: 598), or that they were *overtaken* and *replaced* by electrochemical impulses (Spillane 1981: 112; Flanagan 1991: 3), they should not be taken at their word. The genuine question is about where on the spectrum between reduction and elimination the theory-change over the mechanism of nervous transmission from animal spirits to electricity should be placed. It is not obvious that belief in the electrical nature of the nervous impulse really ended the cheeky spirits' theoretical career.

So Clarke and Jacyna's claim (1987: 160) that theories of hollow nerves and animal spirits were simply 'overthrown by the research on animal electricity first reported by Galvani in 1791' only reveals their desire to separate pre-scientific from progressive views. It is undermined by Galvani's own view, which they quote (1987: 167), that his research actually *explained* the nature of the animal spirits: other historians of animal electricity describe the process as reduction by identification, 'the recognition that the nature of those classical animal spirits was electrical' (Schiller 1982: 1). Though the exact date is disputed, the idea that animal spirits might be *identical* with neural electrical fluid was tentatively suggested by Italian physiologists in the years around 1750 (Pera 1992: 57–60). In 1760 Fontana argued that 'at the moment we cannot decide the identity of the electrical matter and animal spirits' (Pera 1992: 59–60). But after the electric-fish experiments of the 1770s, Galvani interpreted his own work with frogs as proving the existence of an electrical fluid inherent in and specific to animals (Walker 1937; Home 1970; Stevens 1973: ch. 2). Hoff argues (1936: 167) that Galvani simply accepted 'the current theory' of animal spirits, 'and substituted animal electricity for animal spirits', while Kipnis (1987: 141) comments that, to his contemporaries, Galvani 'proved what people had for long conjectured: the existence of the "nervous fluid"'.

Historical judgements about whether particular theoretical entities were eliminated or were reduced by identification are, however, rarely easy. Often the truth lies between, and in this case more detailed examination of the sources is required to understand why some mid- to late eighteenth-century physiologists rejected, and others retained, the concept of spirit (Jackson 1970; Yolton 1991a). But even if the question of whether animal spirits were replaced or simply adopted and adapted does turn out to be merely academic, it remains true that any residual spirits discourse did lose the metaphoric excess of the spirits' heyday. Later eighteenth-century theorists tended to greater caution in neural ontology (Wightman 1958), in a general slippage of neuroscience away from metaphysics. The reference potential of the relevant terms contracted, as animal spirits' old associations with violence, transience, randomness, and excess became less common. One reason for preferring an answer closer to elimination than reduction is that spirits theory did include a considerable irreducible remainder, being in part a set of culturally permeated 'descriptions' of the cognitive phenomena it was meant to explain, which could not be incorporated or assimilated into more sober successor theories. My last two hypotheses about the theory-change are related statements of one perspective on these wider spirituous domains.

Hypothesis 4: the end of the Baroque

Edwin Clarke (1968: 139–41), discussing the modern belief that neuronal axons are hollow after all, ascribes earlier rejections of hollow nerves in favour of 'inflexibly static nervous tissues' to nineteenth-century methodological rigidity: the 'recent replacement' in the twentieth century of this notion 'by a more dynamic conception suggests a tie with the seventeenth century . . . [and] the Baroque demand for movement'. Later twentieth-century physiology and the old hollow-nerve theory 'have fundamental, dynamic features in common'. The neurobiologist Jean-Pierre Changeux (1985: 67–96) chose 'Animal Spirits' as title for the chapter of Neuronal Man which seeks to replace 'a static description' of cerebral wiring with 'knowledge of a different, dynamic order'. But mere invocations of the Baroque in body history do little explanatory work (Duden 1993: 85). It is easy enough to sketch a story of how increasing resistance to turbulence and motion across Enlightenment domains played some part in the taming of the 'Volatile Oeconomy of the Brain' (Mandeville 1711/1976: 131), and I do so here using Foucault's history of madness. But the following paragraphs are as much another statement of the historical problem as they are a solution to it.

The cultural disappointment of eighteenth-century physiology, argued G.S. Rousseau (1969/1991: 1–2, 13–17), was its failure to unite imagination with animal spirits. The thwarting of a promised 'organic marriage' of the spiritual with the material left at sea those who, like Kant and Coleridge, required a strong sense of unity from their theories of mind. The deification of imagination in the art of early Romanticism and idealism was achieved, in part, by removing it from natural philosophical contexts, rejecting the chaotic fluids wandering through brain folds (chapter 9 above). Animal spirits fell victim to this rejection of multiplicity and mixture.

In the central chapters of Histoire de la folie (1972: 181–361, abridged in 1965: 85–198), Foucault evoked the end of inner turbulence, tracing the disappearance in the eighteenth century of 'the image, with all its mechanical and metaphysical implications, of animal spirits in the channels of the nerves' (1965:

126). His analysis of the disappearance of certain 'explanatory myths' hints that the advancing 'morality of sensibility' could not deal with the 'maniacal spirits' and their 'pernicious mobility' (1965: 146, 129, 126). Cognition and physiology had coexisted in the heyday of the animal spirits in realms which were both organic and ethical. In relation to spirit, 'the distinction we make between the scientific and the moral was unnecessary, positively unwanted' (Davie 1963: 59). But in the gradual removal of concepts like sympathy and sensibility (chapter 9 above) from physiology to ethics, the cognitive realm became moralised and its norms narrowed and hardened, its invisible multiplicity of organic forces unified and restrained (Rousseau 1991, 1993; Stafford 1991: 417–36).

In Foucault's scheme, the dynamic of organic and moral penetration, with its indiscriminately permeable body, initially gave way to a 'physiology of corporeal continuity', exemplified by the concepts of sympathy and the complicity of internal parts, and finally to an ethic of nervous sensibility which treated hysteria, for example, as a psychological illness proceeding from a moral fault. English-language commentary on *Madness and Civilization* has focused on the later stages of this scheme, and the consequences for nineteenth- and twentieth-century moral psychiatry (Still and Velody 1992). But in the full French version, and in related early writings like *Mental Illness and Psychology* (1962/1976), Foucault constructs a remarkable positive picture of the earlier theoretical and phenomenological framework, of the jostling of spirits down unmarked inner paths, and of the 'original exuberance' of the early modern 'experience' of madness (Foucault 1962/1976: 65).

If there is naive nostalgia in Foucault's invocation of 'the grovel of flesh in the void' (1965: 279), or in his 'curiously innocent and untamed conception of madness' (Barham 1992: 47), it is not just in describing the 'easy wandering life' of late medieval and Renaissance madmen on their ships of fools (1965: 3–37, 1972: 13–55; Derrida 1978a; Megill 1992), but also in the alien world of 'classical madness' *after* the 'great confinement'. Careful, grey scholarship might find a residue of positive absences, an excess to the experience of madness in the classical age which is not inevitably subsumed in the marks of reason (Foucault 1972: 190–2, 223–5; Sutton 1994b). Awareness of the animal spirits' complex past encourages attention to Foucault's attempts to use old theory (rather than the voices of the mad, impossibly compromised by reason) to articulate something about the 'pre-modern' body, before it was burdened by consciousness with 'its complex coordinations, its intentional openings . . . the tension of the will that adapts and orders the compulsions' (1962/1976: 16–17). A whirl of warring elements, that body was 'a volume traversed by incessant motion whose disorder is . . . a lawless whirlwind in a chaotic space', subject to 'the incoercible agitation of desires'. This body vanished with the 'emergence of *Homo psychologicus*, possessor of internal truth, fleshless, ironical, and positive of all self-consciousness' and of the relation between himself and himself (1962/1976: 87).

Just as 'cures' initially premised on the old physiologies of fluids lost their sense when retained and moralised in the regimes of moral philanthropy (Foucault 1972: 316–61, trans. 1965: 159–98), so the task of the Enlightenment male philosopher concerned with the care of his self became the imposition of docility on his own body fluids: he must come to see cognitive order as natural, denying that memory was reconstructive and vulnerable to interference and confusion. As Foucault explicitly stated, the polymorphous positive experience of the classical age owed more to animal spirits theory than to metaphysical dualism or to 'Descartes' definition of substances'. Body and morality were not split in the scientific revolution, the self not till later pulled apart from its flesh and its fluids: when these schisms did occur, in the early nineteenth century, they did not result from 'a renewed loyalty to the Meditations' (1965: 182).

Hypothesis 5: 'moral Man'

This provocative story can be put together with my account in chapter 9 of the spirits and the self. Even if the self-conscious responsible agents inhabiting quietened static bodies were historically constructed (Richards 1992: 50–4, 242–6, 372–3), they cannot be voluntarily displaced with invocations of turbulence. We inherit the need, as well as the demand, to undertake that progressive integration of past and present, that assimilation of history into identity, which was encouraged by Lockean assumptions about memory and connecting consciousness, and enforced by institutions reliant on the responsible agents which such assumptions produce. It came to seem that a psychophysiology which allowed cognition to rest on volatile inner fluids was incompatible with certain strong assumptions about self and agency. Personal identity, with all its implications for morality and responsibility, requires a connected narrative, founded on memory: so memory must not depend on 'something organic which waxes and wanes and sometimes disappears altogether' (Diderot 1769/1964: 155–6). Distributed representations do not endure unaltered over time, and the instability of the irregular spirits which compose them jeopardised the self which memory was meant to support.

This is a loose claim, requiring evidence in specific contexts. But here is one manifestation: the Scots physician Robert Whytt, who emphatically rejected animal spirits and mocked appeals to them (1765: v–vi), saw no reason to use 'the irregular motion, increasing derivation, repercussion, confusion, or hurry, of the animal spirits, in accounting for the symptoms of nervous hypochondriac or hysteric disorders' (1765: 8, in Yolton 1984b: 187, n. 14).[3] Whytt appeals instead to sympathy, peculiarly appealing in Scotland (Lawrence 1979; Wright

---

3 Yolton (1984b: 168) juxtaposes with surprise this 1765 rejection by Whytt of the spirits with Mandeville's 1711 use and description of them; but it is no shock that texts written over fifty years apart should reveal different attitudes to the same hypothetical constructs. I am trying to explain how such changes occurred over time.

1990). The delicate stability of the 'man of feeling' would be undermined by the fluid machinations of mischievous spirits in his internal passages. If the spirits threaten to enslave the soul, then, in time, it is the spirits which must go. In Scotland at least, medicine was meant 'to calm the mind' (Cunningham 1990): when it failed to do so, when confusion, hurry, or irregular motion seemed to result from particular theoretical commitments, those commitments were vulnerable.

The animal spirits had an intriguing afterlife in metaphor and in the language of character (see the references to Fielding, Austen, and Disraeli in OED, s.v. 'animal spirits'), but they were tamed and officially dead, leaving historians to commend the progress of truly scientific neurophysiology without them. Docility did not, however, come easy. Polarities of order and confusion are still invoked in cognitive science to support particular views on what it is about cognition and memory that needs explaining. The triumph of stasis was partial, and those who fervently desire cognitive discipline must still, like Isaac Watts in sickness, deny the tumult attributed to volatile brains by theorists unnaturally seduced by confusion. The need for a self freely to enforce order on memory and body did not disappear with the animal spirits' demise.

PART III

'The phantasmal chaos of association'

These Subjects are so much involved in each other, that it is difficult, or even impossible, to begin any-where upon clear Ground . . .

(David Hartley, *OM* v, 1.introduction)

Prompting someone to remember their past is akin to forcing them to sneeze at gun-point. The results are fated to disappoint, for true remembering, like sneezing, is not something one can do at will.　　　(Alain de Botton 1995: 89)

Introduction

This has been a long haul through the history of science, through the animal spirits' ragged traces. Ploughing through links between memory and self, widely construed, in early modern neurophilosophy revealed threats which the physiological nature of memory, especially in distributed models, posed to strong forensic conceptions of the person and to allied notions of rationality, autonomy, control, and moral responsibility. Now I begin applying patterns discerned in history to current issues, contrasting criticisms of new connectionist models of memory and mind with attacks on earlier distributed models.

Chapter 11 sketches Jerry Fodor's objections to connectionism, comparing his concern with cognitive discipline in rejecting the plasticity of mind with earlier critiques of associationism. Bergson and recent humanist critics like Stuart Hampshire assume that classical associationism required separate mental 'atoms': in chapter 12 I question this, and argue that dropping atomism to accommodate creativity or complex reconstruction in remembering means rejecting only localist versions of associationism. To support this, chapter 13 gives a detailed account of David Hartley's distributed model, which not only develops the key notions of superposition and causal holism, but applies the basic memory theory to a wide range of psychological phenomena. Criticisms of Hartley by Reid and Coleridge (chapter 14) impose extreme requirements of unity and order on cognitive theory. Insisting on a natural order in cognition, the critics reassert the primacy of the unified self acting freely on and dominating what Coleridge called 'the phantasmal chaos of association'.

Here, then, we leave the animal spirits, but remember their fluid metaphors. The coupling of spirits theory with distributed models of memory saw the rejection of fleeting spirits by moral physiologists who sought more stable continuity of self over time. This shows just how unusual Hartley was: explicitly seeking, not to eliminate, but to subsume animal spirits in his vibrational model of associative memory, he stands out from a period when philosophies of mind, increasingly moralising and transcendentalist, drew further away from neurophysiology.[1]

---

1 My historical choice is again very limited. Different lessons might be learned, for instance, from Kant's complaint that associationism simply threw memories together in accidental heaps, and from the subsequent history of associationism in Germany: but that story is perhaps better known (Hatfield 1990). Kant thought that association allowed only the barren summation of memories, unable to resonate productively as human memory does (Casey 1987: 367–8).

In one sense, part III describes a historical rerun: just as the Cartesian distributed model was rejected by moralising critics, so Hartley's broader development of it received even more reactionary short shrift. But it also reveals a significant and puzzling difference between old and new attitudes to mechanism and associationism. Early modern critics from Glanvill to Coleridge saw distributed models as too chaotic, their unstructured traces too prone to interference to account for the disciplined preservation of past events in proper order. But modern complaints, from perspectives as different as Fodor's and Hampshire's, take associationism to be too passively mechanistic to catch the productivity and generativity of mental life, too reliant on stored items dully interacting by principles of seventeenth-century physics.

How can distributed models be *both* too active *and* too passive, both prone to jumbling confusions *and* devoid of creativity, with tendencies to infidelity *and* to tedium? Analysing the historical sweep of anti-associationist rhetoric reveals deeper motivations: the two forms of hostility are not as distinct as they seem. Both sets of critics require the involvement of an active, autonomous, controlling self in cognitive processes. Associationism, in contrast (whether construed as boring or excessively confused), provides no clear role for an executive self: there is no principled division between memories and their owner, between storage and processing.

The fact that Hartley, like Descartes, believed in a non-physical soul in no way assuaged his critics. Like Descartes, Hartley willingly formed working theories in natural philosophy to answer the cognitive appearances without the insurance of that soul's direct controlling involvement. Thus, as his opponents intuited, he opened up the spectral possibility, disastrous for the moral order, that the bare immanent results of history in different bodies, the merely natural dynamics of experience which sieve through the brain, might displace reason and leave society's norms without a common grip across individuals.

This sets the explanatory agenda. Rationalists and moralists insist on external intervention in the linking and shuffling of ideas, impressed by hard, logical, brittle cognitive processes, which we can sometimes *feel* as effort in conscious calculation. Associationists privilege soft, defeasible, fluid transitions which are less accessible to consciousness (Smolensky 1987/1991), and must show how the mere statistical and causal play of a haphazard world on the mind can produce the faint degree of order that remembering sometimes retains. Even voluntary recall and inventive reminiscence are at stake: if memory is reconstructive rather than reproductive, it is always 'creative', in that pieces of the past do not survive intact but are always transformed, lost, reused.

Cultural assumptions enter cognitive theory here, then, in at least two ways. Changing norms or wishes about control of the personal past affect the explananda for memory theory: and views of personal identity, of the social functions of the self, impose limits on the extent of association. It is not necessary to embrace his dichotomy to sympathise with Deleuze's point (1991: ix), in interpreting Hume, that association was 'a practice of cultural and conventional formations . . . rather than a theory of the human mind': this allows distance, in turn, from the logicist dichotomy in cognitive science between 'true' thinking, modelled on inference and serial reasoning, and 'mere' mental causation figured as inexplicable babble (Fodor 1985a: 12), which itself can be historically situated and queried. The privileged explananda are often intricately linked with each other. The assumptions of common sense so precious to Reid and to Fodor, in their different ways, include not only requirements on the accuracy of memory and the rationality of belief fixation, but also views on free will, unity and continuity of self, responsibility, agency, and autonomy.

Yet attentiveness to culture sanctions no irrationalist anti-scientism. There cannot be a 'hard' set of mature sciences of mind and brain without some concepts evolving with and answering to cultural demands; and it is not as if society runs along leaving brains unchanged. Wriggling across the continuous levels of nature and culture is not interesting only with lab coats off: it is requisite method for better science. This is not to renounce old dreams of generality: rather, with complexity and mechanism back together, it is a plea for refusing to close out individual difference, the background factors which make a single case special even when it does fall, roughly, under general *ceteris paribus* laws. Never are *all* other things equal.

11

Fodor, connectionism, and cognitive discipline

When . . . vibrations occur to the mind in their natural order, and retain their original, natural rational associations and the mind can retard or accelerate their progress, to a certain degree, at pleasure, and can deliberately consider them and compare the past with the present, when of course, memory holds her seat, connecting consciousness, as Hartley terms it, is unimpaired and the associationism of truth and decency and propriety, and virtue remain uninjured; in short when the mind can regulate properly all its operations, it is then a sound and rational state: but in proportion as the reverse takes place, in such proportion is it in a state of unsoundness and insanity.   (Thomas Arnold 1786: 284, in Hoeldtke 1967: 49)

11.1 Fodor, connectionism, and associationism

Jerry Fodor follows up his complaint that cognitive science is 'pathetically out of contact with its own history' (1985a: 8) by employing history in support of his own language of thought hypothesis and representational theory of mind. In The Modularity of Mind (1983: 14–36) he argues against historical association-ism and in favour of a 'vertical' faculty psychology inspired by the phrenologist Gall. The polemical paper 'Connectionism and Cognitive Architecture' (Fodor and Pylyshyn 1988) returns to the attack on associationism. Attention to old shortcomings of associationism undermines new connectionism, a trouble-some alternative to the language of thought.

In this 'enjoyable, but essentially digressive, interlude of Connectionist bashing' (Fodor 1990: ix), Fodor and Pylyshyn present arguments against both classical empiricist association of ideas and modern behaviourism which, they suggest, were decisive in their respective historical contexts, and ought to be decisive now (1988: 6). Even connectionism's vaunted neural fidelity is un-fortunate, only encouraging old errors: 'The idea that the brain is a neural net-work motivates the revival of a largely discredited Associationist psychology' (1988: 63).

Where Fodor and Pylyshyn lament associationism's links with neuro-science, others complain at their absence. Finding little concern with neural mechanisms of memory before the late nineteenth century, Schacter and Tulving (1994: 4) explain the lack of neural influence on cognitive theory thus: 'there was little understanding of the brain at the time . . . the doctrine of associationism held almost universal sway over philosophical and psycholog-ical thinking about memory, rendering any kind of physiologizing superfluous'. So the early modern neurophilosophy I describe in this book is a tradition neglected by some and rejected by others. For the moment, I accept Fodor's connections between old and new forms of associationism, and examine his arguments against both. How convincing is the attempt to blacken connectionism by chaining it to a tainted past?

Fodor is unusual in stressing the implication of weighty cultural and political issues in cognitive science (1985c/1990: 206). He does not deny the links between technical debates about the adequacy of particular theories and broader questions about the nature of psychological explananda and the relative importance of order and disorder in cognition. Reasonably enough as a practising philosopher of psychology, Fodor defends himself against carping doubts about scholarly accuracy with regular disclaimers that he is only 'making up some history', a justifiable practice if, as he says of cognitive science, 'we can see something about where we are and where we're up to if you provide a little backlight' (1985a: 4).[1] So I track this useful target through his entertaining corpus. My treatment of his complex philosophical agenda is sparse (see Loewer and Rey 1991 for an introduction): in this context I am interested less in refuting Fodor's arguments than in questioning his startingpoints. I sketch his historical contentions, before showing how they fit with his views on broader issues about discipline and argument.

The problem with associationism, in Fodor's eyes, is that it cannot explain the parallel between mental processes and *arguments*. According to Fodor, what makes thinking worthwhile 'is that trains of thoughts should be generated by mechanisms that are generally truth-preserving' in the same way as 'argument is generally truth-preserving' (1985b/1991: 40–1). His own representational theory of mind (RTM) is intended to provide 'a theory of mental processes that succeeds where associationism (to say nothing of behaviourism) abjectly failed; a theory which explains how there could regularly be non-arbitrary content relations among causally related thoughts' (1985b/1991: 42).

Since we now know that it is possible to connect semantic properties of *symbols* with their causal properties in computers, we can 'abandon associationism and combine RTM with the "computer metaphor"' by showing 'how to connect semantical with causal properties *for thoughts*' (1985b/1991: 41; compare 1987: 10–21). Fodor's RTM as a theory of *mind* is explicitly based on a theory of *rational* mental processes, of inferring, judging, and the like (see Clark 1988 for an excellent critical account). Rejecting the connectionist claim that we must examine 'lower levels' of the mind/brain to understand higher

---

1 Fodor acknowledges that his use of history is 'no doubt, all pretty loose – a matter less of demonstrative arguments than of elective affinities' (1983: 36). This sensible strategy, based on building up considerations and resemblances rather than on decisive argument, is notable only because it conflicts with his official view that only objectively rational argument deserves assent.

levels of function and processing, Fodor and Pylyshyn think it sufficient to argue that suggested microstructural to macrolevel correspondences or isomorphisms are unlikely to hold when 'the cognitive process under investigation is as abstract as reasoning' (1988: 63).[2] So proponents of RTM take reasoning as the primary explanandum for a cognitive theory. Are those relatively ordered psychological processes in which truth-preserving mechanisms do seem to operate a suitable model for the rest?

It is not surprising that theorists who privilege inference and reasoning find associationism unsatisfactory. Fodor's hero in the history of philosophy is Kant, who, he tells us, 'let the cat out of the bag' by pointing out what associationists had hardly noticed, that 'thought – like argument – involves judging and inferring' (1985b/1991: 41).[3] The leading arguments paraded against connectionism as a cognitive theory follow.[4] The regularity of trains of thought which, like steps in argument, preserve inferential relations is explicable only by attributing to thought the same combinatorial constituent structure as exists in grammatical sentences of language. The combinatorial structure of sentences explains the systematicity of linguistic capacities: only similar constituent structure in thought could explain the systematicity of cognitive capacities (Fodor 1987: 151; Fodor and Pylyshyn 1988: 37–41). If thoughts have constituent structure, there must exist mental representations or symbols, internally structured and capable of arbitrary recombination with other representations, in a language-like internal representational medium: a language of thought.[5] The

---

2 Compare another attack on associationism (Fodor 1986: 319), where the problem is that 'the notion of the form of an inference can get no grip in an associative net' because 'the nodes in a network have no form' and thus cannot distinguish between different but logically equivalent formulae on the basis of, say, the order of their parts, where humans *can* so do.

3 Arguing on these grounds that associationism 'failed to produce a credible mechanism for thinking', Fodor goes on: 'no wonder everybody gave up and turned into a behaviourist'. But this really is C-minus history. Kant failed to prevent associationism's dominance through the nineteenth century as a cognitive theory (on German associationism after Kant see Hatfield 1990: chs. 4–5). Fodor is aware, when convenient, of the survival of associationism in the face of rationalist criticism: when seeking causes of the demise of faculty psychology after Gall, he happily blames the continuing 'promise of an associationistic theory of mind' (1983: 27).

4 I focus on the case for the systematicity of thought, Fodor and Pylyshyn's central argument: they also argue for the productivity of thought and the compositionality of representations (1988: 33–7, 41–6).

5 Officially, Fodor wants to remain neutral on the question of just *how* often the kinds of regularity and systematicity evident in linguistic capacities are also evident in cognitive capacities: see his disclaimers in *Psychosemantics* (1987: 152–3). But he takes the existence of *any* such systematicity in thought as the basic explanandum. Moving to a conclusion, he writes stirringly that 'the key to the nature of cognition is that mental processes preserve semantic properties of mental states; trains of thought, for example, are generally truth preserving, so if you start your thinking with true assumptions you will generally arrive at conclusions that are also true. The central problem about the cognitive mind is to understand how this is so' (1987: 154).

claim that thought is systematic is then said to be confirmed by the intrinsic connection between the ability to think one thought and the ability to think others. In Bechtel and Abrahamsen's example (1991: 212, modifying Fodor and Pylyshyn 1988: 39) 'anyone who can think Joan *loves the florist* can also think the *florist loves Joan*. For this to be so, "the two mental representations, like the two sentences, *must be made of the same parts*".'

But associationism and new connectionism fail to provide the requisite internal structure: therefore neither can be a genuinely cognitive theory. Associationist minds have no true intrinsic structure. The associationist strategy, in Fodor's picture, is to recognise in your ontology only 'the elements among which associations hold – ideas if you're Hume, stimuli and responses if you're Skinner' (1985a: 6–7):

> if you say how the information in long-term storage is articulated, how the bits of information are connected to one another, then you provide the body of structural biases that somewhere has to be posited if one's going to explain the complexity of human achievement. That is good associationist doctrine. The structure that an associationist allows is the relational structure that holds among mental contents: not the structure of the mind, not the structure even of memory, but the structure of the things in memory. And since, of course, associationists are empiricists, they thought that [the] structure of the contents of mind reflects the structure of experience which in turn reflects the state of the organism's environment. That's what an associationist is: He's a guy who thinks that the apparent structure of the mind is really just the structure of the world. (1985a: 8)[6]

Because associationist organisms are slaves of context or creatures of the environment in this way, there is no *guarantee* that what is in their minds will develop the kind of constituent structure which, according to Fodor, is required to support cognitive capacities of inference, reason, and judgement. Learning, for an associationist, is statistical modelling sensitive to the frequency of, for example, co-occurring items presented in experience (Fodor and Pylyshyn 1988: 31). This leaves open the possibility that in a hostile environment, or in an unfavourable context of meagre stimuli, such minds would be unable to generate new combinations of existing items. This is absurd: a theory which allows even the possibility of 'punctate minds', minds which, for example, consist only of 'the ability to think seventy-four unrelated thoughts', without being able to relate them by way of their combinatorial constituent structure, has 'gone not just wrong, but *very profoundly* wrong' (1988: 40). It is not enough to say (Smolensky 1987/1991) that

---

6 Fodor quotes the learning theorist E.L. Thorndike's dissolution of memory to exemplify this exiguous explanatory strategy: 'there is no memory to hold in a uniformly tight and loose grip the experiences of the past. There are only the particular connections between particular mental events and others' (cited from Kline 1970: 662).

connectionist architecture is *compatible* with systematicity, that 'all biologically instantiated networks are, de facto, systematic' (Fodor and Pylyshyn
1988: 50; compare Fodor and McLaughlin 1990; and Clark 1993: 172). Since,
on the connectionist 'no-structure' story, 'gaps are the unmarked case', connectionists require a separate explanation of the 'blatant' systematicity
of 'inferential competencies': so there must be stipulated a mechanism
which 'insures' this systematicity (Fodor and Pylyshyn 1988: 49–50). Only an
architecture like that of RTM which postulates constituent structure as a
primitive property of mental representations can thus *guarantee* systematicity. No diachronic account of contingent evolutionary and experiential
history will count: it is just impossible 'to reconstruct the semantical coherence of thought' without postulating structure-sensitive operations
on structured mental representations: this is 'the problem on which traditional Associationism foundered, and the prospects for solving it now
strike us as not appreciably better than they were a couple of hundred years
ago' (1988: 67).

There are two broad strategies of response to such criticism (see, for
example, Chater and Oaksford 1990; Niklasson and van Gelder 1994). The
associationist can accept the Fodorean requirements on cognitive theory, and
try to mould connectionism so as to satisfy them: or the requirements themselves can be questioned. These are not exclusive strategies, and leaning
different ways may be appropriate on different issues (chapter 17 below).
Connectionist minds, for instance, are not such hostages to the environment
as the traditional sensationalist interpretation of associationism would have it,
and can introduce a 'body of structural biases' which is not dependent on *present*
stimuli. Like the pores and spirits in Cartesian cyborgs, neural nets pick up and
retain complex patterns over time, allowing considerable freedom from the
moment.

There are empirical attempts to model constituent structure in connectionist representations; but other considerations can at the same time be
brought against the central place given to systematicity and to the analogy
with linguistic capacities. The non-existence of punctate minds can be
ascribed to causes other than the mental structure in a language-like representational medium which RTM postulates. The priority of abstract reasoning as an explanandum is open to question. But there are other motivations
for not playing Fodor's game. Mike Oaksford and Nick Chater critically
examine the 'logicist' description (Fodor and Pylyshyn 1988: 29–30) of
(classical) cognitive science as 'an extended attempt to apply the methods of
proof theory to the modelling of thought'. Oaksford and Chater argue
(1991: 2, 8) that this view of cognition as 'an implemented formal logic' is
too rigid to account for looser cognitive processes which are 'inherently
revisable', as any particular conclusion can change on the addition of new

information.[7] I go on to identify further consequences of the logicist desire to model cognition on formal logic. An anti-logicist movement in cognitive science, drawing on distributed representation (Oaksford and Chater 1991: 33–4), will have to overthrow additional assumptions about cognitive control and executive mechanisms, and about the accuracy and adequacy of particular pictures of cognitive processes over time. It is important, then, to examine the fringes of Fodor's thought, by way of a slightly light-headed detour back through Coleridge.

11.2 Coleridge and Fodor on cognitive discipline

Samuel Taylor Coleridge had once been a Hartleian associationist and, going beyond Hartley, had believed in 'the corporeality of *thought*, namely, that it is motion' (Coleridge 1956–71: vol. 1, 137–8; Christensen 1981: 62–76). In *Biographia literaria* (1817), he attacked ugly consequences of Hartley's neuro-philosophical associationism (BL VII: 218–23). The necessitarian laws of association would not only subordinate final to efficient causes in the human being, but would make the will and 'all acts of thought and attention' into mere 'parts and products of this blind mechanism' rather than what Coleridge claims they must be: 'distinct powers, the function of which it is to control, determine, and modify the phantasmal chaos of association' (VII: 218).

For Coleridge, the truth of associationism would be the greatest intellectual catastrophe in history.[8] It would eliminate rationality, purpose, free will, the soul, consciousness, agency, choice and judgement, self, invention and creativity, art and beauty, prudence, ethics, and responsibility as well as theology. Although 'the excellent and pious Hartley' himself, after whom Coleridge had named a son, could surely not have been aware of 'the odium of these consequences', others 'in an unfortunate neighbour nation . . . have embraced this system with a full view of all its moral and religious consequences' (VII: 221). As antidote to evil French materialism, Coleridge quotes his own 1796 poem 'The

---

7 The specific kind of cognitive process which Oaksford and Chater suggest logicists cannot account for is 'non-monotonic' defeasible inference, in which 'it is possible to add premises and lose conclusions' (this contrasts with monotonic inference in which a conclusion, once derived, cannot be invalidated). Defeasible, non-monotonic inference, they argue, 'permeates every area of cognitive activity': if it 'cannot be elucidated within the logicist, proof-theoretic framework, then almost every interesting cognitive phenomenon will fall outside the scope of logicist psychological explanation' (1991: 2, 8–10).

8 This is how Fodor (1987: xii) would describe the collapse of common-sense intentional psychology in eliminative materialism. For Fodor, the end of the supernatural, a major component in Coleridge's fear, was much less disastrous than would be the collapse of belief/desire explanation. Coleridge believed that all the parts of the common-sense psychology of his day, including both the spiritual and the intentional, would stand or fall together.

Destiny of Nations', and vigorously describes how to treat an eliminativistic associationist. There are proud and mean people, the poem announces, who cheat themselves

> With noisy emptiness of learned phrase,
> Their subtle fluids, impacts, essences,
> Self-working tools, uncaus'd effects, and all
> Those blind omniscients, those almighty slaves,
> Untenanting creation of its God!

Coleridge continues in prose: 'Such men need discipline, not argument; they must be made better men, before they can become wiser' (VII: 221).

Those who push too far their belief in the powers of subtle fluids or animal spirits 'that etch and re-etch engravings on the brain' (V: 211) are too far beyond the pale for debate, and must be *forced* into line. Their mistake, in Coleridge's view, is in not taking the controlling and determining powers of will and reason as given in psychological explanation. They give in to phantasmal chaos, to the despotism of the senses and the confusion of senseless memory, and they make all of us victims of jumbled association, in a state of 'complete light-headedness' (VI: 216).

Coleridge reports at length an 'authenticated case' in which will and reason *are* partly suspended, of the light-headedness to which associationism would reduce us all. An illiterate young woman in a Catholic town in Germany, 'seized with a nervous fever' or 'possessed by a very learned devil' (more likely, because of the 'known fact that she was or had been a heretic'), incessantly raved in Latin, Greek, and Hebrew (languages she had never learnt), in sentences 'coherent and intelligible each for itself, but with little or no connection with each other' (VI: 216–17). A 'young medical philosopher' traced her past to find that she once lived with an 'indulgent' Protestant pastor 'as his housekeeper': he read aloud 'out of his favourite books' while walking up and down outside the open kitchen door. Coleridge's diagnosis of the 'feverish state of the brain' in this case illustrates fear of the babble to which we would all be reduced if Hartleian distributed representation really was the ground of cognition. If 'every partial representation recalls the total representation of which it was a part', or 'any one part of [an] impression might recall any other part', the only practical result would be 'mere lawlessness' (VI: 215). Without the discipline imposed internally by the controlling will, only moral discipline will stave off jumble.[9] Yet, as for Isaac Watts (chapter 9 above), surrender is intriguing too:

---

9 Christensen (1981: 110–12) questions Coleridge's aim in telling a story 'which, if it performs any function, reinforces the position of his adversary, albeit in a pathological extreme', and suggests that 'the maidservant in her feverish glossolalia' actually resembles Coleridge himself as writer, inspired by his reading into philosophic collage, a possessed ventriloquist overpowered by language.

in 1802, a trance-like vision while climbing had led Coleridge to speculate on such lightheaded states:

> when the Reason & the Will are away, what remains to us but Darkness & Dimness & a bewildering Shame, and the Pain that is utterly Lord over us, or fantastic Pleasure, that draws the Soul along swimming through the air in many shapes ... (in Holmes 1990: 330)

By 1817 such delightful torments were, officially, to be strictly warded off by asserting the primacy of self.

A perceived need for discipline in cognitive theory drives certain positions too in modern cognitive science, not as background assumption but at the centre of the issues. Again, I focus on Jerry Fodor's picture of cognition and human nature, set out by him with clarity, wit, and eloquence: and again, I am engaged here not in mounting a case against Fodor, but in tracing how his various commitments hang together.

Fodor's central contention was that 'what associationism missed ... was the similarity between trains of thought and *arguments*' (1985b/1991: 39). He gives an example from Conan Doyle's story 'The Speckled Band' in which Sherlock Holmes describes to Watson the reasoning which led him to suspect that 'the Doctor did it with his pet snake'. Reminding us that philosophers are now allowed to treat reasons as causes (Davidson 1963; Fodor 1968a: 32–48), Fodor suggests that the reasoning described by Conan Doyle as characteristic of Holmes, giving premises which allow an inference to a conclusion, is a particularly fine piece of *true* reconstructive psychology.

> Because this train of thoughts is tantamount to an argument, Holmes expects Watson to be *convinced* by the considerations which, when they occurred to him, caused Holmes's own conviction. (Compare the sort of mental history that goes 'Well, I went to bed and slept on it, and when I woke up in the morning found that the problem had solved itself' ... That's mental causation perhaps; but it's not *thinking*.) (Fodor 1985b/1991: 40)

True *thinking* is like arguing: mere mental causation, the mere causal history of cognitive processes, is no use unless the thoughts which figure in the causal history leading to another thought also provide good *grounds* for the subsequent thought. This, for Fodor, is how we profit from thinking: true inferences generally suggest other true inferences (1985b/1991: 40–1). This is what the associationists missed, and so, Fodor judges, 'Conan Doyle was a far deeper psychologist – far closer to what is essential about the mental life – than, say James Joyce (or William James, for that matter)' (Fodor 1985b/1991: 41).

This is telling literary criticism. In *Psychosemantics* (1987: 18) Fodor expands. The normative requirements on cognitive theory entail a vehemently anti-associationist aesthetics:

Exactly what was wrong with Associationism, for example, was that there proved to be no way to get a *rational* mental life to emerge from the sorts of causal relations among thoughts that the 'laws of association' recognized. (See the concluding pages of Joyce's *Ulysses* for a – presumably inadvertent – parody of the contrary view.)

Molly Bloom's dispersed discourse at the end of *Ulysses*, mixing memory and desire, her remembering shot through with bodily intrusions (Joyce 1922/1968: 659–704), from Fodor's point of view merely parodies the essence of the mental life. This psychology could not be more different from Conan Doyle's. In Molly's night thoughts, any part of an impression *can* recall any other part, and so there seems (to a rationalist) no real difference between her train of ruminative cognitions and the 'mere lawlessness' which Coleridge saw in the German woman's raving.

Fodor's wish for cognitive discipline is at work again in his modularity thesis, which divides specialised, genetically determined, superficial, and relatively autonomous 'modules' from deep and rather mysterious central systems. These specialised 'vertical faculties', operating only in limited domains, are what cognitive science can potentially understand (1983: 38–46, 126–7), because their computations do not involve accessing *all* the information available to the organism. They are 'isolated' in being 'computationally encapsulated' (1985a: 12): so scientific psychological explanations can refer to modular processes without having to refer to everything else in the system (Fodor 1989/1990). What is good, for Fodor, about modular 'vertical faculties' is that 'these homunculi are disciplined. They're not allowed to merely *babble*. Gall's picture of the mind is *not* one in which everything connects, in which everybody shouts at the top of his voice, and the guy who produces the migraine first wins' (1985a: 12). Where Joycean mental causation is chaotic babble, to be avoided on pain of headache, disciplined modules provide a basis for rational Holmes-like thinking.

But disciplined homunculi are not enough. Fodor notes that Gall was attacked for dissolving the unity of the soul. There is a 'real issue' in the quest for *something* to integrate the information provided by all these modules which do not talk to each other, a problem to which Gall had no good answer (1985a: 14). But Fodor thinks that *he* has, and says that Gall's faculty psychology and his critics' belief in the unity of the soul 'were *both* right' (1983: 118). After God (evolution) made 'bundles of these fast superficial stimulus-driven mechanisms', says Fodor, he 'created the soul to put them together' (1985a: 18).

The central integrating system is organized in a way that is fundamentally different from the way that input systems are . . . The reason that the central integrator guy is there is the reason that the soul is always there; namely to solve Gall's problem about what puts the peripheral stuff together. (1985a: 14–15; compare 1983: 101–19)[10]

It is no surprise, then, that these higher central processes turn out, on Fodor's view, to be all but inaccessible to science. They exhibit the creativity, non-encapsulation, holism, and 'passion for the analogical' which the high and puzzling processes of the soul were always meant to (1985c/1990: 202). Practically nothing, thinks Fodor, is known of what happens to information after the modules have got it 'into a form appropriate for central processing... The ghost has been chased further back into the machine, but it has not been exorcised' (1983: 127).

Fodor, then, embraces a central executive with a vengeance. While he acknowledges that this may seem a gloomy as well as a tendentious evaluation of the state of cognitive science (1983: 127–9), the rigorous separation of disciplined homunculi from mysterious centre has, for him, distinct advantages. As Fodor regularly informs his audiences, the thing is that he hates relativism, and, sadly, he finds relativism 'affronting intellectual dignity' in far too many areas, permeating the views even of some otherwise respectable philosophers who, he complains 'appalled', tend to take holism, and thus varieties of relativism, for granted these days (1990: xii). His belief that various kinds of holism, both semantic and psychological, lead directly to relativism (1990: xi–xii) leads him to address the arguments which make holism attractive. Only atomist theories of meaning, in which items have their meaning in isolation and can retain the same meaning across uses and contexts, guarantee the possibility of genuine disagreement and democratic argument about the truth (Fodor 1995).

Quine, Goodman, Kuhn, Feyerabend, Putnam, Paul Churchland, 'and many others' make the hateful move from holism to 'anti-Realism (or relativism or Instrumentalism)' (Fodor and Lepore 1992: 11, 211). But Fodor's most extensive efforts in this direction combat the ideas that cognition saturates perception and that theory saturates observation. The modularity thesis separates the work of the vertical faculties, which include the perceptual modules, from the integration of perceptual information which, as Keith Campbell has expressed Fodor's view (1988: 168), 'is the work of the mind's Highest Command'.[11] The theory-neutrality of observation, which Fodor needs if he is to avoid thinking that scientific disputes 'are settled by appeals to coherence, or convention or – worse yet – by mere consensus', is retrievable if modules are insulated and iso-

---

10 Fodor has another argument for a central executive in cognition (1986: 320–1), where he acknowledges that associative networks do not need one. Cam (1988) challenges the idealisation of rationality on which these arguments rest.

11 Campbell's paper is a thoroughgoing application of Fodor's modularity thesis to 'a new and modest vindication of common sense' (1988: 161) against displacements of common sense's epistemic privilege by Quine, Feyerabend, and Paul Churchland.

lated from context and background knowledge (Fodor 1984/1990: 251; see also Fodor 1988/1990). Only thus can 'our agreement on the general character of the perceptual world . . . transcend the particularities of our training and go as deep as our common humanity. Granny and I hope this is so since common humanity is something that we favor.' At least some common-sense judgements, what Campbell dubs the 'Basic Observational Fragment of common sense', can be used regulatively, to impose 'definite, if mild, discipline' on the excesses of theory (Campbell 1988: 170, 174).[12] Within this fragment, common-sense judgements are the same for everybody, 'independent of theorizing . . . preference or prejudice, and not determined by social circumstances' (including, presumably, historical, racial, or cultural situation): if a person is 'deficient in judging of these sorts of things', then they 'are regarded as seriously deficient indeed' (Campbell 1988: 174, 169).[13] Good liberals must uphold common humanity against dangerous jargon-benders who claim that mere persuasion and consensus, and thus not reason, drive conceptual change.

Fodor draws critical conclusions from his arguments against the saturation of perception by cognition. He notes conceptual and historical connections between this view and the corresponding determination not only of observation by theory, but also of values by culture, of science by class affiliations, and of metaphysics by language.[14] All these views are relativistic in suggesting that 'rational criticism of scientific theories, ethical values, metaphysical worldviews, or whatever can take place only within the framework of assumptions that – as a matter of geographical, historical, or sociological accident – the interlocutors happen to share. What you can't do is rationally criticise the framework' (1985c/1990: 205).[15] Fodor hopes that the truth of the modularity thesis will at least be a step towards showing that relativism is false. He upholds

12 This is the fragment of common sense which contains basic categories 'marked by very high, unproblematic, intersubjective agreement' which 'enjoy plainly operable check-up procedures' (1988: 169). It provides a non-foundational yet epistemically privileged 'body of Appearances to which theories must defer and against which they may be tested' (1988: 172).

13 Campbell acknowledges that only empirical research can settle 'just which concepts prove to be basic categories for human beings', but gives some 'likely candidates – parts of the body, the terms by which familiar household artefacts and tools of trade are requested, bought and sold, the genuses (roughly) of biology and geology, explorers' terms for landscape features' (1988: 169). Presumably it is only bad, relativistic theory that leads the anthropologists and psychologists who conduct such research to doubt the universality of classification schemes in these 'basic' categories: but, on the other hand, on the Campbell/Fodor view, their observations are not tainted by bad theory! Who is to go out and prove the existence of such unproblematic agreement?

14 The view Fodor opposes slips, in his characterisation, between the comprehensive determination of (e.g.) values by culture or observation by theory, and the weaker, more plausible permeation of values by culture or observation by theory, which would leave room for the involvement of other causal factors, whether internal or external to the agent.

15 This target is a very extreme incommensurability. There are many intermediate positions which take seriously the influences of theory on observation, class on science, and so on,

what relativists deny, the 'fixed structure of human nature', by insisting on 'the heterogeneity of cognitive mechanisms and on the rigidity of the cognitive architecture that effects their encapsulation. If there are faculties and modules, then not everything affects everything else; not everything is plastic' (1985c/1990: 205–6). The plasticity of mind is a myth: objective information is fed back by relatively stupid domain-specific faculties to an integrating central system which does the strange work of the soul (compare Fodor 1989/1990: 222–5).

Excessive dynamics in cognition would threaten realism, undermining the rationality on which social systems depend: so Fodor seeks cognitive theory which reinstates proper boundaries within the mind. Associationism is not only overly holistic, but also drops the mind's 'central integrator guy' who controls neatly bundled items passed on through the modules. The absence of control in associationism is a target for all its critics. Who will decode the babble?

without contending that criticism from outside the framework is impossible. Historians of science and ethnomethodologists distinguish the versions of a practice or set of beliefs given in 'members' accounts' and those given in 'strangers' accounts' (Shapin and Schaffer 1985: 4–7). If the extreme incommensurability thesis which Fodor attributes to his villains here were accepted, no historical or anthropological study of beliefs which we do not accept could ever get off the ground: there could never be an account by a stranger.

12

Associationism and neo-associationism

... what is stored is not in any sense any sort of item at all. An association is not a link or a path or a bond between two items. It is an unrecognizable aggregate of the two items it relates.   (B.B. Murdock 1982: 625)

Introduction

In any associationist theory of memory, surely, there must exist separate local memories to be associated, 'some number of basic units' (Crovitz 1990: 167) to be related in experience. No! The rigour of empiricist associationism, surely, was in tying transitions between ideas to current stimuli, and excluding all 'cognitive voluntary factors' (Crovitz 1990: 168). No!

Of course most associationists, from Hobbes to Skinner, did accept these obvious foundational principles. But a quite different history of association lurks in the same traditions, and the connectionist return to dynamics in cognitive theory is neither just a triumph of trendy technology nor a blundering surrender to blunt behaviourism.

Atomism's consequences were sad. Bergson eloquently lamented 'the capital error of associationism' (1908/1991: 134):

> it substitutes for this continuity of becoming, which is the living reality, a discontinuous multiplicity of elements, inert and juxtaposed ... the principle of associationism requires that each psychical state should be a kind of atom, a simple element. Hence the necessity for sacrificing, in each of the phases we have distinguished, the unstable to the stable.

Passive minds mechanically shuffle isolated bits of information, responding automatically to immediate stimuli, forever barred from true invention. Associationist minds were the victims of a dull environment with which they could not actively interact. There seemed no room for interesting analysis of interactions between the social and the psychological, for there could be no active cognitive state attuned to particular retrieval conditions: the properties of the dormant trace and of the bare input seemed together wholly to determine remembering, leaving no place for more complex retrieval dynamics (Schacter 1982: 165–70, 1996: 56–71).

Not the most valiant associationist would appropriate its *whole* history. Philosophers sympathetic to connectionism have made a range of responses to the charge that it is too close to old associationism to be a viable model of cognition. Some initially denied the link, but by tending to assimilate associationism to anti-mentalist behaviourism (Bechtel 1985). There are historical puzzles about just how associationism disappeared so wholly into behaviourism: but Hume and Hartley have more in common with Rumelhart and the Churchlands than either does with Watson and Skinner. More recently, Bechtel and Abrahamsen (1991: 102; compare Smolensky 1991: 202) suggest that connectionism is 'not a *return* to associationism; it is not *mere* associationism; but its most obvious ancestor is indeed associationism'.[1] This is a more subtle attitude: acknowledging ancestral relations allows genealogical excavation of aspects of the descent. Bechtel and Abrahamsen list technical developments 'not even conceived of' by classical associationists. They note that hidden units, mathematical models of the dynamics of learning, back-propagation, simulated annealing, and other specific learning mechanisms are new. But they also suggest (1991: 102) that connectionism, 'returning to the original vision of the associationists [and] adopting their powerful idea that contiguities breed connections', has 'an unprecedented degree of sophistication' because distributed representation has been conceived of for the first time. Andy Clark too (1993: 233, n. 1) takes connectionism's non-linear computational functions, 'which compress and dilate a representational space', to mark it off from classical associationism.

But the history in parts I and II already reveals a longer historical background to dynamic distributed memory *within* old associationisms. Before pursuing Hartley's development in chapter 13, I confirm that atomistic, localist associationism is not the only kind.

12.1 Meta-features of associationism

An analysis of conceptual foundations of associationism must be sufficiently general to encompass both twentieth-century learning theory and classical empiricist epistemology as special cases without collapsing the general framework into either. Early cognitivist setting of 'formal limits' on associationist explanation (the ancestors of Fodor and Pylyshyn's (1988) systematicity arguments against connectionism) tended to conflate associationism with behaviourism by allowing only possible descriptions of behaviour to figure as elements between which associations can hold (Bever, Fodor, and Garrett 1968: 583).

But there is a broader standard picture in characterisations by historians as well as philosophers. Initially opposing epistemological nativism and faculty

---

1 Compare van Gelder 1992b: 189–91: connectionism is 'in a deep sense associationist', but is immune to old criticisms because it denies that mind and memory are passive recording devices for independent atoms of information, and allows that minds continually construct environments, rather than forever reflecting them.

psychology, associationists tried 'to reduce faculties to aggregates of elementary sensory units', the union of which 'was accounted for in terms of
mechanical connection, or a chemical analogy of compounding or fusion'
(Young 1970: 95–6). It is possible to extract four broad meta-features of
associationism, which I will then start to whittle down (compare Warren 1921:
ch. 9; Young 1973; Anderson and Bower 1979: ch. 2; Fodor 1983, 1985a):

1 *Reductionism, elementarism, or atomism*: psychological structures are constructed from a set of elements (ideas, sense-data, memory nodes,
   reflexes) out of which psychological structures are constructed. Complex
   elements are decomposable into simple elements.
2 *Sensationalism*: simple elements are sensations.
3 *Connectionism*: elements are associated together through experience, with a
   relation of association defined over the elements.
4 *Laws of association*: mechanistic principles, in virtue of which experience
   determines what gets associated, are used to explain the properties of
   complex associative configurations by reference to the properties of the
   underlying elements.[2]

These meta-features are subject to a range of philosophical objections. I
want to correct the first two before showing in some detail what goes wrong
when they are assumed to characterise *all* associationist views.

12.2 Atomism and sensationalism

Psychological atomism, the view that the basic elements in or of the mind are
primitive, unstructured, independent entities (whether sensations, sense-
data, or raw feels) is *not* an essential part of associationism, and indeed
conflicts with associationist talk of the fusion of memories, with chemical
metaphors for association, and, especially, with the ever-present neurophilosophical or psychophysiological strand in associationism.

Talk of 'simple elements', whether ideas or reflexes, by associationists is
vulnerable to the charge that ultimate primitives, entities which have no
complexity or internal structure, are far from obviously coherent (McMullen
1989, drawing on Anderson 1927/1962). Rumelhart, for example, refers to
'schemata' which are 'elementary in the sense that they do not consist of a
further breakdown in terms of subschemata' (in McMullen 1989: 5). These
look like Hume's 'simple perceptions or impressions and ideas' which 'are

2 Different versions of associationism are distinguished by the combinations of such
   principles which they allow. Possible mechanisms include spatial and temporal contiguity,
   resemblance or similarity, frequency or repetition, causation, inseparability, vividness,
   intensity or degree of strength, attention and degree of readiness, duration, recency, and
   so on. The mathematical learning rules of new connectionism are further examples.

such as admit of no distinction nor separation', and which make up the complex impressions and ideas which can 'be distinguished into parts' (*Treatise* I.i.I: 2). Such an 'ultimate simple' indistinguishable into parts would, it seems, 'have to be something which has no properties, i.e. nothing at all' (McMullen 1989: 6).

There are two linked responses to this point. Firstly, associationists are not now working with totally unstructured primitives: it is just that their 'elements' are not structured *syntactically* as are the combinatorially structured mental representations of Fodor's language of thought. No units or elements in associationist theory are *ontologically* basic as the logical atomists' ontologically neutral sense-data were. What are called associationist 'atoms' are psychological or psychophysiological and supervene on a physical base, and thus are not really atoms at all.

But an even stronger response to the problem about the incoherence of atoms is possible. In one sense, no *things* are associated at all in distributed models. There's no initial stage at which bare impressions float round the mind before they are hooked up with others: traces are always already complex. Effective encoding itself is elaborative, with new information rummaging and arranging existing memories, and old traces shot through with later accretions (Schacter 1996: 44–56). With no part of the system ever inactive, it often makes no sense to ask what items in memory *were* before they were associated with others: in dynamics, 'the beginning point and the endpoint of cognitive processing are usually of only secondary interest, if indeed they matter at all' (van Gelder and Port 1995: 14).

In turn, the second meta-feature of associationism can be challenged. Classical associationists' 'elements' were not always directly tied to sensations. Rather, they could be in systems which mediate between sensory input and behaviour. This is obvious in models of memory: the piled effects of past experience on the present state of the system and thus on current and future behaviour must work by way of long-term internal changes. In new connectionism, and in Hartley's version of classical associationism, relations with the environment are complex, some parts of the system being only remotely connected to the periphery. Of course new connectionists provide much more detail about mediating systems, but only if 'associationism' is assimilated to behaviourism and forced to appeal *only* to direct environmental stimuli will new connectionism appear conceptually new. To the extent that sensationalism *was* adopted by classical associationists, it can be attributed not to the psychological theory itself but to the epistemological anti-nativism of the empiricists (compare Warren 1921: 14).

The distancing of associationism from sensationalism has the advantage that psychological associationism gives no a priori answers about innateness. We cannot decide in advance on the roles of evolution and of early, past, and present environments in teaching the organism. It is an empirical matter to discover which if any sequences of associations may be invariant, given evolution. Certainly, many philosophers of new connectionism retain an anti-nativist slant, and the focus on learning as a natural activity of the organism avoids many pitfalls of extreme nativism: but others consider the issues still more or less open (Clark 1987, 1993: 182–8; O'Brien 1987; Ramsey and Stich 1990).

12.3 Hampshire, Coleridge, and the con/fusions of memory

Reconstruing the history of associationism, then, suggests the dispensability of both atomism and sensationalism. Only *localist* forms of associationism have the tinge of blindness which subjugation to the stimulus brings (compare Bechtel and Abrahamsen 1991: 102). The ongoing dynamics of internal activity, in contrast, give distributed memories considerable independence from the present environment. Now I juxtapose another recent critic with a further strand in Coleridge's attack to reveal clearly the different criticisms which, though considering quite distinct forms of associationism, share a commitment to an active self above and behind the memories themselves.

In *Innocence and Experience*, an extended specimen of 'the enterprise of a moralist', Stuart Hampshire argues that the habit of 'dwelling upon the past' for its own sake is one of 'the distinguishing features of humanity' (1989: 32, 114). Lingering on memories which 'are mine alone' is one way to 'preserve the continuity of my experience and . . . confer some unity and singularity on my life as a whole' (1989: 114). It is this 'appropriately continuous history', rather than the singularity of an individual, which confers true personal identity (1989: 115). Hampshire goes on to seek an explanation for the value we attach to the individuality afforded by memory's 'personal particularity'. In this context he describes memory in terms 'intended to run counter to the famous implications of the association of ideas'. But Hampshire takes localist storehouse models as the pervasive paradigm in the sciences of memory, and so complains that *all* theories of memory are incompatible with the reconstructive nature of human remembering. I concentrate on his specific remarks about associationism.

Hampshire complains that classical associationist theories of memory could not catch the similarities between human memory and a compost heap, in which 'all the organic elements, one after another as they are added, interpenetrate each other and help to form a mixture in which the original ingredients are scarcely distinguishable, each ingredient being at least modified, even transformed, by later ingredients' (1989: 121). Associationistic memories are unnaturally independent of each another, original ingredients still distinguishable, 'their identity and integrity unmodified by their neighbours . . . like beads on a string' or individual stones in a heap. Memory metaphors should 'convey the unmechanical and confused connections which intimately link our memories': Hampshire would prefer 'Heraclitean and William Jamesian metaphors of rivers and streams, which represent our memories fusing with each other to form our consciousness of our own past experience' (1989: 121).[3] There are, he argues, principled barriers to an associationist account of *causal holism* in memory, of how many different memories come together in a present act of remembrance, or of fusions in which encoded items might lose their identity and proliferate in a rich mulch of memory.

Hampshire's historical case is that associationism was *opposed* to the metaphors of rivers and streams which suggest this fusion. But this claim can be neatly refuted by remembering distributed memory: the leading associationist David Hartley suggested exactly such a picture. From Hartley's distributed model, worries Coleridge,

> [it] results inevitably, that the will, the reason, the judgment, and the understanding, instead of being the determining causes of association, must needs be represented as its creatures, and among its mechanical effects. Conceive, for instance, a broad stream, winding its way through a mountainous country with an indefinite number of currents, varying and rushing into each other according as the gusts chance to blow from the opening of the mountains. The temporary union of several currents in one, so as to form the main current of the moment, would present an accurate image of Hartley's theory. (BL VI: 215)[4]

This is exactly the metaphor for memory Hampshire recommends: but whereas he denies it to the associationist, Coleridge is well aware that the winding, gusting course of interfering distributed traces is just what Hartley's associationism catches. Coleridge ascribes to Hartley the very image of shifting control in a distributed model, with storage and processing entwined, which Hampshire had said was impossible for an associationist.[5]

---

3 This is odd: although James thought he had given 'abundant reasons for treating the doctrine of simple ideas or psychic atoms as mythological' (1890b: 552), he clearly did not think associationism was thus ruled out (1890a: 253–79, 1890b: 550–604).

4 This shows that chemical-fusion metaphors for association pre-date James Mill. Coleridge himself distinguished imagination from fancy in parallel terms: as Willey puts it (1949/1973: 24–5), where fancy merely juxtaposes existing images into mechanical mixtures in which the ingredients remain as they were when apart, imagination mingles its elements 'like chemical compounds . . . in which the ingredients lose their separate identities'. But Hartleian fusion occurs *without* the involvement of the will: it does not therefore reduce multiplicity to unity as Coleridge wanted, but confuses. See chapter 14 below.

5 Unintentionally, Hampshire's desiderata for a theory of memory actually read like a manifesto for new connectionism. My 'picture of the past' is 'confused, overlaid by accretions', my memories tend to interpenetrate and display a 'comparative lack of discreteness'. Memory is an 'apparently holistic device installed in the human brain'. He even uses 'network' and 'complex networking' to describe the system by which experience has its effects, and uses as an example 'the phenomenon of "take-off" in language learning' (a child's leap to sudden mastery in understanding and use of language) (Hampshire 1989: 122–3), on which some of the most hotly debated connectionist research has been performed. Hampshire's problems spring from his acceptance of the common assumption that holism is incompatible with mechanism.

It is just because of the contextual dependence of ongoing processing, as various causes conspire in temporary union to form 'the main current of the moment', that Coleridge in contrast sees 'the phantasmal chaos of association' (BL VII: 218) as too prone to fusion, too likely to destroy the identity of the original ingredients, too confusing to be left undisciplined by will and reason. In rejecting associationism, Coleridge requires a central executive or cognitive control system to determine actively the ongoing processing of passive items of memory which are kept cleanly independent of will, reason, and judgement. Perhaps what is more surprising is that although Hampshire, like Fodor, characterises associative memories as too passive, where Coleridge saw them as dangerously active, he shares, in more moderate form, Coleridge's belief in or desire for a strongly role cognitive executive.

Hampshire's critique of some metaphorical and philosophical models of mind and soul is convincing.[6] But in rejecting distinctions which would privilege reflective thought over 'lower domains of thought', he retains a distinction between 'active and passive thought' (1989: 32–41). This distinction, which admits of degrees, is 'an incontestable phenomenon, and is not an invention of philosophical theory' despite the difficulty of formulating or analysing it (1989: 39).[7] Our activities or exercises of skill become thoughtless when 'we' have become passive, when 'one's thought strays or is distracted, and one is no longer directing thought to the task in hand'. It is in this context that Hampshire again refers to associationism, in similar vein. When 'we' are truly thinking, '[when we] assert ourselves and . . . exercise our power of thought . . . we seem not to allow our thought to drift onwards as the immediate effect of external causes and of the association of ideas' (1989: 40). Mere association, mere mental causation, then, makes us passive creatures of the environment and of ideas: the fusion of such ideas, when 'we' are not controlling its pleasant liquid flux, becomes confusion,

---

6 Trying to undermine pervasive philosophical 'dead metaphors' of mind, like that of 'the perpetual conflict of desires, the chaos among the unruly populace, which, like the mob in ancient Rome or in Renaissance Florence, needs to be mastered and controlled' (1989: 35), Hampshire argues that 'the mind, unlike the brain, does not literally have identifiable parts'. This means that 'all pictures or models of the human mind and of its faculties . . . are inventions for a philosophical and moral purpose, and they are all in this sense arbitrary' (1989: 35–6). It looks as if there are then no facts about the mind to be found. But after effectively challenging traditional views of 'the normative implications of the ideology of higher and lower faculties, and of the virtues connected with the obedience of the lower', Hampshire goes on to say that 'one can go behind the ideology and look at the facts'. These facts (about active thought, reflection, and control) have nothing to do with science or theory, but can only be salvaged 'in this context of moral speculation' (1989: 38). The urge towards executive control has many channels.

7 Hampshire's distinction is focused on activity of thought in practical rather than theoretical reasoning, refusing to privilege a concern with truth over a concern with practical skills or social/political engagements.

the surrender of 'the natural dominance of thought within the soul or mind'.[8]

The existence of 'active and directed thought' requires something to direct it, something perhaps identifiable with the first-person pronoun which Hampshire regularly uses. This is 'the thoughtful self' or 'the supervisory self' which looks down on what 'we' are up to, in 'phenomena of consciousness' which give 'a clear sense to the overlordship of thought in the soul' (1989: 40). Critics' opinions on how to treat the associationist have changed in two hundred years. Where Coleridge advised the use of 'discipline, not argument' on those despicable foreigners who denied the sovereignty of will (BL VII: 221), what is now recommended even by a philosopher who retreats from the primacy of reason, is the mild, if definite, discipline of 'stepping back' to supervise the present cognitive processes which 'we' own (Hampshire 1989: 40–1). The maintenance of sufficient order, of creative fusion instead of lawless confusion, requires for all of these critics the separation of the true executive which controls and supervises from the stored items which it manipulates.

Hampshire argues that the true pleasures and value of individuality lie in the contemplation, by this inner executive, of my 'spiritual capital', where that capital has the form of memories which 'are mine alone, the stuff of my inner life', memories selected out of the 'multitude of memories which we know to be ours and no one else's' (1989: 120, 114–15). 'We', unlike 'intelligent but non-human animals' which cannot progress past learned associations, both can and do 'cause [our] minds to linger among memories, or to cherish and to preserve their memories merely as memories' (1989: 114). Hampshire does not explain the nature of this strange causal interaction between an 'I' and a mind, an interaction said to occur whenever I pleasure myself in making it hover among and cherish its (my? our?) truly private memories.

It is too easy to carp, when there is still so much to do, on the oddity of a-empirical speculations. It is still hard to see that models of distributed memories as changes in interrelations between parts can explain how order does, sometimes, erratically, emerge at the psychological level from the phantasmal chaos of multiple nested con/fused memory traces. An actual theoretical model is needed: on, then, to Hartley.

---

8 Phrases like this suggest that Hampshire's critical awareness of the dangers of hierarchical models and metaphors has not been driven far enough. He is happy to acknowledge the normative implication of the distinction between active and passive thought: 'a person actively directing his or her thought is an autonomous agent, fully responsible for what he or she achieves, and in this respect to be praised' (1989: 41). This is an admirably clear demonstration of the intimate connection between issues about, on the one hand, cognitive order or chaos, and on the other, normative conceptions of agency, free will and free action, autonomy, and responsibility, which form the basis for moral praise and blame.

13
Hartley's distributed model of memory

A main characteristic of nervous tissue is memory . . . neurones must be both influenced and also unaltered, unprejudiced. We cannot offhand imagine an apparatus capable of such complicated functioning . . .

(Sigmund Freud 1895/1966: 299)

13.1 Hartley's neurophilosophy

Setting out a theory of brain and mind in part 1 of *Observations on Man, His Frame, His Duty, and His Expectations*, David Hartley claims, ingenuously and appropriately, to provide 'nothing more than hints and conjectures in difficult and obscure matters' (*OM* preface, p. vi).[1] I discuss his general neurophilosophy and distributed model of memory, and its applications to various memory phenomena.

Some historians have emphasised Hartley's influence, and R.M. Young notes that the basic assumptions of physiological psychology 'have thus not changed fundamentally since 1749' (1966: 23; compare Smith 1973: 81; Walls 1982: 261). But little is understood of the detail of his cognitive science as opposed to its sources and development (Rand 1923; Huguelet 1966; Ferg 1981; Webb 1988). Beyond general historical surveys, there are few discussions of his work.[2] One recent history of early modern psychology explicitly sets out to decentre Hartley and associationism from the history of the subject, complaining that he had limited impact on psychology or physiology; that we should privilege Reid and Scots common-sense philosophy instead; and that Hartley was 'a historical curiosity with no direct legacy' (Richards 1992: 237). This, I think, is about right: without attention to the neglected tradition of distributed neurophilosophical models, there would be little cause to care. Hartley is part of a history of connectionism, not of behaviourism.[3]

---

1 The preface, from which this quotation comes, is a resolutely associationist description of influences on Hartley and of the processes by which he 'was led to' write, being 'carried on by a Train of Thoughts from one thing to another, frequently without any express Design, or even any previous Suspicion of the Consequences that might arise'. On the paradoxes of writing associationism, see Christensen 1981: 33–8.

2 Surveys include Warren 1921; Willey 1940/1962: ch. 8; Boring 1950: 193–9: among the more specific studies are Oldfield and Oldfield 1951; Yolton 1984b: 142–3, 180–4, 195–7; Ford 1987; Smith 1987; Lamb 1989: 64–7.

3 Where Walls (1982) criticised Hartley, and the later tradition from Erasmus Darwin to Bain and behaviourism (Young 1970), as a way of berating the ahistorical, acontextual

Hartley is often seen as philosophically unsophisticated, for example, in his compatibilist fudging about free will. He seems to make category mistakes by trying to explicate his psychology (associationism) by way of a psychophysiological theory (of vibrations), in the pervasive kind of early modern muddle which Reid and Kant, in their own ways, are sometimes said to have refuted (Reed 1982: sect. IV).

Hartley's metaphysics of mind is indeed ambiguous. Committed to the immortality of the soul, he needs to ward off the taint of materialism, and tries to retain metaphysical neutrality.[4] He formulates what looks like an epiphenomenalist view: 'One may expect, that *vibrations* should infer *association* as their effect, and *association* point to *vibrations* as its cause' (OM 6, 1.i, introductory note). Vibration and association have a 'mutual dependence' without 'any precise limit' (OM 71, 1.i.2, prop. 11). When worried by materialistic implications, not wanting to 'presume to assert, or intimate, that Matter can be endued with the Power of Sensation', Hartley indulges in the metaphysical profligacy of 'an infinitesimal elementary Body to be intermediate between the Soul and gross Body'. This venerable theological buffer allows him the disclaimer that while his first two (psychophysiological) propositions 'are true, in a very useful and practical Sense, yet they are not so in an ultimate and precise one' (OM 33–4, 1.i.1, prop. 5).

The different metaphysical schemes canvassed by Hartley could just be signs of confusion: but as he clearly thinks that his religious views are not endangered by his psychophysiology, it is possible to think instead that in these sections the working natural philosopher is stressing that metaphysical differences have little or no consequences for detailed theory. All Hartley needs is evidence of regular connection between mind and brain, and his common attitude is that of the second proposition: 'The white medullary Substance of the Brain is also the immediate Instrument, by which Ideas are presented to the Mind: Or, in other Words, whatever Changes are made in this Substance, corresponding Changes are made in our Ideas; and *vice versa*' (OM 8, 1.i.1).

Critics enjoyed pointing out that without the postulated material basis for association, the psychological principles are unfounded: Coleridge thought that without the mechanical basis of vibrations, Hartley's psychology loses both its support and the motive for its adoption (BL VI: 214–15). This is almost

nature of behaviourism, Smith (1987: 123) sees that Hartley's ideas 'prefigure some aspects of contemporary neurophysiology and philosophy of mind and thus provide a further reason for rescuing his vibrationism from oblivion'. Smith refers to Pavlov, but also to recent uses of non-linear mathematics in neurophysiology (1987: 133, 136 n. 78).

4 But he also notes, at the end of a controversial section on the mechanism of the mind (OM 511, conclusion to part 1), that the fact that matter and motion can yield nothing but matter and motion, is no proof of the soul's immateriality, that immateriality has 'little or no connexion with immortality', and that 'it is difficult to know what is meant by the unity of consciousness'.

right. For Hartley, neurophysiology is indispensable, and psychology is not autonomous: but Coleridge is wrong to think that the particular neurophysiology which Hartley has adopted is essential. The psychology could be realised in physiological theories other than Hartley's specific theory of Newtonian vibrations. This is clear, for example, in Hartley's attitude to animal spirits. He prefers Newton's hypothesis of solid nerves to the hollow nerve doctrine, which he attributes to Hermann Boerhaave while praising his work. Hartley thinks that vibrations must be propagated along 'solid Capillaments', but his claim is cautious: the hypothesis of vibrations explains the functions of the brain as easily as would that of nervous fluid or animal spirits (OM 18, 1.i.1, prop. 5). He goes on to say that the vibration hypothesis can accommodate the 'received Doctrines concerning the nervous Fluid, and the Animal Spirits' (OM 20, 1.i.1, prop. 5).[5]

Like a modern connectionist, Hartley is interested in brain structure and function. He locates psychological functions primarily in the white matter of the brain, citing evidence from 'experiments on living animals, from the symptoms of diseases, and from dissections of morbid bodies' (OM 7, 1.i.1, prop. 1). Disorders of memory, attention, and imagination are evidence for the role of the medullary substance in continuing mental life (OM 8–9, I.i.1, prop. 2). The cortex cannot be so important, since injuries done to it seem only to impair function if they extend themselves to the medullary substance (OM 7, I.i.1, prop. 1). But his underlying cognitive theory is independent of these specific assumptions about the brain: there is a looseness in the realisation relation between psychological and physiological levels of explanation. The relevant level of abstraction from neurophysiological detail is that of distributed representation, superpositional storage, and the memory effects which follow. The theory of vibrations accounts for these features: but other psychophysiologies might too (compare Ford 1987: 202–4).

Central to Hartley's neurophilosophy of vibration and association is an account of the preservation of motions in the brain, an account which drives both a general theory of memory and its application to a range of psychological and developmental memory phenomena. Hartley explains 'the agreement of the doctrine of vibrations with the phaenomena of ideas'. When often repeated, sensations leave more permanent effects than mere after-images. What is left are 'Vestiges, Types, or Images, . . . which may be called, Simple Ideas of Sensation' (OM 56, 1.i.2, prop. 8). These ideas can 'recur occasionally, at long distances of time' from the original sensation. Motions preserved in the brain explain what pre-reflectively seems to be action at a temporal distance,

---

5 Priestley, introducing his edition of Hartley's work, notes that while Hartley's theory does not postulate tubular fluid-filled nerves in the animal spirits tradition, it is 'in no way inconsistent with the supposition of their being of that structure' (in Yolton 1984b: 188, n. 28).

when ideas become present to the mind again after gaps. Hartley details the mechanism for this preservation (OM 58–64, 1.i.2, prop. 9): Newton's query about vibration as the basis of the persistence of sensation (Newton 1717/1952: 519, query 16; compare OM 10, 1.i.1, prop. 3 and Hartley 1746/1959: 2) is extended to cover longer-term preservation. Sensory vibrations generate or beget 'traces or dispositions of mind' (OM 58, 1.i.2, prop. 8), dispositions to what Hartley calls 'diminutive Vibrations' or 'Vibratiuncles and Miniatures'. These vibratiuncles preserve patterns of vibration, especially their direction, place, and kind, where kind means, for instance, the rate of recurrence of vibration (OM 58–9, 1.i.2, prop. 9).

Hartley has already spelled out relevant physical variables in the vibrating medullary particles: the 'four sorts of difference' are differences

> in Degree, according as they are more or less vigorous; i.e. as the Particles oscillate to and fro, through a longer or shorter very short Space . . . in Kind, according as they are more or less frequent, i.e. more or less numerous, in the same Space of Time . . . in Place, according as they affect this or that Region of the medullary substance of the Brain primarily . . . in the Line of Direction, according as they enter by different external Nerves. (OM 30–1, 1.i.1, prop. 5)

This reliance on such physical differences to transmit relevant differences in objects perceived is in line with the Cartesian philosophy of the brain. And indeed Hartley acknowledges a 'near relation' between his general plan and the ideas of Descartes, inviting the reader to get some 'entertainment' from a comparison and remarking that

> it seems not improbable to me, that Des Cartes might have had success in the execution of his [plan], as proposed in the beginning of his Treatise of Man, had he been furnished with a proper assemblage of facts from anatomy, physiology, pathology, and philosophy, in general. (OM 111, 1.i.3, prop. 21)

Hartley, then, specifically had Descartes' L'Homme in mind: the tradition of distributed models of memory was known to its participants.

Hartley apostrophises the medullary substance as 'the organ of organs': in 'the exquisite structure of animal bodies', it has 'a proper subtle ultimate structure, for the purpose of retaining a state that is often impressed' (OM 62, 1.i.2, prop. 9). Its function changes during growth, as its texture alters. It is so useful, the ultimate in design, because of its properties of specialisation. Hartley supposes that each medullary region, whence nerves arise, 'has such a texture as to receive, with the greatest facility, the several specific vibrations, which the objects corresponding respectively to these regions, i.e. to their nerves, are most disposed to excite' (OM 60, 1.i.2, prop. 9).

These specialised regions are all in continual motion: 'a very complex set of vibrations, arising from the mixture and combinations of degree, kind, place, and line of direction, exists always in the medullary substance'. The motion is kept going by heat, by the pulsation of arteries, and by incoming vibrations (OM 63–4, 1.i.2, prop. 9).

The incessant set of motions throughout the medullary substance is the key to the superpositional nature of Hartley's model of storage. Laid on top of the natural vibrations which occur in the womb (OM 60, 1.i.2, prop. 9)[6], repeated sensory vibrations in all the sensory regions of the medullary substance immediately overrule the natural state of each region. Many vibrations are propagated incessantly and simultaneously in each region, and, crucially, each inevitably has an effect: 'of the vibrations which are excited in each region, no one can prevail over all the rest, but each must leave an effect, in proportion to its strength and frequency' (OM 63, 1.i.2, prop. 9). This is the causal holism characteristic of distributed models of memory. Diminutive vibrations 'rise in succession in each region', with the actualising or rendering explicit of a particular vibration depending on the incoming vibratory patterns, 'the then present disposition of the nervous system, association . . . and other such-like causes' (OM 63, 1.i.2, prop. 9).[7] Some one vibration will usually 'have a more favourable concurrence of circumstances than the rest' (OM 64, 1.i.2, prop. 9). The processes described are parallel to the way a connectionist model settles gradually into a stable state due to a confluence or 'conspiracy of causes' (Horgan and Tienson 1989: 166; O'Brien 1991). One of all the implicit traces or dispositions left ('stored') in a region of the brain becomes explicit, or is (re)activated when certain contextual causal patterns are present.

Hartley's causal holism, in turn, is the basis for a theory of memory. After discussing the laws and mechanisms of association (OM 65–7, 1.i.2, prop. 10), he notes that, when vibrations are impressed successively, as opposed to being impressed and so associated synchronically, the trace left by the first vibration may be 'modified and altered' by the action of the second, which it in turn modifies and alters 'till at last it be quite overpowered by it, and end in it' (OM 69, 1.i.2, prop. 11). This suggests, firstly, that Hartley has some grasp of both proactive and retroactive interference: and, secondly, that despite talk of

---

6 This shows, as Lamb (1989: 78) sees, that Hartley is not a pure *tabula rasa* empiricist.

7 Hartley gives musical analogies, justified by the observation that, since 'the human body is composed of the same matter as the external world', it is reasonable to expect 'that its component particles should be subjected to the same subtle laws' (OM 61–2, 1.i.2, prop. 9). The accommodated resting state of a musical string depends on its tension, which arises from the mutual influences of its component particles (OM 62). Then the process whereby one vibration prevails over others, becomes active or explicit out of the continuing mass vibratory action of a region of the brain, is compared to the emergence of one musical tone over others out of the complex vibrations of the air during a concert (OM 64, 1.i.2, prop. 9). On Hartley's use of musical models see Kassler 1979: vol. 1, 456–9, and Kassler 1984: 69–70. It is not clear (as Smith 1987: 129 notes) how well Hartley knew eighteenth-century developments in physical theories of propagated waves. Nor is the significance of his use of the concept of frequency as a variable of particulate vibration apparent.

'simple ideas' his is not a strictly atomist theory. Separately impressed vibrations are *not*, as the atomist would have them, intrinsically distinct from and independent of each other.

The mutual modification, alteration, and destruction of traces plays an increasingly central role in Hartley's descriptions of interference in building up complex ideas from simple. This part of his theory, again, initially seems like the combination and recombination of individual elements into larger aggregates. But Hartley explicitly rules out this interpretation. It is only possible for one sensation, associated with a number of others, to elicit all of them distinctly if 'they belong to different regions of the medullary substance'. The production of *distinct* associated sensations will not be possible 'if any two, or more, belong to the same region, *since they cannot exist together in their distinct forms*' (my emphasis). If they are in the same region, says Hartley, then the first sensation will only be able to 'raise something intermediate between them' (OM 73, I.i.2, prop. 12). Only one *explicit* pattern of activation can exist in one (part of a) physical system. If many items are stored superpositionally in the same system, they cannot all be recovered *simultaneously*, even though they can be recovered in succession. When an input associated with two or more patterns stored implicitly in the same system occurs, then a characteristic kind of blending results, and 'something intermediate between them' emerges.

Hartley continues with further suggestions about the mechanisms of 'coalescence' and commixture of different kinds of 'compound miniatures' (OM 73–9, I.i.2, prop. 12; Ford 1987: 204–7). Complex ideas need have little apparent relation to sensory data (OM 75):

> If the number of simple ideas which compose the complex one be very great, it may happen, that the complex idea shall not appear to bear any relation to these its compounding parts, nor to the external senses upon which the original sensations, which gave birth to the compounding ideas, were impressed.

So memories may spill across each other, and the boundary between memory and imagination must be problematic. It is not clear what can count in such a system as continuity of (the identity of) a particular memory trace. Hartley compares compound medicines which have a taste and flavour unlike that of their ingredients, and the colour white, which is not 'the simplest and most uncompounded of all colours', but arises 'from a certain proportion of the seven primary colours' (OM 75). As Smith notes (1987: 129–30), this is not atomism, since the parts compounded are more like waves than billiard balls. The mixing is by fusion rather than by juxtaposition: in a coalescence, as opposed to a mere aggregate or cluster, the single whole 'appears to bear no Relation to its component Parts' (OM 322, I.iii.1, prop. 85): a coalesced idea may seem itself to be 'simple' because its ingredients have lost their identity, but it is in fact complex (*OM* 166, 1.ii.2, prop. 44; see also Ford 1987: 205–7, 220 n. 6).

The overall picture of recurring traces is, Hartley suggests, 'sufficient to explain the chief phaenomena of memory' (*OM* 78, 1.i.2, prop. 12). The distributed model of memory falls easily out of the general account of representation. Even though Hartley thinks his theory allows for the retention of original order in remembering, it does so in the opposite manner to localist theories like Digby's and Hooke's which took the retention of order as a given (chapter 5 above). On a distributed model, regularities, order, and control emerge out of complex continuous processing: and, it turns out, the 'phaenomena of the memory' in which Hartley is interested include not just veridical, order-preserving remembering, but also a variety of departures from such perfection. This leaning of interest away from straightforward cases of 'normal' remembering is characteristic of the neurophilosopher, for whom disorders and differences in function, from minor to major, act as source of correction and new understanding potentially applicable to ordinary cases. Hartley, a physician, was always attentive to the pathological, and would have agreed with Georges Canguilhem (1966/1989: 33; compare Brennan 1989/90: 158; Churchland 1983; Wilkes 1988a):

> Philosophy is a reflection for which all unknown material is good .. It is not necessarily in order to become better acquainted with mental illnesses that a professor of philosophy can become interested in medicine . . . We expected medicine to provide precisely an introduction to concrete human problems.

13.2 Hartley on memory phenomena

Early in the *Observations on Man*, Hartley defines memory as 'that faculty by which traces of sensations and ideas recur, or are recalled, in the same order and proportion, accurately or nearly, as they were once actually presented' (*OM* iii, 1.introduction). But a more detailed later treatment shows that this is a misleading summary of his view. Not only does he soften the requirement of preserved order (see below), but he shows that the 'faculty' of memory is just a name for certain capacities and experiences, the recurrence or recreation of traces in something similar to a previous order (*OM* 374–82, 1.iii.4, prop. 90).

Memory, 'in its full extent', consists of complex compoundings of ideas, or of 'the associations of associations' (*OM* 67, 1.i.2, prop. 10). In proposition 90, Hartley attempts 'to examine how far the Phaenomena of Memory are agreeable to the foregoing Theory' (*OM* 374, 1.iii.4). He refers back to the passages from propositions 8–12 discussed above, saying that the basis of memory is the 'perpetual recurrency of the same impressions, and clusters of impressions', which 'leave traces, in which the order is preserved': these traces can be said to be 'the rudiments or elements of memory'. Given distributed representation, no further deep theorising is required to explain memory, since storage is not separate from ongoing processing. Checking the theory against memory phenomena is all that remains. Memory's dependence on the state of the brain, proved by the effects of diseases, concussions, 'spirituous liquors, and some poisons', is 'peculiarly suitable to the notion of vibrations' (OM 374).

Hartley reaffirms that impressions of memory are correctly ordered. He had distinguished veridical ideas from 'sallies of the fancy' and dreams, on the basis of whether or not order is preserved. What marks some ideas as true 'copies and offsprings' of sensory impressions is that they observe 'the order of place' or 'the order of time', whereas others are variously composed so that 'the order of time and place is different from that of any former impressions' (OM 56–7, I.i.2, prop. 8). This seems to replicate Hume's use of order as a mark by which to distinguish memory from imagination (chapter 9 above). This is rein- forced by the apparently image-based nature of Hartley's theory: the veridical ideal case is couched in terms of accurate copying of impressions, and vibratiuncles differ only in degree from sensory vibrations, as Hume's ideas differed only in force and vivacity from the corresponding impressions. But, while Hartley obviously has much in common with Hume, I want to stress their differences. One is in the different distinctions drawn between memory and imagination, which I discuss below: but there are two other points to make here.

Firstly, Hartley tries to provide mechanistic *explanations* for both retention and loss of order in memory and imagination. Of the trains of ideas of imagination composed of copies of former impressions, 'reasons may be given for the varieties of their compositions' (OM 57, I.i.2, prop. 8). The mech- anisms of association, grounded in vibration theory, are what fix 'these traces or ideas, . . . and their order, in the memory' (OM 374–5, I.iii.4, prop. 90). These mechanisms are psychophysiological, and for this reason Hartley's Humean talk of copies has to be continually reconstrued. This is no simplistic pictorialism by which immaterial minds carry around ideas of ambiguous ontological status which somehow picture objects: rather the isomorphism is between the patterns of vibration in a specialised or dedicated region of the medullary substance at the time of experience and the patterns of traces or vibratiuncles in the same region at later times of remembering or explicit representation.

Secondly, Hartley allows that, in remembering, reproduction of the order of the original experience need not be exact. This is of some importance, for it confirms that any difference between memory and imagination can only, in terms of a *psychological* rather than an *epistemological* theory, be one of degree. The original definition of memory had traces recur in the same order 'accurately *or nearly*' as they were once presented (OM iii, I.introduction, my emphasis). But 'perfect exactness', says Hartley, 'is not to be supposed or required' (OM 375, I.iii.4, prop. 90).[8] In memory for detail, 'many mistakes in the subordinate circumstances are committed in the relations of past facts, if the relater descend to minute particulars' (OM 377).[9] Individual traces can be fuzzy: but gist representations emerge naturally. Hartley understood, then, that faithful reproduction was not a natural consequence of distributed representation and that errors in recall are to be expected when reconstruction is the basis of remembering: 'The mistakes which are committed both on the foregoing account and others, make considerable abatements in the difficulty here to be solved' (OM 377).

When he comes to working out in detail the relations between memory and imagination ('recollection and reverie'), Hartley mentions only briefly Hume's other suggestion, that recollection differs in the vividness of its clusters and the readiness and strength of the associations which cement them together (OM 377). He gives more attention to a range of phenomena which blur these psychological distinctions. Unlike Hume, he forgoes the ideal of finding a guaranteed internal criterion: at the end of his discussion of these cases, he notes, offhand:

> It is not, however, to be here supposed, that we have not many other ways of distinguishing real recollections from mere reveries. For the first are supported by their connexion with known and allowed facts, by various methods of reasoning, and having been related as real recollections, &c. (OM 378)

When there does exist some independent access to the past, then epistemological rather than psychological criteria can differentiate memory from imagination: but this is an external criterion. Hartley's realism was less sceptical than Hume's, so worries about trusting such testimony or independent evidence do not trouble him.

Hartley is more interested in phenomena of disorder in memory and imagination. What was reverie can turn to recollection as we come to believe an oft-told false story, which after many tellings 'hangs as closely together, as an assemblage of past facts recollected by memory' (OM 377). We are all 'sometimes at a loss to know' whether particular ideas which come to mind are recollections or mere reveries.[10] Emotionally laden events, like the death of a

---

8 This is a marked difference of emphasis from that shown by Glanvill in rejecting distributed models (chapter 5 above) on the grounds that they would lead to 'a little Chaos of confusion, where Nature requires the exactest order' (VOD: 36).

9 Such mistakes can easily become associated with the true facts, so that 'the relater himself shall believe that he remembers them distinctly' (OM 377, I.iii.4, prop. 90).

10 Because this depends on the agitation of 'the matter in the mind', persons 'of irritable nervous disposition are more subject to such fallacies than others'. Uncertainty about the provenance of our ideas also occurs in dreams and in madness (OM 377–8, I.iii.4, prop. 90). Proposition 91 (OM 383–95, I.iii.5) then fills out Hartley's account of imagination, reveries, and dreams, and includes a speculation on the utility of dreaming (OM 389) in

friend, seem to have happened more recently: the normal perception of time elapsed can be disturbed (OM 378) in such intrusive traumatic memories.

Hartley's stress on the fragility and uncertainty of memory, and his willingness to take abnormal states seriously as indirect evidence for normal functioning, contrast starkly with Thomas Reid's affirmations of the straightforwardness of memory's deliverances (chapter 14 below). Hartley applies his model to a range of memory phenomena. In discussing retrieval, on top of an orthodox account of decay, he allows for inhibitory effects whereby some memories can exclude others, and for the centrality of visual and verbal memory (OM 375–7, 1.iii.4, prop. 90). He deals at length with developmental aspects of memory in what he calls a 'gross general history of the successive growth of the memory' (OM 379). The imperfections of memory in children and in the aged can be explained psychophysiologically. In old people, for example, dispositions to vibrate are fixed in the brain by the hardening of the medullary substance, leading to lack of flexibility in association, comparable to that which occurs in the obsessed and the passionate (OM 380). After a concussion or 'other disorder of the brain' leading to retrograde amnesia, most former dispositions to vibrate can be gradually recovered, but the vibrations which took place at the time of the trauma are permanently obliterated (OM 380–1). There is an optimum threshold of desire to recall, beyond which performance deteriorates, as excessive desire changes the state of the brain (OM 381–2).

Hartley is aware of the homunculus problems which, philosophers believe, haunt his kind of representationist model of memory. He rejects out of hand the dualist metaphysics which would require a further internal act of recognition to ground and explain human recognition:

> Some persons seem to suppose, that the soul surveys one object, the old for instance, and comparing it with the impressions which a similar new one would excite, calls the old one an object remembered. But this is like supposing an eye within the eye to view the pictures made by objects upon the retina. Not to mention, that the soul cannot in the same instant, during the same 'to nun' [instant] survey both the old and the new, and compare them together; nor is there any evidence, that this is done in fact. (OM 379)[11]

He has strong views on the relation between memory and personal identity. Not only are 'all our voluntary powers of the nature of memory', but 'the whole powers of the soul may be referred to the memory' (OM 381–2, citing evidence

what new connectionists have called 'reverse learning', in 'interrupting and breaking the course of our associations', to avoid the madness of extreme incessant association. Compare Crick and Mitchison 1983, 1986.

11 Compare chapter 16 below on the threats to trace theories posed by homunculus, circularity, and solipsism problems. There I argue that the criticisms only work against localist and/or dualist forms of trace theory.

from 'morbid affections of the memory' in which voluntary powers 'suffer a like change and imperfection'). The details of memory's function in maintaining a sense of self come out, characteristically, in a later section on 'imperfections in the rational faculty', which examines how far 'Deviations from sound Reason, and Alienations of Mind, are agreeable to the foregoing Theory' (OM 390–403, 1.iii.6, prop. 92). In madness, memory is fallacious, and the sufferer loses 'that consciousness . . . by which we connect ourselves with ourselves from time to time' (OM 390). Failures of this Lockean 'connecting consciousness', arising from disorders of memory ('with all the faculties thereon depending'), explain 'the erroneousness of the judgment in children and idiots', 'dotage' and the sluggishness of the brain, deliriums and the effects of various drugs, and fixations due to excessive study (OM 391–8). Violent passions increase vibrations unnaturally, with harmful effects on the 'self, with the peculiar interesting concerns supposed to flow from personal identity': while the forensic, social nature of the concept of person is clear in Hartley's theory of melancholy and 'absurd desires', in which those who have lost the 'connecting consciousness in any great degree' are apt to 'violate the rules of decency and virtue' (OM 398–400). To ward off the impairments of memory which often accompany madness, Hartley recommends the 'constant indefinite hope' afforded by 'religious considerations', along with 'bodily labour' and abstemiousness (OM 402–3).[12]

In summary and conclusion, then, Hartley's distributed model of memory, linked to a neuroscientific theory, is put to work in psychological explanation. While, for him, other neural processes (like animal spirits) could fill the same explanatory roles as do vibrations, there must be some such theory to catch the detail of cognitive phenomena, especially of disorders and irregularities. Hartley shows, too, that associationism can be and was cognitive rather than behaviourist. He does not require all psychological explanation to refer directly to behaviour. There can be complex long-term cognitive processes mediating between sensation and behaviour. The ties to the periphery are loose. Again, Hartley's theory does not display the atomism of the traditional understanding of empiricist associationism. Ideas cannot be strictly distinct, because the vibrations which rise in each region are superpositionally stored: the vibration

---

12 A full study of Hartley's moral physiology would require attention to part II of his work (Willey 1940/1962; Marsh 1959). Hartley's attention to failures of connecting consciousness, the flip side of Lockean continuity of self, is related to his mystical ideal of 'perfect Self-annihilation' (Ford 1987: 215–16). References to bodily labour and abstemiousness derive from Hartley's belief in important links between the psychophysiological and the digestive systems. They are also the final resort recommended against 'gross corporeal gratification', since Hartley thinks that 'the desire of the sexes towards each other', to be 'kept within the confines of virtue', must not be 'allowed and indulged' (OM 239–42, 1.ii.6, prop. 73). These stratagems may work: but for the person 'who desires true chastity and purity of heart', Hartley advises, 'there is no security but in flight' (OM 242).

correlated with each idea is not separate from and independent of the others in the same system.[13]

But, while Hartley shows us further the positive explanatory resources of a distributed model, his critics reveal just as much about its unsettling implications. Thomas Reid and Samuel Taylor Coleridge both attack Hartley's associationism in the course of wider-ranging polemics against traces.

13 Other important aspects of Hartley's neurophilosophy include his ideas on the will and mental causation, on necessity and free will, and on the relevance of associationism to educational practices.

14

Attacks on neurophilosophy: Reid and Coleridge

> To talk of an association between psychical particulars is to utter mere nonsense. These particulars in the first place have got no permanence; their life endures for a fleeting moment . . . There is no Hades where they wait in disconsolate exile, till association announces resurrection and recall . . .
>
> (F.H. Bradley, *Principles of Logic* (1883), in Passmore 1968: 164)

Introduction

In 1824 Dugald Stewart praised his compatriots' attitude to associationism, with its materialistic tendencies: in Scotland, he wrote with pride, the systems of Hartley and Charles Bonnet have been 'uniformly treated with the contempt they deserve' (in Tomaselli 1984b: 435; cf. Hoeldtke 1967: 55–9). But Thomas Reid's attacks on associationism were not driven solely by distaste for materialism. Despite Reid's vast metaphysical and aesthetic differences with Samuel Taylor Coleridge, their critiques of Hartleian neurophilosophy derive from the same horror. Their fear was not the modern one that associationist models of memory and mind are too mechanistic, too passive, to catch the rich personal complexity of cognition: rather, they complain, such models attribute too much activity to memory traces, activity which cannot be controlled by reason, will, or unified self. Mind, Coleridge warned, must not be passive, 'a lazy Looker-on', but must truly govern as a spiritual ruler (in Sysak 1993: 67).

Along with Bentham, says John Skorupski (1993: 3), Reid and Coleridge are the 'great names in the interregnum in British philosophy between Hume and Mill'. I want to show the lengths to which great men would go in fleeing dangerous distributed models of memory.

Reid's interests in science did not extend to sympathy for brain theories. He gave muted praise to Whytt's conclusion that '"true physiology" both proves the existence of an immaterial soul, and "leads us up to the first cause and Supreme Author of all"' (Wood 1995: 21), but was consistently sceptical of '[all existing] hypotheses concerning the nerves and the brain'. Reid correctly took a psychophysiology of 'undulations of animal spirits' to underlie Locke's and Hume's theories of ideas as much as it did Descartes': further, he saw that neurophysiological theories of memory had direct and morally unpleasant implications for personal identity (Reid, Essays II: 245–57, III: 339–60).[1]

My use of Coleridge's critique of Hartley in Biographia literaria requires more justification. His are not the clearest philosophical criticisms, but they reveal a deeply felt rejection of the implications of association for dearly defended values and beliefs, significant in understanding the reception and the perceived threat of neurophilosophical associationism and distributed models then and now.[2]

Coleridge's resistance to mechanism has recently been used to attack all trace theories of memory. Coleridge's critique is 'one of the grandparents of contemporary phenomenological and "humanistic" psychological critiques' in 'the lineage of German Idealism, which never succumbed to the allures of the machine' (Krell 1990: 84–5; compare Walls 1982: 271–3). But to the extent that Coleridge understands the mechanistic models he attacks, his critique rests on exactly the requirements of (allegedly natural) order, rationality, fidelity, and discipline in memory which Krell and other opponents of crude storehouse models otherwise rightly want to reject.

I question the legitimacy of thus simply invoking these critics in support of modern attacks on neurophilosophy, of praising Reid's scepticism about memory traces as 'well ahead of his time' (Wilcox and Katz 1981a: 238; Ben-Zeev 1990), without also embracing his extreme mind/body dualism and his strong views on the unity of the self. If Reid achieved a 'refutation of the storage theory' (Lehrer 1989: ch. 8), it was, as he keenly accepted, at the cost of dropping the idea of explanation and buying into non-physical souls and truly originary free will. Modern critics who wish to dispense with traces must either take on the whole package of incorporeal souls, free will, and inexplicable memory, or find an alternative theory to do the jobs which God, soul, and free will once did.

This historical work is the first step in my attempt to dissolve, bypass, or answer philosophical objections to distributed models of memory traces. As well as criticisms which suggest some internal incoherence or explanatory inadequacy in trace theories (chapter 16 below), a common form of criticism

---

1 As well as Reid's Essays, I use his earlier notes on Joseph Priestley's edition of Hartley (Reid 1775/1995): Wood (1995: 35–6, 249–51) describes the context in which these notes were written, and (1995: 20–56) summarises Reid's other manuscripts on physiology and materialism. Thanks to David Raynor for first sending me copies of this material, and to Derek Brookes (whose outstanding editions of Reid's Inquiry and Essays should soon be published) for conversation and help on Reid.

2 For Coleridge's changing attitudes to Hartley see Christensen 1981: ch. 2. His rejection of associationism is usually dated to 1801, when he wrote to Thomas Poole that he had 'overthrown the doctrine of Association, as taught by Hartley, and with it all the irreligious metaphysics of modern Infidels' (1956–71: vol.2, 706–7): but a more uncertain development is traced by Christensen (1981: 76–95), Holmes (1990: 300), and Sysak (1993: 64–72).

takes the form of a transcendental argument. If Hartleian associationism, say, is true, then, according to the critic, something (x) would be impossible: but we humans have x, so therefore associationism is false. Here x can be any of a number of things, such as continuity of self, free will or free agency, rationality, spiritual unity, control over one's memories, moral responsibility, consciousness, self-consciousness, invention or creativity, individual auton- omy, and so on. When the critics, from Digby and Glanvill through Reid and Coleridge to modern enemies of distributed models, impose require- ments of strict cognitive discipline on psychological theories of memory, they tend to see the only alternative to such order as mere babble or cognitive anarchy.

14.1 The preservation of motions in the brain

Critics of Descartes' theory of memory (chapter 5) denied that either patterns of animal spirit flow or the structure of brain fibres could be enduringly modified by experience. The same worry surfaces in Reid and Coleridge.

'Philosophers suppose, without any evidence, that... the impression on the brain continues, and is permanent' (Reid, Essays III.7: 354a). Although, Reid notes, the brain 'has been dissected times innumerable by the nicest anatomists', it has proved impossible to find any 'vestige of an image of any external object' (II.4: 256b). The brain is 'the most improper substance that can be imagined for receiving or retaining images, being a soft, moist, medullary substance' (II.4: 256b). There is no evidence that 'the impression made upon the brain in perception [even if, contra Reid, there was one] remains after the object is removed' (III.7: 354a). Reid thinks it unlikely that any impressions are permanent, or that, 'when the cause is removed, the effect continues. The brain surely does not appear more fitted to retain an impres- sion than the organ and nerve' (III.7: 354a). He rejects not just mentalistic image theories of memory, but any notion that experience leaves physiological traces.

So no reference to the brain will be truly explanatory. Even if 'a certain constitution or state of the brain is necessary to memory', and even if medicine discovered how to preserve 'that temperament of the brain which is favourable to memory, and [how to remedy] the disorders of that temperament', this knowledge of 'that state of the brain which causes memory' would yet leave us 'as ignorant as before how that state contributes to memory' (III.7: 354a). Knowledge of causes is not understanding: alleged causal explanation is 'to no purpose – memory remains unaccountable', just another series of facts 'inscrutable to the human understanding' (III.7: 354b, 355a; compare Inquiry II.3, Reid 1764/1970: 25). Reid will discuss only 'things obvious and certain with regard to memory', of which there are few: like some other 'direct realists', he allows only for criticism of existing theories, rejecting any possibility of an alternative positive account.[3] Causal theories are rejected to the remarkable extent that Reid sees no differences between our knowledge of the past and of the future.

Reid's attack on neurophilosophical explanation derives from his brand of substance dualism. Reid does not need explanations or theories of cognitive processes: he is more consistent than Descartes, whom he praises as 'the first who drew a distinct line between the material and the intellectual world' (Essays II.8: 270), in refusing to countenance any potentially boundary-blurring scientific hypotheses or theoretical entities. Reid includes far more than Descartes did in the category of the unambiguously mental, and had earlier worried at Descartes' tendency to spiritualize body (Inquiry VII, Reid 1764/ 1970: 260). It must be acknowledged

> that we know not what that State of the Brain is which we call a Sound State, and which is necessary to the exercise of our Mental Powers; nor do we know what are the changes from this sound State by which Memory Reason or any other Mental Power is injured. There may be changes in the Brain that hurt our faculties without producing any Ideas that correspond to those changes . . . (Reid 1775/1995: 153)

This may seem sensible caution: there can be non-cognitive physiological disturbances which make no mental difference. But Reid continues:

> On the other hand although very intense thinking or violent passions of the Mind may sometimes produce changes in the Brain: it by no means follows that every Idea that passes in the Mind has a corresponding change in the Brain which attends it. (1775/1995: 153)

This substance dualism, belief in the possibility of mental differences without any physical differences, is one source of resistance to trace theory which was not so apparent in the earlier critics. It fuels Reid's attacks on theories of brain processes which would allow the blending together of mind and matter, so that it might be 'impossible to say where the one ends and the other

3 John Yolton (1984b: 184–5) contends that 'Reid did not reject all physiology'. He rightly points out Reid's acceptance that physical impressions which correspond to perceptions are *necessary* for perception: but it is exactly the use which Hartley and others make of such correspondences and correlations between physical and mental states to which Reid objects. Reid allows this much to a truly empirical pure neuroscience just to ensure that it will be cordoned off, irrelevant to cognition. Giving necessary and sufficient conditions for perception or cognition is for Reid, as for modern 'direct realists' (Michell 1988: 247; chapter 15 below), not even an approach to an *explanation* of perception or cognition. A proto-functionalist interpretation of Reid's vaunted nescience (Lehrer 1989: ch. 8) is that Reid assumes that operations of the mind, including the 'faculty' of memory, could have been realised in ways other than they in fact are if God had so willed: but this is no reason to claim that we learn *nothing* about them by understanding how they are in fact realised in us. On Reid's philosophy of mind see also Gallie 1989; Smith 1990.

begins' (*Essays* II.8: 270).[4] Before turning to an attack on Hartley's vibration theory, Reid refers to Descartes' use of hollow-nerve theory and animal spirits 'going and returning in the nerves' to explain muscular motion, perception, memory, and imagination. He mocks Descartes' descriptions, 'as if he had been an eye-witness of these operations', and concludes that there is no confirming evidence for spirits and hollow nerves (II.3: 248b). Reid thus devotes critical attention instead to Newtonian models of ether or vibrations in solid nerves. The dualistic motivation for attacking both models is explicit in a later unpublished paper on muscular motion:

> *Animal spirits* . . . and vibrations in an elastick Ether which pervades all Bodies are all Hypotheses, and like all other Hypotheses in Philosophy labour under two defects. First they suppose the Existence of certain things of whose existence we have no Evidence, and Secondly when they are supposed to exist they do not account for the phenomena they are brought to explain . . . [Nervous transmission and muscular motion cannot] be accounted for by any laws of Mechanism we know. It is something beyond Mechanism and of a superior Nature. (In French 1981: 133–4, n. 44)

This is no invitation to vitalism: in addition to the narrow Newtonian strictures on caution with hypotheses, Reid wants to refer sensation and motion directly to the non-physical soul.

Coleridge too rejects the possibility that motions could be preserved in the nervous system. Physical dispositions, central to distributed models of memory, are ridiculed:

> the possibility of such a disposition in a material nerve . . . seems scarcely less absurd than to say, that a weathercock had acquired a habit of turning to the east, from the wind having been so long in that quarter. (BL VI: 214)

This is the culmination of Coleridge's attack on all existing psycho-physiologies. The Cartesian 'theory of nervous fluids and material configurations' merely 'obscured the truth' (BL V: 208), and Descartes' introduction of 'material ideas, or certain configurations of the brain, which were as so many moulds to the influxes of the external world' was a 'fanciful hypothesis' (BL V, 209–10, n. 1). He rejects in one purple passage Hobbes' 'successive particles propagating motion like billiard balls', all 'nervous or animal spirits' or 'living and intelligent fluids, that etch and re-etch engravings on the brain',[5] Hartley's oscillating ether in solid fibres, and two notions of 'yet more recent dreamers'.

---

4 This clearly shows the difference between Reid and, say, Henry More, who was equally concerned with defending the immateriality of the soul. Where More happily accepted churning animal spirits construed merely as instruments of soul (chapter 7, section 7.2 above), Reid rejects all intermediary entities: only God and mind can be active.

5 Coleridge referred only metaphorically to his own 'animal Spirits' which corrected his friend Poole's melancholy (Holmes 1990: 294).

These are the suggestions of 'chemical compositions by elective affinity', and of 'an electric light . . . which rises to the brain . . . and there, disporting in various shapes, as the balance of plus and minus, or negative and positive, is destroyed or re-established, images out both past and present' (BL v, 211). Aristotle's account of association is praised just because it has no spirits or fluids or ethers or chemicals, Coleridge thinking that Aristotle dualistically separated ideas entirely from material motion (BL v, 211).

Coleridge provides one extended argument against Hartley (one, he claims, of 'a hundred possible confutations'), which starts by reminding us that Hartley's ideas are 'appropriate configurative vibrations' (BL VI: 214).[6] The same idea-vibration cannot be produced both (in perception) by an external object and (in memory) by another associated idea-vibration (originally caused by a different object). It cannot be the same idea-vibration, unless 'different causes may produce the same effect'. It becomes clear that Coleridge is thinking here only of a localist storehouse model memory when he goes on to reject 'the pre-existence of the ideas, in any chain of association, as so many differently coloured billiard-balls in contact, so that when an object, the billiard-stick, strikes the first or white ball, the same motion propagates itself through the red, green, blue and black, and sets the whole in motion' (BL VI: 214). But Hartley did not take ideas to pre-exist: they rather are excited or evoked, or 'rise in succession', because many are superpositionally stored in the same physical sub-system. Coleridge's criticism would apply more justly to models of memory like Hooke's coils (chapter 5 above).

When Coleridge grants, for the sake of argument, the possibility of dispositions being acquired by nervous substance, he again addresses a local model (BL VI: 214). If 'every idea has its own nerve and correspondent oscillation' in a one-to-one correspondence, it would have to have an infinity of connections to all other ideas with which it could be associated, and there would be no explanation for the arising of any particular vibration. All predispositions in memory somehow have to be always equally active or present: representations must be explicitly tokened to have causal influence on processing.

Yet Coleridge does have some grasp of distributed memory. He also addresses the case in which every idea does *not* have its own single 'nerve and correspondent oscillation'. Then, 'every nerve having several dispositions, when the motion of any other nerve is propagated into it, there will be no ground or cause present, why exactly the oscillation m should arise, rather than any other to which it was equally predisposed' (BL VI: 214). It would be

---

6 This argument, like much of Coleridge's historical material, was borrowed without acknowledgement directly from a 1797 analysis of associationism by Maass (Christensen 1981: ch. 3). Krell (1990: 84–5) simply quotes the first paragraph of the argument without critical comment as a refutation of the associationist fiction.

inexplicable, Coleridge argues, why a nerve involved in distributed representation, which takes part in the (dispositional) storage of several ideas, should at any particular time take part in the actualising or rendering active and explicit one of those idea-vibrations and not others. He does not acknowledge the particularity of motions which Hartley assumed would evoke idea-vibrations, motions which can arise from sensory input or from elsewhere in the cognitive system. There is no reason to restrict analysis of a distributed-memory system to its activity at a particular time. Just because such memories are mainly implicit as dispositions, explanations will refer to the context and history of the system to discover why particular input or ongoing processing leads to the reconstruction of certain patterns rather than others.[7]

14.2 Reconstruction and the persistence of ideas

Reid had already applied similar concerns in a more thoroughgoing fashion to all existing theories of memory. He reiterates that even the discovery of traces (impossible as that might be) would 'not in any degree account for memory' (Essays III.7: 353b–354a). What is missing is how such persisting impressions, should they exist, would produce their effects. What is the required relation between the trace and retrieval cue? Reid too, at first, takes localist models as his target, assuming that trace theorists require the actual, explicit activation pattern to be continually present from experience to remembering. He complains that on such a view the (permanent) impression or trace should always be causing remembering. How could the effect (the remembering) cease, while the cause (the active trace) remains? The trace, in order not to produce its effect continually, would have to be 'like an inscription which is sometimes covered with rubbish, and on other occasions made legible', to explain the phenomena of remembering after long intervals (III.7: 354a–b). Distributed representation is not considered here, for this would remove the force of Reid's rhetoric: a distributed trace is not like a permanent inscription, for it is not explicit when unactivated, and requires the complicity of the present context.

Reid moves on to examine Locke's account of memory, praising him for speaking 'with more reserve than the ancients' about brain impressions as the cause of memory. Reid takes the repository model of the first edition of Locke's Essay to be merely figurative. He engages seriously with Locke's second account, on which ideas are nothing when not perceived 'and therefore can

---

7 Krell moves from these arguments of Coleridge's straight to a critique of contemporary neurophysiology, including the charge that its models of memory are unable to take time seriously, being stuck in an outdated Newtonian world of 'separate sectors of space and time, atomic units of matter, and linear causality through contiguity' (1990: 86). Krell's neglect of old and new distributed models leads him thus to collapse all trace theories and all sciences of memory into monolithic storehouse models.

neither be laid up in a repository, nor drawn out of it' (III.7: 355a–b). Taking this 'literally and philosophically', Reid notes an ambiguity in Locke's model over the problem of the identity of distributed memory traces, and takes the ambiguity to be sufficient refutation of Locke. He argues that

> [it is] as difficult to revive things that have ceased to be anything, as to lay them up in a repository, or to bring them out of it. When a thing is once annihilated, the same thing cannot be again produced, though another thing similar to it may ... [I]t follows, that an ability to revive our ideas or perceptions, after they have ceased to be, can signify no more but an ability to create new ideas or perceptions similar to those we had before. (III.7: 355b)

Ideas which are 'actually nowhere', in Locke's terms, cannot remain in our memory and actually be themselves *recalled*: they must be other, fresh ideas which are created, and the mind must *really* 'paint them anew upon itself'. This might be construction, but it is not reconstruction.

For Locke's system to elicit true memory, thinks Reid, a further act of the mind is required, to perceive similarity between present and past ideas: the mind needs separate access to the past ideas (it must 'already have the memory of what they were'). But if this is possible, there is no need for the present revived idea, which then drops out, redundant. This circularity objection to trace theories pinpoints the difficulty of reidentifying traces over time which is particularly pressing for distributed models: if ideas or memories have to be reconstructed, in what sense do they persist? How is remembering really connecting with the past?

The problem of the persistence of ideas had consequences for personal identity. If psychological states like ideas and memories do not persist, how could there be any psychological continuity of self ? Reid and Coleridge reject immanent solutions, because the context of memory theory is concern about the permanence of the self, important for its implications for resurrection and eternal accountability. Locke's paradox of ideas which are actually nowhere and yet can be revived is exactly parallel to a 'contradiction' which Reid finds in Priestley, that 'the whole man becomes extinct at death, and yet survives the grave' (1775/1995: 134). Priestley held an unorthodox view that new 'organical structures' are produced at the resurrection: this, complains Reid, is a cue for atheism (and thus social disorder), for it would be impossible to know *whose* organical structure was reconstructed, to be sure that future judgement would justly track current action. 'The doctrine, that a man may survive his total Extinction, and may be drawn forth out of the Limbus of Nonexistence to a second Scene of Existence' depends on the absurd notion of unconscious ideas:

> Whereas other philosophers have held that men have no Ideas when they do not think, the Dr finds that we have Ideas when we think nothing about them.

Now, if Ideas may exist without thought, it seems an easy consequence that Sensations of pleasure or pain may exist when they are not felt, Actions when they are not acted . . . and perhaps our Ideas Sensations and . . . Actions are at Death embalmed and preserved during the State of Nonexistence between Death and the Resurrection, & are then united to the new organical Structure then formed. This seems to be the onely way in which this new-formed being can have an interest in what was thought & done & suffered & enjoyed by its predecessor. (1775/1995: 135–6)

Eschatology is, if anything, more important to philosophy of mind in Reid than it was in the seventeenth century. The alleged survival of ideas ('which were before thought to be as transient as Time itself') in the unconscious, such that a person can have a numerically identical idea on different occasions, is mocked, as Reid argues from the implausibility of feeling the same pain today I did 'half a year ago' to the absurdity of having the same idea now as that I had yesterday. He thinks that unconscious ideas are incompatible with the Hartleian neurophysiology:

Whether Vibrations and Vibratiuncles have the same permanent Nature [as ideas], Dr Priestly does not inform us. Vibrations have hitherto been believed to be Successive & in a perpetual flux. And if that be so it might be expected that Ideas which are the Effects of Vibrations should not be permanent. But however this may be, Ideas retain their Identity. How long we are not told. (1775/1995: 135)[8]

But this is just to ignore Hartley's talk of 'traces or dispositions of mind' (OM 37, I.i.2, prop. 8; chapter 13 above) which are left in the brain after experience and can later cause the reconstruction, the rising in succession, of 'diminutive Vibrations' which have directions, frequencies, oscillations, and places similar to those of the originals.

Opponents of associationism needed some alternative way for present states of mind to gain access to the past. Coleridge bypasses the problems about the persistence of ideas differently, through a spiritual idealism. It is probable, he says, that 'all thoughts are in themselves imperishable' since nothing of the activities of a 'living spirit', of 'that living chain of causes, with all the links of which . . . the free-will, our only absolute Self, is co-extensive and co-present', can ever pass away (BL VI, 217). Hartley's ideals of 'self-annihilation' clashed with Coleridge's belief in this 'absolute Self' (Haven 1959). Again, the denial of memory in motions of matter is backed by resort to a unified non-physical self. Coleridge also makes the same links as Reid here to issues of resurrection and

8 In a passage which is not in the Reid manuscript and so may be an editorial addition, the 'extravagant conceit' that ideas can survive 'independently of the mind's conceptions' is argued to be a great departure from the 'established doctrine of ideas', and incompatible even with Hartley, since Hartley took it that when a vibratiuncle ceases, the idea ceases too (1775/6: 383–4).

responsibility: the bringing before a human soul of 'the collective experience of its whole past existence' may exactly be 'the dread book of judgment, in the mysterious hieroglyphics of which every idle word is recorded' (BL VI: 217).[9] An allegedly firmer, less fragile, incorporeal memory transcendentally guarantees the identity of the absolute self, and ultimate moral responsibility. If the memory process was, as Hartley thought, diminutive vibrations rising in succession in the medullary substance of the brain, the foundations of morality and religion would be undermined.

14.3 Eliminativism and the self

Whereas Hartley was 'a warm friend to religion and morals' (Reid 1775/6: 47), Priestley uses neurophilosophical associationism as ammunition for the elimination of the mind. Seeing mind as 'only an incumbrance to the system' he has thrown it out (Reid 1775/1995: 134). In this section I want to look not at *arguments* against throwing out the mind, but at the interconnectedness of a batch of properties, properties which Reid and Coleridge think it obvious that humans have, and which they think eliminativists deny. It is hard to hive off a narrow part of common-sense psychology, whether as entirely non-theoretical or as embodying easily defensible theory, from wider ranging, culturally embedded beliefs which also seem like 'common sense'. Even to say that the particular religious and ethical concerns which constituted folk psychology in Reid's and Coleridge's times are no longer part of it now is to accept the theoretical and speculative nature of the self-conception evident in the 'common sense' of a historical period.

Ethical issues are central. If a theory of the mind/brain threatens established moral beliefs, the theory is in trouble. Reid believes that the Priestley/Hartley theory would overthrow ethics by removing the possibility of altruism: if 'disinterested passions' were learnt only by association with our interests, in the same way as is love of money, then we should surely 'be ashamed of them in ourselves, and . . . despise or pity them in others' (1775/1995: 140–1). Priestley, complains Reid, simply ignores opposing moral theorists such as 'the best ancient Philosophers, or Shaftesbury Hutcheson Butler and many others among the Moderns' (1775/1995: 140). His system makes evil the work of God, denies the possibility of sin, and overturns distinctions between virtue and vice: the beliefs and practices which keep society together would crumble were associationism true. 'The Love of Parents, Children, Friends, Country, nay of the Supreme Being himself would upon this System be the weaknesses of

---

9 Krell (1990), in his use of Coleridge against trace theories, neglects to mention this alternative location of memories in incorporeal spirit, in 'the body celestial instead of the body terrestrial' (BL VI: 217).

human Nature, and the effect of Associacions which pervert the Judgment . . .'
(1775/1995: 141). Implied, obviously, is the retort that such social bonds are
natural, not merely the effects of association, and so that the associationist
account of their social construction is misguided.[10] By yielding to materialism,
Priestley has been brought 'to think the Mind an Burthen & incumbrance upon
Hartleys scheme' (Reid 1775/1995: 154).

Coleridge too thinks it obvious that associationism leads to the elimination
of the will, of rationality, the soul and the self, art and agency, and to the
destruction of the foundations of morality and religion. Already in an 1803
notebook he had seen the necessary direction of his efforts: 'I will at least make
the attempt to explain to myself the Origin of moral Evil from the *streamy* Nature
of Association' (Coleridge 1957–1961: vol. 1, 1770; Christensen 1981: 90–1,
268). The law of association ('if law it may be called, which would itself be a
slave of chances') makes will, reason, judgement, and understanding mere
creatures of association, subordinating our lives to the despotisms of sensation and passive memory, and reducing us all to the level of the light-headed
(chapter 11 above). It is incompatible 'with even that appearance of rationality
forced upon us by the outward *phaenomena* of human conduct, abstracted from
our own consciousness' (BL VII: 218). Associationism would make thinking
arbitrary, would fail to show the rational patterns which govern sequences of
thoughts. But the implications of association run deeper than the mere disruption of cognitive discipline:

> The process, by which Hume degraded the notion of cause and effect into a
> blind product of delusion and habit, into the mere sensation of proceeding life
> associated with the images of the memory; this same process must be
> repeated to the equal degradation of every fundamental idea in ethics or theol-
> ogy. (BL VII: 220)

So it is not only the bare psychological explanatory scheme of common sense
which is under threat. The eliminativist attack opens doubts about the integrity
and utility of related 'fundamental ideas': soul and self, art and agency, morals
and religion are all at stake. With 'the phantasmal chaos of association'
allowed to reign unchecked, the soul 'as a real separable being' is worthless and
ludicrous, 'present only to be pinched or stroked'. What place is there for 'the

10 Compare a remarkable transcendental argument put forward by Bishop Bramhall against
Hobbes' determinism: Hobbes' 'principles are pernicious both to piety and policy, and
destructive to all relations of mankind, between prince and subject, father and child,
master and servant, husband and wife; and they who maintain them obstinately, are fitter
to live in hollow trees among wild beasts, than in any Christian or political society. So God
bless me' (Bramhall 1841: 23). Determinism and associationism would threaten political
and domestic hierarchical relations, so they must be false. On this form of historical
argument against determinism see Sutton 1991.

poor worthless I', the 'mere quick-silver plating behind a looking-glass' (BL VII: 219)? It follows from Hartley's philosophy, complains Coleridge (BL VII: 220), '[that] We only fancy, that we act from rational resolves, or prudent motives, or from impulses of anger, love, or generosity. In all these cases the real agent is a *something-nothing-everything*, which does all of which we know, and knows nothing of all that itself does.'

These are the passages leading up to advice on how to treat an eliminativist (chapter 11 above). Such nonsense might be true of the deranged: but *we're* not like *that*![11] Coleridge assaults Hartley's theory with all the rhetoric of dignity, humanity, self, soul, and free will. The aim is to convict associationism of self-refutation, by suggesting that authorship, action, and writing, for instance, would be impossible.[12] On the associationist theory, Coleridge complains, his own 'disquisition . . . may be as truly said to be written by Saint Paul's church, as by me', since it would render him a passive victim of external causes (BL VII: 219; he does not mention the role of internal causes in Hartley's system). This is somewhat paradoxical, given the nature of these chapters of the *Biographia literaria*, in which he annexes others' bodies of thought 'into his manuscript to supply a sustaining text that he can cover with marginalia: notes, interpolations, and revisions'. These 'traces left in a book', as Christensen (1981: 104–5, 109) says, allow Coleridge a borrowed home. Coleridge seems to have been led into his methods of juxtaposition, rhetoric, and example, rather than actively fusing them to the command of a sovereign will. For Christensen (1981: 104), Coleridge 'scarcely seems to have composed the *Biographia*, if by compose we mean the act of an intending consciousness bringing disparate materials into equilibrium'.

But in Coleridge's view, all the same, a system which would make 'the existence of an infinite spirit, of an intelligent and holy will . . . be mere articulated motions of the air' refutes itself without need of argument (BL VII: 220). For Coleridge, it is self-evident that association *presupposes* thoughts to be associated and free will to associate them (BL VIII: 226–7). The active mind *acts* on its conditions, sometimes, it is true, yielding, but often resisting, just as a 'small

---

11 At least, we *ought* not to be like that: in a dark mood, in 1801, Coleridge complained that he had always lacked the 'self-directing Principle' and was, 'as an *acting* man, a creature of mere Impact' (Holmes 1990: 315): his later attack on 'billiard-ball' associationism appears in this light as a prescriptive wish to escape the causal nexus.

12 Willey too (1940/1962) is tempted by such a critique of Hartley: he wonders what our role is, how we *choose* courses of action, whence earnestness derives, in a Hartleian world. Compare modern self-refutation arguments, beloved of Popper and Eccles, against determinism, which go roughly like this. If determinism was true, there would be no free will. But then no one could choose to put forward a theory of determinism, no one could write defences of determinism, and, obviously, no one could 'conduct a rational argument'. As Churchland (1981) says in response to this remark of Eccles', the argument begs the question by assuming that philosophy, writing, and reasoned behaviour cannot have causal explanations.

water-insect... wins its way up against the stream, by alternate pulses of active and passive motion' (BL VII: 222). There must be an *active* power of mind, as well as passive powers and the intermediate imagination. Coleridge concludes with an attack on artificial memory schemes, which can only produce 'a confusion and debasement of the fancy' (BL VI: 223).[13] Fusion must be controlled by the will, through the imagination, or confusion results. Coleridge's ideal fusions unite many into one, and subordinate multiplicity, reducing it to unity (Willey 1949/1973: 30–1). Coleridge needed unity, he wrote, for his mind felt 'as if it ached to behold and know something *great*, something *one* and *indivisible*' (in Willey 1949/1973: 12–13). Such unity could be found in the free will, which Coleridge wanted to be the ultimate refutation of Hartley, but which actually makes little argumentative impact on the *Biographia literaria*. Genuine unity, of course, cannot be accessed by Coleridge: 'For if the will be unconditional, it must be inexplicable / for to understand a thing is to see what the conditions of it were, & causes–. But whatever is in the Will, is the Will, & therefore must be equally inexplicable /' (in Christensen 1981: 94–5).

Reid too retreats from the empirical to the solaces of the mysterious interior. The self, for Reid, is a monad, separate from all its faculties.[14] Sometimes he thinks of it as ethereally connected to the organic at some strange neural centre: discussing the 'train of machinery' which God 'has made necessary to our perceiving objects', he follows the path of the physical motions from object via medium to sense organ to nerves to brain, then notes that 'Here the material part ends; at least we can trace it no further; the rest is all intellectual' (*Essays* II.2: 248a). More often the mind is simply asserted to be active and immaterial (*Essays* II.4: 251). A strong conviction of the sameness of 'a man's' identity over time is a necessary accompaniment of memory (III.1: 340b), reaches 'as far back as his memory reaches, [and] needs no aid of philosophy to strengthen it' (III.4: 344a).

The self, for Reid, is permanent, separate from, and behind all mental states: and personal identity, unlike the identity we ascribe to natural or artificial bodies, is perfect, unambiguous, and admits of no degrees. It is just as well that the notion of personal identity is 'fixed and precise', since it 'is the foundation of all rights and obligations, and of all accountableness' (III.4: 345a–346b). Reid's critique of Locke on personal identity is well known. I conclude this chapter by noting one strand of it: Reid's third observation on Locke's doctrine.

13 Coleridge provides an intriguing alternative list of the 'Arts of Memory': to aid remembering it is useful to have sound logic, philosophical knowledge of causal facts, 'a cheerful and communicative temper . . . a quiet conscience; a condition free from anxieties; sound health, and above all (as far as relates to passive remembrance) a healthy digestion' (BL VII: 223).
14 'A person is something indivisible, and is what Leibnitz calls a *monad* . . . I am not thought, I am not action, I am not feeling; I am something that thinks, and acts, and suffers' (Reid, *Essays* III: 4 ('Of Identity'), 345a).

Reid asks: 'Is it not strange that the sameness or identity of a person should consist in a thing which is continually changing, and is not any two minutes the same?' (III.6: 352a). Whether personal identity is located in 'transient and momentary' mental states or in the changing physiological states of body and brain, no self could remain constant over time: identity 'has no fixed nature when applied to bodies', while consciousness and memory are 'still flowing, like the water of a river, or like time itself' (III.4: 346b, III.6: 352a–b). Though Locke himself was of course 'too good a man' to have seen the abhorrent consequences of his views, they would erode the permanence of the self: 'and, as the right and justice of reward and punishment is founded on personal identity, no man could be responsible for his actions' (III.6: 352b).

Reid's belief in a higher centre, separate from specialised cognitive faculties, inaccessible to science, is one example of the entrenchment, after the heyday of early modern neurophilosophy, of those common-sense values and beliefs which their defenders thought would be disproved or undermined by associative models of memory and mind. Social practices which depended on the defeat of cognitive confusion were perhaps under threat: but the strong model of the unified continuous self on which they relied was buttressed and retained, at the cost of a dissociation of philosophy from the empirical sciences of mind and self.

PART IV

Connectionism and the philosophy of memory

A good metaphor would be to imagine what the waves on the surface of a pond would look like after various objects had been dropped in the pond. Say the objects were an automobile tire, a beer bottle, the kitchen sink, and a telephone. The wave action on the surface of the pond shows traces of all but is specific to none. (B.B. Murdock 1982: 611)

It is characteristic of a creature, in contrast to a computer, that nothing is ever precisely repeated or reproduced; there is, rather, a continual revision and reorganization of perception and memory, so that no two experiences (or their neural bases) are ever precisely alike. (Oliver Sacks 1990: 49)

Preexisting knowledge, which often aids in the construction of elaborative encodings, can sometimes seep into and corrupt new memories. Such corrupting influences turn out to be a natural feature of many neural network models of memory. (Daniel Schacter 1996: 104)

Introduction

In part IV I systematically apply to the case of memory some problems about mental representation which are much debated in theories of perception, and go on to defend the postulation of distributed memory traces against objections. Readers unworried by representations may be puzzled by the effort expended in evading dry philosophical complaints against 'those "traces" that still plague psychology' (Grene 1985: 43). But too many mistakenly take any invocation of representation to conflict with common-sense realism, with phenomenology, or even with neurobiology, and are thus tempted to dismiss out of hand the whole set of theories of memory I have described. These final chapters, then, are emphatically underlabouring toil: without clearing the ground by showing that distributed models (unlike static trace theories) do not suffer the conceptual incoherence with which critics charge them, no future and more positive interdisciplinary memory work will be secure. It is sad to have to be negative: but big questions about memory's roles in the interweaving of self and world can barely be sighted while we are repeatedly told that a trace is not a memory.

Yet, despite the shift here to conceptual concerns, these chapters are also continuous with the historical material of the rest of the book. It is not so much that historical theories can *solve* modern worries about the veil of ideas between mind and world, as that historiographical differences in interpreting early modern concerns about representation reveal that apparently technical philosophical debates on traces in fact open up more general and urgent difficulties about the self and the past, or about truth in memory. This also indicates the role of culture: although modern philosophy of memory, obsessed by scepticism in epistemology, has yet had little interest in affect and culture, in asking why specific contexts of recall lead to particular reconstructions of the past, the new cognitive sciences can, if approached with an eye to society and history, transform the way problems are addressed in the philosophy of mind. This is all still promissory: at this stage I am removing obstacles to contextual cognitive science, rather than practising it.

So in chapter 15 I argue that distributed models allow the dissolution of traditional hostilities between 'direct realist' and 'representationist' approaches to memory, and that neither contemporary Gibsonian realism nor direct realist reinterpretations of the history of philosophy offer conclusive challenges to their promise. Chapter 16 centres on a new taxonomy of the many criticisms of trace theories, and suggests that classical objections apply only, if at all, to local and not to distributed models. Finally, in chapter 17 I show how the motivating rhetoric of order and confusion in memory theory which permeates the historical critiques also applies in the methodological twists which connectionism provokes in cognitive science: memory is not a domain in which systematicity or regularity is always apparent.

Notoriously, Wittgenstein demands that we question the assumption that successful remembering must somehow correspond structurally to physiological regularities: 'Why must a trace have been left behind?' The expression of thoughts may be ordered: but 'why should this order not proceed, so to speak, out of chaos?' (1980: paras. 905, 903). From a quite different direction, Christine Skarda, a neurobiologist whose research centres precisely on chaotic brain processes, complains at Patricia Churchland that 'Brains do not represent. Representations are replaced by self-organizing neural processes that achieve a certain end-state of interaction between the organism and its environment in a flexible and adaptive manner' (1986: 187). Retention of the terms 'representation' and 'trace' is unimportant, save for polemic. But I want to show that their use in distributed models does not violate these strictures: although memory is not a notebook and 'the brain is not a writing' (Wittgenstein 1974: para. 131, 1982: para. 806), and although 'the word trace itself seems somewhat disreputable' (Goldmeier 1982: ix), it is still worth retaining it. Sandra Colville-Stewart's massive survey of physico-chemical analogies for memory concludes with the thought (1975: 402) that: 'it is the survival of the memory "trace" concept, some static, permanent, distinct storage form that each experience leaves in the organism, that links together most remarkably the oldest and most modern models'. If this is what traces had to be, then all hail to the critics: who would want them? But traces do not have to be static, permanent, or distinct, or even to be left by 'each experience'. What are conclusive objections to localist versions of the trace do not apply to the superposed traces characteristic of distributed models.

Problems of the self are raised by the historical consideration of representations and realism when, contrasting static and dynamic memory models, we realise that there really is a problematic 'third thing' in the old caricature of ideas barring subject from world. Ryle, Rorty, Grene, and all, encourage us to jettison the nasty intervening representations, hoping thus to rediscover the easy sense of being at home in the world which allegedly disappeared with Cartesian scepticism. But integration with nature need not be so homely: it is possible to argue that the troublesome aspect of the tripartite self/idea/world scheme is the subject rather than the mediating trace. There is a real world, a real past: and there are traces, patterns unfolding through time in complex causal relations with the world and with each other. And that is it: there is no further subject behind and separate from the traces at some deeper inner sanctum (Dennett 1991a), no 'stranger behind the engram', in Daniel Schacter's luscious phrase (1982).

So the developing interdisciplinary connectionistic project needs to find more fragmented and empirically plausible ways of thinking of the self, which do not impose unity and coherence in advance. Memory is a test case for understanding the multiple constraints of body and culture which leave us unable simply to alter our selves at will. Temperament, history, chemistry, belief, and expectation all drive the omissions, inventions, hints and colour of particular acts of remembering (Bartlett 1932: 308–14), and these are precisely the kind of individual differences which make some individuals more susceptible than others to suggestion and false memory. These causes and courses of mixed associations extend to the society in which reconstructions occur (Connerton 1989: 37): 'It is not because thoughts are similar that we can evoke them; it is rather because the same group is interested in those memories, and is able to evoke them, that they are assembled together in our minds.'

If we do not simply possess passive memories, but are in part continually formed by them in ongoing contexts of use, then the sciences of memory must inevitably range across mixed natural and social environments as well as brains. This is how a thoroughgoing materialism actually encourages research on contexts and cultures. Remembering occurs in an inconstant world of 'leaks, holes, escapes and unexpected resistances' (Canguilhem 1966/1989: 198) a world which impinges on aware human bodies. These bodies in turn respond by fallibly shaping both their surroundings and their views of the past. Yet this past so often still drives them, unawares.

15
Representations, realism, and history

We paint the remote past, as it were, upon a canvas in our memory, and yet often imagine that we have direct vision of its depths.   (William James 1890b: 1.643)

It is true that some philosophers have spoken of memory as making us directly acquainted with the past, but all that this comes to is a declaration that they trust their memories.   (A.J. Ayer 1976: 135)

Assumptions of direct access do not obviate the need to specify the mechanisms responsible for such feats.
(J.D. Bransford, N.S. McCarrell, J.J. Franks, and K.E. Nitsch 1977: 445–6)

15.1 Distributed representation and direct realism

Many Anglophone philosophy students coming to the topic of memory find themselves expected to get excited by old debates about representations and realism. My undergraduate assignment was on the role of images in memory, and required me to discuss whether the *concept* of memory was a causal concept or not: the underlying issue I was meant to address was the *direct* or *indirect* nature of cognitive access to the past. Memory would also crop up in discussions of personal identity, and in strange worries about whether I could *know* that the world was not created five minutes ago. Disagreement over the *nature* of memory storage between, say, local and distributed theorists seemed, from these perspectives, to be of minor interest, important only to psychologists: it certainly would not contribute to our understanding of the self. Interdisciplinary contact extended only as far as rude philosophers vainly lamenting conceptual confusion behind empirical assumptions about the trace (Malcolm 1970).

The debate starts roughly like this (Woozley 1949: chs. 2–3; Shoemaker 1972; Locke 1971: chs. 1–4, 8; O'Connor and Carr 1982: ch. 5). Direct realists, hostile to the memory trace, claim that in the act of remembering I am in direct contact with past events. Memory is 'an immediate knowledge of something past' (Reid, *Essays* III.7: 357), or 'the mind's awareness of past things themselves' (Laird 1920: 56). The representationist, in contrast, thinks that an explanation of remembering will include reference to a trace acquired in past experience which somehow 'represents' the events remembered. We do know the real past, says such an *indirect* realist, but only through the mediation of representations which exist in the present.

Neurophilosophical theories of memory, from Descartes to new connectionism, seem at first to fall on the representationist side. According to the Cartesian philosophy of the brain, for instance, traces are left in the fibrous brain substance through which animal spirits flow: remembering is the reconstruction of a patterned flow of spirits relevantly similar to the pattern present at the time of experience. Past experiences are part causes of present remembering:[1] only from, or in, the present events can the past return or become present. Remembering is inference, mediated by traces which represent the past events which partly caused them.

But in fact the relation of distributed models of memory to representationist traditions is far from simple. Both animal spirits and new connectionist models blur alleged boundaries between opposed approaches to memory, and satisfy many of the direct realists' requirements without giving up on science. The local/distributed distinction turns out to be precisely the point on which the philosophical issues hang.

In chapter 1, I mentioned Rumelhart and Norman's suggestion (1981: 2) that distributed models might 'offer an alternative to the "spatial" metaphor of memory storage and retrieval'. They asked (1981: 4): 'Can the theories developed within the place metaphor of memory be translated into a spatially distributed equivalent?' Like them, I have no simple answer: but I show that the distributed models can at least resolve or dissolve many specific problems within the long-running debates.

In this chapter I examine what happens when obstructive representations and nasty traces are jettisoned, arguing that direct realism in psychology and in the historiography of philosophy fails, as a positive alternative, to rule out legitimate questions about the memory processes and mechanisms which underlie our attunement to the past. In chapter 16 I set out a new taxonomy of criticisms of memory traces and suggest that, while existing responses leave residual work for the representationist to do, specifically distributed models can do it.[2] Many criticisms of 'the fiasco of the theory of traces' (Straus 1962/1966: 99) depend on the mistaken assumption that traces must be local, independent atoms which faithfully store and reproduce the past.

---

1 Many other causal factors are involved: the state of the system at the time of the original experience, the effects of experience in the interim, and the context of reconstruction in the present all influence the fate of the trace.

2 In the case of perception, Gardner (1985: 321–2) suggests that connectionism might reconcile Gibsonian realism and representationism (compare Humphreys and Riddoch 1986; Hatfield 1988b, 1989; O'Brien 1988). The problem in perception is whether we see objects directly, or only through representations partly caused by those objects. The object of perception is usually present, whereas that of memory is, on most views, usually not: direct realism is thus harder to accept for memory. I transfer and adapt arguments from the (extensive) literature on perception to the case of memory.

But I am not only out to confirm for the case of memory 'how prone anti-representationalists are to attacking imaginary opponents' (Wright 1993: 1). There is a stronger reason for reassessing this dry literature. The orthodox presentation of indirect realism includes assumptions about the nature of the self whose access to world or past is mediated by representations. Some objections to the trace are misplaced attacks on these implicit pictures of subjectivity. The different form of representationism I defend must find alternative descriptions not only of the trace but also of the self.

The link between memory and self can be relocated by way of two initial responses to the traditional debate. Firstly, I show that the trace theories I have described evade some old notions about representations.[3] Then I query the notion of a bounded inner world of pure subjectivity into which only representational proxies of objects intrude.

Firstly, there is no direct awareness of a trace or an idea from which the subject then indirectly infers the past. Representations were once meant to be immaterial or ontologically ambiguous mental items scanned, in turn, by a non-physical soul. Indirect realism was thus often seen as a form of dualism (Woozley 1949: 21–2, 29–34, 38, 53; Gibson 1979a: 223). When representations are thought of as brain states, it is clear that they are not immediate objects of experience which a subject then consciously puts to use. Some critics, keen to convict Descartes of incoherence, took him to accept direct consciousness of images etched on the pineal gland: but there is no good evidence for this interpretation and ample reason to reject it (Rozemond 1989: 228–43).

But when, secondly, 'inference' in perception or memory is unconscious, there can be no incorrigible awareness in the present of a private object (idea, image, sense-datum) from which the past is read off (Shoemaker 1972: 268; Harrison 1976). If the notion of privileged access to transparent mental entities was all the direct realist rejected, there would be no conflict with traces (Pitson 1986; Schwartz 1994: 10–17). 'Inference' in distributed models is an immanent computational process, as a system settles into a stable state, with no subject scanning input and itself computing conclusions from pure sensory data. The base worry about a representation acting as a veil or iron curtain, a useless third thing between subject and object, needs to be twisted by dropping, not the representation, but the separate subject. Without a unitary subject behind the traces, there is no principled way to distinguish input from transformed computational representation, data from hypothesis, or 'the given' from its supplementation (Schwartz 1994: 116–21, 142).

3   Important related attempts to clarify these issues include Cornman 1972; Armstrong 1976/1980; Wright 1984; Gigerenzer and Murray 1987: 61–105; Snowdon 1992; Schwartz 1994: 10–17, 84–124.

15.2 Gibson and Gibsonians on remembering

J. J. Gibson (1979a: 254) criticises the concept of 'memory':

> Because we are led to separate the present from the past, we find ourselves
> involved in what I have called the 'muddle of memory'. We think that the past
> ceases to exist unless it is preserved in memory. We assume that memory is the
> bridge between the past and the present. We assume that memories accumu-
> late and are stored somewhere; that they are images, or pictures, or repre-
> sentations of the past; or that memory is actually physiological, not mental,
> consisting of engrams, or traces; or that it actually consists of neural connec-
> tions, not engrams; that memory is the basis of all learning; that memory is the
> basis of habit; that memories live on in the unconscious; that heredity is a
> form of memory; that cultural heredity is another form of memory; that any
> effect of the past on the present is memory, including hysteresis. If we cannot
> do any better than this, we should stop using the word.

The rhetoric of this summary dismissal of all theories of memory, apparently
on the basis that they differ from each other, is not untypical of Gibsonian
ecological psychology. 'Direct realists' have written much less about memory
than about perception, and most is only critical. I concentrate on Gibson and
his followers, neglecting other positive anti-representationist approaches to
memory only through constraints of space, and construct a positive view.
Distributed representationists *also* complain about static traces, logicist cognitive science, and the theoretical over-intellectualising of cognition: perhaps
Merlin Donald (1991: 362) is correct to judge that in neo-associationism
'Gibson's neo-Gestalt perceptual ideas were given a neural foundation', or
perhaps this cross-classifying of the old distinctions over which controversy
raged shows that they had outlived their usefulness (Schwartz 1996: 90).

Gibsonian realism has been incorporated into the history of the new dynamics in cognitive science (van Gelder and Port 1995: 38–9). But the edge is taken
off its polemical tang, as if Gibson was recommending only a *temporary* shift of
attention away from 'models of internal mechanisms when the structure of
stimulus information remained so poorly understood' (1995: 38). In fact
memory research led the way in integrating ecological care for real-world set-
tings into psychology. After a period of debilitating tension between lab-based
cognitive psychologists and 'everyday-memory' theorists (Banaji and Crowder
1989; Edwards and Middleton 1990), the combined effects of Neisser's wise
unifying work (1982, 1988), of increased attention to autobiographical remembering (Rubin 1986), and of a need to find disciplinary consensus and relevance
in controversies over recovered memories have produced more naturalistic
research on interactions between rememberer and environment (see Koriat
and Goldsmith 1996 for an extensive critical review of recent theories,
methods, and metaphors).

Even though complaints about mainstream cognitivism made by early connectionists were very close to those in some Gibsonian work (Jenkins 1977; Carello *et al.* 1984), other Gibsonians adopted a messianic tone in calling for the salvation of psychology from representationist errors (Reed 1983, 1986), or for refutations of 'the traditional conception of memory' (Wilcox and Katz 1981a: 227).[4] Gibson himself dealt with memory only in passing, with 'tentative proposals' to replace 'the outworn theory of past experience, memory, and mental images' (1979a: 263): his supporters admit that a Gibsonian approach to remembering needs to be judged with some lenience (Michaels and Carello 1981: 185–6). But selective analysis of Gibson's later writings, in fact, raises doubt about whether there really is room in his approach for the explanations of long-term memory which the reviled traces were postulated to provide. Like Steen Larsen (1988: 338–9) I argue that an 'ecological mnemonics' analogous to Gibson's view of perception 'would have to take into account that most of the information that in the past specified states and events in the world is not available in the environment at the time of remembering' and might thus have persisted internally.

Occluding edges and the perception/memory dichotomy

For Gibson, perceiving organisms are 'eye-head-brain-body system[s]' (1979b/1982: 222) in direct contact with objects in their environment. The laws of *ecological optics* are 'regularities known to common sense', learnt simply by observing everyday events, and 'not by mastering a discipline in school' like laws of physical optics. Of these 'laws, rules, or regularities', one is particularly telling, both for Gibson because it 'probably cannot be formulated at all in the usual terms of physical optics' (1979b/1982: 217–19), and for me because of its applicability to memory theory. 'The discovery of the occluding edge' (1979a: 189) was, thought Gibson, a radical challenge to inferential paradigms in perception. Contrary to the assumption that you can only see what you see *now*, an object or a surface can be perceived *without* being 'present to the senses'. How is this so?

> The occluding edge of an opaque object of sheet screens (hides, conceals, or puts *out of sight*) part of the background, all of the far side of the object itself, and any other object that is temporarily positioned within the envelope of its solid visual angle. But occlusion is progressive and reversible. The occluding edge can be seen as such and hence to that extent, the hidden as well as the unhidden surfaces can be seen. (Gibson 1979b/1982: 218–19)[5]

4 Overall assessments of Gibson (which focus, as he does, on perception) include Richards 1976/7; Fodor and Pylyshyn 1981; Aurell 1984; Morss 1989; Stroll 1989; Hamlyn 1990: ch. 4; and Schwartz 1994: 125–52. For the view that Gibson's official hostility to processes and mechanisms does not render his work in principle incompatible with them see Marr 1982: 29–31; and Manfredi 1986.

5 Compare Gibson 1975/1982: 393–6, 1979a: ch. 11; Arcaya 1989: 105.

Since an object occluded in this way does not have to be a source of sensory stimulation in order to be perceived, Gibson says, traditional dichotomies between perception and memory and between present and past experience break down. It is, says Gibson, just a relic of old faculty psychology to think that perception is in and of the present, while memory is of the past (1966b/1982). Seeing what is hidden when 'the occluding edge is seen as such' suggests instead that perceiving, remembering, and expecting are all activities with duration, but that the question of what duration each has makes no sense. There is no moment at which a present percept becomes a memory (1979a: 253–5). Indeed, there is no basis to the naive trichotomy between remembrance, perception, and expectancy, between hindsight, sight, and foresight: perception, in a sense, includes all three, for what actually occurs when the present 'hides' past and future in the fact of occluding edges is that 'of course one simply apprehends the environment' (1966a: 276–7; 1975/1982: 396; note the characteristic rhetorical qualifiers).

Gibson's realisation that percepts do not need to be converted into memory traces leads him to claim that past objects and events themselves remain with us as objects of remembering. This encourages both negative polemic and positive trace-less approaches to memory. I look at the two directions in turn.

Memory traces, attunement, and the luxury of long-term memory

Gibson ridicules all non-Gibsonian memory theory, from static engrams to neural connections, because they locate memory information in organisms rather than in the world. Since, for Gibson, percepts are not converted after a momentary stimulus period into traces, no 'short-term memory' system is required. Perception requires no intellectual operations of integration, combination, unification, or comparison of initially discrete sensory images. New perceptions do not need to be compared with existing memories in an act of judgement, because they already contain all the significant information the organism needs (1979a: 221–2, 246–9, 251–3; Gibson and Gibson 1955/1982). Internal differences between organisms are not cognitive differences. The point of the claim that there is no shunting of information from a perceptual faculty to a storage system is not that encoding is already elaborative, new input already feeding the same system in which it will persist: it is that there are no such cognitive systems to hold information in the mind.

In an important paper on temporal order, Gibson discusses Lashley's search for the physiological basis of memory. Noting his rejection of storehouse models and existing trace theories, Gibson picks up an alternative. Lashley had suggested (1950/1988: 63) that 'the learning process must consist of the attunement of the elements of a complex system in such a way that a particular combination or pattern of cells responds more readily than before the experience'. Impressed, Gibson marvels at the novelty of Lashley's idea:

> If learning is a kind of *resonance* in the nervous system, a tuning of the system to certain inputs, then it is not any sort of storage of engrams or depositing of traces ... It seems to me an astonishing idea, that learning does not necessarily depend on memory as it has always been conceived. (Gibson 1966b/1982: 172)

This naive passage is significant, for Gibson was about to develop the key concept of 'affordance', describing what it is in environments to which organisms are attuned (the manuscript 'Notes on Affordances' dates from August 1967). But the dichotomy set up here by Gibson is a false one. Trace theories and resonance theories are not incompatible. Hartley's vibration theory of memory (chapter 13 above) is a resonance theory if any is: and yet there is clearly a use for the term 'trace' for Hartley, *even though* it does not name an entity permanently and passively stored at a fixed memory address. The same goes for new connectionist models, which talk of resonance in more detail, and yet continue to use the concept of trace *outside* the crude localist spatial metaphor: traces are the means by which the system attunes itself to certain inputs. Gibson is blind to the historical existence of anything other than faithful local reproductive computer-like models of memory traces.

But Gibson, trying to bypass 'the muddle of memory', then claims that an explanatory theory of information pickup will not refer to memory. Lashley's 'hypothesis of tuning or resonance ... suggests a surprising possibility – that learning does not depend on memory at all, at least not on the re-arousal of traces or the remembering of the past' (1966a: 275). The state of a system is altered or 'sensitized' when attuned to information of a certain sort. But, says Gibson, this learning, this 'altered state need not be thought of as depending on a memory, an image, an engram, or a trace. An image of the past, if experienced at all, would be only an incidental symptom of the altered state' (1979a: 254). As well as the usual assimilation of quite distinct targets here, Gibson denies that there can be further questions about *how* attunement occurs, about what its mechanisms might be. The danger of obscurantism in this form of direct realism is marked.

Images, said Gibson, are only incidental accompaniments of attunement. Clearly he is not seeking a form of representation which does not rely on resemblance, as indirect realists who reject the necessity for images might. Instead he is disclaiming any need to explain phenomena of long-term memory. The rejection of traditional theories of memory runs deep: there is to be no account of 'recollection' understood as, for instance, voluntary recall of events long in the personal past. The only phenomena admitted will be forms of habit memory where an organism is sensitised to new information and 'differences are noticed that were previously not noticed. Features become distinctive that were formerly vague' (1979a: 254). One can accept the importance of these phenomena, especially in ethological psychology: but that is not to say that they are all that an approach to learning and memory needs to explain.

Yet this is what Gibson intends: 'what we call memory and recognition is often only a special case of invariant-detection. *Recollection* is then a sort of human luxury, an incidental ability to contemplate the past' (1966b/1982: 178). This is strange science for one concerned with biological plausibility, for the human ability to contemplate the past can hardly have had an incidental evolutionary importance. Gibson refers to recollection again only to say that it is *not* explained by 'the traditional hypothesis of mental imagery' (1979a: 256). After discussing the perception of occluded surfaces again, he notes that 'one kind of remembering' is 'an awareness of surfaces that have ceased to exist or events that will not recur, such as items in the story of one's own life. There is no point of observation at which such an item will come into sight' (1979a: 255). The information gained in such activity is 'further detached from stimulation' than is perceptual information: and other than the polemical reminder that '[this] is still an activity of the system, not an appearance in the theater of consciousness' (1979a: 256), that is all we are told. This is not a replacement theory of memory but a denial of its relevance or importance. Gibson felt little need to extend treatment of his proprietary domain, perception, to cover remembering: perceiving, for him, was 'the simplest and best kind of knowing' (1979a: 263).

Gibson's followers likewise displace human long-term memory as an explanandum. Turvey and Shaw (1979) set out to prove that Gibson's work provides better directions 'for understanding memory' than does 'the legacy of the past five centuries'. Yet, remarkably, in a 55–page paper they refer to memory only in the three concluding pages, which propose only a view of memory 'as knowledge that persists by analogical extension (generalization) from earlier to later situations' (1979: 219)![6] Michaels and Carello, also dispensing with any 'concept of memory' which requires 'the storage or retrieval of information', give no alternative other than a plea for relating ontogeny to phylogeny by collapsing individual learning and memory into evolutionary adaptation. They complain that traditional sciences 'never view the evolutionary concept of experience as the amassing of memories while they rarely view the consequences of an animal's personal history as anything but the amassing of

---

6 Turvey and Shaw argue that memory is a property of an ecosystem, and not of an organism. They are thus forced vigorously to deny that the causal processes which support memory are relevant to an understanding of 'the epistemic act of remembering as such'. These claims, however, are supported only with quasi-formal 'postulates' which already assume the attribution of memory only to ecosystems (1979: 217–19). But even before pushing the criticism that the neo-Gibsonian formalisms are misleading in failing significantly to constrain possibilities (Cutting 1982: 211–13), one may doubt the force of Turvey and Shaw's rejection of memory traces. They deny that traces left by experience could be things which 'enter into a recipe whose product is perception', but they accept that experience, which is 'preparatory to perceiving', 'attunes or sensitizes perceptual systems to the information that specifies affordances' (1979: 216–17). The dichotomy between trace theory and attunement or sensitisation is, again, unfounded.

memories' (1981: 77). This is an astonishing suggestion: cultural change and its effects on individual learning are to be understood in exactly the same terms as the effects of evolutionary history on the individual's adaptation (compare Schacter 1982: 105–47; and Otis 1994 on 'organic memory'). Both evolution and individual learning produce 'a new animal that is better able to cope with its environment'. Experience, we are told, actually leads to a *new* machine: 'the consequence of personal experience is *not* that the old animal has new knowledge, but that *it is a new animal that knows better*' (Michaels and Carello 1981: 78; emphasis is in the original). This is a strange way to argue either for biological plausibility in psychology or for the disunity and discontinuity of personal identity. Any more detailed attempt to explain the phenomena of long-term memory would have to start looking for mechanisms: but the hostility of Gibsonians to psychophysiological explanation prevents them from taking such phenomena seriously. If traces and attunement are mutually exclusive, then denying traces looks sensible. But there is no good reason to accept the antecedent.

Temporal order and the specification of the past

The Gibsonian programme encourages reconsideration of temporal structure in the explanation of remembering. Asserting that we are aware of persistence in change, that we do not have to *construct* stability out of a sensory flux, Gibson says that perception is of sequences, not of discrete images. The stability is out there, in the invariants of the optical array (1975/1982; 1979a: 221–2, 248–9). He rejects the Humean picture of atomic sensations succeeding one another like snapshots without real connections (1979a: 250). Sequential and temporal structures are just as real as spatial structures.

The representationist theory of memory, in contrast, 'fits harmoniously with the common sense, Western idea of time', which is an unfortunate inheritance of philosophical tradition (Wilcox and Katz 1981a: 233). The supposed need for traces stems from seeing time as 'linear and absolute', and allowing the past no independent ontological status. Stored mental representations are then hypothesised to keep the past in mind. Gibson's scepticism (1966b/1982) about cognitive experiments which rely on the presentation of successions of static patterns is generalised to an attack on the need to bridge alleged temporal gulfs between discrete units of time.

This argument is also in the philosophical literature. John Laird (1920: 46), responding to the attempt to join temporal gaps with traces, claims that all perceptions are of 'an enduring slab of time or a stretch of change'. Such a stretch has an objective order of earlier and later embedded in it. Past events have their determinate place in a series, and so the past 'is neither trackless nor unknown' (1920: 59). Laird asserts that this is enough to show there to be no contradiction in the notion of direct apprehension of the past. Wilcox and Katz in similar vein envisage time as ordered sequential structure, of which past events are part. Sequential structure, as in a melody, is temporally constrained: before and after, earlier and later, are real distinctions within it. A melody will not be perceived as that melody if its sequential elements are disordered (1981a: 235; compare Earle 1956/7: 22–6; Jenkins 1977: 428; Arcaya 1989: 103–4, 1992). Whole stretches of temporal structure can be apprehended in the present without the need (impossibly) to jump to other instants.

There's ample reason to accept that, for systems like us, time comes in slabs or stretches rather than discrete and unconnected instants. But questions remain about the effects of a rememberer's specific location within such a temporal structure. Even Gibsonians need some account of individual differences in the effects of learning history and experience, and in memory capacities and abilities, if stretches of time are 'simply' directly accessible (Sanders 1985: 512–5; for controversy over individual difference in perception see Heil 1979, 1981, against Reed and Jones 1981, and Wilcox and Katz 1981b). Representationist cognitive theories are good at this, for background memory representations acquired in individual experience have causal effects as context on the nature of particular acts of remembering. The present environment alone fails uniquely to specify the past for *any* individual. Remembering is underdetermined by either cue or engram alone: differences in past experience affect it through the effects of experience on internal states. Remembering, produced by the interaction of meagre stimulus and internal context, if accurate, is so contingently (Rock 1991; Searle 1991).

I argue in chapter 16 that connectionist theories of memory are not only compatible with, but require careful stress on information about the past being available in the present. Sometimes, indeed, retrieval cues must be highly specific to elicit remembering: memory is not simply 'an activated picture of a past event' (Schacter 1996: 60–4, 71). But present hints and cues do not work on air: 'a neural network combines information in the present environment with patterns that have been stored in the past, and the resulting mixture of the two is what the network remembers' (Schacter 1996: 71). Gibsonians deny that this mixing occurs in the brain or mind, rejecting arguments from the poverty of the stimulus (Michaels and Carello 1981: ch. 1), and claim that the past is uniquely specified in enduring information which somehow remains in the environment. Explaining how this could be so is the central task in the application of Gibsonian theory to memory. Yet existing attempts produce alternatives only to static localist storehouse models of memory, and are, despite their proponents' wishes, compatible with distributed models.

To take one example, Bransford and colleagues, sensitive to Gibson's thought, rejected the 'searching for traces conceptualization' (Bransford *et al.* 1977: 432). Yet, invoking Bartlett, they suggested instead only a 're-creation metaphor of remembering' (1977: 449–56) not unlike dynamic connectionism. Past experience 'sets the stage' for later experience through the education or attunement of an organism, without being faithfully stored in an internal system (1977: 434–9). This stage-setting can be thought of as an imposition through attunement of constraints on creative and (re)constructive processes (1977: 441–3). Perception and recognition are said to be direct *given* the attunement (1977: 435). One can accept the need for 'an account of the global level of "attunement" set by the context of the situation', a level which 'will affect the nature of the experiences afforded by potential cues' (1977: 443). But why does one individual reconstruct the past in this way, and another quite differently? Because of their different existing levels of attunement (1977: 450). Here hypotheses about what it is that *grounds* or *underpins* the differing attunements which set constraints on resonance are hard to rule out of court on conceptual grounds.

To repeat, there is no reason to think the opposition between storage and reconstruction on which Bransford *et al.* rely (1977: 453) to be a true dichotomy. Of course the aspects of the world to which an organism is currently attuned matter for remembering: internal states do not just reactivate in a vacuum. Yet caricatures of storage as faithful reproduction continually encourage anti-theory rhetoric (Arcaya 1989: 104; Ben-Zeev 1986). Direct realists, from Reid on, are drawn to reject all analysis and explanation of the phenomena of remembering. Laird (1920: 59) complained that 'it is quite unreasonable to be dissatisfied with the analysis and description of apprehension as we find it. We can perceive the present and recollect the past; and we are not required to explain the inexplicable.' Joel Michell (1988: 247) quotes this passage to deny that representationist theories can explain 'the emergence of cognition'. He agrees that 'the occurrence of cognition will have its necessary and sufficient physical and physiological conditions', but denies that specifying them explains how cognition is 'generated by these conditions' (Michell 1988: 247). Apart from the fact that many representationists do not believe that there are *necessary* physical conditions for cognition, this blanket rejection of explanation is unnecessary caution, disallowing common ground. Michell is deploying a powerful critique of cognitivism by John Maze (1983): but Maze, in contrast, is willing to wonder on the nature of brain traces. Maze marvels at the intricacy of the neural mechanisms underpinning cognition, mechanisms which must operate in a variable 'context-related' way, without there being 'one separate neural trace for each proposition known' (Maze 1983: 91). The possibility of reconciling a *distributed* connectionist approach to memory with direct realism could not be clearer.[7]

---

7 I have not touched on the problems which direct realists face in accounting for error (compare Cutting 1982: 209–11). Gibson himself allowed for rare perceptual errors, when for example 'a thing may not look like what it is' (1979a: 143), but his followers sometimes deny the intelligibility of misperceiving and misremembering. Turvey and

15.3 Gibsonian history

Polemic against representations is also prominent in interpretations of early modern philosophy. Descartes' indirect realism, complains Marjorie Grene (1985: 211) is responsible for 'disastrous, science-fiction philosophising'. Rejecting Descartes' internal processing of visual information, Grene (1985: 205–12) invokes the full Gibsonian story about the existence of information in the ambient light which uniquely specifies what is seen. As I suggested in section 15.2, it is not easy to apply this picture to remembering. Grene recommends as 'a more reasonable beginning' the attempt, with Gibson or Merleau-Ponty, 'to put intellectual activities back into their place in our natures as living things, and thereby also to put meaning back into the natural world', a world in which, 'though in a complicated and often messy way, things make sense' (Grene 1985: 212, 208–9). It is hard to disagree with such wisdom! But obviously I deny that the attainment of genuinely 'full-bodied' perspectives on psychology requires exposure of a 'crippling Cartesian heritage' (Grene 1985: 199, 95).

Grene addresses conceptions of time, arguing with Gibson that we are sensitive to processes, 'not snapshot-like presentations' (1985: 202). As well as bringing temporal context into the perceptual process, Grene insists on the importance of personal/historical contexts, and on the activity of the embodied organism with its needs. This is all laudable: but there is no reason why a context-sensitive distributed representationism cannot accommodate it, and no reason but for fear of mechanism to deny even that Descartes' model of memory allows it (chapter 3 above). Grene moves easily from care for contexts to the rejection of mechanism.[8] But mechanism is not refuted by pointing out

Shaw (1979: 213) note that 'to say that perception it is direct, rather than indirect, is to say that it necessarily provides information about how things are (in reference to the effectivities of a given animal) and not merely about how they appear'. The fact that indirect realism fails to guarantee the veridicality of perception is, for them, an argument against it (1979: 178, 182 n. 2, 214)! On memory, Wilcox and Katz (1981a: 235–7) suggest that, since memory is just 'the apprehension of elements that are part of a sequential structure', the notion of error must be 'relativistic', and has sense only as 'the perception of an element in a sequential structure that has changed as we discover more about the world'. Denying error in remembering is unacceptable to many who are otherwise sympathetic to direct realism, for on most views the possibility of error is the price of realism. For a complaint that Gibsonian observer-dependence in perception buys its directness at the cost of a relativistic loss of the independence of perceiver and environment, breaking down a needed 'distinction between objects in themselves and objects as known', see Yolton 1987: 329–30; compare Yolton 1996: 21–30.

8 This is evident in an earlier essay on Hobbes (Grene 1976), in which to Hobbes' materialism and representationism are quickly assimilated all the 'barbarisms' and 'computer-ridden speculations' of scientistic modern philosophy, from the loss of God and the denial of significance in the universe, through ignorance of the 'higher realities' of human culture, to reductionism, determinism, and the rejection of teleology, of 'oughts', laws, reason, and choice. One might wonder why, again, it is the anti-reductionist who assimilates many quite different things.

that organisms are not passive, for internal causes can be explained mechanistically just as can external stimuli. Neither is it refuted by pointing to the importance of the personal past (Grene 1985: 202–3), for the personal past has its effects by way of superposed memory traces which interact, blend, and form again according to the present situation.

Responding further to historians' uses of Descartes as exemplar and originary sources of persistent representationist errors allows me to sketch a more naturalistic reading of historical indirect realism. Like John Yolton, I hope that history 'may even offer some resolutions to questions about representation and realism' (1990b: 516).[9] Yolton, attuned to Gibson's work for some time (Yolton 1968/9), has led a different reinterpretation by revivifying Arnauld's act theory of representative perception, which drops representational entities in favour of a significatory relation between perceiver and world (Yolton 1984a: ch. 1, 1987, 1990a). I conclude with a brief response.

These historians focus almost exclusively on perception, with theories of memory, let alone those postulating distributed representations, barely featuring. It is hard to interpret early modern philosophers as accepting the action at a temporal distance which non-mechanistic theories of memory require. Yolton (1987: 327) notes that 'the influence of memory' is one of the numerous details not covered by writers in the 'way of ideas' tradition. Yet some of them, I have shown, did have neurophilosophical theories of memory.

Representation and world

For Edward Reed, Gibson's biographer, Gibson offers 'the first truly new theory' in psychology 'for the last 400 years' (Reed 1988: 2), allowing escape from 'Cartesian themata' which are disastrous 'intellectual straitjackets' (Reed 1990: 101–2, 1989). Recently Reed questions the assumption or hope that a self can move or control its own physiological processes. As I showed in parts I and II, the idea of the mind 'slyly affecting' bodily movements by way of animal spirits leads to the Cartesian moral injunctions to keep the will in line, to maintain inner discipline by 'conquering the passions' (Reed 1990: 119, 112–13). The will is meant to be limitless but is actually bound within the body: since physical objects are transformed into representations which do not resemble their causes, the will acts only on the internal proxies, not on the external objects which common sense takes to be the objects of volition. We are unaware of mental action on the animal spirits, so 'much or all of volition must be unconscious' (1990: 109, 116–17). Where Reed thinks this the absurd legacy of Descartes' refusal to understand volition as directed at the environment, from

9 Compare Yolton 1987: 330. Yolton 1996 impressively integrates early modern and contemporary accounts of perception and representation: I regret being unable to use it more fully. It is not clear how memory would fit Yolton's schema. My thanks to John Yolton for helpful correspondence and discussion about this material.

which only Gibson offers escape, I have taken it to be a roughly accurate approach to the plight of cognition.

Reed's rejection of representations relies on a slippage between two formulations of Descartes' position. One is that 'all existing thoughts are consequences of the motions of the brain'; the other that 'all awarenesses are awarenesses of brain states' (Reed 1982: 733). But these are not equivalent: the former can be accepted while the latter is denied. The hardest materialist reductionist claims only that awarenesses *are* brain states, not that they are *of* brain states. Descartes' insistence that ideas do not resemble their objects, that the world of appearances differs from the physical world, does not entail that we only ever see our own brains, but does drive his rejection of direct realism (Gaukroger 1990: 37–9). But Descartes explicitly allows for a number of different relations of representation which do not require resemblance, and which together will explain why the appearances are as they are.

Descartes's distinction between representation and resemblance, as Larmore observes (1980: 13–16), derives from his physiology: the relation between patterns of animal spirits motions and perceptible qualities of objects cannot, obviously, be simply pictorial. Representation by resemblance would be incompatible with science as well as superfluous (Meyering 1989: 82–4, 105–6; Hatfield 1990: 52–3). Descartes outlines a general notion of representation, by which words represent what they signify, laughter and tears represent joy and sadness, two-dimensional engravings represent three-dimensional objects, *and* brain patterns represent objects and their properties.

Nancy Maull, in turn, shows that Descartes' account of distance perception explains *why* we are unaware of the unconscious processes which underpin it (Maull 1980: 27–30, 30–4).[10] Maull takes natural geometry to be algorithms for generating judgements about distant objects, objects which are *indirectly* accessible 'because of the intervention of geometry or reasoning about [visual] cues'. This 'elaborate optical plumbing . . . does not imply that the soul is aware of a pineal pattern' (1980: 30, 34; compare on distance perception Lennon 1980; and Gaukroger 1990: 18–26). Ann Mackenzie, summarising passages on different 'representational situations', identifies three main elements of the theory of representation. Brain events, specifically corporeal ideas, 'are viewed as *vehicles of representation*; physical objects and/or their properties are viewed as the *objects of representation*; and the whole causal nexus which links registration events in the brain to objects and properties represented constitutes the *background system* by virtue of which the vehicles represent their objects to the mind' (Mackenzie 1989: 179). This interpretation allows for (indirect, fallibilist)

---

10 Maull diagnoses scholarly failure to attend to 'the peculiarities of Descartes' version of representative perception' as partly due to 'an orthodoxy of misplaced emphasis on Descartes' more "philosophical" texts' (1980: 40, 35). Compare chapter 3 above.

realism, and takes seriously the contextual role of the causal background. It still requires, as Mackenzie acknowledges, an unexplained external user of the representational system in the form of the mind (Mackenzie 1989: 190).

In another recent invocation of Gibson, Emily Grosholz draws on his dichotomy between (mere) physical causation and 'a revised and extended notion of causality appropriate to biology' to accuse Descartes of confusion because animal spirits are described at both physiological and psychological levels (Grosholz 1991: 129–31).[11] The distinction between, on the one hand, physical-causal relations between perceiver and world and, on the other, some quite different kind of relation is developed further by Yolton. But where Grosholz complains that Descartes failed to keep them separate, Yolton sees in Descartes at least hints of a distinction between different relations.

The standard history of philosophy, on which Descartes 'invented the mind' and inserted a veil of ontologically ambiguous ideas between knower and known (Rorty 1980: ch. 1), is questioned by Yolton who also examines the source of this standard interpretation in Reid (Yolton 1984a: ch. 11). In contrast Yolton argues that evidence is slim for the allegedly widespread early modern commitment to the view that perceivers are only ever directly aware of reified intermediary 'third things'; slim too for a consequent sudden concern with epistemological scepticism because of the gap thus opened between subject and reality (Yolton 1981, 1990a: 67–70; compare Jolley 1989: 1–11; Hatfield 1990: 46–60).

Instead of the naturalistic reinterpretation of indirect realism offered by historians sympathetic to new connectionism such as Hatfield and Meyering, with which I have been working throughout these studies, Yolton and others seek to break the impasse in modern debates with a form of direct realism which yet retains a role for both cognitive and causal processes. The key is in Arnauld's development of Descartes, whereby 'all our perceptions are essentially representative modalities' (Arnauld 1683/1990: 66). Where Malebranche took ideas (in the mind of God) to be the objects of perception, Arnauld understood them as acts of perception, and thus not intermediary objects at all. An idea just is a perception or, better, a perceiving (on the Arnauld/Malebranche dispute see Laird 1920: ch. 1; Cook 1974; Radner 1976; Wahl 1988). So Arnauld was a direct realist (Nadler 1989; Cook 1991), who saw that when the relation of representation holds, not between an idea-object and a physical object, but between an act of

---

11 This kind of mistake ('confounding levels of description') allegedly also permeates 'contemporary materialist accounts in epistemology and cognitive psychology'. Grosholz's brief invocation (1991: 129, 131 n. 21) of Gibson's work, whence she draws 'some of [her] theoretical orientation', supports the negative claim that a pattern with cognitive significance 'cannot be physically-causally transmitted' but 'must be recognized, interpreted, cognitively grasped, by a consciousness'. See on this chapter 3 above, and compare Gaukroger 1990: 39.

perceiving and a physical object, 'the indirectness traditionally associated with representative theories disappears' (Yolton 1991b: 111).[12] Since ideas are acts of perceiving, modifications of mind, 'perception' can be used to designate a perception-idea in relation to the mind which they modify, and 'idea' the same perception-idea in relation to a physical object as it is in the mind (Yolton 1984a: 61–2).

Yolton traces Arnauld's direct but representative realism back to Descartes (1984a: ch. 1, 1987: 323–5, 1996: 183–214; compare O'Neil 1974). I discuss briefly just two strands of this reinterpretation: the account of natural signs; and the distinction between causal and cognitive relations. In each case I merely query whether this interpretation is incompatible with naturalism and causal theories of perception and cognition.

Descartes hints that natural signs are instituted by nature or God to occasion perceptual responses. Without internalised copies of objects, a natural geometry makes us respond in a particular way to a particular sign, 'even if the sign contained nothing in itself which is similar to this sensation' (Le Monde 1, AT xi.4, CSM 1.81). Yolton's great insight is to see that ideas themselves are not signs. Ideas are merely 'the interpretations of, or cognitive responses to' the signs, where the signs are physical (physiological) motions in nerves and brain (Yolton 1990a: 62; compare 1984a: 22–31). So we do not require a self separate from its ideas to read information about objects off from its idea-signs. This is why Descartes insists that our responses to all perceptible differences in objects are occasioned by differences in the motions in the brain: these motions, not ambiguous ideas, do the signifying.

But Yolton keenly distinguishes his view from causal or information-theoretic accounts, by which corporeal motions encode information about the external objects which caused them. Descartes *rejects* 'any causal relation between the physical activity of objects on our sense and the perceptual ideas in our minds' (Yolton 1984a: 18): the point of using natural-sign language in 'describing the act of perceptual cognition ... is to avoid the language of causation' (Gaukroger 1990: 24).

I focus on this incompatibilist account of causal and cognitive relations below: but even within the natural-sign doctrine there are reasons for resisting it. The 'teachings of nature' formed in childhood are habitual judgements made on the basis of natural signs (sixth set of Replies, AT vii.438–9, CSM 11.295–6), instituted by God for the preservation of the body, not the

12 Yet Yolton resists the excessive claims of Gibsonian realism, questioning the complete rejection of physiology and the wish to dispense entirely with psychological *processes* (1987: 327–30). No realism can be *so* direct, Yolton acknowledges, as to 'escape from the cognitive, psychological, and representative nature of perceptual awareness'. Unless the perceiver's mind is, impossibly, just out there physically wandering among objects to seize their being, there must be cognitive terms in an account of perception (1987: 329–30).

perception of truths (Fourth Meditation, AT vii.82, CSM 11.56–7; compare Hatfield 1986). The judgements of Descartes' third grade of sense are unnoticed responses. But now, to explain the possibility of error in these responses, might it not be that we have to look at deviant causal processes between object, sense organs, and brain? Where Descartes, reluctant to allow non-conscious cognitive processing, simply spoke of automatic responses instituted by nature, Malebranche and later cognitive theorists would fill out different ways in which these irresistible God-given responses occur (Meyering 1989: 89–105).[13] What determines differences in perceptual or cognitive response to natural signs are differences in the signs themselves, caused by different physical-causal relations between the perceiver and the physical object.

Indeed Yolton's own account is sometimes often couched in terms which look like those of a causal theory. Awareness is 'a result of the cognitive activity of the mind working in conjunction with (even attending to) physiological processes in the brain' (Yolton 1984a: 39): but perceptual discriminations are made 'on the basis of sensations felt by the perceiver', sensations which are 'a response to or an interpretation of natural signs' (1984a: 39, 1990a: 62). Elsewhere the nature of the cognitive reaction to physical events is said to be 'translatory' (1987: 325). How does this interpretation or translation of natural signs differ from the 'reading off' of properties of the world which Yolton officially rejects (1984a: 26)? When he does accept that 'the mind reads the physical motions [in nerves or brain], as it does the tears and smiles of a face' (1984a: 30), the only distance kept between this view and a naturalistic causal theory is the negative point that this reading, translation, or interpretation is not causal. To this I now turn.

Although Yolton on occasion wonders if, in the psychology which Descartes outlines 'to link cognition with physiology' (1984a: 21), causal and cognitive relations between perceiver and object could go together,[14] he generally maintains the incompatibilist view that 'for Descartes there is no causal relation in perception between physical objects and ideas' (1987: 325).[15] The interaction is

13 For Meyering, Descartes' ideas on natural geometry and natural signs suggest that the cues ordained by nature to occasion responses in us are being automatically 'decoded and interpreted' in subcognitive information processing (1989: 85–6). Even Malebranche's God must obey the fixed laws of mind/body union: as Meyering says (1989: 104), 'only changes that are physiologically imprinted upon the senses can occasion God's incredible production of exact psychic responses'.

14 Some possibilities he canvasses are that causal and physiological relations, while being 'inadequate for cognition' (1990a: 62–3), are supplemented by (1987: 323), or work in tandem with (1990a: 62), or even are (1984a: 39) significatory, cognitive, or semantic relations.

15 Ideas are not causal effects of motions (1984a: 19); Descartes rejects 'causation between brain and cognitive activity' (1984a: 21), and tries to preserve an 'interaction between body and mind which is not causal, or which is more than causal' (1990a: 62); 'motion in my body does not cause but signifies my sensations' (1990a: 62). Yolton now suggests (1996: conclusion) that, after his correspondence with Princess Elizabeth, Descartes replaced his

not causal, but 'significatory'. There is a connection between mind and world, but it is 'precisely that which is proper to cognition: significatory, not resemblance or causation' (1984a: 30, see also 1996: 183–214). Yolton acknowledges that Descartes' brief hints at a 'doctrine of signification' are 'far from clear' (1984a: 30–1, 19).[16] Without here going into Yolton's positive development of such a doctrine,[17] I want to note how strange it is to deny that minds as well as brains enter into causal relations, especially in the case of memory. Creative or reconstructive cognitive remembering, even on Yolton's view, is an interpretation of the physical traces which stand in causal relations to past events. The language of interpretation and signification reminds us that the trace itself cannot uniquely determine the remembering, that the current cognitive context counts: but, that said, it is hard to see what is lost in saying that the trace is a cause (among others) of the cognitive episode. What explanation could there be of the way memories blend, mix, and interfere if the past is directly signified?

Yolton accurately pinpoints the problems of causal interaction over a substantial distinction between mind and body as the residual sticking-point for early modern causal theories (Yolton 1984a: 22, 1987: 326). However, reinterpreting history for philosophical use, an alternative to rejecting the causal explanation of world/representation relations is to seek dis/solution of the problems of a 'third thing' by rejecting the mental subject behind the traces.

substance dualism 'by a dualism of processes: physical causality between objects and brain, signification between brain and mind, and perhaps representation between mind and external objects' (1996: 216).

16 For the related view that a theory of action should be not a causal theory but an account of the 'significance of action' see Yolton 1984b: 145–50. This strong incompatibilism between the causal and the significatory seems surprising for one who had previously complained at the 'curious reluctance' of recent action theorists 'to employ the notion of cause' (1966: 17): but in fact the mental causes to which Yolton then referred were incompatible with physical causation (1966: 22–4).

17 For responses to Yolton's account of the significatory relation see Costa 1983; Michael and Michael 1985; Ayers 1986; Matthews 1986; Cook 1987; Kelly 1987.

16

Attacks on traces

A basic problem in understanding the organization of memory in a biological system is to understand how a vast quantity of information can be stored and recalled by a system composed of vulnerable and relatively unreliable elements, with no knowledge of where the information has been filed.   (Leon Cooper 1980: 7)

16.1 A taxonomy of criticisms of trace theory

In chapter 15, seeking positive accounts of memory which dispensed with traces, I ran through a number of direct realist and Gibsonian objections to trace theory. Now I attempt a more extensive account of the criticisms which many readers will have felt rumbling beneath my descriptions of historical theories. Here, rather than hypothesising on critics' motives, I finally try to reply to their arguments.

Arguments against traces are bewilderingly abundant: many who hold quite different *positive* views about memory share broadly the same negative complaints. So, in moving towards an exhaustive taxonomy, I synthesise the polemics of Gibsonian ecological realists, phenomenological philosophers, Wittgensteinians, historians of philosophy, and direct-realist analytic philosophers under four broad headings: here I omit only more technical differences over reduction and levels of explanation, and a set of more extreme Wittgensteinian complaints, both of which I address elsewhere (Sutton 1993, 1995). The underlabouring character of this task is pronounced: only by a slow enumeration of possible reasons to reject traces and a careful explanation of the strategies of evasion by which distributed models avoid refutation can tedious philosophical overgrowth be cleared, and shared attempts to mix keen phenomenology with explanation be rejoined.

This survey of objections to traces catches the most troubling issues. But a range of less clearly articulated complaints lurks under them, around the discomfort critics feel about apparent scientism. Many critics cited in this chapter oppose the materialism and determinism of causal theories.[1] Many reject the

---

1 Here I just ignore complaints about scientists' alleged reduction of all the diversity of remembering to one causal model, and about its unanalysable nature (Malcolm 1977; Bursen 1978). As I have shown throughout, science and complexity must coexist in memory theory, with social and personal levels of analysis as important as biological. Two suggestive treatments of the *variety* of memory phenomena which do not polemically rule out causal analyses are Deutscher 1989: 53–7 and Fentress and Wickham 1992: 1–40.

use of concepts unavailable to the subject in explanations of memory (Sanders 1985: 511–13). Some who do not explicitly address problems of reduction and levels mistake their preference for demonstration. Here I just give one example, as warning, of how difficult issues can simply be ignored.

Don Locke's introduction to the philosophy of memory begins:

> Our first questions are obvious. What precisely is memory? What is it to remember something? These philosophical questions need to be distinguished from the similar questions that might be asked by a psychologist or neurologist. There are problems about how memory operates, about what goes on in our body or brain when we remember, about what physical and psychological factors help or hinder our remembering, and so on. These are the concern of the scientist, who investigates the functioning of the human capacity we call memory. But our question is different: we are asking what memory is in itself, what that human capacity consists in, however it may operate. We want to explain not the mechanisms of memory, but its nature; not how it works, but what it is. The question is, in effect, what it is we are talking about when we talk about memory. (Locke 1971: 1)

This is a defensible philosophical position: but to dissent from it is certainly not to stop doing philosophy. Locke makes, without argument, a specific claim about the autonomy of the mental from the levels which realise or constitute it. It cannot be ruled conceptually impossible that the *nature* of memory, what it is we are talking about, *cannot* be understood independently of its mechanisms, what it is independently of how it works.[2]

16.2 The role of empirical evidence

The importance of empirical evidence for or against the memory trace is far from clear. It did not, I suggested in part II, exclusively determine the fate of the animal spirits version of trace theory. Could the *discovery* of memory traces ever settle the issue? What would such a discovery involve? What is the status of the claim that traces exist? Is a trace theorist claiming that there *must* be a trace

---

2 O'Connor and Carr (1982: 116) agree that 'questions about physical mechanisms are not problems for the philosopher' and that the 'scientific theories [of memory] established by experiment . . . are not part of philosophy' and do not 'have to be considered by philosophers': but they at least acknowledge that 'anything that philosophers may say about memory must at least be consistent with well established scientific theories'. I have suggested throughout this book that fruitful interactions as well as tensions have long characterised theories of memory. Johnson (1983: 377–8) argues that scientific evidence for the reconstructive rather than duplicatory nature of human (as opposed, say, to ant or beetle) memory is 'the most important problem' for the traditional analysis of memory as retained knowledge. Even those with untarnished faith in the analytic project need to heed Johnson's warning that 'no philosopher of memory can afford to ignore such scientific results, because they tell him what the phenomenon is, which he is trying to explain in philosophical terms'.

spanning the temporal gap between experience and remembering, and assuming that empirical research just fleshes out the particular way it is realised in the brain?

Critics argue on conceptual or 'logical' grounds against this whole empirical research programme. Bursen's *Dismantling the Memory Machine* is meant to demonstrate philosophically the absurdity of neuropsychology (1978: xii; cf. Krell 1990: xi). Maze describes as 'gratifying' the work on perception by the Gibsonians Turvey and Shaw, who show that 'empirical research *cannot* establish the truth of an indirect [representationist] theory of perception; of course, it cannot establish the truth of a direct one, either, since the issue is one of logical rather than empirical tenability' (1983: 78).

This is not the defensive position of the practitioner of conceptual analysis cordoning off areas of honest philosophical concern from the aggressive march of the sciences. It is, rather, polemical invasion, on a priori grounds, of the terrain of empirical science with arguments to show that alleged *philosophical* preconceptions of these sciences are ill-founded. For Sanders (1985: 507), 'the technical or theoretical accounts of memory that have been given are spurious': Wilcox and Katz (1981a: 238) claim that Gibsonian realism explains the phenomena of remembering, but that 'it does not, unlike the representative theory, accomplish [this] at the expense of logic'. If concepts like structural isomorphism, encoding, storage, and retrieval are logically incoherent, no amount of empirical research can save trace theory.

Some defenders of the trace seek, in reaction, to drain it of empirical content. The article on animal spirits in Chambers' *Cyclopaedia* noted that 'the existence of the *animal spirits* is controverted [disputed]: but the infinite use they are of in the animal oeconomy and the exceedingly lame account we should have of any of the animal functions without them, will keep the greatest part of the world on their side' (in Myer 1984: 103). Doubt about traces is to be dispelled by reference to the sheer difficulty of psychological explanation without them. Some modern trace theorists, seeking a notion of the trace which does not commit them to predictions about future neuroscience, put the existence of traces beyond the empirical. Johnson uses 'trace' 'in a content-less, functional way to mean simply 'that by means of which someone's past influences his present, in the course of remembering' (1983: 381, n. 6). And Deborah Rosen (1975: 3) develops a 'logical notion of the memory trace' which is 'independent of its physical realization', and is distanced 'from specialized scientific notions for which the logical notion provides only a philosophical underpinning' (compare Gomulicki 1953: vii).

Local and distributed traces, then, would be subspecies of this general notion which *do* involve specific claims about physical realisation. The bare, content-less concept of trace does some work: but unfortunately critics are tempted too easily to think that it still implies the crude sacks-in-storehouse image. So arguments which purport to reject traces in general often in fact make a case only against localist traces.

Critics use counterexamples to remove the aura of necessity from the concept: 'If I say, rightly, "I remember it", the *most different things* can happen, and even merely this: that I say it' (Wittgenstein 1974: para. 131; Malcolm 1977: chs. 6–10). Nothing here tells against distributed-memory theorists, who make no claims about what *must* happen in every episode of remembering. But it is natural to explain such a theory in terms which render the characterisation of the trace more specific. Critics fulminate against mechanism by repeating that the trace cannot be the memory (since, for example, it would be possible for someone who cannot remember an event nevertheless to have a trace of it).

> An event leaves a trace in the memory: one sometimes imagines this as if it consisted in the event's having left a trace, an impression, a consequence, in the nervous system. As if one could say: even the nerves have a memory. But then when someone remembered an event, he would have to *infer* it from this impression, this trace. Whatever the event does leave behind, it isn't the memory. (Wittgenstein 1980: para. 220)[3]

The trace is not the occurrent remembering: but the trace theorist, if required, can agree to restrict the use of the word 'memory' to the act of remembering, or even, if philosophers decide that ordinary language so leads us, to restrict it further, as a 'success-word', to the act of remembering *truly*, although both historians and psychologists have provided ample reason to work on veridical and non-veridical 'memory' together.[4] But there can still be underlying dispositions which underpin the occurrent act of remembering.

So 'the engram (the stored fragments of an episode) and the memory . . . are not the same thing' (Schacter 1996: 70). Rather, the trace provides one kind of continuity between past event and present remembering. As Max Deutscher argues, it is not the stored trace which triggers or prompts present recall, nor is it the past event itself: the event recalled

---

3 Wittgenstein's followers outdo him in attributing ludicrous views to their opponents. But in context, this remark (which can be compared to Gibson's at the start of section 15.2 above) is aimed at the notion of memory traces as faithful reproductions or copies of past experience. Wittgenstein continues, mockingly: 'The organism compared with a dictaphone spool; the impression, the trace, is the alteration in the spool that the voice leaves behind. Can one say that the dictaphone (or the spool) is remembering what was spoken all over again, when it reproduces what it took?' There is a genuine target here, but it is Wittgenstein's earlier self (Sutton 1993). Distributed models, in contrast, are not high fidelity reproduction systems.

4 Compare McCauley 1988: 129, complaining that the 'epistemic honor' we associate with 'remember' as opposed to 'believe' is irrelevant to arguments about the extent of reconstruction in memory. Likewise, facts about the justification of memory claims and 'the concept of memory', or that 'our everyday verifications of whether some person does or does not remember that *p* are not bound up with any questions about what is and has been going on in this brain' (Malcolm 1963: 237; also Munsat 1967: 9), do not mean that there are, in fact, no memory traces (Rosen 1975: 2).

did its work in the past in laying down a trace which now makes [it] possible that the present mnemonic, the prompting, elicits recall. The 'causation' which is involved in memory is that of laying something down; it is a 'causation' as sedimentation which makes a capacity possible later on. (Deutscher 1989: 61)[5]

This formulation is sufficiently neutral that those opposed to literal copying by traces of the structure of experience can find alternative senses for the concept. 'Causation as sedimentation' does not imply that what is left after experience must remain permanently fixed. Bartlett, theorising on the basis of his evidence for the reconstructive and context-based nature of remembering, wrote (1932: 211–12) that

> though we may still talk of traces, there is no reason in the world for regarding these as made complete at one moment, stored up somewhere, and then re-excited at some much later moment. The traces that our evidence allows us to speak of are interest-determined, interest-carried traces. They live with our interests and with them they change.[6]

Experiment, explanation, and theory continue even if context, culture, and change are relevant to the memory trace. But for the trace to be a legitimate construct, it must be connected to what it is a trace of only contingently. It must be a 'distinct existence' in order to stand in causal relations with the past, and it must be identifiable independently of its nature as a trace of that past event (Malcolm 1963; Warnock 1987: 43–6). So talk of the as-yet-not-understood substrate of remembering, whatever that should be, cannot be the whole story. Some independent account of what a trace is will ultimately be required of a developed science. The philosophical and scientific projects cannot be isolated, and at some point more specific claims about physical realisation are required.

In chapter 4 I discussed the problem of action at a temporal distance, suggesting that animal spirits explanations of physical continuity in remembering appealed to seventeenth-century natural philosophers who denied occult action at a temporal distance. Their memory theory, in this respect, had to cohere with the rest of their sciences: and the situation is similar now.[7] But the postulation

---

5 Shope (1973: 322), complaining that arguments for traces should be scientific not philosophical, acknowledges that the trace will not be the only causally relevant factor involved in acts of remembering. The contexts of retrieval which interact with the trace, as I have stated before, do not fall beyond the ambit of scientific psychology.

6 Causal theories of memory do not, as Zemach (1983: 32–3) complains, 'dictate to science what to discover in the brain'. Interesting scientific possibilities, like the 'holographic principles' which Zemach cites as challenges to localised codes, are not rejecting memory traces tout court, merely elucidating their (distributed) nature.

7 Malcolm, trying to expose the 'confusion' behind this route to trace theory, acknowledges that 'our strong desire for a mechanism (either physical or mental) of memory arises from an abhorrence of the notion of action at a distance-in-time' (1963: 238; compare 1977: ch. 6).

of memory traces in some neutral sense might be empirical without being empirical *within* psychology. The relevant empirical domain lies elsewhere, in the *physical* assumption of no action at a distance, of continuity between a cause and its effect when the effect is temporally subsequent. The assumption, verified in ordinary experience, is that mechanisms underlie apparent cases of direct action between temporally remote events (see Rosen 1975 on the 'principle of temporal contiguity'). It may be mistaken: it is shared by folk physics and classical physics, but challenged in quantum physics. Challenges to it must meet certain constraints. Firstly, they require more than negative complaints about science's lack of success in identifying the trace.[8] Secondly, they require more than the bare point that the postulation of traces is not logically *necessary*.[9] Action at a temporal distance would conflict with basic assumptions about the physical world: this is of course conceivable (quantum non-locality, for example, *might* turn out to have applications to psychophysiology), but would be an attack from within another powerful theoretical and scientific framework. Assumptions are rarely ditched without replacement, and purely negative complaints are doomed to be ignored. The positivist prudery which prohibits the postulation of intervening unobservables is one temperamental preference (Hesse 1961/1970: 291–2), and 'suspicion of the hypothetical' can play a useful whistle-blowing role in curbing scientistic excess: but investigation of processes and mechanisms underpinning capacities will not just stop.

Indeed, as Frank Jackson points out to me, there is a specific difficulty in postulating action at a temporal distance in the case of memory. Without causal continuity, a past event would not only have to leap to the present to cause my

---

8 For there may, for instance, be good empirical reasons why empirical research into memory traces is very hard. For sensible remarks about why, within the context of the history of the brain sciences, it should have taken so long to get any grip on identifying the trace, see Horn 1985: ch. 1 and Rose 1993.

9 In *The Analysis of Mind* Russell suggested that there is no a priori objection to the immediate causation of present events by past events, even when this means that 'part of the cause has ceased to exist' (1921: 89). A special, unique *mnemic causation* might operate directly over remote times. But Russell is only arguing against the logical necessity of traces: while, he wrote, 'in the present state of physiology, the introduction of the engram does not serve to simplify the account of mnemic phenomena' (1921: 85), there is no suggestion here that a full positive scientific theory of memory which did postulate traces would be conceptually incoherent. Russell's words have been used to encourage acceptance of the possibility of action at a temporal distance in remembering by Anscombe (1974/1981: 126–7, in a defence of memory as 'an original phenomenon of causation'), and Heil (1978: 66–9; compare Beardsmore 1989). But the bare possibility that mnemic causation might be completely unlike any other causation is no reason to think that it actually might be. For defences of trace theory on this count see Broad 1925: 456–60, Warnock 1987: 46–52. Shope (1973: 318–21) is hostile to the use of traces in an analysis of remembering, but acknowledges that a developing scientific theory of traces could generate support for a causal theory of memory. Shope's defence of mnemic action at a temporal distance is mild, boiling down to a preference for the 'economy of postulating the existence of fewer relations of causal relevance among phenomena' (1973: 321).

memory activity; further, it would somehow have to track my spatiotemporal path, to ensure that it could at any time become causally active as I moved around. Such long-distance tracking of rememberer by past event seems unlikely to be 'direct' in any intuitive sense.

So another way of making space for traces while retaining direct-realist intuitions is by asking *how* in remembering I am in contact with the remote past. The problem is reminiscent of the 'time-lag' argument in the perceptual case. Events we perceive might have occurred before we perceive them, and the states of objects which we perceive might be temporally prior to their states at the exact time we perceive them. Orion, as we see it, is centuries old (Laird 1920: 45). Sound and light waves from the external world take time to reach our sensory transducers. Does the temporal gap between the occurrence of thunder and the hearing of the thunder not entail that perception of thunder is indirect, mediated, or inferred from the present stimuli? Not necessarily, for anti-representationists assert that we're just directly aware of something existing or occurring at a time earlier than the present (Woozley 1949: 55–8; Heil 1983: 128; Ben-Zeev 1986: 299; Snowdon 1992: 76–7). This response, however, seems harder to maintain in the case of memory. It is not just that the temporal gulf in memory can be much greater than the barely perceptible gap between a distant axe striking its target and the sound of the blow reaching our ears: it is that the causal connections between remote past and current remembering are often more devious and twisted, enmeshed in more mixed causal fields and passing through more media, than the simple transmission of light or sound over time through a single medium. Some Wittgensteinian approaches, as I have noted, hide or deny the apparent temporal gap to be bridged between past experience or present remembering (Malcolm 1963: 238).[10] It is hard to find clear alternative accounts: for John Laird, in remembering certain 'peaks in the past' do 'stand out in relief where everything else is a bland or a crapulous haze'. This is metaphor, as Laird acknowledges, and 'falls short of demonstration' (1920: 52–3). Even if 'direct acquaintance' with what is temporally remote is a human capacity, questions remain about *how* it occurs. There is no obvious reason why memory traces might not be just what underpin such capacities.[11]

10 Malcolm claims to have disproved all candidates like the trace which might have filled such a gap, and concludes that 'in a sense, therefore, we do not know what it means to speak of a *gap* here' (1963: 238). Warnock (1987: 45) comments that 'in spite of the authoritative echoes of Wittgenstein . . . what Malcolm says is great rubbish', because the temporal gap between the past and the present 'is the most obvious gap in the world'.

11 Shanon argues (1991: 92) that the bizarreness of action at a distance is attenuated by attention to the context of action in the world, in which memory is used as a temporal tool with which to gain access to remote events. But, while acknowledging that, on this view, 'memory is a process that enables one to remember', he suggests that how this is achieved may not be 'the subject of psychological theory at all'. The ecological wishes are laudable: but legislation over disciplinary boundaries is unlikely to succeed, certainly without support from a principled defence of the autonomy of psychology from other sciences.

16.3 Retention and storage

Critics of the spatial metaphor and traces claim that the *retention* involved in memory (whether this is the retention of knowledge, beliefs, dispositions, abilities, or whatever[12]) does *not* require any physical *storage* or causal continuity across time. Therefore the postulation of traces or representations spatially located in the brain between past experience and present remembering, is unwarranted speculation and should be dropped (Squires 1969; Malcolm 1977; Schumacher 1975/6; Lewis 1983).

Malcolm notes, for example, that people can retain their good looks without keeping the good looks in storage. I can retain a sunny disposition after hardship without my disposition being stored (1977: 197). The fact that indigo curtains have kept their colour does not entail any causal connection between their previous states and their present state (Squires 1969: 178). So while memories, like beliefs, have duration in time, duration does not imply storage: 'retention and storage are different concepts . . . Storage implies retention, but retention does not imply storage' (Malcolm 1977: 197–8). The confused identification of retention with storage mars not just philosophical but also neuropsychological writing on memory, which has created a 'mythology of traces' (Malcolm 1977: 199ff.). Again, think (says Squires) of a teddy bear in the attic which has retained its squeak. Even though six months ago, in the damp winter attic, the bear remained silent when poked, now that it is summer again the bear responds. This case of the retention of the ability to squeak, on Squires' view, proves that no continuous causal chain over time is required for retention. 'It is usually incorrect to claim that a toy that has kept its squeak squeaks now because it could squeak before' (Squires 1969: 181). Memories, analogously, can be kept without a trace (Squires 1969: 196).

These critics feel something magical in the notion of causal processes operating over time (Bursen 1978: 19–47). A straightforward response for the trace theorist is to point to the permeation of ordinary thought and language by assumptions of causal continuity. Causal talk is restricted neither by requirements that instances of causation must be covered by general causal laws, nor by the specific metaphor of the serial causal chain from which Squires wanted to unchain memory. Talk of the 'sources' of a person's present memory knowledge presumes some kind of historical continuity (Warnock 1987: 50–2). Normally, the precise nature of the continuity is unknown, for, as Deutscher says (1989: 60), 'common sense and the thought expressed in common language requires only that there be some such [underlying] process'. The trace theorist does not have to say, as Squires seemed to think, that it is the retention

---

12 I cannot go into conceptual debates over whether memory is adequately analysed as the retention of knowledge, and whether it can also be a source of knowledge: see Ryle 1949/1963: 257–63; von Leyden 1961: chs. 1–2.

of the indigo colour by the curtains yesterday which 'causes' them to be indigo today. This is ludicrous (and Deutscher is 'happy to join in the joke'): and yet there are causal explanations for their retention of colour, to do perhaps with the effects of sunlight on particular dyes.[13] The relevant causal conditions, those which explain the present colour of the curtains, the present squeakiness of the bear, or a present act of remembering, can be made more complex and inclusive, to cover, for instance, the causal effects of the environment over time, the teddy bear's causal field.

Behind this line of attack on causal theories is the view, associated with Ryle, that the dispositions which support counterfactual conditionals are pure powers, not grounded in any physical facts which make them true.[14] There are many more or less respectable positions on the metaphysics of dispositions, and I only want here to point to the fact that there are views of dispositions which will allow explanations of memory capacities in terms of the nature of underlying states and processes.[15] It does seem odd, even within common-sense understanding, 'to fancy that the retentive power of memory consists in nothing and subsists as "pure power"' (Deutscher 1989: 60).

But, even if room can be made for the quest for the exact nature of the operative involvement of the trace in remembering, and if some such criteria can be made to work along Martin and Deutscher's (1966) lines, this only goes to defend a very general causal account of memory. Yet there is no *general* issue of the links between retention and storage: it all depends on what it is that is stored or retained. So work still has to be done in spelling out just what is meant by saying that traces are 'stored' between experience and remembering. There *are* forms of (literal) storage which are not implied by retention: but Malcolm was mistaken in thinking retention in memory is possible without *any* causal continuity.

This is where the specifically distributed model of memory helps. If remembering involves the retention of capacities over time, does it require brute physical storage? The distinction within distributed models, familiar by now between explicit and implicit representation (chapter 6; O'Brien 1993) operates here.

The point of the distinction between transient activity patterns and enduring dispositional traces is that there is no need for representation which is both

---

13 As Deutscher points out (1989: 60), while the details of the chemical processes involved are the province of experts, the existence of such processes is commonly accepted, since, for example, 'knowing that dyes are complex chemicals is part of the everyday practice of following recipes'.

14 'To possess a dispositional property is not to be in a particular state, or to undergo a particular change; it is to be bound or liable to be in a particular state, or to undergo a particular change, when a particular condition is realized' (Ryle 1949/1963: 43).

15 Gerard O'Brien is currently developing a promising non-relational account of dispositions in connectionist networks, using the anti-Rylean views of David Armstrong (Armstrong 1966/1980: 1–15, 1973: 11–16).

continuous and explicit, for memories retaining their form in local boxes, as in cruder causal theories of memory (the teddy bear is not *always* squeaking). Context, in the form of the effects of past experience and new input on connection weights, automatically influences the transient explicit activation pattern which is evoked on presentation of a new input. What is retained and, implicitly, 'stored' in weights or pores after experience is a disposition. The actualisation, or rendering explicit, of an activity pattern at a given time depends on the global state of the system, the individual connection weights, the present patterns of input to the system, and thus on contextual environmental factors like winter damp in the teddy bear's attic.

So it is true that retention in memory does not require the literal, faithful storage of past experiences such that, if you open a door, they are just there. Patterns which are not active exist only potentially in the changed weights of the system. Remembering of course depends on many factors other than the nature of what is 'stored'. But retention in memory requires *some* theoretically explicable causal continuity over time through physical processes in which the system takes part. The processes underlying our capacities may be much more chaotic than any that sets of stored copies could pursue. Intuitions not hooked on high fidelity or on the paradigms of print will cleave to traces which inevitably mingle. No critique of trace theory can legitimately fail to deal with implicit distributed traces.

16.4 Isomorphism and resemblance

How is it that traces *represent* past events, experiences, or whatever? What is it about these 'representations' that allows them to latch on to the world and the past? How can they have *content*, and what kind of content is it?

No philosophy of mind has a fully satisfactory account of the meaning of mental representations. But specific problems seem to arise for the kinds of mechanistic causal models I have described. There seems no coherent way to spell out the required structural resemblance between the trace and what it is a trace of. This resemblance relation between experienced order in space and time and functional order in correlated mind/brain processes rests on unanalysed and incoherent metaphors of imprinting, engraving, copying, coding, or writing (felicitously dubbed typography, iconography, and engrammatology by Krell 1990: 3–7). What does it mean to say that a trace is 'similar to' that of which it is a trace?

Some critics focus on the assumption that the world, the past, or experience *has* a structure to be somehow encoded into the brain. They claim, on the contrary, that the world *has* no single, natural, non-arbitrary structure of elements to stand in isomorphic relations to internal traces (Malcolm 1977: ch. 10; Bursen 1978; Heil 1978: 61–6; compare Wittgenstein 1958: para. 47, satirising the idea that there are simple consituent parts of a chair). But the notion of the trace as a 'structural analogue' is sufficiently unclear to question without having to suggest in turn that all categorisation is arbitrary.

Neither do critics need to rely on assimilating all representations to images which picture the past: it is misguided to announce that trace theorists' materialistic 'dogma makes the copy theory indispensable' (Straus 1970: 54; compare Locke 1971: ch. 1; and Hass 1991). 'The traditional attraction with the image as the nerve of recall' (Deutscher 1989: 71) only confuses the issue by demanding representation by resemblance.[16] It is implausible that we carry round whole sets of mental pictures in our heads. Even apart from the difficulties of representing abstractions by resemblance, the mental image in fact sits badly with even a moderate physicalism. Brain states can hardly be similar to furry tabby cats or big rubber balls (Cummins 1989: 31–2).

So weaker notions of the trace are sought. Martin and Deutscher (1966: 189, 191) included in their analysis of remembering the requirement that, to the extent remembering succeeds, 'the state or set of states produced by the past experience must constitute a structural analogue of the thing remembered'. Only this condition, they felt, would get around problem cases in which, for instance, present knowledge of something past is caused by a route other than memory. Martin and Deutscher did not want to commit themselves to the trace as a perfect analogue, 'mirroring all the features of a thing', or to there being any 'sense in the notion of all the features of anything': but, they believed, the trace must contain 'at least as many features as there are details which a given person can relate about something he has experienced' (1966: 190).

Even this now looks too strong. Some details which crop up in remembering an experience need not have been permanently encoded in the same trace as that experience. We tell more than we remember: later inferences creep into the telling. Even where memory for the gist of an event is roughly accurate, details may shift as the trace is filtered through other beliefs, dreams, fears, or wishes (Schacter 1996: 101–13). Less accurate verbal memories, such as attempted descriptions of faces or of wines, can overshadow more precise non-verbal traces (Schooler and Engstler-Schooler 1990). No psychological evidence suggests that remembering can be explained *without* causal connections between events and traces, and between traces and recollection: but it does encourage us to think of those causal connections as multiple, indirect, and context-dependent. So details remembered need not have been contained in the same trace in unchanging form.

Representation by explicit resemblance has often been specifically denied by

---

16 Malcolm says, rudely, that although the terms image, picture, idea, copy and representation 'all tend to be equivalent terms in the philosophy of memory', most memory theorists prefer 'representation . . ., since its greater vagueness gives [their] thesis better protection against refutation' (1970: 67).

trace theorists. Descartes rejected 'little pictures formed in our heads', which would require there 'to be yet other eyes in our brain', with which to perceive them (*Dioptrics* IV, AT vi.112, CSM 1.165; *Dioptrics* VI, AT vi.130, CSM 1.167). He noticed instead the significatory utility of things like words and signs, engravings, laughter and tears, which 'bear no resemblance to the things they signify' (*Le Monde* I, AT xi.3–4, CSM 1.81; see also *Principles* IV.189–98, AT viii(a). 315–23, CSM 1.279–85; compare Gaukroger 1990: 14–26; and Slezak 1990). Brain traces are the *vehicles* of representation, but they require a causal nexus involving body and environment as their background system (Mackenzie 1989). The only 'resemblance' in play is between different traces, with some grouped together by, for example, being located in proximity in an internal state space,[17] not between the structure of traces and the structure of the world: yet the world's structure is still part cause of the structure of the traces.

Some contemporary critics of representation-by-resemblance who wish to retain representation instead follow Fodor's account of the discrete storage of abstract symbols in a language-like representational medium (Pylyshyn 1984). But pictorialism and logicism do not exhaust possible forms of representation (compare Tye 1991): distributed representation could be a distinct third genus, neither image nor symbol (Haugeland 1991; van Gelder 1991b). Computations are defined over dynamic activation patterns rather than icons or syntactic strings (Kosslyn and Hatfield 1984; Hatfield 1989; Horgan and Tienson 1989; Cussins 1990). For Hatfield, for example, the relevant kind of structural isomorphism is simply the complex physiological transduction of, say, visual information into the visual system. There's obviously immense difficulty in forcing a theory of *content* from such alternatives:[18] But here I only need claim that metaphors of writing, imprinting, and copying do not exhaust the ways of getting isomorphism between past events and experience and encoded trace. If

17 'An activation space will also be a similarity space, inasmuch as similar vectors will define adjacent regions in space. This means that similarity between objects represented can be reflected by similarity in their representations, that is, proximity of positions in activation space. Similarity in representations is thus not an accidental feature, but an intrinsic and systematic feature' (Churchland and Sejnowski 1992: 169). This is not a simple two-term resembling relation between image and object, but a four-term relation in which the similarity between two traces maps non-accidentally on to similarity between two objects or events.

18 The biggest new problem with this kind of approach (which looks like the right problem in this area) is in finding a principled way to distinguish which of all the subsequent activity patterns in the system are truly psychological visual memories, truly representational states, and which are mere physiological responses, merely causal/correlational relations between world and brain. It is for lack of a solution to this difficulty that Hatfield rejects the Churchlands' notion of calibrational content, and prefers to tie representational content to the functional role played by the activity patterns in the system, and to those theories of content which make reference to the biological idea of normal function (1989: 269–76, 284 n. 41). But it is not altogether clear that a principled distinction between psychophysiological states and merely physiological states is necessary for good theory (Schwartz 1994).

there is any hope of more strictly neurophilosophical accounts of the isomorphism of patterns then some criticisms of trace theory may not get a grip
and the notion of a structural analogue can be successfully generalised or
weakened. To note that the structures which underpin retention need not
remain the same over time, or might not even involve determinate forms over
time, is not to refute the very concept of a trace.[19]

16.5 The four-pronged fork: homunculus/regress/ circularity/solipsism

Thus far I have tried to answer or deflect various hostilities to the trace. But a
fourth set of objections, synthesised from the critical literature on memory and
perception, has direct reflections in different options and possibilities within
connectionist theory.

The four prongs of the fork which I will describe are not mutually exclusive:
according to many critics of representationism, many trace theorists are
confusedly pinioned on all four simultaneously. It is convenient to present the
problems in the context of the retrieval process. How does the stored trace of
the past come to play a part in the present act of recognition or recall?

Encoded traces, it is said, require an internal interpreter or reader to recognise a new input as matching an existing trace, or to know in advance which
trace to search for and recall for a given purpose. But who is this inner subject
behind the engram? Such an intelligent homunculus, merely shifting the problems of retrieval one step deeper inside, is the first prong of the four-pronged
fork (Gibson 1970/1982: 95, 1979a: 256).

If it is avoided by having further internal mechanisms, in some 'corporeal
studio' (Ryle 1949/1963: 36), pick out the relevant trace, a vicious Rylean regress,
the second prong, is generated: each of these mechanisms will need a further
mechanism to do its interpretative job for it. The problem of representation has
been pushed further inside, not clarified.

Or if the homunculus is avoided by allowing that the remembering subject
can somehow just choose the right trace, or match a new input to an existing
encoded trace, then the trace would be redundant, for the subject has direct independent access to the past to know what a trace is a trace of. If the subject can
just inspect the past in order to check and compare a representation against it,

19 As Shope, for instance, thought it did: 'it is the functional relation of something to its
sources and effects which makes it a trace, not its structure' (1973: 317). But, clearly, the
sciences of memory would already be using the notion of function in identifying traces
and in teasing out specific kinds of function/structure relationships. Function is a
necessary, not an alien, concept for the mind/brain sciences (Wilkes 1981). For another
case of the mistaken assumption that rejection of that precise isomorphism found in
localised codes entails the falsity of causal theories in general, see Zemach 1983: 32–4.

the facts which traces were meant to explain have not been explained, and trace theory is *circular* (Earle 1956/7: 5–6; Bursen 1978: 52–60; Lyons 1981: 152–3; Wilcox and Katz 1981a: 229–32; Sanders 1985: 508–10; Arcaya 1989: 102–5; Krell 1990: 17–18, 89). This redundancy or circularity objection is the third prong of the fork.

If, finally, it is claimed that no independent access to the past is in fact assumed by representationism, and that no interpretations are being checked against another somehow guaranteed veridical memory, then, the critic argues, *solipsism* or *scepticism* results. There is no guarantee that *any* act of remembering does provide access to the past at all: remembering is all inference, and nothing gives us confidence in its accuracy. Representationism, it seems, cuts the subject off from the past behind a murky veil of traces (Wilcox and Katz 1981a: 231; Ben-Zeev 1986: 296; Maze 1991).

Handling the fork

These four prongs, homunculus, regress, circularity, and solipsism/scepticism await the unwary trace theorist. Having the recognition of traces done by a little internal recogniser merely pushes the problem inside, and homunculus or regress arguments ensue. But if such inner recognition does not occur, then either the subject has circular independent access to the past to compare with the trace, or there is no guarantee of *any* access to the real past, and solipsism threatens.

To some extent these repeated worries are just ignored by memory theorists in the cognitive sciences, who continue to seek existence proofs that remembering is possible with representationist assumptions. Defences depend on the particular version of representationism being fortified (Shoemaker 1970; Rakover 1983; Rock 1991). Localist models of memory like Hooke's (chapter 5 above), with atomic items independently stored at separate addresses, require a central processor to extract and manipulate them, an executive Chairperson of the Board of Mental Modules (Krell 1990: 89), and some defend this homunculus (Rock 1983: 39; Fodor 1986: 320–1). But I do not pursue this defence, since central executives are exactly what I hope to dispense with.

Others deny the force of the regress prong, claiming that the ability to 'interpret' sequences of on- and off-currents can be decomposed by subdividing the tasks involved and attributing each to an ever smaller 'team or committee of *relatively* ignorant, narrow-minded, blind homunculi to produce the intelligent behavior of the whole' (Dennett 1978: 123) and that there is no illegitimate intelligence in mere mechanisms (Fodor 1968b: 627–30).[20] This

---

20 As Dennett argues, 'homunculi are *bogeymen* only if they duplicate *entire* the talents they are rung in to explain', which is not the case when the nested levels of homuncular function are decomposable to, for instance, simple stupid binary mechanisms: 'one discharges fancy homunculi from one's scheme by organizing armies of such idiots to do the work' (Dennett 1978: 124).

decompositional strategy for innocent homuncularism has been connected with recent work on function-analytical explanation to accommodate connectionism (Lycan 1991). It has attractive consequences in stressing the continuity of levels of nature which rejects the simple 'two-levelism' of earlier philosophical functionalism (Lycan 1987: 37–48, 1991: 265–8). But while it may be that biting the homunculus and regress prongs will eventually blunt the four-pronged fork, it is not immediately obvious that functional decompositions explain *how* stored traces get matched to inputs or how retrieval in general works.

Perhaps a more promising response is to deny the force of the final, solipsistic/sceptical prong of the fork.[21] In distributed models, there is no internal central processor which searches, inspects, or otherwise manipulates items stored passively in discrete memory locations. The only connections within the system are local, and processing and storage occur in the same parts of the system. There is no internal reading, decoding, or interpreting of memory traces. Behaviour mediated by cognitive activity is the result not of an intelligent homunculus' calculations, but of numerous relatively independent but interacting systems computing best-fit solutions in parallel. But, without a homunculus, how *do* recognition and learning happen? Can the past in fact play any role in the causation of present retrieval episodes? In the context of the right kind of causal theory, the world itself must partly drive the learning and remembering process.

So the direct realist's circularity charge contains an element of truth important for the connectionist. As Gibsonians argue, information about the past is in the present environment for the attuned subject to extract. The past is not forever concealed: sequential orders in time allow veridical remembering on the prompting of present inputs. The connectionist is enough of a representationist to think that accepting the *unique* specification of the past by present input alone would be to ignore the internal and cognitive effects of past experience (chapter 15 above). The same present input or cue will not produce the

---

21 Compare Fodor 1976: 204–5 on how, as a representationist, to avoid thinking of 'the mind as somehow caged in a shadow show of representations unable, in the nature of the thing, to get in contact with the world outside'. The *causal* nature of the sequence of events from objects to representations cuts off a degeneration into solipsism, so that 'epistemic relations are typically immediate in whatever sense causal relations are, and that ought to be immediate enough for anybody'. But Fodor's representational theory, attributing much to innate mental structure, does not say more about the role of the world in the formation of representations: the connectionist response which I am adumbrating does. It also deflects John Maze's case (1991: 164–8) that Fodor's representationism cannot avoid the 'decline into solipsism'. Maze (1991: 167–8) complains that, while Fodor (1976: 204) is right in saying that solipsism cannot be true because representations must have causes, his representationism does not allow him to talk about these causes. This is not true of the representationism I am defending, according to which it is not that we are only ever aware of representations, but that we can sometimes be aware of the actual external causes of the representations.

same response in two different rememberers with different learning histories, or in one rememberer at different times or in different contexts. Input comes from elsewhere within a system or organism as well as from the environment. But while the connectionist does take memory to involve inference in an important way, realism is maintained by arguing that the 'teacher' of the connectionist model or mind is the environment, plus evolution.[22] This needs some cashing out.

Circularity and supervised learning

The final two prongs of the philosophical fork, the circularity and solipsism objections, have direct empirical realisations in the options available within connectionist theory. 'Supervised' learning rules require circular independent access to reality, the past, or the right answer, making the postulation of representations redundant. 'Unsupervised' learning rules, on the other hand, render the system's contact with the world problematic.

Connectionist models employ a variety of learning rules (Hinton 1989; Bechtel and Abrahamsen 1991: ch. 3). These are algorithms by which the weights on connections between units change over time. The error margin, in a simple case, between an actual output and the 'correct' output can be used over a series of trials to alter the weights on the units which together compute the output value. Such *supervised* learning rules, like the delta rule, back-propagation, and Boltzmann learning with simulated annealing (Churchland and Sejnowski 1992: 82–96) are common, since they allow easier management of ongoing processing: 'the network is provided with explicit feedback as to what output pattern was desired for a particular input pattern', and desired output is compared to actual output in order to change the weights (Bechtel and Abrahamsen 1991: 314).

The importance of supervised learning in human development should not be underestimated: as well as learning by ostension and schooling, explicit correction by external teachers is one mechanism for the internalisation of a culture's social and moral categories. But supervised-learning techniques have major shortcomings if considered as complete models of human cognition. Paul Churchland, writing on back-propagation in particular, notes:

> First, the requirement that the correct output be available to the learning network in every case is clearly unrealistic. After failing to solve a problem, real brains do not generally get to look at the correct answers at the back of the book. Second, the brain shows no plausible mechanisms for computing and

22 What seems a really robust realism is the possibility that we could be globally mistaken about the way that the world (or the past) is. Global realism must allow for large-scale error (Churchland 1988; Pettit 1991). While, I shall argue, scepticism does not follow from this, Gibsonian 'direct' realism does not seem to even allow for the possibility of significant error (see note 7 to chapter 15 above).

distributing such globally informed adjustments to its myriad weights. And third, the back-propagation procedure scales upward to large networks only very poorly. (Churchland 1989a: 243–4)

Churchland's first complaint about supervised learning is the empirical version of the circularity prong. As he notes, we need 'to escape the unreality of an omniscient teacher' (1989a: 246).

The biological implausibility of supervised learning realises in empirical form the circularity or redundancy prong of the direct realist's four-pronged fork. A system outside the system of traces already knows the answer, identifying whether a candidate stored trace is the appropriate one for current input. In human remembering, then, these models would be circular, for they require external access to the past to perform their retrieval operations.

Solipsism and unsupervised learning

Just as the circularity prong of the philosophers' fork has an empirical realisation in connectionist research, so too does the solipsism prong, on which impaling must be risked. 'Unsupervised learning' labels a range of biologically more plausible learning algorithms. Without an internal interpreter, and without independent access to the past, neural networks must somehow maintain genuine causal contact with the world. This was the perceived problem with animal spirits models of memory, for the fleeting spirits were pre-eminently unsupervised, and threatened to blunt confidence in the possibility of veridical recall. The key, then, is the input. In unsupervised learning, networks 'evolve processing strategies that . . . maximise their capacity for identifying salient information in the . . . input vectors . . . [and] find similarities among the inputs so that they are taxonomised into potentially useful groupings' (Churchland 1989a: 246).[23] The partitioning of hidden units groups inputs into similarity classes. The network becomes increasingly sensitive to complex regularities, through a 'progressive accommodation to the objective statistical distribution among inputs' (Churchland 1989a: 248).[24] If something like this

23 Bechtel and Abrahamsen (1991: 314) describe the way a network using unsupervised learning 'gradually achieves, without feedback, a weight matrix that allows it to classify a set of inputs (by discovering the regularities exhibited by subsets of the input patterns)'. The terminology here needs some care or modification, as P.S. Churchland and Sejnowski have pointed out (1992: 96–7): in unsupervised learning a network has no access to external feedback as from a programmer, but it can have internal error messages either from other parts of the system or in using its own previous states retained in some form in extra context layers (compare Jordan and Jacobs 1992). They suggest the term 'monitored' learning when there is some internal measure of error. For the philosophical issue at hand, unsupervised systems face the solipsism charge whether or not they are monitored: only systems with supervised learning have independent access to the answer.

24 It is for this reason that connectionist models promise better performance than expert systems over some complex task domains. Human experts' skills need not be accessible to conscious, linguistic or explicit formulation (Dreyfus 1990). Nevertheless skill is no accident: experts respond to objective regularities in the world.

occurs in biological networks, the connectionist has some hope of blunting the solipsist/sceptical prong of the direct realists' dilemma, since the world itself can 'exert a robust influence on the process' (1989a: 248; P.S. Churchland and Sejnowski 1992: 202–21).

It is worth spelling out the philosophical dialectic here. The charge was that no representationist theory which avoids the other three prongs can avoid solipsism. The critics are not sceptics or solipsists themselves, and no ultimate *refutation* of solipsism is specifically required in answer. There is room for an empirical response which shows that in fact particular representationist trace theories do allow for genuine contact with the past: if this is so, the objection that the theory does not allow reality to impinge on the rememberer loses its grip.

But not all realist critics are content with the fallible, corrigible processes which such empirical answers provide. There is a tendency to demand not *probable* causal contact with reality, but *certainty* in remembering as in perceiving, *incorrigible* contact with the world. Turvey and Shaw, for example, complain that 'the muddle' arising in perceptual representationism is due to 'a failure to uncover . . . any legitimate kind of knowing that is epistemologically unquestionable' (1979: 178). They acknowledge the suggestion, from Fodor and others, 'that such epistemic incorrigibility is not really needed' and that there need merely be some causal process or 'algorithm' which in fact underpins contact with the world although it is not ultimately 'unquestionable'. They reject this solution because it 'bears the traces of legerdemain; an unquestioned but incorrect algorithm as a bench mark could hardly guarantee that other algorithms will be adjusted in the direction of a truer fit to reality' (1979: 178). But the demand for a *guarantee* of incorrigible access to reality is terribly strong foundationalism: as Schwartz (1996: 89) complains, it is hard to be convinced by the Gibsonian view that 'unless there is a one–one, lawlike, correlation between the environment and some single aspect of the stimulus array perception would be indirect' in a metaphysically troubling way. The imposition of certainty should be rejected. Why look beyond the empirical likelihood, given natural selection, that contact with an objective world does, sometimes, occur? The cost of a robust realism just is the bare logical possibility of scepticism. But bare logical possibility is insufficient ground for concern or action.

A fallibilist defence of the reality of the external causes of representations is hostage to the empirical success of the theory in which it is embedded. Neurobiological research on long-term potentiation may show how unsupervised learning is realised in some brain regions (Goddard 1980; Lynch 1986; Sejnowski and Tesauro 1990; Alkon 1992): connectivity is adjusted locally at independent synaptic sites without a global, omniscient teacher. The different mechanisms involved at different temporal stages of consolidation are driven only by environmental effects and the current state of brain and body, arising from evolution and past experience (Thorpe and Imbert 1989; Churchland and Sejnowski 1992: 254–95).

Distributed models extract information from inputs, becoming attuned, in context-dependent fashion, to what the environment affords. Despite the promissory tone of this discussion, there are good philosophical reasons to look in these directions. We attune ourselves to our environments, sometimes through explicit tuition but more often by picking up patterns in experience, revising and transforming internal models as we go. It would be strange if empirical theories described the mind/brain as faithfully reflecting the world in its full presence, or the past in its full transparency, as the demand for epistemologically unquestionable remembering requires. Better metaphors are those of the continual filtering, deformation, and melding of representations over time (Churchland 1993: 220–1). Body, brain, and memory do actively alter perceptual input, not by a dualistic inferential imposition of constructed or innate structure on impoverished data, but through ongoing rearrangement and moulding of representations in the interaction with, and 'interpretation' of, new experience.

To put it another way, of course truth in memory is a problem. Just as Descartes and Malebranche realised that the same processes operate in animal spirits across memory, imagination, and dreaming (chapters 3 and 9 above), so connectionism allows multiple causal inputs in any act of remembering. There is seldom a simple, direct transmission from a single past experience through discretely stored informational items to a cleanly defined moment of recall, for 'each memory is many memories' (Matsuda 1993: 24; Schechtman 1994: 9–10). Outside philosophy and the courtroom, we only recognise human memory as operating 'normally' when it is 'malfunctioning', shot through with forgetting, selection, condensation, interference, and distortion. Yet, outside contexts in which truth is so desired that it is enforced, this rarely elicits worries about solipsism. The experienced sedimentations of memory in the body and of affect in memories make it blindly obvious that the past, for all its obscurity and opacity to *conscious* capture, does affect the present in multiple, skewed ways.

17

Order, confusion, remembering

Memory can be compared with a storehouse only so far as it fulfils the same
purpose. Where it does not, we could not say whether the things stored up may
not constantly change their nature and so could not be stored at all.

> (Ludwig Wittgenstein, 'Notes for the "Philosophical Lecture"',
> MS 166 (1935/6), in Stern 1991: 204)

... our personal identity is not simply a molecular formula of continual knowledge
and skills; it is a singular compound of fragmentary systems of knowledge,
incomplete stocks of information and discontinuous paradigms, disjoint fantasy
fields, personal repetition cycles and intermittent rituals.

> (Alphonso Lingis 1994a: 148)

17.1 The vulnerability of distributed memory

I responded to the 'four-pronged fork' in chapter 16 by suggesting that distributed models with unsupervised learning rules can extract objective statistical
regularities out of input deriving from the world without external control. But
apart from the difficulty of scaling up from toy network models competent in
restricted domains to psychologically realistic networks (Churchland and
Sejnowski 1992: 125–37), the vaunted context-sensitivity of distributed models
might go too far.[1] Just because they pick up these regularities in input, they are
liable to being misled by ambiguities or idiosyncrasies of particular input sets.
As Andy Clark, who calls this the 'hostage problem', says (1993: 171), 'the price
of this sensitivity is an apparent vulnerability to the whims of a potentially
hostile environment'. Networks which develop in good Gibsonian fashion by
attunement to environmental regularities require 'the continued presence of a
friendly training environment in which appropriate data are presented in an
appropriate order' (1993: 173).

Connectionist practice demonstrates the difficulty of extracting relatively
ordered partitions in representational space from certain kinds of input patterns. Elman, developing models of the representation of grammatical structure in which memory is 'inextricably bound up with the rest of the processing
mechanism' and in which polysemy is a continuum with meanings differing
naturally according to context (1990: 208, 191), had to reorder the training

---

1 Thanks to the audiences at cognitive science seminars at the universities of Melbourne,
Sydney, and New South Wales for helpful discussions of earlier drafts of this material.

input so that more complex inputs were presented only later. In earlier versions, 'the network was unable to learn the task when given the full range of complex data from the beginning of training. However, when the network was permitted to focus on the simpler data first, it was able to learn the task quickly and then move on successfully to more complex patterns' (Elman 1989: 11–12). Exposure to full complex input from the start meant that no useful partitions were made, and the system could not learn. The problem exemplified here is that, without the artificial control of input complexity and order which Elman had to impose, distributed representational space will be too chaotic, too buffeted by complex inputs when the system has not yet developed internal structure of sufficient richness, to learn successfully over time. If this is so, Fodor's systematicity objection (chapter 11 above) gains force, and classical cognitivists can retort that only language-like symbolic structure will allow flexible capacities to develop in the face of poor or ambiguous input (Clark 1993: 172).

In response to the worry, connectionists can, firstly, design more powerful and stable networks, using recurrent nets and extra context layers to rival symbolic models in hard domains (Pollack 1990); and secondly, with Clark (1993: 173–88), look to evolutionary shields between networks and world. But historical attention to perceived dichotomies between order and chaos in human remembering supports the additional, complementary strategy of treating the vulnerability of distributed models as a virtue, to encourage re-evaluations of the explananda in memory theory. Where critics from Glanvill to Fodor require and impose intrinsic order in memory and cognition, supporters of superposition merely want their theory to allow for the emergence of order. Indeed thinking about the notion of *sequence* in remembering encourages suspicion about the very idea, or ideal, of order. The phenomenology of continuous flow between memories seems to gel with dynamic systems operating in real time, in which processes unfold and the variables change 'smoothly and continuously': in contrast, time in serial classical models 'is not real time, it is mere order' (van Gelder and Port 1995: 19–20). Connectionism does have a 'largely unnoticed capacity to illuminate our phenomenology' (Lloyd 1996: 61).

So it may be possible to bolster auto-associative mechanisms by clever design or with extra innate structures against environmental vagary. But just as useful is suspicion about critics' focus on abstract cognitive competences, their treatment of irregularities in performance as deviations from norms set out in tacit internal rules. Bechtel and Abrahamsen (1991: 254) complain that those 'impressed with the abstract regularities in behavior' captured in linguistic competence theories just talk past those whose concern is with variations in actual performance. In distributed models, a competence theory, expressing the structure of a task analysis, only approximates performance. As Smolensky puts it in the context of connectionist harmony theory, the competence theory gives the functions relating a system's input to an ideal output, whereas the performance theory is a 'differential equation governing the system's moment-to-moment evolution' (1988: 20). Regularity emerges from ongoing processing: but because it is not guaranteed, the theory will better extend to cover performance irregularities.

These points make sense of the historical debates on distributed memory. Glanvill's complaint that the ongoing processing of active memory trace motions and patterns, when they are not kept in a distinct storage system, will 'raise a little Chaos of confusion, where Nature requires the exactest order' (VOD: 36) and Coleridge's fears of 'the phantasmal chaos of association' (BL VII: 218) (chapters 5 and 14 above) are just older examples of the rationalist ploy of requiring regularity. Hartley acknowledged that in remembering 'perfect exactness is not to be supposed or required' (OM 375, 1.iii.4, prop. 90), claiming that the many actual mistakes made in human performance make his distributed model of memory more plausible (chapter 13). In similar fashion, connectionists, attending to a fuller range of normal and abnormal cognitive and behavioural phenomena, seek to understand the common microstructure of cognition, and only afterwards ask if 'some order in the confusion might be forthcoming' (Churchland and Sejnowski 1992: 85).

Connectionists have already changed the explananda in specific psychological debates, on prototypes and exemplars, or on the acquisition of past tenses by English speakers, where initial connectionist modelling spurred new developmental research on just when children tend to stop over-regularising endings on irregular verbs (Rumelhart and McClelland 1986; Bechtel and Abrahamsen 1991: 194–200; Clark 1993: 155–62). Not only might actual performance be simulated without a mechanism governed by the explicit rules of the task domain: but the interaction of model and data can reveal that there is less order in later usage than was once thought.

The methodological strategy, then, is not only to challenge the task analyses of logicist cognitive science (Chater and Oaksford 1990), but to specify positive prospects for connectionist psychological explanation in domains where our cognitive capacities are not, in fact, all that systematic. Clark (1990: 195, 208) drives home the gap between competence and processing which connectionism opens up, where competence theories can only be idealised fixes 'on certain stable states of the system' which do not reveal 'the dynamics, or actual processing strategies'. Instead of implementing a prior theory of the structure of a task domain, connectionists must work backwards to trace the shape of a cognitive space after performance. Only thus do we 'avoid imposing the form of our conscious, sentential thought on our models of unconscious processing' (Clark 1990: 215–18).

Decentring requirements of order forces accounts of how cognitive regularity ever exists. 'How can we do logic if [our] basic operations are not logical at all?' (Rumelhart et al. 1986: 44): how does memory sometimes track past events reliably? Some of the work is done by *external* structures and symbol-systems. When your theory suggests that there is chaos or mush inside, you have to look for order outside the mind/brain. Despite the tendency of Wittgenstein and his followers to reject all sciences of mind out of hand, this strategy is precisely in line with his cautions against projecting expressed regularities on to mysteriously structured inner processes. The 'system of impulses going out from my brain' when I talk or write need not itself 'continue further in the direction of the centre' (Wittgenstein 1980: para. 903; compare Davies 1991: 230–1; Shotter 1991: 205). Evolution and experience teach us to manipulate the environment and to supplement memory, turning hard cognitive problems into tractable ones: as Clark has recently put it, 'advanced cognition depends crucially on our abilities to *dissipate* reasoning' by building 'designer environments' in which 'the brain in its bodily context' can interact with a complex world (Clark 1997: 180, 191; see also pp. 59–69).[2] External symbols and recording devices, obviously, are culturally and historically specific, and the many senses of the past in different cultures and periods develop partly through different social uses of material and cultural artefacts and practices (Burke 1989; Lowenthal 1989; Radley 1990; Cole 1993; Munn 1995). So, again, it is not just that distributed traces are compatible with the attention to context, environment, and society which many critics of static traces demand: it is that the broadening of cognitive science beyond the mind/brain alone is specifically required by them.

17.2 Self, memory, confusion

One of the most obvious phenomenological features of memory seems untouched by all this cognitive and social scientism. The fears about memory's access to the real past which early modern thinkers projected on to animal spirits (chapter 9 above), their worry that they might be tricked by sly fluids into 'remembering' falsely, were about the intrusion of confabulation into memory. But there is a different subjective distinction available, relying on the sense of imagination which does not mean 'failed memory': do I not just know immediately when I am remembering as opposed to merely fantasising, when (as Reid would say) belief is inexorably attached? I may be misled in some way, but there is still a great difference between personal memory of an event and merely thinking that it happened.

Yet one secure finding in recent psychology of memory is that our 'remember/know' judgements, in deciding for instance whether we experienced

2 'One element frequently left out of cognitive modeling is the element of culture, that is, shared patterns of acquired behavior characteristic of a species. But the cognitive capacities of animals directly affect the kinds of culture they produce, and in the case of humans, the opposite is also true: specific types of human culture have direct effects upon individual cognition' (Donald 1991: 9–10; compare Hutchins 1995: 353–74).

something personally or just know that it occurred, are surprisingly malleable (Schacter 1996: 22–6, 114–21). Failures in 'source monitoring' (Johnson and Raye 1981; Belli and Loftus 1996: 174–5; Roediger 1996: 87–9) lead us to infer a likely cause in personal memory for beliefs, images, or other mental states which in fact derive from other sources. On one account, judgement of whether we subjectively remember something or just know it is determined not just by the real past experience but also, in particular, by fluency heuristics which make us attribute an image, say, to personal memory if it plausibly and quickly integrates with background knowledge (Kelley and Jacoby 1990, 1996). The conscious experience of remembering is not, as critics of trace theory complain, somehow contained in the trace itself: it is a result of constructive attribution in which conscious states can, but need not, be causally involved (Kelley and Jacoby 1990: 53; Mandler 1989).

Such constructions in turn influence future processing, and we can influence our memories and thus our selves within the causal nexus, abetted by whatever benevolent checks the social and natural environment affords. But the nature of the subjectivity and the control involved may not match pre-theoretical intuition. Intimately subjective beliefs about the relations between our current mental states and the past are no more transparent, no less accessible to science, than are beliefs about the voluntary origin of action, where the lack of immediate introspective awareness of the mechanisms involved does not mean that there are none: it is only 'the cognitive impenetrability of one's own actions which makes them appear autonomous and uncaused' (Slezak 1986: 431). The relevant sciences, again, will refer to the social as well as to the brain, for we spin tales about our past selves in linguistic and other narratives which suit particular purposes, shoring up some fragile coherence against pandemonium in story and autobiographical thoughts.

Neither neurophilosophy nor lab psychology alone will drive vast conceptual change, or force the elimination of common-sense self-conceptions. You can only revise what you can replace, and whirling revisionary schemes require independent motivation before evidence from cognitive science is to convince. But fragmentation has its seductions too (Churchland 1983: 85):

> If our conception of control changes, then our conception of the self changes *pari passu*, and this possibility may initially produce a kind of dizziness, tainted perhaps with anxiety. The warm antiquity of self, as Wallace Stevens calls it, binds us profoundly . . . The self, in the event, may turn out to be not so much a unified coherent entity, but a disconnected collection of wants, needs, and whatnots, flying in loose formation.

Regularity, order, and coherence in memory and cognition are fragile, temporary achievements: no less real for that, but more rare, less common, than we think.

The dream of memory as re-presenting the past in its full presence, anyway, may always have been more a philosopher's phantom than part of folk psychology. Experience was never fully captured even at the time, and the things 'stored up . . . constantly change their nature' in the superpositional mix. The act of autobiographical remembering obliterates by reducing the past to only one current context: but it also exceeds, as the early modern theorists struggling to keep the past in place realised, by creating a past which was never present. As one activity pattern flickers across brain pores, others subside, alter irretrievably, slip: but the animal spirits gather new wishes too in playing down their haphazard paths. Again, if traces are distributed fragments rather than monolithic containers, memory theory is not immune to loss, time, melding, and productive confusion.

This chapter has described the methodological shift which both connectionism and history encourage, and drawn on further psychological accounts of ordinary confusion, in which rigid control over memories is not required. This final part of the book has attacked the cogency of blanket refusals to countenance memory traces. Without prudish conceptual legislation, broader memory theory can perhaps recover tinges of both the sadness and the lightness of talk and theorising about the nimble animal spirits. We are, inevitably, more mixed within ourselves than we know.

References

Aaron, Richard I. (1955) *John Locke*, 2nd edn (Oxford: Clarendon).

Aarsleff, Hans (1994) 'Locke's Influence', in V. Chappell (ed.), *The Cambridge Companion to Locke* (Cambridge University Press), 252–89.

Alexander, Peter (1985) *Ideas, Qualities, and Corpuscles: Locke and Boyle on the External World* (Cambridge University Press).

Alkon, Daniel (1992) *Memory's Voice* (New York: HarperCollins).

Allison, Henry E. (1966/1977) 'Locke's Theory of Personal Identity: A Re-examination', in I.C. Tipton (ed.), *Locke on Human Understanding* (Oxford University Press), 105–22.

Alquié, Ferdinand (1966) *La Découverte métaphysique de l'homme chez Descartes*, 2nd edn (Paris: P.U.F.).

(1974) *Le Cartesianisme de Malebranche* (Paris: Vrin).

Alston, W. and Bennett, J. (1988) 'Locke on People and Substances', *Philosophical Review* 97, 25–46.

Anderson, James A. and Hinton, Geoffrey E. (1981) 'Models of Information Processing in the Brain', in G.E. Hinton and J.A. Anderson (eds.), *Parallel Models of Associative Memory* (Hillsdale, NJ: Erlbaum), 9–48.

Anderson, John (1927/1962) 'The Knower and the Known', repr. in his *Studies in Empirical Philosophy* (Sydney: Angus and Robertson), 27–40.

Anderson, John R. (1995) *Learning and Memory: An Integrated Approach* (New York: Wiley).

Anderson, John R. and Bower, Gordon H. (1979) *Human Associative Memory*, revised edn (Hillsdale, NJ: Erlbaum).

Anderson, Robert F. (1966) *Hume's First Principles* (Lincoln: Nebraska University Press).

(1976) 'The Location, Extension, Shape, and Size of Hume's Perceptions', in D.W. Livingston and J.T. King (eds.), *Hume: A Re-evaluation* (New York: Fordham University Press), 153–71.

Anderson, Ruth L. (1927) *Elizabethan Psychology and Shakespeare's Plays* (Iowa University Press).

Annas, Julia (1992) 'Aristotle on Memory and the Self', in M. Nussbaum and A. Rorty (eds.), *Essays on Aristotle's 'De Anima'* (Oxford: Clarendon), 297–311.

(1993) *Hellenistic Philosophy of Mind* (Berkeley and Los Angeles: California University Press).

Anscombe, G.E.M. (1974/1981) 'Memory, "Experience", and Causation', in her *Collected Philosophical Papers*, vol. II: *Metaphysics and the Philosophy of Mind* (Oxford: Blackwell), 120–30.

Anstey, Peter R. (1996) 'Qualities, Causes and Laws: A Study in the Corpuscular Philosophy of Robert Boyle', Ph.D. thesis, University of Sydney.

(forthcoming) 'A Study in the Reception of Cartesian Physiology in England: Descartes on the Movement of the Heart', in S. Gaukroger and J. Sutton (eds.), *Descartes' Natural Philosophy*, vol. II: *Cognition and Physiology* (forthcoming).

Arcaya, Jose M. (1989) 'Memory and Temporality: A Phenomenological Alternative',
    Philosophical Psychology 2, 101–10.
    (1992) 'Why is Time not Included in Modern Theories of Memory?', *Time and Society* 1,
    301–14.
Armogathe, Jean-Robert (1984) 'Note brève sur le vocabulaire de l'âme au dix-septième
    siècle', in M. Fattori and M. Bianchi (eds.), *Spiritus* (Rome: Edizioni dell'Ateneo),
    325–31.
Armstrong, David M. (1966/1980) 'The Nature of Mind', repr. in his *The Nature of Mind* (St
    Lucia: Queensland University Press), 1–15.
    (1973) *Belief, Truth and Knowledge* (Cambridge University Press).
    (1976/1980) 'Immediate Perception', repr. in his *The Nature of Mind* (St Lucia:
    Queensland University Press), 119–31.
Arnauld, Antoine (1683/1990) *On True and False Ideas*, trans. S. Gaukroger (Manchester
    University Press).
Arnold, Thomas (1786) *Observations on the Nature, Kinds, Causes and Prevention of Insanity,
    Lunacy, or Madness* (2 vols., London: G. Ireland).
Artaud, Antonin (1947/1976) 'Van Gogh, The Man Suicided by Society', in S. Sontag (ed.),
    Selected Writings of Antonin Artaud (New York: Farrar, Straus, and Giroux), 483–512.
Atherton, Margaret (1983) 'Locke's Theory of Personal Identity', *Midwest Studies in
    Philosophy* 8, 273–93.
Aubrey, John (1949) *Aubrey's Brief Lives*, ed. O.L. Dick (London: Secker and Warburg).
Aurell, Carl G. (1984) 'Note on Gibson's Direct Visual Perception', *Perceptual and Motor
    Skills* 58, 540–2.
Ayer, A.J. (1976) *The Central Questions of Philosophy* (Harmondsworth: Penguin).
Ayers, Michael (1986) 'Are Locke's "Ideas" Images, Intentional Objects, or Natural
    Signs?', *Locke Newsletter* 17, 3–36.
    (1988) *Locke*, vol.I: *Epistemology*, vol. II: *Ontology* (London: Routledge).
    (1993) 'Voluntarism and Naturalism in Physics from Descartes to Hume',
    K. Haakonssen and U. Thiel (eds.), *History of Philosophy Yearbook* 1 (Canberra:
    Australasian Society for the History of Philosophy), 41–65.
    (1994) 'Belief without Reason', forthcoming in *The Cambridge History of Philosophy*.
Babb, Lawrence (1951) *The Elizabethan Malady: A Study of Melancholia in English Literature from
    1580 to 1642* (East Lansing: Michigan State University Press).
Baker, Gordon and Morris, Katherine J. (1996) *Descartes' Dualism* (London: Routledge).
Bakhtin, Mikhail (1965/1984) *Rabelais and his World*, trans. H. Iswolsky (Bloomington:
    Indiana University Press).
Balz, Albert G.A. (1951) *Cartesian Studies* (New York: Columbia University Press).
Banaji, M.R. and Crowder, R.G. (1989) 'The Bankruptcy of Everyday Memory', *American
    Psychologist* 44, 1183–95.
Barclay, Craig R. (1996) 'Autobiographical Remembering: Narrative Constraints on
    Objectified Selves', in D.C. Rubin (ed.), *Remembering our Past: Studies in Autobiographical
    Memory* (Cambridge University Press), 94–125.
Barclay, Craig R. and Smith, Thomas S. (1992) 'Autobiographical Remembering: Creating
    Personal Culture', in M.A. Conway, D.C. Rubin, H. Spinnler, and W.A. Wagenaar
    (eds.), *Theoretical Perspectives on Autobiographical Memory* (Dordrecht: Kluwer), 75–97.
Barham, Peter (1992) 'Foucault and the Psychiatric Practitioner', in A. Still and I. Velody
    (eds.), *Rewriting the History of Madness* (London: Routledge), 45–50.

Barkan, Leonard (1975) Nature's Work of Art: The Human Body as Image of the World (New Haven: Yale University Press).

(1980) 'Diana and Actaeon: The Myth as Synthesis', English Literary Renaissance 10, 317–59.

Barker, Francis (1984) The Tremulous Private Body: Essays on Subjection (London: Methuen).

(1994) The Culture of Violence (Chicago University Press).

Barker, Peter (1991) 'Stoic Contributions to Early Modern Science', in M.J. Osler (ed.), Atoms, 'Pneuma', and Tranquillity (Cambridge University Press), 135–54.

Barker, Peter and Goldstein, Bernard R. (1984) 'Is Seventeenth Century Physics Indebted to the Stoics?', Centaurus 27, 148–64.

Barnouw, Jeffrey (1992) 'Passion as "Confused" Perception or Thought in Descartes, Malebranche, and Hutcheson', Journal of the History of Ideas 53, 397–424.

Barsalou, Lawrence W. (1988) 'The Content and Organisation of Autobiographical Memories', in U. Neisser and E. Winograd (eds.), Remembering Reconsidered: Ecological and Traditional Approaches to the Study of Memory (Cambridge University Press), 193–243.

Bartlett, Frederic C. (1932) Remembering: A Study in Experimental and Social Psychology (Cambridge University Press).

Beardsmore, R.W. (1989) 'Autobiography and the Brain', British Journal of Aesthetics 29, 261–9.

Bechtel, William (1985) 'Contemporary Connectionism: Are The New Parallel Distributed Processing Models Cognitive or Associationist?', Behaviourism 13, 53–61.

Bechtel, William and Abrahamsen, Adele (1991) Connectionism and the Mind: An Introduction to Parallel Processing in Networks (Oxford: Blackwell).

Bedini, Silvio A. (1964) 'The Role of Automata in the History of Technology', Technology and Culture 5, 24–42.

Behan, D.P. (1979) 'Locke on Persons and Personal Identity', Canadian Journal of Philosophy 9, 53–75.

Beier, Lucinda McCray (1989) 'Experience and Experiment: Robert Hooke, Illness, and Medicine', in M. Hunter and S. Schaffer (eds.), Robert Hooke: New Studies (Woodbridge: Boydell Press), 235–52.

Bell, Robert H. (1975) 'David Hume's Fables of Identity', Philological Quarterly 54, 471–83.

Belli, Robert F. (1986) 'Mechanist and Organicist Parallels between Theories of Memory and Science', Journal of Mind and Behavior 7, 63–86.

Belli, Robert F. and Loftus, Elizabeth F. (1996) 'The Pliability of Autobiographical Memory: Misinformation and the False Memory Problem', in D.C. Rubin (ed.), Remembering Our Past: Studies in Autobiographical Memory (Cambridge University Press), 157–79.

Belsey, Catherine (1985) The Subject of Tragedy (London: Methuen).

Ben-Zeev, Aaron (1986) 'Two Approaches to Memory', Philosophical Investigations 9, 288–301.

(1989) 'Reid's Opposition to the Theory of Ideas', in M. Dalgarno and E. Matthews (eds.), The Philosophy of Thomas Reid (Dordrecht: Kluwer), 91–101.

(1990) 'Reid and the Cartesian Framework', Journal of the History of the Behavioral Sciences 26, 38–47.

Benjamin, Andrew (1993) 'Descartes' Body of Forgetting', in his The Plural Event: Descartes, Hegel, Heidegger (London: Routledge), 34–53.

Bergson, Henri (1908/1991) Matter and Memory, 5th edn, trans. N.M. Paul and W.S. Palmer (New York: Zone Books).

Berrios, German E. (1990) 'Memory and the Cognitive Paradigm of Dementia during the 19th Century: A Conceptual History', in R. Murray and J. Turner (eds.), *Lectures on the History of Psychiatry* (London: Royal College of Physicians), 194–211.

(1996) *The History of Mental Symptoms: Descriptive Psychopathology since the Nineteenth Century* (Cambridge University Press).

Berthoud, J. (1984) 'Shandeism and Sexuality', in V. Grosvenor Myer (ed.), *Laurence Sterne: Riddles and Mysteries* (London: Barnes and Noble), 24–38.

Bever, Thomas G., Fodor, Jerry A., and Garrett, Merrill (1968) 'A Formal Limitation of Associationism', in T.R. Dixon and D.L. Horton (eds.), *Verbal Behavior and General Behavior Theory* (Englewood Cliffs, NJ: Prentice Hall), 582–5.

Beyssade, Michelle (1994) 'Descartes' Doctrine of Freedom', in J. Cottingham (ed.), *Reason, Will, and Sensation: Studies in Descartes' Metaphysics* (Oxford: Clarendon), 191–206.

Bitbol-Hespériès, Annie (1990) *Le Principe de vie chez Descartes* (Paris: Vrin).

Blackmore, Richard (1725) *A Treatise of the Spleen* (London: Pemberton).

Bloch, Maurice (1996) 'Internal and External Memory: Different Ways of Being in History', in P. Antze and M. Lambek (eds.), *Tense Past: Cultural Essays in Trauma and Memory* (London: Routledge), 215–33.

Blok, F.F. (1976) *Caspar Barlaeus (1584–1648): From the Correspondence of a Melancholic* (Amsterdam/Assen: van Gorcum).

Bolles, Edmund Blair (1988) *Remembering and Forgetting* (New York: Walker & Co.).

Bolzoni, Lina (1991) 'The Play of Images: The Art of Memory from its Origins to the Seventeenth Century', in P. Corsi (ed.), *The Enchanted Loom: Chapters in the History of Neuroscience* (Oxford University Press), 16–26.

Bono, James J. (1984) 'Medical Spirits and the Medieval Language of Life', *Traditio* 40, 91–130.

(1995) *The Word of God and the Languages of Man: Interpreting Nature in Early Modern Science and Medicine* (Madison, WI: Wisconsin University Press).

Boring, Edwin G. (1950) *A History of Experimental Psychology*, 2nd edn (New York: Appleton-Century-Crofts).

Bowers, Kenneth S. and Farvolden, Peter (1996) 'Revisiting a Century-Old Freudian Slip: From Suggestion Disavowed to the Truth Repressed', *Psychological Bulletin* 119, 355–80.

Boyer, Pascal (ed.) (1993) *Cognitive Aspects of Religious Symbolism* (Cambridge University Press).

Boyle, Robert (1772/1965) *The Works of the Honourable Robert Boyle*, ed. T. Birch (London; repr. Hildesheim: Georg Olms).

Bramhall, John (1841) *A Vindication of True Liberty from Antecedent Extrinsical Necessity*, in W. Molesworth (ed.), *The English Works of Thomas Hobbes* (London: J. Bohn), vol. v.

Bransford, J.D., McCarrell, N.S., Franks, J.J., and Nitsch, K.E. (1977) 'Toward Unexplaining Memory', in R. Shaw and J.D. Bransford (eds.), *Perceiving, Acting, and Knowing: Towards an Ecological Psychology* (Hillsdale, NJ: Erlbaum), 431–66.

Brazier, Mary A.B. (1958) 'The Evolution of Concepts relating to the Electrical Activity of the Nervous System, 1600–1800', in F.N.L. Poynter (ed.), *The History and Philosophy of Knowledge of the Brain and its Functions* (Oxford: Blackwell), 191–222.

(1984) *A History of Neurophysiology in the Seventeenth and Eighteenth Centuries* (New York: Raven Press).

Brennan, Andrew (1989/90) 'Fragmented Selves and the Problem of Ownership', *Proceedings of the Aristotelian Society* 90, 143–58.

Brewer, William F. (1996) 'What is Recollective Memory?', in D.C. Rubin (ed.), *Remembering our Past: Studies in Autobiographical Memory* (Cambridge University Press), 19–66.

Brewin, Chris R. (1996) 'Scientific Status of Recovered Memories', *British Journal of Psychiatry* 169, 131–4.

Broad, C.D. (1925) *The Mind and its Place in Nature* (London: Routledge and Kegan Paul).

Brooke, John (1991) *Science and Religion: Some Historical Perspectives* (Cambridge University Press).

Brown, Theodore M. (1968/1982) *The Mechanical Philosophy and the 'Animal Oeconomy': A Study in the Development of English Physiology in the Seventeenth and Early Eighteenth Centuries* (Ann Arbor: University Microfilms).

(1971) 'Introduction' to *The Posthumous Works of Robert Hooke*, ed. R. Waller (London: Frank Cass), 1–13.

(1974) 'From Mechanism to Vitalism in Eighteenth-Century English Physiology', *Journal of the History of Biology* 7, 179–216.

(1977) 'Physiology and the Mechanical Philosophy in Mid-Seventeenth Century England', *Bulletin of the History of Medicine* 51, 25–54.

(1985) 'Descartes, Dualism, and Psychosomatic Medicine', in W.F. Bynum, R. Porter, and M. Shepherd (eds.), *The Anatomy of Madness* (London: Tavistock), vol. 1, 40–62.

(1987) 'Medicine in the Shadow of the Principia', *Journal of the History of Ideas* 48, 629–48.

Bruyn, G.W. (1982) 'The Seat of the Soul', in F.C. Rose and W.F. Bynum (eds.), *Historical Aspects of the Neurosciences* (New York: Raven Press), 55–81.

Burke, Peter (1989) 'History as Social Memory', in T. Butler (ed.), *Memory: History, Culture, and the Mind* (Oxford: Blackwell), 97–113.

Burnham, William H. (1888) 'Memory, Historically and Experimentally Considered', *American Journal of Psychology* 2, 39–90, 255–70, 431–64, 566–622.

Bursen, Howard A. (1978) *Dismantling the Memory Machine: A Philosophical Investigation of Machine Theories of Memory* (Dordrecht: D. Reidel).

Burthogge, Richard (1694/1976) *An Essay Upon Reason and the Nature of Spirits* (London: John Dunton; repr. New York: Garland).

Burton, Robert (1621/1989) *The Anatomy of Melancholy*, ed. T.C. Faulkner, N.K. Kiessling, R.L. Blair, vol. 1 (Oxford: Clarendon).

Burtt, E.A. (1932) *The Metaphysical Foundations of Modern Physical Science* (London: Routledge and Kegan Paul).

Burwood, Steve and Jagger, Gill (1994), call for papers for Body Matters conference, University of Hull, 4–5 April 1995.

Bynum, Caroline W. (1992), 'Material Continuity, Personal Survival, and the Resurrection of the Body', in her *Fragmentation and Redemption: Essays on Gender and the Human Body in Medieval Religion* (New York: Zone Books), 239–97.

(1995a) 'Why All the Fuss about the Body? A Medievalist's Perspective', *Critical Inquiry* 22, 1–33.

(1995b), 'Reassemblage and Regurgitation: Ideas of Bodily Resurrection in Early Scholasticism', in her *The Resurrection of the Body* (New York: Columbia University Press), 117–55.

Bynum, William F. (1973) 'The Anatomical Method, Natural Theology, and the Functions of the Brain', *Isis* 64, 445–68.

Cam, Philip (1988) 'Modularity, Rationality, and Higher Cognition', *Philosophical Studies* 53, 279–94.

Campbell, Keith (1970) *Body and Mind* (London: Macmillan).

—— (1986) 'Can Intuitive Psychology Survive the Growth of Neuroscience?', *Inquiry* 29, 143–52.

—— (1988) 'Philosophy and Common Sense', *Philosophy* 63, 161–74.

Camus, Albert (1942/1975) 'Philosophical Suicide', in his *The Myth of Sisyphus*, trans. J. O'Brien (Harmondsworth: Penguin), 32–51.

Canguilhem, Georges (1937/1994) 'Descartes et la technique', in Canguilhem 1994: 219–26.

—— (1952/1994) 'Machine et organisme', in his *La Connaissance de la vie* (Paris: Hachette), 124–59; extracts in Canguilhem 1994: 227–32.

—— (1955/1977) *La Formation du concept de réflexe aux XVIIe et XVIIIe siècles*, 2nd edn (Paris: Vrin).

—— (1966/1989) *The Normal and the Pathological*, trans. Carolyn B. Fawcett (New York: Zone Books).

—— (1977) *Idéologie et rationalité dans l'histoire des sciences de la vie* (Paris: Vrin).

—— (1994) *A Vital Rationalist: Selected Writings from Georges Canguilhem*, ed. F. Delaporte (New York: Zone Books).

Carello, Claudia, Turvey, M.T., Kugler, P.N., and Shaw, R. (1984) 'Inadequacies of the Computer Metaphor', in M. Gazzaniga (ed.), *Handbook of Cognitive Neuroscience* (New York: Plenum Press), 229–48.

Carey, John (1990) *John Donne: Life, Mind and Art*, 2nd edn (London: Faber).

Carlson, Eric T. and Simpson, Meribeth M. (1969) 'Models of the Nervous System in Eighteenth Century Psychiatry', *Bulletin of the History of Medicine* 43, 101–15.

Carruthers, Mary (1990) *The Book of Memory* (Cambridge University Press).

Carter, Richard B. (1983) *Descartes' Medical Philosophy: The Organic Solution to the Mind–Body Problem* (Baltimore: Johns Hopkins University Press).

—— (1985/1991) 'Descartes' Bio-Physics', repr. in G. Moyal (ed.), *René Descartes* (London: Routledge), vol. IV, 194–219.

Casey, Edward S. (1987) 'The World of Nostalgia', *Man and World* 20, 361–84.

Castle, Terry (1988) 'Phantasmagoria: Spectral Technology and the Metaphorics of Modern Reverie', *Critical Inquiry* 15, 26–61.

Changeux, Jean-Pierre (1985) *Neuronal Man: The Biology of Mind* (Oxford University Press).

Chappell, Vere (1994) 'Descartes' Compatibilism', in J. Cottingham (ed.), *Reason, Will, and Sensation: Studies in Descartes' Metaphysics* (Oxford: Clarendon), 177–90.

Chater, Nick and Oaksford, Mike (1990) 'Autonomy, Implementation, and Cognitive Architecture: A Reply to Fodor and Pylyshyn', *Cognition* 34, 93–107.

Cherniak, Christopher (1986) *Minimal Rationality* (Cambridge, MA: MIT Press).

Cheyne, George (1715) *Philosophical Principles of Religion* (1705) 2nd edn (London).

—— (1733/1976) *The English Malady: or, A Treatise of Nervous Diseases of All Kinds . . .* (London: Strahan and Leake; repr. New York: Scholars' Facsimiles and Reprints).

Chomsky, Noam (1966) *Cartesian Linguistics: A Chapter in the History of Rationalist Thought* (New York: Harper and Row).

Christensen, Jerome (1981) *Coleridge's Blessed Machine of Language* (Ithaca, NY: Cornell University Press).

Churchland, Patricia S. (1981) 'Is Determinism Self-refuting?', *Mind* 90, 99–101.

—— (1983) 'Consciousness: The Transmutation of a Concept', *Pacific Philosophical Quarterly* 64, 80–95.

(1986a) *Neurophilosophy: Towards a Unified Science of the Mind/Brain* (Cambridge, MA: MIT Press).

(1986b) 'Replies to Comments', *Inquiry* 29, 241–72.

(1989) 'From Descartes to Neural Networks', *Scientific American* 261 (1), 100.

Churchland, Patricia S. and Sejnowski, Terrence J. (1989) 'Neural Representation and Neural Computation', in L. Nadel, L.A. Cooper, P. Culicover, and R.M. Harnish (eds.), *Neural Connections, Mental Computation* (Cambridge, MA: MIT Press), 15–48.

(1992) *The Computational Brain* (Cambridge, MA: MIT Press).

Churchland, Paul M. (1982) 'Is "Thinker" a Natural Kind?', *Dialogue* 21, 223–38.

(1985) 'The Ontological Status of Observables: In Praise of the Superempirical Virtues', in C.A. Hooker and P.M. Churchland (eds.), *Images of Science* (Chicago University Press), 35–47.

(1988) 'Perceptual Plasticity and Theoretical Neutrality', *Philosophy of Science* 55, 167–87.

(1989a) 'Learning and Conceptual Change', in Churchland 1989c: 231–53.

(1989b) 'Reductionism, Connectionism, and the Plasticity of Human Consciousness', in Churchland 1989c: 129–35.

(1989c) *A Neurocomputational Perspective: The Nature of Mind and the Structure of Science* (Cambridge, MA: MIT Press).

(1993) 'Evaluating our Self Conception', *Mind and Language* 8, 211–20.

(1995) *The Engine of Reason, the Seat of the Soul* (Cambridge, MA: MIT Press).

Clark, Andy (1987) 'From Folk Psychology to Naive Psychology', *Cognitive Science* 11, 139–54.

(1988) 'Thoughts, Sentences, and Cognitive Science', *Philosophical Psychology* 1, 263–78.

(1989) *Microcognition: Philosophy, Cognitive Science, and Parallel Distributed Processing* (Cambridge, MA: MIT Press).

(1990) 'Connectionism, Competence, and Explanation', *British Journal for the Philosophy of Science* 41, 195–222.

(1993) *Associative Engines: Connectionism, Concepts, and Representational Change* (Cambridge, MA: MIT Press).

(1996) 'Connectionism, Moral Cognition, and Collaborative Problem Solving', in L. May, M. Friedman, and A. Clark (eds.), *Mind and Morals: Essays on Cognitive Science and Ethics* (Cambridge, MA: MIT Press), 109–27.

(1997) *Being There: Putting Brain, Body, and World Together Again* (Cambridge, MA: MIT Press).

Clarke, Desmond (1982) *Descartes' Philosophy of Science* (Manchester University Press).

(1989) *Occult Powers and Hypotheses* (Oxford: Clarendon).

Clarke, Edwin (1968) 'The Doctrine of the Hollow Nerve in the Seventeenth and Eighteenth Centuries', in L.G. Stevenson and R.P. Multhauf (eds.), *Medicine, Science, and Culture* (Baltimore: Johns Hopkins University Press), 123–41.

(1978) 'The Neural Circulation: The Use of Analogy in Medicine', *Medical History* 22, 291–307.

Clarke, Edwin and Dewhurst, Kenneth (1973) *An Illustrated History of Brain Function* (Berkeley and Los Angeles: California University Press).

Clarke, Edwin and Jacyna, L.S. (1987) *Nineteenth Century Origins of Neuroscientific Concepts* (Berkeley and Los Angeles: California University Press).

Clericuzio, Antonio (1994) 'The Internal Laboratory: The Chemical Reinterpretation of Medical Spirits in England (1650–1680)', in P. Rattansi and A. Clericuzio (eds.), *Alchemy and Chemistry in the 16th and 17th Centuries* (Dordrecht: Kluwer), 51–83.

Coady, C.A.J. (1992) *Testimony: A Philosophical Study* (Oxford: Clarendon).

Cole, Michael (1993) 'Remembering the Future', in G. Harman (ed.), *Conceptions of the Human Mind* (Hillsdale, NJ: Erlbaum), 247–65.

Coleman, Janet (1992) *Ancient and Medieval Memories: Studies in the Reconstruction of the Past* (Cambridge University Press).

Coleman, William (1970) 'Mechanical Philosophy and Hypothetical Physiology', in R. Palter (ed.), *The 'Annus Mirabilis' of Sir Isaac Newton* (Cambridge, MA: MIT Press), 322–32.

Coleridge, Samuel T. (1801/1990), Letters to the Wedgewoods, in Jean S. Yolton (ed.), *A Locke Miscellany* (Bristol: Thoemmes Press), 261–92.

(1817/1985) *Biographia literaria*, in H.J. Jackson (ed.), *Samuel Taylor Coleridge* (Oxford University Press), 155–482.

(1956–71) *Collected Letters of Samuel Taylor Coleridge*, ed. E.L. Griggs (6 vols., Oxford: Clarendon).

(1957–61) *The Notebooks of Samuel Taylor Coleridge*, ed. Kathleen Coburn (3 vols., New York: Pantheon).

Colie, Rosalie (1960/1990) 'John Locke in the Republic of Letters', in Jean S. Yolton (ed.), *A Locke Miscellany* (Bristol: Thoemmes Press), 55–74.

Collins, A.F. and Hay, D.C. (1994) 'Connectionism and Memory', in P. Morris and M. Gruneberg (eds.), *Theoretical Aspects of Memory*, 2nd edn (London: Routledge), 196–237.

Colville-Stewart, Sandra B. (1975) 'Physico-Chemical Models of the Memory Storage Process: The Historical Role of Argument from Analogy', Ph.D. thesis, University of London.

Connerton, Paul (1989) *How Societies Remember* (Cambridge University Press).

Conway, Anne (1690/1982) *The Principles of the Most Ancient and Modern Philosophy*, ed. P. Loptson (The Hague: Martinus Nijhoff).

Cook, Harold J. (1990) 'The New Philosophy and Medicine in Seventeenth-Century England', in D.C. Lindberg and R. Westman (eds.), *Reappraisals of the Scientific Revolution* (Cambridge University Press), 397–436.

Cook, John (1969) 'Human Beings', in P. Winch (ed.), *Studies in the Philosophy of Wittgenstein* (London: Routledge).

Cook, Monte (1974) 'Arnauld's Alleged Representationalism', *Journal of the History of Philosophy* 12, 53–62.

(1987) 'Descartes' Alleged Representationalism', *History of Philosophy Quarterly* 4, 179–95.

(1991) 'Malebranche versus Arnauld', *Journal of the History of Philosophy* 29, 183–99.

Cooper, Leon A. (1980) 'Source and Limits of Human Intellect', *Daedalus* 109, no. 2: 1–17.

Cope, Jackson I. (1956) *Joseph Glanvill: Anglican Apologist* (St Louis: Washington University Press).

Copenhaver, Brian P. (1990) 'Natural Magic, Hermetism, and Occultism in Early Modern Science', in D.C. Lindberg and R.S. Westman (eds.), *Reappraisals of the Scientific Revolution* (Cambridge University Press), 261–301.

(1991) 'A Tale of Two Fishes: Magical Objects in the Scientific Revolution', *Journal of the History of Ideas* 52, 373–98.

Cornman, James W. (1972) 'On Direct Perception', *Review of Metaphysics* 26, 38–56.

Costa, Michael J. (1983) 'What Cartesian Ideas are Not', *Journal of the History of Philosophy* 21, 317–37.

Cottingham, John (1986) *Descartes* (Oxford: Blackwell).

Cottingham, John (ed.) (1992) *The Cambridge Companion to Descartes* (Cambridge University Press).

Cowan, J.D. and Sharp, D.H. (1988) 'Neural Nets and Artificial Intelligence', in S.R. Graubard (ed.), *The AI Debate: False Starts, Real Foundations* (Cambridge, MA: MIT Press), 85–121.

Cox, Stephen D. (1980) *'The Stranger Within Thee': Concepts of the Self in Late Eighteenth Century Literature* (Pittsburgh: Pittsburgh University Press).

Crick, Francis and Mitchison, Graeme (1983) 'The Function of Dream Sleep', *Nature* 304, 111–14.

(1986) 'REM Sleep and Neural Nets', *Journal of Mind and Behavior* 7, 229–49.

Crocker, Robert (1990) 'Mysticism and Enthusiasm in Henry More', in S. Hutton (ed.), *Henry More: 1614–1687* (Dordrecht: Kluwer), 137–55.

Croone, William (1664) *De ratione motus musculorum* (London: Hayes).

Crovitz, Herbert F. (1990) 'Association, Cognition, and Neural Networks', in M.G. Johnson and T.B. Henley (eds.), *Reflections on 'The Principles of Psychology': William James After a Century* (Hillsdale, NJ: Erlbaum), 167–82.

Crowder, Robert G. (1993) 'Systems and Principles in Memory Theory: Another Critique of Pure Memory', in A. Collins, S.E. Gathercole, M.A. Conway, and P.E. Morris (eds.), *Theories of Memory* (Hillsdale, NJ: Erlbaum), 139–61.

Cudworth, Ralph (1678/1743), *The True Intellectual System of the Universe*, 2nd edn (London: J. Walthoe).

Cummins, Robert (1989) *Meaning and Mental Representation* (Cambridge, MA: MIT Press).

Cunningham, Andrew (1990) 'Medicine to Calm the Mind: Boerhaave's Medical System, and Why it was Adopted in Edinburgh', in A. Cunningham and R. French (eds.), *The Medical Revolution of the Eighteenth Century* (Cambridge University Press), 40–66.

Curley, Edwin (1982), 'Leibniz on Locke on Personal Identity', in M. Hooker (ed.), *Leibniz: Critical and Interpretative Essays* (Minneapolis: Minnesota University Press), 302–26.

Cussins, Adrian (1990) 'The Connectionist Construction of Concepts', in M.A. Boden (ed.), *The Philosophy of Artificial Intelligence* (Oxford University Press), 368–440.

(1993) 'Nonconceptual Content and the Elimination of Misconceived Composites!', *Mind and Language* 8, 234–52.

Cutting, James E. (1982) 'Two Ecological Perspectives: Gibson vs. Shaw and Turvey', *American Journal of Psychology* 95, 199–222.

D'Andrade, Roy (1995) *The Development of Cognitive Anthropology* (Cambridge University Press).

Daston, Lorraine J. (1982) 'The Theory of Will and the Science of Mind' in W.R. Woodward and M.G. Ash (eds.), *The Problematic Science: Psychology in Nineteenth Century Thought* (New York: Praeger), 88–115.

Davidson, Donald (1963) 'Actions, Reasons, and Causes'.

Davie, Donald (1963) *The Language of Science and the Language of Literature, 1700–1740* (London: Sheed and Ward).

Davies, Martin (1991) 'Concepts, Connectionism, and the Language of Thought', in W. Ramsey, S.P. Stich, and D.E. Rumelhart (eds.), *Philosophy and Connectionist Theory* (Hillsdale, NJ: Erlbaum), 229–57.

Davis, Audrey B. (1973) *Circulation Physiology and Medical Chemistry in England 1650–1680* (Lawrence, Kansas: Coronado Press).

Davis, Stephen (1988) 'Traditional Christian Belief in the Resurrection of the Body', *New Scholasticism* 62, 72–87.

Day, W.G. (1984) 'Tristram Shandy: Locke may not be the Key', in V. Grosvenor Myer (ed.), *Laurence Sterne: Riddles and Mysteries* (London: Barnes and Noble), 75–83.

De Botton, Alain (1995) *Kiss and Tell* (London: Macmillan).

De Caus, Isaac (1659) *New and Rare Inventions of Water-Works . . . (a work both usefull profitable and delightfull for all sorts of people)* trans. J. Leak (London: Joseph Moxon).

De Solla Price, Derek (1964) 'Automata and the Origins of Mechanism and the Mechanical Philosophy', *Technology and Culture* 5, 9–23.

Debus, Allen G. (1984) 'Chemistry and the Quest for a Material Spirit of Life in the Seventeenth Century', in M. Fattori and M. Bianchi (eds.), *Spiritus* (Rome: Edizioni dell'Ateneo), 245–63.

Decyk, Betsy (forthcoming) 'Descartes' Theory of the Imagination as Illustrated by Concurrent Developments in Perspectival Art', in S. Gaukroger and J. Sutton (eds.), *Descartes' Natural Philosophy*, vol. II: *Cognition and Physiology* (forthcoming).

Delatte, Louis, Govaerts, Suzanne, and Denooz, Joseph (1984) 'Note sur *Spiritus*', in M. Fattori and M. Bianchi (eds.), *Spiritus* (Rome: Edizioni dell'Ateneo), 55–62.

Deleuze, Gilles (1991) 'Preface to the English edition', *Empiricism and Subjectivity: An Essay on Hume's Theory of Human Nature*, trans. C.V. Boundas (New York: Columbia University Press).

(1993) *The Fold: Leibniz and the Baroque* (Minneapolis: Minnesota University Press).

Dennett, Daniel C. (1978) 'Artificial Intelligence as Philosophy and as Psychology', in his *Brainstorms* (Brighton: Harvester), 109–26.

(1991a) *Consciousness Explained* (New York: Little Brown).

(1991b) 'Real Patterns', *Journal of Philosophy* 88, 27–51.

Dennett, Daniel C. and Kinsbourne, Marcel (1992) 'Time and the Observer: The Where and When of Consciousness in the Brain', *Behavioral and Brain Sciences* 15, 183–247.

DePorte, Michael V. (1974) *Nightmares and Hobbyhorses: Swift, Sterne, and Augustan Ideas of Madness* (San Marino: Huntington Library).

Derrida, Jacques (1978a) 'Cogito and the History of Madness', in his *Writing and Difference*, trans. A. Bass (London: Routledge), 31–63.

(1978b) 'Freud and the Scene of Writing', in his *Writing and Difference*, trans. A. Bass (London: Routledge), 196–231.

(1996) *Archive Fever: A Freudian Impression*, trans. E. Prenowitz (Chicago University Press).

Des Cartes, Renatus (1662) *De homine figuris et latinitate donatus a Florentio Schuyl* (Lugduni Batavorum: Leffen and Moyardum).

Descartes, René (1662/1972) *Treatise of Man: René Descartes*, trans. T.S. Hall (Cambridge, MA: Harvard University Press).

(1664) *L' Homme de René Descartes et un traitté de la formation du foetus du mesme autheur*, with commentary by Louis de La Forge (Paris: Charles Angot).

(1963) *Descartes: oeuvres philosophiques*, vol. 1: 1618–1637, ed. F. Alquié (Paris: Editions Garnier Frères).

(1970) *Descartes: Philosophical Letters*, trans. A. Kenny (Oxford: Clarendon).

(1985) *The Philosophical Writings of Descartes*, trans. J. Cottingham, R. Stoothoff, and D. Murdoch (2 vols., Cambridge University Press).

(1991) *The Philosophical Writings of Descartes*, vol. III: *Correspondence*, trans. J. Cottingham, R. Stoothoff, D. Murdoch, and A. Kenny (Cambridge University Press).

(1996) *Oeuvres de Descartes*, ed. C. Adam and P. Tannery (12 vols., Paris: Vrin).

Deutsch, Helen (1994) 'Symptomatic Correspondences: Engendering the Author in Eighteenth-century England', paper read at the UCLA/Clark Library workshop 'Life Studies', November 1994.

Deutscher, Max (1989) 'Remembering "Remembering"', in J. Heil (ed.), *Cause, Mind, and Reality: Essays Presented to C.B. Martin* (Dordrecht: Kluwer), 53–72.

Dewhurst, Kenneth (1963) *John Locke (1632–1704), Physician and Philosopher: A Medical Biography* (London: Wellcome Historical Medical Library).

(1966) *Dr. Thomas Sydenham (1624–1689): His Life and Original Writings* (Berkeley and Los Angeles: California University Press).

Dewhurst, Kenneth and Clarke, Edwin (1973) *An Illustrated History of Brain Function* (Berkeley and Los Angeles: California University Press).

Diamond, Solomon (1969) 'Seventeenth-Century French Connectionism: La Forge, Dilly, and Regis', *Journal of the History of the Behavioral Sciences* 5, 3–9.

Dicker, George (1992) *Descartes: An Analytical and Historical Introduction* (Oxford University Press).

Dickinson, Emily (1968) *A Choice of Emily Dickinson's Verse*, ed. T. Hughes (London: Faber & Faber).

Diderot, Denis (1769/1964) *Conversation between Diderot and D'Alembert*, in *D'Alembert's Dream*, trans. L. Tancock (Harmondsworth: Penguin), 149–64.

Digby, Kenelm (1644/1978) *Two Treatises: in the one of which, the nature of bodies; in the other, the nature of man's soule; is looked into: in way of discovery, of the Immortality of Reasonable Soules* (Paris: Gilles Blaizot; repr. New York and London: Garland).

Djørup, Frans (1968) 'Steno's Ideas on Brain Research', in G. Scherz (ed.), *Nicolaus Steno and Brain Research in the Seventeenth Century* (Oxford: Pergamon), 111–14.

Dobbs, Betty Jo (1971, 1973, 1974) 'Studies in the Natural Philosophy of Sir Kenelm Digby', *Ambix* 18, 1–25; 20, 143–63; 21, 1–28.

Dollimore, Jonathan (1984/1989) *Radical Tragedy*, 2nd edn (Brighton: Harvester).

Donald, Merlin (1991) *Origins of the Modern Mind: Three Stages in the Evolution of Culture and Cognition* (Cambridge, MA: Harvard University Press).

Douglas, Mary (1992) 'The Person in an Enterprise Culture', in S.H. Heap and A. Ross (eds.), *Understanding the Enterprise Culture* (Edinburgh University Press), 41–62.

Dreyfus, Hubert L. (1990) 'Socratic and Platonic Roots of Cognitivism', in J.-C. Smith (ed.), *Historical Foundations of Cognitive Science* (Dordrecht: Kluwer), 1–17.

Dreyfus, Hubert L. and Dreyfus, Stuart E. (1988) 'Making a Mind versus Modeling the Brain', in S.R. Graubard (ed.), *The Artificial Intelligence Debate* (Cambridge, MA: MIT Press), 15–41.

Duden, Barbara (1991) *The Woman Beneath the Skin: A Doctor's Patients in Eighteenth-century Germany*, trans. Thomas Dunlap (Cambridge, MA: Harvard University Press).

(1993) *Disembodying Women: Perspectives on Pregnancy and the Unborn*, trans. Lee Hoinacki (Cambridge, MA: Harvard University Press).

Earle, William (1956/7) 'Memory', *Review of Metaphysics* 10, 3–27.

Easlea, Brian (1980) *Witch-Hunting, Magic, and the New Philosophy* (Brighton: Harvester Press).

Easton, Patricia, Lennon, T.M., and Sebba, G. (1992), *Bibliographia Malebranchiana* (Carbondale, IL: Southern Illinois University Press).

Eccles, John (1994) *How the SELF Controls its BRAIN* (Berlin: Springer-Verlag).

Edwards, D. and Middleton, D. (1990) 'Conversational Remembering: A Social

Psychological Approach', in D. Middleton and D. Edwards (eds.), *Collective Remembering* (London: Sage), 23–45.

Elman, Jeff (1989) *Representation and Structure in Connectionist Models*, University of California, San Diego CRL Technical Report 8903.

—— (1990) 'Finding Structure in Time', *Cognitive Science* 14, 179–211.

—— (1993) 'Learning and Development in Neural Networks: The Importance of Starting Small', *Cognition* 48, 71–99.

Enc, Berent (1983) 'In Defense of the Identity Theory', *Journal of Philosophy* 80, 279–98.

'Espinasse, Margaret (1956) *Robert Hooke* (London: Heinemann).

Fearing, Franklin (1929) 'René Descartes', *Psychological Review* 36, 375–88.

Fentress, James and Wickham, Chris (1992) *Social Memory* (Oxford: Blackwell).

Ferg, S. (1981) 'Two Early Works by David Hartley', *Journal of the History of Philosophy* 19, 173–89.

Feyerabend, Paul (1988) 'Knowledge and the Role of Theories', *Philosophy of the Social Sciences* 18, 157–78.

—— (1989) 'Realism and the Historicity of Knowledge', *Journal of Philosophy* 86, 393–406.

Figlio, Karl (1975) 'Theories of Perception and the Physiology of Mind in the Late Eighteenth Century', *History of Science* 12, 177–212.

Fivush, Robyn and Reese, Elaine (1992) 'The Social Construction of Autobiographical Memory', in M.A. Conway, D.C. Rubin, H. Spinnler, and W.A. Wagenaar (eds.), *Theoretical Perspectives on Autobiographical Memory* (Dordrecht: Kluwer), 115–32.

Flage, Daniel (1985a) 'Hume on Memory and Causation', *Hume Studies* supplement, 168–88.

—— (1985b) 'Perchance to Dream: A Reply to Traiger', *Hume Studies* 11, 173–82.

—— (1990) *David Hume's Theory of Mind* (London: Routledge).

Flanagan, Owen (1991) *The Science of the Mind*, 2nd edn (Cambridge, MA: MIT Press).

Flemyng, Malcolm (1751) *The Nature of the Nervous Fluid, or Animal Spirits, Demonstrated* (London: A. Millar).

Flew, Anthony (1951/1968) 'Locke and the Problem of Personal Identity', repr. in C.B. Martin and D.M. Armstrong (eds.), *Locke and Berkeley* (New York: Anchor Books), 155–78.

Flynn, Carol H. (1990) 'Running Out of Matter: The Body Exercised in Eighteenth-Century Fiction', in G.S. Rousseau (ed.), *The Languages of Psyche: Mind and Body in Enlightenment Thought* (Berkeley and Los Angeles: California University Press), 147–85.

Fodor, Jerry A. (1968a) *Psychological Explanation* (New York: Random House).

—— (1968b) 'The Appeal to Tacit Knowledge in Psychological Explanation', *Journal of Philosophy* 65, 627–40.

—— (1976) *The Language of Thought* (New York: Thomas Crowell).

—— (1983) *The Modularity of Mind* (Cambridge, MA: MIT Press).

—— (1984/1990) 'Observation Reconsidered', repr. in Fodor 1990: 231–52.

—— (1985a) 'The Modularity of Mind', in Z. Pylyshyn and W. Demopoulos (eds.), *Meaning and Cognitive Structure* (Cambridge, MA: MIT Press), 3–18.

—— (1985b/1991) 'Fodor's Guide to Mental Representation: the intelligent auntie's vademecum', in J.D. Greenwood (ed.), *The Future of Folk Psychology: Intentionality and Cognitive Science* (Cambridge University Press), 22–50.

—— (1985c/1990) 'Précis of Modularity of Mind', repr. in Fodor 1990: 195–206.

(1986) 'Information and Association', *Notre Dame Journal of Formal Logic* 27, 307–23.

(1987) *Psychosemantics: The Problem of Meaning in the Philosophy of Mind* (Cambridge, MA: MIT Press).

(1988/1990) 'Perceptual Plasticity and Theoretical Neutrality: A Reply to Churchland', repr. in Fodor 1990: 253–64.

(1989/1990) 'Why Should the Mind be Modular?', repr. in Fodor 1990, 207–30.

(1990) *A Theory of Content and Other Essays* (Cambridge, MA: MIT Press).

(1995) 'Rationality: The Arguments from Meaning Holism', paper presented to rationality conference, Santa Clara University, March 1995.

Fodor, Jerry A. and Lepore, Ernest (1992) *Holism: A Shopper's Guide* (Oxford: Blackwell).

Fodor, Jerry A. and McLaughlin, Brian (1990) 'Connectionism and the Problem of Systematicity: Why Smolensky's Solution Doesn't Work', *Cognition* 35, 183–204.

Fodor, Jerry A. and Pylyshyn, Zenon (1981) 'How Direct is Visual Perception? Some Reflections on Gibson's 'Ecological Approach'', *Cognition* 9, 139–96.

(1988) 'Connectionism and Cognitive Architecture: A Critical Analysis', *Cognition* 28, 3–71.

Fogelin, Robert (1985) *Hume's Skepticism in the 'Treatise of Human Nature'* (London: Routledge).

Ford, Stephen H. (1987) '*Coalescence*: David Hartley's "Great Apparatus"', in C. Fox (ed.), *Psychology and Literature in the Eighteenth Century* (New York: AMS Press), 199–223.

Foster, Michael (1901/1970) *Lectures on the History of Physiology during the Sixteenth, Seventeenth, and Eighteenth Centuries* (New York: Dover).

Foti, Veronique (1986a) 'Presence and Memory: Derrida, Freud, Plato, Descartes', *The Graduate Faculty Philosophy Journal* 11 (New York: New School for Social Research), 67–81.

(1986b) 'The Cartesian Imagination', *Philosophy and Phenomenological Research* 46, 631–42.

Foucault, Michel (1962/1976) *Mental Illness and Psychology*, trans. A. Sheridan (New York: Harper and Row).

(1965) *Madness and Civilisation: A History of Insanity in the Age of Reason*, trans. by R. Howard (New York: Random House).

(1972) *Histoire de la folie à l'âge classique*, 2nd edn (Paris: Gallimard).

(1977) *Discipline and Punish: The Birth of the Prison*, trans. A. Sheridan (London: Allen Lane).

(1985) *The Use of Pleasure*, trans. R. Hurley (New York: Random House).

(1986) *The Care of the Self*, trans. R. Hurley (New York: Random House).

(1988) 'Technologies of the Self', in L. Martin, H. Gutman, and P. Hutton (eds.), *Technologies of the Self* (Amherst, MA: Massachusetts University Press), 16–49.

Fox, Christopher (1988) *Locke and the Scriblerians: Identity and Consciousness in Early Eighteenth-century Britain* (Berkeley and Los Angeles: California University Press).

Frank, Robert G. (1980) *Harvey and the Oxford Physiologists* (Berkeley and Los Angeles: California University Press).

(1990) 'Thomas Willis and his Circle: Brain and Mind in Seventeenth-Century Medicine', in G.S. Rousseau (ed.), *The Languages of Psyche: Mind and Body in Enlightenment Thought* (Berkeley and Los Angeles: California University Press), 107–46.

Frankfurt, Harry G. (1970) *Demons, Dreamers, and Madmen* (Indianapolis: Bobbs-Merrill).

French, Robert M. (1992) 'Semi-distributed Representations and Catastrophic Interference in Connectionist Networks', *Connection Science* 4, 365–77.

French, Roger K. (1969) *Robert Whytt, the Soul, and Medicine* (London: Wellcome Institute for the History of Medicine).

— (1981) 'Ether and Physiology', in G.N. Cantor and M.J.S. Hodge (eds.), *Conceptions of Ether: Studies in the History of Ether Theories 1740–1900* (Cambridge University Press), 111–34.

Freud, Sigmund (1895/1966) *Project for a Scientific Psychology*, in the *Standard Edition of the Complete Psychological Works of Sigmund Freud*, vol. I, trans. James Strachey (London: Hogarth Press).

Freudenthal, Gad (1995) *Aristotle's Theory of Material Substance: Heat and Pneuma, Form and Soul* (Oxford: Clarendon).

Furlong, E.J. (1951) *A Study in Memory* (London: Thomas Nelson).

Gabbey, Alan (1980) 'Force and Inertia in the Seventeenth Century: Descartes and Newton', in S. Gaukroger (ed.), *Descartes: Philosophy, Mathematics, Physics* (Brighton: Harvester), 230–320.

— (1982) 'Philosophia Cartesiana Triumphata: Henry More (1646–1671)', in T.M. Lennon, J.M. Nicholas, and J.W. Davies (eds.), *Problems of Cartesianism* (Kingston and Montreal: McGill-Queen's University Press), 171–250.

— (1985) 'The Mechanical Philosophy and its Problems: Mechanical Explanations, Impenetrability, and Perpetual Motion', in J.C. Pitt (ed.), *Change and Progress in Modern Science* (Dordrecht: Reidel), 9–67.

— (1990) 'Henry More and the Limits of Mechanism', in S. Hutton (ed.), *Henry More (1614–1687)* (Dordrecht: Kluwer), 19–35.

— (1992) 'Cudworth, More, and the Mechanical Analogy', in R. Kroll, R. Ashcraft and P. Zagorin (eds.), *Philosophy, Science, and Religion in England 1640–1700* (Cambridge University Press), 109–27.

Gallagher, Shaun (1995) 'Body Schema and Intentionality', in J.L. Bermudez, A. Marcel, and N. Eilan (eds.), *The Body and the Self* (Cambridge, MA: MIT Press), 225–44.

Gallie, Roger D. (1989) *Thomas Reid and the 'Way of Ideas'* (Dordrecht: Kluwer).

Gardner, Howard (1985) *The Mind's New Science* (New York: Basic Books).

Gaukroger, Stephen (1989) *Cartesian Logic* (Oxford: Clarendon).

— (1990) 'Introduction: The Background to the Problem of Perceptual Cognition', in A. Arnauld: On True and False Ideas, trans. S. Gaukroger (Manchester University Press), 1–41.

— (1993a) 'Descartes: Methodology', in G.H.R. Parkinson (ed.), *Routledge History of Philosophy*, vol. IV: *The Renaissance and Seventeenth Century Rationalism* (London: Routledge), 167–200.

— (1993b) 'Nature without Reason: Cartesian Automata and Perceptual Cognition', K. Haakonssen and U. Thiel (eds.), *History of Philosophy Yearbook* I (Canberra: Australasian Society for the History of Philosophy), 26–40.

— (1995) *Descartes: An Intellectual Biography* (Oxford: Clarendon).

Geary, Patrick J. (1994) *Phantoms of Remembrance: Memory and Oblivion at the End of the First Millenium* (Princeton University Press).

Gibson, J.J. (1966a) *The Senses Considered as Perceptual Systems* (Boston: Houghton Mifflin).

— (1966b/1982) 'The Problem of Temporal Order in Stimulation and Perception', in Gibson 1982: 171–9.

(1970/1982) 'A History of the Ideas behind Ecological Optics', in Gibson 1982: 90–101.

(1975/1982) 'On the New Idea of Persistence and Change and the Old Ideas that it Drives Out', in Gibson 1982: 393–6.

(1979a) *The Ecological Approach to Visual Perception* (Boston: Houghton Mifflin).

(1979b/1982) 'Ecological Physics, Magic, and Reality', in Gibson 1982: 217–23.

(1982) *Reasons for Realism: Selected Essays of James J. Gibson*, ed. E.S. Reed and R. Jones (Hillsdale, NJ: Erlbaum).

Gibson, J.J. and Gibson, E.J. (1955/1982) 'Perceptual Learning: Differentiation or Enrichment?', in Gibson 1982: 317–32.

Gigerenzer, Gerd and Murray, David J. (1987) *Cognition as Intuitive Statistics* (Hillsdale, NJ: Erlbaum).

Ginzburg, Carlo (1966/1983) *The Night Battles: Witchcraft and Agrarian Cults in the Sixteenth and Seventeenth Centuries*, trans. J. and A. Tedeschi (Baltimore: Johns Hopkins University Press).

Glanvill, Joseph (1661/1970) *The Vanity of Dogmatizing . . .* (London: Henry Eversden); repr. in Glanvill 1970.

(1665/1970) *Scepsis scientifica* (London: Henry Eversden); repr. in Glanvill 1970.

(1676/1970) *Essay against Confidence in Philosophy*, in *Essays on Several Important Subjects in Philosophy and Religion* (London: John Baker & Henry Mortlock); repr. Glanvill 1970.

(1970) *The Vanity of Dogmatizing: The Three 'Versions'*, ed. S. Medcalf (Brighton: Harvester Press).

Glover, Jonathan (1988) *I: The Philosophy and Psychology of Personal Identity* (Harmondsworth: Penguin).

Goddard, Graham V. (1980) 'Component Properties of the Memory Machine: Hebb revisited', in P.W. Jusczyk and R.M. Klein (eds.), *The Nature of Thought* (Hillsdale, NJ: Erlbaum), 231–47.

Goldmeier, Erich (1982) *The Memory Trace: Its Formation and its Fate* (Hillsdale, NJ: Erlbaum).

Gomulicki, Bronislaw R. (1953) *The Development and Present Status of the Trace Theory of Memory* (Cambridge University Press/ British Journal of Psychology supplement 24).

Goodfield, G. June (1960) *The Growth of Scientific Physiology: Physiological Method and the Mechanist–Vitalist Controversy* (London: Hutchinson).

Gouk, Penelope (1980) 'The Role of Acoustics and Music Theory in the Scientific Work of Robert Hooke', *Annals of Science* 37, 573–605.

Gould, Stephen Jay (1983/1990) 'The Titular Bishop of Titiopolis', in his *Hen's Teeth and Horse's Toes* (Harmondsworth: Penguin), 69–78.

Grene, Marjorie (1976) 'Hobbes and the Modern Mind', in her *Philosophy In and Out of Europe* (Berkeley and Los Angeles: California University Press), 155–65.

(1985) *Descartes* (Brighton: Harvester Press).

Grosholz, Emily R. (1991) *Cartesian Method and the Problem of Reduction* (Oxford: Clarendon).

Gueroult, Martial (1980) 'The Metaphysics and Physics of Force in Descartes', in S. Gaukroger (ed.), *Descartes: Philosophy, Mathematics, and Physics* (Brighton: Harvester), 196–229.

Guerrini, Anita (1987) 'Archibald Pitcairne and Newtonian Medicine', *Medical History* 31, 70–83.

(1989) 'The Ethics of Animal Experimentation in Seventeenth Century England', *Journal of the History of Ideas* 50, 391–407.

Hacking, Ian (1983) *Representing and Intervening: Introductory Topics in the Philosophy of Natural Science* (Cambridge University Press).

(1994) 'Memoro-Politics, Trauma, and the Soul', *History of the Human Sciences* 7, 29–52.

(1995) *Rewriting the Soul: Multiple Personality and the Sciences of Memory* (Princeton University Press).

Hagstrum, Jean (1987) 'Towards a Profile of the Word "Conscious" in Eighteenth-Century Literature', in C. Fox (ed.), *Psychology and Literature in the Eighteenth Century* (New York: AMS Press), 23–50.

Hahm, David E. (1977) *The Origins of Stoic Cosmology* (Columbus, OH: Ohio State University Press).

Hahn, Rahel (1995) 'The Representation of the Diseased Body in Early Modern Autobiographical Narrative: The Case of Syphilis', paper presented to UCLA workshop 'Life Studies', April 1995.

Hakfoort, Casper (1988) 'Newton's Optics', in J. Fauvel, R. Flood, M. Shortland, and R. Wilson (eds.), *Let Newton Be!* (Oxford University Press), 81–99.

Hall, A. Rupert (1990) *Henry More: Magic, Religion and Experiment* (Oxford: Blackwell).

Hall, Thomas S. (1969) 'Microbiomechanics', in his *Ideas of Life and Matter* (Chicago University Press), vol. I, 250–63.

(1970) 'Descartes' Physiological Method: Position, Principles, Examples', *Journal of the History of Biology* 3, 53–79.

Hamlyn, David (1990) *In and Out of the Black Box* (Oxford: Blackwell).

Hampshire, Stuart (1989) *Innocence and Experience* (Cambridge, MA: Harvard University Press).

Hansen, Harriet M. (1992) 'A Traveller in Neuroanatomy: Stensen, 1664–1670', *Journal of the History of Neuroscience* 1, 219–26.

Haraway, Donna (1989/1991) 'The Biopolitics of Postmodern Bodies', in Haraway 1991b: 203–30.

(1991a) 'A Cyborg Manifesto', in Haraway 1991b: 149–81.

(1991b) *Simians, Cyborgs, and Women: The Reinvention of Nature* (London: Free Association Books).

Harding, Jennifer (1996) 'Sex and Control: The Hormonal Body', *Body and Society* 2, 99–111.

Harrington, Anne (1987) *Medicine, Mind, and the Double Brain* (Princeton University Press).

Harrison, John and Laslett, Peter (1971) *The Library of John Locke*, 2nd edn (Oxford: Clarendon).

Harrison, Jonathan (1976) 'Direct Perception and the Sense-Datum Theory', in H.D. Lewis (ed.), *Contemporary British Philosophy*, 4th series (London: Allen and Unwin), 132–51.

Harth, Erica (1992) *Cartesian Women: Versions and Subversions of Rational Discourse in the Old Regime* (Ithaca, NY: Cornell University Press).

Hartley, David (1746/1959) *Various Conjectures on the Perception, Motion, and Generation of Ideas*, trans. R.E.A. Palmer, ed. M. Kallich (Berkeley and Los Angeles: California University Press).

(1749/1971) *Observations on Man, His Frame, His Duty, and His Expectations* (London; repr. New York: Garland).

Harvey, E. Ruth (1975) *The Inward Wits: Psychological Theory in the Middle Ages and the Renaissance* (London: Warburg Institute).

Harvey, William (1649/1990) 'Second Letter to Riolan', in his *The Circulation of the Blood and other writings*, trans. K.J. Franklin, ed. A. Wear (London: Everyman), 111–39.

Hass, Lawrence (1991) 'The Antinomy of Perception: Merleau-Ponty and Causal Representation Theory', *Man and World* 24, 13–25.

Hatfield, Gary (1979) 'Force (God) in Descartes' Physics', *Studies in the History and Philosophy of Science* 10, 113–40.

(1985) 'First Philosophy and Natural Philosophy in Descartes', in A.J. Holland (ed.), *Philosophy: Its History and Historiography* (Dordrecht: Reidel), 149–64.

(1986) 'The Senses and the Fleshless Eye: The *Meditations* as Cognitive Exercises', in A.O. Rorty (ed.), *Essays on Descartes' 'Meditations'* (Berkeley and Los Angeles: California University Press), 45–79.

(1988a) 'Neuro-philosophy meets Psychology: Reduction, Autonomy, and Physiological Constraints', *Cognitive Neuropsychology* 5, 723–46.

(1988b) 'Representation and Content in Some (Actual) Theories of Perception', *Studies in History and Philosophy of Science* 2, 175–214.

(1989) 'Computation, Representation, and Content in Noncognitive Theories of Perception', in S. Silvers (ed.), *Rerepresentation* (Dordrecht: Kluwer), 255–88.

(1990) *The Natural and the Normative: Theories of Spatial Perception from Kant to Helmholtz* (Cambridge, MA: MIT Press).

(1991) 'Representation and Rule-Instantiation in Connectionist Systems', in T. Horgan and J. Tienson (eds.), *Connectionism and the Philosophy of Mind* (Dordrecht: Kluwer), 281–308.

(1992) 'Descartes' Physiology and its Relation to his Psychology', in J. Cottingham (ed.), *The Cambridge Companion to Descartes* (Cambridge University Press), 335–70.

(1995) 'Remaking the Science of Mind: Psychology as Natural Science', in C. Fox, R. Porter, and R. Wokler (eds.), *Inventing Human Science: Eighteenth-century Domains* (Berkeley and Los Angeles: California University Press), 184–231.

Hatfield, Gary and Epstein, William (1979) 'The Sensory Core and the Medieval Foundations of Early Modern Perceptual Theory', *Isis* 70, 363–84.

Haugeland, John (1991) 'Representational Genera', in W. Ramsey, S.P. Stich, and D.E. Rumelhart (eds.), *Philosophy and Connectionist Theory* (Hillsdale, NJ: Erlbaum), 61–78.

Haven, Richard (1959) 'Coleridge, Hartley, and the Mystics', *Journal of the History of Ideas* 20, 477–94.

Hawley, Judith (1993) 'The Anatomy of *Tristram Shandy*', in M.M. Roberts and R. Porter (eds.), *Literature and Medicine during the Eighteenth Century* (London: Routledge), 84–100.

Hawthorne, John (1989) 'On the Compatibility of Connectionist and Classical Models', *Philosophical Psychology* 2, 5–15.

Heil, John (1978) 'Traces of Things Past', *Philosophy of Science* 45, 60–72.

(1979) 'What Gibson's Missing', *Journal for the Theory of Social Behaviour* 9, 265–9.

(1981) 'Gibsonian Sins of Omission' *Journal for the Theory of Social Behaviour* 11, 307–11.

(1983) *Perception and Cognition* (Berkeley and Los Angeles: California University Press).

Heilbron, John L. (1982) *Elements of Early Modern Physics* (Berkeley and Los Angeles: California University Press).

Henry, John (1982) 'Atomism and Eschatology: Catholicism and Natural Philosophy in the Interregnum', *British Journal for the History of Science* 15, 211–39.

(1986a) 'Occult Qualities and the Experimental Philosophy: Active Principles in Pre-Newtonian Matter Theory', *History of Science* 24, 335–81.

(1986b) 'A Cambridge Platonist's Materialism: Henry More and the Concept of Soul', *Journal of the Warburg and Courtauld Institutes* 49, 172–95.

(1987) 'Medicine and Pneumatology: Henry More, Richard Baxter, and Francis Glisson's Treatise on the Energetic Nature of Substance', *Medical History* 31, 15–40.

(1988) 'Newton, Matter, and Magic', in J. Fauvel, R. Flood, M. Shortland, and R. Wilson (eds.), *Let Newton Be!* (Oxford University Press), 127–45.

(1989a) 'Robert Hooke, the Incongruous Mechanist', in M. Hunter and S. Schaffer (eds.), *Robert Hooke: New Studies* (Woodbridge: Boydell Press), 149–80.

(1989b) 'The Matter of Souls: Medical Theory and Theology in Seventeenth-century England', in R.K. French and A. Wear (eds.), *The Medical Revolution of the Seventeenth Century* (Cambridge University Press), 87–113.

(1990) 'Magic and Science in the Sixteenth and Seventeenth Centuries', in R.C. Olby, G.N. Cantor, M.J.S. Hodge, and J.R.R. Christie (eds.), *Companion to the History of Modern Science* (London: Routledge), 583–96.

Herrmann, Douglas J. and Chaffin, Roger (eds.) (1988) *Memory in Historical Perspective: The Literature before Ebbinghaus* (New York: Springer-Verlag).

Hesse, Mary (1961/1970) *Forces and Fields: The Concept of Action at a Distance in the History of Physics* (London: Thomas Nelson).

Heyd, Michael (1981) 'The Reaction to Enthusiasm in the Seventeenth Century: Towards an Integrative Approach', *Journal of Modern History* 53, 258–80.

Hill, John (1766/1969) *Hypochondriasis: A Practical Treatise*, ed. G.S. Rousseau (Los Angeles: Clark Library).

Hilmy, Stephen S. (1987) *The Later Wittgenstein: The Emergence of a New Philosophical Method* (Oxford: Blackwell).

Hine, William L. (1984) 'Mersenne, Naturalism, and Magic', in B. Vickers (ed.), *Occult and Scientific Mentalities in the Renaissance* (Cambridge University Press), 165–76.

Hinton, Geoffrey E. (1989) 'Connectionist Learning Systems', *Artificial Intelligence* 4, 185–234.

Hinton, Geoffrey E., McClelland, James L., and Rumelhart, David E. (1986) 'Distributed Representation', in D.E. Rumelhart and J.L. McClelland (eds.), *Parallel Distributed Processing: Explorations in the Microstructure of Cognition* (Cambridge, MA: MIT Press), vol. I, 77–109.

Hobbes, Thomas (1651/1968) *Leviathan*, ed. C.B. Macpherson (Harmondsworth: Penguin).

Hoeldtke, Robert (1967) 'The History of Associationism and British Medical Psychology', *Medical History* 11, 46–65.

Hoff, Hebbel E. (1936) 'Galvani and the Pre-Galvanian Electrophysiologists', *Annals of Science* 1, 157–72.

Hoffman, Friedrich (1695/1971) *Fundamenta Medicinae*, trans. L. King (New York: Elsevier).

Hoffman, R.R., Cochran, E.L., and Nead, J.M. (1990) 'Cognitive Metaphors in Experimental Psychology', in D.E. Leary (ed.), *Metaphors in the History of Psychology* (Cambridge University Press), 173–229.

Hogarth, William (1753/1971) *Analysis of Beauty* (London; repr. Menston: Scolar Press).

Holmes, Richard (1990) *Coleridge: Early Visions* (London: Penguin).

Home, Roderick W. (1970) 'Electricity and the Nervous Fluid', *Journal of the History of Biology* 3, 235–51.

Hooke, Robert (1705/1971) *Lectures of Light*, in *The Posthumous Works of Robert Hooke*, ed. R.

Waller (London, 1705); reprint with an introduction by T.M. Brown (London: Frank Cass and Co.).

Horgan, Terence and Tienson, John (1989) 'Representations without Rules', *Philosophical Topics* 17, 147–74.

Horn, Gabriel (1985) *Memory, Imprinting, and the Brain* (Oxford University Press).

Hoyles, John (1971) *The Waning of the English Renaissance, 1640–1740: Studies in the Thought and Poetry of Henry More, John Norris and Isaac Watts* (The Hague: Martinus Nijhoff).

Huet, Marie-Helene (1993) *Monstrous Imagination* (Cambridge, MA: Harvard University Press).

Huguelet, Theodore (1966) Introduction to reprint of David Hartley, *Observations on Man* (Gainesville: Scholars' Facsimiles and Reprints), v–xvii.

Hume, David (1734/1993a) 'A Kind of History of My Life', in D.F. Norton (ed.), *The Cambridge Companion to Hume* (Cambridge University Press), 345–50.

(1739/1978) *A Treatise of Human Nature*, ed. L.A. Selby-Bigge and P.H. Nidditch (Oxford: Clarendon).

(1776/1993b) 'My Own Life', in D.F. Norton (ed.), *The Cambridge Companion to Hume* (Cambridge University Press), 351–6.

(1948) 'Hume's Early Memoranda 1729–1740: The Complete Text', ed. E.C. Mossner, *Journal of the History of Ideas* 9, 492–518.

Humphreys, Glyn and Riddoch, Jane (1986) 'Information Processing Systems which Embody Computational Rules: The Connectionist Approach', *Mind and Language* 1, 201–11.

Hunter, Michael (1981) *Science and Society in Restoration England* (Cambridge University Press).

(1994) *The Royal Society and its Fellows 1660–1700: The Morphology of an Early Scientific Institution*, 2nd edn (Oxford: British Society for the History of Science Monograph 4).

Hunter, Michael and Schaffer, Simon (eds.) (1989), *Robert Hooke: New Studies* (Woodbridge: Boydell Press).

Hutchins, Edwin (1995) *Cognition in the Wild* (Cambridge, MA: MIT Press).

Hutchison, Keith (1982) 'What Happened to Occult Qualities in the Scientific Revolution?', *Isis* 73, 233–53.

(1983) 'Supernaturalism and the Mechanical Philosophy', *History of Science* 21, 297–333.

(1991) 'Dormitive Virtues, Scholastic Qualities, and the New Philosophies', *History of Science* 29, 245–78.

Iliffe, Rob (1995) '"That puzleing Problem": Isaac Newton and the Political Physiology of Self', *Medical History* 39, 433–58.

Irigaray, Luce (1974/1985a) '. . . And If, Taking the Eye of a Man Recently Dead, . . . ', in her *Speculum of the Other Woman*, trans. Gillian Gill (New York: Cornell University Press), 180–90.

(1974/1985b) 'The "Mechanics" of Fluids', in her *This Sex which is Not One*, trans. C. Porter with C. Burke (Ithaca, NY: Cornell University Press), 106–18.

Jackson, Stanley W. (1970) 'Force and Kindred Notions in Eighteenth Century Neurophysiology and Medical Psychology', *Bulletin of the History of Medicine* 44, 397–410, 539–54.

(1986) *Melancholia and Depression* (New Haven: Yale University Press).

Jacob, James R. (1978) 'Boyle's Atomism and the Restoration Assault on Pagan Naturalism', *Social Studies of Science* 8, 211–33.

Jacob, James R. and Jacob, Margaret (1980) 'The Anglican Origins of Modern Science: The Metaphysical Foundations of the Whig Constitution', *Isis* 71, 251–67.

Jacoby, Larry L. (1988) 'Memory Observed and Memory Unobserved', in U. Neisser and E. Winograd (eds.), *Remembering Reconsidered: Ecological and Traditional Approaches to the Study of Memory* (Cambridge University Press), 145–77.

Jacquart, Danielle and Thomasset, Claude (1985/1988) *Sexuality and Medicine in the Middle Ages*, trans. M. Adamson (Oxford: Polity Press).

Jacquot, Jean (1974) 'Harriot, Hill, Warner and the New Philosophy', in J.W. Shirley (ed.), *Thomas Harriot: Renaissance Scientist* (Oxford: Clarendon), 107–28.

Jacyna, L.S. (1995) 'Animal Spirits and Eighteenth-Century British Medicine', in Y. Kawakita, S. Sakai, and Y. Otsuka (eds.), *The Comparison between Concepts of Life-Breath in East and West* (Tokyo and St Louis: Ishiyaku Euro-America), 139–61.

James, William (1890a) *Psychology (Briefer Course)* (New York: Holt).

(1890b) *The Principles of Psychology* (London: Macmillan), vol. 1.

Jardine, Lisa (1974) *Francis Bacon: Discovery and the Art of Discourse* (Cambridge University Press).

Jaynes, Julian (1970) 'The Problem of Animate Motion in the Seventeenth Century', *Journal of the History of Ideas* 31, 219–34.

(1976) *The Origin of Consciousness in the Breakdown of the Bicameral Mind* (Boston: Houghton Mifflin).

Jefferson, Geoffrey (1949) 'René Descartes on the Localisation of the Soul', *Irish Journal of Medical Science* 285, 6th series, 691–706.

Jenkins, James J. (1977) 'Remember That Old Theory of Memory? Well, Forget It!', in R. Shaw and J.D. Bransford (eds.), *Perceiving, Acting, and Knowing: Towards an Ecological Psychology* (Hillsdale, NJ: Erlbaum), 413–29.

Jobe, Thomas H. (1976) 'Medical Theories of Melancholia in the Seventeenth and Early Eighteenth Centuries', *Clio Medica* 11, 217–31.

(1981) 'The Devil in Restoration Science: The Glanvill–Webster Witchcraft Debate', *Isis* 72, 343–56.

Johnson, D.M. (1983) 'Memory and Knowledge: The Epistemological Significance of Biology', *American Philosophical Quarterly* 20, 375–82.

Johnson, Marcia and Raye, C.L. (1981) 'Reality Monitoring', *Psychological Review* 88, 3–28.

Johnson, Mark (1991) 'The Imaginative Basis of Memory and Cognition', in S. Kuchler and W. Melion (eds.), *Images of Memory: On Remembering and Representation* (Washington: Smithsonian Institute), 74–86.

Johnson, Oliver (1987) '"Lively" Memory and "Past" Memory', *Hume Studies* 13, 343–59.

Jolley, Nicolas (1989) *The Light of the Soul: Theories of Ideas in Leibniz, Malebranche and Descartes* (Oxford: Clarendon).

Jones, Howard (1989) *The Epicurean Tradition* (London: Routledge).

Jordan, Michael I. and Jacobs, Robert A. (1992) 'Modularity, Unsupervised Learning, and Supervised Learning', in S. Davis (ed.), *Connectionism: Theory and Practice* (Oxford University Press), 21–9.

Jordanova, Ludmilla (1989) *Sexual Visions: Images of Gender in Science and Medicine between the Eighteenth and Twentieth Centuries* (Brighton: Harvester).

Joyce, James (1922/1968) *Ulysses* (Harmondsworth: Penguin).

Judowitz, Dalia (1988) *Subjectivity and Representation in Descartes* (Cambridge University Press).

Kagan, Jerome (1989) *Unstable Ideas: Temperament, Cognition, and Self* (Cambridge, MA: Harvard University Press).

Kallich, M. (1970) *The Association of Ideas and Critical Theory in Eighteenth Century England* (The Hague: Mouton).

Kardel, Troels (1994a) 'Stensen's Myology in Historical Perspective', in T. Kardel (ed.), *Steno on Muscles* (Philadelphia: American Philosophical Society), 1–57.

(1994b) *Steno: Life, Science, Philosophy* (Copenhagen: Danish National Library of Science and Medicine).

Kassler, Jamie C. (1979) *The Science of Music in Britain, 1714–1830: A Catalogue of Writings, Lectures and Inventions* (2 vols., New York and London: Garland).

(1984) 'Man – A Musical Instrument: Models of the Brain and Mental Functioning before the Computer', *History of Science* 24, 59–92.

(1991) 'The Paradox of Power: Hobbes and Stoic Naturalism', in S. Gaukroger (ed.), *The Uses of Antiquity: The Scientific Revolution and the Classical Tradition* (Dordrecht: Kluwer), 53–78.

(1995) *Inner Music: Hobbes, Hooke, and North on Internal Character* (London: Athlone Press).

(1997) 'On the Stretch: Hobbes, Mechanics, and the Shaking Palsy', in A. Corones and G. Freeland (eds.), *1543 and All That: Word and Image in the Proto-scientific Revolution* (Dordrecht: Kluwer).

(1998) 'Thomas Willis and the Passions as Wind', in S. Gaukroger (ed.), *The Soft Underbelly of Reason: The Passions in the Seventeenth Century* (London: Routledge).

Kassler, Jamie C. and Oldroyd, David R. (1983) 'Robert Hooke's Trinity College "Musick Scripts", his Music Theory and the Role of Music in his Cosmology', *Annals of Science* 40, 559–95.

Kearns, Michael S. (1987) *Metaphors of Mind in Fiction and Psychology* (Lexington, KY: Kentucky University Press).

Keele, K.D. (1967) 'Thomas Willis on the Brain', *Medical History* 11, 194–200.

Kelley, Colleen M. and Jacoby, Larry L. (1990) 'The Construction of Subjective Memory Attributions', *Mind and Language* 5, 49–65.

(1996) 'Misremembering on Cue', paper presented to international memory conference, Abano Terme, July 1996.

Kelly, James S. (1987) review of Yolton 1984a, *Noûs* 21, 55–9.

Kemp, Martin (1997) 'Vision and Visualization in Art and Anatomy', in A. Corones and G. Freeland (eds.), *1543 and All That: Word and Image in the Proto-scientific Revolution* (Dordrecht: Kluwer).

Kemp, Simon (1990) *Medieval Psychology* (Westport, CT: Greenwood Press).

Kemp, Wolfgang (1991) 'Visual Narratives, Memory, and the Medieval *Esprit du System*', in S. Kuchler and W. Melion (eds.), *Images of Memory: On Remembering and Representation* (Washington: Smithsonian Institute), 87–108.

Kemp Smith, Norman (1952) *New Studies in the Philosophy of Descartes* (London: Macmillan).

Kenny, Anthony (1968) *Descartes* (New York: Random House).

Kessler, Eckhard (1988) 'The Intellective Soul', in C.B. Schmitt and Q. Skinner (eds.), *The Cambridge History of Renaissance Philosophy* (Cambridge University Press), 485–534.

Kihlstrom, John F. and Barnhardt, Terrence M. (1993) 'The Self-Regulation of Memory: For Better and For Worse, With and Without Hypnosis', in D. Wegner and D.

Pennebaker (eds.), *Handbook of Mental Control* (Englewood Cliffs, NJ: Prentice-Hall), 88–125.

King, Lester S. (1970) *The Road to Medical Enlightenment 1650–1695* (London: Macdonald).

(1978) *The Philosophy of Medicine: The Early Eighteenth Century* (Cambridge, MA: Harvard University Press).

Kinneir, David (1739) *A New Essay on the Nerves, and the Doctrine of the Animal Spirits Rationally Considered . . .* , 2nd edn (London and Bath: Innys and Manby).

Kipnis, Naum (1987) 'Luigi Galvani and the Debate on Animal Electricity, 1791–1800', *Annals of Science* 44, 107–42.

Kirsh, David (1990) 'When is Information Explicitly Represented?', in P.P. Hanson (ed.), *Information, Language, and Cognition* (Vancouver: University of British Columbia Press), 340–65.

Kitcher, Philip (1978) 'Theories, Theorists, and Theoretical Change', *Philosophical Review* 87, 519–47.

(1992) 'The Naturalists Return', *Philosophical Review* 101, 53–114.

(1993a) *The Advancement of Science: Science without Legend, Objectivity without Illusions* (Oxford University Press).

(1993b) 'Knowledge, Society, and History', *Canadian Journal of Philosophy* 23, 155–77.

Klibansky, Raymond, Panofsky, Erwin, and Saxl, Fritz (1964) *Saturn and Melancholy: Studies in the History of Natural Philosophy, Religion, and Art* (London: Thomas Nelson).

Kline, D.B. (1970) *A History of Scientific Psychology* (New York: Basic Books).

Knoespel, Kenneth J. (1992) 'Gazing on Technology: Theatrum Mechanorum and the Assimilation of Renaissance Technology', in M.L. Greenberg and L. Schachterle (eds.), *Literature and Technology* (Bethlehem: Lehigh University Press), 99–124.

Kofman, Sarah (1976/1991) 'Descartes Entrapped', trans. K. Aschheim, in E. Cadava, P. Connor, and J.-L. Nancy (eds.), *Who Comes After the Subject?* (London: Routledge), 178–97.

Koriat, Asher and Goldsmith, Morris (1996) 'Memory Metaphors and the Real-Life/Laboratory Controversy: Correspondence versus Storehouse Conceptions of Memory', *Behavioral and Brain Sciences* 19, 167–228.

Kosslyn, Stephen and Hatfield, Gary (1984) 'Representation without Symbol Systems', *Social Research* 51, 1019–45.

Krell, David Farrell (1988) 'Paradoxes of the Pineal: From Descartes to George Bataille', in A. Phillips Griffiths (ed.), *Contemporary French Philosophy*, special issue of *Philosophy* 21 (Cambridge University Press), 215–28.

(1990) *Of Memory, Reminiscence, and Writing: On the Verge* (Bloomington, IN: Indiana University Press).

Kuriyama, Shigehisa (1995) 'Pneuma, Qi, and the Problematic of Breath', in Y. Kawakita, S. Sakai, and Y. Otsuka (eds.), *The Comparison between Concepts of Life-Breath in East and West* (Tokyo and St Louis: Ishiyaku Euro-America), 1–31.

La Forge, Louis de (1664) notes to *L'Homme de René Descartes . . .* (Paris: Charles Angot).

Laird, John (1920) *A Study in Realism* (Cambridge University Press).

Lamb, Jonathan (1989) *Sterne's Fiction and the Double Principle* (Cambridge University Press).

Lambek, Michael and Antze, Paul (1996) 'Introduction: Forecasting Memory', in P. Antze and M. Lambek (eds.), *Tense Past: Cultural Essays in Trauma and Memory* (London: Routledge), xi–xxxviii.

Lamprecht, S.P. (1935) 'The Role of Descartes in Seventeenth Century England', *Studies in* the History of Ideas, vol. III (New York: Columbia University Dept of Philosophy), 178–240.

Landormy, Paul (1902) 'La Mémoire corporelle et la mémoire intellectuelle dans la philosophie de Descartes', Bibliothèque du Congrès Internationale de Philosophie 4, 259–98.

Lang, Helen S. (1980) 'On Memory: Aristotle's Corrections of Plato', Journal of the History of Philosophy 18, 379–93.

Laqueur, Thomas (1990) Making Sex: Body and Gender from the Greeks to Freud (Cambridge, MA: Harvard University Press).

Larmore, Charles (1980) 'Descartes' Empirical Epistemology', in S. Gaukroger (ed.), Descartes: Philosophy, Mathematics, Physics (Brighton: Harvester), 6–22.

Larsen, Steen F. (1988) 'Remembering without Experiencing: Memory for Reported Events', in U. Neisser and E. Winograd (eds.), Remembering Reconsidered: Ecological and Traditional Approaches to the Study of Memory (Cambridge University Press), 326–55.

(1992) 'Personal Context in Autobiographical and Narrative Memories', in M.A. Conway, D.C. Rubin, H. Spinnler, and W.A. Wagenaar (eds.), Theoretical Perspectives on Autobiographical Memories (Dordrecht: Kluwer), 53–71.

Larsen, Steen F., Thompson, Charles P., and Hansen, Tia (1996) 'Time in Autobiographical Memory', in D.C. Rubin (ed.), Remembering our Past: Studies in Autobiographical Memory (Cambridge University Press), 129–56.

Lashley, Karl (1950/1988) 'In Search of the Engram', extracts repr. in J.A. Anderson and E. Rosenfeld (eds.), Neurocomputing: Foundations of Research (Cambridge, MA: MIT Press), 59–63.

Lawrence, Christopher (1979) 'The Nervous System and Society in the Scottish Enlightenment', in B. Barnes and S. Shapin (eds.), Natural Order (London: Sage), 19–40.

Lawson, E. Thomas (1993) 'Cognitive Categories, Cultural Forms and Ritual Structures', in P. Boyer (ed.), Cognitive Aspects of Religious Symbolism (Cambridge University Press), 188–206.

Leder, Drew (1990) The Absent Body (Chicago University Press).

Lehrer, Keith (1989) Thomas Reid (London: Routledge).

Lennon, Thomas M. (1980) 'Representationalism, Judgment and Perception of Distance: Further to Yolton and McRae', Dialogue 19, 151–62.

Levin, David M. and Solomon, George F. (1990) 'The Discursive Formation of the Body in the History of Medicine', Journal of Medicine and Philosophy 15, 515–37.

Lewandowsky, Stephan (1991) 'Gradual Unlearning and Catastrophic Interference: A Comparison of Distributed Architectures', in W. Hockley and S. Lewandowsky (eds.), Relating Theory and Data (Hillsdale, NJ: Erlbaum), 445–76.

Lewis, Delmas (1983) 'Dualism and the Causal Theory of Memory', Philosophy and Phenomenological Research 44, 21–30.

Lindeboom, G.A. (1974) Boerhaave and Great Britain (Leiden: Brill).

(1979) Descartes and Medicine (Amsterdam: Rodopi).

Lingis, Alphonso (1994a) 'Lust', in S. Shamdasani and M. Munchow (eds.), Speculations after Freud (London: Routledge), 133–49.

(1994b) Foreign Bodies (London: Routledge).

Lloyd, Dan (1989) Simple Minds (Cambridge, MA: MIT Press).

(1996) 'Consciousness, Connectionism, and Cognitive Neuroscience: A Meeting of the Minds', Philosophical Psychology 9, 61–79.

Lloyd, G.E.R. (1983) *Science, Folklore, and Ideology* (Cambridge University Press).

Lloyd, G.E.R. (ed.) (1978) *Hippocratic Writings*, trans. J. Chadwick and W.N. Mann (Harmondsworth: Penguin).

Lloyd, Genevieve (1993a) 'Maleness, Metaphor, and the "Crisis" of Reason', in L. Antony and C. Witt (eds.), *A Mind of One's Own* (Boulder, CO: Westview Press), 69–83.

(1993b) *Being in Time: Selves and Narrators in Philosophy and Literature* (London: Routledge).

Locke, Don (1971) *Memory* (London: Macmillan).

Locke, John (1690/1975) *An Essay Concerning Human Understanding*, ed. P.H. Nidditch (Oxford: Clarendon).

(1979) *The Correspondence of John Locke*, vol. v, ed. E.S. De Beer (Oxford: Clarendon).

(1990) *Drafts for the 'Essay Concerning Human Understanding' and Other Philosophical Writings*, vol. 1, ed. P.H. Nidditch and G.A.J. Rogers (Oxford: Clarendon).

Loewer, Barry and Rey, Georges (1991), 'Introduction', in B. Loewer and G. Rey (eds.), *Meaning in Mind: Fodor and his Critics* (Oxford: Blackwell), xi–xxxvii.

Loftus, Elizabeth F. and Loftus, Geoffrey R. (1980) 'On the Permanence of Stored Information in the Human Brain', *American Psychologist* 35, 409–20.

Loftus, Elizabeth F., Feldman, Julie, and Dashiell, Richard (1995) 'The Reality of Illusory Memories', in D.L. Schacter (ed.), *Memory Distortion* (Cambridge, MA: Harvard University Press), 47–68.

Lowenthal, David (1989) 'The Timeless Past: Some Anglo-American Historical Preconceptions', *Journal of American History* 75, 1263–80.

Lycan, William G. (1987) *Consciousness* (Cambridge, MA: MIT Press).

(1991) 'Homuncular Functionalism Meets PDP', in W. Ramsey, S. Stich, and D.E. Rumelhart (eds.), *Philosophy and Connectionist Theory* (Hillsdale, NJ: Erlbaum), 259–86.

Lynch, Gary (1986) *Synapses, Circuits, and the Beginnings of Memory* (Cambridge, MA: MIT Press).

Lyons, Bridget G. (1971) *Voices of Melancholy: Studies in Literary Treatments of Melancholy in Renaissance England* (London: Routledge and Kegan Paul).

Lyons, Joseph (1981) 'Memory Traces and Infantile Amnesia: A Reconsideration of the Work of Erwin Straus', *Journal for the Theory of Social Behaviour* 11, 147–65.

McCann, Edwin (1987) 'Locke on Identity: Matter, Life, and Consciousness', *Archiv für Geschichte der Philosophie* 69, 54–77.

McCauley, Robert N. (1988) 'Walking in our own Footsteps: Autobiographical Memory and Reconstruction', in U. Neisser and E. Winograd (eds.), *Remembering Reconsidered: Ecological and Traditional Approaches to the Study of Memory* (Cambridge University Press), 126–44.

McClelland, James L. (1995) 'Constructive Memory and Memory Distortions: A Parallel-distributed Processing Approach', in D.L. Schacter (ed.), *Memory Distortion: How Minds, Brains, and Societies Reconstruct the Past* (Cambridge, MA: Harvard University Press), 69–90.

McClelland, James L. and Rumelhart, David E. (1986) 'A Distributed Model of Human Learning and Memory', in J.L. McClelland and D.E. Rumelhart (eds.), *Parallel Distributed Processing: Explorations in the Microstructure of Cognition*, vol. 11: *Psychological and Biological Models* (Cambridge, MA: MIT Press), 170–215.

McClelland, James L., Rumelhart, David E., and Hinton, Geoffrey E. (1986) 'The Appeal of Parallel Distributed Processing', in D.E. Rumelhart and J.L. McClelland (eds.), *Parallel*

Distributed Processing: Explorations in the Microstructure of Cognition, vol. 1: Foundations (Cambridge, MA: MIT Press), 3–44

McCloskey, M. and Cohen, N.J. (1989) 'Catastrophic Interference in Connectionist Networks: The Sequential Learning Problem', Psychology of Learning and Motivation 24, 109–65.

McCracken, Charles J. (1983) Malebranche and British Philosophy (Oxford: Clarendon).

Macdonald, Michael (1981) Mystical Bedlam: Madness, Anxiety, and Healing in Seventeenth-century England (Cambridge University Press).

McGuire, J.E. (1972) 'Boyle's Conception of Nature', Journal of the History of Ideas 33, 523–42.

McGuire, J.E. and Tamny, M. (eds) (1983) Certain Philosophical Questions: Newton's Trinity Notebook (Cambridge University Press).

MacIntosh, J.J. (1983) 'Perception and Imagination in Descartes, Boyle, and Hooke', Canadian Journal of Philosophy 13, 327–52.

Mackenzie, Ann W. (1975) 'A Word about Descartes' Mechanistic Conception of Life', Journal of the History of Biology 8, 1–13.

(1989) 'Descartes on Life and Sense', Canadian Journal of Philosophy 19, 163–92.

(1992) 'Descartes on Sensory Representation', Canadian Journal of Philosophy supplement 16, 127–46.

Mackenzie, Henry (1771/1987) The Man of Feeling (Oxford University Press).

Mackie, John L. (1976) Problems from Locke (Oxford: Clarendon).

MacLean, Ian (1980) The Renaissance Notion of Woman (Cambridge University Press).

McMullen, Terry (1989) 'The Impossibility of Associationism', unpublished paper, Department of Psychology, University of Sydney.

Macnabb, D.G.C. (ed.) (1962) David Hume, A Treatise of Human Nature, book 1 (London: Fontana/Collins).

Maestroni, Georges J.M. and Conti, Ario (1991) 'Role of the Pineal Neurohormone Melatonin in the Psycho-Neuroendocrine-Immune Network', in R. Ader, D.L. Felten, and N. Cohen (eds.), Psychoneuroimmunology, 2nd edn (San Diego: Academic Press), 495–513.

Malcolm, Norman (1963) 'A Definition of Factual Memory', in his Knowledge and Certainty (Ithaca: Cornell University Press), 222–40.

(1970) 'Memory and Representation', Noûs 4, 59–70.

(1977) Memory and Mind (Ithaca, NY: Cornell University Press).

Malebranche, Nicolas (1674/1980) The Search After Truth, trans. T.M. Lennon and P.J. Olscamp (Columbus, OH: Ohio State University Press).

Mandelbaum, Maurice (1964) 'Locke's Realism', in his Philosophy, Science, and Sense Perception (Baltimore: Johns Hopkins University Press), 1–60.

Mandeville, Bernard (1711/1976) A Treatise of the Hypochondriack and Hysterick Passions . . . in Three Dialogues (London: Dryden Leach and W. Taylor; repr. New York: Arno Press).

Mandler, George (1989) 'Memory: Conscious and Unconscious', in P. Solomon, G.R. Goethals, C.M. Kelley, and B.R. Stephens (eds.), Memory: Interdisciplinary Approaches (New York: Springer-Verlag), 84–106.

Manfredi, Pat A. (1986) 'Processing or Pickup: Conflicting Approaches to Perception', Mind and Language 1, 181–200.

Marr, David (1982) Vision (New York: Freeman).

Marsh, Robert (1959) 'The Second Part of Hartley's System', Journal of the History of Ideas 20, 264–73.

Marshall, John C. and Fryer, David M. (1978) 'Speak, Memory! An Introduction to Some Historic Studies of Remembering and Forgetting', in M.M. Gruneberg and P. Morris (eds.), *Aspects of Memory* (London: Methuen), 1–25.

Marston, John (1600/1965) *Antonio's Revenge*, ed. G.K. Hunter (London: Edward Arnold).

Martensen, Robert L. (1992) '"Habit of Reason": Anatomy and Anglicanism in Restoration England', *Bulletin of the History of Medicine* 66, 511–35.

Martin, C.B. and Deutscher, Max (1966) 'Remembering', *Philosophical Review* 75, 161–96.

Mascuch, Michael (1997) *The Origins of the Individualist Self: Autobiographical Practice and Self-identity in Britain, 1591–1791* (Cambridge: Polity Press).

Matsuda, Matt Keoki (1993) 'The Memory of the Modern', Ph.D. dissertation, Dept of History, UCLA.

Matthews, Eric (1986) 'Mind and Matter in the Eighteenth Century', *Philosophical Quarterly* 3, 420–9.

Maull, Nancy L. (1980) 'Cartesian Optics and the Geometrization of Nature', in S. Gaukroger (ed.), *Descartes: Philosophy, Mathematics, Physics* (Brighton: Harvester), 23–40.

Mayow, John (1674/1957) *Medico-Physical Works of John Mayow*, trans. A.C.B.and L.D. (Edinburgh: The Alembic Club).

Mayr, Otto (1980) 'A Mechanical Symbol for an Authoritarian World', in K. Maurice and O. Mayr (eds.), *The Clockwork Universe: German Clocks and Automata 1550–1650* (Washington: Smithsonian Institute), 1–8.

—— (1986) *Authority, Liberty, and Automatic Machinery in Early Modern Europe* (Baltimore: Johns Hopkins University Press).

Maze, John R. (1983) *The Meaning of Behaviour* (London: Allen and Unwin).

—— (1991) 'Representationism, Realism, and the Redundancy of "Mentalese"', *Theory and Psychology* 1, 163–85.

Mazzolini, Renato G. (1991) 'Schemes and Models of the Thinking Machine (1662–1762)', in P. Corsi (ed.), *The Enchanted Loom: Chapters in the History of Neuroscience* (Oxford University Press), 68–83.

Medcalf, Stephen (1970) introduction to Joseph Glanvill, *The Vanity of Dogmatizing* (Brighton: Harvester Press).

Megill, Alan (1992) 'Foucault, Ambiguity, and the Rhetoric of Historiography', in A. Still and I. Velody (eds.), *Rewriting the History of Madness* (London: Routledge), 86–104.

Melion, Walter and Kuchler, Suzanne (1991) 'Introduction: Memory, Cognition, and Image Production', in S. Kuchler and W. Melion (eds.) *Images of Memory: On Remembering and Representation* (Washington: Smithsonian Institute), 1–46.

Merchant, Carolyn (1980) *The Death of Nature: Women, Ecology, and the Scientific Revolution* (New York: Harper and Row).

Metcalfe Eich, Janet (1982) 'A Composite Holographic Associative Recall Model', *Psychological Review* 89, 627–61.

Metcalfe, Janet (1989) 'Composite Holographic Associative Recall Model (CHARM) and Blended Memories in Eyewitness Testimony', *Proceedings of the 11th Annual Conference of the Cognitive Science Society*, 307–14.

Metraux, Alexandre (1996) 'Impure Epistemology and the Search for the Nervous Agent: A Case Study in Seventeenth- and Eighteenth-century Neurophysics', *Science in Context* 9, 57–78.

Meyer, Alfred and Hierons, Raymond (1965) 'On Thomas Willis' Concepts on Neurophysiology', *Medical History* 9, 1–15, 142–55.

Meyering, Theo C. (1989) *Historical Roots of Cognitive Science* (Dordrecht: Kluwer).

Micale, Mark (1995) *Approaching Hysteria: Disease and its Interpretations* (Princeton University Press).

Michael, Emily and Michael, Fred S. (1989) 'Corporeal Ideas in Seventeenth-century Psychology', *Journal of the History of Ideas* 50, 31–48.

Michael, Fred S. and Michael, Emily (1985) review of Yolton 1984a, *Philosophical Books* 26, 214–17.

Michaels, Claire and Carello, Claudia (1981) *Direct Perception* (Englewood Cliffs, NJ: Prentice-Hall).

Michell, Joel (1988) 'Maze and Direct Realism', *Australian Journal of Psychology* 40, 227–49.

Mignon, Maurice (1934) 'La Théorie des esprits animaux exposée dans un manuscrit anonyme du XVIIIe siècle: commentaires sur l'évolution des idées concernant cette théorie et le problème vital', *Bulletin de Société Française d'Histoire de la Medicine* 28, 5–26.

Miller, Jonathan (1978) *The Body in Question* (London: Jonathan Cape).

Mintz, Samuel I. (1962) *The Hunting of Leviathan: Seventeenth-century Reactions to the Materialism and Moral Philosophy of Thomas Hobbes* (Cambridge University Press).

Monro, Alexander (1783) *Observations on the Structure and Functions of the Nervous System* (Edinburgh: William Creech and Joseph Johnson).

Monro, Hector (1975) *The Ambivalence of Bernard Mandeville* (Oxford: Clarendon).

More, Henry (1647/1969) *Philosophical Poems* (reprint Menston: Scholar Press).

(1662) *The Immortality of the Soul*, in *A Collection of Several Philosophical Writings*, vol. II (repr. New York and London: Garland).

(1662/1978) *A Collection of Several Philosophical Writings* (2 vols., repr. New York and London: Garland).

Morgan, Vance G. (1994) *Foundations of Cartesian Ethics* (Atlantic Highlands, NJ: Humanities Press).

Morris, John (1969) 'Pattern Recognition in Descartes' Automata', *Isis* 60, 451–60.

Morris, P.E. (1994) 'Theories of Memory: An Historical Perspective', in P. Morris and M. Gruneberg (eds.), *Theoretical Aspects of Memory*, 2nd edn (London: Routledge), 1–28.

Morss, John R. (1989) 'Misconceiving Gibson', *New Ideas in Psychology* 7, 223–8.

Mulligan, Lotte (1992) 'Robert Hooke's "Memoranda": Memory and Natural History', *Annals of Science* 49, 47–61.

Mundy, Jean and Gorman, Warren (1969) 'The Image of the Brain', in W. Gorman, *Body Image and the Image of the Brain* (St Louis: Warren Green), 187–251.

Munn, Nancy D. (1995) 'An Essay on the Symbolic Construction of Memory in the Kaluli Gisalo', in D. de Coppet and A. Iteanu (eds.), *Cosmos and Society in Oceania* (Oxford: Berg), 83–104.

Munsat, Stanley (1967) *The Concept of Memory* (New York: Random House).

Murdock, B.B. (1982) 'A Theory for the Storage and Retrieval of Item and Associative Information', *Psychological Review* 89, 609–26.

Murray, D.J. (1976) 'Research on Human Memory in the Nineteenth Century', *Canadian Journal of Psychology* 30, 201–20.

Myer, Valerie Grosvenor (1984) 'Tristram and the Animal Spirits', in V. Grosvenor Myer (ed.), *Laurence Sterne: Riddles and Mysteries* (London: Barnes and Noble), 99–112.

Nadler, Steven M. (1989) *Arnauld and the Cartesian Philosophy of Ideas* (Manchester University Press).

(1992) *Malebranche and Ideas* (Oxford University Press).

Nayler, Margaret A. (1993) 'The Insoluble Problem: Muscle in the Mid to Late Seventeenth Century', Ph.D. thesis, University of Melbourne.

Neisser, Ulric (1988) 'Time Present and Time Past', in M.M. Gruneberg, P.E. Morris, and R.N. Sykes (eds.), *Practical Aspects of Memory: Current Research and Issues*, vol. II (Chichester: Wiley), 545–60.

Neisser, Ulric (ed.) (1982), *Memory Observed* (San Francisco: Freeman).

Newton, Isaac (1717/1952) *Optics*, 2nd edn (Chicago: Encyclopaedia Britannica).

Niebyl, Peter H. (1971) 'The Non-Naturals', *Bulletin of the History of Medicine* 45, 486–92.

(1973) 'Science and Metaphor in the Medicine of Restoration England', *Bulletin of the History of Medicine* 47, 356–74.

Niklasson, Lars F. and van Gelder, Tim (1994) 'On Being Systematically Connectionist', *Mind and Language* 9, 288–302.

Nussbaum, Martha (1978) *Aristotle's 'De Motu Animalium'* (Princeton University Press).

Nutton, Vivian (1981) 'Pneuma', in W.F. Bynum, E.J. Browne, and R. Porter (eds.), *Dictionary of the History of Science* (Princeton University Press), 331.

(1995) 'Medicine in Medieval Western Europe, 1000–1500', in L.I. Conrad, M. Neve, V. Nutton, R. Porter, and A. Wear, *The Western Medical Tradition* (Cambridge University Press), 139–205.

O'Brien, Gerard (1987) 'Eliminative Materialism and our Psychological Self-knowledge', *Philosophical Studies* 52, 49–70.

(1988) 'Visual Perception and the Mind-Brain', in 'Parallel Distributed Processing: An Overview and Discussion', unpublished draft, Oxford University, 94–156.

(1991) 'Is Connectionism Common Sense?', *Philosophical Psychology* 4, 165–78.

(1993) 'The Computational Theory of Mind: An Exploration in the Conceptual Foundations of Cognitive Science', D.Phil. thesis, Oxford University.

O'Brien, Gerard and Opie, Jon (forthcoming), 'A Connectionist Theory of Phenomenal Experience', *Behavioral and Brain Sciences* (forthcoming).

O'Connor, D.J. and Carr, Brian (1982) *Introduction to the Theory of Knowledge* (Brighton: Harvester).

O'Neil, Brian (1974) *Epistemological Direct Realism in Descartes' Philosophy* (Albuquerque, NM: New Mexico University Press).

Oaksford, Mike and Chater, Nick (1991) 'Against Logicist Cognitive Science', *Mind and Language* 6, 1–38.

Oldfield, R.C. and Oldfield, Lady Kathleen (1951) 'Hartley's *Observations on Man*', *Annals of Science* 7, 371–81.

Oldroyd, David (1980) 'Some "Philosophical Scribbles" attributed to Robert Hooke', *Notes and Records of the Royal Society of London* 35, 17–32.

Oppenheim, Janet (1991) *'Shattered Nerves': Doctors, Patients, and Depression in Victorian England* (Oxford University Press).

Otis, Laura (1994) *Organic Memory* (Lincoln, NE: Nebraska University Press).

Pagel, Walter (1958) 'Medieval and Renaissance Contributions to the Knowledge of the Brain and its Functions', in F.N.L. Poynter (ed.), *The History and Philosophy of Knowledge of the Brain and its Functions* (Oxford: Blackwell), 95–114.

Parfit, Derek (1984) *Reasons and Persons* (Oxford: Clarendon).

Park, Katherine (1988) 'The Organic Soul', in C.B. Schmitt and Q. Skinner (eds.), *The Cambridge History of Renaissance Philosophy* (Cambridge University Press), 464–84.

—— (1992) 'Medicine and Society in Medieval Europe, 500–1500', in A. Wear (ed.), *Medicine in Society* (Cambridge University Press), 59–90.

Passmore, John (1968) *A Hundred Years of Philosophy* (Harmondsworth: Penguin).

Paster, Gail Kern (1993) *The Body Embarrassed: Drama and the Disciplines of Shame in Early Modern England* (Ithaca, NY: Cornell University Press).

Patton, Paul (1994) 'Translator's Preface' to Gilles Deleuze, *Difference and Repetition* (New York: Columbia University Press), xi–xiii.

Pears, David (1990) *Hume's System* (Oxford University Press).

Pera, Marcello (1992) *The Ambiguous Frog: The Galvani–Volta Controversy on Animal Electricity*, trans. J. Mandelbaum (Princeton University Press).

Petersson, R.T. (1956) *Sir Kenelm Digby: The Ornament of England, 1603–1665* (London: Jonathan Cape; Cambridge, MA: Harvard University Press).

Pettit, Philip (1991) 'Realism and Response-Dependence', *Mind* 100, 587–626.

Pine, Martin L. (1986) *Pietro Pomponazzi: Radical Philosopher of the Italian Renaissance* (Padua: Editions di Antinori).

Pitson, Tony (1986) 'The New Representationalism', *Philosophical Papers* 15, 41–9.

Pliny (1962) *The Natural History*, trans. P. Holland (1601), ed. P. Turner (New York: McGraw-Hill).

Pocock, J.G.A. (1971) 'Time, History and Eschatology in the Thought of Thomas Hobbes', in his *Politics, Language, and Time* (New York: Athenaeum), 148–201.

Pollack, Jordan B. (1990) 'Recursive Distributed Representations', *Artificial Intelligence* 46, 77–105.

Pomponazzi, Pietro (1516/1948) *The Immortality of the Soul*, trans. W.H. Hay in E. Cassirer, P.O. Kristeller, and J.H. Randall (eds.), *The Renaissance Philosophy of Man* (Chicago University Press), 280–381.

Poole, Ross (1992) 'On National Identity: A Response to Jonathan Rée', *Radical Philosophy* 62, 14–19.

—— (1996), 'On Being A Person', *Australasian Journal of Philosophy* 74, 38–56.

Porter, Roy (1984) 'Against the Spleen', in V. Grosvenor Myer (ed.), *Laurence Sterne: Riddles and Mysteries* (London: Barnes and Noble), 84–98.

—— (1987) *Mind-Forg'd Manacles: A History of Madness in England from the Restoration to the Regency* (London: Athlone Press).

—— (1995) 'The Eighteenth Century', in L.I. Conrad, M. Neve, V. Nutton, R. Porter, and A. Wear, *The Western Medical Tradition, 800 BC to AD 1800* (Cambridge University Press), 371–475.

Pouchelle, Marie-Christine (1983/1990) *The Body and Surgery in the Middle Ages*, trans. R. Morris (New Brunswick: Rutgers University Press).

Pribram, Karl (1971) *Languages of the Brain* (Englewood Cliffs, NJ: Prentice-Hall).

Prudovsky, Gad (1989) 'The Confirmation of the Superposition Principle: On the Role of a Constructive Thought Experiment in Galileo's *Discorsi*', *Studies in the History and Philosophy of Science* 20, 453–68.

Putscher, Marielene (1973) *Pneuma, Spiritus, Geist: vorstellungen vom Lebensantrieb in ihren Geschichtlichen Wandlungen* (Wiesbaden: Franz Steiner Verlag).

Pye, Christopher (1988) 'The Sovereign, the Theater, and the Kingdome of Darknesse:

Hobbes and the Spectacle of Power', in S. Greenblatt (ed.), *Representing the English Renaissance* (Berkeley and Los Angeles: California University Press), 279–301.

Pylyshyn, Zenon (1984) *Computation and Cognition* (Cambridge, MA: MIT Press).

Radley, Alan (1990) 'Artefacts, Memory, and a Sense of the Past', in D. Middleton and D. Edwards (eds.), *Collective Remembering* (London: Sage), 46–59.

Radner, Daisie (1976) 'Representationalism in Arnauld's Act Theory of Perception', *Journal of the History of Philosophy* 14, 96–8.

(1978) *Malebranche: A Study of a Cartesian System* (Amsterdam: Van Gorcum).

Rakover, Sam (1983) 'In Defense of Memory Viewed as Stored Mental Representations', *Behaviorism* 11, 53–62.

Ramsey, William and Stich, Stephen P. (1990) 'Connectionism and Three Levels of Nativism', *Synthese* 82, 177–205.

Ramsey, William, Stich, Stephen, and Garon, Joseph (1991) 'Connectionism, Eliminativism, and the Future of Folk Psychology', repr. in J. Greenwood (ed.), *The Future of Folk Psychology* (Cambridge University Press), 93–119.

Rand, Benjamin (1923) 'The Early Development of Hartley's Doctrine of Association', *Psychological Review* 30, 306–20.

Ratcliff, R. (1990) 'Connectionist Models of Recognition Memory: Constraints Imposed by Learning and Forgetting Function', *Psychological Review* 97, 285–308.

Rather, L.J. (1965) *Mind and Body in Eighteenth Century Medicine: A Study based on Jerome Gaub* (London: Wellcome Historical Medical Library).

(1968) 'The "Six Things Non-Natural": A Note on the Origins and Fate of a Doctrine and a Phrase', *Clio Medica* 3, 337–47.

(1982) 'On the Source and Development of Metaphorical Language in the History of Western Medicine', in L.G. Stevenson (ed.), *A Celebration of Medical History* (Baltimore: Johns Hopkins University Press), 135–53.

Rattansi, Piyo (1988) 'Newton and the Wisdom of the Ancients', in J. Fauvel, R. Flood, M. Shortland, and R. Wilson (eds.), *Let Newton Be!* (Oxford University Press), 185–201.

Raynor, David (1990) 'Hume and Berkeley's Three Dialogues', in M.A. Stewart (ed.), *Studies in the Philosophy of the Scottish Enlightenment* (Oxford University Press), 231–50.

Rée, Jonathan (1995) 'Subjectivity in the Twentieth Century', *New Literary History* 26, 205–17.

Reed, Edward S. (1982) 'Descartes' Corporeal Ideas Hypothesis and the Origins of Scientific Psychology', *Review of Metaphysics* 35, 731–52.

(1983) 'Two Theories of the Intentionality of Perceiving', *Synthese* 54, 85–94.

(1986) 'James J. Gibson's Revolution in Perceptual Psychology: A Case Study of the Transformation of Scientific Ideas', *Studies in the History and Philosophy of Science* 17, 65–98.

(1988) *James J. Gibson and the Psychology of Perception* (New Haven: Yale University Press).

(1989) 'Theory, Concept, and Experiment in the History of Psychology: An Old Tradition Behind a "young" Science', *History of the Human Sciences* 2, 333–57.

(1990) 'The Trapped Infinity: Cartesian Volition as Conceptual Nightmare', *Philosophical Psychology* 3, 101–21.

Reed, Edward S. and Jones, Rebecca (1981) 'Is Perception Blind?', *Journal for the Theory of Social Behaviour* 11, 87–91.

Reiche, Harald A.T. (1960) *Empedocles' Mixture, Eudoxan Astronomy, and Aristotle's Connate Pneuma* (Amsterdam: Hakkert).

Reid, Thomas (1764/1970), *An Inquiry into the Human Mind*, ed. T. Duggan (Chicago University Press).

(1775–6) review of Joseph Priestley, *Hartley's Theory of the Human Mind*, in *Monthly Review* 53 (1775), 380–90; 54 (1776), 41–7.

(1775/1995) 'Miscelaneous Reflections on Priestly's Account of Hartleys Theory of the Human Mind', Aberdeen University Library (AUL) MS 3061/9; repr. in Wood 1995: 132–54.

(1785/1849) *Essays on the Intellectual Powers of Man*, in *The Works of Thomas Reid*, ed. W. Hamilton (Edinburgh: MacLachlan, Stewart, & Co.).

Reiss, Timothy (1996) 'Denying the Body? Memory and the Dilemmas of History in Descartes', *Journal of the History of Ideas* 57, 587–607.

René Descartes: vie, philosophie, et oeuvre (1996), available on the internet at: http://members.aol.com/fabgueho/fg001.htm or from JoliCiel, 3 square Jacques Menier, F-77186 Noisiel, France.

Richards, Graham (1992) *Mental Machinery: The Origins and Consequences of Psychological Ideas*, vol. I, 1600–1850 (London: Athlone Press).

Richards, Robert J. (1976/7) 'James Gibson's Passive Theory of Perception: A Rejection of the Doctrine of Specific Nerve Energies', *Philosophy and Phenomenological Research* 37, 218–33.

Richardson, Linda Deer (1985) 'The Generation of Disease: Occult Causes and Diseases of the Total Substance', in A. Wear, R.K. French, and I.M. Lonie (eds.), *The Medical Renaissance of the Sixteenth Century* (Cambridge University Press), 175–94.

Riese, Walther (1958) 'Descartes' Ideas of Brain Function', in F.N.L. Poynter (ed.), *The History and Philosophy of Knowledge of the Brain and its Functions* (Oxford: Blackwell), 115–34.

(1959) *A History of Neurology* (New York: MD Publications).

Rist, John M. (1985) 'On Greek Biology, Greek Cosmology, and Some Sources of Theological Pneuma', in D. Dockrill and G. Tanner (eds.), *The Concept of Spirit* (Auckland University Press), 27–47.

Robinet, Andre (1984) 'Spiritus/Esprit chez Spinoza et Malebranche', in M. Fattori and M. Bianchi (eds.), *Spiritus* (Rome: Edizioni dell'Ateneo), 333–43.

Rock, Irvin (1983) *The Logic of Perception* (Cambridge, MA: MIT Press).

(1991) 'Explanation in Psychology', in E. Lepore and B. McLaughlin (eds.), *John Searle and his Critics* (Oxford: Blackwell), 311–22.

Rodis-Lewis, Genevieve (1978) 'Limitations of the Mechanical Model in the Cartesian Conception of the Organism', in M. Hooker (ed.), *Descartes: Critical and Interpretive Essays* (Baltimore: Johns Hopkins University Press), 152–70.

Roe, Shirley A. (1981) *Matter, Life, and Generation: Eighteenth Century Embryology and the Haller–Wolff Debate* (Cambridge University Press).

Roediger, Henry L. (1980) 'Memory Metaphors in Cognitive Psychology', *Memory and Cognition* 8, 231–46.

(1996) 'Memory Illusions', *Journal of Memory and Language* 35, 76–100.

Roediger, Henry L. and McDermott, Kathleen B. (1995) 'Creating False Memories: Remembering Words not Presented in Lists', *Journal of Experimental Psychology: Learning, Memory, and Cognition* 21, 803–14.

Roger, Jacques (1980) 'The Living World', in G.S. Rousseau and R. Porter (eds.), *The Ferment of Knowledge* (Cambridge University Press), 255–83.

Rogers, G.A.J. (1985) 'Descartes and the English', in J.D. North and J.J. Roche (eds.), *The Light of Nature* (The Hague: Martinus Nijhoff), 281–302.

Rohault, Jacques (1723/1969) *Rohault's System of Natural Philosophy*, trans. J. Clarke (reprint New York: Johnson Reprints).

Romanell, Patrick (1984) *John Locke and Medicine: A New Key to Locke* (New York: Prometheus Books).

Rome, Dom R. (1956) 'Nicolas Sténon et la Royal Society of London', *Osiris* 12, 244–68.

Rorty, Amelie (1992) 'Descartes on Thinking with the Body', in J. Cottingham (ed.), *The Cambridge Companion to Descartes* (Cambridge University Press), 371–92.

Rorty, Richard (1980) *Philosophy and the Mirror of Nature* (Oxford: Blackwell).

(1989) 'The Contingency of Selfhood', in his *Contingency, Irony, and Solidarity* (Cambridge University Press), 23–43.

Rose, Stephen (1993) *The Making of Memory: From Molecules to Mind* (New York: Anchor Books).

Rosen, Deborah (1975) 'An Argument for the Logical Notion of a Memory Trace', *Philosophy of Science* 42, 1–10.

Ross, Don (1991) 'Hume, Resemblance, and the Foundations of Psychology', *History of Philosophy Quarterly* 8, 343–56.

Rostenberg, Leona (1989) *The Library of Robert Hooke: The Scientific Book Trade of Restoration England* (Santa Monica: Modoc Press).

Roth, Michael S. (1989) 'Remembering Forgetting: Maladies de la mémoire in Nineteenth Century France', *Representations* 26, 49–68.

(1991) 'Dying of the Past: Medical Studies of Nostalgia in Nineteenth Century France', *History and Memory* 3, 5–29.

(1992) 'The Time of Nostalgia: Medicine, History, and Normality in Nineteenth Century France', *Time and Society* 1, 271–86.

Rothschuh, Karl E. (1953/1973) *History of Physiology*, trans. G.B. Risse (Huntington, NY: Robert E. Krieger).

(1958) 'Vom Spiritus animalis zum Nervenaktionsstrom', *CIBA-Zeitschrift* 89, 2949–80.

Rousseau, G.S. (1969/1991), 'Towards a Social Anthropology of the Imagination', in his *Enlightenment Crossings* (Manchester University Press), 1–25 (first published as 'Science and the Discovery of the Imagination').

(1976) 'Nerves, Spirits, and Fibres: Towards Defining the Origins of Sensibility', in R.F. Brissenden and J.C. Eade (eds.), *Studies in the Eighteenth Century* 3 (Toronto and Buffalo: Toronto University Press), 137–57.

(1980) 'Psychology', in G.S. Rousseau and R. Porter (eds.), *The Ferment of Knowledge* (Cambridge University Press), 143–210.

(1989) 'Discourses of the Nerve', in F. Amrine (ed.), *Literature and Science as Modes of Expression* (Dordrecht: Kluwer), 29–60.

(1991) 'Towards a Semiotics of the Nerve: The Social History of Language in a New Key', in P. Burke and R. Porter (eds.), *Language, Self, and Society* (Cambridge: Polity Press), 213–75.

(1993) 'A Strange Pathology: Hysteria in the Early Modern Period, 1500–1800' in S. Gilman, H. King, R. Porter, G.S. Rousseau, and E. Showalter, *Hysteria Beyond Freud* (Berkeley and Los Angeles: California University Press), 91–221.

Rozemond, Maria H. (1989) 'Descartes' Conception of the Mind', Ph.D. dissertation, UCLA.

Rubin, David C. (1995) *Memory in Oral Traditions: The Cognitive Psychology of Epic, Ballads, and Counting-out Rhymes* (Oxford University Press).

Rubin, David C. (ed.) (1986) *Autobiographical Memory* (Cambridge University Press).

Ruestow, Edward G. (1996) *The Microscope in the Dutch Republic: The Shaping of Discovery* (Cambridge University Press).

Rumelhart, David E. (1980) 'Schemata: The Building Blocks of Knowledge', in R. Spiro, B. Bruce, and W. Brewer (eds.), *Theoretical Issues in Reading Comprehension* (Hillsdale, NJ: Erlbaum), 33–58.

(1992) 'Towards a Microstructural Account of Human Reasoning', in S. Davis (ed.), *Connectionism: Theory and Practice* (Oxford University Press), 69–83.

Rumelhart, David E. and McClelland, James L. (1986) 'On Learning the Past Tenses of English Verbs', in J.L. McClelland and D.E. Rumelhart (eds.), *Parallel Distributed Processing: Explorations in the Microstructure of Cognition*, vol. II: *Psychological and Biological Models* (Cambridge, MA: MIT Press), 216–71.

Rumelhart, David E. and Norman, Donald A. (1981) 'Introduction', in G.E. Hinton and J.A. Anderson (eds.), *Parallel Models of Associative Memory* (Hillsdale, NJ: Erlbaum), 1–7.

Rumelhart, David E., Smolensky, Paul, McClelland, James L. and Hinton, Geoffrey E. (1986) 'Schemata and Sequential Thought Processes', in J.L. McClelland and D.E. Rumelhart (eds.), *Parallel Distributed Processing: Explorations in the Microstructure of Cognition*, vol. II: *Psychological and Biological Models* (Cambridge, MA: MIT Press), 7–57.

Rupp, Jan C.C. (1990) 'Matters of Life and Death: The Social and Cultural Conditions of the Rise of Anatomical Theatres, with Special Reference to Seventeenth Century Holland', *History of Science* 28, 263–87.

(1992) 'Foucault, Body Politics, and the Rise of Modern Anatomy', *Journal of Historical Sociology* 5, 31–60.

Russell, Bertrand (1921) *The Analysis of Mind* (London: Allen and Unwin).

Ryle, Gilbert (1949/1963) *The Concept of Mind* (Harmondsworth: Penguin).

Sabra, A.I. (1967/1981) *Theories of Light from Descartes to Newton*, 2nd edn (Cambridge University Press).

Sacks, Oliver (1990) 'Neurology and the Soul', *New York Review of Books*, 22 November, 44–50.

Salmon, Vivian (1972) *The Works of Francis Lodwick* (London: Longman).

Sambursky, Shmuel (1959) *Physics of the Stoics* (London: Routledge and Kegan Paul).

Sanchez-Gonzalez, M.A. (1990) 'Medicine in John Locke's Philosophy', *Journal of Medicine and Philosophy* 15, 675–95.

Sanders, John T. (1985) 'Experience, Memory, and Intelligence', *Monist* 68, 507–21.

Sawday, Jonathan (1995) *The Body Emblazoned: Dissection and the Human Body in Renaissance Culture* (London: Routledge).

Scarry, Elaine (1985) *The Body in Pain: The Making and Unmaking of the World* (Oxford University Press).

(1988) 'Donne: "but yet the body is his booke"', in E. Scarry (ed.), *Literature and the Body* (Baltimore: Johns Hopkins University Press), 70–105.

Schacter, Daniel L. (1982) *Stranger Behind the Engram: Theories of Memory and the Psychology of Science* (Hillsdale, NJ: Erlbaum).

(1995) 'Memory Distortion: History and Current Status', in D.L. Schacter (ed.) *Memory Distortion: How Minds, Brains, and Societies Reconstruct the Past* (Cambridge, MA: Harvard University Press), 1–43.

(1996) *Searching for Memory: The Mind, the Brain, and the Past* (New York: Basic Books).

Schacter, Daniel L. and Tulving, Endel (1994) 'What are the Memory Systems of 1994?', in D.L. Schacter and E. Tulving (eds.), *Memory Systems 1994* (Cambridge, MA: MIT Press), 1–38.

Schaffer, Simon (1980) 'Natural Philosophy', in G.S. Rousseau and R. Porter (eds.), *The Ferment of Knowledge* (Cambridge University Press), 55–91.

(1987) 'Godly Men and Mechanical Philosophers: Souls and Spirits in Restoration Natural Philosophy', *Science in Context* 1, 55–85.

(1990) 'Newtonianism', in R.C. Olby, G.N. Cantor, J.R.R. Christie, and M.J.S. Hodge (eds.), *Companion to the History of Modern Science* (London: Routledge), 610–26.

Schechtman, Marya (1994) 'The Truth About Memory', *Philosophical Psychology* 7, 3–18.

Scherz, Gustav (1965) 'Introduction', *Nicolaus Steno's Lecture on the Anatomy of the Brain* (Copenhagen), 61–103.

(1976) 'Steno, Nicolaus', *Dictionary of Scientific Biography*, vol. XIII, 30–5.

Schiller, Francis (1982) 'Neurology: The Electrical Root', in F.C. Rose and W.F. Bynum (eds.), *Historical Aspects of the Neurosciences* (New York: Raven Press), 1–11.

Schofield, Robert (1970) *Mechanism and Materialism: British Natural Philosophy in an Age of Reason* (Princeton University Press).

Schooler, J.W. and Engstler-Schooler, T.Y. (1990) 'Verbal Overshadowing of Visual Memories: Some Things are Better Left Unsaid', *Cognitive Psychology* 22, 36–71.

Schouls, Peter A. (1989) *Descartes and the Enlightenment* (Kingston and Montreal: McGill-Queen's University Press).

Schreter, Zoltan (1994) 'Distributed and Localist Representation in the Brain and in Connectionist Models', in J. Wiles, C. Latimer, and C. Stevens (eds.), *Connectionist Models and Psychology*, Technical report 289, Dept of Computer Science, University of Queensland, 93–100.

Schulte, B.P.M. (1968) 'Swammerdam and Steno', in G. Scherz (ed.), *Steno and Brain Research in the Seventeenth Century* (Oxford: Pergamon), 35–41.

Schulte-Sasse, Jochen (1987) 'Imagination and Modernity, or the Taming of the Human Mind', *Cultural Critique* 5, 23–48.

(1995) 'From the Body's to the Mind's Imagination: Discursive Intersections of 18th-century Medicine and Aesthetics', paper read at the UCLA/Clark Library workshop 'Life Studies', April 1995.

Schumacher, John A. (1975/6) 'Memory Unchained Again', *Analysis* 36, 101–4.

Schuster, John (1977) 'Descartes and the Scientific Revolution, 1618–1634: An Interpretation', Princeton University Ph.D. dissertation.

(1990) 'The Scientific Revolution', in R.C. Olby, G.N. Cantor, J.R.R. Christie, and M.J.S. Hodge (eds.), *Companion to the History of Modern Science* (London: Routledge), 217–42.

(1993) 'Whatever Should We do with Cartesian Method? Reclaiming Descartes for the History of Science', in S. Voss (ed.), *Essays on the Philosophy and Science of René Descartes* (Cambridge University Press), 195–223.

Schwartz, Hillel (1978) *Knaves, Fools, Madmen, and the Subtile Effluvium: A Study of the Opposition to the French Prophets in England, 1706–1710* (Gainesville, FL: Florida University Press).

Schwartz, Robert (1994) *Vision: Variations on Some Berkeleian Themes* (Oxford: Blackwell).

(1996) 'Directed Perception', *Philosophical Psychology* 9, 81–91.

Screech, M.A. (1980) *Erasmus: Ecstasy and the Praise of Folly* (London: Penguin).

Searle, John (1991) 'Reply to Rock', in E. Lepore and B. McLaughlin (eds.), *John Searle and his Critics* (Oxford: Blackwell), 338–41.

Sejnowski, Terrence J. and Tesauro, Gerald (1990) 'Building Network Learning Algorithms from Hebbian Synapses', in J.L. McGaugh, N.M. Weinberger, and G. Lynch (eds.), *Brain Organisation and Memory: Cells, Systems, and Circuits* (Oxford University Press), 338–55.

Sepper, Dennis L. (1988) 'Imagination, Phantasms, and the Making of Hobbesian and Cartesian Science', *Monist* 71, 526–42.

(1989) 'Descartes and the Eclipse of Imagination, 1618–1630', *Journal of the History of Philosophy* 27, 379–403.

(1993) 'Ingenium, Memory Art, and the Unity of Imaginative Knowing in the Early Descartes' in S. Voss (ed.), *Essays on the Philosophy and Science of René Descartes* (Cambridge University Press), 142–61.

(1996) *Descartes's Imagination: Proportion, Images, and the Activity of Thinking* (Berkeley and Los Angeles: California University Press).

Seris, Jean-Pierre (1993) 'Language and Machine in the Philosophy of Descartes', in S. Voss (ed.), *Essays on the Philosophy and Science of René Descartes* (Cambridge University Press), 177–92.

Serres, Michel (1982) 'Platonic Dialogue', in *Hermes: Literature, Science, Philosophy*, trans. J. Harari and D. Bell (Baltimore: Johns Hopkins University Press), 65–72.

Shanon, Benny (1991) 'Memory as a Tool: An Analogy with the Guiding Stick', *New Ideas in Psychology* 9, 89–93.

Shapin, Steven (1980) 'Social Uses of Science', in G.S. Rousseau and R. Porter (eds.), *The Ferment of Knowledge* (Cambridge University Press), 93–193.

(1992) 'Discipline and Bounding: The History and Sociology of Science as Seen through the Externalism–Internalism Debate', *History of Science* 30, 333–69.

Shapin, Steven and Schaffer, Simon (1985) *Leviathan and the Air-Pump: Hobbes, Boyle, and the Experimental Life* (Princeton University Press).

Shapiro, Alan E. (1973) 'Kinematic Optics: A Study of the Wave Theory of Light in the Seventeenth Century', *Archives for the History of the Exact Sciences* 11, 134–272.

(1974) 'Light, Pressure, and Rectilinear Propagation: Descartes' Celestial Optics and Newton's Hydrostatics', *Studies in the History and Philosophy of Science* 5, 239–96.

(1994) 'Artists' Colours and Newton's Colours', *Isis* 85, 600–30.

Sharpe, R.A. (1991) 'Minds Made Up', *Inquiry* 34, 91–106.

Shea, William R. (1991) *The Magic of Numbers and Motion: The Scientific Career of René Descartes* (Canton, MA: Science History Publications).

Shelley, Mary (1818/1974) *Frankenstein, or The Modern Prometheus*, ed. J. Rieger (Chicago University Press).

Shoemaker, Sydney (1963) *Self-Knowledge and Self-Identity* (Ithaca NY: Cornell University Press).

(1970) 'Persons and their Pasts', *American Philosophical Quarterly* 7, 269–85.

(1972) 'Memory', in P. Edwards (ed.), *Encyclopaedia of Philosophy* (New York: Macmillan), vol. v, 265–74.

Shope, R.K. (1973) 'Remembering, Knowledge, and Memory Traces', *Philosophy and Phenomenological Research* 33, 303–22.

Shotter, John (1991) 'Wittgenstein and Psychology: On Our "Hook-up" to Reality', in A.P. Griffiths (ed.), *Wittgenstein: Centenary Essays* (Cambridge University Press), 193–208.

Siegel, Rudolph E. (1973) *Galen on Psychology, Psychopathology, and Function and Diseases of the Nervous System* (Basle: S. Karger).

Singer, B.R. (1976) 'Robert Hooke on Memory, Association, and Time Perception', *Notes and Records of the Royal Society of London* 31, 115–31.

Singer, Charles (1952) *Vesalius on the Human Brain* (Oxford University Press).

Singer, Charles and Underwood, E.A. (1962) *A Short History of Medicine*, 2nd edn (Oxford: Clarendon).

Siraisi, Nancy (1990) *Medieval and Early Renaissance Medicine: An Introduction to Knowledge and Practice* (Chicago University Press).

Skarda, Christine (1986) 'Bringing the Brain Back In', *Inquiry* 29, 187–202.

Skinner, Quentin (1991) 'Who are "We"? Ambiguities of the Modern Self', *Inquiry* 34, 133–53.

Skorupski, John (1993) *English-Language Philosophy 1750–1945* (Oxford University Press).

Skulsky, H. (1968) 'Paduan Epistemology and the Doctrine of One Mind', *Journal of the History of Philosophy* 6, 341–61.

Slaughter, M.M. (1982) *Universal Languages and Scientific Taxonomy in the Seventeenth Century* (Cambridge University Press).

Slezak, Peter (1986) 'Actions, Cognition, and the Self', *Synthese* 66, 405–35.

(1990) 'Reinterpreting Images', *Analysis* 50, 235–43.

Sloan, Philip R. (1977) 'Descartes, the Sceptics, and the Rejection of Vitalism in Seventeenth-Century Physiology', *Studies in the History and Philosophy of Science* 8, 1–28.

Smith, C.U.M. (1987) 'David Hartley's Newtonian Neuropsychology', *Journal of the History of the Behavioral Sciences* 23, 123–36.

Smith, John (1660/1979) 'Discourse demonstrating the Immortality of the Soul', in his *Select Discourses* (London: W. Morden; repr. with an introduction by C.A. Patrides, New York: Scholars' Facsimiles and Reprints).

Smith, John-Christian (1990) 'Reid and the Contemporary View of Consciousness', in J.-C. Smith (ed.), *Historical Foundations of Cognitive Science* (Dordrecht: Kluwer), 139–59.

Smith, Roger (1973) 'The Background of Physiological Psychology in Natural Philosophy', *History of Science* 11, 75–123.

(1992) *Inhibition: History and Meaning in the Sciences of Mind and Brain* (Berkeley and Los Angeles: California University Press).

Smolensky, Paul (1987/1991) 'The Constituent Structure of Connectionist Mental States: A Reply to Fodor and Pylyshyn', repr. in T. Horgan and J. Tienson (eds.), *Connectionism and the Philosophy of Mind* (Dordrecht: Kluwer), 281–308.

(1988) 'On the Proper Treatment of Connectionism', *Behavioral and Brain Sciences* 11, 1–73.

(1991) 'Connectionism, Constituency, and the Language of Thought', in B. Loewer and G. Rey (eds.), *Meaning in Mind: Fodor and his Critics* (Oxford: Blackwell), 201–27.

Snowdon, Paul (1992) 'How to Interpret "Direct Perception"', in T. Crane (ed.), *The Contents of Experience* (Cambridge University Press), 48–78.

Solmsen, Friedrich (1961) 'Greek Philosophy and the Discovery of the Nerves', *Museum Helveticum* 18, 150–67, 169–97.

Sorabji, Richard (1972) *Aristotle on Memory* (London: Duckworth).

Southgate, Beverly C. (1992) '"The Power of Imagination": Psychological Explanations in Mid-seventeenth-century England', *History of Science* 30, 281–94.

Spacks, Patricia Meyer (1976) *Imagining a Self: Autobiography and Novel in Eighteenth-century England* (Cambridge, MA: Harvard University Press).

Spence, Donald P. (1988) 'Passive Remembering', in U. Neisser and E. Winograd (eds.), *Remembering Reconsidered: Ecological and Traditional Approaches to the Study of Memory* (Cambridge University Press), 311–25.

Sperber, Dan (1996) *Explaining Culture: A Naturalistic Approach* (Oxford; Blackwell).

Spillane, John D. (1981) *The Doctrine of the Nerves: Chapters in the History of Neurology* (Oxford University Press).

Squires, Roger (1969) 'Memory Unchained', *Philosophical Review* 78, 178–96.

Stafford, Barbara Maria (1991) *Body Criticism: Imaging the Unseen in Enlightenment Art and Medicine* (Cambridge, MA: MIT Press).

Stallybrass, Peter (1987) 'Reading the Body: *The Revenger's Tragedy* and the Jacobean Theater of Consumption', *Renaissance Drama* 18, 121–48.

Stallybrass, Peter and White, Allon (1986) *The Politics and Poetics of Transgression* (London: Methuen).

Starobinski, Jean (1966) 'Note sur l'histoire des fluides imaginaires (des esprits animaux à la libido)', *Gesnerus* 23, 176–87.

Steneck, Nicholas H. (1976) *Science and Creation in the Middle Ages: Henry of Langenstein on Genesis* (Notre Dame University Press).

Steno, Nicolaus (1669/1965) *Discours sur l'anatomie de cerveau* (Paris: Robert de Ninville).

Stent, Gunther (1990) 'The Poverty of Neurophilosophy', *Journal of Medicine and Philosophy* 15, 539–57.

Stern, David (1991) 'Models of Memory: Wittgenstein and Cognitive Science', *Philosophical Psychology* 4, 203–18.

Sterne, Laurence (1759/1983) *The Life and Opinions of Tristram Shandy, Gentleman*, ed. I.C. Ross (Oxford University Press).

Stevens, Leonard (1973) *Explorers of the Brain* (London: Angus and Robertson).

Stewart, Susan (1984/1993) *On Longing: Narratives of the Miniature, the Gigantic, the Souvenir, the Collection* (Durham, NC: Duke University Press).

Stich, Stephen P. (1996) *Deconstructing the Mind* (Oxford University Press).

Still, Arthur and Velody, Irving (eds.) (1992) *Rewriting the History of Madness: Studies in Foucault's 'Histoire de la Folie'* (London: Routledge).

Straker, Stephen M. (1985) 'What is the History of Theories of Perception the History Of?', in M.J. Osler and P.L. Farber (eds.), *Religion, Science, and Worldview: Essays in Honor of Richard S. Westfall* (Cambridge University Press), 245–73.

Strathern, Andrew J. (1996) *Body Thoughts* (Ann Arbor: Michigan University Press).

Straus, Erwin W. (1962/1966) 'Memory Traces', in his *Phenomenological Psychology* (New York: Basic Books), 75–100.

  (1970) 'Phenomenology of Memory', in E.W. Straus and R. Griffith (eds.), *Phenomenology of Memory* (Pittsburgh: Duquesne University Press), 45–63.

Stroll, Avrum (1989) 'Wittgenstein's Nose', in B. McGuinness and R. Haller (eds.), *Wittgenstein in Focus* (Amsterdam: Rodopi), 395–413.

Summers, David (1987) *The Judgement of Sense: Renaissance Naturalism and the Rise of Aesthetics* (Cambridge University Press).

Sutton, John (1990) 'Where Was Thought? Notes Towards a Genealogy of Mind', *Hermes 1990* (Sydney: University of Sydney Union Publications), 99–109.

  (1991) 'Religion and the Failures of Determinism', in S. Gaukroger (ed.), *The Uses of*

Antiquity: The Scientific Revolution and the Classical Tradition (Dordrecht: Kluwer),
   25–51.

(1993) 'Wittgenstein, Memory, and Neurophilosophy', in 'Connecting Memory Traces',
   Ph.D. thesis, University of Sydney, 487–550.

(1994a) 'Angel Sex and Angel Memory: Interpenetration, Mixture, and Spirits in
   Restoration Natural Philosophy and Literature', paper presented to Australasian
   Association for History and Philosophy of Science conference, Griffith University,
   July 1994.

(1994b) 'Nervous Turbulence and Psychological Control: Foucault, Early Modern
   Bodies, and the Moral Physiology of Self', paper presented to Foucault conference,
   Queensland University of Technology, July 1994.

(1995) 'Reduction and Levels of Explanation in Connectionism', in P. Slezak, T. Caelli,
   and R. Clark (eds.), Perspectives on Cognitive Science: Theories, Experiments, and Foundations
   (Norwood, NJ: Ablex), 347–68.

(1996) 'Uncanny Innards', review of Sawday 1995, Metascience 9, 179–82.

(1997) 'Body, Mind, and Order: Local Memory and the Control of Mental
   Representations in Medieval and Renaissance Sciences of Self', in A. Corones and
   G. Freeland (eds.), 1543 and All That: Word and Image in the Proto-scientific Revolution
   (Dordrecht: Kluwer).

(1998) 'Controlling the Passions: Passion, Memory, and the Moral Physiology of Self in
   Seventeenth-century Neurophilosophy', in S. Gaukroger (ed.), The Soft Underbelly of
   Reason: The Passions in the Seventeenth Century (London: Routledge), 115–46.

Suzuki, Akihito (1992) 'Mind and its Disease in Enlightenment British Medicine', Ph.D.
   thesis, University of London.

Swift, Jonathan (1704/1984) A Discourse concerning the Mechanical Operation of the Spirit. In a
   Letter to a Friend, in Jonathan Swift, ed. A. Ross and D. Woolley (Oxford University
   Press), 165–80.

Sydenham, Thomas (1682/1685) 'Dissertatio epistolaris ad . . . Guileilmum Cole, M.D.', in
   Thomae Sydenham, M.D., Opera Universa (London: Walter Kettilby), 75–176 (paginated
   separately).

(1697) 'Dissertatio epistolaris ad . . . Guileilmum Cole, M.D.', in The Whole Works of that
   Excellent Practical Physician Dr. Thomas Sydenham (London: Wellington), 374–447
   (translation of Sydenham 1682/1685).

(1850) 'Dissertatio epistolaris ad . . . Guileilmum Cole, M.D.', in The Works of Thomas
   Sydenham, M.D., ed. R.D. Latham (London: Sydenham Society), vol. II, 51–118
   (translation of Sydenham 1682/1685).

Sysak, Janusz (1993) 'Coleridge's Construction of Newton', Annals of Science 50, 59–81.

Tamny, Martin (1990) 'Atomism and the Mechanical Philosophy', in R.C. Olby, G.N.
   Cantor, J.R.R. Christie, and M.J.S. Hodge (eds.), Companion to the History of Modern
   Science (London: Routledge), 597–609.

Tanner, Godfrey (1985) 'Early Greek Origins of the Idea of Pneuma: Notes Towards a
   Theory', in D. Dockrill and G. Tanner (eds.), The Concept of Spirit (Auckland University
   Press), 49–53.

Tarrant, Harold (1985) 'Pneuma-related Concepts in Platonism', in D. Dockrill and
   G. Tanner (eds.), The Concept of Spirit (Auckland University Press), 55–60.

Taylor, Charles (1989) Sources of the Self: The Making of the Modern Identity (Cambridge
   University Press).

Taylor, D.W. (1988) '"Discourses on the Human Physiology" by Alexander Monro Primus', *Medical History* 32, 65–81.

Temkin, Owsei (1951/1977), 'On Galen's Pneumatology', in his *The Double Face of Janus and Other Essays in the History of Medicine* (Baltimore: Johns Hopkins University Press), 154–61.

(1973) *Galenism: Rise and Decline of a Medical Philosophy* (Ithaca, NY: Cornell University Press).

Tennant, R.C. (1982) 'The Anglican Response to Locke's Theory of Personal Identity', *Journal of the History of Ideas* 43, 73–90.

Terdiman, Richard (1993) *Present Past: Modernity and the Memory Crisis* (Ithaca, NY: Cornell University Press).

Terrall, Mary (1996) 'Salon, Academy, and Boudoir: Generation and Desire in Maupertuis' Science of Life', *Isis* 87, 217–29.

Thiel, Udo (1981) 'Locke's Concept of a Person', in R. Brandt (ed.), *John Locke: Symposium Wolfenbüttel 1979* (Berlin: de Gruyter), 181–92.

(1991) 'Cudworth and Seventeenth Century Theories of Consciousness', in S. Gaukroger (ed.), *The Uses of Antiquity: The Scientific Revolution and the Classical Tradition* (Dordrecht: Kluwer), 79–99.

Thorpe, Simon J. and Imbert, Michel (1989) 'Biological Constraints on Connectionist Modelling', in R. Pfeifer, Z. Schreter, F. Fogelman-Soulié, and L. Steele (eds.), *Connectionism in Perspective* (North-Holland: Elsevier), 63–92.

Tomaselli, Sylvana (1984a) 'The First Person: Descartes, Locke, and Mind–Body Dualism', *History of Science* 22, 185–205.

(1984b) 'The Torrent and the Brook: A Juxtaposition of Diderot and Hume', *British Journal for Eighteenth Century Studies* 7, 229–39.

Toulmin, Stephen (1990) *Cosmopolis: The Hidden Agenda of Modernity* (Chicago University Press).

Touretzky, David S. and Pomerleau, Dean A. (1989) 'What's Hidden in the Hidden Layers?', *Byte*, August, 227–33.

Tourneur, Cyril (1611/1976) *The Atheist's Tragedy*, ed. B. Morris and R. Gill (London: Benn).

Tracy, Theodore J. (1969) *Physiological Theory and the Doctrine of the Mean in Plato and Aristotle* (The Hague: Mouton).

Traiger, Saul (1985) 'Flage on Hume's Account of Memory', *Hume Studies* 11, 166–72.

Trevor-Roper, Hugh (1989) 'James Ussher, Archbishop of Armagh', in his *Catholics, Anglicans, and Puritans* (London: Fontana), 120–65.

Tryon, Warren W. (1993) 'Neural Networks I: Theoretical Unification Through Connectionism', *Clinical Psychology Review* 13, 341–52.

Tulving, Endel (1983) *Elements of Episodic Memory* (Oxford: Clarendon).

Turnbull, H.W. (ed.) (1959) *The Correspondence of Isaac Newton*, vol. 1: *1661–1675* (Cambridge University Press).

Turvey, M.T. and Shaw, R. (1979) 'The Primacy of Perceiving: An Ecological Reformulation of Perception for Understanding Memory', in L.-G. Nilsson (ed.), *Perspectives on Memory Research* (Hillsdale, NJ: Erlbaum), 167–222.

Tuveson, Ernest (1962) 'Locke and Sterne', in J.A. Mazzeo (ed.), *Reason and Imagination: Studies in the History of Ideas, 1600–1800* (New York: Columbia University Press), 255–77.

Tye, Michael (1991) 'Representation in Pictorialism and Connectionism', in T. Horgan and J. Tienson (eds.), *Connectionism and the Philosophy of Mind* (Dordrecht: Kluwer), 309–30.

Valentine, Elizabeth R. (1989) 'Neural Nets: From Hartley and Hebb to Hinton', *Journal of Mathematical Psychology* 33, 348–57.

Van Gelder, Tim (1991a) review of Churchland 1989c, *Connection Science* 3, 91–3.

(1991b) 'What is the "D" in "PDP"? A Survey of the Concept of Distribution', in W. Ramsey, S.P. Stich, and D.E. Rumelhart (eds.), *Philosophy and Connectionist Theory* (Hillsdale, NJ: Erlbaum), 33–59.

(1991c) 'Classical Questions, Radical Answers: Connectionism and the Structure of Mental Representations', in T. Horgan and J. Tienson (eds.), *Connectionism and the Philosophy of Mind* (Dordrecht: Kluwer), 355–81.

(1992a) 'Defining "Distributed Representation"', *Connection Science* 4, 175–91.

(1992b) 'Making Conceptual Space', in S. Davis (ed.), *Connectionism: Theory and Practice* (Oxford University Press), 179–94.

(1995) 'What Could Cognition Be, If Not Computation?', *Journal of Philosophy* 91, 345–81.

Van Gelder, Tim and Port, Robert (1995) 'It's About Time: An Overview of the Dynamical Approach to Cognition', in R. Port and T. van Gelder (eds.), *Mind as Motion: Explorations in the Dynamics of Cognition* (Cambridge, MA: MIT Press), 1–43.

Van Sant, Ann Jessie (1993) *Eighteenth-Century Sensibility and the Novel* (Cambridge University Press).

Vartanian, Aram (1953) *Diderot and Descartes: A Study of Scientific Naturalism in the Enlightenment* (Princeton University Press).

Verbeke, G. (1945) *L'Evolution de la doctrine du pneuma du stoïcisme à S. Augustin* (Paris and Louvain: de Brouwer).

Vickers, Brian (ed.) (1987) *English Science: Bacon to Newton* (Cambridge University Press).

Vickers, Nancy (1982) 'Diana Described: Scattered Woman and Scattered Rhyme', in E. Abel (ed.), *Writing and Sexual Difference* (Brighton: Harvester Press), 95–109.

Von Leyden, W. (1961) *Remembering: A Philosophical Problem* (London: Duckworth).

Voss, Stephen (1993) 'Simplicity and the Seat of the Soul', in S. Voss (ed.), *Essays on the Philosophy and Science of René Descartes* (Cambridge University Press), 128–41.

(1994) 'Descartes: The End of Anthropology', in J. Cottingham (ed.), *Reason, Will, and Sensation: Studies in Descartes' Metaphysics* (Oxford: Clarendon), 273–306.

Wahl, Russell (1988) 'The Arnauld–Malebranche Controversy and Descartes' Ideas', *Monist* 71, 560–72.

Waldby, Catherine (1992) 'AIDS and the Immunology of the Body Politic', unpublished paper, HIV Social Research Centre, Macquarie University.

Walker, D.P. (1953/1985) 'Ficino's *Spiritus* and Music', in Walker, 1985c; also in Walker 1958/1975: ch. 1.

(1958/1975) *Spiritual and Demonic Magic from Ficino to Campanella* (repr. University of Notre Dame Press).

(1981) *Unclean Spirits: Possession and Exorcism in France and England in the Late Sixteenth and Early Seventeenth Centuries* (Philadelphia: Pennsylvania University Press).

(1984) 'Medical Spirits and God and the Soul', in M. Fattori and M. Bianchi (eds.), *Spiritus* (Rome: Edizioni dell'Ateneo), 223–244; also in Walker 1985c as 'Medical Spirits in Philosophy and Theology from Ficino to Newton'.

(1985a) 'Francis Bacon and Spiritus', in Walker 1985c.

(1985b) 'The Astral Body in Renaissance Medicine', in Walker 1985c.

(1985c) Music, Spirit, and Language in the Renaissance, ed. P. Gouk (London: Variorum Reprints).

Walker, W. Cameron (1937) 'Animal Electricity before Galvani', Annals of Science 2, 84–113.

Wallace, Karl R. (1967) Francis Bacon on the Nature of Man (Urbana, IL: Illinois University Press).

Walls, Joan (1982) 'The Psychology of David Hartley and the Root Metaphor of Mechanism: A Study in the History of Psychology', Journal of Mind and Behavior 3, 259–74.

Warnock, Mary (1987) Memory (London: Faber).

Warren, Howard C. (1921) A History of the Association Psychology (London: Constable and Co.).

Watts, Isaac (1734) Reliquiae Juveniles: Miscellaneous Thoughts in Prose and Verse, on Natural, Moral, and Divine Subjects; Written chiefly in Younger Years (London: Ford and Hett).

Wear, Andrew (1995) 'Medicine in Early Modern Europe, 1500–1700', in L.I. Conrad, M. Neve, V. Nutton, R. Porter, and A. Wear, The Western Medical Tradition (Cambridge University Press), 215–361.

Webb, Martha Ellen (1988) 'A New History of Hartley's Observations on Man', Journal of the History of the Behavioral Sciences 24, 202–11.

Webster, Charles (1982) From Paracelsus to Newton: Magic and the Making of Modern Science (Cambridge University Press).

Wedeking, Gary (1990) 'Locke on Personal Identity and the Trinity Controversies of the 1690s', Dialogue 29, 163–88.

Wells, G.A. (1985) 'A Characteristic of Mechanical Theories of the Mind and its Probable Explanation', British Journal for Eighteenth Century Studies 8, 79–82.

West, Robert H. (1955) Milton and the Angels (Athens, GA: Georgia University Press).

(1969) The Invisible World: A Study of Pneumatology in Elizabethan Drama, 2nd edn (New York: Octagon Books).

Westfall, Richard (1971) Force in Newton's Physics: The Science of Dynamics in the Seventeenth Century (London: Macdonald).

Whigham, Frank (1988) 'Reading Social Conflict in the Alimentary Tract: More on the Body in Renaissance Drama', ELH 55, 333–50.

Whittaker, E.W. (1951) A History of the Theories of Aether and Electricity: The Classical Theories (London: Thomas Nelson and Sons).

Whyte, Lancelot L. (1962) The Unconscious Before Freud (London: Tavistock Publications).

Whytt, Robert (1765) Observations on the Nature, Causes, and Cure of those Disorders which have been commonly called Nervous, Hypochondriac, or Hysteric (Edinburgh: Becket and du Hondt).

Wieand, Jeffrey (1980) 'Locke on Memory', The Locke Newsletter 11, 63–75.

Wiggins, David (1976) 'Locke, Butler and the Stream of Consciousness: And Men as a Natural Kind', in A.O. Rorty (ed.), The Identities of Persons (Berkeley and Los Angeles: California University Press), 139–73.

Wightman, W.P.D. (1958) 'Wars of Ideas in Neurological Science', in F.N.L. Poynter (ed.), The History and Philosophy of Knowledge of the Brain and its Functions (Oxford: Blackwell), 135–45.

Wilcox, Stephen and Katz, Stuart (1981a) 'A Direct Realist Alternative to the Traditional Conception of Memory', Behaviorism 9, 227–39.

(1981b) 'What Gibson is not Missing After All: A Reply to Heil', *Journal for the Theory of Social Behaviour* 11, 313–17.

Wiles, Janet (1994) 'The Connectionist Modeler's Toolkit: A Review of Some Basic Processes over Distributed Memories', in J. Wiles, C. Latimer, and C. Stevens (eds.), *Connectionist Models and Psychology*, Technical report 289, Dept of Computer Science, University of Queensland, 74–87.

Wiles, Janet and Ollila, Mark (1993) 'Intersecting Regions: The Key to Combinatorial Structure in Hidden Unit Space', in S. Hanson, J.D. Cowan, and C.L. Giles (eds.), *Advances in Neural Information Processing Systems* 5 (San Mateo, CA: Morgan Kaufman).

Wilkes, Kathleen V. (1975) 'Anthropomorphism and Analogy in Psychology', *Philosophical Quarterly* 25, 126–37.

(1980) 'Brain States', *British Journal for the Philosophy of Science* 31, 111–29.

(1981) 'Functionalism, Psychology, and Philosophy of Mind', *Philosophical Topics* 12, 147–67.

(1984) 'Is Consciousness Important?', *British Journal for the Philosophy of Science* 35, 223–43.

(1988a) *Real People: Personal Identity without Thought Experiments* (Oxford: Clarendon Press).

(1988b) '——, yishi, duh, um, and consciousness', in A. Marcel and E.J. Bisiach (eds.), *Consciousness in Contemporary Science* (Oxford: Clarendon), 16–41.

(1990) 'Modelling the Mind', in K. Mohyeldin Said, W.H. Newton-Smith, R. Viale, and K.V. Wilkes (eds.), *Modelling the Mind* (Oxford: Clarendon), 63–82.

Willey, Basil (1934/1962) *The Seventeenth Century Background*, 2nd edn (Harmondsworth: Penguin).

(1940/1962) *The Eighteenth-Century Background: Studies on the Idea of Nature in the Thought of the Period* (Harmondsworth: Penguin).

(1949/1973) *Nineteenth-Century Studies* (Harmondsworth: Penguin).

Williams, Bernard (1978) *Descartes: The Project of Pure Enquiry* (Harmondsworth: Penguin).

(1994) 'Descartes and the Historiography of Philosophy', in J. Cottingham (ed.), *Reason, Will, and Sensation: Studies in Descartes' Metaphysics* (Oxford University Press), 19–27.

Williams, Katherine (1990) 'Hysteria in Seventeenth Century Case Records', *History of Psychiatry* 1, 383–401.

Williams, Raymond (1976) *Keywords*, 2nd edn (London: Flamingo).

Wilson, Catherine (1995) *The Invisible World: Early Modern Philosophy and the Invention of the Microscope* (Princeton University Press).

Wilson, Leonard G. (1959) 'Erasistratus, Galen, and the Pneuma', *Bulletin of the History of Medicine* 33, 293–314.

(1961) 'William Croone's Theory of Muscular Contraction', *Notes and Records of the Royal Society* 16, 158–78.

Wilson, Margaret D. (1978) *Descartes* (London: Routledge and Kegan Paul).

Wilson, Philip K. (1992) '"Out of Sight, Out of Mind?": The Daniel Turner–James Blondel Dispute over the Power of the Maternal Imagination', *Annals of Science* 49, 63–85.

Winkler, Kenneth P. (1991) 'Locke on Personal Identity', *Journal of the History of Philosophy* 29, 201–26.

Winsor, Mary P. (1976) 'Swammerdam, Jan', in *Dictionary of Scientific Biography*, vol. XIII, 168–75.

Wittgenstein, Ludwig (1958) *Philosophical Investigations*, trans. G.E.M. Anscombe (Oxford: Blackwell).

(1967) *Zettel*, ed. G.E.M. Anscombe and G.H. von Wright, trans. G.E.M. Anscombe (Oxford: Blackwell).

(1974) *Philosophical Grammar*, ed. R. Rhees, trans. A. Kenny (Oxford: Blackwell).

(1980) *Remarks on the Philosophy of Psychology*, vol. 1, ed. G.E.M. Anscombe and G.H. von Wright, trans. G.E.M. Anscombe (Oxford: Blackwell).

(1982) *Last Writings on the Philosophy of Psychology*, vol. 1, ed. G.H. von Wright and H. Nyman, trans. C.G. Luckhardt and M.A.E. Aue (Oxford: Blackwell).

Wood, Paul B. (1995) *Thomas Reid and the Animate Creation: Papers Relating to the Life Sciences* (Edinburgh University Press).

Woollam, D.H.M. (1958), 'Concepts of the Brain and its Functions in Classical Antiquity', in F.N.L. Poynter (ed.), *The History and Philosophy of Knowledge of the Brain and its Functions* (Oxford: Blackwell), 5–18.

Woozley, A.D. (1949) *Theory of Knowledge: An Introduction* (London: Hutchinson).

Woozley, A.D. (ed.) (1964/1977) Locke, *An Essay Concerning Human Understanding* (London: Fontana).

Wright, Edmond (1984) 'Recent Work in Perception', *American Philosophical Quarterly* 21, 17–30.

(1993) 'Introduction', in E. Wright (ed.), *New Representationalisms: Essays in the Philosophy of Perception* (Aldershot: Avebury Press), 1–12.

Wright, John P. (1980) 'Hysteria and Mechanical Man', *Journal of the History of Ideas* 41, 233–47.

(1983) *The Sceptical Realism of David Hume* (Manchester University Press).

(1985) 'Matter, Mind and Active Principles in Mid Eighteenth-Century British Physiology', *Man and Nature* 4, 17–27.

(1987) 'Association, Madness, and the Measures of Probability in Locke and Hume', in C. Fox (ed.), *Psychology and Literature in the Eighteenth Century* (New York: AMS), 103–27.

(1990) 'Metaphysics and Physiology: Mind, Body, and the Animal Economy in Eighteenth-century Scotland', in M.A. Stewart (ed.), *Studies in the Philosophy of the Scottish Enlightenment* (Oxford University Press), 251–301.

(1991a) 'Locke, Willis, and the Seventeenth-century Epicurean Soul', in Margaret J. Osler (ed.), *Atoms, 'Pneuma', and Tranquillity: Epicurean and Stoic Themes in European Thought* (Cambridge University Press), 239–58.

(1991b) 'Hume's Rejection of the Theory of Ideas', *History of Philosophy Quarterly* 8, 149–62.

Yates, Frances (1966) *The Art of Memory* (London: Routledge and Kegan Paul).

Yolton, John W. (1956) *John Locke and the Way of Ideas* (Oxford University Press).

(1966) 'Agent Causality', *American Philosophical Quarterly* 3, 14–26.

(1968/9) 'Gibson's Realism', *Synthese* 19, 400–7.

(1981) 'Phenomenology and Pragmatism: Review of Rorty [1980]', *Philosophical Books* 22, 129–34.

(1984a) *Perceptual Acquaintance from Descartes to Reid* (Minneapolis: Minnesota University Press).

(1984b) *Thinking Matter: Materialism in Eighteenth Century Britain* (Oxford: Blackwell).

(1987) 'Representation and Realism: Some Reflections on the Way of Ideas', *Mind* 96, 318–30.

(1990a) 'Mirrors and Veils, Thoughts and Things: The Epistemological Problematic', in A. Malachowski (ed.), *Reading Rorty: Critical Responses to 'Philosophy and the Mirror of Nature'* (Oxford: Blackwell), 58–73.

(1990b) 'The Way of Ideas: A Retrospective', *Journal of Philosophy* 87, 510–16.

(1991a) *Locke and French Materialism* (Oxford: Clarendon).

(1991b) review of Nadler 1989, *Journal of Philosophy* 88, 109–12.

(1993) *A Locke Dictionary* (Oxford: Blackwell).

(1996) *Perception and Reality: A History from Descartes to Kant* (Ithaca, NY: Cornell University Press).

Young, Dudley (1991/1993) *Origins of the Sacred: The Ecstasies of Love and War* (London: Abacus).

Young, Robert M. (1966) 'Scholarship and the History of the Behavioural Sciences', *History of Science* 5, 1–51.

(1970) *Mind, Brain, and Adaptation in the Nineteenth Century: Cerebral Localisation and its Biological Context from Gall to Ferrier* (Oxford: Clarendon).

(1973) 'Association of Ideas', in P.P. Wiener (ed.), *Dictionary of the History of Ideas* (New York: Scribner), vol. I, 111–18.

Zemach, E.M. (1983) 'Memory: What it Is, and What it Cannot Possibly Be', *Philosophy and Phenomenological Research* 44, 31–44.

Index